INTERNATIONAL
POLITICAL
ECONOMY

PERSPECTIVES ON
GLOBAL POWER
AND WEALTH

FOURTH EDITION

Jeffry A. Frieden
Harvard University

David A. Lake
University of California, San Diego

London and New York

For Bedford/St. Martin's

Political Science Editor: James R. Headley
Senior Editor, Publishing Services: Douglas Bell
Production Supervisor: Joe Ford
Project Management: Stratford Publishing Services, Inc.
Cover Design: Lucy Krikorian
Cover Photo: CORBIS/Stuart Westmorland
Composition: Stratford Publishing Services, Inc.
Printing and Binding: Haddon Craftsman, an R.R. Donnelley & Sons Company

President: Charles H. Christensen
Editorial Director: Joan E. Feinberg
Director of Editing, Design, and Production: Marcia Cohen
Manager, Publishing Services: Emily Berleth

First published 2000 by Bedford/St. Martin's. Simultaneously published and distributed outside North America by
Routledge
11 New Fetter Lane, London, EC4P 4EE
and representatives throughout the world.

Reprinted 2004

Library of Congress Catalog Card Number: 99-62343

Printed and bound by Antony Rowe Ltd, Eastbourne

5 4 3 2 1 0
f e d c b a

For information, write: Bedford/St. Martin's, 75 Arlington Street, Boston, MA 02116
(617-426-7440)

British Library Cataloguing in Publication Data

A catalogue record for this book is available from the British Library.

ISBN: 0-415-22279-6

Acknowledgments

PREFACE

The readings in *International Political Economy: Perspectives on Global Power and Wealth* are primarily intended to introduce the study of international political economy to those with little or no prior knowledge of it. The book is designed for use in courses in international political economy, international relations, and international economics. The selections present both clear and identifiable theoretical arguments and important substantive material. Fifteen of the 31 articles are new to this fourth edition of our book, and the theoretical approach has been updated to reflect the changing state of both the world and the field of international political economy.

Although the selections can be read in any order, they are grouped in seven parts, which reflect some of the more common organizing principles used in international political economy courses. Each part begins with an introduction by the editors that provides background information and highlights issues raised in the readings. Each reading is preceded by an abstract summarizing its specific arguments and contributions. The readings were edited to eliminate extraneous or dated information, and most footnotes were removed.

The introduction defines the study of international political economy, summarizes major analytical frameworks in the field, and identifies several current debates. In earlier editions, the introduction and readings were largely structured around three analytic perspectives: Realism, Marxism, and Liberalism. This framework is substantially downplayed in this edition. The field of international political economy has made significant progress over the last two decades, and this division — while useful as a pedagogic device — has become increasingly obsolete. To capture the most important work and current debates in the international political economy, we now highlight the analytic tensions between international and domestic explanations, on the one hand, and institutionalist- and society-centered explanations, on the other. These two dimensions create four distinct views, which we refer to as the international political, international economic, domestic institutionalist, and domestic societal approaches. Part I presents examples of these different perspectives on international political economy. The readings in this part are intended to suggest the underlying logic and types of arguments used by proponents of each approach. Although they are representative of their respective schools, they do not necessarily capture the wide range of opinion within each approach.

Part II, which reviews the history of the international economy since the nineteenth century, provides the background and perspective necessary to understand the contemporary international political economy. The selections describe the major developments in the history of the modern international economy from a variety of different theoretical viewpoints.

The remainder of the book is devoted to the modern international political economy. Separate sections on production, money and finance, and trade look at the principal broad issue areas associated with the politics of international economic relations. Part VI focuses on the particular political and economic problems of developing and transitional economies. Finally, Part VII examines current problems in the politics of international economics.

The selections in this volume have been used successfully in our courses on international political economy at the University of California, Los Angeles; Harvard University; and the University of California, San Diego (UCSD). In our own research, we approach the study of international political economy from very different perspectives. Yet we find that this set of readings accommodates our individual approaches to the subject matter while simultaneously covering the major questions of the field.

For this edition, Patricia Lindenboim and Michael Spence at Harvard and Angela O'Mahony at UCSD provided valuable research and editorial assistance. Leslie S. Connor of Stratford Publishing Services prepared the manuscript for publication. We want to thank our respective spouses, Anabela Costa and Wendy K. Lake, for their continuing encouragement.

Jeffry A. Frieden
David A. Lake

CONTENTS

ABOUT THE EDITORS

Jeffry A. Frieden (Ph.D., Columbia University) is professor of government at Harvard University. He specializes in the political economy of international monetary and financial relations. His book publications include *Debt, Development, and Democracy: Modern Political Economy and Latin America, 1965–1985* (Princeton: Princeton University Press, 1991) and *Banking on the World: The Politics of American International Finance* (New York: Harper & Row, 1987), which has been issued in both Japanese and British editions.

David A. Lake (Ph.D., Cornell University) is professor of political science at the University of California, San Diego, and coeditor of the journal *International Organization*. He has published widely in the field of international relations and international political economy. His principal book publications include *Power, Protection, and Free Trade: International Sources of U.S. Commercial Strategy, 1887–1939* (Ithaca: Cornell University Press, 1988) and *Entangling Relations: American Foreign Policy in its Century* (Princeton: Princeton University Press, 1999).

Introduction

INTERNATIONAL POLITICS AND INTERNATIONAL ECONOMICS

Over the past thirty years, the study of international political economy underwent a remarkable resurgence. Virtually nonexistent before 1970 as a field of study, international political economy is now a popular area of specialization for both undergraduates and graduate students, as well as the source of much innovative and influential scholarship. The revival of international political economy after nearly forty years of dormancy enriched both social science and public debate, and promises to continue to do both.

International political economy is the study of the interplay of economics and politics in the world arena. In the most general sense, the economy can be defined as the system of producing, distributing, and using wealth; politics is the set of institutions and rules by which social and economic interactions are governed. *Political economy* has a variety of meanings. For some, it refers primarily to the study of the political basis of economic actions, the ways in which government policies affect market operations. For others, the principal preoccupation is the economic basis of political action, the ways in which economic forces mold government policies. The two focuses are, in a sense, complementary, for politics and markets are in a constant state of mutual interaction.

Most markets are governed by certain fundamental laws that operate more or less independently of the will of firms and individuals. Any shopkeeper knows that an attempt to raise the price of a readily available and standardized product — a pencil, for example — above that charged by nearby and competing shopkeepers will rapidly cause customers to stop buying pencils at the higher price. Unless the shopkeeper wants to be left with piles of unsold pencils, he or she will have to bring the price back into line with "what the market will bear." The shopkeeper will have learned a microcosmic lesson in what economists call *market-clearing equilibrium,* the price at which the number of goods supplied equals the number demanded — the point at which supply and demand curves intersect.

At the base of all modern economics is the general assertion that, within certain

1

carefully specified parameters, markets operate in and of themselves to maintain balance between supply and demand. Other things being equal, if the supply of a good increases far beyond the demand for it, the good's price will be driven down until demand rises to meet supply, supply falls to meet demand, and market-clearing equilibrium is restored. By the same token, if demand exceeds supply, the good's price will rise, thus causing demand to decline and supply to increase until the two are in balance.

If the international and domestic economies functioned as perfectly competitive markets, they would be relatively easy to describe and comprehend. But such markets are only highly stylized or abstract models, which are rarely reproduced in the real world. A variety of factors influence the workings of domestic and international markets in ways that a focus on perfectly competitive and unchanging market forces does not fully capture. Consumer tastes can change — how large is the American market for spats or sarsaparilla today? — as can the technology needed to make products more cheaply, or even to make entirely new goods that displace others (stick shifts for horsewhips, calculators for slide rules). Producers, sellers, or buyers of goods can band together to try to raise or lower prices unilaterally, as the Organization of Petroleum Exporting Countries (OPEC) did with petroleum in 1974 and 1979. And governments can act, consciously or inadvertently, to alter patterns of consumption, supply, demand, prices, and virtually all other economic variables.

This last fact — the impact of policy and politics on economic trends — is the most visible, and probably the most important, reason to look beyond market-based, purely economic explanations of social behavior. Indeed, many market-oriented economists are continually surprised by the ability of governments or of powerful groups pressuring governments to contravene economic tendencies. When OPEC first raised oil prices in December 1973, some market-minded pundits, and even a few naive economists, predicted that such naked manipulation of the forces of supply and demand could last only a matter of months. However, what has emerged from the past thirty years' experience with oil prices is the recognition that they are a function of both market forces and the ability of OPEC's member states to organize concerted intervention in the oil market.

Somewhat less dramatic are the everyday operations of local and national governments, which affect prices, production, profits, wages, and almost every other aspect of the economy. Wage, price, and rent controls; taxation; incentives and subsidies; tariffs and other barriers to trade; and government spending all serve to mold modern economies and the functioning of markets themselves. Who could understand the suburbanization of the United States after World War II without taking into account government tax incentives to home mortgage–holders, government-financed highway construction, and politically driven patterns of local educational expenditures? How many American (or Japanese or European) farmers would be left if agricultural subsidies were eliminated? How many Americans would have college educations were it not for public universities, government scholarships and publicly subsidized student loans, and tax exemptions for private universities? Who could explain the proliferation of nonprofit groups in the United States without knowing the tax incentives given to charitable donations?

In these instances and many more, political pressure groups, politicians, and government bureaucrats have at least as much effect on economic outcomes as do the laws of the marketplace. Social scientists, especially political scientists, have spent decades trying to understand how these political pressures interact to produce government policy. Many of the results provide as elegant and stylized a view of politics as the economics profession has developed of markets. As in economics, however, social science models of political behavior are little more than didactic devices whose accuracy depends on a wide variety of unpredictable factors, including underlying economic trends. If an economist would be equally foolish to dismiss the possibilities of intergovernmental producers' cartels (such as OPEC) out of hand, a political scientist would be foolish not to realize that the economic realities of modern international commodity markets ensure that successful producers' cartels will be few and far between.

It is thus no surprise that political economy is far from new. Indeed, until a century ago, virtually all thinkers concerned with understanding human society wrote about political economy. For individuals as diverse as Adam Smith, John Stuart Mill, and Karl Marx, the economy was eminently political and politics was obviously tied to economic phenomena. Few scholars before 1900 would have taken seriously any attempt to describe and analyze politics and economics independently of each other.

Around the turn of the century, however, professional studies of economics and politics became increasingly divorced from one another. Economic investigation began to focus on understanding more fully the operation of specific markets and their interaction; the development of new mathematical techniques permitted the formalization of, for example, laws of supply and demand. By the time of World War I, an economics profession per se was in existence, and its attention was focused on understanding the operation of economic activities in and of themselves. At the same time, other scholars were looking increasingly at the political realm in isolation from the economy. The rise of modern representative political institutions, mass political parties, more politically informed populations, and modern bureaucracies all seemed to justify the study of politics as an activity that had a logic of its own.

With the exception of a few isolated individuals and an upsurge of interest during the politically and economically troubled Depression years, the twentieth century saw an increasing separation of the study of economics from that of politics. Economists developed ever more elaborate and sophisticated models of how economies work, and similarly, political scientists spun out ever more complex theories of political development and activity.

The resurgence of political economy after 1970 had two, interrelated sources. The first was dissatisfaction among academics with the gap between abstract models of political and economic behavior, on the one hand, and the actual behavior of polities and economies, on the other. Theory had become more ethereal and seemed less realistic. Many scholars therefore questioned the intellectual justifications for a strict analytic division between politics and economics. Second, as the stability and prosperity of the first twenty-five postwar years started to disintegrate in the early 1970s, economic issues became politicized while political systems became increasingly preoccupied with economic affairs. In August 1971, President Richard Nixon ended the gold–dollar standard, which had formed the basis for postwar monetary relations; two and a half years later, OPEC, a previously little-known group, succeeded in substantially raising the price of oil. In 1974 and 1975, the industrial nations of Western Europe, North America, and Japan fell into the first worldwide economic recession since the 1930s; unemployment and inflation were soon widespread realities and explosive political issues. In the world arena, the underdeveloped countries — most of them recently independent — burst onto center stage as the Third World and demanded a fairer division of global wealth and power. If in the 1950s and 1960s, economic growth was taken for granted and politics occupied itself with other matters, in the 1970s and 1980s, economic stagnation fed political strife while political conflict exacerbated economic uncertainty.

For both intellectual and practical reasons, then, social scientists began seeking, once more, to understand how politics and economics interact in modern society. As interest in political economy grew, a series of fundamental questions was posed and a broad variety of contending approaches arose.

To be sure, today's political economists have not simply reproduced the studies of earlier (and perhaps neglected) generations of scholars in the discipline. The professionalization of both economics and political science led to major advances in both fields, and scholars now understand both economic and political phenomena far better than they did a generation ago. It is on this improved basis that the new political economy has been constructed, albeit with some long-standing issues in mind.

Just as in the real world, where politicians pay close attention to economic trends and economic actors keep track of political tendencies, those who would understand the political process must take the economy into account, and vice versa. A much richer picture of social processes emerges from an integrated understanding of both political and economic affairs than from the isolated study of politics and economics as separate realms. This much is, by now, hardly controversial; it is in application that disagreements arise. Government actions may influence economic trends, but these actions themselves may simply reflect the pressures of economic interest groups. Economic interest groups may be central in determining government policy, yet the political system — democratic or totalitarian, two-party or multiparty, parliamentary or presidential — may crucially color the outlooks and influence of economic interests. In the attempt to arrive at an integrated view of how politics and economics interact, we must disentangle economic and political causes from effects. In this effort, different scholars have different approaches, with different implications for the resulting views of the world.

CONTENDING PERSPECTIVES ON INTERNATIONAL POLITICAL ECONOMY

Analysts of the international political economy must understand the interaction of many disparate forces. It is possible to simplify many such factors so that they can be arrayed on two dimensions. These two dimensions also capture many of the theoretical disagreements that characterize scholarship on the politics of international economic relations. One set of disagreements has to do with the relationship between the international and domestic political economies; another set concerns the relationship between the state and social forces.

The first dimension of interest concerns the degree to which the causes of international political and economic trends are to be found at the domestic or international level. All observers agree that in a complex world, both global and national forces are important. But different analysts place different emphases on the importance of one or the other. Some focus on how international forces tend to overpower domestic interests; others emphasize the degree to which national concerns override global considerations.

It should surprise no one that, for example, American trade policy, Japan's financial goals, and South Korean development strategies are important in the world's political economy. Disagreements arise, however, over how best to explain the sources of the foreign economic policies of individual nations, or of nation-states in general. At one end of the spectrum, some scholars believe that nations' foreign economic policies are essentially determined by the global environment. The actual room for national maneuver of even the most powerful of states, these scholars believe, is limited by characteristics inherent in the international system. At the other end of the spectrum are scholars who see foreign economic policies primarily as the outgrowth of nations' domestic-level political and economic processes. For them, the international system exists only as a jumble of independent nation-states, each with its own political and economic peculiarities.

The international–domestic division is at the base of many debates within international political economy, as in the world at large. While some argue, for example, that the cause of Third World poverty is in the unequal global economic order, others blame domestic politics and economics in developing nations. Similarly, many scholars see multinational corporations as a powerful independent force in the world — whether working for good or for evil — while others see international firms as extensions of their home countries. Moreover, for some analysts, global geopolitical relations among nations dominate the impulses that arise from their domestic social orders.

The distinction between the two approaches can be seen quite clearly, for example, in explanations of trade policy. To take a specific instance, starting in the early 1980s the United States and many European governments imposed restrictions on the import of Japanese automobiles. The form of the controls varied widely: the U.S. and Japanese governments negotiated "voluntary" export restraints, with which Japanese producers agreed to comply, while in some European countries, quantitative quotas were imposed unilaterally. Concerned about stiff Japanese competition, which was reducing profits and employment, European and North American automakers and the trade unions that represent their employees provided key support for these policies.

From this example, one clear analytic conclusion would be that domestic political and economic pressures — the electoral importance of the regions where auto industries are concentrated; the economic centrality of that sector to the European and North American economies; government concern about the broad, national ramifications of the auto industry; the political clout of the autoworkers' unions —

led to important foreign economic measures involving the restriction of Japanese automobile imports. Indeed, many scholars saw the restrictions as confirmation of the primacy of domestic concerns in the making of foreign economic policy.

Yet analysts who search for the causes of national foreign economic policies in the international rather than the domestic arena could also find support in the auto import restrictions. After all, the policies were responsive to the rise of Japan as a major manufacturer and exporter of automobiles, a fact that had little to do with the domestic scene in the United States or Europe. Many North American and European industries had lost competitive ground to rapidly growing overseas manufacturers, a process that is complex in origin but clearly one of worldwide proportions. Some have argued that trade policies are a function of realities inherent in the international system, such as the existence of a leading, hegemonic power and the eventual decline of that state (see Krasner, Reading 1). In this view, the decline of American power set the stage for a proliferation of barriers to trade.

The internationally minded scholar might also argue that it is important to understand why the European and American measures took the relatively mild form they did in simply limiting the Japanese to established (and, often, very appreciable) shares of the markets. If the measures had been adopted solely to respond to the distress of local auto industries, the logical step would have been to exclude foreign cars from the markets in question. Yet the positions of Europe and the United States in the global economic and political system — including everything from world finance to international military alliances — dictated that European and North American policymakers not pursue overly hostile policies toward the Japanese.

More generally, scholars have explained long-term changes in trade policy in very different ways. During the period between World Wars I and II, and especially in the 1930s, almost all European nations and the United States were highly protectionist. After World War II, on the other hand, the North American and Western European markets were opened gradually to one another and to the rest of the world.

Scholars whose theoretical bent is international point out that domestic politics in Europe and the United States did not change enough to explain such a radical shift. But the postwar role of the United States and Western Europe in the international political and economic system has indeed been different from what it was during the 1930s: after 1945, North American and Western European countries were united in an American-led military and economic alliance against the Soviet Union. Some internationally oriented analysts argue that the causes of postwar foreign economic policies in North America and Western Europe can be found in international geopolitical positions of these regions — the increase in American power, the decline of Europe, the Soviet challenge, and the rise of the Atlantic Alliance. Others point to broad technological and economic developments, such as dramatic improvements in telecommunications and transportation, that have altered governments' incentives to either protect or open their economies.

Scholars who promote domestic-level explanations take the opposite tack. For them, the postwar system was itself largely a creation of the United States and the major Western European powers. To cite the modern international political economy as a source of American or British foreign economic policy, these scholars argue, is to put the cart before the horse in that the United States and its allies had created the institutions — the Marshall Plan, the Bretton Woods agreement, the European Union — of today's international political economy. We must therefore search within these nations for the true roots of the shift in trade policy in North America and Western Europe.

The example of trade policy illustrates that serious scholars can arrive at strikingly different analytic conclusions on the basis of the same information. For some, domestic political and economic pressures caused the adoption of auto import restrictions, whereas for others, geopolitical, economic, or technological trends in the international environment explain the same action.

The second dimension along which analysts differ in their interpretation of trends in the international political economy has to do with the relative importance of politicians and political institutions, on the one hand, and private social actors, on the other. The interaction between state and society — between national governments and the social forces they, variously, represent, rule, or ignore — is indeed another dividing line within the field of international political economy. In studying the politics of the world economy, questions continually arise about the relative importance of independent government action and institutions versus a variety of societal pressures on the policy-making process.

The role of the state is at the center of all political science; international political economy is no exception. Foreign economic policy is made, of course, by foreign economic policymakers; this much is trivial. But just as scholars debate the relative importance of overseas and domestic determinants of foreign economic policies, so, too, they disagree over whether policymakers represent a logic of their own or instead reflect domestic socioeconomic interest groups or classes. According to one view, the state is relatively insulated or autonomous from the multitude of social, political, and economic pressures that emanate from society. The most that pluralistic interest groups can produce is a confused cacophony of complaints and demands; coherent national policy comes from the conscious actions of national leaders and those who occupy positions of political power and from the institutions in which they operate. The state, in this view, molds society, and foreign economic policy is one part of this larger mold.

The opposing school of thought asserts that policymakers are little more than the transmitters of underlying societal demands. At best, the political system can organize and regularize these demands, but the state is essentially a tool in the hands of socioeconomic and political interests. Foreign economic policy, like other state actions, evolves in response to social demands; it is society that molds the state, and not the other way around.

We can illustrate the difference in focus with the previously discussed example of trade policy in North America and Western Europe before and after World War II. Many of those who look first and foremost at state actors would emphasize the dramatic change in the overall foreign policy of these governments after World War II, starting with the Atlantic Alliance, which was formed to meet the demands of European reconstruction, and the Cold War, which required that the American market be opened to foreign goods in order to stimulate the economies of the country's allies. Eventually, the European Union arose as a further effort to cement the Atlantic Alliance and bolster it against the Soviet Union.

According to this view, trade liberalization arose out of national security concerns, as understood and articulated by a very small number of individuals in the American and Western European governments, who then went about "selling" the policies to their publics. Alternatively, it might be argued that the traumas of the Great Depression taught the managers of nation-states that a descent into protectionism could lead to intolerable social tensions. In this context, political leaders may have developed a strong belief in the desirability of trade relations that are generally open. In this view of the world, explanatory precedence goes to the opinions, beliefs, and desires of national political leaders — in short, to the state.

Other scholars, for whom society is determinant, emphasize the major socioeconomic and political changes that had been gaining force within the industrial capitalist nations after World War I. Corporations became more international, and thus came to fear overseas competition less. For important groups, trade protection was counterproductive because it limited access to the rest of the world economy; on the other hand, freer trade and investment opened broad and profitable new horizons for major economic actors in North America and Western Europe.

By the same token, socioeconomic trends at a global level were also pushing toward international trade liberalization. The rise of internationally integrated financial markets and global corporations, for example, created private interests that oppose interference with the free movement of goods and capital across national borders. This new group of social forces has, in the opinion of some analysts (see, for example, Strange, Reading 4), fundamentally transformed the very nature of economic policy making in all nations.

When combined, these two dimensions give rise to four different perspectives in international political economy. An *international political* view emphasizes the constraints imposed on national states by the global geostrategic and diplomatic environment within which they operate. It focuses on the inherent conflict among states in a hostile world, within which cooperation, although often desirable and feasible, can be difficult to achieve.

The *international economic* perspective similarly emphasizes the importance of constraints external to individual nations, but it highlights global socioeconomic factors rather than political ones. Accordingly, international developments in technology, telecommunications, finance, and production fundamentally affect the setting within which national governments make policy. Indeed, these developments can matter to the point of making some choices practically impossible to implement and others so attractive as to be impossible to resist.

Domestic approaches look inside nation-states for explanations of the international political economy. The *domestic institutional* view turns its attention to states, as does the international political perspective, but it emphasizes the role and institutions of the state in a domestic setting rather than in the global system. This view, which at times is called simply *institutionalism,* tends to downplay the impact of constraints emanating both from the international system and from domestic societies. National policymakers, and the political institutions within which they operate, are thus seen as the predominant actors in determining national priorities and implementing policies to carry out these goals. Some variants of institutionalism emphasize the autonomy of states from societal actors, while others focus on how state institutions mediate and alter social forces.

The *domestic societal* perspective shares with domestic institutionalism an emphasis on developments within national borders but looks first and foremost at economic and sociopolitical actors rather than political leaders. This view, which at times is known simply as *societal,* tends to minimize international constraints and to emphasize socioeconomic pressures that originate at home. Accordingly, the determinants of national policy are the demands made by individuals, firms, and groups rather than independent action by policymakers.

The contending perspectives can once again be illustrated by recalling their approaches to the example of trade policy tendencies. International political interpretations would rely on geopolitical trends among states at the global level to explain changing patterns of trade relations. An international economic view would emphasize trends in market forces, technologies, and the like that alter the environment in which governments make trade policy. The domestic institutional approach focuses on the goals and actions of the government within the national political system, for which foreign trade can represent ways to help politicians stay in power. Finally, a domestic societal perspective looks primarily at the pressures brought to bear on policy by various socioeconomic groups, some desirous of trade liberalization and others interested in protection from imports.

It should be noted that these simplistic categories hardly describe the nuance and complexity of actual theoretical approaches; all scholars recognize that the foreign economic policies of all countries are constrained by both international and domestic — and by both political and economic — factors. It may indeed be the case that one set of forces matters more or less in some issue areas rather than others, in some times rather than others, and in some countries rather than others. In particular, international geopolitical concerns will presumably have more impact on a small, weak country surrounded by enemies than a large, powerful nation far from any threat. Similarly, domestic concerns, whether institutional or societal, may have more effect on policy in times of great social and political conflict than in less turbulent times.

Nonetheless, analysts of the international political economy do differ in their interpretations. Rather than being absolute, the disagreements concern relative weights to be assigned to each set of causes. Some scholars assign primacy to social forces, others to autonomous state action; some to global factors, others to domestic ones.

These perspectives can lead to widely different explanations of specific events and general processes within the international political economy. Their differences have generated numerous debates in the field, many of which are contained in the readings in this volume.

THREE ALTERNATIVE VIEWS OF
INTERNATIONAL POLITICAL ECONOMY

In addition to the perspectives already mentioned, some scholars attempt to classify interpretations of global political and economic developments in a somewhat different manner. Many theories of international political economy can also be categorized into one of three perspectives: Liberalism, Marxism, and Realism.

Note that in international political economy, advocates of free trade and free markets are still referred to as Liberals. In twentieth-century American domestic politics, on the other hand, the term has come to mean something different. In the United States today, whereas "conservatives" generally support free markets and less government intervention, "liberals" advocate greater governmental intervention in the market to stimulate growth and mitigate inequalities. These contradictory usages of the term *Liberal* may seem confusing, but the context will usually make an author's meaning clear.

The Liberal argument emphasizes how both the market and politics are environments in which all parties can benefit by entering into voluntary exchanges with others. If there are no impediments to trade among individuals, Liberals reason, everyone can be made as well off as possible, given the existing stocks of goods and services. All participants in the market, in other words, will be at their highest possible level of utility. Neoclassical economists, who are generally Liberals, believe firmly in the superiority of the market as a mechanism for allocating scarce resources.

Liberals therefore reason that the economic role of government should be quite limited. Many forms of government intervention in the economy, they argue, intentionally or unintentionally restrict the market and thereby prevent potentially rewarding trades from occurring.

Liberals do generally support the provision by government of certain "public goods" — goods and services that benefit society and that would not be provided by private markets.[1] The government, for example, plays an important role in supplying the conditions necessary for the maintenance of a free and competitive market. Governments must provide for the defense of the country, protect property rights, and prevent any unfair collusion or concentration of power within the market. The government should also, according to most Liberals, educate its citizens, build infrastructure, and provide and regulate a common currency. The proper role of government, in other words, is to provide the necessary foundation for the market.

At the level of the international economy, Liberals assert that a fundamental harmony of interests exists between, as well as within, countries. They argue that all countries are best off when goods and services move freely across national borders in mutually rewarding exchanges. If universal free trade were to exist, all countries would enjoy the highest level of utility and there would be no economic basis for international conflict or war. Liberals also believe that governments should manage the international economy in much the same way as they manage their domestic economies. They should establish rules and regulations, often referred to as "international regimes," to govern exchanges between different national currencies and ensure that no country or domestic group is damaged by "unfair" international competition.

Marxism originated with the writings of Karl Marx, a nineteenth-century political economist and perhaps the severest critic of capitalism and its Liberal supporters. Marx saw capitalism and the market as creating extremes of wealth for capitalists and poverty for workers. While the entire populace may have been better off than before, the capitalists were clearly expanding their wealth more rapidly than everyone else. Marx rejected the assertion that exchange between individuals necessarily maximizes the welfare of the whole society. Accordingly, he perceived capitalism as an inherently conflictual system that both should, and will, be inevitably overthrown and replaced by socialism.

Marxists believe that classes are the dominant actors in the political economy. Specifically, they identify as central two economically determined aggregations of individuals, or classes: capital, or the owners of the means of production, and labor, or the workers. Marxists assume that classes act in their economic interests, that is, to maximize the economic well-being of the class as a whole. Accordingly, the basis of the capitalist economy is the exploitation of labor by capital: capitalism, by its very nature, denies labor the full return for its efforts.

Marxists see the political economy as necessarily conflictual, since the relationship between capitalists and workers is essentially antagonistic. Because the means of production are controlled by a minority within society — the capitalists — labor does not receive its full return; conflict between the classes is inevitably caused by this exploitation. Marxists also believe that capitalism is inherently prone to periodic economic crises, which will, they believe, ultimately lead to the overthrow of capitalism by labor and the erection of a socialist society in which the means of production will be owned jointly by all members of society and exploitation will cease.

V. I. Lenin, the Russian revolutionary who founded the Soviet Union, extended Marx's ideas to the international political economy to explain imperialism and war. Imperialism, Lenin argued, was endemic to modern capitalism. As capitalism decayed in the most developed nations, capitalists would attempt to solve their problems by exporting capital abroad. As this capital required protection from both local and foreign challengers, governments would colonize regions to safeguard the interests of their foreign investors. Eventually, capitalist countries would compete for control over these areas and intracapitalist wars would follow.

Today, Marxists who study the international political economy are primarily concerned with two issues. The first is the fate of labor in a world of increasingly internationalized capital. The growth of multinational corporations and the rise of globally integrated financial markets appear to have weakened labor's economic and political power. If workers in a particular country demand higher wages or improved health and safety measures, for example, the multinational capitalist can simply shift production to another country where labor is more compliant. As a result, many Marxists fear that labor's ability to negotiate with capital for a more equitable division of wealth has been significantly undermined.

Second, Marxists are concerned with the poverty and continued underdevelopment of the Third World. Some Marxists argue that development is blocked by domestic ruling classes, which pursue their own, narrow interests at the expense of national economic progress. Others, known as "dependency" theorists, extend class analysis to the level of the international economy. According to these Marxists, the global system is stratified into a wealthy area (the "core," or First World) and a region of oppression and poverty (the "periphery," or Third World). International capitalism, in this view, exploits the periphery and benefits the core, just as capitalists exploit workers within a single country. The principal questions here focus on the mechanisms of exploitation — whether they be multinational corporations, international financial markets and organizations, or trade — and the appropriate strategies for stimulating autonomous growth and development in the periphery.

Realism traces its intellectual roots back to Thucydides' writings in 400 B.C.E., as well as those of Niccoló Machiavelli, Thomas Hobbes, and the Mercantilists Jean-Baptiste Colbert and Friedrich List. Realists believe that nation-states pursue power and shape the economy to this end. Moreover, they are the dominant actors within the international political economy. According to Realists, the international system is anarchical, a condition under which nation-states are sovereign, the sole judges of their own behaviors, and subject to no higher authority. If no authority is higher than the nation-state, Realists believe, then all actors must be subordinate to it. While private citizens can interact with their counterparts in other countries, Realists assert that the basis for this interaction is legislated by the nation-state. Thus, where Liberals focus on individuals and Marxists on classes, Realists concentrate on nation-states.

Realists also argue that nation-states are fundamentally concerned about international power relations. Because the international system is based on anarchy, the use of force or coercion by other nation-states is always a possibility and no higher authority is obligated to come to the aid of a nation-state under attack. Nation-states are thus ultimately dependent on their own resources for protection. For Realists, then, each nation-state must always be prepared to defend itself to the best of its ability. For Realists, politics is largely a zero-sum game and by necessity conflictual. In other words, if one nation-state is to win, another must lose.

Realists also believe that nation-states can be thought of as rational actors in the same sense that other theorists assume individuals to be rational. Nation-states are assumed to operate according to cost-benefit analyses and choose the option that yields the greatest value, especially regarding the nation's international geopolitical and power positions.

It is the emphasis on power that gives Realism its distinctive approach to international political economy. While economic considerations may often complement power concerns, the former are, in the Realist view, subordinate to the latter. Realists allow for circumstances in which nation-states sacrifice economic gain to weaken their opponents or strengthen themselves in military or diplomatic terms. Thus, trade protection, which might reduce a country's overall income by restricting the market, may nonetheless be adopted for reasons of national political power.

Realist political economy is primarily concerned with how changes in the distribution of international power affect the form and type of international economy. The best known Realist approach to this question is the *theory of hegemonic stability,* which holds that an open international economy — that is, one characterized by the free exchange of goods, capital, and services — is most likely to exist when a single dominant or hegemonic power is present to stabilize the system and construct a strong regime (see Krasner, Reading 1, and Lake, Reading 8). For Realists, then, the pursuit of power by nation-states shapes the international economy.

Each of these three perspectives features different assumptions and assertions. Liberals assume that individuals are the proper unit of analysis, while Marxists and Realists make similar assumptions for classes and nation-states, respectively. The three perspectives also differ on the inevitability of conflict within the political economy. Liberals believe economics and politics are largely autonomous spheres, Marxists maintain that economics determines politics, and Realists argue that politics determines economics.

This tripartite division of international political economy is useful in many ways, especially as it highlights differing evaluations of the importance of economic efficiency, class conflict, and geostrategic considerations. However, the lines between the three views are easily blurred. Some Marxists agree with the Realist focus on interstate conflict; others, with the Liberal emphasis on economic interests. Likewise, there are many Liberals who use neoclassical tools to analyze interstate strategic interaction in much the same way Realists do or to investigate the clash of classes as do the Marxists. Such substantial overlap, in our view, helps clarify the two-dimensional categorization outlined here. We also believe that these two dimensions — international–domestic and state–society — most accurately characterize analytical differences among scholars and observers of the international political economy.

THE CONTEMPORARY INTERNATIONAL POLITICAL ECONOMY: AN OVERVIEW

Following initial sections on theoretical perspectives and historical background, the remainder of this book of readings concerns the politics of international economic relations since World War II. Developments since 1945 have, indeed, raised a wide variety of theoretical, practical, and policy issues.

The contemporary international political economy is characterized by unprecedented levels of multinational production, cross-border financial flows, and international trade. It is also plagued by increasing political conflict as individuals, groups, classes, and countries clash over the meaning and implications of these economic transactions. The contradiction between increasing economic integration and the wealth it produces, on the one hand, and the desire for political control and national autonomy, on the other, defines much of what happens in the global political economy.

For the first thirty years after World War II, the general pattern of relations among noncommunist nations was set by American leadership, and this pattern continues to influence the international political economy today. In the political arena, formal and informal alliances tied virtually every major noncommunist nation into an American-led network of mutual support and defense. In the economic arena, a wide-ranging set of international economic organizations — including the International Monetary Fund (IMF), the General Agreement on Tariffs and Trade (GATT), and the International Bank for Reconstruction and Development (World Bank) — grew up under a protective American "umbrella," and often as a direct American initiative. The world economy itself was heavily influenced by the rise of modern multinational corporations and banks, whose contemporary form is largely of U.S. origin.

American plans for a reordered world economy go back to the mid-1930s. After World War I, the United States retreated into relative economic insularity, for reasons explored in Part II, "Historical Perspectives." When the Great Depression hit, American political leaders virtually ignored the possibility of international economic cooperation in their attempts to stabilize the domestic economy. Yet even as the Franklin Roosevelt administration looked inward for recovery, by 1934 new American initiatives were signaling a shift in America's traditional isolation. Roosevelt's secretary of state, Cordell Hull, was a militant free trader, and in 1934 he convinced Congress to pass the Reciprocal Trade Agreements Act, which allowed the executive to negotiate tariff reductions with foreign nations. This important step toward trade liberalization and international economic cooperation was deepened as war threatened in Europe and the United States drew closer to Great Britain and France.

The seeds of the new international order, which had been planted in the 1930s, began to grow even as World War II came to an end. The Bretton Woods agreement, reached among the Allied powers in 1944, established a new series of international economic organizations that became the foundation for the postwar American-led system. As the wartime American–Soviet alliance began to shatter, a new economic order emerged in the noncommunist world. At its center were the three pillars of the Bretton Woods system: international monetary cooperation under the auspices of the IMF, international trade liberalization negotiated within the GATT, and investment in the developing countries stimulated by the World Bank. All three pillars were essentially designed by the United States and dependent on its support.

As it developed, the postwar capitalist world reflected American foreign policy in many of its details. One principal concern of the United States was to build a bulwark of anti-Soviet allies; this was done with a massive inflow of American aid under the Marshall Plan and the encouragement of Western European cooperation within a new Common Market. At the same time, the United States dramatically lowered its barriers to foreign goods and American corporations began to invest heavily in foreign nations. Of course, the United States was not acting altruistically: European recovery, trade liberalization, and booming international investment helped ensure great prosperity within its own borders as well.

American policies, whatever their motivation, had an undeniable impact on the international political economy. Trade liberalization opened the huge American market to foreign producers. American overseas investment provided capital, technology, and expertise for both Europe and the developing world. American governmental economic aid, whether direct or channeled through such institutions as the World Bank, helped finance economic growth abroad. In addition, the American military umbrella allowed anti-Soviet governments in Europe, Japan, and the developing world to rely on the United States for security and to turn their attentions to encouraging economic growth.

All in all, the noncommunist world's unprecedented access to American markets and American capital provided a major stimulus to world economic growth, not to mention to the profits of American businesses and general prosperity within the United States. For over twenty-five years after World War II, the capitalist world experienced impressive levels of economic growth and development, all within a general context of international cooperation under American political, economic, and military tutelage.

This period is often referred to as the *Pax Americana* because of its broad similarity to the British-led international economic system that operated from about 1820 until World War I, which was known as the Pax Britannica. In both instances, general political and economic peace prevailed under the leadership of an overwhelming world power — the United Kingdom in one case, the United States in the other. There were, nonetheless, major differences between the two eras (see Lake, Reading 8).

Just as the Pax Britannica eventually ended, however, the Pax Americana gradually eroded. By the early 1970s, strains were developing in the postwar system. Between 1971 and 1975, the postwar international monetary system, which had been based on a gold-backed U.S. dollar, fell apart and was replaced by a new, improvised pattern of floating exchange rates in which the dollar's role was still strong but no longer quite so central. At the same time, pressures for trade protection from uncompetitive industries in North America and Western Europe began to mount; and, although tariff levels remained low, a variety of nontariff barriers to world trade, such as import quotas, soon proliferated. In the political arena, détente between the United States and the Soviet Union seemed to make the American security umbrella less relevant for the Japanese and Western Europeans; in the less developed countries, North–South conflict appeared more important than East–West strife. In short, during the 1970s, as American economic strength declined, the Bretton Woods institutions weakened, and the Cold War thawed, the Pax Americana drew to a close.

The quickening pace of change in the Soviet Union and its allies eventually culminated in the collapse of former Soviet bloc nations in the late 1980s and early 1990s, and ultimately in the disintegration of the former Soviet Union. The end of the Cold War did not, of course, mean an end to international conflict, but it did put an end to the East–West divide that had dominated global politics for so long. To some extent, some of the former centrally planned economies, especially in Central Europe, moved successfully into the ranks of the developed nations, albeit as relatively poor ones. Others, however, became most similar to the developing nations as they struggled to overcome poverty and privation. Russia, although it shares many typical Third World problems, is unique in its mix of underdevelopment, size, and military might.

Within a rapidly changing environment, the United States remains the most important country within the contemporary international political economy, but it is no longer dominant. The era of American hegemony has been replaced by a new, multilateral order based on the joint leadership of Western Europe, Japan, and the United States. Together, these countries have successfully managed — or, some would say, muddled through — the "oil shocks" of the 1970s, the debt crisis of the early 1980s, the transition to the market of the former centrally planned economies after 1989, and the currency and other financial volatility of the 1990s.

Despite greater success than many thought possible, multilateral leadership and the liberal international order remain fragile. Conflicts of interest and economic tensions remain muted, but they could erupt at any time.

As might be expected, the rise and decline of the Pax Americana and the emergence of the new, multilateral order, along with the end of the Cold War, have led to great scholarly controversy. For some analysts, America's global dominance and the East–West divide were the principal determinants of Western interests and policies and, in turn, of the liberal international economy. In this view, the decline of the United States in a post–Cold War world presages the eventual collapse of international openness. For other observers, the policies of the United States and other countries were affected in more important ways by domestic economic and political pressures; from this perspective, the decline of American hegemony is expected to have little effect on international openness. For still others, the consequences of the liberal order have fundamentally altered the interests of the United States and other countries; the internationalization of production and finance and the rise of economic interdependence have created vested interests in favor of the free flow of goods, services, and capital across national borders.

The remainder of this book is devoted to understanding the contemporary international political economy and its likely future. In the sections that follow, a variety of thematic issues are addressed; in each cluster of issues, alternative theoretical and analytical perspectives compete. The selections in this reader serve both to provide information on broad trends in the politics of international economic relations and to give an overview of the contending approaches to be found within the discipline.

NOTE

1. More specifically, a public good is one that, in its purest form, is *nonrival in consumption* and *nonexcludable*. The first characteristic means that consumption of the good by one person does not reduce the opportunities for others to consume that good; for example, clean air can be breathed by one individual without reducing its availability to others. The second characteristic means that nobody can be prevented from consuming the good: Those who do not contribute to pollution control are still able to breathe clean air. These two conditions are fully met only rarely, but goods whose characteristics come close to meeting them are generally considered public goods.

I

CONTENDING
PERSPECTIVES ON
INTERNATIONAL
POLITICAL ECONOMY

As outlined in the Introduction, two principal theoretical dimensions can be used to organize debates within international political economy. The first addresses the relative importance of international and domestic variables in accounting for trends in the international political economy; the second, the significance of institutional and societal factors. Part I contains four selections, one representing each approach as applied to a specific issue. In a classic example of an international political approach, Stephen D. Krasner (Reading 1) examines patterns of trade openness within the international economy over the nineteenth and twentieth centuries. Barry Eichengreen (Reading 2) uses a domestic society–centered theory to account for the Smoot-Hawley Tariff, which contained some of the highest duties in history. Douglass C. North (Reading 3) emphasizes the effect of domestic institutions on economic growth. Finally, Susan Strange (Reading 4) explores how international economic factors have altered both the relationship between states and firms and the nature of diplomacy between countries. As exemplars of their respective approaches, these essays are intended only to illustrate basic themes and arguments; all four approaches contain a rich diversity of styles and conclusions, and the essays selected here are only a sample. Nonetheless, they serve to highlight key analytic debates and provide a useful empirical introduction to critical trends and cases in international political economy.

1

State Power and the Structure
of International Trade
STEPHEN D. KRASNER

In this essay, Stephen D. Krasner addresses the relationship between the interests and power of major states and the trade openness of the international economy. In this international political analysis, he identifies four principal goals of state action: political power, aggregate national income, economic growth, and social stability. He then combines the goals with different national abilities to pursue them, relating the international distribution of potential economic power to alternative trade regimes. Krasner maintains, most significantly, that the hegemony of a leading power is necessary for the creation and continuance of free trade. He applies his model to six periods. Krasner's analysis in this 1976 article is a well-known attempt to use international political theory, and Realism more generally, to explain international economic affairs. The theory he propounds, which has been dubbed the "theory of hegemonic stability," has influenced many subsequent analyses.

INTRODUCTION

In recent years, students of international relations have multinationalized, transnationalized, bureaucratized, and transgovernmentalized the state until it has virtually ceased to exist as an analytic construct. Nowhere is that trend more apparent than in the study of the politics of international economic relations. The basic conventional assumptions have been undermined by assertions that the state is trapped by a transnational society created not by sovereigns, but by nonstate actors. Interdependence is not seen as a reflection of state policies and state choices (the perspective of balance-of-power theory), but as the result of elements beyond the control of any state or a system created by states.

This perspective is at best profoundly misleading. It may explain developments within a particular international economic structure, but it cannot explain the structure itself. That structure has many institutional and behavioral manifestations. The central continuum along which it can be described is openness. International economic structures may range from complete autarky (if all states prevent movements across their borders), to complete openness (if no restrictions exist). In this paper I will present an analysis of one aspect of the international economy — the structure of international trade; that is, the degree of openness for the movement of goods as opposed to capital, labor, technology, or other factors of production. Since the beginning of the nineteenth century, this structure has gone through several changes. These can be explained, albeit imperfectly, by a state-power theory: an approach that begins with the assumption that the structure of international trade is determined by the interests and power of states acting to maximize national goals. The first step in this argument is to relate four basic state interests — aggregate national income, social stability, political power, and economic growth — to the degree of openness for the movement of goods. The relationship between these interests and openness depends upon the potential economic power of any given state. Potential economic power is operationalized in terms of the relative size and level of economic development of the state. The second step in the argument is to relate different distributions of potential power, such as multipolar and hegemonic, to different international trading structures. The most important conclusion of this theoretical analysis is that a hegemonic distribution of potential economic power is likely to result in an open trading structure. That argument is largely, although not completely, substantiated by empirical data. For a fully adequate analysis it is necessary to amend a state-power argument to take account of the impact of past state decisions on domestic social structures as well as on international economic ones. The two major organizers of the structure of trade since the beginning of the nineteenth century, Great Britain and the United States, have both been prevented from making policy amendments in line with state interests by particular societal groups whose power had been enhanced by earlier state policies.

THE CAUSAL ARGUMENT: STATE INTERESTS, STATE POWER, AND INTERNATIONAL TRADING STRUCTURES

Neoclassical trade theory is based upon the assumption that states act to maximize their aggregate economic utility. This leads to the conclusion that maximum global welfare and Pareto optimality are achieved under free trade. While particular countries might better their situations through protectionism, economic theory has generally looked askance at such policies. . . . Neoclassical theory recognizes that trade regulations can . . . be used to correct domestic distortions and to promote infant industries, but these are exceptions or temporary departures from policy conclusions that lead logically to the support of free trade.

State Preferences

Historical experience suggests that policy makers are dense, or that the assumptions of the conventional argument are wrong. Free trade has hardly been the norm. Stupidity is not a very interesting analytic category. An alternative approach to explaining international trading structures is to assume that states seek a broad range of goals. At least four major state interests affected by the structure of international trade can be identified. They are: political power, aggregate national income, economic growth, and social stability. The way in which each of these goals is affected by the degree of openness depends upon the potential economic power of the state as defined by its relative size and level of development.

Let us begin with aggregate national income because it is most straightforward. Given the exception noted above, conventional neoclassical theory demonstrates that the greater the degree of openness in the international trading system, the greater the level of aggregate economic income. This conclusion applies to all states regardless of their size or relative level of development. The static economic benefits of openness are, however, generally inversely related to size. Trade gives small states relatively more welfare benefits than it gives large ones. Empirically, small states have higher ratios of trade to national product. They do not have the generous factor endowments or potential for national economies of scale that are enjoyed by larger — particularly continental — states.

The impact of openness on social stability runs in the opposite direction. Greater openness exposes the domestic economy to the exigencies of the world market. That implies a higher level of factor movements than in a closed economy, because domestic production patterns must adjust to changes in international prices. Social instability is thereby increased, since there is friction in moving factors, particularly labor, from one sector to another. The impact will be stronger in small states than in large, and in relatively less developed than in more developed ones. Large states are less involved in the international economy: a smaller percentage of their total factor endowment is affected by the international market at any given level of openness. More developed states are better able to adjust factors: skilled workers can more easily be moved from one kind of production to another than can unskilled laborers or peasants. Hence social stability is, *ceteris paribus*, inversely related to openness, but the deleterious consequences of exposure to the international trading system are mitigated by larger size and greater economic development.

The relationship between political power and the international trading structure can be analyzed in terms of the relative opportunity costs of closure for trading partners. The higher the relative cost of closure, the weaker the political position of the state. Hirschman has argued that this cost can be measured in terms of direct income losses and the adjustment costs of reallocating factors. These will be smaller for large states and for relatively more developed states. Other things being equal, utility costs will be less for large states because they generally have a smaller proportion of their economy engaged in the international economic system. Reallocation costs will be less for more advanced states because their factors are more mobile. Hence a state that is relatively large and more developed will find its political power enhanced by an open system because its opportunity costs of closure are less. The large state can use the threat to alter the system to secure economic or noneconomic objectives. Historically, there is one important exception to this generalization — the oil-exporting states. The level of reserves for some of the states, particularly Saudi Arabia, has reduced the economic opportunity costs of closure to a very low level despite their lack of development.

The relationship between international economic structure and economic growth is elusive. For small states, economic growth has generally been empirically associated with openness. Exposure to the international system makes possible a much more efficient allocation of resources. Openness also probably furthers the rate of growth of large countries with relatively advanced technologies because they do not need to protect infant industries and can take advantage of expanded world markets. In the long term, however, openness for capital and technology, as well as goods, may hamper the growth of large, developed countries by diverting resources from the domestic economy and by providing potential competitors with the knowledge needed to develop their own industries. Only by maintaining its technological lead and continually developing new industries can even a very large state escape the undesired consequences of an entirely open economic system. For medium-size states, the relationship between international trading structure and growth is impossible to specify definitively, either theoretically or empirically. On the one hand, writers from the mercantilists through the American protectionists and the German historical school, and more recently analysts of *dependencia,* have argued that an entirely open system can undermine a state's effort to develop, and even lead to underdevelopment. On the other hand, adherents of more conventional neoclassical positions have maintained that exposure to international competition spurs economic transformation. The evidence is not yet in. All that can confidently be said is that openness furthers the economic growth of small states and of large ones so long as they maintain their technological edge.

From State Preferences to International Trading Structures

The next step in this argument is to relate particular distributions of potential economic power, defined by the size and level of development of individual states, to the structure of the international trading system, defined in terms of openness.

Let us consider a system composed of a large number of small, highly developed states. Such a system is likely to lead to an open international trading structure. The aggregate income and economic growth of each state are increased by an open system. The social instability produced by exposure to international competition is mitigated by the factor mobility made possible by higher levels of development. There is no loss of political power from openness because the costs of closure are symmetrical for all members of the system.

Now let us consider a system composed of a few very large, but unequally developed states. Such a distribution of potential economic power is likely to lead to a closed structure. Each state could increase its income through a more open system, but the gains would be modest. Openness would create more social instability in the less developed countries. The rate of growth for more backward areas might be frustrated, while that of the more advanced ones would be enhanced. A more open structure would leave the less developed states in a politically more vulnerable position, because their greater factor rigidity would mean a higher relative cost of closure. Because of these disadvantages, large but relatively less developed states are unlikely to accept an open trading structure. More advanced states cannot, unless they are militarily more powerful, force large backward countries to accept openness.

Finally, let us consider a hegemonic system — one in which there is a single state that is much larger and relatively more advanced than its trading partners. The costs and benefits of openness are not symmetrical for all members of the system. The hegemonic state will have a preference for an open structure. Such a structure increases its aggregate national income. It also increases its rate of growth during its ascendancy — that is, when its relative size and technological lead are increasing. Further, an open structure increases its political power, since the opportunity costs of closure are least for a large and developed state. The social instability resulting from exposure to the international system is mitigated by the hegemonic power's relatively low level of involvement in the international economy and the mobility of its factors.

What of the other members of a hegemonic system? Small states are likely to opt for openness because the advantages in terms of aggregate income and growth are so great, and their political power is bound to be restricted regardless of what they do. The reaction of medium-size states is hard to predict; it depends at least in part on the way in which the hegemonic power utilizes its resources. The potentially dominant state has symbolic, economic, and military capabilities that can be used to entice or compel others to accept an open trading structure.

At the symbolic level, the hegemonic state stands as an example of how economic development can be achieved. Its policies may be emulated, even if they are inappropriate for other states. Where there are very dramatic asymmetries, military power can be used to coerce weaker states into an open structure. Force is not, however, a very efficient means for changing economic policies and it is unlikely to be employed against medium-size states.

Most importantly, the hegemonic state can use its economic resources to create an open structure. In terms of positive incentives, it can offer access to its large domestic market and to its relatively cheap exports. In terms of negative ones, it can withhold foreign grants and engage in competition potentially ruinous for the weaker state in third-country markets. The size and economic robustness of the hegemonic state also enable it to provide the confidence necessary for a stable international monetary system, and its currency can offer the liquidity needed for an increasingly open system.

In sum, openness is most likely to occur during periods when a hegemonic state is in its ascendancy. Such a state has the interest and the resources to create a structure characterized by lower tariffs, rising trade proportions, and less regionalism. There are other distributions of potential power where openness is likely, such as a system composed of many small, highly developed states. But even here, that potential might not be realized because of the problems of creating confidence in a monetary system where adequate liquidity would have to be provided by a negotiated international reserve asset or a group of national currencies. Finally, it is unlikely that very large states, particularly at unequal levels of development, would accept open trading relations.

**CHART 1. Probability of an Open Trading Structure
with Different Distributions of Potential Economic Power**

Level of Development of States	Size of States		
	Relatively Equal		Very Unequal
	Small	Large	
Equal	Moderate–High	Low–Moderate	High
Unequal	Moderate	Low	Moderate–High

These arguments, and the implications of other ideal typical configurations of potential economic power for the openness of trading structures, are summarized in [Chart 1].

THE DEPENDENT VARIABLE: DESCRIBING THE STRUCTURE OF THE INTERNATIONAL TRADING SYSTEM

The structure of international trade has both behavioral and institutional attributes. The degree of openness can be described both by the flow of goods and by the *policies* that are followed by states with respect to trade barriers and international payments. The two are not unrelated, but they do not coincide perfectly.

In common usage, the focus of attention has been upon institutions. Openness is associated with those historical periods in which tariffs were substantially lowered: the third quarter of the nineteenth century and the period since the Second World War.

Tariffs alone, however, are not an adequate indicator of structure. They are hard to operationalize quantitatively. Tariffs do not have to be high to be effective. If cost functions are nearly identical, even low tariffs can prevent trade. Effective tariff rates may be much higher than nominal ones. Nontariff barriers to trade, which are not easily compared across states, can substitute for duties. An undervalued exchange rate can protect domestic markets from foreign competition. Tariff levels alone cannot describe the structure of international trade.

A second indicator, and one which is behavioral rather than institutional, is trade proportions — the ratios of trade to national income for different states. Like tariff levels, these involve describing the system in terms of an agglomeration of national tendencies. A period in which these ratios are increasing across time for most states can be described as one of increasing openness.

A third indicator is the concentration of trade within regions composed of states at different levels of development. The degree of such regional encapsulation is determined not so much by comparative advantage (because relative factor endowments would allow almost any backward area to trade with almost any developed one), but by political choices or dictates. Large states, attempting to protect themselves from the vagaries of a global system, seek to maximize their interests by creating regional blocs. Openness in the global economic system has in effect meant greater trade among the leading industrial states. Periods of closure are associated with the encapsulation of certain advanced states within regional systems shared with certain less developed areas.

A description of the international trading system involves, then, an exercise that is comparative rather than absolute. A period when tariffs are falling, trade proportions are rising, and regional trading patterns are becoming less extreme will be defined as one in which the structure is becoming more open.

Tariff Levels

The period from the 1820's to 1879 was basically one of decreasing tariff levels in Europe. The trend began in Great Britain in the 1820's, with reductions of duties and other barriers to trade. In 1846 the abolition of the Corn Laws ended agricultural protectionism. France reduced duties on some intermediate goods in the 1830's, and on coal, iron, and steel in 1852. The *Zollverein* established fairly low tariffs in 1834. Belgium, Portugal, Spain, Piedmont, Norway, Switzerland, and Sweden lowered imposts in the 1850's. The golden age of free trade began in 1860, when Britain and France signed the Cobden-Chevalier Treaty, which virtually eliminated trade barriers. This was followed by a series of bilateral trade agreements between virtually all European states. It is important to note, however, that the United States took little part in the general movement toward lower trade barriers.

The movement toward greater liberality was reversed in the late 1870's. Austria-Hungary increased duties in 1876 and 1878, and Italy also in 1878; but the main breach came in Germany in 1879. France increased tariffs modestly in 1881, sharply in 1892, and raised them still further in 1910. Other countries followed a similar pattern. Only Great Britain, Belgium, the Netherlands, and Switzerland continued to follow free-trade policies through the 1880's. Although Britain did not herself impose duties, she began establishing a system of preferential markets in her overseas Empire in 1898. The United States was basically protectionist throughout the nineteenth century. The high tariffs imposed during the Civil War continued with the exception of a brief period in the 1890's. There were no major duty reductions before 1914.

During the 1920's tariff levels increased further. Western European states protected their agrarian sectors against imports from the Danube region, Australia, Canada, and the United States, where the war had stimulated increased output. Great Britain adopted some colonial preferences in 1919, imposed a small number of tariffs in 1921, and extended some wartime duties. The successor states of the Austro-Hungarian Empire imposed duties to achieve some national self-sufficiency. The British dominions and Latin America protected industries nurtured by wartime demands. In the United States the Fordney-McCumber Tariff Act of 1922 increased protectionism. The October Revolution removed Russia from the Western trading system.

Dramatic closure in terms of tariff levels began with the passage of the Smoot-Hawley Tariff Act in the United States in 1930. Britain raised tariffs in 1931 and definitively abandoned free trade at the Ottawa Conference of 1932, which introduced extensive imperial preferences. Germany and Japan established trading blocs within their own spheres of influence. All other major countries followed protectionist policies.

Significant reductions in protection began after the Second World War; the United States had foreshadowed the movement toward greater liberality with the passage of the Reciprocal Trade Agreements Act in 1934. Since 1945 there have been seven rounds of multilateral tariff reductions. The first, held in 1947 at Geneva, and the Kennedy Round, held during the 1960's, have been the most significant. They have substantially reduced the level of protection.

The present situation is ambiguous. There have recently been some new trade controls. In the United States these include a voluntary import agreement for steel, the imposition of a 10 per cent import surcharge during four months of 1971, and export controls on agricultural products in 1973 and 1974. Italy imposed a deposit requirement on imports during parts of 1974 and 1975. Britain and Japan have engaged in export subsidization. Nontariff barriers have become more important. On balance, there has been movement toward greater protectionism since the end of the Kennedy Round, but it is not decisive. The outcome of the multilateral negotiations that began in 1975 remains to be seen.

In sum, after 1820 there was a general trend toward lower tariffs (with the notable exception of the United States), which culminated between 1860 and 1879; higher tariffs from 1879 through the interwar years, with dramatic increases in the 1930's; and less protectionism from 1945 through the conclusion of the Kennedy Round in 1967.

Trade Proportions

With the exception of one period, ratios of trade to aggregate economic activity followed the same general pattern as tariff levels. Trade proportions increased from the early part of the nineteenth century to about 1880. Between 1880 and 1900 there was a decrease, sharper if measured in current prices than constant ones, but apparent in both statistical series for most countries. Between 1900 and 1913 — and here is the exception from the tariff pattern — there was a marked increase in the ratio of trade to aggregate economic activity. This trend brought trade proportions to levels that have generally not been reattained. During the 1920's and 1930's the importance of trade in national economic activity declined. After the Second World War it increased.

. . . There are considerable differences in the movement of trade proportions among states. They hold more or less constant for the United States; Japan, Denmark, and Norway . . . are unaffected by the general decrease in the ratio of trade to aggregate economic activity that takes place after 1880. The pattern described in the previous paragraph does, however, hold for Great Britain, France, Sweden, Germany, and Italy.

. . . Because of the boom in commodity prices that occurred in the early 1950's, the ratio of trade to gross domestic product was relatively high for larger states during these years, at least in current prices. It then faltered or remained constant until about 1960. From the early 1960's through 1972, trade proportions rose for all major states except Japan. Data for 1973 and 1974 show further increases. For smaller countries the trend was more erratic, with Belgium showing a more or less steady increase, Norway vacillating between 82 and 90 per cent, and Denmark and the Netherlands showing higher figures for the late 1950's than for more recent years. There is then, in current prices, a generally upward trend in trade proportions since 1960, particularly for larger states. The movement is more pronounced if constant prices are used.

Regional Trading Patterns

The final indicator of the degree of openness of the global trading system is regional bloc concentration. There is a natural affinity for some states to trade with others because of geographical propinquity or comparative advantage. In general, however, a system in which there are fewer manifestations of trading within given blocs, particularly among specific groups of more and less developed states, is a more open one. Over time there have been extensive changes in trading patterns between particular areas of the world whose relative factor endowments have remained largely the same.

Richard Chadwick and Karl Deutsch have collected extensive information on international trading patterns since 1890. Their basic datum is the relative acceptance indicator (RA), which measures deviations from a null hypothesis in which trade between a pair of states, or a state and a region, is precisely what would be predicted on the basis of their total share of international trade. When the null hypothesis holds, the RA indicator is equal to zero. Values less than zero indicate less trade than expected; greater than zero more trade than expected. For our purposes the critical issue is whether, over time, trade tends to become more concentrated as shown by movements away from zero, or less as shown by movements toward zero. . . .

There is a general pattern. In three of the four cases, the RA value closest to zero — that is the least regional encapsulation — occurred in 1890, 1913, or 1928; in the fourth case (France and French West Africa), the 1928 value was not bettered until 1964. In every case there was an increase in the RA indicator between 1928 and 1938, reflecting the breakdown of international commerce that is associated with the Depression. Surprisingly, the RA indicator was higher for each of the four pairs in 1954 and in 1938, an indication that regional patterns persisted and even became more intense in the postwar period. With the exception of the Soviet Union and Eastern Europe, there was a general trend toward decreasing RA's for the period after 1954. They still, however, show fairly high values even in the late 1960's.

If we put all three indicators — tariff levels, trade proportions, and trade patterns — together, they suggest the following periodization.

Period I (1820–1879): Increasing openness — tariffs are generally lowered; trade proportions increase. Data are not available for trade patterns. However, it is important to note that this is not a universal pattern. The United States is largely unaffected; its tariff levels remain high (and are in fact increased during the early 1860's) and American trade proportions remain almost constant.

Period II (1879–1900): Modest closure — tariffs are increased; trade proportions decline modestly for most states. Data are not available for trade patterns.

Period III (1900–1913): Greater openness — tariff levels remain generally unchanged; trade proportions increase for all major trading states except the United States. Trading patterns become less regional in three out of the four cases for which data are available.

Period IV (1918–1939): Closure — tariff levels are increased in the 1920's and again in the 1930's; trade proportions decline. Trade becomes more regionally encapsulated.

Period V (1945–c. 1970): Great openness — tariffs are lowered; trade proportions increase, particularly after 1960. Regional concentration decreases after 1960. However, these developments are limited to non-Communist areas of the world.

THE INDEPENDENT VARIABLE: DESCRIBING THE DISTRIBUTION OF POTENTIAL ECONOMIC POWER AMONG STATES

Analysts of international relations have an almost pro forma set of variables designed to show the distribution of potential power in the international *political* system. It includes such factors as gross national product, per capita income, geographical position, and size of armed forces. A similar set of indicators can be presented for the international economic system.

Statistics are available over a long time period for per capita income, aggregate size, share of world trade, and share of world investment. They demonstrate that, since the beginning of the nineteenth century, there have been two first-rank economic powers in the world economy — Britain and the United States. The United States passed Britain in aggregate size sometime in the middle of the nineteenth century and, in the 1880's, became the largest producer of manufactures. America's lead was particularly marked in technologically advanced industries turning out sewing machines, harvesters, cash registers, locomotives, steam pumps, telephones, and petroleum. Until the First World War, however, Great Britain had a higher per capita income, a greater share of world trade, and a greater share of world investment than any other state. The peak of British ascendance occurred around 1880, when Britain's relative per capita income, share of world trade, and share of investment flows reached their highest levels. Britain's potential dominance in 1880 and 1900 was particularly striking in the international economic system, where her share of trade and foreign investment was about twice as large as that of any other state.

It was only after the First World War that the United States became relatively larger and more developed in terms of all four indicators. This potential dominance reached new and dramatic heights between 1945 and 1960. Since then, the relative position of the United States has declined, bringing it quite close to West Germany, its nearest rival, in terms of per capita income and share of world trade. The devaluations of the dollar that have taken place since 1972 are reflected in a continuation of this downward trend for income and aggregate size.

The relative potential economic power of Britain and the United States is shown in [Tables I and II].

TABLE I. Indicators of British Potential Power
(ratio of British value to next highest)

	Per Capita Income	Aggregate Size	Share of World Trade	Share of World Investment*
1860	.91(U.S.)	.74(U.S.)	2.01(FR)	n.a.
1880	1.30(U.S.)	.79(1874–83 U.S.)	2.22(FR)	1.93(FR)
1900	1.05(1899 U.S.)	.58(1899 U.S.)	2.17(1890 GERM)	2.08(FR)
1913	.92(U.S.)	.43(U.S.)	1.20(U.S.)	2.18(1914 FR)
1928	.66(U.S.)	.25(1929 U.S.)	.79(U.S.)	.64(1921–29 U.S.)
1937	.79(U.S.)	.29(U.S.)	.88(U.S.)	.18(1930–38 U.S.)
1950	.56(U.S.)	.19(U.S.)	.69(U.S.)	.13(1951–55 U.S.)
1960	.49(U.S.)	.14(U.S.)	.46(1958 U.S.)	.15(1956–61 U.S.)
1972	.46(U.S.)	.13(U.S.)	.47(1973 U.S.)	n.a.

*Stock, 1870–1913; Flow, 1928–1950.

Note: Years are in parentheses when different from those in first column. Countries in parentheses are those with the largest values for the particular indicator other than Great Britain. n.a. = not applicable.

TABLE II. Indicators of U.S. Potential Power
(ratio of U.S. value to next highest)

	Per Capita Income	Aggregate Size	Share of World Trade	Share of World Investment Flows
1860	1.10(GB)	1.41(GB)	.36(GB)	Net debtor
1880	.77(GB)	1.23(1883 GB)	.37(GB)	Net debtor
1900	.95(1899 GB)	1.73(1899 GB)	.43(1890 GB)	n.a.
1913	1.09(GB)	2.15(RUS)	.83(GB)	Net debtor
1928	1.51(GB)	3.22(USSR)	1.26(GB)	1.55(1921–29 UK)
1937	1.26(GB)	2.67(USSR)	1.13(GB)	5.53(1930–38 UK)
1950	1.78(GB)	3.15(USSR)	1.44(GB)	7.42(1951–55 UK)
1960	2.05(GB)	2.81(USSR)	2.15(1958 GB)	6.60(1956–61 UK)
1972	1.31(GERM)	n.a.	1.18(1973 GERM)	n.a.

Note: Years are in parentheses when different from those in first column. Countries in parentheses are those with the largest values for the particular indicator other than the United States. n.a. = not applicable.

In sum, Britain was the world's most important trading state from the period after the Napoleonic Wars until 1913. Her relative position rose until about 1880 and fell thereafter. The United States became the largest and most advanced state in economic terms after the First World War, but did not equal the relative share of world trade and investment achieved by Britain in the 1880's until after the Second World War.

TESTING THE ARGUMENT

The contention that hegemony leads to a more open trading structure is fairly well, but not perfectly, confirmed by the empirical evidence presented in the preceding sections. The argument explains the periods 1820 to 1879, 1880 to 1900, and 1945 to 1960. It does not fully explain those from 1900 to 1913, 1919 to 1939, or 1960 to the present.

1820–1879

The period from 1820 to 1879 was one of increasing openness in the structure of international trade. It was also one of rising hegemony. Great Britain was the instigator and supporter of the new structure. She began lowering her trade barriers in the 1820's, before any other state. The signing of the Cobden-Chevalier Tariff Treaty with France in 1860 initiated a series of bilateral tariff reductions. It is, however, important to note that the United States was hardly involved in these developments, and that America's ratio of trade to aggregate economic activity did not increase during the nineteenth century.

Britain put to use her internal flexibility and external power in securing a more open structure. At the domestic level, openness was favored by the rising industrialists. The opposition of the agrarian sector was mitigated by its capacity for adjustment: the rate of capital investment and technological innovation was high enough to prevent British agricultural incomes from falling until some thirty years after the abolition of the Corn Laws. Symbolically, the Manchester School led by Cobden and Bright provided the ideological justification for free trade. Its influence was felt throughout Europe where Britain stood as an example to at least some members of the elite.

Britain used her military strength to open many backward areas: British interventions were frequent in Latin America during the nineteenth century, and formal and informal colonial expansion opened the interior of Africa. Most importantly, Britain forced India into the international economic system. British military power was also a factor in concluding the Cobden-Chevalier Treaty, for Louis Napoleon was more concerned with cementing his relations with Britain than he was in the economic consequences of greater openness. Once this pact was signed, however, it became a catalyst for the many other treaties that followed.

Britain also put economic instruments to good use in creating an open system. The abolition of the Corn Laws offered continental grain producers the incentive of continued access to the growing British market. Britain was at the heart of the nineteenth-century international monetary system which functioned exceptionally well, at least for the core of the more developed states and the areas closely associated with them. Exchange rates were stable, and countries did not have to impose trade barriers to rectify cyclical payments difficulties. Both confidence and liquidity were, to a critical degree, provided by Britain. The use of sterling balances as opposed to specie became increasingly widespread, alleviating the liquidity problems presented by the erratic production of gold and silver. Foreign private and central banks increasingly placed their cash reserves in London, and accounts were cleared through changing bank balances rather than gold flows. Great Britain's extremely sophisticated financial institutions, centered in the City of London, provided the short-term financing necessary to facilitate the international flow of goods. Her early and somewhat fortuitous adherence to the gold — as opposed to the silver or bimetallic — standard proved to be an important source of confidence as all countries adopted at least a *de facto* gold standard after 1870 because of the declining relative value of silver. In times of monetary emergency, the confidence placed in the pound because of the strength of the British economy allowed the Bank of England to be a lender of last resort.

Hence, for the first three-quarters of the nineteenth century, British policy favored an open international trading structure, and British power helped to create it. But this was not a global regime. British resources were not sufficient to entice or compel the United States (a country whose economy was larger than Britain's by 1860 and whose technology was developing very rapidly) to abandon its protectionist commercial policy. As a state-power argument suggests, openness was only established within the geographical area where the rising economic hegemony was able to exercise its influence.

1880–1900

The last two decades of the nineteenth century were a period of modest closure which corresponds to a relative decline in British per capita income, size, and share of world trade. The event that precipitated higher tariff levels was the availability of inexpensive grain from the American Midwest, made possible by the construction of continental railways. National responses varied. Britain let her agricultural sector decline, a not unexpected development given her still dominant economic position. Denmark, a small and relatively well-developed state, also refrained from imposing tariffs and transformed its farming sector from agriculture to animal husbandry. Several other small states also followed open policies. Germany, France, Russia, and Italy imposed higher tariffs, however. Britain did not have the military or economic power to forestall these policies. Still, the institutional structure of the international monetary system, with the city of London at its center, did not crumble. The decline in trade proportions was modest despite higher tariffs.

1945–1960

The third period that is neatly explained by the argument that hegemony leads to an open trading structure is the decade and a half after the Second World War, characterized by the ascendancy of the United States. During these years the structure of the international trading system became increasingly open. Tariffs were lowered; trade proportions were restored well above interwar levels. Asymmetrical regional trading patterns did begin to decline, although not until the late 1950's. America's bilateral rival, the Soviet Union, remained — as the theory would predict — encapsulated within its own regional sphere of influence.

Unlike Britain in the nineteenth century, the United States after World War II operated in a bipolar political structure. Free trade was preferred, but departures such as the Common Market and Japanese import restrictions were accepted to make sure that these areas remained within the general American sphere of influence. Domestically, the Reciprocal Trade Agreements Act, first passed in 1934, was extended several times after the war. Internationally the United States supported the framework for tariff reductions provided by the General Agreement on Tariffs and Trade. American policy makers used their economic leverage over Great Britain to force an end to the imperial preference system. The monetary system established at Bretton Woods was basically an American creation. In practice, liquidity was provided by the American deficit; confidence by the size of the American economy. Behind the economic veil stood American military protection for other industrialized market economies — an overwhelming incentive for them to accept an open system, particularly one which was in fact relatively beneficial.

The argument about the relationship between hegemony and openness is not as satisfactory for the years 1900 to 1913, 1919 to 1939, and 1960 to the present.

1900–1913

During the years immediately preceding the First World War, the structure of international trade became more open in terms of trade proportions and regional patterns. Britain remained the largest international economic entity, but her relative position continued a decline that had begun two decades earlier. Still, Britain maintained her commitment to free trade and to the financial institutions of the city of London. A state-power argument would suggest some reconsideration of these policies.

Perhaps the simplest explanation for the increase in trade proportions was the burst of loans that flowed out of Europe in the years before the First World War, loans that financed the increasing sale of goods. Germany and France as well as Britain participated in this development. Despite the higher tariff levels imposed after 1879, institutional structures — particularly the monetary system — allowed these capital flows to generate increasing trade flows. Had Britain reconsidered her policies, this might not have been the case.

1919–1939

The United States emerged from the First World War as the world's most powerful economic state. Whether America was large enough to have put an open system in place is a moot question. As Table II indicates, America's share of world trade and investment was [respectively] only 26 and 55 per cent greater than that of any other state, while comparable figures for Great Britain during the last part of the nineteenth century are 100 per cent. What is apparent, though, is that American policy makers made little effort to open the structure of international trade. The call for an open door was a shibboleth, not a policy. It was really the British who attempted to continue a hegemonic role.

In the area of trade, the U.S. Fordney-McCumber Tariff of 1922 increased protection. That tendency was greatly reinforced by the Smoot-Hawley Tariff of 1930 which touched off a wave of protective legislation. Instead of leading the way to openness, the United States led the way to closure.

In the monetary area, the American government made little effort to alter a situation that was confused and often chaotic. During the first half of the 1920's, exchange rates fluctuated widely among major currencies as countries were forced, by the inflationary pressures of the war, to abandon the gold standard. Convertibility was restored in the mid-twenties at values incompatible with long-term equilibrium. The British pound was overvalued, and the French franc undervalued. Britain was forced off the gold standard in September 1931, accelerating a trend that had begun with Uruguay in April 1929. The United States went off gold in 1933. France's decision to end convertibility in 1936 completed the pattern. During the 1930's the monetary system collapsed.

Constructing a stable monetary order would have been no easy task in the political environment of the 1920's and 1930's. The United States made no effort. It refused to recognize a connection between war debts and reparations, although much of the postwar flow of funds took the form of American loans to Germany, German reparations payments to France and Britain, and French and British war-debt payments to the United States. The Great Depression was in no small measure touched off by the contraction of American credit in the late 1920's. In the deflationary collapse that followed, the British were too weak to act as a lender of last resort, and the Americans actually undercut efforts to reconstruct the Western economy when, before the London Monetary Conference of 1933, President Roosevelt changed the basic assumptions of the meeting by taking the United States off gold. American concern was wholly with restoring the domestic economy.

That is not to say that American behavior was entirely obstreperous; but cooperation was erratic and often private. The Federal Reserve Bank of New York did try, during the late 1920's, to maintain New York interest rates below those in London to protect the value of the pound. Two Americans, Dawes and Young, lent their names to the renegotiations of German reparations payments, but most of the actual work was carried out by British experts. At the official level, the first manifestation of American leadership was President Hoover's call for a moratorium on war debts and reparations in June 1931; but in 1932 the United States refused to participate in the Lausanne Conference that in effect ended reparations.

It was not until the mid-thirties that the United States asserted any real leadership. The Reciprocal Trade Agreements Act of 1934 led to bilateral treaties with twenty-seven countries before 1945. American concessions covered 64 per cent of dutiable items and reduced rates by an average of 44 per cent. However, tariffs were so high to begin with that the actual impact of these agreements was limited. There were also some modest steps toward tariff liberalization in Britain and France. In the monetary field, the United States, Britain, and France pledged to maintain exchange-rate stability in the Tripartite Declaration of September 1936. These actions were not adequate to create an open international economic structure. American policy during the interwar period, and particularly before the mid-thirties, fails to accord with the predictions made by a state-power explanation of the behavior of a rising hegemonic power.

1960–Present

The final period not adequately dealt with by a state-power explanation is the last decade or so. In recent years, the relative size and level of development of the U.S. economy has fallen. This decline has not, however, been accompanied by a clear turn toward protectionism. The Trade Expansion Act of 1962 was extremely liberal and led to the very successful Kennedy Round of multilateral tariff cuts during the mid-sixties. The protectionist Burke-Hartke Bill did not pass. The 1974 Trade Act does include new protectionist aspects, particularly in its requirements for review of the removal of nontariff barriers by Congress and for stiffer requirements for the imposition of countervailing duties, but it still maintains the mechanism of presidential discretion on tariff cuts that has been the keystone of postwar reductions. While the Voluntary Steel Agreement, the August 1971 economic policy, and restrictions on agricultural exports all show a tendency toward protectionism, there is as yet no evidence of a basic turn away from a commitment to openness.

In terms of behavior in the international trading system, the decade of the 1960's was clearly one of greater openness. Trade proportions increased, and traditional regional trade patterns became weaker. A state-power argument would predict a downturn or at least a faltering in these indicators as American power declined.

In sum, although the general pattern of the structure of international trade conforms with the predictions of a state-power argument — two periods of openness separated by one of closure — corresponding to periods of rising British and American hegemony and an interregnum, the whole pattern is out of phase. British commitment to openness continued long after Britain's position had declined. American commitment to openness did not begin until well after the United States had become the world's leading economic power and has continued during a period of relative American decline. The state-power argument needs to be amended to take these delayed reactions into account.

AMENDING THE ARGUMENT

The structure of the international trading system does not move in lockstep with changes in the distribution of potential power among states. Systems are initiated and ended, not as a state-power theory would predict, by close assessments of the interests of the state at every given moment, but by external events — usually cataclysmic ones. The closure that began in 1879 coincided with the Great Depression of the last part of the nineteenth century. The final dismantling of the nineteenth-century international economic system was not precipitated by a change in British trade or monetary policy, but by the First World War and the Depression. The potato famine of the 1840's prompted abolition of the Corn Laws; and the United States did not assume the mantle of world leadership until the world had been laid bare by six years of total war. Some catalytic external event seems necessary to move states to dramatic policy initiatives in line with state interests.

Once policies have been adopted, they are pursued until a new crisis demonstrates that they are no longer feasible. States become locked in by the impact of prior choices on their domestic political structures. The British decision to opt for openness in 1846 corresponded with state interests. It also strengthened the position of industrial and financial groups over time, because they had the opportunity to operate in an international system that furthered their objectives. That system eventually undermined the position of British farmers, a group that would have supported protectionism, if it had survived. Once entrenched, Britain's export industries, and more importantly the City of London, resisted policies of closure. In the interwar years, the British rentier class insisted on restoring the prewar parity of the pound — a decision that placed enormous deflationary pressures on the domestic economy — because they wanted to protect the value of their investments.

Institutions created during periods of rising ascendancy remained in operation when they were no longer appropriate. For instance, the organization of British banking in the nineteenth century separated domestic and foreign operations. The Court of Directors of the Bank of England was dominated by international banking houses. Their decisions about British monetary policy were geared toward the international economy. Under a different institutional arrangement more attention might have been given after 1900 to the need to revitalize the domestic economy. The British state was unable to free itself from the domestic structures that its earlier policy decisions had created, and continued to follow policies appropriate for a rising hegemony long after Britain's star had begun to fall.

Similarly, earlier policies in the United States begat social structures and institutional arrangements that trammeled state policy. After protecting import-competing industries for a century, the United States was unable in the 1920's to opt for more open policies, even though state interests would have been furthered thereby. Institutionally, decisions about tariff reductions were taken primarily in congressional committees, giving virtually any group seeking protection easy access to the decision-making process. When there were conflicts among groups, they were resolved by raising the levels of protection for everyone. It was only after the cataclysm of the depression that the decision-making processes for trade policy were changed. The presidency, far more insulated from the entreaties of particular societal groups than congressional committees, was then given more power. Furthermore, the American commercial banking system was unable to assume the burden of regulating the international economy during the 1920's. American institutions were geared toward the domestic economy. Only after the Second World War, and in fact not until the late 1950's, did American banks fully develop the complex institutional structures commensurate with the dollar's role in the international monetary system.

Having taken the critical decisions that created an open system after 1945, the American government is unlikely to change its policy until it confronts some external event that it cannot control, such as a worldwide deflation, drought in the great plains, or the malicious use of petrodollars. In America perhaps more than in any other country "new policies," as E.E. Schattschneider wrote in his brilliant study of the Smoot-Hawley Tariff in 1935, "create new politics,"[1] for in America the state is weak and the society strong. State decisions taken because of state interests reinforce private societal groups that the state is unable to resist in later periods. Multinational corporations have grown and prospered since 1950. International economic policy making has passed from the Congress to the Executive. Groups favoring closure, such as organized labor, are unlikely to carry the day until some external event demonstrates that existing policies can no longer be implemented.

The structure of international trade changes in fits and starts; it does not flow smoothly with the redistribution of potential state power. Nevertheless, it is the power and the policies of states that create order where there would otherwise be chaos or at best a Lockian state of nature. The existence of various transnational, multinational, transgovernmental, and other nonstate actors that have riveted scholarly attention in recent years can only be understood within the context of a broader structure that ultimately rests upon the power and interests of states, shackled through they may be by the societal consequences of their own past decisions.

NOTE

1. E.E. Schattschneider, *Politics, Pressures and the Tariff: A Study of Free Enterprise in Pressure Politics as Shown in the 1929–1930 Revision of the Tariff* (New York: Prentice-Hall, 1935), p. 288.

2

The Political Economy
of the Smoot-Hawley Tariff
BARRY EICHENGREEN

Barry Eichengreen presents a domestic societal explanation of the passage of the Smoot-Hawley Tariff Act of 1930. Eichengreen argues that economic interest groups were the key actors underlying the passage of the act. Specifically, he asserts that certain sectors of agriculture and industry supported each other's desire for protection and together pressured the government to pass the highly restrictive Smoot-Hawley Tariff. He shows both how the actions of self-interested groups in national societies affect the making of foreign economic policy and how international political and market forces can influence the interests of societal actors.

The intimate connection between the Great Depression and the Smoot-Hawley Tariff of 1930 was recognized by contemporaries and continues to be emphasized by historical scholars. But just as contemporaries, while agreeing on its importance, nonetheless viewed the tariff in a variety of different ways, historians of the era have achieved no consensus on the tariff's origins and effects. The definitive study of the Smoot-Hawley's origins, by Schattschneider [1935], portrays the tariff as a classic example of pork-barrel politics, with each member of Congress after his particular piece of pork. Revisionist treatments characterize it instead as a classic instance of party politics; protectionism being the household remedy of the Republican Party, the tariff's adoption is ascribed to the outcome of the 1928 election. Yet proponents of neither interpretation provide an adequate analysis of the relationship of Smoot-Hawley to the Depression. . . .

POLITICS, PRESSURES AND THE TARIFF

The debate surrounding the passage of the Tariff Act of 1930 remains a classic study in the political economy of protection. A number of theories have been developed to explain Smoot-Hawley's adoption, starting with that advanced in Schattschneider's [1935] classic monograph whose title this section bears.

Schattschneider's influential study "set the tone for a whole generation of political writing on pressure groups. . . ." and "cut the lens through which Americans have since visualized the making of U.S. foreign trade policy. . . ."[1] Schattschneider focused on the influence of special interest groups. In his account, the actions of lobbyists and special interests were responsible for both the tariff's adoption and its form.

Schattschneider dubbed the principle around which the tariff coalition organized "reciprocal noninterference." The coalition was assembled by offering limited protection to everyone involved. Since only moderate protection was provided and no single import-competing sector reaped extraordinary benefits at the expense of others, they could combine in support of tariff legislation. In addition, under provisions of the original House and Senate bills, credits (or "debentures") were to be made available to exporters, extending the coalition beyond the import-competing to the export-producing sector. Not just the number of duties raised but the very process by which the bill was passed is invoked in support of the log-rolling interpretation. Passage required 14 months from when Hoover called a special session of Congress to when the final bill was signed. The record of public hearings in which the bill was discussed ran to 20,000 pages, while the final bill provided tariff schedules for more than 20,000 items. Since insurgency was easier under Senate than House rules, log-rolling was more conspicuous there: the Senate amended the House bill over 1,200 times, most of them on the Senate floor. Still other changes were engineered in conference committee.

If the distinguishing feature of the Tariff Act of 1930 was the dominance of special interests, one must ask why they had grown so much more powerful. Schattschneider provides no explicit answer, although he indicts Hoover for failing to guide the legislation through Congress. But the systematic explanation implicit in his analysis is the rise of the "new lobby." Although fraternal, religious, social, and economic groups had always been part of the American scene, they had never been so well organized or visible in the Capitol as in the 1920s. . . .

A number of influences prompted the rise of the new lobby. First, the activities of the "muckrakers" in the first decade of the twentieth century had intensified public scrutiny of political affairs. Second, whereas businessmen had traditionally dealt with government in "a spasmodic and haphazard fashion," the panic of 1907 spurred them to cultivate more systematic representation. Simultaneously, the U.S. Chamber of Commerce took a more prominent role in representing the interests of business. . . . Finally, much as the Chamber of Commerce represented business's general interests, trade associations filled this role for more specialized groups. A Department of Commerce publication listed some 1,500 organizations classified as trade associations, nearly double the number known to exist in 1914. Some were organized by products produced, others by materials used, still others by markets in which sales took place. Like the other three influences, the growth of trade associations was a distinctively twentieth-century development, but in contrast to other trends, which had been underway in the early years of the century, the sudden rise to prominence of trade associations was attributable to World War I. The war effort required closer ties between government and industry, but upon attempting to establish them the authorities found it difficult to deal with individual enterprises and requested that associations be formed. If the war occasioned the formation and growth of trade associations, the armistice by no means signalled their demise. Once formed into an association the process of mar-

shalling a constituency was no longer so difficult. Improvements in communication, notably the telephone, reinforced these advantages, and associations quickly
learned to use pamphlets and other media to publicize their case. The adoption of
new Congressional rules made it more difficult for powerful individuals to dictate
policy, opening the legislative process to competing interests.

The same forces tending to promote effective representation of industrial interests in Washington encouraged the formation of effective organizations representing farmers and labor. The American farm movement had long been distinguished
by its inability to organize effectively and represent its interests before Congress.
The ad hoc methods of agricultural organizations, such as sending a representative
to Washington in response to specific developments, had proven ineffectual. For
agriculture as for industry, World War I and the impetus it provided for the formation of the War Trade Board and the Food Administration permitted farmers' organizations to assume new importance. In 1918 the National Grange opened a
permanent legislative office in Washington, and the militant American Farm
Bureau Federation, founded in 1919, lobbied actively for farm legislation. In 1921
a bipartisan Farm Bloc of senators and congressmen from the South and West was
formed, and it acquired a pivotal position in the balance of power in the 66th and
67th Congresses. Although it had at best mixed success in passing farm legislation
before falling into disarray, the prominence of the Farm Bloc did much to alert
agricultural interests to the advantages of effective congressional representation.

By encouraging the development of direct government-labor relations, the war
had a similar impact on the American Federation of Labor. While maintaining its
distance from party politics, by the 1920s the AFL was commonly acknowledged
as the most formidable group in the United States other than the political parties.
Thus, in the 1920s the three principal American interest groups — business, agriculture, and labor — were for the first time ably represented in Washington.

The rise of the new lobby is consistent with Schattschneider's characterization
of Smoot-Hawley as an instance of pork-barrel politics. But his theory of reciprocal noninterference — that the Smoot-Hawley bill by offering something for
everyone, garnered widespread support — fails to confront the question of why
the vote on the final bill so closely followed party lines, with only 5 Democratic
Senators voting in favor and 11 Republicans against. Neither does it explain why
tariff-rate increases differed so widely by schedule.

An alternative explanation, recently advanced by Pastor [1980], is that Smoot-
Hawley is simply an instance of party politics. Protection in general and for industry in particular was regularly advocated by the Republican Party. With the White
House occupied by a Republican President and the Senate in Republican hands,
there were few obstacles to revising upward existing tariff schedules. It is curious
that this straightforward explanation has attracted so little attention. It may be that
partisan aspects of the debate were disguised by the absence of a change in party
in 1928 like that following the 1920 election which preceded the 1922 Fordney-
McCumber Tariff Act. Moreover, the issue of protection had not been hotly disputed
in the 1928 campaign. Although the Democrats had traditionally campaigned on
the basis of staunch opposition to protectionist measures, in 1928 they moderated
their position and joined the Republicans in endorsing protection, albeit in vague

and reserved terms. . . . Given the extent of consensus, there was little debate in the subsequent Congress over principles of free trade and protection. Hence even Free Traders among the Democrats were ill positioned to mount effective opposition to tariff increases.

The problem with this partisan interpretation is that it provides no explanation for Smoot-Hawley's timing or its form. It is suggested that Congress was simply accustomed to engaging in tariff revision every seven years (the average life of a tariff law between the Acts of 1883 and 1930), and that by 1929 Congress and the public had recovered from the exhausting Fordney-McCumber deliberations of 1920–22. But this mechanical explanation neither recognizes links between protectionist pressure and economic events nor provides an explanation for the observed variation in import duty levels.

The explanation coming closest to satisfying these requirements is the view of Smoot-Hawley as a response to the problems of American agriculture. The explanation runs as follows. While the 1920s were boom years for the country as a whole, prosperity was unevenly distributed. After benefiting from high prices from 1917 to 1920, American agriculture failed to recover from the recession of 1920–21. For much of the decade, farm gate prices declined relative to the prices of nonagricultural goods. . . . In 1926, a relatively favorable year for farmers when average wholesale prices were 51 percent above their 1913 levels, the prices of farm products were only 42 percent above those levels. The explanation for lagging prices was that World War I had prompted the expansion of agricultural production outside Europe. While European sugar production, for example, fell by 50 percent during the war, the shortfall was offset by expanding output in Cuba, Java, and South America. Once European production recovered, often under cover of import duties or production subsidies, world prices were depressed. Similarly, wartime disruptions of the global wheat market greatly stimulated production in Argentina, Australia, Canada, and the United States. The consequent decline in prices was magnified in the second half of the 1920s by the imposition of import duties on wheat by Germany, Italy, and France.

Agrarian distress in the United States took various forms, notably farm foreclosures, which, after averaging 3.2 per thousand farms between 1913 and 1920, rose to 10.7 per thousand in 1921–25 and 17.0 per thousand in 1926–29. Foreclosure reflected not just the declining relative price of agricultural products but overall price level trends; since much agricultural land had turned over between 1917 and 1920 when prices were high, the subsequent deflation greatly augmented the burden of mortgage debt. The value of total farm mortgage debt rose by 45 percent between 1917 and 1920 and by a further 28 percent between 1920 and 1923 despite the deflation that set in after the beginning of the decade. The foreclosures of the second half of the 1920s were most heavily concentrated in Idaho, Montana, North and South Dakota, Colorado, and Arizona, the sources of strongest pressure for agrarian relief.

In the 1928 presidential campaign Hoover laid stress on tariff protection for agriculture. Previously, agriculture had been the recipient of only modest tariffs, in part because duties on farm imports would have been ineffective given U.S. status as a net exporter of most agricultural goods (sugar, wool and hides being the principal exceptions). In 1922, for reasons detailed above, the U.S. balance of trade in farm products turned negative, where it remained except in 1925 for the duration of the decade. Hence an expanding segment of American agriculture grew to appreciate the relevance of tariff protection.

By this interpretation, Smoot-Hawley was predominantly a form of agricultural relief. . . . Farm interests were well positioned to press their case. Although the United States had grown increasingly urbanized over preceding decades, Congress had not been reapportioned following the 1920 Census. Consequently, farm interests were overrepresented in the House, just as, on the two senator per state rule, they were overrepresented in the Senate.

This characterization of Smoot-Hawley as an agricultural measure won by the West over the opposition of the East is consistent not only with the partisan interpretation, given the regional concentration of Democratic and Republican voters, but it explains a number of defections from party ranks. To the extent that agricultural distress intensified with the onset of the Depression, it links the tariff to macroeconomic conditions. Where it falls short is in explaining why tariffs on manufactured imports were raised as part of an agrarian relief measure, or why the tariff was supported not only by representatives of agricultural districts but by those of industrial regions as well. Many accounts emphasize the extent of discord between agriculture and industry. . . . What explains the pattern of voting and the tariff schedule that emerged from Congressional debate?

A MODEL OF THE TARIFF-MAKING PROCESS

The framework I use to analyze the adoption of Smoot-Hawley is a variant of Gerschenkron's [1943] model of the political economy of protection. This is a member of the class of "interest-group models" of tariff formation. . . . I first review Gerschenkron's application of his model to Bismarckian Germany before adapting it to analysis of the Smoot-Hawley Tariff.

In Gerschenkron's model, a tariff is adopted when narrow yet well-placed interest groups combine in its support. Gerschenkron divides German society not merely along sectorial lines but into heavy industry (producers of basic products such as coal, iron and steel), light industry (manufacturers of consumer goods, along with whom might be included artisans and shopkeepers), large agriculture (the Junkers, or estate owners of the east), and small agriculture (commercial producers located primarily west of the Elbe). He explains the Bismarckian tariff as a coalition of iron and rye, allying large agriculture and heavy industry.

In the 1870s as in the 1920s, the impetus for agrarian protection was the fall in grain prices. The position of traditional German agriculture, which specialized in grain, was seriously undermined. The alternative to continued grain production behind tariff walls was to shift into the production of high quality foodstuffs such as dairy products and meat for rapidly expanding urban markets. Cheap imported grain could serve as an input into such production. But, crucially, large and small agriculture differed in their capacity to adjust. Variations in soil quality and proximity to urban markets provided greater scope for the production of dairy products and meat west of the Elbe. In addition, dairy products, meats and vegetables were most efficiently produced on small owner-managed farms. Hence costs of adjustment were lowest where long-term leaseholders and small owner-managed farms predominated — west of the Elbe — and highest where landless laborers worked large estates. The model predicts that small agriculture should have opposed agricultural protection due to its impact on costs, while large agriculture should have favored it.

Neither light nor heavy industry, with the possible exception of yarn spinning, desperately required protection from import competition. Under competitive conditions, Germany probably would have imported grain and exported both light manufactures and the products of the basic industries. While it is not clear that import duties on industrial goods would have succeeded in raising the prices of domestically-produced goods, given competition at home but the net export position of German manufacturers, heavy industry in fact supported the imposition of a tariff on manufactured goods. One interpretation is that, with high levels of fixed capital, heavy industry was exceptionally susceptible to cyclical fluctuations. Tariffs may have reduced the risk of falling prices, thereby encouraging the fixed investments which permitted scale economies to be reaped. A more compelling interpretation is that barriers to cheap imports were a necessary condition for firms producing basic goods to combine and extract monopoly profits from domestic users. Consistent with this interpretation, producers of final goods like stoves, pots and pans, shovels and rakes opposed tariffs on the products of basic industries because of their impact on production costs.

What is relevant for our purposes is that no group favored the final outcome: high tariffs on both agricultural and industrial goods. But because of the dispersion of interests, action required compromise. The two likely outcomes were a coalition of large industrialists and landowners obtaining general protection, and a coalition of small manufacturers and farmers successfully defending free trade. Gerschenkron ascribes the victory of the protectionist coalition to institutional factors. The Junkers, as members of the squirearchy, occupied a privileged position in the political system. Not only did they staff the bureaucracy and judiciary but, like the wealthy industrialists, they benefitted from the structure of the electoral system. Heavy industry, aided by smaller numbers, organized more effectively than small manufacturing. Managers of large enterprises formed new associations and worked to convert existing ones to protectionism. Their cause was not hurt by the fact that the Chancellor found protection a useful tool for achieving his political goals and played an active role in forging the alliance of iron and rye.

Gerschenkron's model can be applied to the case of the Smoot-Hawley Tariff by again distinguishing industry by size and agriculture by region. Naturally, the interests of the groups and the coalitions are entirely different from those observed in Bismarckian Germany — So is the role of national leadership. Nonetheless, distinctions of region and scale shed considerable light on the American case.

In the case of Smoot-Hawley, it is useful to distinguish sheltered from unsheltered agriculture and, as in Germany, light from heavy industry, where it is light industry and unsheltered agriculture that combined to support protection. As noted previously, critics of the Smoot-Hawley Tariff argued that duties on agricultural products would not be "effective" in raising prices because the United States was a net exporter of these goods. . . . The problem with this contention is that net trade may not be the appropriate indicator of the effectiveness of a tariff. It may mislead either if there existed segmented regional markets or if products were heterogeneous. For goods such as wheat with a high ratio of value to volume, there existed not merely a national but an international market. But wheat was not a homogeneous product, and the United States both imported and exported different grades of what was often regarded in policy debate as a single commodity. Since, for example, little if any exportable surplus of high grade milling wheat was produced in the United States, it was argued that a tariff would therefore be effective in raising the Minneapolis price relative to that prevailing in Winnipeg. Even if the product was homogeneous, for perishable products the United States was sufficiently large geographically that transport costs might impede the equalization of prices across regions. . . . Northern states like Minnesota and Eastern seaboard states like Massachusetts might find their markets flooded by cheap Canadian potatoes, milk, cream, butter and eggs. Since these goods could not penetrate further into the interior because of their high ratio of volume to value or due to the danger of spoilage, inland producers remained insulated from imports. Moreover, Southern farmers who engaged in the production of cotton (other than the long staple variety, which was imported and received a generous increase in tariff protection under the 1930 Act) were oriented toward the export market. Northern farmers close to the Canadian border had reason to favor protection to a much greater extent than their counterparts in the interior or the South.

There existed equally sharp divisions within manufacturing. The pressure for protection was greatest in light industry concentrating in the batch production of goods tailored to market. Heavy industry and manufacturers of standardized products had mechanized their operations and largely held their own against foreign competition. But labor-intensive industries dominated by small-scale firms experienced growing competition from abroad. In the bottle-making industry, producers of "fancy ware" such as perfume and toilet water bottles suffered from an increasing volume of French imports. Manufacturers of watches faced Swiss competition and producers of jewelry complained of German imports. Eastern glove manufacturers experienced difficulty in matching the prices of foreign goods. The New England shoe industry experienced competition from Czechoslovak producers. Some producers were sheltered by relatively generous Fordney-McCumber duties. But, for most, foreign trends such as the desperate attempts of English mills to hold onto market share exacerbated their woes. Still, only a minority of American industries were seriously injured by competition from foreign goods.

In opposition stood heavy industries producing standardized products, particularly segments which relied on the assembly line, mass production, the latest technology and the multi-divisional form. By the turn of the century, the United States had gained a competitive advantage in many of the industries of the Second Industrial Revolution, automobiles being a prime example. In 1929 motor cars and parts comprised 10 percent of total U.S. merchandise exports, while imports were negligible, due only partially to a modicum of tariff protection. Given the importance of export sales and the anticipated impact of a tariff on production costs, the automobile producers, led by Henry Ford, made clear their opposition to the tariff bill. The same was true of producers of farm machinery, iron and steel bars, sheet, rails and metal manufactures.

The banking community had traditionally supported the protectionist system. Bankers doing business in industrial regions where firms depended on the tariff favored the maintenance of protection. But in the 1920s their support was tempered by events. World War I had transformed the United States from a debtor to a creditor nation and reoriented America's banking business abroad. Already in 1923 spokesmen for the financial community acknowledged that Europe's continued ability to service its dollar debt hinged upon foreign industries' access to American markets.

The opposite shift was evident in the attitudes of organized labor. Traditionally, labor had opposed protection for its impact on the cost of living. Those groups of workers injured by import competition were incapable of changing this policy. For half a century the AFL's position on the tariff had been one of carefully cultivated neutrality. Although individual unions might lobby for protection against imported goods or for lower duties on raw materials, the Federation's policy was to take no position on the issue. In 1930 it went only so far as to accede to individual unions' requests for legislative assistance. However, at the November 1928 AFL convention the first official caucus of pro-tariff unions was formed. This "Wage Earners Protective Conference" represented 8 or 9 percent of the federation's membership, the leading participants including the photo-engravers, wallpaper craftsmen, glass-bottle blowers and potters. Clearly, labor's traditional opposition to protection was attenuated by the success of pro-tariff unions in organizing to lobby for a change in policy.

In sum, the situation in 1930 appeared as follows. Farmers along the Canadian border and Eastern seaboard desired higher protection but, comprising only a minority of American agriculture, found it difficult to obtain alone. Light industries producing goods tailored to market also desired protection but similarly composed only a portion of American manufacturing. In principle, neither group favored protection for the other, but each was willing to support the claims of its counterpart in return for participation in the coalition. While agriculture received generous protection under the final Smoot-Hawley bill, so did light industry producing goods tailored to market. . . .

This interpretation has advantages over the view of Smoot-Hawley that divides the American economy into monolithic agricultural and industrial blocs. It explains why sections of the industrial Midwest and East should have complained about the height of agricultural tariffs, and why certain agrarian interests, notably in the South, should have complained of industrial protection. It is consistent also with the observed alliance of industrial and agricultural protectionists and explains why the Smoot-Hawley Tariff, originally conceived as agricultural relief, evolved into a bill extending protection to portions of both industry and agriculture. It is consistent with Schattschneider's emphasis on log-rolling aspects of the legislative process, but rather than characterizing log-rolling as entirely general suggests that "reciprocal noninterference" should have favored border agriculture and light industry. It is consistent with the notion that Hoover lost control of the legislative process by permitting the debate to extend beyond the question of agricultural relief and with the inference that Hoover failed to take forceful action on the grounds that he saw the small businesses which dominated light industry as his constituency, but not necessarily with the opinion of Senator Borah that a narrowly agricultural tariff could have passed in 1929 had Hoover taken the bit in his teeth. National leadership, while important in both Gerschenkron's and this paper's application of the model, plays opposite roles in the two instances, since Bismarck favored widespread protection and played a prominent role in obtaining it, while Hoover personally opposed blanket protection but failed to effectively guide the legislative process. Finally, by invoking the rise of the trade association, the model can be used to explain how diverse agricultural and industrial interests succeeded in influencing the legislative process.

The model can be elaborated in various directions. One extension would introduce the long history of protectionism in the United States and the country's habit of neglecting the impact of its economic policies on the rest of the world. Another would build on the tendency of the Depression to undermine confidence in the self-equilibrating nature of the market. In many countries, the depth of the Depression provided a rationale for the extension of economic planning. In Britain, for example, Keynes went so far for a time as to argue for central planning along Soviet lines. In the United States this desire for intervention and control was most clearly manifest in the New Deal, but the same tendencies contributed to the pressure for tariff protection in 1930. . . .

At the same time the Depression worked to promote Smoot-Hawley by undermining confidence in the stability of the market, it altered the costs and benefits of protection as perceived by interest groups. By further lowering already depressed agricultural prices, it increased the pressure agricultural interests brought to bear on elected officials. By further undermining the already tenuous position of light industries engaged in the production of specialty products, it reinforced their efforts to acquire insulation from foreign competition. . . .

CONCLUSION

. . . Economic histories view the Great Depression and the Smoot-Hawley Tariff as inextricably bound up with one another. They assign a central role to the Depression in explaining the passage of the 1930 Tariff Act and at the same time emphasize the role of the tariff in the singular depth and long duration of the slump. This paper has reexamined the historical evidence on both points. It is not hard to identify relationships linking the tariff to the Depression and vice versa. But the evidence examined here suggests that previous accounts have conveyed what is at best an incomplete and at worst a misleading impression of the mechanisms at work. It is clear that the severity of the initial business cycle downturn lent additional impetus to the campaign for protection. But it is equally clear that the impact of the downturn on the movement for protection worked through different channels than typically posited. Rather than simply strengthening the hand of a Republican Executive predisposed toward protection, or increasing the burden borne by a depressed agricultural sector which had long been agitating for tariff protection, the uneven impact of the Depression occasioned the birth of a protectionist coalition comprising producers particularly hard hit by import competition: border agriculture and small-scale industry engaged in the production of specialty goods. That coalition was able to obtain for its members substantial increases in levels of tariff protection because of an unusual conjuncture of distinct if related developments including reforms of Congressional procedure, the rise of trade associations and the growth of interventionist sentiment. The experience of Smoot-Hawley documents how macroeconomic distress accompanied by import penetration gives rise to protectionist pressure, but does so only once the analysis transcends the model of monolithic agricultural and industrial blocs. . . .

NOTE

1. The first quote is from Bauer et al. [1972: 25], the second from Pastor [1980: 70].

REFERENCES

Bauer, de Sola Pool, and Dexter [1972]. Raymond Bauer, Ithiel de Sola Pool, and L.A. Dexter. *American Business and Public Policy.* Aldine-Atherton, 1972.
Gerschenkron [1943]. Alexander Gerschenkron. *Bread and Democracy in Germany.* University of California Press, 1943.
Pastor [1980]. Robert A. Pastor. *Congress and the Politics of U.S. Foreign Economic Policy, 1929–1976.* University of California Press, 1980.
Schattschneider [1935]. E.E. Schattschneider. *Politics, Pressures and the Tariff.* Prentice-Hall, 1935.

3

Institutions and Economic Growth: A Historical Introduction

DOUGLASS C. NORTH

In this essay, Nobel prize–winning economist Douglass C. North argues for the importance of domestic political institutions as determinants of economic growth. For North, institutions comprise both sets of formal rules, like constitutions, and informal norms of behavior. Moving beyond the traditional economic focus on population and savings, North examines how political institutions affect property rights and, in turn, the efficiency of economic exchange. In England, according to North, the rise of Parliament beginning in the sixteenth century constrained the powers of the king, ultimately leading to more secure rights to property and a relatively efficient market economy. In Spain, by contrast, the king augmented his power and created a large bureaucracy, which produced revenues for the crown but impeded economic growth. The divergent paths of institutional development in Europe were replicated in the British and Spanish empires in the New World, with important long-term consequences for growth in North and South America.

The objective of this essay is two-fold: (1) to develop a theoretical framework which focuses on the historical obstacles to economic growth; and (2) to briefly apply this framework to explore the contrasting characteristics of institutional change in early modern Britain and Spain and the downstream implications for North and Latin America. In the sections that follow, I explore (1) the issues; (2) the nature of institutions; (3) the sources of institutional change; (4) the initial historical conditions in England and Spain; (5) English development; (6) Spanish development; and finally (7) the consequences for the New World. Of necessity, the historical sections are little more than outlines, illustrating the framework developed in the first sections.

1. THE ISSUES

I begin with one of the most cited but still misunderstood essays of our time. It is 25 years since Ronald Coase published "The Problem of Social Cost" (1960), but the impact of that essay has still not really penetrated the economics profession, or the development literature. Coase pointed out that the neoclassical model, which has served as the basis of economic reasoning for most scholars in the Western world, holds only under the severely restrictive assumption of zero transaction costs; but that with positive transaction costs, institutions matter. There are no institutions in the neoclassical world; and indeed in such a world growth is not a problem, its rate being simply a function of the number of children people have and the rate of saving.

Ever since Adam Smith, economists have recognized that gains from trade are the key to the wealth of nations. Specialization and division of labor have made possible the improved productivity that arises from technological change, better resource allocation, and specialized production, the key underlying features of modern economies. What economists have not realized until recently is that the exchange process is not costless. Economists still misunderstand key dilemmas of economies and ignore the costs involved in exchange, assuming (as the standard neoclassicists do) that exchange is costless or unproductive (i.e., the classical notion of unproductive labor), or contending that such costs exist but are passive and therefore not important, or are neutral with respect to their consequences for economies.

In fact, the costs of transacting are the key to the performance of economies. There have always been gains from trade, as classical international trade theory has taught, but so too have there been obstacles to realizing these gains. If transport costs were the only obstacle, then we would observe through history an inverse relationship between transport costs, on the one hand, and trade and exchange and the well-being of societies on the other. But recall that as early as the Roman Empire of the first two centuries AD trade was possible over a vast area, even with the transport costs of the time; and that after the end of the Roman Empire trade declined and probably the well-being of societies and individual groups declined as well. It was not that transport costs had risen; but that the costs of transacting had risen as regions expanded, and unified political systems that could effectively enforce rules and laws disappeared.

From the evidence of history, let us turn to the economies of the world today and observe the enormous disparity between the rich countries of the Western world and the poor countries of the Third World. It is not transport costs but the costs of transacting that are the key obstacles that prevent economies and societies from realizing well-being. We can understand why when we examine analytically the costs of transacting in different situations.

We begin with a simple model of personal exchange. In personal exchange, individuals either engage in repeat dealings with others or otherwise have a great deal of personal knowledge about the attributes, characteristics, and features of each other. The measured transaction costs of a society where there is a dense social network of interaction are very low. Cheating, shirking, opportunism, all features that underlie modern industrial organization theory, are limited or indeed absent, because they simply do not pay. Under such conditions, norms of behavior are seldom written down. Formal contracting does not exist, and there are few formal specific rules. However, while measured transaction costs in such societies are low (although unmeasured costs of societal cooperation in tribal societies may indeed be high), production costs are high, because specialization and division of labor are limited to the extent of markets that can be defined by personal exchange.

At the other extreme from personal exchange is a world of specialized interdependence in which the well-being of individuals depends upon a complex structure characterized by individual specialization and hence by exchange ties that extend both in time and space. A pure model of this world of impersonal exchange is one in which goods and services or the performance of agents is characterized by many valued attributes, in which exchange takes place over time, and in which there are not repeat dealings. Under these forms of exchange, the costs of transacting can be high, because there are problems both in measuring the attributes of what is being exchanged and problems of enforcing the terms of exchange; in consequence there are gains to be realized by engaging in cheating, shirking, opportunism, etc. In order to prevent such activity, elaborate institutional structures must be devised that constrain the participants and so minimize the costly aspects I have just described. As a result, in modern Western societies we have devised formal contracts, bonding of participants, guarantees, brand names, elaborate monitoring systems, and effective enforcement mechanisms. In short, we have well-specified and well-enforced property rights. The result of all this is that resources devoted to transacting (although small per transaction) are large, while the productivity associated with the gains from trade is even greater; and high rates of growth and development have characterized Western societies. Of course these institutions depend on a much more complex institutional structure that makes possible the specification and enforcement of property rights, which in turn allow transactions to occur and productivity gains from modern technology to be realized.

Increasing specialization and division of labor necessitate the development of institutional structures that permit individuals to take actions that involve complex relationships with other individuals both in terms of personal knowledge and over time. The evolution of more complex social frameworks will not occur if such institutional structures cannot reduce the uncertainties associated with such situations. So, institutional reliability is essential, because it means that even as the network of interdependence caused by the growth of specialization widens we can have confidence in outcomes that are necessarily increasingly remote from our personal knowledge.

The institutional requirements that are necessary in order to be able to realize the productivity gains associated with the model of impersonal exchange outlined above entail both the development of efficient products and factor markets and of a medium of exchange with reliable features. The establishment of such a set of property rights will then allow individuals in highly complex interdependent situations to be able to have confidence in their dealings with individuals of whom they have no personal knowledge and with whom they have no reciprocal and ongoing exchange relationships. This is only possible as the result, first, of the development of a third party to exchanges, namely government, which specifies property rights and enforces contracts; and second of the existence of norms of behavior to constrain the parties in interaction, which will permit exchange where high measurement costs, even with third party enforcement, pose problems with respect to opportunism, cheating, etc.

But why isn't it automatic to develop more and more complex institutions that will enable us to handle more complex interdependence? Indeed, much of the literature of game theory and stories of institutional development imply that the progress of primitive societies to the status of modern Western societies should be automatic and unilinear. The answer is quite clear. The breakdown of personal exchange is not just the breakdown of a dense communication network, but is the breakdown of communities of common ideologies and of a common set of rules in which all believe. The rise of impersonal rules and contracts means the rise of the state, and with it unequal distribution of coercive power. This provides the opportunity for individuals with superior coercive power to enforce the rules to their advantage, regardless of their effects on efficiency. That is, rules will be devised and enforced on behalf of the interests of the politically advantaged but they will not necessarily lower the costs of transacting in total.

In fact, one of the most evident lessons from history is that political systems have an inherent tendency to produce inefficient property rights which result in stagnation or decline. There are two basic reasons for this result. First, the revenue that can be raised by rulers may be greater with an inefficient structure of property rights that can, however, be effectively monitored, and therefore taxed, than with an efficient structure of property rights with high monitoring and collection costs. Second, rulers can seldom afford efficient property rights, since such rights can offend many of their constituents and hence jeopardize the security of others' rights. That is, even when rulers wish to promulgate rules on the basis of their efficiency consequences, survival will dictate a different course of action, because efficient rules can offend powerful interest groups in the polity.

2. THE NATURE OF INSTITUTIONS

Institutions are rules, enforcement characteristics of rules, and norms of behavior that structure repeated human interaction. Hence, they limit and define the choice set of neoclassical theory. We are interested not in the institutions *per se,* but in their consequences for the choices individuals actually make.

Constitutions, statute and common laws, and contracts specify in formal terms the rules of the game, from the most general constitutional ones, to the specific terms of a particular exchange. Rules (and their enforcement) are constrained by the costliness of measuring the characteristics or attributes of what constitutes rule compliance or violation. Hence, the technology of measurement of all the dimensions (sight, sound, taste, etc.) of the human senses has played a critical role in our ability to define property rights and other types of rules. Moreover, since we receive utility from the various attributes of goods and services rather than from the entities themselves, it is the costliness of measuring the separable dimensions that is critical in this study. The relationship between the benefits derived from rule specification and the costs of measurement not only has been critical in the history of property rights (common property vs. private property) but is at the heart of many of the issues related to the structure and effectiveness of enforcement.

If it were costless to measure the performance of agents or the attributes of goods and services as well as the terms of exchange, then enforcement would not be a problem. We would be back in the neoclassical world of the instantaneous exchange of a unidimensional good or service. But because measurement is costly and the parties to exchange stand to gain by receiving the benefits without incurring all of the costs of exchange, not only is enforcement typically imperfect, but the structure of the enforcement process will affect outcomes and hence choices. Let me elaborate both points.

Enforcement is typically imperfect for two reasons: measurement is costly; and the interests of principals and agents are not identical. The costliness of measurement implies that at the margin, the benefits from additional monitoring or policing will be balanced against the incremental costs. Moreover . . . the marginal benefits and costs of policing will be weighed against those of investing at the margin in ideological persuasion. Rules are enforced by agents (police, foremen, judges, juries, etc.), and therefore the standard problems of agency theory obtain. It is important to stress here that both the structure of the enforcement mechanism and the degree of imperfection of enforcement are important in the choices that are made.

Rules and their (imperfect) enforcement are not the complete story. If they were, the modeling of institutions and hence the costs of transacting could be made, at this stage of our knowledge, much more precise. But norms of behavior also matter; and we know very little about them.

As a first approximation, norms are informal constraints on behavior that are in part derivative of formal rules; that is they are extensions of such rules and apply to specific issues. These informal procedures, deriving as they do from formal organizational structures and agendas, are important but still relatively easy to analyze. Much more important, norms are codes of conduct, taboos, standards of behavior, that are in part derived from perceptions that all individuals form, both to explain and to evaluate the world around them. Some of these perceptions are shaped and molded by organized ideologies (religions, social and political values, etc.). Others are honed by experience, which leads to the reaffirmation or rejection of earlier norms.

However they are formed, and however they evolve, norms play a critical role in constraining the choice set at a moment of time and in the evolution of institutions through time. They are important at a moment of time precisely because of the costliness of measurement and the imperfect enforcement of rules. To the degree that individuals believe in the rules, contracts, property rights, etc., of a society, they will be willing to forego opportunities to cheat, steal or engage in opportunistic behavior. In short, they live up to the terms of contracts. Conversely, to the degree that individuals do not believe in the rules, regard them as unjust, or simply live up to the standard wealth-maximizing behavioral assumption we typically employ in neoclassical economics, the costs of contracting, that is transaction costs, will also increase. . . .

The foregoing paragraphs suggest that ideas and values matter at a moment of time. They do so because of "slack in the system," "agency costs," "consumption on the job," etc., all of which result from the costliness of measurement and enforcement. But how do they change through time? Certainly fundamental changes in relative prices lead not only to rule (and enforcement) changes; but to changes in ideas and values, and the rate of these two kinds of change may be markedly different. This subject will be explored below, but first let me raise some specific issues about institutions, transaction costs, and the consequent choices of the "players," which bear on the subject of this essay. . . .

Rules themselves are not a sufficient condition for determining outcomes even though they are, on occasion, critical. . . . [I]t is important to remember that a number of Latin American countries patterned their constitutions after that of the United States with radically different results.

It may be a slight exaggeration to assert that enforcement is always imperfect, but this statement focuses our attention on a critical and neglected aspect of economic history, which is the essential role that third-party enforcement of contracts has played in human economic progress. There is a large literature in the new industrial organization on self-enforcing contracts, etc.; but as with so much of modern economics, it misses the larger issues involved in exchange in a specialized world. Personal exchange solves the problems of contract fulfillment by repeat dealings and a dense network of social interaction. But the key to the high-income societies of the Western world is still the one that Adam Smith propounded more than 200 years ago. Increasing specialization and division of labor necessitate the development of institutional structures that permit individuals to take actions involving complex relationships with other individuals far removed from any personal knowledge and extending over long periods of time. This is only possible with a third party to exchange, government, which specifies property rights and enforces contracts.

Let me emphasize that while third-party enforcement is far from perfect, there are vast differences in the relative certainty and effectiveness of contract enforcement, temporally over the past five centuries in the Western world, and more currently between modern Western and Third World countries. The evolution of government from its medieval, Mafia-like character to that embodying modern legal institutions and instruments is a major part of the history of freedom. It is a part that tends to be obscured or ignored because of the myopic vision of many economists, who persist in modeling government as nothing more than a gigantic form of theft and income redistribution.

. . . While some norms are externally forced, others are internally enforced codes of conduct, like honesty or integrity. It would be an immense contribution to have a testable general theory of the sociology of knowledge and therefore an understanding of the way overall ideologies emerge and evolve. In the absence of such a theory, we can still derive an important and potentially testable implication about norms at a more specific microlevel of analysis, which is derived from an understanding of institutions. Specifically, the structure of rules and their enforcement help define the costs we bear for ideologically determined choices; the lower the costs, the more will ideas and ideologies matter. . . .

However possible it is to show that ideas matter, it is much more difficult to trace the way they have evolved. For example, the demise of slavery is simply not explicable in an interest group model. Surely the micro argument described above is important to understanding its end. That is, most of those who voted for its elimination, either directly or indirectly, paid few or no costs; they could simply express their abhorrence of one human being owning another. There was no institutional way for the slave owner to buy off the voters. On the other hand, the *way* in which the anti-slavery movement grew (and frequently was used by interest groups) so that it could lead to these votes is a much more complex story. . . .

3. THE SOURCES OF INSTITUTIONAL CHANGE

There are two issues I wish to address on institutional change: what causes the change; and what determines its path? In neither case have I a completely satisfactory answer.

Before we can turn to these two issues, we must examine the role institutions play in reducing uncertainty in human interaction, since it is this stabilizing role of institutions which separates clearly the framework of analysis being developed here from the traditional neoclassical approach. We can most readily understand the difference if we have ever visited foreign countries and attempted to "do business" with them. We will find that of necessity we must learn their "way of doing things." The structural forms of human interaction that characterize societies are a combination of rules, enforcement features, and norms of behavior. Until we learn what these are, the costs of transacting are high. Once we understand them, we can effectively communicate and engage in varieties of social, political, and economic exchange. The function of institutions is to provide certainty in human interaction, and this is accomplished by the inherent features of rules and norms. Rules are typically nested in a hierarchical structure, each more costly to change. But even in the absence of the hierarchical institutional structure, the status quo typically has an advantage over changes in a variety of political structures, as a consequence of agenda control and committee structure.

It is norms of behavior, however, that probably provide the most important sources of stability in human interaction. They are extensions, elaborations, and qualifications of rules that have tenacious survival ability, because they become an integral part of habitual behavior. The reduction of uncertainty, in consequence, makes possible regular human interaction; but it in no way implies that the institutions are efficient, only that they dampen the consequences of relative price changes.

But institutions do change, and fundamental changes in relative prices do lead to institutional change. Historically, population change has been the single most important source of relative price changes, though technological change (including and importantly, changes in military technology) and changes in the costs of information have also been major sources. Moreover, as briefly noted in the previous section, changes in norms of behavior, while certainly influenced by relative price changes, are also influenced by the evolution of ideas and ideologies.

A stylized characterization of the process of institutional change could proceed as follows: as a result of a relative price change, one or both parties to an exchange (political or economic) perceives that he (they) could do better with an altered agreement (contract). Depending on his relative (and presumably changed) bargaining power, he will, as a consequence of the changed prices, renegotiate the contract. However, contracts are nested in a hierarchy of rules. If the renegotiation involves alteration of a more fundamental rule, he (or they) may find it worthwhile to devote resources to changing the rule; or gradually, over time, the rule or custom may simply become ignored and/or unenforced. Agenda power, free-rider problems, and norms of behavior will add meat (and lots of complications) to this skeletal outline.

An important distinction in this argument is made between absolute bargaining power and changes at the margin. To illustrate this distinction, I turn to the medieval world. The "agreement" between lord and serf on the medieval manor reflected the overwhelming power of the lord vis-à-vis the serf. But changes at the margin, as a consequence of 14th century population decline, altered the opportunity costs, increased the relative bargaining power of serfs, and led to the gradual evolution of copyhold. . . .

A special note should be made of the role of military technology in institutional change. Not only have changes in military technology resulted in different, efficient (survival) sizes of political units, but, as in the story that follows, they have consequently induced fundamental changes in other institutions, so that fiscal revenues essential to survival could be realized.

The second issue of institutional change is what determines the direction of change. From what must have been quite common origins several million years ago or even as recently as the hunting and gathering societies that predate the "agricultural revolution" in the 8th millenium BC, we have evolved in radically different directions (and at radically different rates). How have we evolved such divergent patterns of social, political, and economic organization? To consider a specific example, as I will do in the subsequent sections of this paper, how do we explain the divergent paths of British and Spanish development, both at home and in the contrasting histories of North and South America?

I believe the answer lies in the way that institutional structures evolve. The closest (although by no means perfect) analogy is the way we perceive that the common law evolved. It is precedent-based law: past decisions become embedded in the structure of rules, which marginally change as cases arise evolving some new or, at least in the terms of past cases, unforeseen issue, which when decided becomes, in turn, a part of the legal framework. However, I don't intend to imply by this analogy that the result is "efficient." In fact, as we shall see, Spanish institutional evolution moved in the direction of stagnation. . . .

. . . The larger point . . . is that we can only understand historical change by modeling the way institutions evolved through time. That brings us to the following brief outline of English and Spanish institutional change, from the 1500s to the 19th century in North America and Latin America.

4. INITIAL HISTORICAL CONDITIONS IN ENGLAND AND SPAIN

Despite the similarities between England and Spain (discussed below) at the beginning of the 16th century, the two countries had evolved very differently. Spain had just emerged from seven centuries of Moorish domination of the peninsula. It was not really a unified country. Although the marriage of Ferdinand and Isabella brought Castile and Aragon together, they continued to maintain separate rules, Cortes (parliaments), and policies. England, in contrast, had developed a relatively centralized feudalism as a result of the Norman conquest and, with the Battle of Bosworth (1485), had recently established the power of the Tudors.

Yet, in common with the rest of the emerging European nation states, they each faced a problem with far-reaching consequences: that a ruler required additional revenue to survive. The tradition was that a king was supposed to live on his own, which meant that the income from his estates, together with the traditional feudal dues, were his total revenue. The changes in military technology associated with the effective use of the cross-bow, long-bow, pike, and gunpowder enormously increased the cost of warfare and led to a fiscal crisis. . . . In order to get more revenue, the king had somehow to make a bargain with constituents. In both countries, this initially led to the development of some form of representation on the part of the constituents in return for revenue, and in both countries, the wool trade became a major source of crown revenue. Thereafter, the stories diverge. We can better appreciate this divergence in the framework of a very simple model of the state, consistent with the framework developed in the previous sections of this essay.

The king acts like a discriminating monopolist, offering to different groups of constituents "protection and justice," or at least the reduction of internal disorder and the protection of property rights, in return for tax revenue. Since different constituent groups have different opportunity costs and bargaining power with the ruler, there result different bargains. But economies of scale also exist in the provision of these (semi)public goods of law and enforcement. Hence, total revenue is increased, but the division of the incremental gains between ruler and constituents depends on their relative bargaining power; changes at the margin in either the *violence* potential of the ruler or the opportunity costs of the constituents will result in redivisions of revenue increments. Moreover, the rulers' gross and net revenues differ significantly as a result of the necessity of developing agents (a bureaucracy) to monitor, meter, and collect the revenue; and all the inherent consequences of agency theory obtain here. The initial institutional structure that emerged in order to solve the fiscal crisis therefore looked similar in all the emerging nation states of Europe. A representative body (or bodies) of constituents, designed to facilitate exchanges between the two parties, was created. To the ruler it meant the development of a hierarchical structure of agents, which was a major transformation from the simple (if extensive) management of the king's household and estates to a bureaucracy monitoring the wealth and/or income of the king's constituents. Let us see how this initial framework evolved in the two cases.

5. ENGLISH DEVELOPMENT

The tension between rulers and constituents (although that would hardly describe the situation at Runnymede in 1215) surfaces with the Magna Carta; but the fiscal crises come to a head with Edward I and Edward III during the Hundred Years War. . . . A logical consequence was that in the sixteenth century under the Tudors the structure of Tudor government was revolutionized. . . . This revolution transformed the government from an elaborate household structure into a bureaucracy increasingly concerned with overseeing and regulating the economy. It had early on been the wool trade which had served as the basis for a good deal of tax revenue; and . . . the wool trade involved a three-way relationship between the exporters, the wool growers as represented in Parliament, and the Crown. In this agreement, the Merchants of the Staple achieved a monopoly of the export trade as well as a depot in Calais. Parliament received the right to set the tax and the Crown obtained the revenue. In England the combined mix of the growth of the wool trade, the development of fee-simple ownership in land, and the development of arable lands and new crops imported from the Dutch contributed to an expansion of agriculture. At the same time, in the nonagricultural sector the economy became increasingly diversified. Although the Tudors continued to attempt to control the economy and to freeze the structure of economic activity into guilds and monopolistic activities, their efforts were relatively ineffective. They were ineffective because (1) the statutes only covered existing industries, so that new industries escaped rule; (2) despite opposition by town guilds, industries moved to the countryside and effectively escaped guild control; (3) the control of wages and laborers in the Statute of Artificers of 1563 was only partially and sporadically enforced; and (4) enforcement in the countryside was typically in the hands of unpaid justices of the peace who had little incentive to enforce the law.

The cloth trade therefore grew in the countryside. The interplay between the expansion of diverse economic activities escaping from guild restrictions and the pressures for the development of parliamentary control over the sovereign came to a head with the Stuarts, with the fumbling efforts of James I, the continuing fiscal crises that occurred under Charles I, and the articulate opposition of Coke and others. It was Coke who insisted that the common law was the supreme law of the land, and who repeatedly incurred the anger of James I. It was Coke who led the parliamentary opposition in the 1620s, which established common-law control over commercial law. By the end of Elizabeth's reign, a changing benefit-cost pattern of economic activity was emerging with the widening of domestic and foreign markets; the result was the expansion of voluntary organizations in the form of joint stock companies, and growing resentment against the crown-sponsored monopolies which excluded private companies from many of these growing markets. *Darcy vs. Allein* was only the most celebrated case reflecting this ongoing struggle to create a set of rights that would be outside the control of the monarchy. Passing the Statute of Monopolies was just another step in the ongoing process.

Yet the issue of the supremacy of Parliament hung in the balance for much of the 17th century. As the struggle continued, Parliament not only attempted to wrest from the king's control the granting of monopolies (as in the Statute of

Monopolies), but also to protect itself from the King's wrath by establishing religious, civil, and political freedoms as well (such as the Petition of Right in 1628). It distorts the story, however, to think of it as a clear-struggle between an absolutist "oriented" king and a unified Parliament concerned with economic, civil, and political liberties. As the Civil War attests, a complex of religious, economic, and political interests coalesced into armed camps. Moreover, the winning coalition one day could be in the minority the next day. Hence, there was persistent interest and concern with broadly based and impersonally guarded rights.

The final triumph of Parliament was produced in 1689, and in rapid consequence came a set of economic institutions reflecting the relatively increasing security of property rights. The creation of the Bank of England (1694) and the development of new financial instruments led to a dramatic decline in the cost of transacting and have been described as the English financial revolution. Both institutions and consequent failing transaction costs reflect increased security of the time dimension of property rights, a dimension critical to both a long-term capital market and to economic growth itself. . . .

6. SPANISH DEVELOPMENT

While the major steps in Spanish institutional evolution are not in question, nor is the final result, I do not believe that the specific steps along the way have been as clearly delineated as in the English story. . . . However, some sketch is possible.

Prior to the union of Ferdinand and Isabella, the kingdom of Aragon (comprising approximately Valencia, Aragon, and Catalonia) had a very different character than Castile. Aragon had been reconquered from the Arabs in the last half of the 13th century and had become a major commercial empire extending into Sardinia, Sicily, and part of Greece. The Cortes, reflecting the interests of merchants "had already secured the power to legislate and even to limit the king's power to issue legislation under certain conditions" (Veliz, 1980, p. 34). In contrast, Castile was continually engaged in warfare, either against the Moors or in internal strife. While the Cortes existed, it was seldom summoned. . . . In the 15 years after their union, Isabella succeeded in gaining control not only over the unruly warlike barons but over church policy in Castile as well. The result was a centralized monarchy in Castile; and it was Castile that defined the institutional evolution of both Spain and Latin America.

A major source of fiscal revenues was the Mesta (the sheep-herders guild), which in return for the right to migrate with their sheep across Castile provided the Crown with a secure source of revenue, but also with consequences adverse to the development of arable agriculture and the security of property rights, as well as with soil erosion.

Within Castile the other chief source of revenue was the *alcaba,* a sales tax. But as the Spanish empire grew to become the greatest empire since Roman times, its major sources of revenue were increasingly external, derived from Sicily, Naples, the low countries, and the New World. Control internally over the economy and externally over the far-flung empire entailed a large and elaborate hierarchy of bureaucrats armed with an immense outpouring of royal edicts. Over 400,000 decrees had been issued concerning the governance and economy of the Indies by 1635, an average of 2,500 a year since Columbus sailed first to the Indies. Designed to provide minute regulation of the economy, guilds also provided a vehicle for internal economic regulation. Price ceilings were imposed on grain and state-owned trading companies, and monopolistic grants provided control of external trade.

As the military costs of controlling the empire outstripped revenues (which declined with the revolt of the Netherlands and the gradual decrease in receipts of treasure), the Crown raised the internal tax (*alcaba*) from 1.2% to 10% and repeatedly went into bankruptcy, which is resolved through the seizure of properties and financial assets. The consequence was the decline of the Spanish economy and economic stagnation.

In terms of the foregoing model of the polity, the bargaining position of the Crown, vis-à-vis the Cortes, shifted in favor of the Crown and consequently resulted in the decline of the Cortes. The governance structure then became a large and elaborate bureaucracy, and there were endless efforts by the Crown to control its far-flung agents. Indeed, the history of the control of the Indies is an elaborate story in agency theory, beginning as early as Isabella's recision of Columbus' policies toward the Indians in 1502. Distance magnified the immense problem of monitoring agents in the New World; but despite the dissipation of rent at every level of the hierarchical structure, the Crown maintained effective control over the polity and over the economy of the New World.

7. CONSEQUENCES FOR THE NEW WORLD

It is likewise much easier to trace the institutional evolution of the English North American colonies than their Latin American counterpart. The initial conditions are in striking contrast. English America was formed in the very century when the struggle between Parliament and the Crown was coming to a head. Religious diversity, as well as political diversity in the mother country, was paralleled in the colonies. In the Spanish Indies, conquest came at the precise time that the influence of the Castilian Cortes was declining. The conquerers imposed a uniform religion and a uniform bureaucratic administration on the existing agricultural society.

In the English colonies there was substantial diversity in the political structure of crown proprietary and charter colonies. But the general development in the direction of local political control and the growth of assemblies was clear and unambiguous. Similarly, the Navigation Acts placed the colonies within the framework of overall British imperial policy, and within that broad framework the colonists were free to develop the economy. Indeed, the colonists themselves frequently imposed more restrictions on property rights than did the mother country. (The exception was the effort of proprietors to obtain quit-rents from settlers in proprietary colonies, such as that of Lord Penn. The problem of enforcement and collection in the context of the availability of land resulted in very indifferent success.) . . .

The French and Indian War (1755–63) is the familiar breaking point in American history. British efforts to impose (very modest) taxes on colonial subjects, as well as to curb westward migration, produced a violent reaction that led through a sequence of steps to the Revolution, the Declaration of Independence, the Articles of Confederation, the Northwest Ordinance, and the Constitution: a sequence of institutional expressions that formed a consistent evolutionary institutional pattern, despite the precariousness of the process.

In the Spanish Indies the recurrent crises were over the efficiency and control of the bureaucratic machinery. The decline under the Hapsburgs and the revival efforts under the Bourbons led to restructuring of the bureaucracy and even some liberalization of trade (under the Bourbons) within the empire. But the control of agents was a persistent problem, compounded by efforts of the Creoles to take over the bureaucracy in order to pursue their own interests. To whatever degree the wars of independence in Latin America were a struggle between colonial control (of the bureaucracy and consequent polity and economy) and imperial control, the struggle was imbued with ideological overtones that stemmed for the American and French revolutions. Independence brought United States-inspired constitutions, but with radically different consequences. . . .

The contrasting histories of North and South America are perhaps the best comparative case that we have of the consequences of divergent institutional paths for political and economic performance. We are only just beginning to extend economic and political theory to the study of institutions. I hope this historical introduction gives some indication of the promise of this approach for the study of economic history and economic growth.

REFERENCE

Coase, Ronald. "The Problem of Societal Cost." *Journal of Law and Economics* 3 (1960), pp. 1–44.

4

States, Firms, and Diplomacy

SUSAN STRANGE

Susan Strange argues that changes in the international economy have altered the relationship between states and multinational corporations and have given rise to new forms of diplomacy in the international arena. Highlighting the crucial importance of international economic factors, Strange points out how such world-wide trends as technological development, the growing mobility of capital, and the decreasing costs of communication and transportation have led increasing numbers of firms to plan their activities on a global basis. This has increased competition among states as they encourage firms to locate within their territories. The international economic environment within which all states operate has been fundamentally transformed, and governments are being forced to adapt to this new reality.

... Three propositions will be advanced here. First, that many seemingly unrelated developments in world politics and world business have common roots and are the result in large part of the same structural changes in the world economy and society. Second, that partly in consequence of these same structural changes, there has been a fundamental change in the nature of diplomacy. Governments must now bargain not only with other governments, but also with firms or enterprises, while firms now bargain both with governments and with one another. As a corollary of this, the nature of the competition between states has changed, so that macroeconomic management and industrial policies may often be as or even more important for governments than conventional foreign policies as conventionally conceived. The third proposition follows from the second, and concerns the significance of firms as actors influencing the future course of transnational relations — not least for the study of international relations and political economy.

STRUCTURAL CHANGE

Most commentators on international affairs have in our opinion paid far too little attention to structural change, particularly to change in the structure of production in the world economy. Our recent work argues that most of the recent changes in world politics, however unrelated they may seem on the surface, can be traced back in large part to certain common roots in the global political economy. We see common driving forces of structural change behind the liberation of Central Europe, the disintegration of the former Soviet Union, the intractable payments deficit of the United States, the Japanese surpluses, the rapid rise of the East Asian newly industrialized countries, and the U-turns of many developing country governments from military or authoritarian government to democracy, and from protection and import substitution towards open borders and export promotion.

These common driving forces of change, in brief, are the accelerating rate and cost of technological change, which has speeded up in its turn the internationalization of production and the dispersion of manufacturing industry to newly industrialized countries; increased capital mobility, which has made this dispersion of industry easier and speedier; and those changes in the structure of knowledge that have made transnational communications cheap and fast and have raised people's awareness of the potential for material betterment in a market economy. These common roots have resulted, at the same time and in many countries, in the demand for democratic government and for the economic flexibility that is impossible in a command economy. . . .

Technological Change, Mobile Capital, Transborder Communications

Most obvious of the structural changes acting as the driving force on firms and governments alike were those in the technology of industrial and agricultural production; related to them were changes in the international financial structure. The accelerating pace of technological change has enhanced the capacity of successful producers to supply the market with new products, and/or to make them with new materials or new processes. At the same time, product and process lifetimes have shortened, sometimes dramatically. Meanwhile, the costs to the firm of investment in R&D, research and development — and therefore of innovation — have risen. The result is that all sorts of firms that were until recently comfortably ensconced in their home markets have been forced, whether they like it or not, to seek additional markets abroad in order to gain the profits necessary to amortize their investments in time to stay up with the competition when the next technological advance comes along. It used to be thought that internationalism was the preserve of the large, privately owned Western "multinational" or transnational corporations. Today, thanks to the imperatives of structural change, these have been joined by many smaller firms, and also by state-owned enterprises and firms based in developing countries. Thus it is not the phenomenon of the transnational corporation that is new, but the changed balance between firms working only for a local or domestic market, and those working for a global market and in part producing in countries other than their original home base.

Besides the accelerating rate of technological change, two other critical developments contributed to the rapid internationalization of production. One was the liberalization of international finance, beginning perhaps with the innovation of Eurocurrency dealing and lending in the 1960s, and continuing unchecked with the measures of financial deregulation initiated by the United States in the mid-1970s and early 1980s. As barriers went down, the mobility of capital went up. The old difficulties of raising money for investment in offshore operations and moving it across the exchanges vanished. It was either unnecessary for the transnational corporations to find new funds, or they could do so locally.

The third contributing factor to internationalization has often been overlooked — the steady and cumulative lowering of the real costs of transborder transport and communication. Without them, central strategic planning of far-flung affiliates would have been riskier and more difficult, and out-sourcing of components as in car manufacture would have been hampered.

Broader Perspectives

These structural changes have permeated beyond finance and production to affect global politics at a deep level. They have, for instance, significantly affected North-South relations. The so-called Third World no longer exists as a coalition of developing countries ranged, as in UNCTAD (the UN Conference on Trade and Development), in opposition to the rich countries. Developing countries are now acutely aware that they are competing against each other, the laggards desperately trying to catch up with the successful newly industrialized countries. The transnational corporations' search for new markets was often a major factor leading them to set up production within those markets. Sometimes this was done for cost reasons. Other times it was done simply because the host government made it a condition of entry. The internationalization of production by the multinationals has surely been a major factor in the accelerated industrialization of developing countries since the 1950s. For it is not only the Asian newly industrialized countries whose manufacturing capacity has expanded enormously in the last two or three decades, but also countries like India, Brazil, Turkey and Thailand.

At the same time, the internationalization of production has also played a major part in the U-turn taken in economic policies by political leaders in countries as diverse and far apart as Turkey and Burma, Thailand and Argentina, India and Australia. Structural change, exploited more readily by some than others, has altered the perception of policy-makers in poor countries both about the nature of the system and the opportunities it opens to them for the present and the future. In the space of a decade, there has been a striking shift away from policies of import-substitution and protection towards export promotion, liberalization and privatization.

It is no accident that the "dependency school" writers of the 1970s have lost so much of their audience. Not only in Latin America (where most of this writing was focused), we see politicians and professors who were almost unanimous in the 1970s in castigating the multinationals as agents of American imperialism who now acknowledge them as potential allies in earning the foreign exchange badly needed for further development.

Nor, we would argue, is the end of the Cold War, the détente in East-West relations and the liberation of Central Europe from Soviet rule and military occupation to be explained by politics or personalities alone. Here too there are ways in which structural change has acted, both at the level of government and the bureaucracy, and at the popular level of consumers and workers.

In the production structure, even in the centrally planned economies, industrialization has raised living standards from the levels of the 1930s and 1940s, at least for the privileged classes of society. Material progress has not been as fast as in the market economy, but in the socialist countries as in Latin America or Asia, the ranks have multiplied of a middle class of managers, professional doctors, lawyers, engineers and bureaucrats, many of whom are significantly better educated than their parents. With this *embourgeoisement* has come greater awareness of what is going on in other countries, and of the widening gap between living standards in the affluent West and their own.

In the world market economy, competition among producers has lowered costs to consumers and widened their choice of goods, while raising their real incomes. Under the pressures of shortening product life cycles, heavier capital costs and new advances in technologies, rivalry among producers has unquestionably contributed to material wealth for the state as well as for consumers. Witness the spread down through income groups of cars, colour TVs, washing machines, freezers, video recorders, telephones, personal computers. In any Western home, a high proportion of these consumer goods carries the brand names of foreign firms.

By contrast, the Soviet consumer has suffered the deprivation consequent on the economy's insulation from the fast-changing global financial and production structures. But the information about what others enjoyed in the West could not altogether be kept from people even in the Soviet Union, let alone in Central Europe. The revolution in communications, and thus in the whole global knowledge structure, helped to reveal the widening gap between standards of living for similar social groups under global capitalism and under socialism.

At the same time, the new bourgeoisie, aware of the inefficiencies of the command economy, saw that economic change was being blocked by the entrenched apparatus of centralized government and could only be achieved through political change and wider participation. While the burden of defence spending certainly played a part in both East and West in furthering détente and making possible the liberation of Central Europe, political change was accelerated within the socialist countries by the rise of a new middle class and their perception of the gap in living standards and of the apparent inability of centrally planned systems to respond to the structural change in technologies of production.

We would argue that similar structural forces also lie behind the worldwide trend to democratic government and the rejection of military and authoritarian rule. In short, people have become better off and better educated and are making their material dissatisfaction and their political aspirations strongly felt. We would argue that this wave of political change has the same universal roots, whether in Greece, Portugal or Spain, in Turkey, or in Burma, Brazil, or Argentina. . . .

TWO NEW SIDES TO DIPLOMACY

State-Firm Diplomacy

The net result of these structural changes is that there now is greatly intensified competition among states for world market shares. That competition is forcing states to bargain with foreign firms to locate their operations within the territory of the state, and with national firms not to leave home, at least not entirely. . . .

... The transnational firm has command of an arsenal of economic weapons that are badly needed by any state wishing to win world market shares. The firm has, first, command of technology; second, ready access to global sources of capital; third, ready access to major markets in America, Europe and, often, Japan. If wealth for the state, as for the firm, can be gained only by selling on world markets — for the same reason that national markets are too small a source of profit for survival — then foreign policy should now begin to take second place to industrial policy; or perhaps, more broadly, to the successful management of society and the efficient administration of the economy in such a way as to outbid other states as the preferred home to the transnational firms most likely to win and hold world market shares.

While the bargaining assets of the firm are specific to the enterprise, the bargaining assets of the state are specific to the territory it rules over. The enterprise can operate in that territory — even if it just sells goods or services to people living there — only by permission and on the terms laid down by the government. Yet it is the firm that is adding value to the labour, materials and know-how going into the product. States are therefore competing with other states to get the value-added done in their territory and not elsewhere. That is the basis of the bargain.

Firm-Firm Diplomacy

A third dimension, equally the product of the structural changes noted earlier, is the bargaining that goes on between firms. This too may lead to partnerships or alliances in which, while they may be temporary or permanent, each side contributes something that the other needs, so that both may enhance their chances of success in the competition for world market shares. Firms involved in this third dimension of diplomacy may be operating in the same sector (as in aircraft design, development, and manufacturing) or in different sectors (where, for instance, one party may be contributing its expertise in computer electronics, the other in satellite communications).

For scholars of international relations, both new dimensions are important. The significance of the state-firm dimension is that states are now competing more for the means to create wealth within their territory than for power over more territory. Power, especially military capability, used to be a means to wealth. Now it is more the other way around. Wealth is the means to power — not just military power, but the popular or electoral support that will keep present ruling groups in their jobs. Without this kind of support, even the largest nuclear arsenals may be of little avail. Nowadays, except perhaps for oilfields and water resources, there is little material gain to be found in the control of more territory. As Singapore and Hong Kong have shown, world market shares — and the resulting wealth — can be won with the very minimum of territory. Even where, as in Yugoslavia or the Soviet Union, there is a recurrence of conflict over territory, the forces behind it are not solely ethnic nationalism of the old kind. Many Slovenes, Croats, Russians or Georgians want to wrest control over their territory from the central power because they believe they would be able to compete better in the world economy on their own than under the control of their old federal bosses. Autonomy is seen as a necessary condition for economic transformation and progress.

Successfully Managing Society and Economy

Having got control over territory, government policy-makers may understand well enough what is needed to bargain successfully with foreign firms to locate with them. But they may not always be able to deliver. For though the forces of structural change affect everyone, even the old centrally planned economies, the capacity of governments to respond are extremely diverse. . . .

. . . The diversity of government responses to structural change usually reflects the policy dilemmas peculiar to the government of that society. But precisely because of increased integration in the world market economy, it is more and more difficult for governments to "ring-fence" a particular policy so that implementing it does not directly conflict with, perhaps negate, some other policy. . . .

Contemplation of the diversity of host-country policies in monetary management, trade and competition policy very soon brings home the fact that there are no shortcuts and no magic tricks in wooing foreign firms. However, some general advice is still possible. One piece of advice is obviously to pinpoint the policy dilemmas where objectives clash. Another is to cut out the administrative delays and inefficiencies that bedevil the work of local managers. . . . Another good piece of advice, already stressed in the growing literature on the management of international business, is to break up monopolies and enforce competition among producers. . . .

. . . The diversity of government responses . . . is surely due not only to mulish stupidity or ignorance of the keys to success. Governments are, after all, political systems for the reconciliation of conflicting economic and social, and sometimes ethnic, interests. Moreover, the global structural changes that affect them all do so very differently, sometimes putting snakes, sometimes ladders in their path. Some small boats caught by a freak low tide in an estuary may escape grounding on the mud by alert and skillful management; others may be saved by luck. Our research suggests that the crucial difference between states these days is not, as the political scientists used to think, that between "strong" states and "weak" ones, but between the sleepy and the shrewd. States today have to be alert, adaptable to external change, quick to note what other states are up to. The name of the game, for governments just as for firms, is competition.

FIRMS AS DIPLOMATS

Our third general point — the importance of firms as major actors in the world system — will be obvious enough to leaders of finance and industry. They will not need reminding that markets may be moved, governments blown off course and balances of power upset by the big oil firms, by the handful of grain dealers, by major chemical or pharmaceutical makers. It will come as no surprise to them that the game of diplomacy these days has two extra new dimensions as well as the conventional one between governments.

But while I have scratched the surface of one of these — the bargaining between firms and governments — I have not said much about the third, bargaining between firms. This deserves to be the subject of a whole new research programme. Examples have recently multiplied of firms which were and may remain competitors but which under the pressures of structural change have decided to make strategic or even just tactical alliances with other firms in their own or a related sector of business. In the study of international relations it is accepted as normal that states should ally themselves with others while remaining competitors, so that the bargaining that takes place between allies is extremely tough about who takes key decisions, how risks are managed and how benefits are shared.

The implications for international relations analysis of the three-sided nature of diplomacy are far-reaching. The assertion that firms are major actors is at odds with the conventions of international relations as presently taught in most British universities and polytechnics. The standard texts in the subject subscribe to the dominant "realist" school of thought, which holds that the central issue in international society is war between territorial states, and the prime problematic therefore is the maintenance of order in the relations between these states. This traditional view of international relations also holds that the object of study is the behaviour of states towards other states, and the outcome of such behaviour *for states:* whether they are better or worse off, less or more powerful or secure. Transnational corporations may be mentioned in passing, but they are seen as adjuncts to or instruments of state policy.

Our contention is that transnational corporations should now be put centre stage; that their corporate strategies in choosing host countries as partners are already having great influence on the development of the global political economy, and will continue increasingly to do so. In common with many contemporary political economists, our interest is not confined to the behaviour of states or the outcomes for states. Who-gets-what questions must also now be asked — about social groups, generations, genders, and not least, about firms and the sectors in which they operate. Ten years from now we anticipate that the conventions and limitations of what has sometimes been called the British school of international relations will be regarded as impossibly dated, its perceptions as démodé as 1950s fashions. This is not to say, of course, that there are no lessons to be learned by economic ministries and corporate executives from the diplomatic history of interstate relations. Only that the study of international relations must move with the times, or be marginalized as a narrow specialism. . . .

To sum up. Much more analytical work is needed on firm-firm bargaining as well as on state-firm bargaining in all its multivariant forms. It needs recognizing that both types of bargaining are interdependent with developments in state-state bargaining (the stock in trade of international relations), and that this in turn is interdependent with the other two forms of transnational diplomacy. In the discipline of management studies, corporate diplomacy is becoming at least as important a subject as analysis of individual firms and their corporate strategies for finance, production and marketing. In the study of international relations, an interest in bargaining is already beginning to supplant the still-fashionable analysis of international regimes.

A focus on bargaining, and the interdependence of the three sides of diplomacy that together constitute transnational bargaining, will necessarily prove more flexible and better able to keep up with change in global structures. No bargain is for ever, and this is generally well understood by anyone with hands-on experience of negotiation. The political art for corporate executives, as for government diplomats, is to devise bargains that will hold as long as possible, bargains that will not easily be upset by changes in other bargaining relationships. This is true for political coalitions between parties, or between governments and social groups, such as labour; and it is equally true for bargains between governments and foreign firms, and between firms and other firms. The multiplicity of variables in the pattern of any one player's interlocking series of bargains is self-evident.

A final point about the interlocking outcomes of transnational bargaining relates to theories of international relations and political economy. Social scientists like to think that the accumulation of more and more data, the perfecting of analytical tools and their rigorous application according to scientific principles will some day, somehow, produce a general theory to explain political and economic behaviour. They are a bit like peasants who still believe there is a pot of gold buried at the end of the rainbow despite their repeated failures to track it down. Today, the complexity of the factors involved in each of the three forms of transnational bargaining, and the multiplicity of variables at play, incline us to deep scepticism about general theories. Not only are economics — *pace* the economists — inseparable from the real world of power and politics, but outcomes in the global political economy, the product of this complex interplay of bargains, are subject to the great divergences that we have observed.

II

HISTORICAL PERSPECTIVES

A truly international economy first emerged during the "long sixteenth century," the period from approximately 1480 to 1650. In its earliest form, the modern international economy was organized on the basis of mercantilism, a doctrine asserting that power and wealth were closely interrelated and were legitimate goals of national policy. Thus, wealth was necessary for power, and power could be used to obtain wealth. Power is a relative concept because one country can gain it only at the expense of another; thus, mercantilist nations perceived themselves to be locked in a zero-sum conflict in the international economy.

During this period countries pursued a variety of policies intended to expand production and wealth at home while denying similar capabilities to others. Six policies were of nearly universal importance. First, countries sought to prevent gold and silver, common mercantilist measures of wealth, from being exported. At the beginning of the sixteenth century, Spain declared the export of gold or silver punishable by death. Similarly, France declared the export of coined gold and silver illegal in 1506, 1540, 1548, and 1574, thereby demonstrating the difficulties of enforcing such laws. Second, regulations (typically, high tariffs) were adopted to limit imports to necessary raw materials. Importing raw materials was desirable because it lowered prices at home and thereby reduced costs for manufacturers. By limiting imports of manufactured and luxury items, on the other hand, countries sought to stimulate production at home while reducing it abroad. Third, exports of manufactured goods were encouraged for similar reasons. Fourth, just as they sought to encourage imports of raw materials, countries aimed to limit the export of these goods so as to both lower prices at home and limit the ability of others to develop a manufacturing capability of their own. Fifth, exports of technology — including both machinery and skilled artisans — were restricted in order to inhibit potential foreign competitors. Finally, many countries adopted navigation laws mandating that a certain percentage of their foreign trade had to be carried in native ships. This last trade regulation was intended to stimulate the domestic shipping and shipbuilding industries — both of which were necessary resources for successful war making.

By the early nineteenth century, mercantilist trade restrictions were coming under widespread attack, particularly in Great Britain. Drawing on the Liberal writings of Adam Smith and David Ricardo, Richard Cobden and other Manchester industrialists led the fight for free trade, which culminated in 1846 in the abolition of the "Corn Laws" (restrictions on grain imports), the last major mercantilist impediment to free trade in Britain. Other countries soon followed example. Indeed, under Britain's leadership, Europe entered a period of free trade that lasted from 1860 to 1879 (see Kindleberger, Reading 5). However, this trend toward freer trade was reversed in the last quarter of the nineteenth century. The purported causes of this reversal are many, including the decline of British hegemony, the onset of the first Great Depression (of 1873–1896), and the new wave of industrialization on the Continent, which led to protection for domestic manufacturers from British competition (see Gourevitch, Reading 6). For whatever reason — and the debate continues even today — by 1890, nearly all the major industrialized countries except Great Britain had once again imposed substantial restrictions on imports.

Coupled with this trend toward increased protection was a new wave of international investment and formal colonialism (see Frieden, Reading 7). Britain had already begun to expand its holdings of foreign territory during the period of free trade, and after 1880, it was joined by Germany and France. In 1860, Great Britain possessed 2.5 million square miles of colonial territory, and France, only .2 million square miles; Germany had not yet entered the colonial race. By 1899, Britain's holdings had expanded to 9.3 million square miles, France's to 3.7 million, and Germany's to 1.0 million, an expansion that occurred primarily in Africa and the Pacific. In 1876, slightly less than 11 percent of Africa and nearly 57 percent of Polynesia were colonized, yet by 1900, over 90 percent of Africa and almost 99 percent of Polynesia were controlled by European colonial powers and the United States.

World War I, which many analysts believe to have been stimulated by the race for colonies, and in particular by Germany's aggressive attempt to catch up with Great Britain, destroyed the remaining elements of the Pax Britannica. The mantle of leadership, which had previously been borne by Britain, was now divided between Britain and the United States. Yet neither country could — or desired to — play the leadership role previously performed by Britain (see Lake, Reading 8).

World War I was indeed a watershed in American international involvement. The terrible devastation caused by the war in Europe served to weaken the traditional world powers, while it brought the United States a period of unexpected prosperity. The Allies, which were short of food and weapons, bought furiously from American suppliers. To finance their purchases, they borrowed heavily from American banks and, once the United States entered the war, from the U.S. government. As a result, American factories and farms hummed as the war dragged on; industrial production nearly doubled during the war years. Moreover, because the war forced the European powers to neglect many of their overseas economic activities, American exporters and investors were also able to move into areas they had never before influenced. When the war began, the United States was a net debtor of the major European nations; by the time it ended, however, it was the world's principal lender and all the Allies were deeply in debt to American banks and the U.S. government.

Despite the position of political and economic leadership that the United States shared with Great Britain after World War I, the former country rapidly retreated into its traditional inward orientation. To be sure, many American banks and corporations continued to expand abroad very rapidly in the 1920s and the country remained an important world power, but the United States refused to join the League of Nations or any of the other international organizations created in the period. American tariff levels, which had been reduced on the eve of World War I, were once again raised. The reasons for the country's post–World War I *isolationism,* as it is often called, are many and controversial. Chief among them were the continued insularity of major segments of the American public, which were traditionally inward-looking in political and economic matters; the resistance to American power of such European nations as Great Britain and France; and widespread revulsion at the apparently futile deaths that had resulted from involvement in the internecine strife of the Old World.

Whatever the reasons for the isolationism of the 1920s, these tendencies were heightened as the world spiraled downward into depression after 1929. In the Smoot-Hawley Act of 1930, the United States dramatically increased its tariffs, and by 1933 the world was engulfed in a bitter trade and currency conflict. In 1933, desperate to encourage domestic economic recovery, U.S. president Franklin Roosevelt significantly devalued the dollar, thus effectively sounding the death knell of what remained of the nineteenth-century international economic order.

During the nearly four centuries summarized here, the international economy underwent several dramatic transformations. From a closed and highly regulated mercantilist system, the international economy evolved toward free trade in the middle of the nineteenth century. However, after a relatively brief period of openness, the international economy reversed direction and, starting with the resurgence of formal imperialism and accelerating after World War I, once again drifted toward closure. This historical survey highlights the uniqueness of the contemporary international political economy, which is the focus of the rest of this reader; David A. Lake compares the central characteristics of the international economy in the nineteenth and twentieth centuries. This survey also raises a host of analytic questions, many of which appear elsewhere in the book as well. Particularly important here is the question of what drives change in the international economy. In the readings that follow, Charles Kindleberger, in a domestic society–centered approach, focuses on interest groups and ideology; Peter Alexis Gourevitch examines interest groups and domestic institutions; Jeffry A. Frieden focuses on the evolving nature of international investment and its impact on the need for direct, colonial control over peripheral regions; and Lake emphasizes changes in the international political and economic systems.

5

The Rise of Free Trade
in Western Europe
CHARLES P. KINDLEBERGER

Charles P. Kindleberger, a leading economic historian, examines the process by which mercantilist trade restrictions were dismantled and evaluates several of the best-known theses concerning the ascendance of free trade in Western Europe. Presenting a domestic society–centered argument, Kindleberger contends that free trade in many instances arose as individual entrepreneurs pressured their governments to lift restrictions on international trade and finance so that they could pursue overseas business opportunities. Yet Kindleberger points out that political activity by entrepreneurs cannot explain the rapid expansion of free trade in Europe after 1850. He suggests that this "second wave" of free trade may have been motivated by ideology rather than by economic or political interests. This important article offers a persuasive explanation of how and why the market principle gained dominance within the international economy during the nineteenth century.

I

. . . The beginnings of free trade internationally go back to the eighteenth century. French Physiocratic theory enunciated the slogan *laisser faire, laisser passer* to reduce export prohibitions on agricultural products. Pride of place in practice, however, goes to Tuscany, which permitted free export of the corn of Sienese Maremma in 1737, after the Grand Duke Francis had read Sallustio Bandini's *Economical Discourse*. Beset by famine in 1764, Tuscany gradually opened its market to imported grain well before the Vergennes Treaty of 1786 between France and Britain put French Physiocratic doctrine into practice. Grain exports in Tuscany had been restricted under the "policy of supply," or "provisioning," or "abundance," under which the city-states of Italy limited exports from the surrounding countryside in order to assure food to the urban populace. Bandini and Pompeo Neri pointed out the ill effects this had on investment and productivity in agriculture.

The policy of supply was not limited to food. In the eighteenth and early nineteenth century exports were restricted in, among others, wool and coal (Britain), ashes, rags, sand for glass and firewood (Germany), ship timbers (Austria), rose madder (the Netherlands), and silk cocoons (Italy). The restrictions on exports of ashes and timber from Germany had conservation overtones. The industrial revolution in Britain led further to prohibitions on export of machinery and on emigration of artisans, partly to increase the supply for local use, but also to prevent the diffusion of technology on the Continent. We return to this below.

What was left in the policy of supply after the Napoleonic Wars quickly ran down. Prohibition of export of raw silk was withdrawn in Piedmont, Lombardy, and Venetia in the 1830's, freedom to export coal from Britain enacted in the 1840's. Details of the relaxation of restrictions are recorded for Baden as part of the movement to occupational freedom. The guild system gradually collapsed under the weight of increasing complexity of regulations by firms seeking exceptions for themselves and objecting to exceptions for others. A number of Prohibitions and export taxes lasted to the 1850's — as industrial consumers held out against producers, or in some cases, like rags, the collectors of waste products. Reduction of the export tax on rags in Piedmont in 1851 produced a long drawnout struggle between Cavour and the industry which had to close up thirteen plants when the tax was reduced. To Cavour salvation of the industry lay in machinery and the substitution of other materials, not in restricting export through Leghorn and Messina to Britain and North America.

Elimination of export taxes and prohibitions in nineteenth-century Europe raises doubt about the universal validity of the theory of the tariff as a collective good, imposed by a concentrated interest at the expense of the diffuse. The interest of groups producing inputs for other industries are normally more deeply affected than those of the consuming industries, but it is hardly possible that the consuming is always less concentrated than the producing industry.

II

The question of export duties sought by domestic manufacturers on their raw materials, and of import duties on outputs demanded by producers for the domestic market, was settled in the Netherlands in the eighteenth century in favor of mercantile interests. These were divided into the First Hand, merchants, shipowners and bankers; the Second Hand, which carried on the work of sorting and packing in staple markets, and wholesaling on the Continent; and the Third Hand, concerned with distribution in the hinterland. Dutch staple trade was based partly on mercantile skills and partly on the pivotal location of Amsterdam, Rotterdam, and other staple towns dedicated to trade in particular commodities, largely perishable, nonstandardized and best suited to short voyages. The First Hand dominated Dutch social and political life and opposed all tariffs on export or import goods, above a minimum for revenue, in order to maximize trade and minimize formalities. From 1815 to 1830 when Holland and Belgium were united as the Low Countries, the clash between the Dutch First Hand and Belgian producers in search of import protection from British manufactures was continuous and heated.

The First Hand objected to taxes for revenue on coffee, tea, tobacco, rice, sugar, and so on, and urged their replacement by excises on flour, meat, horses and servants. Tariffs for revenue must be held down to prevent smuggling and to sustain turnover. The safe maximum was given variously as three percent, five percent, and on transit even as one-half percent. Transit in bond, and transit with duty-cum-drawback were thought too cumbersome. The Dutch made a mistake in failing to emulate London which in 1803 adopted a convenient entrepôt dock with bonding. Loss of colonies and of overseas connections in the Napoleonic Wars made it impossible from early in the period to compete with Britain in trade. Equally threatening was Hamburg which supplied British and colonial goods to Central Europe in transit for one-half percent revenue duty maximum, many products free, and all so after 1839. More serious, however, was the rise of direct selling as transport efficiency increased. Early signs of direct selling can be detected at the end of the seventeenth century when Venice and Genoa lost their role as intermediary in traffic between Italy and the West. By the first half of the nineteenth century, they were abundant. "By the improved intercourse of our time (1840), the seller is brought more immediately into contact with the producer." Twenty years earlier, the Belgian members of a Dutch Belgian fiscal commission argued that "there was no hope of restoring Holland's general trade. Owing to the spread of civilization, all European countries could now provide for themselves in directly trading."[1]

It is a mistake to think of merchants as all alike. As indicated, First, Second and Third Hands of the Netherlands had different functions, status and power. In Germany, republican merchants of Hamburg differed sharply from those of the Imperial city, Frankfurt, and held out fifty years longer against the Zollverein. Within Frankfurt there were two groups, the English-goods party associated with the bankers, and the majority, which triumphed in 1836, interested in transit, forwarding, retail and domestic trade within the Zollverein. In Britain a brilliant picture had been drawn of a pragmatic free trader, John Gladstone, father of William, opposed to timber preferences for Canada, enemy of the East India Company monopoly on trade with China and India, but supportive of imperial preference in cotton and sugar, and approving of the Corn Laws on the ground of support for the aristocracy he hoped his children could enter via politics. The doctrinaire free traders of Britain were the cotton manufacturers like Gladstone's friend, Kirman Finlay, who regarded shipowners and corn growers as the two great monopolists.

The doctrinaire free trade of the Dutch merchants led to economic sclerosis, or economic sickness. Hamburg stayed in trade and finance and did not move into industry. In Britain, merchants were ignorant of industry, but were saved by the coming of the railroad and limited liability which provided an outlet for their surplus as direct trading squeezed profits from stapling. The economic point is simple: free trade may stimulate, but again it may lead to fossilization.

III

The movement toward freer trade in Britain began gross in the eighteenth century, net only after the Napoleonic Wars. In the initial stages, there was little problem for a man like Wedgewood advocating free trade for exports of manufactures under the Treaty of Vergennes with France, but prohibitions on the export of machinery and emigrations of artisans. Even in the 1820's and 1830's, a number of the political economists — Torrens, Baring, Peel, Nassau Senior — favored repeal of the Corn Laws but opposed export of machinery. The nineteenth century is seen by Brebner not as a steady march to *laisser-faire* but as a counterpoint between Smithian *laisser-faire* in trade matters and, after the Reform Bill, Benthamic intervention of 1832 which produced the Factory, Mines, Ten Hours and similar acts from 1833 to 1847.

First came the revenue aspect, which was critical to the movement to freer trade under Huskisson in the 1820's, Peel in the 1840's, and Gladstone in the 1850's. Huskisson and Gladstone used the argument that the bulk of revenue was produced by taxes on a few items — largely colonial products such as tea, coffee, sugar, tobacco, and wine and spirits — and that others produced too little revenue to be worth the trouble. Many were redundant (for example, import duties on products which Britain exported). Others were so high as to be prohibitory or encouraged smuggling and reduced revenue. When Peel was converted to free trade, it was necessary to reintroduce the income tax before he could proceed with repeal of 605 duties between 1841 and 1846, and reductions in 1,035 others. The title of Sir Henry Parnell's treatise on freer trade (1830) was *Financial Reform.*

But Huskisson was a free trader, if a cautious one. He spoke of benefits to be derived from the removal of "vexatious restraints and meddling interference in the concerns of internal industry and foreign commerce."[2] Especially he thought that imports stimulated efficiency in import-competing industry. In 1824 the prohibition on silk imports had been converted to a duty of thirty percent regarded as the upper limit of discouragement to smuggling. In a speech on March 24, 1826, said by Canning to be the finest he had heard in the House of Commons, Huskisson observed that Macclesfield and Spitalfield had reorganized the industry under the spur of enlarged imports, and expanded the scale of output. Both Michel Chevalier and Count Cavour referred to this positive and dynamic response to increased imports in England.

Restrictions on export of machinery and emigration of artisans went back, as indicated, to the industrial revolution. Prohibition of export of stocking frames was enacted as early as 1696. Beginning in 1774 there was a succession of restrictions on tools and utensils for the cotton and linen trades and on the emigration of skilled artisans. The basis was partly the policy of supply, partly naked maintenance of monopoly. Freedom had been granted to the emigration of workmen in 1824. After the depression of the late 1830's, pressure for removal of the prohibition came from all machinery manufacturers. Following further investigation by a Select Committee of Parliament, the export prohibition was withdrawn.

The main arguments against prohibition of the export of machinery and emigration of artisans were three: they were ineffective, unnecessary, and harmful. Ineffectuality was attested to by much detail in the Select Committee reports on the efficiency of smuggling. Machinery for which licenses could not be obtained could be dispatched illegally in one of a number of ways — by another port; hidden in cotton bales, in baggage or mixed with permitted machinery and in a matter of hours. Guaranteed and insured shipments could be arranged in London or Paris for premia up to thirty percent.

That prohibition was unnecessary was justified first by the inability of foreigners, even with English machinery and English workmen, to rival English manufacturers. Britain had minerals, railways, canals, rivers, better division of labor, "trained workmen habituated to all industrious employments."[3] "Even when the Belgians employed English machines and skilled workers, they failed to import the English spirit of enterprise, and secured only disappointing results."[4] In 1825, the Select Committee concluded it was safe to export machinery, since seven-year-old machinery in Manchester was already obsolete.

In the third place it was dangerous. Restriction on emigration of artisans failed to prevent their departure, but did inhibit their return. Restriction of machinery, moreover, raised the price abroad through the cost of smuggling, and stimulated production on the Continent. Improvement in the terms of trade through restriction of exports (but failure to cut them off altogether) was deleterious for its protective effect abroad.

Greater coherence of the Manchester cotton spinners over the machinery makers spread over Manchester, Birmingham and London may account for the delay from 1825 to 1841 in freeing up machinery, and support Pincus' theory on the need of concentrated interests. But the argument of consistency was telling. In 1800 the Manchester manufacturers of cloth had demanded a law forbidding export of yarn, but did not obtain it. The 1841 Second Report concluded that machinery making should be put on the same footing as other departments of British industry. It is noted that Nottingham manufacturers approved free trade but claim an exception in regard to machinery used in their own manufacture. Babbage observed that machinery makers are more intelligent than their users, to whose imagined benefits their interests are sacrificed, and referred to the "impolicy of interfering between two classes."[5] In the end, the Manchester Chamber of Commerce became troubled by the inconsistency and divided; the issue of prohibition of machinery was subsumed into the general attack on the Corn Laws. In the 1840's moreover, the sentiment spread that Britain should become the Workshop of the World, which implied the production of heavy goods as well as cotton cloth and yarn.

Rivers of ink have been spilled on the repeal of the Corn Laws, and the present paper can do little but summarize the issues and indicate a position. The questions relate to the Stolper-Samuelson distribution argument, combined with the Reform Bill of 1832 and the shift of political power from the landed aristocracy to the bourgeois; incidence of the Corn Laws and of their repeal, within both farming and manufacturing sectors; the potential for a dynamic response of farming to lower prices from competition; and the relation of repeal to economic development on the Continent, and especially whether industrialization could be halted by expanded and assured outlets for agricultural produce, a point of view characterized by Gallagher and Robinson as "free-trade imperialism." A number of lesser issues may be touched upon incidentally: interaction between the Corn Laws and the Zollverein, and its tariff changes in the 1840's; the question of whether repeal of the Corn Laws and of the Navigation Acts would have been very long delayed had it not been for the potato famine in Ireland and on the Continent; and the question of whether the term "free-trade imperialism" is better reserved for Joseph Chamberlain's Empire preference of fifty years later.

In the normal view, the Reform Bill of 1832 shifted power from the land and country to the factory and city, from the aristocratic class to the bourgeois, and inexorably led to changes in the trade policies which had favored farming and hurt manufacturing. One can argue that repeal of the Corn Laws represented something less than that and that the Reform Bill was not critical. The movement to free trade had begun earlier in the Huskisson reforms: speeches in Parliament were broadly the same in 1825 when it was dominated by landed aristocrats as in the 1830's and 1840's. Numbers had changed with continued manufacturing expansion, but nothing much more. Or one can reject the class explanation, as Polanyi does, and see something much more ideological. "Not until the 1830's did economic liberalism burst forth as a crusading passion." The liberal creed involved faith in man's secular salvation through a self-regulating market, held with fanaticism and evangelical fervor. French Physiocrats were trying to correct only one inequity, to break out of the policy of supply and permit export of grain. British political economists of the 1830's and 1840's who won over Tories like Sir Robert Peel and Lord Russell, and ended up in 1846 with many landlords agreeable to repeal of the Corn Laws, represented an ideology. "Mere class interests cannot offer a satisfactory explanation for any long-run social process."[6]

Under a two-sector model, free trade comes when the abundant factor acquires political power and moves to eliminate restrictions imposed in the interest of the scarce factor which has lost power. In reality factors of production are not monolithic. Some confusion in the debate attached to the incidence of the tax on imported corn within both farming and manufacturing. The Anti-Corn Law League of Cobden and Bright regarded it as a tax on food, taking as much as twenty percent of the earnings of a hand-loom weaver. Cobden denied the "fallacy" that wages rose and fell with the price of bread. Benefits, moreover, went to the landlord and not to the farmer or farm-laborer, as rents on the short leases in practice rose with the price of corn. There are passages in Cobden which suggest that hurt of the Corn Laws fell upon the manufacturing and commercial classes rather than labor but the speeches run mainly in terms of a higher standard of living for the laborer who would spend his "surplus of earnings on meat, vegetables, butter, milk and cheese," rather than on wheaten loaves. The Chartists were interested not in repeal, but in other amenities for the workers. Peel's conversion waited on his conclusion that wages did not vary with the price of provision, and that repeal would benefit the wage earner rather than line the pockets of the manufacturer.

In any event, with Gladstone's reductions in duties on meat, eggs and dairy products, with High Farming, and an end to the movement off the farm and out of handwork into the factory real wages did rise in the 1850's, but so did profits on manufacturing. As so often in economic debates between two alternatives, history provides the answer which economists abhor, both. Nor did repeal bring a reduction in incomes to landlords — at least not for thirty years — as the farm response to repeal, and to high prices of food produced by the potato famine, was more High Farming.

Cobden may have only been scoring debating points rather than speaking from conviction when on a number of occasions he argued that the repeal would stimulate landlords "to employ their capital and their intelligence as other classes are forced to do in other pursuits" rather than "in sluggish indolence," and to double the quantity of grain, or butter, or cheese, which the land is capable of providing, with "longer leases, draining, extending the length of fields, knocking down hedgerows, clearing away trees which now shield the corn" and to provide more agricultural employment by activity to "grub up hedges, grub up thorns, drain, ditch." Sir James Caird insisted that High Farming was the answer to the repeal of the Corn Laws and many shared his view. The fact is, moreover, that the 1850's were the Golden Age of British farming, with rapid technical progress through the decade though it slowed thereafter. Repeal of the Corn Laws may not have stimulated increased efficiency in agriculture, but it did not set it back immediately, and only after the 1870's did increases in productivity run down.

The political economists in the Board of Trade — Bowring, Jacob, MacGregor — sought free trade as a means of slowing down the development of manufacturing on the Continent. They regarded the Zollverein as a reply to the imposition of the Corn Laws, and thought that with its repeal Europe, but especially the Zollverein under the leadership of Prussia, could be diverted to invest more heavily in agriculture and to retard the march to manufacturing. There were inconsistencies between this position and other facts they adduced: Bowring recognized that Germany had advantages over Great Britain for the development of manufacturing, and that Swiss spinning had made progress without protection. The 1818 Prussian tariff which formed the basis for that of the Zollverein was the lowest in Europe when it was enacted — though the levying of tariffs on cloth and yarn by weight gave high effective rates of protection despite low nominal duties to the cheaper constructions and counts. Jacob noted that the export supply elasticity of Prussian grain must be low, given poor transport. "To export machinery, we must import corn,"[7] but imports of corn were intended to prevent the development of manufacturers abroad, whereas the export of machinery assisted it. The rise and progress of German manufacturing was attributed to restrictions on the admission of German agricultural products and wood, imposed by France and England, but also to "the natural advantages of the several states for manufacturing industry, the genius and laborious character and the necessities of the German people, and . . . especially the unexampled duration of peace, and internal tranquility which all Germany enjoyed."[8]

The clearest statements are those of John Bowring. In a letter of August 28, 1839, to Lord Palmerston he asserted that the manufacturing interest in the Zollverein "is greatly strengthened and will become stronger from year to year unless counteracted by a system of concessions, conditional upon the gradual lowering of tariffs. The present state of things will not be tenable. The tariffs will be elevated under the growing demands and increasing power of the manufacturing states, or they will be lowered by calling into action, and bringing over to an alliance, the agricultural and commercial interests."[9] In his testimony before the Select Committee on Import Duties in 1840 he went further: "I believe we have created an unnecessary rivalry by our vicious legislation; that many of these countries never would have dreamed of being manufacturers."

On this showing, the repeal of the Corn Laws was motivated by "free-trade imperialism," the desire to gain a monopoly of trade with the world in manufactured goods. Zollverein in the 1830's merely indicated the need for haste. Torrens and James Deacon Hume, among others, had been pushing for importing corn to expand exports in the 1820's, before Zollverein was a threat.

Reciprocity had been a part of British commercial policy in the Treaty of Vergennes in 1786, in treaties reducing the impact of the Navigation Laws in the 1820's and 1830's. The French were suspicious, fearing that they had been out-traded in 1786. They evaded Huskisson's negotiations in 1828. But reciprocity was unnecessary, given David Hume's law. Unilateral reduction of import duties increased exports. Restored into the British diplomatic armory in 1860, reciprocity later became heresy in the eyes of political economists, and of the manufacturing interest as well.

The view that ascribes repeal of the Corn Laws to free-trade imperialism, however, fails adequately to take account of the ideology of the political economists, who believed in buying in the cheapest market and selling in the dearest, or of the short-run nature of the interests of the Manchester merchants themselves. It was evident after the 1840's that industrialization on the Continent could not be stopped, and likely that it could not be slowed down. The Navigation Acts were too complex; they had best be eliminated. The Corn Laws were doomed, even before the Irish potato famine, though that hastened the end of both Corn Laws and Navigation Acts, along with its demonstration of the limitation of market solutions under some circumstances.

"A good cause seldom triumphs unless someone's interest is bound up with it."[10] Free trade is the hypocrisy of the export interest, the clever device of the climber who kicks the ladder away when he has attained the summit of greatness. But in the English case it was more a view of the world at peace, with cosmopolitan interests served as well as national.

It is difficult in this to find clear-cut support for any of the theories of tariff formation set forth earlier. Free trade as an export-interest collective good, sought in a representative democracy by concentrated interests to escape the free rider, would seem to require a simple and direct connection between the removal of the tariff and the increase in rents. In the repeal of the Corn Laws, and the earlier tariff reductions of Huskisson and Peel, the connection was roundabout — through Hume's law, which meant that increased imports would lead to increased prices or quantities (or both) exported on the one hand, and/or through reduced wages, or higher real incomes from lower food prices on the other. Each chain of reasoning had several links.

Johnson's view that free trade is adopted by countries with improving competitiveness is contradictory to the free-trade-imperialism explanation, that free trade is adopted in an effort to undermine foreign gains in manufacturing when competitiveness has begun to decline. The former might better account in timing for Adam Smith's advocacy of free trade seventy years earlier—though that had large elements of French Physiocratic thought — or apply to the 1820's when British productivity was still improving, before the Continent had started to catch up. In turn, free-trade imperialism is a better explanation for the 1830's than for the end of the 1840's, since by 1846 it was already too late to slow, much less to halt, the advance of manufacturing on the Continent.

Vested interests competing for rents in a representative democracy, thrusting manufacturers seeking to expand markets, or faltering innovators, trying as a last resort to force exports on shrinking markets — rather like the stage of foreign direct investment in Vernon's product cycle when diffusion of technology has been accomplished — none of these explanations seems free of difficulties as compared with an ideological explanation based on the intellectual triumph of the political economists, their doctrines modified to incorporate consistency. The argument took many forms: static, dynamic, with implicit reliance on one incidence or another, direct or indirect in its use of Hume's law. But the Manchester School, based on the political economists, represented a rapidly rising ideology of freedom for industry to buy in the cheapest and sell in the dearest market. It overwhelmed the Tories when it did not convert them. Britain in the nineteenth century, and only to a slightly lesser extent the Continent, were characterized by a "strong, widely-shared conviction that the teachings of contemporary orthodox economists, including Free Traders, were scientifically exact, universally applicable, and demanded assent."[11] In the implicit debate between Thurman Arnold who regarded economic theorists (and lawyers) as high priests who rationalize and sprinkle holy water on contemporary practice, and Keynes who thought of practical men as responding unconsciously to the preaching of dead theorists, the British movement to free trade is a vote, aided by the potato famine, for the view of Keynes.

IV

France after 1815 was a high-tariff country which conformed to the Pincus model for a representative democracy with tariffs, for various interests, except that (a) there were tariffs for all, and (b) it was not a democracy. The Physiocratic doctrine of *laisser-faire* agricultural exports had been discredited in its reciprocal form by the disaster wreaked by imports up to 1789 under the Treaty of Vergennes. The Continental system, moreover, provided strong protection to hothouse industries, which was continued in the tariff of 1816, and elaborated in 1820 and 1822. To the principles of Turgot, that there should be freedom of grain trade inside France but no imports except in periods of drought, were added two more: protection of the consumer by regulating the right of export of wheat — a step back from Physiocratic doctrine — and protecting the rights of producers by import tariffs. In introducing the tariff of 1822 for manufactures, Saint-Cricq defended prohibitions, attacked the view that an industry could not survive with a duty of twenty percent should perish, saying that the government intended to protect all branches together: "agriculture, industry, internal commerce, colonial production, navigation, foreign commerce finally, both of land and of sea."[12]

It was not long, however, before pressures for lower duties manifested themselves. Industries complained of the burden of the tariff on their purchases of inputs, and especially of the excess protection accorded to iron. It was calculated that protection against English iron cost industrial consumers fifty million francs a year and had increased the price of wood — used for charcoal, and owned by the many noble *maîtres de forges* — by thirty percent on the average and in some places fifty percent. Commissions of inquiry in 1828 and 1834 recommended modifications in duties, especially to enlarge supplies which local industry was not in a position to provide, and to convert prohibitions into tariffs. A tumult of conflict broke out in the Chamber among the export interests of the ports, the textile interests of Alsace and Normandy, the *maîtres de forges,* and the consumers of iron, with no regard, says the protectionist Gouraud, for the national interest. The Chambers were then dissolved by the cabinet, and tariffs adjusted downward, in coal, iron, copper, nitrates, machinery, horses. Reductions of the 1830's were followed in the peaks of business by similar pressure for reductions in prosperous phases of the cycle of the 1840's and 1850's.

A troubling question that involved conflicting interests in this period was presented by sugar, for which it was impossible to find a solution agreeable at the same time to colonial planters, shipowners, port refiners, consumers and the treasury. Colonial supply was high cost and a 55 francs per 100 kilograms duty on foreign supplies was needed to keep the sugar ports content. This, however, made it economical to expand beet-sugar production, begun during the Continental blockade, and the sugar ports turned to taxing this domestic production, less heavily at first, but with full equality in 1843. By this time it was too late, and with the freeing of the slaves in 1848, French colonial sugar production no longer counted.

The free-trade movement in France had its support in Bordeaux, the wine-exporting region; Lyon, interested in silk; and Paris, producer of so-called Paris articles for sale abroad (cabinet ware, perfumes, imitation jewelry, toys, and so on). Later Norman agricultural interests in the export of butter and eggs to London teamed up with Bordeaux in wine to resist the attempts by textile interests to enlist agriculture in favor of higher tariffs.

Intellectual support to free trade led by Bastiat from Bordeaux, and with Michel Chevalier as its most prestigious member, is dismissed by Lévy-Leboyer as unimportant. Nonetheless, Chevalier had an important part in the negotiation of the treaty, and in persuading Napoleon III to impose it on France in the face of the united opposition of the Chamber of Deputies. Some attention to his thought is required.

The prime interest of the *Société d'Economie Politique* and of Chevalier was growth. His two-year visit to the United States in 1833–1835 impressed him with the contribution of transport to economic growth and contributed to his 1838 major work on *The Material Interests of France in Roads, Canals and Railroads.* American protectionist doctrine of Henry Carey seems not to have affected him. Polytechnician, graduate of the *Ecole des Mines,* Chevalier's first interest in freer trade came from a project to establish woolen production in the Midi, and to obtain cheaper wool. Much of his later reasoning was in terms of the penalty to industry from expensive materials: Charging 35 francs for a quintal of iron worth 20 imposes on industry "the labor of Sisyphus and the work of Penelope."[13] His major argument, at the *College de France,* and in his *Examen du Système Commercial,* cited the success of Spitalfield and Macclesfield when Huskisson permitted competition of imports; and the experience of the manufacturers of cotton and woolen textiles in Saxony, who were worried by the enactment of

Zollverein but sufficiently stimulated by import competition so that in two or three years their industry was flourishing. The letter of Napoleon III to Fould talks in specifics of the need to abolish all duties on raw materials essential to industry to encourage production, and to reduce by stages the duties on goods which are consumed on a large scale. In the more general introduction it states that "lack of competition causes industry to stagnate," echoing the Chevalier view. Chevalier himself was one of the judges of the Universal Exposition of 1855 in Paris and noted that France received so many prizes that no one dared confess to being a protectionist.

There were economic purposes behind the Anglo-French treaty, as evidenced by the proposal in France in 1851 for tariffs of twenty percent, ten percent and a duty-free on wholly manufactured goods, semi-finished manufactures and raw materials; by actual reductions in duties on coal, iron and steel in 1852 as the railroad boom picked up; and by the legislative proposal designed by Napoleon III in 1855, but not put forward until after the Crimean War, to admit 241 items duty free, reduce tariffs on 19 others, remove all prohibitions and set a top limit of thirty percent. This last was turned down by the Chamber and Napoleon promised not to submit a new tariff proposal before 1861.

Economic interests were involved, and the theories of great men like Cobden and Chevalier. However, there was more: Napoleon III was starting to engage in foreign adventure. He wanted to rid Italy of Austrian rule by use of arms. The British opposed his military measures, despite their recent use of force in Crimea. The treaty was used to hold British neutrality, as much as or more than to stimulate growth in France. Moreover, it did not need to be submitted to the Chamber. Under the Constitution of 1851, the Emperor had the sole power to make treaties, and such treaties encompassed those dealing with trade.

The move was successful both politically and economically. With the help of the French armies, Italy was unified under the leadership of Piedmont, and French growth never faltered under the impetus of increased imports. French industries met competition successfully and checked the growth of imports after two years. While its effects are intermingled with those of the spread of the French railroad network, it "helped to bring about the full development of the industrial revolution in France."

Further, it added impetus to the free-trade movement in Europe. This was under way in the early 1850's, following repeal of the Corn Laws. The Swiss constitution of 1848 had called for a tariff for revenue only and protective duties were reduced progressively from 1851 to 1855. The Netherlands removed a tariff on ship imports and a prohibition against nationalization of foreign ships. Belgium plugged gap after gap in its protective system in the early 1850's, only to turn around at the end of the decade and adopt free trade down the line. Piedmont, as we shall see, and Spain, Portugal, Norway and Sweden (after 1857) undertook to dismantle their protective and prohibitive restrictions. With the Anglo-French treaty the trickle became a flood. France, Germany, Italy and Britain engaged in negotiating reciprocal trade treaties with the most-favored nation clause.

Following French defeat at Sedan in 1870 and the abdication of Louis Napoleon, the Third Republic brought in the protectionist Thiers. The Cobden treaty was denounced in 1872. Reversal of policy waited upon the repeal of the Le Chapelier law of 1791, taken in the heat of the French revolution against associations, which forbade economic interests from organizing. Dunham claims that a country with leadership would have accepted a moderate tariff in 1875, but that the free traders had neither organization nor conviction, that is, too many free riders.

The French movement to free trade was taken against the weight of the separate interests, in the absence of strong export interests, with an admixture of economic theory of a dynamic kind, and imposed from above. The motivation of that imposition was partly economic, partly, perhaps even mainly, political. Moreover, it had a bandwagon effect in spreading freer trade.

In the French case, the leadership overwhelmed the concentrated economic interests. That leadership earned its surplus, to use Frohlich, Oppenheimer and Young's expression, in a coin different than economic, that is, in freedom to maneuver in foreign policy. It may be possible to subsume increases in leadership surplus in this form into an "economic theory of national decision-making" with costs to vested interests accepted in exchange for political benefits to a national leader, ruling by an imposed constitution, the legitimacy of which is not questioned. The effort seems tortured.

V

As mentioned earlier, the Prussian tariff of 1818 was regarded when it was enacted as the lowest in Europe. But the duties on coarse yarns and textiles were effectively high, since the tariff was levied by weight. Jacob in 1819 noted that the "system of the Prussian government has always been of manufacturing at home everything consumed within the Kingdom; of buying from others, nothing that can be dispensed with," adding "As scarcely any competition exists, but with their own countrymen, there is little inducement to adopt the inventions of other countries, or to exercise their facilities in perfecting their fabrics; none of these have kept pace. . . ."[14] Baden, on joining the Zollverein which adopted the Prussian tariff for the totality, believed itself to be raising its tariff level when it joined. What Baden did, however, was to acquire enforcement: its long border had previously been effectively open.

The Prussian tariff dominated that of the Zollverein, organized in the years from 1828 to 1833, primarily because Prussia took a very liberal view of tariff revenues. Most goods by sea entered the German states via Prussia, directly or by way of the Netherlands, but the text of the Zollverein treaty of 1833 provided that the revenues from the duties after deduction of expenses would be divided among the contracting states according to population. Prussia thus received 55 percent, Bavaria 17 percent, Saxony 6.36 percent, Wurtemberg 5.5 percent, and so on, and [Prussia] was said in 1848 to have sacrificed about two million talers a year, exclusive of the fiscal loss sustained by smuggling along the Rhine and Lake Constance. This can be regarded as a side-payment made by the beneficiary of income-distribution under Pareto-optimal conditions to gain its policy, or as the disproportionate share of overhead costs of the collective good saddled on the party that most wanted it.

Despite adjustments made in Prussian customs duties between 1819 and 1833, the tariff remained low by British standards. Junker grain growers were hopeful of importing British manufactures in order to sell Britain more grain. Junker bureaucrats, brought up on Adam Smith and free trade by instinct, were fearful that highly protective rates would reduce the revenue yield.

Outside of Prussia plus Hamburg and Frankfurt and the other grain-growing states of Mecklenburg, Pomerania, and so on, there was interest in higher tariffs, but apart from the Rhineland, little in the way of organized interests. Von Delbrück comments that Prussia and Pomerania had free trade interests and shipping interests, but that outside the Rhineland, which had organized Chambers of Commerce under the French occupation, there were few bureaucrats, or organs with views on questions of trade and industry. Nor did the Prussian government see a need to develop them.

Saxony was sufficiently protected by its interior location so as not to feel threatened by low tariffs, which, as mentioned, were not really low on coarse cloths. On joining the Zollverein, Baden was concerned over raising its tariff, and worried lest it be cut off from its traditional trading areas of Switzerland and Alsace. It fought with the Zollverein authorities over exemptions for imported capital equipment, but gradually evolved into a source of pressure, with Bavaria and Wurtemberg, for higher tariffs on cotton yarns and iron. Fischer points out the request for lifting the duty on cotton yarns from two talers per centner to five was resisted by the weavers of Prussia (the Rhineland) and Silesia.

Cotton yarns and iron were the critical items. Shortly after the formation of the Zollverein, a trend toward protection was seen to be under way. The Leipsig consul reported a new duty on iron to the Board of Trade in February 1837 and observed that the switch from imports of cotton cloth to imports of yarn pointed in the direction of ultimate exclusion of both. Bowring's letter of August 1839 noted that the manufacturing interest was growing stronger, that the existing position was untenable, and that tariffs would be raised under the growing demands and increasing power of the manufacturing states, or would be lowered by an alliance between the agricultural and commercial interests.

Open agitation for protection began two and one-half years after the formation of the Zollverein when the South pushed for duties on cotton yarns. Linen yarns and cloth went on the agenda in 1839 and iron, protection for which was sought by Silesian and west German ironwork owners, beginning in 1842. But these groups lacked decisive power. The Prussian landed nobility covered their position by citing the interests of the consumers, and Prince Smith, the expatriate leader of the doctrinaire free traders, in turn tried to identify free trade and low tariffs with the international free-trade movement rather than with the export interests of the Junkers. The tariff on iron was raised in 1844, those on cotton yarns and linen yarns in 1846. Von Delbrück presents in detail the background of the latter increases, starting with the bureaucratic investigations into linen, cotton, wool, and soda, with their negative recommendations; continuing through the negotiations, in which Prussia was ranged against any increase and all the others in favor; and concluding that the Prussian plenipotentiary to the Zollverein conference was right in not vetoing the increases, as he could have done, operating on the theory that a compromise was more important than the rationally correct measure of this or that tariff. The head of the Prussian Handelsamt was not satisfied with the outcome of the conference but had to accept it.

From 1846 on, the direction of Zollverein tariffs was downward, aided first by the repeal of the Corn Laws and secondly by the Cobden-Chevalier treaty. With the increases of the 1840's and English reductions, the Zollverein tariff from one of the lowest in Europe had become relatively high. Von Delbrück was one of the doctrinaire free traders in the Prussian civil service and notes that in 1863 he had been trying for a reduction on the tariff in pig iron for seven years, since the tariff reform of 1856, which reordered but did not lower duty schedules. He also wanted a reduction in the tariff on cotton cloth; duties on woolens were no longer needed. The opportunity came with the announcement of the Anglo-French treaty. He noted that Austria had gone from prohibitions to tariffs, that the Netherlands had reformed its tariffs with a five percent maximum on industrial production, and that the levels of Italian duties were lower than those in Germany. "Could we stay away from this movement? We could not."[15]

Bismarck was no barrier to the Junker bureaucracy. His view about tariff negotiations was expressed in 1879 in the question: "Who got the better of the bargain?" Trade treaties, he believed, were nothing in themselves but an expression of friendship. His economic conscience at this time, he said later, was in the hands of others. Moreover, he had two political ends which a trade treaty with France might serve: to gain her friendship in the Danish question, and to isolate Austria, which was bidding for a role in the German Confederation. Austrian tariffs were high. The lower the levels of the Zollverein the more difficulty she would have in joining it and bidding against Prussia for influence. The Zollverein followed the 1863 treaty with France with a series of others.

Exports of grain from Prussia, Pomerania, and Mecklenberg to London as a percentage of total English imports hit a peak in 1862 at the time of the Civil War and proceeded down thereafter as American supplies took over. The free-trade movement nonetheless continued. Only hesitation prevented a move to complete free trade at the peak of the boom in 1873. There is debate whether the crash later in the year triggered off the return to protection in 1879 or not. Victory in 1871 had enlarged competition in iron and cotton textiles by including Alsace and Lorraine in the new German Empire. Radical free traders and large farmers achieved the reduction in duties on raw iron in 1873 and passed legislative provision for their complete removal in 1877. But Lambi notes that *Gewerbefreiheit* (freedom of occupation) had caused dissatisfaction and in some versions subsumed free trade. By 1875 the iron interests are organizing to resist the scheduled elimination of iron duties in 1877.

The difference between the 1873 depression which led to tariffs, and the 1857 crisis which did not lay in (a) the fact that the interests were not cohesive in the earlier period and (b) that Britain did not keep on lowering duties in the later period as it had in the first. On the first score the Verein Deutscher Eisen und Stahl-Industrielle was formed in 1873 after vertical integration of steel back to iron mining had removed the opposition between the producers and consumers of iron. This much supports the view of the effectiveness of concentrated interests achieving their tariff goals when scattered interests will not — though again it has nothing to do with representative democracy. On the other hand, the free traders also organized; in 1868 the Kongress Nord-Deutscher Landwirte was organized, and in 1871 it was broadened to cover all Germany. In 1872, a Deutsche Landwirtschaftsrat was formed. Many of these organizations and the once free-trade Congress of German Economists were subverted and converted to protection after 1875, but a new Union for the Promotion of Free Trade was formed in September 1876. German economic interests as a whole became organized, and the struggle was among interests concentrated on both sides.

Abandonment of the opposition of the landed interests is perhaps critical. Consumers of iron in machinery, they opposed tariffs on iron up to 1875, but with the decline in the price of grain and the threat of imports, their opposition collapsed. It might have been possible to support tariffs for grain and free trade for iron, but inconsistency is open to attack. After von Delbrück's resignation or discharge in April 1876, Bismarck forged the alliance of bread and iron. As widely recounted, he had strong domestic political motives for higher tariffs on this occasion, as contrasted with his international political gains from lower tariffs up to 1875.

In general, however, the German case conforms to the Stolper-Samuelson explanation: the abundant factor wants free trade; when it becomes relatively scarce, through a gain in manufacturing at home and an expansion of agriculture abroad, it shifts to wanting tariffs. Doctrine was largely on the side of free trade. List's advocacy of national economy had little or no political force. His ultimate goal was always free trade, and his early proposal of ten percent duties on colonial goods, fifteen percent on Continental and fifty percent on British was more anti-British than national. In the 1840's he was regarded in Germany, or at least by the Prussians, as a polemicist whose views were offered for sale. Bismarck is often regarded as the arch-villain of the 1879 reversal of Zollverein low tariffs, but it is hard to see that his role was a major one. . . .

VI

My first conclusion reached from this survey was that free trade in Europe in the period from 1820 to 1875 had many different causes. Whereas after 1879, various countries reacted quite differently to the single stimulus of the fall in the price of wheat — England liquidating its agriculture; France and Germany imposing tariffs, though for different political and sociological reasons; Italy emigrating (in violation of the assumptions of classical economics); and Denmark transforming from producing grain for export to importing it as an input in the production of dairy products, bacon, and eggs — before that the countries of Europe all responded to different stimuli in the same way. Free trade was part of a general response to the breakdown of the manor and guild system. This was especially true of the removal of restrictions on exports and export taxes, which limited freedom of producers. As more and conflicting interests came into contention, the task of sorting them out became too complex for government (as shown in *Gewerbeförderung* in Baden, and the refinement of the Navigation Laws in England), and it became desirable to sweep them all away.

Part of the stimulus came from the direct self-interest of particular dominant groups, illustrated particularly by the First Hand in the Netherlands. In Britain, free trade emerged as a doctrine from the political economists, with a variety of rationalizations to sustain it in particular applications: anti-monopoly, increases to real wages, higher profits, increased allocative efficiency, increased productivity through innovation required by import competition. In France, the lead in the direction of free trade came less from the export interests than from industrial interests using imported materials and equipment as inputs, though the drive to free trade after 1846 required the overcoming of the weight of the vested interests by strong governmental leadership, motivated by political gain in international politics. The German case was more straightforward: free trade was in the interest of the exporting grain- and timber-producing classes, who were politically dominant in Prussia and who partly bought off and partly overwhelmed the rest of the country. The Italian case seems to be one in which doctrines developed abroad which were dominant in England and in a minority position in France, were imported by strong political leadership and imposed on a relatively disorganized political body.

Second thoughts raise questions. The movement to free trade in the 1850's in the Netherlands, Belgium, Spain, Portugal, Denmark, Norway, and Sweden, along with the countries discussed in detail, suggests the possibility that Europe as a whole was motivated by ideological considerations rather than economic interests. That Louis Napoleon and Bismarck would use trade treaties to gain ends in foreign policy suggests that free trade was valued for itself, and that moves toward it would earn approval. Viewed in one perspective, the countries of Europe in this period should not be considered as independent economies whose reactions to various phenomena can properly be compared, but rather as a single entity which moved to free trade for ideological or perhaps better doctrinal reasons. Manchester and the English political economists persuaded Britain which persuaded Europe, by precept and example. Economic theories of representative democracy, of constitutional monarchy, or even absolute monarchy may explain some cases of tariff changes. They are little help in Western Europe between the Napoleonic Wars and the Great Depression.

NOTES

1. H.R.C. Wright, *Free Trade and Protection in the Netherlands, 1816–1830: A Study of the First Benelux* (Cambridge: Cambridge University Press, 1955) p. 124.

2. *William Huskisson, (The Speeches of the Right Honorable)* (London: John Murray, 1832), 11, p. 328.

3. Report of the Select Committee on the Laws Relating to the Export of Tools and Machinery, 30 June 1825, in *Parliamentary Papers, Reports of Committee,* (1825), 5, p. 12.

4. Wright, *Free Trade and Protection*, p. 130.

5. Charles Babbage, *The Economy of Machinery and Manufactures* (London: Charles Knight, 4th ed., 1835), p. 364.

6. Karl Polanyi, *The Great Transformation* (New York: Farrar & Rinehart, 1944), pp. 152–153.

7. Testimony of Thomas Ashton, in *First Report of the Select Committee,* para. 235.

8. John McGregor, *Germany, Her Resources, Government, Union of Customs and Power under Frederick William IV* (London: Whittaker and Co., 1948), p. 68.

9. John Bowring, "Report on the Prussian Commercial Union 1840," *Parliamentary Papers,* 1840, 21, p. 287.

10. Mill, cited by Bernard Semmel, *The Rise of Free Trade Imperialism: Classical Political Economy, The Empire of Free Trade and Imperialism, 1750–1850* (Cambridge: Cambridge University Press, 1970), p. 207.

11. Kenneth Fielden, "The Rise and Fall of Free Trade," in C.J. Bartlett, ed., *Britain Pre-eminent: Studies in British World Influence in the Nineteenth Century* (London: Macmillan, 1969), p. 78.

12. Charles Gouraud, *Histoire de la politique commerciale de la France et son influence sur le progrès de la richesse publique depuis le moyen age jusqu'à nos jours, 1, 11* (Paris: Auguste Durand, 1854), p. 208.

13. Michel Chevalier, *Cours d'economie politique, Fait au Collège de France, 1, 11, 111* (2nd ed., Paris: n.p., 1855), p. 538.

14. William Jacob, *A View of the Agriculture, Manufactures, Statistics and Society in the State of Germany and Parts of Holland and France* (London: John Murray, 1820), pp. 201–212.

15. Rudolph von Delbrück, *Lebenserinnerungen, I* (Leipsig: Duncker u. Humblot, 1905), p. 200.

6

International Trade, Domestic Coalitions, and Liberty: Comparative Responses to the Crisis of 1873–1896

PETER ALEXIS GOUREVITCH

Peter Alexis Gourevitch examines the impact upon the trade policies and political coalitions of four countries of the Great
Depression of 1873–1896, during which Germany and France
adopted high tariffs on both agricultural and industrial products,
Great Britain maintained its historic policy of free trade, and the
United States protected industry but not agriculture. In attempting to explain this pattern of response, Gourevitch compares four
alternative hypotheses: economic explanations, emphasizing
domestic societal interests; political system explanations, focusing on domestic statist variables; international system explanations, combining international political and economic factors;
and economic ideology explanations. Domestic societal interests
supplemented by a concern with state structures, he concludes,
provide the most persuasive account of these four cases.
Gourevitch not only gives a detailed and informative history of
the trade policies of the four great economic powers of the late
nineteenth century, he also provides a useful test of several of the
main approaches in international political economy.

For social scientists who enjoy comparisons, happiness is finding a force or event
which affects a number of societies at the same time. Like test-tube solutions that
respond differently to the same reagent, these societies reveal their characters in
divergent responses to the same stimulus. One such phenomenon is the present
worldwide inflation/depression. An earlier one was the Great Depression of
1873–1896. Technological breakthroughs in agriculture (the reaper, sower, fertilizers, drainage tiles, and new forms of wheat) and in transportation (continental
rail networks, refrigeration, and motorized shipping) transformed international
markets for food, causing world prices to fall. Since conditions favored extensive
grain growing, the plains nations of the world (the United States, Canada, Australia,

Argentina, and Russia) became the low-cost producers. The agricultural populations of Western and Central Europe found themselves abruptly uncompetitive.

In industry as well, 1873 marks a break. At first the sharp slump of that year
looked like an ordinary business-cycle downturn, like the one in 1857. Instead,
prices continued to drop for over two decades, while output continued to rise.
New industries — steel, chemicals, electrical equipment, and shipbuilding —
sprang up, but the return on capital declined. As in agriculture, international competition became intense. Businessmen everywhere felt the crisis, and most of
them wanted remedies.

The clamour for action was universal. The responses differed: vertical integration, cartels, government contracts, and economic protection. The most visible
response was tariffs. . . .

Although the economic stimuli were uniform, the political systems forced
to cope with them differed considerably. Some systems were new or relatively
precarious: Republican France, Imperial Germany, Monarchical Italy, Reconstruction America, Newly Formed Canada, Recently Autonomous Australia. Only
Britain could be called stable. Thirty years later when most of these political systems had grown stronger, most of the countries had high tariffs. The importance of
the relation between the nature of the political system and protection has been
most forcefully argued by Gershenkron in *Bread and Democracy in Germany*.
The coalition of iron and rye built around high tariffs contributed to a belligerent
foreign policy and helped to shore up the authoritarian Imperial Constitution of
1871. High tariffs, then, contributed to both world wars and to fascism, not a
minor consequence. It was once a commonly held notion that free trade and
democracy, protection and authoritarianism, went together. . . .

These basic facts about tariff levels and political forms have been discussed by
many authors. What is less clear, and not thoroughly explored in the literature, is
the best way to understand these outcomes. As with most complex problems, there
is no shortage of possible explanations: interest groups, class conflict, institutions,
foreign policy, ideology. Are these explanations all necessary though, or equally
important? This essay seeks to probe these alternative explanations. It is speculative; it does not offer new information or definitive answers to old questions.
Rather, it takes a type of debate about which social scientists are increasingly conscious (the comparison of different explanations of a given phenomenon) and
extends it to an old problem that has significant bearing on current issues in political economy — the interaction of international trade and domestic politics. The
paper examines closely the formation of tariff policy in late nineteenth-century
Germany, France, Britain, and the United States, and then considers the impact of
the tariff policy quarrel on the character of each political system.

EXPLAINING TARIFF LEVELS

Explanations for late nineteenth-century tariff levels may be classified under four
headings, according to the type of variable to which primacy is given.

1. *Economic Explanations.* Tariff levels derive from the interests of economic groups able to translate calculations of economic benefit into public policy. Types of economic explanations differ in their conceptualization of groups (classes vs. sectors vs. companies) and of the strategies groups pursue (maximizing income, satisfying, stability, and class hegemony).
2. *Political System Explanations.* The "statement of the groups" does not state everything. The ability of economic actors to realize policy goals is affected by political structures and the individuals who staff them. Groups differ in their access to power, the costs they must bear in influencing decisions, prestige, and other elements of political power.
3. *International System Explanations.* Tariff levels derive from a country's position in the international state system. Considerations of military security, independence, stability, or glory shape trade policy. Agriculture may be protected, for example, in order to guarantee supplies of food and soldiers, rather than to provide profit to farmers (an explanation I would suggest).
4. *Economic Ideology Explanations.* Tariff levels derive from intellectual orientations about proper economic and trade policies. National traditions may favor autarchy or market principles; faddishness or emulation may induce policy makers to follow the lead given by successful countries. Such intellectual orientations may have originated in calculations of self-interest (explanation 1), or in broader political concerns (explanation 2) or in understandings of international politics (explanation 3), but they may outlive the conditions that spawned them.

These explanations are by no means mutually exclusive. The German case could be construed as compatible with all four: Junkers and heavy industry fought falling prices, competition, and political reformism; Bismarck helped organize the iron and rye coalition; foreign policy concerns over supply sources and hostile great powers helped to create it; and the nationalist school of German economic thought provided fertile ground for protectionist arguments. But were all four factors really essential to produce high tariffs in Germany? Given the principle that a simple explanation is better than a complex one, we may legitimately try to determine at what point we have said enough to explain the result. Other points may be interesting, perhaps crucial for other outcomes, but redundant for this one. It would also be useful to find explanations that fit the largest possible number of cases.

Economic explanation offers us a good port of entry. It requires that we investigate the impact of high and low tariffs, both for agricultural and industrial products, on the economic situation of each major group in each country. We can then turn to the types of evidence — structures, interstate relations, and ideas — required by the other modes of reasoning. Having worked these out for each country, it will then be possible to attempt an evaluation of all four arguments.

GERMANY

Economic Explanations

What attitude toward industrial and agricultural tariffs would we predict for each of the major economic groups in German society, if each acted according to its economic interests? A simple model of German society contains the following groups: small peasants; Junkers (or estate owners); manufacturers in heavy, basic industries (iron, coal, steel); manufacturers of finished goods; workers in each type of industry; shopkeepers and artisans; shippers; bankers; and professionals (lawyers, doctors). What were the interests of each in relation to the new market conditions after 1873?

Agriculture, notes Gerschenkron, could respond to the sharp drop in grain prices in two ways: modernization or protection. Modernization meant applying the logic of comparative advantage to agriculture. Domestic grain production would be abandoned. Cheap foreign grain would become an input for the domestic production of higher quality foodstuffs such as dairy products and meat. With rising incomes, the urban and industrial sectors would provide the market for this type of produce. Protection, conversely, meant maintaining domestic grain production. This would retard modernization, maintain a large agricultural population, and prolong national self-sufficiency in food.

Each policy implied a different organization for farming. Under late nineteenth-century conditions, dairy products, meats, and vegetables were best produced by high-quality labor, working in small units, managed by owners, or long-term leaseholders. They were produced least well on estates by landless laborers working for a squirearchy. Thus, modernization would be easier where small units of production already predominated, as in Denmark, which is Gerschenkron's model of a modernizing response to the crisis of 1873. The Danish state helped by organizing cooperatives, providing technology, and loaning capital.

In Germany, however, landholding patterns varied considerably. In the region of vast estates east of the Elbe, modernization would have required drastic restructuring of the Junkers' control of the land. It would have eroded their hold over the laborers, their dominance of local life, and their position in German society. The poor quality of Prussian soil hindered modernization of any kind; in any case it would have cost money. Conversely, western and southern Germany contained primarily small- and medium-sized farms more suited to modernization.

Gerschenkron thinks that the Danish solution would have been best for everyone, but especially for these smaller farmers. Following his reasoning, we can impute divergent interests to these two groups. For the Junkers, protection of agriculture was a dire necessity. For the small farmers, modernization optimized their welfare in the long run, but in the short run, protection would keep them going. their interests, therefore, can be construed as ambivalent.

What were the interests of agriculture concerning industrial tariffs? Presumably the agricultural population sought to pay the lowest possible prices for the industrial goods that it consumed, and would be opposed to high industrial tariffs. Farmers selling high-quality produce to the industrial sector prospered, however, when that sector prospered, since additional income was spent disproportionately on meat and eggs. Modernizing producers might therefore be receptive to tariff and other economic policies which helped industry. For grain, conversely, demand was less elastic. Whatever the state of the industrial economy, the Junkers would be able to sell their output provided that foreign sources were prevented from undercutting them. Thus, we would expect the Junkers to be the most resolutely against high industrial tariffs, while the smaller farmers would again have a less clear-cut interest.

Neither were the interests of the industrial sector homogeneous. Makers of basic materials such as iron and steel wanted the producers of manufactured products such as stoves, pots and pans, shovels, rakes, to buy supplies at home rather than from cheaper sources abroad. Conversely the finished goods manufacturers wanted cheap materials; their ideal policy would have been low tariffs on all goods except the ones that they made.

In theory, both types of industries were already well past the "infant industry" stage and would have benefited from low tariffs and international specialization. Indeed, German industry competed very effectively against British and American products during this period, penetrating Latin America, Africa, Asia, and even the United States and United Kingdom home markets. Low tariffs might not have meant lower incomes for industry, but rather a shift among companies and a change in the mix of items produced.

Nevertheless tariffs still offered certain advantages even to the strong. They reduced risk in industries requiring massive investments like steel; they assured economies of scale, which supported price wars or dumping in foreign markets; and to the extent that cartels and mergers suppressed domestic production, they allowed monopoly profits. Finally, iron and steel manufacturers everywhere faced softening demand due to the declining rate of railroad building, not wholly offset by shipbuilding. As we shall see, steelmen were in the vanguard of protectionist movements everywhere including Britain (their only failure).

All industrialists (except those who sold farm equipment) had an interest in low agricultural tariffs. Cheap food helped to keep wages down and to conserve purchasing power for manufactured goods.

The interests of the industrial workforce were pulled in conflicting directions by the divergent claims of consumer preoccupations and producer concerns. As consumers, workers found any duties onerous, especially those on food. But as producers, they shared an interest with their employers in having their particular products protected, or in advancing the interests of the industrial sector as a whole.

Shippers and their employees had an interest in high levels of imports and exports and hence in low tariffs of all kinds. Bankers and those employed in finance had varied interests according to the ties each had with particular sectors of the economy. As consumers, professionals and shopkeepers, along with labor, had a general interest in keeping costs down, although special links (counsel to a steel company or greengrocer in a steel town) might align them to a high-tariff industry.

This pattern of group interests may be represented diagrammatically. Table 1 shows each group's position in relation to four policy combinations, pairing high and low tariffs for industry and agriculture. The group's intensity of interest can be conveyed by its placement in relation to the axis: closeness to the origin suggests ambiguity in the group's interest; distance from the intersection suggests clarity and intensity of interest.

Notice that no group wanted the actual policy outcome in Germany — high tariffs in both sectors. To become policy, the law of 1879 and its successors required trade-offs among members of different sectors. This is not really surprising. Logrolling is expected of interest groups. Explanation 1 would therefore find the coalition of iron and rye quite normal.

TABLE 1. Interests of Different Groups in Relation to Industrial and Agricultural Tariffs (Germany)

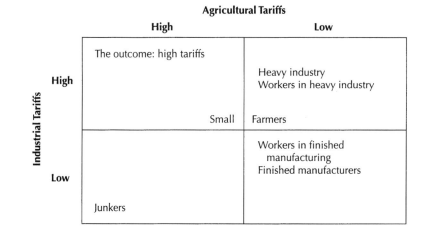

Nevertheless, a different outcome — low tariffs on both types of goods — also would have been compatible with an economic interest group explanation. Logrolling could also have linked up those parts of industry and agriculture that had a plausible interest in low tariffs: finished goods manufacturers, shippers and dockworkers, labor, professionals, shopkeepers, consumers, and farmers of the West and South. This coalition may even have been a majority of the electorate, and at certain moments managed to impose its policy preferences. Under Chancellor Georg von Caprivi (1890–1894), reciprocal trade treaties were negotiated and tariffs lowered. Why did this coalition lose over the long run? Clearly because it was weaker, but of what did this weakness consist?

Political Explanations

One answer looks to aspects of the political system which favored protectionist forces at the expense of free traders: institutions (weighted voting, bureaucracy); personalities who intervened on one side or another; the press of other issues (socialism, taxation, constitutional reform, democratization); and interest group organization.

In all these domains, the protectionists had real advantages. The Junkers especially enjoyed a privileged position in the German system. They staffed or influenced the army, the bureaucracy, the judiciary, the educational system, and the Court. The three-class voting system in Prussia, and the allocation of seats, helped overrepresent them and propertied interests in general.

In the late 1870s, Bismarck and the emperor switched to the protectionists' side. Their motives were primarily political. They sought to strengthen the basic foundations of the conservative system (autonomy of the military and the executive from parliamentary pressure; a conservative foreign policy; dominance of conservative social forces at home; and preservation of the Junkers). For a long time, industry and bourgeois elements had fought over many of these issues. Unification had helped to reconcile the army and the middle classes, but many among the latter still demanded a more liberal constitution and economic reforms opposed by the Junkers. In the 1870s Bismarck used the Kulturkampf to prevent a revisionist alliance of Liberals, Catholics, and Federalists. In the long run, this was an unsatisfactory arrangement because it made the government dependent on unreliable political liberals and alienated the essentially conservative Catholics.

Tariffs offered a way to overcome these contradictions and forge a new, conservative alliance. Industrialists gave up their antagonism toward the Junkers, and any lingering constitutionalist demands, in exchange for tariffs, anti-Socialist laws, and incorporation into the governing majority. Catholics gave way on constitutional revision in exchange for tariffs and the end of the Kulturkampf (expendable because protection would now carry out its political function). The Junkers accepted industry and paid higher prices for industrial goods, but maintained a variety of privileges, and their estates. Peasants obtained a solution to their immediate distress, less desirable over the long run than modernization credits, but effective nonetheless. Tariff revenues eased conflicts over tax reform. The military obtained armaments for which the iron and steel manufacturers received the contracts. The coalition excluded everyone who challenged the economic order and/or the constitutional settlement of 1871. The passage of the first broad protectionist measure in 1879 has aptly been called the "second founding" of the Empire.

Control of the Executive allowed Bismarck to orchestrate these complex trade-offs. Each of the coalition partners had to be persuaded to pay the price, especially that of high tariffs on the goods of the other sector. Control of foreign policy offered instruments for maintaining the bargain once it had been struck. . . . The Chancellor used imperialism, nationalism, and overseas crises to obscure internal divisions, and particularly, to blunt middle-class criticism. Nationalism and the vision of Germany surrounded by enemies, or at least harsh competitors, reinforced arguments on behalf of the need for self-sufficiency in food and industrial production and for a powerful military machine. . . .

The protectionists also appear to have organized more effectively than the free traders. In the aftermath of 1848, industry had been a junior partner, concerned with the elimination of obstacles to a domestic German free market (such as guild regulations and internal tariffs). Its demands for protection against British imports were ignored. . . . The boom of the 1860s greatly increased the relative importance of the industrialists. After 1873, managers of heavy industry, mines and some of the banks formed new associations and worked to convert old ones: in 1874 the Association of German Steel Producers was founded; in 1876, the majority of the Chambers of Commerce swung away from free trade, and other associations began to fall apart over the issue. These protectionist producers' groups were clear in purpose, small in number, and intense in interest. Such groups generally have an easier time working out means of common action than do more general and diffuse ones. Banks and the state provided coordination among firms and access to other powerful groups in German society.

The most significant of these powerful groups — the Junkers — became available as coalition allies after the sharp drop in wheat prices which began in 1875. Traditionally staunch defenders of free trade, the Junkers switched very quickly to protection. They organized rapidly, adapting with remarkable ease, as Gerschenkron notes, to the *ère des foules*. Associations such as the Union of Agriculturalists and the Conservative Party sought to define and represent the collective interest of the whole agricultural sector, large and small, east and west. Exploiting their great prestige and superior resources, the Junkers imposed their definition of that interest — protection as a means of preserving the status quo on the land. To legitimate this program, the Junker-led movements developed many of the themes later contained in Nazi propaganda: moral superiority of agriculture; organic unity of those who work the land; anti-Semitism; and distrust of cities, factories, workers, and capitalists. . . .

The alternative (Low/Low) coalition operated under several political handicaps. It comprised heterogeneous components, hence a diffuse range of interests. In economic terms, the coalition embraced producers and consumers, manufacturers and shippers, owners and workers, and city dwellers and peasants. Little in day to day life brought these elements together, or otherwise facilitated the awareness and pursuit of common goals; much kept them apart — property rights, working conditions, credit, and taxation. The low tariff groups also differed on other issues such as religion, federalism, democratization of the Constitution, and constitutional control of the army and Executive. Unlike the High/High alliance, the low-tariff coalition had to overcome its diversity without help from the Executive. Only during the four years of Caprivi was the chancellor's office sympathetic to low-tariff politics, and Caprivi was very isolated from the court, the kaiser, the army, and the bureaucracy.

Despite these weaknesses, the low-tariff alliance was not without its successes. It did well in the first elections after the "refounding" (1881), a defeat for Bismarck which . . . drove him further toward social imperialism. From 1890, Caprivi directed a series of reciprocal trade negotiations leading to tariff reductions. Caprivi's ministry suggests the character of the programmatic glue needed to keep a low-tariff coalition together: at home, a little more egalitarianism and constitutionalism (the end of the antisocialist laws); in foreign policy, a little more internationalism — no lack of interest in empire or prestige, but a greater willingness to insert Germany into an international division of labor.

International System Explanations

A third type of explanation for tariff levels looks at each country's position in the international system. Tariff policy has consequences, not only for profit and loss for the economy as a whole or for particular industries, but for other national concerns, such as security, independence, and glory. International specialization means interdependence. Food supplies, raw materials, manufactured products, markets become vulnerable. Britain, according to this argument, could rely on imports because of her navy. If Germany did the same, would she not expose her lifeline to that navy? If the German agricultural sector shrank, would she not lose a supply of soldiers with which to protect herself from foreign threats? On the other hand, were there such threats? Was the danger of the Franco-British-Russian alliance an immutable constituent fact of the international order, or a response to German aggressiveness? This brings us back to the Kehr-Wehler emphasis on the importance of domestic interests in shaping foreign policy. There were different ways to interpret the implications of the international system for German interests: one view, seeing the world as hostile, justified protection; the other, seeing the world as benevolent, led to free trade. To the extent that the international system was ambiguous, we cannot explain the choice between these competing foreign policies by reference to the international system alone.

A variant of international system explanations focuses on the structure of bargaining among many actors in the network of reciprocal trade negotiations. Maintenance of low tariffs by one country required a similar willingness by others. One could argue that Germany was driven to high tariffs by the protectionist behavior of other countries. A careful study of the timing of reciprocal trade treaties in this period is required to demonstrate this point, a type of study I have been unable to find. The evidence suggests that at least in Germany, the shift from Caprivi's low tariff policy to Bernhard Bulow's solidarity bloc (protection, naval-building, nationalism, antisocialism) did not come about because of changes in the behavior of foreign governments. Rather, the old Bismarckian coalition of heavy industry, army, Junkers, nationalists, and conservatives mobilized itself to prevent further erosion of its domestic position.

Economic Ideology

A fourth explanation for the success of the protectionist alliance looks to economic ideology. The German nationalist school, associated with Friedrich List, favored state intervention in economic matters to promote national power and welfare. Free trade and laissez-faire doctrines were less entrenched than they were in Britain. According to this explanation, when faced with sharp competition from other countries, German interests found it easier to switch positions toward protection than did their British counterparts. This interpretation is plausible. The free trade policies of the 1850s and 1860s were doubtless more shallowly rooted in Germany and the tradition of state interventionism was stronger.

All four explanations, indeed, are compatible with the German experience: economic circumstances provided powerful inducements for major groups to support high tariffs; political structures and key politicians favored the protectionist coalition; international forces seemed to make its success a matter of national security; and German economic traditions helped justify it. Are all these factors really necessary to explain the protectionist victory, or is this causal overkill? I shall reserve judgment until we have looked at more examples.

FRANCE

The French case offers us a very different political system producing a very similar policy result. As with Germany, the causes may explain more than necessary. The High/High outcome (Table 1) is certainly what we would expect to find looking at the interests of key economic actors. French industry, despite striking gains under the Second Empire and the Cobden-Chevalier Treaty, was certainly less efficient than that of other "late starters" (Germany and the United States). Hence manufacturers in heavy industry, in highly capitalized ones, or in particularly vulnerable ones like textiles had an intense interest in protection. Shippers and successful exporters opposed it.

Agriculture, as in Germany, had diverse interests. France had no precise equivalent to the Junkers; even on the biggest farms the soil was better, the labor force freer, and the owners less likely to be exclusively dependent on the land for income. Nonetheless, whether large or small, all producing units heavily involved in the market were hard hit by the drop in prices. The large proportion of quasi-subsistence farmers, hardly in the market economy, were less affected. The prevalence of small holdings made modernization easier than in Prussia, but still costly. For most of the agriculture sector, the path of least resistance was to maintain past practice behind high tariff walls.

As we would expect, most French producer groups became increasingly protectionist as prices dropped. In the early 1870s Adolphe Thiers tried to raise tariffs, largely for revenue purposes but failed. New associations demanded tariff revision. In 1881, the National Assembly passed the first general tariff measure, which protected industry more than agriculture. In the same year American meat products were barred as unhealthy. Sugar received help in 1884, grains and meats in the tariffs of 1885 and 1887. Finally, broad coverage was given to both agriculture and industry in the famous Méline Tariff of 1892. Thereafter, tariffs drifted upwards, culminating in the very high tariff of 1910.

This policy response fits the logic of the political system explanation as well. Universal suffrage in a society of small property owners favored the protection of units of production rather than consumer interests. Conflict over nontariff issues, although severe, did not prevent protectionists from finding each other. Republican, Royalist, Clerical, and anti-Clerical protectionists broke away from their free trade homologues to vote the Méline Tariff. Méline and others even hoped to reform the party system by using economic and social questions to drive out the religious and constitutional ones. This effort failed but cross-party majorities continued to coalesce every time the question of protection arose and high tariffs helped reconcile many conservatives to the Republic.

In France, protection is the result we would expect from the international system explanation: international political rivalries imposed concern for a domestic food supply and a rural reservoir of soldiers. As for the economic ideology explanation, ideological traditions abound with arguments in favor of state intervention. The Cobden-Chevalier Treaty had been negotiated at the top. The process of approving it generated no mass commitment to free trade as had the lengthy public battle over the repeal of the Corn Laws in Britain. The tariffs of the 1880s restored the *status quo ante*.

Two things stand out in the comparison of France with Germany. First, France had no equivalent to Bismarck, or to the state mechanism which supported him. The compromise between industry and agriculture was organized without any help from the top. Interest groups and politicians operating through elections and the party system came together and worked things out. Neither the party system, nor the constitution, nor outstanding personalities can be shown to have favored one coalition over another.

Second, it is mildly surprising that this alliance took so long to come about — perhaps the consequence of having no Bismarck. It appears that industry took the lead in fighting for protection, and scored the first success. Why was agriculture left out of the Tariff of 1881 (while in Germany it was an integral part of the Tariff of 1879), when it represented such a large number of people? Why did it take another eleven years to get a general bill? Part of the answer may lie in the proportion of people outside the market economy; the rest may lie in the absence of leaders with a commanding structural position working to effect a particular policy. In any case, the Republic eventually secured a general bill, at about the same time that the United States was also raising tariffs.

GREAT BRITAIN

Britain is the only highly industrialized country which failed to raise tariffs on either industrial or agricultural products in this period. Explanation 1 appears to deal with this result quite easily. British industry, having developed first, enjoyed a great competitive advantage over its rivals and did not need tariffs. International specialization worked to Britain's advantage. The world provided her with cheap food; she supplied industrial products in exchange and made additional money financing and organizing the exchange. Farmers could make a living by modernizing and integrating their units into this industrial order. Such had been the logic behind the repeal of the Corn Laws in 1846.

Upon closer inspection, British policy during the Great Depression seems less sensible from a materialist viewpoint. Conditions had changed since 1846. After 1873, industry started to suffer at the hands of its new competitors, especially American and German ones. Other countries began to substitute their own products for British goods, compete with Britain in overseas markets, penetrate the British domestic market, and erect tariff barriers against British goods. Britain was beginning that languorous industrial decline which has continued uninterrupted to the present day.

In other countries, industrial producers, especially in heavy industry, led agitation for protection in response to the dilemma of the price slump. Although some British counterparts did organize a Fair Trade league which sought protection within the context of the Empire (the policy adopted after World War I), most industrialists stayed with free trade.

If this outcome is to be consistent with explanation 1, it is necessary to look for forces which blunted the apparent thrust of international market forces. British producers' acceptance of low tariffs was not irrational if other ways of sustaining income existed. In industry, there were several. Despite Canadian and Australian tariff barriers, the rest of the Empire sustained a stable demand for British goods; so did British overseas investment, commercial ties, and prestige. International banking and shipping provided important sources of revenue which helped to conceal the decline in sales. Bankers and shippers also constituted a massive lobby in favor of an open international economy. To some degree, then, British industry was shielded from perceiving the full extent of the deterioration of her competitive position.

In agriculture, the demand for protection was also weak. This cannot be explained simply by reference to 1846. Initially the repeal of the Corn Laws affected farming rather little. Although repeal helped prevent sharp price increases following bad harvests, there was simply not enough grain produced in the world (nor enough shipping capacity to bring it to Europe) to provoke a major agricultural crisis. The real turning point came in the 1870s, when falling prices were compounded by bad weather. Why, at this moment, did the English landowning aristocracy fail to join its Junker or French counterpart in demanding protection? The aristocrats, after all, held a privileged position in the political system; they remained significantly overrepresented in the composition of the political class, especially in the leadership of Parliament; they had wealth and great prestige.

As with industry, certain characteristics of British agriculture served to shield landowners from the full impact of low grain prices. First, the advanced state of British industrial development had already altered the structure of incentives in agriculture. Many landowners had made the change from growing grain to selling high-quality foodstuffs. These farmers, especially dairymen and meat producers, identified their interests with the health of the industrial sector and were unresponsive to grain growers' efforts to organize agriculture for protection.

Second, since British landowners derived their income from a much wider range of sources than did the Junkers the decline of farming did not imply as profound a social or economic disaster for them. They had invested in mining, manufacturing, and trading and had intermarried with the rising industrial bourgeoisie. Interpenetration of wealth provided the material basis for their identification with industry. This might explain some Tories' willingness to abandon protection in 1846, and accept that verdict even in the 1870s.

If repeal of the Corn Laws did not immediately affect the British economy it did profoundly influence politics and British economic thought in ways, following the logic of explanations 2 and 4, that are relevant for explaining policy in the 1870s. The attack on the Corn Laws mobilized the Anti-Corn Law League (which received some help from another mass movement, the Chartists). Over a twenty-year period, the League linked the demand for cheap food to a broader critique of landed interest and privilege. Its victory, and the defection of Peel and the Tory leadership, had great symbolic meaning. Repeal affirmed that the British future would be an industrial one, in which the two forms of wealth would fuse on terms laid down for agriculture by industry. By the mid-1850s even the backwoods Tory rump led by Disraeli had accepted this; a decade later he made it the basis for the Conservative revival. To most of the ever larger electorate, free trade, cheap food, and the reformed political system were inextricably linked. Protection implied an attack on all the gains realized since 1832. Free trade meant freedom and prosperity. These identifications inhibited the realization that British economic health might no longer be served by keeping her economy open to international economic forces.

Finally, British policy fits what one would expect from analysis of the international system (explanation 3). Empire and navy certainly made it easier to contemplate dependence on overseas sources of food. It is significant that protection could be legitimated in the long run only as part of empire. People would do for imperialism what they would not do to help one industry or another. Chamberlain's passage from free trade to protection via empire foreshadows the entire country's actions after World War I.

UNITED STATES

Of the four countries examined here, only the United States combined low-cost agriculture and dynamic industry within the same political system. The policy outcome of high industrial tariffs and low agricultural ones fits the logic of explanation 1. Endowed with efficient agriculture, the United States had no need to protect it; given the long shadow of the British giant, industry did need protection. But despite its efficiency (or rather because of it) American agriculture did have severe problems in this period. On a number of points, it came into intense conflict with industry. By and large industry had its way.

> *Monetary Policy.* The increasing value of money appreciated the value of debt owed to Eastern bankers. Expanding farm production constantly drove prices downward, so that a larger amount of produce was needed to pay off an ever increasing debt. Cheap money schemes were repeatedly defeated.
>
> *Transportation.* Where no competition among alternative modes of transport or companies existed, farmers were highly vulnerable to rate manipulation. Regulation eventually was introduced, but whether because of the farmers' efforts or the desire of railroad men and other industrialists to prevent ruinous competition — as part of their "search for order" — is not clear. Insurance and fees also helped redistribute income from one sector to the other.
>
> *Tariffs.* The protection of industrial goods required farmers to sell in a free world market and buy in a protected one.
>
> *Taxation.* Before income and corporate taxes, the revenue burden was most severe for the landowner. Industry blocked an income tax until 1913.
>
> *Market Instability.* Highly variable crop yields contributed to erratic prices, which could have been controlled by storage facilities, government price stabilization boards, and price supports. This did not happen until after World War I.
>
> *Monopoly Pricing Practices.* Differential pricing (such as Pittsburgh Plus, whereby goods were priced according to the location of the head office rather than the factory) worked like an internal tariff, pumping money from the country into the Northeast. The antitrust acts addressed some of these problems, but left many untouched.
>
> *Patronage and Pork-Barrel.* Some agrarian areas, especially the South, fared badly in the distribution of Federal largesse.

In the process of political and industrial development, defeat of the agricultural sector appears inevitable. Whatever the indicator (share of GNP, percentage of the workforce, control of the land) farmers decline; whether peasants, landless laborers, family farmers, kulaks, or estate owners, they fuel industrialization by providing foreign exchange, food, and manpower. In the end they disappear.

This can happen, however, at varying rates: very slowly, as appears to be the case in China today, slowly as in France, quickly as in Britain. In the United States, I would argue, the defeat of agriculture as a *sector* was swift and thorough. This may sound strange in light of the stupendous agricultural output today. Some landowners were successful. They shifted from broad attacks on the system to interest group lobbying for certain types of members. The mass of the agricultural population, however, lost most of its policy battles and left the land.

One might have expected America to develop not like Germany, . . . but like France: with controlled, slower industrial growth, speed sacrificed to balance, and the preservation of a large rural population. For it to have happened the mass of small farmers would have to have found allies willing to battle the Eastern banking and industrial combine which dominated American policy-making. To understand their failure it is useful to analyze the structure of incentives among potential alliance partners as was done for the European countries. If we take farmers' grievances on the policy issues noted above (such as money and rates) as the functional equivalent of tariffs, the politics of coalition formation in the United States become comparable to the equivalent process in Europe.

Again two alliances were competing for the allegiance of the same groups. The protectionist core consisted of heavy industry, banks, and textiles. These employers persuaded workers that their interests derived from their roles as producers in the industrial sector, not as consumers. To farmers selling in urban markets, the protectionists made the familiar case for keeping industry strong.

The alternative coalition, constructed around hostility toward heavy industry and banks, appealed to workers and farmers as consumers, to farmers as debtors and victims of industrial manipulation, to the immigrant poor and factory hands against the tribulations of the industrial system, . . . and to shippers and manufacturers of finished products on behalf of lower costs. Broadly this was a Jackson-type coalition confronting the Whig interest — the little man versus the man of property. Lower tariffs and more industrial regulation (of hours, rates, and working conditions) were its policies.

The progressive, low-tariff alliance was not weak. Agriculture employed by far the largest percentage of the workforce. Federalism should have given it considerable leverage: the whole South, the Midwest, and the trans-Mississippi West. True, parts of the Midwest were industrializing, but then much of the Northeast remained agricultural. Nonetheless the alliance failed: the explanation turns on an understanding of the critical realignment election of 1896. The defeat of Populism marked the end of two decades of intense party competition, the beginning of forty years of Republican hegemony and the turning point for agriculture as a sector. It will be heuristically useful to work backwards from the conjuncture of 1896 to the broader forces which produced that contest.

The battle of 1896 was shaped by the character and strategy of William Jennings Bryan, the standard bearer of the low-tariff alliance. Bryan has had a bad historical press because his Populism had overtones of bigotry, anti-intellectualism, archaism, and religious fundamentalism. Politically these attributes were flaws because they made it harder to attract badly needed allies to the farmers' cause. Bryan's style, symbols, and program were meaningful to the trans-Mississippi and southern farmers who fueled Populism, but incomprehensible to city dwellers, immigrants, and Catholics, to say nothing of free-trade oriented businessmen. In the drive for the Democratic nomination and during the subsequent campaign, Bryan put silver in the forefront. Yet free coinage was but a piece of the Populist economic analysis and not the part with the strongest appeal for nonfarmers (nor even the most important element to farmers themselves). The city dweller's grievances against the industrial economy were more complex. Deflation actually improved his real wages, while cheap money threatened to raise prices. In the search for allies other criticisms of the industrial order could have been developed but Bryan failed to prevent silver from overwhelming them.

Even within the agrarian sector, the concentration on silver and the fervid quality of the campaign worried the more prosperous farmers. By the 1890s, American agriculture was considerably differentiated. In the trans-Mississippi region, conditions were primitive; farmers were vulnerable, marginal producers: they grew a single crop for the market, had little capital, and no reserves. For different reasons, Southern agriculture was also marginal. In the Northeast and the Midwest farming had become much more diversified; it was less dependent on grain, more highly capitalized, and benefited from greater competition among railroads, alternative shipping routes, and direct access to urban markets. These farmers related to the industrial sector, rather like the dairymen in Britain, or the Danes. Bryan frightened these farmers as he frightened workers and immigrants. The qualities which made him attractive to one group antagonized others. Like Sen. Barry Goldwater and Sen. George McGovern, he was able to win the nomination, but in a manner which guaranteed defeat. Bryan's campaign caused potential allies to define their interests in ways which seemed incompatible with those of the agricultural sector. It drove farmers away rather than attracting them. Workers saw Bryan not as an ally against their bosses but as a threat to the industrial sector of the economy of which they were a part. To immigrants, he was a nativist xenophobe. Well-to-do Midwestern farmers, southern Whigs, and Northeast-shippers all saw him as a threat to property.

The Republicans, on the other hand, were very shrewd. Not only did they have large campaign funds, but, as Williams argues, James G. Blaine, Benjamin Harrison, and William McKinley understood that industrial interests required allies, the support of which they must actively recruit. Like Bismarck, these Republican leaders worked to make minimal concessions in order to split the opposition. In the German coalition the terms of trade were social security for the workers, tariffs for the farmers and the manufacturers, guns and boats for the military. In America, McKinley, et al., outmaneuvered President Grover Cleveland and the Gold Democrats on the money issue; when Cleveland repealed the Silver Purchase Act, some of the Republicans helped pass the Sherman Silver Purchase Act. The Republican leaders then went after the farmers. Minimizing the importance of monetary issues, they proposed an alternative solution in the form of

overseas markets: selling surpluses to the Chinese or the Latin Americans, negotiating the lowering of tariff levels, and policing the meat industry to meet the
health regulations Europeans had imposed in order to keep out American imports.
To the working class, the Republicans argued that Bryan and the agrarians would
cost them jobs and boost prices. Social security was never mentioned —
McKinley paid less than Bismarck.

In 1896, the Republican candidate was tactically shrewd and the Democratic
one was not. It might have been the other way around. Imagine a charismatic
Democrat from Ohio, with a Catholic mother, traditionally friendly to workers,
known for his understanding of farmers' problems, the historical equivalent of
Senator Robert Kennedy in the latter's ability to appeal simultaneously to urban
ethnics, machine politicians, blacks, and suburban liberals. Unlikely but not
impossible: had he existed, such a candidate would still have labored under severe
handicaps. The difference between Bryan and McKinley was more than a matter
of personality or accident. The forces which made Bryan the standard bearer were
built into the structure of American politics. First, McKinley's success in constructing a coalition derives from features inherent in industrial society. As in
Germany, producers' groups had a structural advantage. Bringing the farmers,
workers, and consumers together was difficult everywhere in the industrial world
during that period. In America, ethnic, geographic, and religious differences made
it even harder.

Second, the industrialists controlled both political parties. Whatever happened
at the local level, the national Democratic party lay in the firm grip of Southern
conservatives and Northern businessmen. Prior to 1896, they wrote their ideas
into the party platforms and nominated their man at every convention. The Gold
Democrats were not a choice but an echo. . . . A Bryan-type crusade was structurally necessary. Action out of the ordinary was required to wrest the electoral
machine away from the Gold Democrats. But the requirements of that success
also sowed seeds for the failure of November, 1896.

Why, in turn, did the industrialists control the parties? The Civil War is crucial.
At its inception, the Republican party was an amalgam of entrepreneurs, farmers,
lawyers, and professionals who believed in opportunity, hard work, and self-help;
these were people from medium-sized towns, medium-sized enterprises, medium-
sized farms. These people disliked the South not because they wished to help the
black race or even eliminate slavery, but because the South and slavery symbolized the very opposite of "Free Soil, Free Labor, Free Men." By accelerating the
pace of industrialization, the Civil War altered the internal balance of the Party,
tipping control to the industrialists. By mobilizing national emotions against the
South, the Civil War fused North and West together, locking the voter into the
Republican Party. Men who had been antibusiness and Jacksonian prior to 1860
were now members of a coalition dominated by business.

In the South, the Old Whigs, in desperate need of capital, fearful of social
change, and contemptuous of the old Jacksonians looked to the Northern industrialists for help in rebuilding their lands and restoring conservative rule. What
would have been more natural than to have joined their Northern allies in the
Republican party? In the end, the hostility of the Radical Republicans made this

impossible, and instead the Old Whigs went into the Democratic Party where they eventually helped sustain the Gold Democrats and battled with the Populists for control of the Democratic organization in the South.

There were, then, in the American system certain structural obstacles to a low-tariff coalition. What of economic ideology (explanation 4) and the international system (explanation 3)? Free trade in the United States never had the ideological force it had in the United Kingdom. Infant industries and competition with the major industrial power provided the base for a protectionist tradition, as farming and distrust of the state provided a base for free trade. Tariffs had always been an important source of revenue for the Federal government. It is interesting that the "Free Soil, Labor and Men" coalition did not add Free Trade to its program.

Trade bore some relation to foreign policy. . . . Nonetheless, it is hard to see that the international political system determined tariff policy. The United States had no need to worry about foreign control of resources or food supply. In any case the foreign policy of the low-tariff coalition was not very different from the foreign policy of the high-tariff coalition.

In conclusion, four countries have been subjected to a set of questions in an attempt to find evidence relevant to differing explanations of tariff levels in the late nineteenth century. In each country, we find a large bloc of economic interest groups gaining significant economic advantages from the policy decision adopted concerning tariffs. Hence, the economic explanation has both simplicity and power. But is it enough? It does have two weaknesses. First, it presupposes a certain obviousness about the direction of economic pressures upon groups. Yet, as the argumentation above has sought to show, other economic calculations would also have been rational for those groups. Had farmers supported protection in Britain or opposed it in Germany and France, we could also offer a plausible economic interpretation for their behavior. The same is true for industrialists: had they accepted the opposite policy, we could find ways in which they benefited from doing so. We require an explanation, therefore, for the choice between two economic logics. One possibility is to look at the urgency of economic need. For protectionists, the incentive for high tariffs was intense and obvious. For free traders, the advantages of their policy preference, and the costs of their opponents' victory, were more ambiguous. Those who wanted their goals the most, won.

Second, the economic explanation fails to flesh out the political steps involved in translating a potential alliance of interest into policy. Logrolling does take some organization, especially in arranging side payments among the partners. The iron-rye bargain seems so natural that we forget the depth of animosity between the partners in the period preceding it. To get their way, economic groups had to translate their economic power into political currency.

The political structures explanation appears to take care of this problem. Certain institutions and particular individuals helped to organize the winning coalition and facilitate its victory. Looking at each victory separately, these structures and personalities bulk large in the story. Yet viewed comparatively, their importance washes out. Bismarck, the Junkers, the authoritarian constitution, the character of the German civil service, the special connections among the state, banking, and industry—these conspicuous features of the German case have no equivalents elsewhere. Méline was no Bismarck and the system gave him no particular leverage. Mobilization against socialism did not occur in the United States, or even in Britain and France. Yet the pattern of policy outcomes in these countries was the same, suggesting that those aspects of the political system which were *idiosyncratic* to each country (such as Bismarck and regime type) are not crucial in explaining the result. In this sense the political explanation does not add to the economic one.

Nonetheless, some aspects of the relation between economic groups and the political system are *uniform* among the countries examined here and do help explain the outcome. There is a striking similarity in the identity of victors and losers from country to country: producers over consumers, heavy industrialists over finished manufacturers, big farmers over small, and property owners over laborers. In each case, a coalition of producers' interests defined by large-scale basic industry and substantial landowners defeated its opponent. It is probable, therefore, that different types of groups from country to country are systematically not equal in political resources. Rather, heavy industrialists and landowners are stronger than peasants, workers, shopkeepers, and consumers. They have superior resources, access to power, and compactness. They would have had these advantages even if the regimes had differed considerably from their historical profiles. Thus a republicanized or democratized Germany would doubtless have had high tariffs (although it might have taken longer for this to come about, as it did in France). A monarchist France (Bourbon, Orleanist, or Bonapartist) would certainly have had the same high tariffs as Republican France. An authoritarian Britain could only have come about through repression of the industrialists by landowners, so it is possible a shift in regime might have meant higher tariffs; more likely, the industrialists would have broken through as they did in Germany. Certainly Republican Britain would have had the same tariff policy. In the United States, it is possible (although doubtful) that without the critical election of 1896, or with a different party system altogether, the alternation between protectionist Republicans and low-tariff Democrats might have continued.

Two coalitions faced each other. Each contained a variety of groups. Compared to the losers, the winners comprised: (1) groups for which the benefits of their policy goal were intense and urgent, rather than diffuse; (2) groups occupying strategic positions in the economy; and (3) groups with structurally superior positions in each political system. The uniformity of the winners' economic characteristics, regardless of regime type, suggests that to the extent that the political advantages derive from economic ones, the political explanation is not needed. The translation of economic advantage into policy does require action, organization, and politics; to that extent, and to varying degrees, the economic explanation by itself is insufficient. It is strongest in Germany, where the rapidity of the switch from free trade to protection is breathtaking, and in France where economic slowness made the nation especially vulnerable to competition. It works least well for Britain, where the policy's advantages to the industrialists seem the least clear, and for the United States, where the weakness of agriculture is not explicable without the Civil War. Note that nowhere do industrialists fail to obtain their preferences.

In this discussion, we have called the actors groups, not classes, for two reasons. First, the language of class often makes it difficult to clarify the conflicts of interest (e.g., heavy industry vs. manufacture) which exist within classes, and to explain which conception of class interest prevails. Second, class analysis is complex. Since interest group reasoning claims less, and works, there is no point in going further.

The international system and economic ideology explanations appear the least useful. Each is certainly compatible with the various outcomes, but has drawbacks. First, adding them violates the principle of parsimony. If one accepts the power of the particular economic-political explanation stated above, the other two explanations become redundant. Second, even if one is not attracted by parsimony, reference to the international system does not escape the difficulty inherent in any "unitary actor" mode of reasoning: why does a particular conception of the national interest predominate? In the German case, the low-tariff coalition did not share Bismarck's and Bulow's conception of how Germany should relate to the world. Thus the international system explanation must revert to some investigation of domestic politics.

Finally, the economic ideology explanation seems the weakest. Whatever its strength in accounting for the free trade movement of the 1850s and 1860s, this explanation cannot deal with the rapid switch to protection in the 1870s. A national culture argument cannot really explain why two different policies are followed within a very short span of time. The flight away from free trade by Junkers, manufacturers, farmers, and so on was clearly provoked by the price drop. For the United Kingdom, conversely, the continuity of policy makes the cultural argument more appropriate. Belief in free trade may have blunted the receptivity of British interest groups toward a protectionist solution of their problems. The need for the economic ideology explanation here depends on one's evaluation of the structure of economic incentives facing industry: to whatever extent empire, and other advantages of having been first, eased the full impact of the depression, ideology was superfluous. To whatever extent industry suffered but avoided protection, ideology was significant.

7

International Investment and Colonial Control: A New Interpretation
JEFFRY A. FRIEDEN

The origins of colonial imperialism have long been a topic of intense debate. In this article, Jeffry Frieden examines the relationship between different forms of international investment and varying political ties among developed and developing countries. Frieden argues that direct colonial control was likely when international investments were particularly easy to seize or protect unilaterally, as was the case with raw materials or agricultural investments. Where investments were more difficult to seize or protect, as with multinational manufacturing affiliates, colonialism was less likely to take hold. Frieden does not claim that international investment caused imperialism. Rather, he argues only that colonialism and site-specific international investments coincided historically and were mutually reinforcing. In the twentieth century, as imperialism came under challenge and as manufacturing superseded extractive investments, colonialism gradually became obsolete.

. . . This article recasts the relationship between international investment and colonialism in a more general context. Putative ties between metropolitan investment and colonial control are one subset of a problem associated with the monitoring and enforcement of property rights across national jurisdictions. Cross-border investment involves an implicit or explicit contract between the host country and the investor. The arrangements developed to monitor and enforce these contracts — from gunboat diplomacy to private negotiations — are varied institutional forms responding to different characteristics of the investments and the environment. Colonialism is a particular, perhaps particularly noxious, form that the "resolution" of these quasi-contractual issues can take: the use of force by a home government to annex the host region and so eliminate the interjurisdictional nature of the dispute.

This approach leads to two principal dimensions of variation in overseas investments expected to be associated with different levels of interstate conflict and the propensity for such investments to have been involved in colonialism. The first is the ease with which rents accruing to investments can be appropriated by the host country, or protected by the home country, by coercive means. Everything else being equal, the more easily rents are seized, the more likely the use of force by home countries. The second dimension is the difference between the net expected benefits of cooperation among home countries as compared with unilateral action by a single home country. This is a function both of the degree to which interinvestor cooperation facilitates monitoring and enforcing property rights to the investment and of the cost of organizing and sustaining such concerted action by home countries. All else being equal, the lower the net expected benefits of cooperation, the more likely are home countries to engage in unilateral action, including colonialism.

Certain types of investments appear to have lent themselves more easily than others to protection by the unilateral use of force by home governments. This is especially true for investments with site-specific and easily appropriated rents, such as raw materials extraction and agriculture. For such investments, colonial control resolved inherent property rights problems that arose in its absence. This is not to say that these investments caused colonialism, for the reverse might have been the case — the greater security colonialism offered might have attracted disproportionate amounts of certain kinds of investments; it is, however, to argue for an affinity between certain cross-border investments and colonialism. I do not claim that these factors exhaust all explanation. Clearly geopolitical, technological, ideological, and other forces were important; but the sorts of differentiated economic variables discussed here often have been neglected in studies of colonialism. Further, their importance appears confirmed by historical evidence. . . .

COLONIALISM AND INTERNATIONAL INVESTMENT: THE ISSUES

. . . Most controversy over colonialism and foreign investment has to do with the so-called economic theory of imperialism. The debate seems peculiar to the student of political economy, for it revolves around the simple question of whether economic considerations were important to colonial imperialism or not. As such it is not about an economic theory as normally understood but rather about the relative importance of the totality of economic concerns and the "contending" totality of noneconomic concerns, even though all scholars agree that both were present. This confusion is compounded by all sides in the debate. Supporters of the "economic approach" point to instances in which nationals of a colonial power made money as a result of colonialism, while opponents call upon examples of colonial possessions devoid of economic significance. If the question were whether colonialism was solely and entirely motivated by expectations of direct and measurable economic profits, this might be appropriate; inasmuch as this is manifestly not the question scholars ask, it is not.

In general, an economic theory of political behavior tries to correlate different kinds of economic activity with different kinds of policy or political outcomes.

For example, some common economic theories of politics hypothesize a relation-ship between firm and industry characteristics on the one hand and levels of sup-port for trade protection, regulatory outcomes, or other government actions on the other. Typically, an economic explanation is not about the relationship between the economy and politics in general but rather about the relationship of a specific economic independent variable to a specific political or policy dependent variable. It is variation in the economic variable that is purported to explain corre-sponding variation in the political or policy outcome. If so desired, confrontation with noneconomic theories can then be made by seeing whether noneconomic variables outperform economic variables in explaining outcomes; more com-monly, scholars accept that economic and noneconomic factors are not mutually exclusive. In any case, the appropriate test of a typical economic theory is not whether or not economic considerations matter, but whether they matter in the ways hypothesized by the theory in question. An economic theory of colonialism, in this context, would correlate particular kinds of economic activities with the likelihood of colonial rule.

It is also useful to get a clearer sense than is usually provided in the debate over colonialism of what is being explained by contending theories. Colonial rule is but one possible outcome of relations between and among countries — one value that the dependent variable can take. Its uniqueness is twofold. First, it involves the explicit or implicit use of force by the colonial power over the annexed region. Second, the relationship is exclusive; that is, the colonial power acts unilaterally and not in concert with other powers (and often explicitly to exclude them).

To express the thing to be explained more generally, colonialism is simply one example of interstate interaction occurring along two dimensions. [For ease of exposition, I refer to potential colonial powers as "home countries" (that is, sources of foreign investment) and to potential colonized regions as "host coun-tries" (that is, sites of foreign investment).] The first dimension of variation is the extent to which a home country engages in the use or threat of military force in its relations with the host country. Variation along this dimension runs from military intervention at one limit to the absence of government involvement at the other. The second dimension is the degree to which home countries act in concert toward a host country. Variation along this dimension runs from unilateral and exclusion-ary action by a home country at one limit to cooperative multilateral action by many home countries at the other. . . . In this context, colonialism (the unilateral use of force) is one possible outcome. Other potential outcomes include multi-lateral use of force, bilateral arms-length negotiations, or multilateral negotia-tions — and gradations in between. . . .

INTERNATIONAL INVESTMENT, PROPERTY RIGHTS, AND INTERNATIONAL CONFLICT

The international politics of international investment are largely organized around two broad problems. The first is the desire of investors to monitor and enforce the host country's respect for cross-border property rights. The second is the degree to which different foreign investors engage in collective action to carry out these monitoring and enforcement activities.

The security of property across borders is in essence a contractual problem. Overseas investment involves an implicit or explicit contract between the investor and the host state. This contract may commit a host government to repay a loan, to allow a firm to mine copper, or to permit the establishment of a local branch factory of a multinational corporation. If the host government breaks the contract — by not servicing the loan, expropriating the mine, or closing down the factory— foreign investors have no direct recourse. This requires investors to devise some mechanism to monitor and enforce their property rights. In this sense home-country military force is one choice among a number of devices to protect overseas assets. . . .

Regarding the security of property across borders as a problem in relational contracting directs attention to characteristics of the assets, product markets, and informational environment that affect the ability of the parties to monitor and enforce their contract. Variation in such contractual problems in turn gives rise to different organizational or political responses.

In addition to underlying contractual questions, the need for investors to monitor and enforce host-country compliance can lead to problems of collective action. In many cases, of course, property rights can be secured on a purely individual basis so that there is no incentive for investor collaboration. All investors may have a common interest in ensuring stable rights to private property, but this does not mean that such stable rights must necessarily be provided to all investors. Each investor is first concerned about the investor's own property rights, and an investor can, in fact, benefit by receiving exclusive property rights. Where secure property rights can be supplied on a specific basis to specific investors, there is little reason for cooperation among investors.

On the other hand, the protection of foreign property may be made substantially more effective if investors cooperate. Whenever the combined action of many investors reduces the cost of protecting their property to each investor, cooperation would be desirable to them. This might be the case, for example, when evaluating the host government's compliance with contractual commitments can be costly — such as when it is difficult to separate the impact of exogenous events from straightforward cheating. In this case, crucially important accurate information about the host government's actions and intentions serve all interested investors, and it is in the interest of all to cooperate in obtaining the information. . . .

However, the circumstances that can make cooperation attractive to investors can also make it difficult. If the benefits of joint action accrue to larger groups of (or all) foreign investors, such protection may come to take on the characteristics of a public good. Under these circumstances, a host government's commitment to respect the property of foreign investors (or a class of foreign investors) is indivisible, inherently available to all investors (or all members of a class of investors). When monitoring and enforcing compliance with quasi-contractual commitments to property rights serves a large class of (or even all) investors, there may be collective action problems associated with the provision of this public good. Because the public good would benefit a large group of actors, actors have an incentive to cooperate to help provide it; cooperation is hindered by the fact that noncooperators cannot be excluded from benefiting from the provision of the public good.

The more the protection of property requires joint action to accomplish, the greater the potential gains from cooperation; but the more difficult collective action, the less likely such cooperation is to succeed. Where joint action by international investors to monitor and enforce property rights improves their welfare, the probability of successful cooperation is a function of free-rider problems. To summarize: cooperation among investors becomes more likely as the potential return to investor collaboration increases (i.e., the more monitoring and enforcement are public goods). And as collaboration among investors becomes more likely, the easier it is to organize collective contribution to monitoring and enforcement. Emphasizing these considerations is not to downplay the importance of other, noneconomic, elements; it is to argue for the anticipated political implications of these economic factors, all else being equal.

Thus the two dimensions of variation in the characteristics of international investment that I expect will affect the probability that such investment will be associated with colonial rule may be summarized as follows: the first is the ability of the investment to be protected by force; the second is the degree to which monitoring and enforcing a host government's respect for foreign property has the character of a public good, and (if it does) the difficulties in overcoming collective action problems to supply the public good.

INTERNATIONAL INVESTMENT AND CONFLICT: ANALYTICAL EXPECTATIONS

The preceding discussion is only useful inasmuch as it leads to otherwise non-obvious analytical expectations. In what follows, I summarize features of cross-border investments and of the markets in which those investments operate, both of which I expect will affect the character of the monitoring and enforcement of international property rights and the degree of collaboration among international investors in pursuit of this monitoring and enforcement. In other words, variation in these factors should be associated with (1) variation in home-state use of force against a host state and (2) the degree of home-state cooperation over investments of this type. Once again, these should be taken as potentially contributory rather than necessarily competing variables, in a complex explanation that includes a wide variety of economic, political, military, cultural, and other considerations. For my more limited purposes, the factors relevant to this evaluation of the use of force by and cooperation among investing countries can be grouped into the two categories described above and then can be applied to particular classes of investments.

Site Specificity and the Costs of Physical Protection

Some assets can be more easily protected, and some contracts more easily enforced, by the use or threat of force than others. Put another way, the rents accruing to some assets can be more easily appropriated or protected by force than the rents accruing to other assets. To some extent, the appropriability of the asset and its income stream is related to the asset's specificity to a particular site or corporate network. For example, the income stream created by a copper mine is specific to the place where the copper is located. The mine, and the resource rents associated with it, can be seized by a host country with relative ease. On the other hand, the income stream accruing to a branch plant of a manufacturing multinational corporation typically is specific to its participation in a global enterprise — it relies on managerial, marketing, or technological inputs available only within the firm. While the host government can seize the factory, it cannot appropriate the rents.

By the same token, site-specific assets can be protected by force on the part of investors or their home countries. A mine or plantation can be retaken from a host government by force, and it can continue to earn income once retaken, especially if it is producing for export. While a branch factory can be retaken by force, inasmuch as it is integrated into the local economy — perhaps with networks of suppliers and customers — it would be unlikely to continue to earn income in such circumstances.

This leads me to expect that investing country governments will tend to use or threaten force more the easier it is for the income accruing to the asset in question to be physically seized or protected. The more the rents earned by an asset are site-specific, the more the use of force will serve to protect them, and hence the more likely it is to be used.

Net Expected Benefits of Investor Cooperation

Leaving aside whether or not investors and their home countries use force, we want to understand the circumstances under which investors cooperate with one another instead of pursuing unilateral solutions (including colonialism). I assume the goal of cooperation would be to monitor and enforce the host country's compliance with explicit or implicit contractual commitments. I expect cooperation among investors to be more common when the net expected benefits of collaborative action compare favorably with those of private enforcement by a single investor.

As discussed above, one important determinant of the benefits of collective action is the degree to which monitoring and enforcement become easier for each investor as more investors participate. At one extreme, the cost of monitoring an agreement can be the same for each investor no matter how many there are. This might be the case when each firm must observe aspects of the contract specific to itself; no matter how many firms are in similar situations, no one firm's efforts affect those of any other firm. At the other extreme, there may be significant economies of scale in monitoring and enforcing an agreement, such that the cost per firm declines steeply with the number of investors.

This continuum applies to monitoring and enforcement costs. If a debtor threatens default on foreign loans, information about the government's solvency, macroeconomic conditions, and other contingencies may be valuable to all creditors. This information is essentially the same for all creditors, and if they each contribute a small amount toward a common effort to obtain the information, they will be better off than if each goes about trying to gather the data on its own. By the same token, in some instances each investor has effective ways of punishing a host government that violates a contract. The owner of a mine that is nationalized might withhold technological information without which the mine cannot run and which is not available elsewhere. In other instances, however, cooperation among investors may be necessary to ensure effective enforcement. Perhaps the technology in question is available to a dozen foreign mining firms; all would need to participate in withholding this technology for the sanctions to bind.

Monitoring and enforcement both may be characterized by diminishing costs (increasing returns) for many reasons. For my purposes, it is enough to observe that the incentives for investors to cooperate in monitoring and enforcing contractual compliance by host governments increase the more such efforts are characterized by diminishing costs (increasing returns); the specifics of each case can be examined separately.

Nevertheless, it is also necessary to look at the costs of organizing such beneficial cooperation. As the number of investors rises, if the increased benefits of monitoring are outweighed by the increased costs of holding an ever more fractious group of investors together, then cooperation will not be stable.

The costs of obtaining and sustaining cooperation are a function of well-known collective action considerations. As mentioned above, the cooperative monitoring and enforcement of cross-border contractual commitments by a host country can have characteristics of a public (or at least a club) good. Using the earlier example of creditors who agree to cooperate to monitor a troubled debtor, if all the creditors expect the information to be gathered by others and shared with them, no single creditor has an incentive to contribute toward its gathering. Similarly, creditors who agree to impose sanctions on a recalcitrant debtor face the problem that while all benefit from successful sanctions, no one creditor alone has an incentive to impose the sanction.

Many circumstances conduce toward reducing free riding. These include relatively small numbers, so that all members of the group can observe which members are not contributing and try to design effective sanctions; selective incentives, by which those who contribute can be rewarded; and long time horizons, which increase incentives to cooperate by increasing the expected benefits of cooperation. All of these conditions vary from international investment to international investment; collective action will be easier among some investors than among others. The greater the ability to control free riding, the more I expect cooperation among investors. . . .

Primary Production for Export   Overseas investments in primary production for export include both extractive industries and agriculture: for example, the mining of precious metals, copper, and oil, and the raising of sugar, cotton, and tea. Such assets are quite specific as to site and can be protected (or attacked) by force relatively easily. I expect force to be linked to them more than to other investments.

Monitoring and enforcing property rights to extractive and agricultural investments are not, in most instances, characterized by increasing returns. One mine or plantation owner seldom benefits from efforts by other owners to protect their own investments. There may be gains from cooperation when investors can boycott the output of a seized facility. If copper-mining corporations control the world copper market, they can collude to make it impossible for a host government that nationalizes a mine to sell its product. Among other things, this will depend on how differentiated the product is (the more differentiated, the easier the embargo), how large spot markets are (the larger, the easier for the host government to evade the embargo), and other conditions. However, collective action among overseas investors in primary production cannot be assumed. It will depend on how many producers there are; on whether they are linked on some other dimension (such as marketing the product); and on other such collective action considerations.

The prediction, then, is that overseas investments in primary production for export will be more likely to be associated with the use of force. Except where an embargo of the product is technically feasible and free riding can be readily combated, these investments also will be more likely to be associated with unilateral action by home countries. In addition to the use of force, such investment will be correlated with other unilateral action, such as intervention or colonial annexation.

Affiliates of Manufacturing Multinational Corporations   Modern theories emphasize that foreign direct investment, especially in manufacturing, is but a special case of the internalization of economic activities within one corporate entity. In this sense, a local affiliate is an integral part of a corporate network, and if separated from this network it loses most of its value. The assets of the local affiliate are specific to their use within a broader international enterprise, generally for technological, managerial, or marketing reasons. Most of the value of an overseas Ford affiliate, for example, is inseparable from the affiliate's connection with Ford. This may be because the affiliate makes parts (or requires inputs) which are used (or supplied) only by the parent company, or because the affiliate depends on the reputation and managerial expertise of the international firm. The host government could not appropriate most of the rents that accrue to these assets; once the assets are separated from the integrated corporation, they lose much of their value.

Host governments have little incentive to take assets whose value disappears with the takeover. For this reason, affiliates of integrated multinational corporations have relatively secure property rights. The more specific the assets to a corporate network, the less likely is the host government to threaten the asset, and the less likely is the firm to require home country involvement.

The limited incentive to take such affiliates is paralleled by the difficulties a home country would have in defending a manufacturing affiliate. Unlike the typical mine, the typical branch plant is integrated into the local economy; it cannot function in protected isolation, ringed by a protective force. Similarly, because the assets of affiliates are quite specific to the global firms, there are few externalities created by the defense of one such affiliate — thus the incentive to cooperate is limited. For all these reasons, I expect very little home country political involvement in foreign direct investment in manufacturing and hence little cooperation among home countries.

Public Utilities   International investment in public utilities was especially important during the century before World War II. Foreign-owned railroads, water and power plants, and urban transportation were common throughout the developing world. Such facilities are in a sense intermediate between primary production for export and manufacturing affiliates. On the one hand, like manufacturing affiliates, utilities are often fully integrated into the local economy, so that physical protection by a home government would not assure the investment's earning power: for a railroad to pay off, it has to be used by local customers. In addition, some utilities are technically sophisticated enough that local operators in developing economies might have difficulty running them. However, in many instances, utilities are site-specific and can be seized by force: this might be true of a railroad line or power plant. Force might be useful in some cases — where, for example, the railroad line serves only to transport bananas from foreign-owned plantations to the coast — but in many others it is less likely to be practical.

Scale economies are rare in monitoring and enforcing contracts involving utilities. Each facility is likely to face specific conditions, such as rates for a power company, that in themselves have little impact on other investors in the sector. Even when different utilities face similar problems, such as foreign railroads, the returns from cooperation appear relatively low. For example, railroad companies have little with which to threaten a boycott and similarly little on which to collaborate. Information sharing might be useful, but it is likely to be limited by the different conditions faced by different firms.

For all these reasons, I expect that utilities may be seized by host countries but are unlikely to cause a use of force by home countries. I also expect little cooperation among the home countries of utilities investors. The expected pattern, then, is one of voluntary contracts and negotiations between host countries and individual owners of utilities.

Loans to Governments   The practice of lending to foreign sovereigns is probably as old as the nation-state, and problems in monitoring and enforcing sovereign compliance with such loan contracts are just as old. They remain important today, although their economic form has changed over the years. The loan contract comprises a government's promise to pay and is easy for the host government to violate. Since the asset is an intangible contract, it is difficult to protect by force. An exception might arise when the lender or its home government are able to seize the income stream accruing to a debtor's asset (such as a government-owned airplane or, in earlier days, a customs house), but these are strictly limited: governments with large external assets are unlikely to need to borrow heavily.

On the other hand, the returns from cooperation are enormous. Financial markets, especially international financial markets, rely on debtor fears that default will impede future borrowing. For this threat of future borrowing difficulty to be credible, financial markets must cooperate in refusing to lend to a debtor in default. The more potential lenders are expected to boycott an errant debtor, the greater the debtor's incentive to maintain debt service. In this sense, cooperation among financial institutions to monitor and enforce foreign debt contracts is crucial, and the benefits of such sanctions to each creditor rise dramatically with the scale of the cooperative effort.

There are many obstacles to collective action among creditors. Their numbers are often large and credit is undifferentiated, to name but two. However, financial institutions tend to have many connections among themselves, from correspondent banking to joint ventures, so that their reputations with each other may be important. This will conduce to cooperation.

In the case of foreign lending, then, I expect the use of force by home countries against debtors in default to be relatively rare. However, I expect to find a great deal of cooperation among creditors, for the benefits of creditor unity are large. Collaboration also will depend on circumstances that affect the costs of collective action, such as how close the ties among the creditors are along other dimensions.

To summarize, I expect foreign investment in primary production for export to be most closely associated with the unilateral use of force by the home country. I expect public utilities to be less tied to the use of force, although characterized by home-country unilateralism. Foreign loans should seldom be linked to military intervention, and I expect home governments to be relatively cooperative. Multinational manufacturing affiliates are unlikely to be seized by force and are therefore unlikely to become the focus of violent disputes and unlikely to lead to home-country cooperation. . . .

These analytical expectations do . . . lead to some straightforward predictions about the relationship and different forms of foreign investment. I expect colonial rule to be most commonly found in association with foreign investment whose problems can be resolved most easily by unilateral intervention, for colonialism is unilateral and interventionist. Thus, I expect colonialism to be especially strongly associated, not with foreign investments in general, but rather with foreign investments in primary production. . . .

COLONIALISM AND INVESTMENT

Evidence from the British Empire

The analytical considerations presented above lead, most concretely, to hypotheses correlating colonialism with foreign investment in primary production. Although it is theoretically possible to evaluate the other hypotheses presented above, such as the likelihood that foreign lending is associated with private lender cooperation but not military intervention, colonialism is the most easily measured outcome. It is to an evaluation of this claim that I now turn. . . .

The most straightforward way to weigh my approach is to see whether colonial control is correlated with the investments I anticipate will be associated with the use of force and home country unilateralism. Some data along these lines are available for the United Kingdom. However, almost no analogous data are available for other European colonial experiences. Hence, my statistical analysis is confined to the British case.

It is worth starting with some consideration of evidence that colonialism could and did affect the composition of foreign investment in the colonial area.

Although this is a controversial topic, one study shows that investors from the colonial powers systematically were overrepresented in foreign direct investments in their colonies — in 1938 by a factor of 2.2 for British colonies and 11.9 for French colonies. That is, there was 2.2 times as much investment by British investors in British colonies as would have been predicted given Britain's share of total global investment, and 11.9 times as much French investment in French colonies. Another study by the same scholar indicates that British direct investment in British colonies earned higher rates of return than British investment in non-British developing regions. This dovetails with the general revival among historians of the view that economic motives played a role in colonial expansion, albeit not in the simple way posited by earlier critics.

Recently compiled quantitative evidence can be used more directly to assess my argument about the political implications of different sorts of foreign investments. . . . [By looking at British overseas investments inside and outside the British Empire from 1865 to 1914, it becomes clear that investment] in transport, manufacturing, and public utilities was overrepresented outside the empire, while investment in primary production was overrepresented inside the empire. Overrepresentation in this context means that a larger proportion of British investment in the region was of this particular type compared with overall British foreign investment; or, stated another way, that more of this type of investment was made in the region than would be expected given the region's overall share of total British foreign investment. For example, . . . primary investment made up 16.5 percent of British investment inside the empire but only 11.9 percent of British investment outside the empire. By this criterion, colonial areas had proportionally greater shares of investment in primary production, while independent areas had greater shares of investment in utilities (including railroads) and manufacturing. Data on government loans run counter to my expectations, which are discussed below. (British gross national product in the 1890s was approximately £1.7 billion, so the amounts involved were very substantial by contemporary standards.)

[It is important] to avoid comparing areas at strikingly different stages of growth, for it could easily be argued that the differences between foreign investment in Kenya and the United States, say, are more easily attributed to level of development than to form of rule. [Looking at the sectoral breakdown of British investment in different types of less developed areas (LDAs), government] lending is disproportionately concentrated in the developing empire, which is a problem for my approach. However, for the less developed empire as a whole, the relative preponderance of primary investments is clear: 46.9 percent of private-sector British investment (i.e., excluding loans to governments) in the empire went to primary activities, while 23.7 percent of British investment in the private sector in non-empire developing areas went to such agricultural and extractive investments. By the same token, transport (overwhelmingly railroads) comprised 42.0 percent of all British private-sector investment in the developing empire but 68.2 percent outside it. Again, in the terms used above, there is a clear overrepresentation of (that is, bias toward) primary investment, and a clear underrepresentation of (that is, bias against) transport investment, inside the empire. . . .

The dependent developing areas, that is the developing empire without India and South Africa, tend to confirm my expectations even more strongly. Loans to governments comprise only 27 percent of British investment in these regions. Of private-sector investment in the dependent colonies, primary production accounted for an enormous 74 percent of the total. This is a very substantial overrepresentation of (that is, bias toward) primary investment in the dependent empire. Public utilities are slightly overrepresented, while manufacturing and transport are underrepresented. In fact, taken as a whole and expressed slightly differently . . . government loans, railroads, manufacturing, and utilities combined made up 45 percent of British investment in the dependent colonies, compared with 86 percent in noncolonial LDAs.

[Looking at the empire's share of each sector's investment] shows the heavy concentration of primary investment in the empire and especially in the dependent colonies. In other words, while the dependent colonies accounted for just 11.3 percent of all British private investment in the developing world, they took 27.2 percent of all primary investment. . . .

The overrepresentation of extractive and agricultural investments in the dependent colonial areas is striking and tends to confirm my hypothesis about the correlation between colonialism and primary investment. . . .

[Data on the sectoral breakdown of British investment in Latin America in 1913 indicate,] again as expected and in many ways contrary to received wisdom, that in these independent countries raw materials investments were quite insignificant, while British investments were concentrated in government loans, railroads, and utilities.

. . . During [the interwar] period colonial governments . . . borrowed substantially more than independent states; the proximate reason was that the British government restricted borrowing by nonsterling areas in order to defend the pound. Looking at private investment alone, we continue to see a substantial colonial preference for primary production and a foreign preference for utilities and railroads. Oil is treated separately here, since much British oil investment was in areas under semiformal British control (such as League of Nations mandates).

Although there are many problems with the statistical data at our disposal, they do indicate the systematic bias expected by my analysis. That is, colonialism was strongly associated with foreign investment in primary production. It is not possible to determine from these data which way the causal arrow may have run, for time series are sorely inadequate. Only qualitative evidence, if that, can help clarify the direction of causation in particular cases. Nonetheless, it does appear that British overseas investment in manufacturing and utilities was correlated with independent status, and investment in primary production, with colonial rule.

Other Evidence

Quantitative evidence on the British case, which is suggestive but hardly conclusive, can be supplemented with other evidence, especially that based on historical case or country studies. It is useful to discuss this by sector, to parallel the analytical predictions presented above. Of course, this information is at best impressionistic.

Primary Production for Export   The approach described herein leads to an expectation that primary investment will be correlated with the use of force by home countries and with a relative lack of cooperation among investors. In many historical episodes, indeed, primary investors were at the forefront of interventionist agitation; additionally, primary investment is substantially overrepresented in virtually every colonial setting. The role of mining in sub-Saharan Africa, from the Congo to the cape, is frequently remarked upon. So, too, are the colonialist proclivities of those involved in plantation agriculture in East Africa, the Indian subcontinent, and Southeast Asia. Again, whether the prior existence of primary investments gave rise to demands for annexation or prior colonial control made the area attractive to primary investors is immaterial for the theory presented here — my argument is about the affinity of a form of investment for a form of political governance.

The interventionist tendencies of the oil industry in the decades before the Organization of Petroleum Exporting Countries (OPEC) was formed are well-known. Evidence about the degree of cooperation among oil investors is less clear-cut. In some instances, oil companies procured and secured exclusive access to particular territories: especially within the colonial empires, rights to mine oil often were reserved explicitly or implicitly for metropolitan firms. However, in other instances, oil firms cooperated in the joint exploitation of the resource and presented a united front to local rulers. This was true in parts of the Middle East: the Red Line Agreement of 1928, for example, reserved much of the former Ottoman Empire for a few Anglo-Dutch, British, French, and U.S. firms. Cooperation was repeated elsewhere, as in conflict between oil producers and a nationalist Iranian regime in the early 1950s. Cooperation among oil investors — rare among other primary investors — was a function of the very small number of global oil companies and their dense and longstanding networks of economic and other linkages. As more independent producers arose, cooperation among oil investors gradually eroded, although the private cartel was largely replaced by OPEC's cartel of governments.

The overrepresentation of British primary investment in the colonies was noted above. Although similarly well-developed statistics are not available for other colonial powers, what evidence there is reinforces the impression of the British data. Some 42 percent of investment in French West Africa was in primary production; most of the rest (39 percent) was in commercial services, an important category that we ignore here. Over three-quarters of the Belgian investment in the Congo apparently was in mines and the railways connected directly to them. Japan's overseas investment before World War II was concentrated in China and its colonies. Assets in Japan's possessions — Korea, Kwantung, Taiwan, and the South Pacific — were concentrated almost exclusively in agriculture and raw materials production. It also may not be coincidental that Japanese investment in Manchuria, where Japanese political influence (later, direct rule) was strongest, was concentrated in primary production, while investments in other parts of China were more diversified and included many manufacturing firms.

A particularly interesting and a difficult case to explain is that of American overseas investors. Elsewhere I have attempted to show that those most prone to demand U.S. government intervention in Latin America were primary investors. Indeed, many U.S. overseas lenders and manufacturing multinational corporations opposed gunboat diplomacy, and as U.S. investment in the region diversified toward government lending and manufacturing, demands for intervention subsided, as did intervention itself.

Affiliates of Multinational Manufacturing Corporations   I expect that manufacturing investment will not be strongly associated with the use of force (i.e., with colonial control); nor will it see much cooperation among investors. On the use of force, recent nationalist ambivalence about manufacturing multinational corporations has obscured prior historical experience. Indeed, in interwar South America it was common to distinguish between "bad" foreign direct investments in primary production and railroads (which were mostly British) and "good" foreign investments in manufacturing (which were mostly American). Parallel phenomena have been noted in many societies in the process of decolonization: the end of colonial rule is associated with a relative decline in foreign investment in primary production and a significant rise in the share of foreign investment going into manufacturing industries. . . .

The Indian experience is interesting in this regard. After World War I the colonial government secured substantial economic policy autonomy, and as this took place foreign investment in manufacturing rose continually (in part, due to increased Indian tariffs). The leading scholar of the economics of Indian decolonization draws a direct connection between the increasing likelihood of independence and the growth of foreign interest in local manufacturing (and the relative decline of primary investments). It should be recalled that for my purposes the chronology is not important: I argue simply that foreign investment in manufacturing is less dependent upon colonial ties than is investment in primary production, and the Indian experience appears to confirm this. . . .

. . . Rarely have manufacturing multinational corporations attempted to bring their home governments into conflict with host countries (such spectacular cases as ITT in Chile are clearly exceptions). Nor have manufacturing investors commonly cooperated with each other in their dealings with host countries. The general rule, as expected, is direct firm-to-host-government bargaining, and sometimes private or quasi-public insurance schemes.

Public Utilities   My approach leads to the expectation that, although host governments might appropriate a utility, home governments are not likely to use force to defend it and cooperation among utility investors will be difficult (because the benefits are limited and the costs, high). By far the most historically important type of utility in which foreign investment was significant is the railroad. . . . British railroad and utilities investment was heavily biased toward independent states, and historical evidence does not provide any obvious case of military intervention in defense of either a utility or a railroad.

Cooperation among utilities investors, especially railroad investors, was also very fragile. The spectacular divisions among Western nations over railroad development in Africa and the Near East — the Berlin to Baghdad, cape to Cairo, and trans-Saharan routes all became real or potential sources of conflict — are well-known. Strife was not due to lack of attempts to cooperate. Joint railroad ventures, typically to finance the development of new lines with loans from several national financial centers, were tried in China and the Ottoman Empire but with little success. Even where investors all were British, with similar interests — as in negotiations with the Argentine government over railroad warrantees in the 1890s — cooperation was almost impossible to sustain.

Private Loans to Governments   The argument presented here, namely, that foreign loans to governments will tend not to be associated with home-country use of force and will tend to be associated with cooperation among home countries, is perhaps the most divergent from traditional impressions and received wisdom. The logic, nonetheless, is clear. A loan is a promise, and if unmet it cannot be seized by force. The principal penalty available to creditors against an errant debtor is to deny it the ability to borrow again; in this case, enforcement depends almost entirely upon cooperation among potential international lenders.

None of this is pure and simple. The use of force can help lenders, as it can help almost anyone. Although a home country might seize assets of a country in default, as mentioned above, such overseas assets of debtor nations are typically vastly outweighed by their liabilities. Creditors or their governments might seize income-earning property (such as a customs house) without the debtor government's consent, but this historically has been both extremely costly to accomplish and often useless. Nor is cooperation the only way of ensuring a return on foreign lending. Creditors use various mechanisms to cover default risk and can demand some sort of recoverable collateral from the debtor. However, my general argument still holds: relative to other investments, for international lenders the utility of military force is low and the gains from investor cooperation, high.

The myriad examples of creditor cooperation in dealings with debtors throughout history include the private creditor committees formed to monitor the finances of shaky LDA debtors during the century before World War I. Private financiers, generally with the support of their home governments, established such committees in Egypt, Greece, Morocco, Persia, Serbia, Tunisia, and elsewhere.

The Ottoman Public Debt Administration exemplifies this financial cooperation. In 1875, after fifteen years of borrowing, the Ottoman Empire began to default on its obligations. Six years later, after laborious negotiations among the empire, private bondholders' groups, and the European powers, the Decree of Mouharrem established a Public Debt Administration to be run by a Council of the Public Debt. The council had seven members: one representative of the British and Dutch bondholders, one representative apiece of the French, German, and Austro-Hungarian bank syndicates, an appointee of the Rome Chamber of Commerce, a representative of the Priority Bondholders appointed by the Anglo-French Ottoman Imperial Bank, and one representative of the Ottoman bondholders.

By 1898 the Public Debt Administration controlled about one-quarter of all Ottoman government revenues; its mandate gradually had expanded to include responsibility for new bank loans and railroad guarantees. Certainly the administration's establishment and success owed much to the empire's importance in the prewar balance of power. However, it is striking that financial cooperation was achieved with relative ease, even as the great powers were engaged in bitter rivalry within the same empire over raw materials, railroads, and other concessions. And this curious combination of financial cooperation and conflict on other economic dimensions recurred throughout the decades before World War I. More generally, the historical literature indicates quite clearly that the norm in cases of sovereign debt problems was market-based renegotiation in which creditors typically cooperated among themselves with little difficulty.

Roughly the same pattern held in the interwar period, during which the primary lending institutions were based in New York and London. Many of the postwar financial stabilization loans in Europe were arranged by committees made up of representatives of the governments and financial communities of Britain, France, and the United States, often under the aegis of the Financial Committee of the League of Nations. The Dawes and Young plans each represented collaborative international financial efforts, and the Young Plan included the formation of the Bank for International Settlements (BIS) as a supranational agency to supervise German reparations payments and, more generally, help manage intra-European capital movements. . . .

Fledgling attempts at regularizing creditor unity before World War II pale in comparison to the extraordinarily important (if generally indirect) role the International Monetary Fund has played in the complex process of monitoring and enforcing international loan agreements since the 1950s. Creditor cooperation also has been solid as regards government or government-guaranteed lending, and private financial institutions generally have cooperated among themselves in their interaction with troubled debtors.

If it is not hard to show that creditor cooperation has been common, it is more difficult to demonstrate that force has been used rarely, for the nonexistence of something is hard to document. Nonetheless, most studies that address the issue find few instances of military intervention on behalf of bondholders. Indeed, some of the cases commonly used to support the charge of debt-related gunboat diplomacy are mischaracterized. The United States had few or no financial interests in the Caribbean nations in which it intervened before 1930, while primary investments were quite substantial. The 1902 joint European blockade of Venezuela was prompted by threats to resident foreigners and their property by a capricious dictator; the debt issue was insignificant.

Two well-known historical cases do present something of a problem for my analysis: Egypt and India. As noted above, India and the Dominions were frequent borrowers, a fact that contradicts my argument that colonial control not be associated with disproportionately high levels of borrowing. In the case of the Dominions, it is likely that the effects of colonial rule on investment decisions were swamped by two factors. First, by most calculations the governments of Australia, Canada, and New Zealand were independent, and Dominion status meant little from the standpoint of property rights. Second, these areas were not typical of other capital-importing regions: they were high-income and politically very stable. These factors, and several others of a related nature, could easily explain the preference of British investors for Dominion government bonds. Investment in India and Egypt is less clearly explicable.

The analytical problem is different for the two countries. India was a heavy borrower despite its underdeveloped and colonial status: according to one set of figures, 55 percent of British investment in India between 1865 and 1914 was in government bonds. Two obvious explanations suggest themselves. First, the British government implicitly subsidized Indian bond issues (primarily by allowing them to be used for trust accounts), which increased their attractiveness. Second, India's strategic importance to the British Empire required a massive railroad network, most of which was publicly owned and much of which the British government encouraged to be financed in London. Accurate as these explanations may be, they do not represent support for my approach in this instance; at best, they reflect the potential importance of other factors, which is indubitable.

The relationship between foreign economic interests (including bondholders) and the extension of British control to Egypt is a complex and hotly contested issue. It is clear enough that Egypt's foreign debt (largely to British and French bondholders) was an important irritant in the country's relations with the European powers and that Egyptian finances were regularized, to the benefit of foreign bondholders, after the British occupation in 1882. Several considerations, however, mitigate the quick conclusion that the country's foreign debt was the sole or principal cause of the British intervention. The first is the obvious importance of other economic interests in the area — cotton cultivation and exports, the large community of resident investors, and the Suez Canal — all of which contributed to British concern. Indeed, it might well be argued that the Suez Canal was the ultimate example of an overseas asset whose value was site-specific and whose protection by the use of force was particularly feasible. The second consideration is that the Egyptian saga began, like that of the Ottoman Empire, with a joint creditors' committee, in this case an Anglo-French dual control commission. British occupation came as the French left the field, and British unilateralism may have been spurred by the gradual failure of cooperation. In any event, more work needs to be done before all the case's analytical implications are clear. It is, in fact, striking that, while loans represented roughly half of all foreign investment in the developing world before World War I, there are few cases in which even the boldest historians argue for a connection between lending and intervention.

Despite gaps, then, it does appear that sovereign lending was seldom associated with the use of force by home governments. It also appears that such lending typically involved multilateral cooperation among private creditors or their governments.

CONCLUSION

By putting forth a relatively simple set of hypotheses such as those discussed here, I do not mean to imply that these variables are the sole or even the most important explanations of colonialism or North-South relations more generally. Everything from relative military capabilities, through geostrategic considerations, to norms of sovereignty would need to be included in a full discussion of the determinants of variation in colonial policy over time and across regions. I do nonetheless argue (1) that economic characteristics of cross-border investments had certain systematic effects on the use of force against host countries and on cooperation among home countries, and vice versa and (2) that the evidence tends to support the validity of this first assertion.

The most direct purpose of this article has been to bring new analytical and empirical evidence to bear on an old debate about the relationship between foreign investment and colonialism. In the interests of analytical clarity, I reframed both the questions and the proposed answers. In so doing, I pointed out that the relevant question is not whether "the economy mattered" but under what circumstances economic considerations had predictable effects on political outcomes. I believe that the hypotheses put forth help clarify the analytical issues and the evidence adduced provides at least some indication of the plausibility of my arguments.

Apart from its relevance to explaining the relationship between colonialism and foreign investment, one potential implication of my argument has to do with change over time. It may indeed not be coincidental that the movement away from colonialism has been correlated with a continual decline in the importance of primary investment in the Third World and an increase in sovereign lending and foreign direct investment in manufacturing. The causal arrows may go in either direction, or their direction may vary from case to case. Nonetheless, there appears to be a strong historical association between colonial rule and foreign investment in primary production for export and between independence and foreign borrowing and foreign investment in manufacturing. . . .

8

British and American Hegemony Compared: Lessons for the Current Era of Decline

DAVID A. LAKE

Analysts often look to the precedent of British decline, which is said to have contributed to international political and economic unrest, in attempting to understand the impact of America's relative decline. In this essay, David A. Lake points out that the analogy is deeply flawed. International political and economic structures were fundamentally different in the two hegemonic eras, as were the specific processes associated with the relative decline of Britain and of the United States. Lake summarizes the salient characteristics of the two periods and on this basis projects a continuation of past international economic openness even as American hegemony wanes.

America's decline has gained new prominence in the current political debate. There is little doubt that the country's economic competitiveness has, in fact, waned since its hegemonic zenith in the 1950s. The immediate post–Second World War era was anomalous; with Europe and Japan devastated by the war, the United States enjoyed a period of unchallenged economic supremacy. As other countries rebuilt their economies, this lead had to diminish. Yet, even in the 1970s and 1980s, long after the period of "catch up" had ended, America's economy continued to weaken relative to its principal trading partners.

Popular attention has focused on the appropriate policy response to this self-evident decline. One critical issue, which cuts across the traditional liberal-conservative spectrum, is America's relations with its allies. Should the United States maintain a policy of free trade premised on broad reciprocity as in the General Agreement on Tariffs and Trade (GATT), or must it "get tough" with its trading partners, demand equal access industry-by-industry to foreign markets, balance trade between specific countries, and retaliate if others fail to abide by America's understanding of the international trade regime? This is a question which all present and future American governments will have to address — and the answer is by no means ideologically predetermined or, for that matter, clear.

The issue of American decline is not new, despite the recent attention devoted to it. It has been a topic of lively academic debate for almost twenty years — a debate which, while not directly focused on such issues, can shed considerable light on the question of America's relations with its trading partners. The so-called theory of hegemonic stability was developed in the early 1970s to explain the rise and fall of the *Pax Britannica* and *Pax Americana,* periods of relative international economic openness in the mid-nineteenth and mid-twentieth centuries respectively. In its early form, the theory posited that hegemony, or the existence of a single dominant economic power, was both a necessary and sufficient condition for the construction and maintenance of a liberal international economy. It followed that once the hegemon began to decline, the international economy would move toward greater conflict and closure. The theory has since been refined and extended, with nearly all revisions concluding that a greater potential exists — for non-hegemonic international economic cooperation than was allowed for in the original formulation. All variants of the theory of hegemonic stability suggest, nonetheless, that Britain's relative decline after 1870 is the closest historical analogy to the present era and a fruitful source of lessons for American policy. Many have drawn pessimistic predictions about the future of the liberal international economy on the basis of this comparison, with the implication that a more nationalist foreign economic policy is necessary to halt the breakdown of the open international economy into a series of regional trading blocs. To understand and judge this, one must recognize and begin with the parallels between the *Pax Americana* and the *Pax Britannica* and their subsequent periods of decline. Yet, one must also recognize that the differences between these two cycles of hegemony are just as important as the similarities. The two periods of declining hegemony are similar, but not identical—and the differences have tremendous import for the future of the liberal international economic order and the nature of American policy.

THE HISTORICAL ANALOGY

From the sixteenth to the eighteenth centuries, the international economy was dominated by mercantilism — a pervasive set of state regulations governing the import and export of goods, services, capital, and people. Britain was no exception to this general trend and, in fact, was one of its leading proponents. While restrictions on trade may have been adopted largely as a result of rent-seeking by domestic groups, they also stimulated home production and innovation and allowed Britain to build an industrial base from which to challenge Dutch hegemony.

With the industrial revolution, and the resulting economic take-off, Britain slowly began dismantling its mercantilist system. Various restraints were removed, and by the 1830s few industrial tariffs and trade restrictions remained. Agricultural protection persisted, however, until industry finally triumphed over landed interests in the repeal of the Corn Laws in 1846. Britain's shift to free trade ushered in a period of international economic liberalization. For reasons discussed below, the repeal of the Corn Laws facilitated the rise of free trade coalitions in both the emerging Germany and the United States. Moreover, Britain finally induced France to join in the emerging free trade order in 1860, trading its acquiescence in France's military excursions into Northern Italy for lower tariffs in a bargain which underlay the important Cobden-Chevalier Treaty. Interlocking trade treaties premised on the unconditional most-favored-nation principle then served to spread these reductions throughout Europe.

British hegemony peaked in approximately 1870, after which its national product, trade and labor productivity — while continuing to grow in absolute terms — began to shrink relative to its principal economic rivals. With Britain's decline, the free trade order began to unravel. The United States returned to a policy of high protection after the Civil War. Germany adopted high tariffs in its coalition of Iron and Rye in 1879. France followed suit in the Méline Tariff of 1892.

Just as Britain had used mercantilism as a weapon against Dutch hegemony, the United States and Germany used protection to build up their infant industries, which were then able to challenge and defeat British industry in global competition. Despite a large measure of protectionist rent-seeking by various uncompetitive groups in both countries, this strategy of industrial stimulation was successful. By the late 1890s, the United States surpassed Britain in relative labor productivity and other key indicators of industrial production. Germany also emerged as a major threat to British economic supremacy, particularly in the race for colonies in the developing world.

Despite these threats, Britain continued to dominate and manage the international economy until the outbreak of the First World War. With its industrial base slipping, Britain moved into services — relying on shipping, insurance and international finance to offset its increasing trade deficits. The British pound remained the international currency and the City of London the core of the international financial system.

British weakness, however, was revealed and exacerbated by the First World War. Britain sold off many of its overseas assets to pay for the necessary wartime supplies. As a result, repatriated profits were no longer sufficient to offset its trade deficit. Moreover, the war generated several deep and insidious sources of international economic instability — war debts, German reparations, America's new status as a net creditor nation, and, at least partly through Britain's own mistakes, an overvalued pound.

Eventually, the international economy collapsed under the weight of its own contradictions, despite futile efforts at joint Anglo-American international economic leadership in the 1920s. American capital, previously channeled to Germany, which in turn used its international borrowings to pay reparations to Britain and France, was diverted to the stock market after 1927, feeding the speculative fever and precipitating a wave of bank closures in Austria and Germany. As the banking panic spread across Europe and eventually across the Atlantic, the stock market became its own victim. While the crash of 1929 did not cause the Great Depression, it certainly exacerbated the underlying instabilities in international commodity markets. As the depression worsened, each country turned inward upon itself, adopting beggar-thy-neighbor policies in a vain attempt to export the pain to other states.

The roots of American hegemony lie in the period following the Civil War. With the defeat of the South, government policy shifted in favor of the North and industrialization. By the First World War, the United States had emerged as Britain's equal. The two competed for international economic leadership (and occasionally for the abdication of leadership) throughout the inter-war period.

The United States began the process of liberalization in 1913 with the passage of the Underwood Tariff Act. While pressure for freer trade had been building for over a decade, this was the first concrete manifestation of reform. This nascent liberalism, however, was aborted by the war and the international economic instability it engendered; tariffs were raised in 1922 and again in 1930. The United States returned to international liberalism in the Reciprocal Trade Agreements Act of 1934. While free trade remained politically tenuous throughout the 1930s and early 1940s, it was locked securely in place as the centerpiece of American foreign economic policy by the end of the Second World War.

Like Britain, the United States was the principal impetus behind international economic liberalization. It led the international economy to greater economic openness through the GATT, the International Monetary Fund (IMF), the World Bank, and a host of United Nations–related organizations. The United States also made disproportionately large reductions in its tariffs and encouraged discrimination against its exports as a means of facilitating economic reconstruction. Real trade liberalization was delayed until the 1960s, when the Kennedy Round of the GATT substantially reduced tariffs in all industrialized countries. This success was soon followed by the equally important Tokyo Round, which further reduced tariffs and rendered them essentially unimportant impediments to trade.

Despite these successes, and in part because of them, challenges to international liberalism began to emerge in the late 1960s. As America's economic supremacy receded, the exercise of international power became more overt and coercive. This was especially true in the international monetary arena, where the series of stopgap measures adopted during the 1960s to cope with the dollar overhang were abandoned in favor of a more unilateral approach in the appropriately named "Nixon Shocks" of August 1971. More importantly, as tariffs were reduced and previously sheltered industries were exposed to international competition, new pressures were placed on governments for trade restrictions. These pressures have been satisfied, at least in part, by the proliferation of nontariff barriers to trade, the most important of which take the form of "voluntary" export restraints by foreign producers. While the net effect of reduced tariffs and increased nontariff barriers to trade is difficult to discern, it is clear that domestic political support for free trade in the United States and other advanced industrialized countries has eroded.

In summary, during their hegemonic ascendancies, both Britain and the United States played leading roles in opening the international economy. And in both cases, brief successes were soon followed by increasing challenges to global liberalism. The parallels are clear. The historical analogy suggests a period of increasing economic conflict, a slide down the "slippery slope of protection," and a return to the beggar-thy-neighbor policies of the inter-war period.

THE HISTORICAL REALITY

Despite the plausibility and attractiveness of this historical analogy, it is deeply flawed. The similarities between the *Pax Britannica* and *Pax Americana* have overshadowed the differences, but those differences may in the end prove to be more important. The points of contrast between the two periods of hegemony can be grouped into four categories.

I. International Political Structures

In the nineteenth century, and throughout the period of British hegemony, the United Kingdom, France, and then Germany all pursued empire as a partial substitute for trade within an open international economy. No country relied entirely on intra-empire trade, but as the international economy became more competitive in the late nineteenth century all three countries turned toward their colonies. This stimulated a general breakdown of the international economy into regional trading blocs and substituted government legislation and regulations for international market forces.

At the height of its hegemony, for instance, Britain pursued an open door policy within its colonies. Parliament repealed the mercantilist Navigation Laws in 1828 and soon thereafter opened the trade of the colonies to all countries on equal terms. Despite the absence of formal trade restrictions in the colonies, however, Britain continued to dominate their trade through informal means, counting on the ties between colonial administrators and the home state to channel trade in the appropriate directions.

Beginning in the late 1890s, however, Britain began to accept and, later, actively to promote preferential trade measures within the empire. While the earliest preferences took the form of unilateral reductions in colonial tariffs on British exports, by the First World War, Britain, under pressure from the colonies, began to reciprocate. The McKenna Duties, passed in 1915, and the Safeguarding of Industry Duties, enacted after the war, all discriminated against non-empire trade. In 1932, Britain returned to protection and adopted a complete system of Imperial Preference. In short, as its economic strength deteriorated in the late nineteenth century, even Britain, the paragon of international liberalism, turned inward to its empire.

Since 1945, on the other hand, formal imperialism has all but disappeared. Instead of a system of geographically dispersed empires, there now exists a system of sovereign states. As the American-dominated "Dollar bloc" of the 1930s attests, a formal empire is not necessary for the creation of a regional trade bloc. Yet the present international system is less likely to break down into regional economic blocs for two reasons.

As Hobson, Lenin and other theorists of late nineteenth-century imperialism correctly pointed out, imperialism is a finite process, the end point of which is determined by the quantity of available land. Once the hinterland is exhausted, countries can expand only through the redistribution of existing colonies. Thus, the quest for imperial trading blocs transforms exchange, at least in part, from a positive into a zero-sum game and increases the level of economic conflict endemic in the international system. Despite the decline of American hegemony, the gains from trade today are both more visible and less exclusive, helping to make the liberal international economy more durable than in the past.

In addition, colonies are not fully sovereign and have, at best, abridged decision-making powers. As a result, intra-imperial trade and trade agreements are not subject to the same possibilities for opportunism as are trade arrangements between independent states. Today, even if two countries undertake a bilateral trade treaty, as in the case of the United States and Canada, each remains fully sovereign and capable of cheating and exploiting the other. Indeed, as regional specialization expands, the quasi-rents potentially appropriable by either party will also increase, thereby raising the gains from opportunism. The higher the gains and, therefore, the risk of opportunism, the less likely it is that two countries will enter into binding bilateral relationships. As a result, trade blocs between sovereign states will always be more fragile, less beneficial and, it follows, less prevalent than those based upon imperial preference.

II. International Economic Structures

A. The Bases of British and American Hegemony   While both Britain and the United States enjoyed a position of international economic dominance, the bases of their economic hegemony differed in important ways. Britain's share of world *trade* was substantially larger than that obtained by the United States, while America's share of world *product* was far larger than Britain's.

In 1870, Britain controlled approximately 24 per cent of world trade, declining to less than 15 per cent by the outbreak of the First World War. The United States, however, accounted for only 18.4 per cent of world trade in 1950, and its share fell to less than 15 per cent by the mid 1960s. Collective goods theory suggests that Britain had a stronger interest in acting as a benevolent hegemon and, specifically, in regulating and maintaining an open international economy. This interest in providing the international economic infrastructure, furthermore, was reinforced by Britain's higher dependence on trade, which reached 49 per cent of national product in 1877–85 and 52 percent in 1909–13. For the United States, trade accounted for only 17 per cent of national product in the 1960s, although this ratio has risen in recent years. These figures indicate that Britain also faced considerably higher opportunity costs of international economic closure.

While British hegemony was based upon control of international trade, the United States — still the largest trader of its era — relied on the relatively greater size of its domestic economy. Throughout its hegemonic rise and decline, the British economy (measured in terms of national product) was relatively small compared to its trading rivals, and to that of the United States at a similar stage in its hegemonic cycle. In 1860, Britain's economy was only three-quarters the size of America's. Conversely, in 1950, the domestic economy of the United States was over three times larger than the Soviet Union's, its next largest rival. This difference between British and American hegemony, while highlighting variations in the opportunity costs of closure, also has important implications for the international political processes discussed below.

B. The Trajectories of Decline   Not only were the economic bases of British and American hegemony different, but their respective declines have also followed alternative trajectories. In the late nineteenth century, Britain was confronted by two dynamic, vibrant and rapidly growing rivals: the United States and Germany. Perhaps because of its latecomer status or its geographical position in Europe, Germany was singled out as Britain's principal challenger for hegemony. With the eventual assistance of the United States, Britain defeated Germany in war, and Germany was eliminated as an important economic actor.

The waning of British hegemony thus found the United States and the United Kingdom in roughly equal international economic positions. In the years immediately before the First World War, an economic *modus vivendi,* grounded in substantial tariff reductions in the United States, appeared possible between these two powers. Yet, Anglo-American cooperation and the potential for joint leadership of the international economy were cut short by the war and its aftermath. The breakdown of the international economy during the war created difficult problems of reconstruction and generated high international economic instability, which shortened time horizons in both the United States and Britain and rendered post-war cooperation substantially more difficult. In the absence of such cooperation, the conflicts over reconstruction were insoluble, and the international economy eventually collapsed in the Great Depression.

The decline of American hegemony has occurred primarily through a general levelling of international economic capabilities among the Western powers. Today, the international economy is dominated by the United States, the Federal Republic of Germany, France, and Japan, all substantial traders with a strong interest in free trade, even if they desire some protection for their own industries. The greatest structural threat to continued cooperation is not the absence of partners capable of joint management, but too many partners and the corresponding potential for free riding that this creates.

Despite the instability generated by the oil shocks of the 1970s, moreover, these four economic powers have successfully managed the international economy — or at least muddled through. They have coped with a major change in the international monetary regime, the rise of the Euromarkets, and the Third World debt crisis. The most immediate threats to continued cooperation are the large and, apparently, endless budget and trade deficits of the United States. Barring any further increase in international economic instability, however, even these problems may be manageable.

III. International Political Processes

A. The Three Faces of Hegemony   Elsewhere, Scott James and I have distinguished three "faces" or strategies of hegemonic leadership.[1] The first face of hegemony, as we define it, is characterized by the use of positive and negative sanctions aimed directly at foreign governments in an attempt to influence their choice of policies. Through inducements or threats, the hegemon seeks to alter the international costs and benefits of particular state actions. Economic sanctions, foreign aid and military support (or lack thereof) exemplify the strategic use of direct and overt international power central to this first face.

In the second face, the hegemon uses its international market power, or the ability to influence the price of specific goods, to alter the incentives and political influence of societal actors in foreign countries. These individuals, firms, sectors, or regions then exert pressure upon their governments for alternative policies, which — if the hegemon has used its market power correctly — will be more consistent with the interests of the dominant international power. This is a "Trojan Horse" strategy in which the hegemon changes the constellation of interests and political power within other countries in ways more favorable to its own interests.

The third face focuses on the hegemon's use of ideas and ideology to structure public opinion and the political agenda in other countries so as to determine what are legitimate and illegitimate policies and forms of political behavior. In other words, the hegemon uses propaganda, in the broadest sense of the word, to influence the climate of opinion in foreign countries.

In the mid-nineteenth century, Britain used its dominance of world trade to pursue an essentially second face strategy of hegemonic leadership. By repealing its Corn Laws, and allowing unfettered access to its markets, Britain effectively restructured the economic incentives facing producers of raw materials and food-stuffs. Over the long term, by altering factor and sector profit rates, and hence investment patterns, Britain augmented and mobilized the political influence of the interests within non-hegemonic countries most amenable to an international division of labor. All this was premised on complementary production and the free exchange of primary goods for British manufactures. Thus, in the United States, repeal of the Corn Laws facilitated the rise of a free trade coalition between Southern cotton growers, the traditional force for international economic openness in American politics, and Western grain producers who had previously allied themselves with the more protectionist northeastern industrialists. This South-West coalition was reflected in almost two decades of freer trade in the United States, begun with the passage of the Walker Tariff in 1846. A similar process can be identified in Prussia, where the repeal of the Corn Laws reinforced the political power and free trade tendencies of the Junkers. This is not to argue, of course, that Britain relied exclusively on the second face of hegemony, only that it was an important theme in British trade policy and international leadership.

The United States, as noted above, has never dominated international trade to the same extent as Britain, but instead bases its leadership and influence upon its large domestic market. American strategy follows from this difference. Where Britain used its trade dominance to pursue a second face strategy, the United States relies to a larger extent on a first face strategy, trading access to its own market for reciprocal tariff reductions abroad. Accordingly, the United States did not unilaterally reduce tariffs, except for the period immediately after the Second World War, but instead linked reductions in, at first, bilateral treaties under the Reciprocal Trade Agreements Act and, later, in the GATT.

The explicitly reciprocal nature of American trade policy facilitates greater multilateral openness. British liberalization was spread throughout Europe by the unconditional most-favored-nation principle, but free trade remained fragile. As soon as alternative political coalitions obtained power, as in the United States in the aftermath of the Civil War and in Germany in the coalition of Iron and Rye, liberal trade policies were quickly jettisoned in favor of protection. Committed to free trade, Britain made clear its reluctance to retaliate against new protectionism by its trading partners. As a result, it allowed countries like the United States and Germany to free ride on its leadership — specifically, to protect their domestic industries while continuing to take advantage of British openness. The reciprocal trade policy adopted by the United States has brought more countries into the fold, so to speak, by linking access to American markets to participation in the GATT system. This system of generalized reciprocity, as well as the increasing willingness of the United States to retaliate against unfair foreign trade practices, acts to restrain protectionism in foreign countries. Paradoxically, a trade strategy based upon the first face of hegemony, despite its more overt use of international power, may prove more resilient.

B. International Regimes   A second and related difference in the international political processes of British and American hegemony is the latter's greater reliance upon international institutions and international economic regimes. Britain led the international economy in the nineteenth century without recourse to any formal international institutions and with few international rules governing exchange relations between countries. The nineteenth century, in other words, was a period of weak or, at best, implicit international economic regimes.

In the present period, on the other hand, international economic regimes are highly prevalent, even pervasive. The GATT, the IMF, the World Bank, and many United Nations organizations all give concrete — and lasting — substance to America's global economic leadership. As a result, international liberalism has been institutionalized in international relations.

As Robert Keohane has persuasively argued, international regimes are instruments of statecraft and are created to facilitate cooperation, specifically, by (a) providing a legal liability framework, (b) reducing transactions costs, and (c) reducing uncertainty by providing information and constraining moral hazard and irresponsibility. States comply with their dictates, Keohane continues, because of reputational considerations, because regimes provide a service which is of value, and because they are easier to maintain than to create. For these same reasons, Keohane suggests, international regimes are likely to persist even though the interests which brought them into being change. International regimes are thus important because they create more consistent, routinized, and enduring international behavior.[2]

To the extent that this argument is correct, the greater reliance of American hegemony on international regimes can be expected to preserve the liberal international economic order for some unspecifiable period, not only in the United States but throughout the international economy as well. America's hegemonic "afterglow" may well be longer than Britain's.

C. Issue Linkage   The "low" politics of trade have always been linked with the "high" politics of national security — the views of certain liberal economists notwithstanding. Military issues have been linked with trade treaties, as in the

Cobden-Chevalier treaty between Britain and France in 1860. Trade policy also impinges upon economic growth and the basis for long-term military strength.

The free trade order constructed under British leadership bridged the political divide by including both allies and antagonists, friends and foes. In this system, not only was British influence over its military competitors limited, but the free trade order benefited all participants, often stimulating growth in antagonists and undermining the long-term strength of the United Kingdom. As Robert Gilpin noted, perhaps the most important contradiction of a free trade order, and international capitalism more generally, is that it develops rather than exploits potential competitors for international leadership.[3]

The liberal international economic regimes of American hegemony, on the other hand, have been built exclusively on one side of a bipolar political divide. All of America's important trading partners are also its allies. This provides great potential leverage for the United States in trade issues. America's contributions to the public good of common defense can be diplomatically and tactically linked to liberal trade policies. In addition, the greater benefits derived from specialization and the international division of labor are confined to allies of the United States. All economic benefits, in other words, reinforce America's security needs. As a result, challengers to American hegemony are less likely to emerge. And the United States, in turn, may be willing to make greater economic sacrifices to maintain the long-term strength and stability of the Western alliance.

IV. International Economic Processes

A. The Pattern of Specialization   The nineteenth-century international economy was built upon a pattern of complementary trade. Britain, and later a handful of other industrialized countries, exported manufactured goods and imported raw materials and foodstuffs. To the extent that complementary products were not available within any particular economy, or available only at a substantially higher cost, this system of North-South trade created conditions of mutual dependence between core and peripheral states and, in turn, high opportunity costs of closure. As the Great Depression of the early 1930s clearly demonstrated, the economic costs of international closure were considerable.

The largest and most rapidly growing area of international trade after 1945, on the other hand, has been intra-industry trade — or the exchange of similar commodities between similarly endowed countries. Accordingly, the United States is both a major importer and exporter of chemicals, machine tools and numerous other products. Similar patterns can be found in Europe and, to a lesser extent, for Japan.

This pattern of intra-industry trade creates two important but offsetting pressures, the net impact of which is unclear. First, intra-industry trade has a lower opportunity cost of closure than does complementary trade. The welfare loss of trade restraints on automobiles in the United States, for instance, is considerably less than it would be in the absence of a significant domestic car industry. In short, countries can more easily do without intra-industry trade. Second, the primary stimulus for intra-industry trade is economies of scale in production. To the extent that these economies are larger than the domestic market, and can be satisfied only by exporting to foreign countries, they create important domestic political interest in favor of free trade and international openness. This restraint on protection, of course, will vary across countries, weighing more heavily in, say, Switzerland, than in the United States.

B. International Capital Flows   In both the mid-nineteenth and mid-twentieth centuries, Britain and the United States, respectively, were the centers of the international financial system and the primary source of foreign investment. Both hegemons invested considerable sums abroad, perhaps at the expense of their own domestic economies. Nonetheless, an important difference exists between the two cases. Britain engaged almost exclusively in portfolio investment; the United States relied to a greater extent upon foreign direct investment.

During the period of British decline, a deep conflict emerged between the City of London, the primary source of international capital, and British manufacturers. As the latter found themselves less competitive within the international economy, they began to demand and lobby for a return to protection. The protectionists, or so-called tariff reformers, had grown strong enough to split the Conservative Party by 1903, costing it the parliamentary election of January 1906. By 1912, the tariff reformers dominated the party and, before the trade issue was displaced on the political agenda by Irish home rule, appeared likely to win the next legislative battle. The City, on the other hand, remained solidly liberal. Increasingly, financial profits depended upon new capital outflows and prompt repayment of loans made to developing countries. With an international horizon stretched before it, the City would bear the costs of protection in the form of higher domestic prices and, more importantly, in the reduced ability of exporting countries to repay their loans, but would receive few if any benefits. Where the manufacturers desired to return to an industrially based economy and a trade surplus, the City was content with the reliance on services and recognized the need for Britain to run a trade deficit for the foreseeable future. This conflict lasted throughout the inter-war period, with the City emerging triumphant with the return of pre-war parity in 1925, only to be defeated on the question of protection in 1932.

Until the 1970s, on the other hand, the United States engaged primarily in foreign direct investment. The export of both capital and ownership alters the nature of America's political cleavages, creating intra-industry and capital-labor conflicts rather than an industry-finance division. The overseas manufacturing assets, globally integrated production facilities, and enhanced trade dependence of multinational corporations reduce the demands for protection by firms engaged in foreign investment, but not by labor employed in those sectors. In this sense, the trade interests of multinational corporations are more similar to those of the international financial community than they are to domestic or non-internationalized firms. While nationally oriented firms and labor may still seek rents through domestic protection, the presence of a large multinational sector creates offsetting trade policy pressures within manufacturing and, indeed, often within the same sector, thereby strengthening the free trade lobby in the United States.

WHITHER THE *PAX AMERICANA*?

The differences between British and American hegemony are considerable, and serve to call into question the appropriateness of the historical analogy. The decline of the *Pax Americana* will not follow the same path blazed by the decline of the *Pax Britannica*. Simplistic historical analogies fully deserve the scepticism with which they are greeted. What then is the likely future of the international economic order? Will openness endure, or is closure imminent?

The international constraints discussed above point in different directions. The absence of formal imperialism, the emerging structure of the post-hegemonic international economy, the moderate (so far) level of international economic instability, greater American reliance on a first face strategy of explicit reciprocity, the institutionalization of liberal international economic regimes, the overlap between the security and economic issue areas, and the importance of foreign direct investment, all suggest that international liberalism is robust and likely to endure. The potential for free riding among the great economic powers, the pattern of economic specialization, and the growing importance of intra-industry trade, are the most important challenges to the liberal international economy — and are a source of caution about the future.

While certainly more fragile than in, say, the 1960s, the open international economy has several underlying sources of resiliency. Even though America's economic competitiveness has declined, relatively free and unrestricted commerce is likely to remain the international norm. The international economy is not being held open simply through inertia; there are real interests supporting international liberalism.

This relatively optimistic view of the future of the international trading order supports continued commitment by the United States to free trade and generalized reciprocity as found in the GATT. Japan- or Korea-bashing is unnecessary; other countries share America's interest in maintaining free trade within the international economy. The United States does not carry the burden of maintaining international openness alone.

Narrow policies of reciprocity, which seek equal access industry-by-industry or balanced trade between specific countries, may prove counterproductive, encouraging a decline into bilateralism that will redound to everyone's disadvantage and create the result which pessimists fear. As recent work on iterated prisoners' dilemma shows, cooperation can be sustained best by reciprocating cooperation. To the extent that the United States is perceived as defecting from the open international economy, it encourages similar behavior in others. Economic instability enhanced this problem in the 1920s, but it is inherent in the current system as well.

On the other hand, the United States cannot benefit by being the "sucker" in international trade. It must make clear that the continued openness of the American market is contingent upon similar degrees of openness in other countries. A broad or generalized policy of reciprocity is sufficient for this task, and promises to calm rather than exacerbate international economic tensions.

CONCLUSION

Statesmen and stateswomen undoubtedly base their decisions on theories of international politics, even if such theories are so implicit and amorphous as to resemble nothing more than "world views." No policy is made in a theoretical vacuum. Rather, beginning from selected assumptions or principles of human action, all policy-makers rely upon means-ends relationships and estimates of costs and benefits either derived from or validated by historical experience. These theories can be quite wrong or poorly understood, in which case the policy is likely to fail. Good theories, well employed, lead to more positive outcomes — or at least one hopes they do.

Scholars are an important source of the theories upon which decision-makers base their policies. This is especially true of the theory of hegemonic stability. Developed just as the first signs of American decline were becoming apparent and long before the pattern and its implications were recognized in diplomatic circles, the theory of hegemonic stability has slowly crept out of the ivory tower and into the public consciousness. It has helped spark a debate on the limits of American power in the late twentieth century. It has also led to demands for more aggressive trade policies under the generally accepted but nonetheless dangerous standard of "specific reciprocity."

No theory is widely accepted unless it has some empirical support and intuitive plausibility. The danger is, however, that even theories that meet these criteria may be underdeveloped and inadequately specified by their scholarly progenitors or oversimplified by those who translate academic jargon and subtlety into the language of public debate. The theory of hegemonic stability has been poorly served on both counts, leading to overly pessimistic predictions on the future of the international economy and to far too aggressive trade policies which threaten to bring about the results they are supposedly designed to prevent.

NOTES

1. Scott C. James and David A. Lake, "The Second Face of Hegemony: Britain's Repeal of the Corn Laws and the American Walker Tariff of 1846," *International Organization* 43, 1 (1989): 1–29.

2. Robert O. Keohane, *After Hegemony: Cooperation and Discord in the World Political Economy* (Princeton: Princeton University Press, 1984).

3. Robert Gilpin, *U.S. Power and the Multinational Corporation: The Political Economy of Foreign Direct Investment* (New York: Basic Books, 1975).

III

PRODUCTION

Productive activity is at the center of any economy. Agriculture, mining, and manufacturing are the bases on which domestic and international commerce, finance, and other services rest. No society can survive without producing. Thus, production is crucial to both the domestic and international political economies.

In the international arena, production abroad by large corporations gained enormously in importance after World War I. The establishment of productive facilities in foreign lands was nothing new, however. The planters who settled the southern portion of the Thirteen Colonies under contract to, and financed by, British merchant companies were engaging in foreign direct investment in plantation agriculture. Indeed, before the twentieth century, foreign investment in primary production — mining and agriculture — was quite common. In particular, European and North American investors financed copper mines in Chile and Mexico, tea and rubber plantations in India and Indochina, and gold mines in South Africa and Australia, among other endeavors.

Around the turn of the century, and especially after World War I, a relatively novel form of foreign direct investment arose: the establishment of overseas branch factories of manufacturing corporations. In its origin the phenomenon was largely North American, and it remained so until the 1960s, when European, and then Japanese, manufacturers also began investing in productive facilities abroad. These internationalized industrial firms were called multinational or transnational corporations or enterprises (MNCs/TNCs or MNEs/TNEs), usually defined as firms with productive facilities in three or more countries. Such corporations have been extraordinarily controversial for both scholars and politicians.

By the late 1990s, there were some 53,000 MNCs in the world, with 450,000 foreign affiliates. Most are relatively small, but the top several hundred are so huge and so globe straddling as to dominate major portions of the world economy. MNCs' foreign affiliates are worth about $3.5 trillion, and they produce goods worth $9.5 trillion every year. These foreign affiliates account for one-third of world exports and a very substantial proportion of world output. Indeed, the largest MNCs have annual sales larger than the gross national product (GNP) of all but a few of the world's nations.[1]

One major analytic task is to explain the very existence of multinational manufacturing corporations. It is, of course, simple to understand why English investors would finance tea plantations in Ceylon — they could hardly have grown tea in Manchester. Yet, in the abstract, there is little logic in Bayer producing aspirin in the United States. If the German aspirin industry were more efficient than the American, Bayer could simply produce the pills in its factories at home and export them to the United States. Why, then, does Ford make cars in England, Volkswagen make cars in the United States, and both companies make cars in Mexico instead of simply shipping them, respectively, across the Atlantic or the Rio Grande?

For the answer, students of the MNC have examined both economic and political factors. The political spurs to overseas direct investment are straightforward. Many countries maintain trade barriers in order to protect local industry; this makes exporting to these nations difficult, and MNCs choose to "jump trade barriers" and produce inside protected markets. Similar considerations apply where the local government uses such policies as "Buy American" regulations, which favor domestic products in government purchases, or where, as in the case of Japanese auto investment in the United States, overseas producers fear the onset of protectionist measures.

Economic factors in the spread of MNCs are many and complex. The simplest explanation is that foreign direct investment moves capital from more-developed regions, where it is abundant and cheap, to less-developed nations, where it is scarce and expensive. This captures some of the story, but it also leaves much unexplained. Why, for example, does this transfer of capital not take the form of foreign lending rather than the (much more complex) form of foreign direct investment? Furthermore, why is most foreign direct investment among developed countries with similar endowments of capital rather than between developed and developing nations?

Economists have often explained foreign direct investment by pointing to certain size-related characteristics of multinational corporations. Because MNCs are very large in comparison to local firms in most countries, they can mobilize large amounts of capital more easily than local enterprises. Foreign corporations may then, simply by virtue of their vast wealth, buy up local firms in order to eliminate competitors. In some lines of business, such as large-scale production of appliances or automobiles, the initial investment necessary to begin production may be prohibitive for local firms, giving MNCs a decisive advantage. Similarly, MNC access to many different currencies from the many markets in which they operate may give them a competitive advantage over firms doing business in only one nation and currency. Moreover, the widespread popularity of consumption patterns formed in North America and Western Europe and then transplanted to other nations — a process that often leads to charges of "cultural imperialism" — may lead local consumers to prefer foreign brand names to local ones: for example, much of the Third World population brushes their teeth with Colgate and drinks Coke, American brands popularized by literature, cinema, television, and advertising. However, though these points may be accurate, they do not amount to a systematic explanation of foreign direct investment.

The first step in the search for a more rigorous explanation of foreign direct investment was the "product cycle theory" developed by Raymond Vernon.[2] Vernon pointed out that products manufactured by MNCs typically follow similar patterns or cycles. A firm begins by introducing a new product that it manufactures and sells at home; over time, it expands exports to foreign markets; as the product becomes more widely known, it eventually engages in foreign investment; and finally, as production of the good is standardized, the firm begins exporting back to the home market. This jibes with observations that MNCs tend to operate in oligopolistic markets (those dominated by a few firms); that their products often are produced with new technologies; and that they tend to have important previous exporting experience.

The product cycle theory did not answer all the economic questions, however. There was still no explanation of why firms would invest abroad instead of simply exporting from their (presumably more congenial) home base or licensing the production technology, trademark, or other distinguishing market advantage to local producers. In the past twenty-five years most economists have come to regard the multinational corporation as a special case of the vertically or horizontally integrated corporation. In this view, large companies come to organize certain activities inside the firm rather than through the marketplace because some transactions are difficult to carry out by normal market means — especially in cases where prices are hard to calculate or contracts hard to enforce. When applied to MNCs, this approach suggests that foreign direct investment takes place because these firms have access to unique technologies, managerial skills, or marketing expertise that is more profitable when maintained within the corporate network than when sold on the open market. In Reading 9, economist Richard E. Caves surveys the modern economic theories of MNCs.

If the origins of MNCs are analytically controversial, their effects are debated with even more ferocity. In the 1950s and 1960s, as American-based corporations expanded rapidly into Western Europe, protests about foreigners buying up the European economies were common. At the time, most Americans regarded these protests as signs of retrograde nationalism, as they had traditionally taken MNCs for granted — few even realized that such firms as Shell, Universal Studios, Bayer, Saks Fifth Avenue, Nestlé, and Firestone Tires were foreign owned. However, as investment in the United States by firms from the rest of the world grew, some critics began to argue that this represented a threat to American control over the U.S. economy. Thus, even in the United States, the most important home base of MNCs, the role of foreign direct investment is hotly debated. American MNCs employ 6 million people around the world, while foreign firms employ 5 million Americans, which means that foreign direct investment is, directly or indirectly, relevant to many people at home and abroad.

While foreign direct investment is controversial in the developed countries, it is far more contentious in the Third World. Developed nations, after all, have technically advanced regulatory agencies and relatively large economies. However, most of the less developed countries (LDCs) have economies smaller than the largest MNCs, with governmental regulatory bureaucracies that are no match for MNC executives. In many LDCs, then, the very presence of MNCs is viewed with suspicion. MNCs have been known to interfere in local politics, and local businesspeople often resent the competition created by huge foreign enterprises. Over the years many LDCs have imposed stringent regulations on foreign direct investors, although most of them continue to believe that on balance, MNCs have a beneficial impact on national economic and political development. In the section that follows, the articles by Shah M. Tarzi (Reading 10) and David Fieldhouse (Reading 11) evaluate the arguments in favor of, and opposed to, multinational corporations in the Third World.

Foreign direct investment is closely related to international trade, and over the years, governments have developed policies to try to take advantage of the unique characteristics of MNCs. Among the more common, and more controversial, are strategic trade and investment policies. In Reading 12, Jeffrey A. Hart and Aseem Prakash describe and analyze these measures, which typically involve a mix of trade and industrial policies to encourage investment in activities regarded as critical to economic growth, and which usually are directly related to the role of multinational corporations.

NOTES

1. United Nations Conference on Trade and Development, *World Investment Report 1998: Trends and Determinants* (New York and Geneva: United Nations, 1998), p. xvii.

2. Raymond Vernon, "International Investment and International Trade in the Product Cycle," *Quarterly Journal of Economics* 80, 2 (1966): 190–207.

9

The Multinational Enterprise as an Economic Organization
RICHARD E. CAVES

Richard E. Caves, a neoclassical economist, provides a survey of economic explanations of the multinational enterprise (MNE). He focuses on how certain circumstances can make it difficult to carry out transactions in the marketplace. For example, it is hard to measure or establish a "fair" price for assets such as new technologies or managerial expertise. In these cases, firms, including MNEs, can overcome the problems of market transactions involving such hard-to-price assets by carrying out transactions internally, within the corporation. This reading presents the predominant economic explanation for the rise and existence of MNEs.

The multinational enterprise (MNE) is defined here as an enterprise that controls and manages production establishments — plants — located in at least two countries. It is simply one subspecies of multiplant firm. We use the term "enterprise" rather than "company" to direct attention to the top level of coordination in the hierarchy of business decisions; a company, itself multinational, may be the controlled subsidiary of another firm. The minimum "plant" abroad needed to make an enterprise multinational is, as we shall see, judgmental. The transition from a foreign sales subsidiary or a technology licensee to a producing subsidiary is not always a discrete jump, for good economic reasons. What constitutes "control" over a foreign establishment is another judgmental issue. Not infrequently a MNE will choose to hold only a minor fraction of the equity of a foreign affiliate. Countries differ in regard to the minimum percentage of equity ownership that they count as a "direct investment" abroad, as distinguished from a "portfolio investment," in their international-payments statistics.

. . . [T]he definition does identify the MNE as essentially a multiplant firm. We are back to Coase's (1937) classic question of why the boundary between the administrative allocation of resources within the firm and the market allocation of resources between firms falls where it does. In a market economy, entrepreneurs are free to try their hands at displacing market transactions by increasing the scope of allocations made administratively within their firms. The Darwinian tradition holds that the most profitable pattern of enterprise organization should ultimately prevail: Where more profit results from placing plants under a common administrative control, multiplant enterprises will predominate, and single-plant

145

firms will merge or go out of business. In order to explain the existence and prevalence of MNEs, we require models that predict where the multiplant firm enjoys advantages from displacing the arm's-length market and where it does not. In fact, the prevalence of multiplant (multinational) enterprises varies greatly from sector to sector and from country to country, affording a ready opportunity to test models of the MNE.

The models of the multiplant firm potentially relevant to explaining the presence of MNEs are quite numerous and rather diverse in their concerns. It proves convenient to divide them into three groups: (1) One type of multiplant firm turns out broadly the same line of goods from its plants in each geographic market. Such firms are common in domestic industries with fragmented local markets such as metal containers, bakeries, and brewing. Similarly, the many MNEs that establish plants in different countries to make the same or similar goods can be called horizontally integrated. (2) Another type of multiplant enterprise produces outputs in some of its plants that serve as inputs to its other activities. Actual physical transfer of intermediate products from one of the firm's plants to another is not required by the definition; it needs only to produce at adjacent stages of a vertically related set of production processes. (3) The third type of multiplant firm is the diversified company whose plants' outputs are neither vertically nor horizontally related to one another. As an international firm it is designated a diversified MNE.

1. HORIZONTAL MULTIPLANT ENTERPRISES AND THE MNE

We start by equating the horizontal MNE to a multiplant firm with plants in several countries. Its existence requires, first, that *locational forces* justify dispersing the world's production so that plants are found in different national markets. Given this dispersion of production, there must be some *governance* or *transaction-cost advantage* to placing the plants (some plants, at least) under common administrative control. This abstract, static approach provides the most general and satisfying avenue to explaining the multinational company. . . . We assume at first that plant A was located in southeast England because that was the lowest-cost way to serve the market it in fact serves. We also assume that this locational choice was not essentially influenced by whether the plant was built by an MNE, bought by an MNE, or not owned by an MNE at all. The static approach also puts aside the vital question of why a company grows into MNE status — something more readily explained after the static model is in hand.

The transaction-cost approach asserts, quite simply, that horizontal MNEs will exist only if the plants they control and operate attain lower costs or higher revenue productivity than the same plants under separate managements. Why should this net-revenue advantage arise? Some of the reasons have to do with minimizing costs of production and associated logistical activities of the firm. The more analytically interesting reasons — and, we shall see, the more important ones empirically — concern the complementary nonproduction activities of the firm.

Proprietary Assets

The most fruitful concept for explaining the nonproduction bases for the MNE is that of assets having these properties: The firm owns or can appropriate the assets or their services; they can differ in productivity from comparable assets possessed by competing firms; the assets or their productivity effects are mobile between national markets; they may be depreciable (or subject to augmentation), but their lifespans are not short relative to the horizon of the firm's investment decision. Successful firms in most industries possess one or more types of such assets. An asset might represent knowledge about how to produce a cheaper or better product at given input prices, or how to produce a given product at a lower cost than competing firms. The firm could possess special skills in styling or promoting its product that make it such that the buyer differentiates it from those of competitors. Such an asset has a revenue productivity for the firm because it signifies the willingness of some buyers to pay more for that firm's product than for a rival firm's comparable variety. Assets of this type are closely akin to product differentiation, a market condition in which the distinctive features of various sellers' outputs cause each competing firm to face its own downward-sloping demand curve. The proprietary asset might take the form of a specific property — a registered trademark or brand — or it might rest in marketing and selling skills shared among the firm's employees. Finally, the distinctiveness of the firm's marketing-oriented assets might rest with the firm's ability to come up with frequent innovations; its proprietary asset then might be a patented novelty, or simply some new combination of attributes that its rivals cannot quickly or effectively imitate. This asset might vary greatly in tangibility and specificity. It could take the specific form of a patented process or design, or it might simply rest on know-how shared among employees of the firm. It is important that the proprietary asset, however it creates value, might rest on a set of skills or repertory of routines possessed by the firm's team of human (and other) inputs.

The proprietary assets described by these examples evidently share the necessary conditions to support foreign investment. They are things that the firm can use but not necessarily sell or contract upon. Either the firm can hold legal title (patents, trademarks) or the assets are shared among the firm's employees and cannot be easily copied or appropriated (by other firms or by the employees themselves). They possess either the limitless capacities of public goods (the strict intangibles) or the flexible capacities of the firm's repertory of routines. Especially important for the MNE, while the productive use of these assets is not tightly tied to single physical sites or even nations, arm's-length transfers of them between firms are prone to market failures. These failures deter a successful one-plant firm from selling or renting its proprietary assets to other single-plant firms and thereby foster the existence of multiplant (and multinational) firms. Proprietary assets are subject to a daunting list of infirmities for being detached and transferred by sale or lease:

1. They are, at least to some degree, *public goods*. Once a piece of knowledge has been developed and applied at a certain location, it can be put to work elsewhere at little extra cost and without reducing the capacity available at the original site. From society's point of view, the marginal conditions for

efficient allocation of resources then require that the price of the intangible asset be equal to its marginal cost, zero or approximately zero. But no one gets rich selling bright ideas for zero. Therefore, intangible assets tend to be underprovided or to be priced inefficiently (at a net price exceeding their marginal cost) or both.

2. Transactions in intangibles suffer from *impactedness* combined with *opportunism.* This problem is best explained by examples: I have a piece of knowledge that I know will be valuable to you. I try to convince you of this value by describing its general nature and character. But I do not reveal the details, because then the cat would be out of the bag, and you could use the knowledge without paying for it unless I have a well-established property right. But you therefore decline to pay me as much as the knowledge would in fact be worth to you, because you suspect that I am opportunistic and overstate my claims.

3. A proprietary asset might be diffuse and therefore incapable of an enforceable lease or sale contract. The owning firm might readily contract with a customer to achieve a specific result using some competence that it possesses, but be unable to contract to install that competence within another firm. Even with well-defined intangibles, various sources of uncertainty can render contractual transfers infeasible or distort the terms of viable deals.

This application of modern transaction-cost analysis underlies a framework widely used in research on the MNE. It asserts the existence of three necessary conditions for the appearance of horizontal foreign investments: (1) The firm can appropriate some value-creating proprietary asset ("ownership"); (2) production processes that employ or apply the value-creating asset are efficiently dispersed among several national markets ("location"); and (3) the decentralized application of the proprietary asset is more efficiently managed within the owning firm than by renting it at arm's length to another firm ("internalization"). . . .

Empirical Evidence: Prevalence of Horizontal Foreign Investment

Hypotheses about horizontal MNEs have received many statistical tests. The usual strategy of research involves relating the prevalence of MNEs in an industry to structural traits of that industry: If attribute x promotes the formation of MNEs, and successful firms in industry A have a lot of x, then MNEs should be prevalent in industry A. These tests have been performed on two dependent variables: foreign operations of firms in a source country's industries normalized by their total activity level in those industries (hereafter "outbound" foreign investment), and foreign subsidiaries' share of activity in a host country's markets normalized by total transactions in those markets (hereafter "inbound" foreign investment). The exogenous variables are chosen to represent features of industries' structures that should either promote or deter foreign direct investment. . . .

. . . There is considerable agreement on the major results among studies of both outbound and inbound investment, among studies of a given type for each country, and among studies based on different countries. Therefore we offer here some generalizations about the principal conclusions without referring extensively to the conclusions reached in individual studies or about particular countries. . . .

. . . [Research] results confirm, first and foremost, the role of proprietary assets inferred from the outlays that firms make to create and maintain these assets. Research and development intensity (R&D sales ratio) is a thoroughly robust predictor. Advertising intensity has proved nearly as robust, even though most studies have lacked an appropriately comprehensive measure of firms' sales-promotion outlays. The literature also consistently finds a significant positive influence for an industry's intensive use of skilled managerial labor; this variable seems to confirm the "repertory of routines" basis for foreign investment, independent of the strictly intangible proprietary assets. . . . A third result that also supports a role for the firm's general coordinating capacity is the positive influence of multiplant operation within large countries such as the United States. . . .

Multinationals in Service Industries

Horizontal MNEs in banking and other services have received increased attention from researchers. The proprietary-assets hypothesis again makes a good showing — especially when extended to the transaction-specific assets of an ongoing semicontractual relationship between the service enterprise and its customer. A bank, advertising agency, or accounting firm acquires a good deal of specific knowledge about its client's business, and the parties' sustained relationship based on trust lowers the cost of contracting and the risks of opportunistic behavior. The service firm enjoying such a quasi-contractual relation with a parent MNE holds a transaction-cost advantage for supplying the same service to the MNE's foreign subsidiaries. If the service must be supplied locally, the service firm goes multinational to follow its customer.

Much casual evidence reveals this transaction-specific asset behind service industries' foreign investments, especially in the banking sector. . . . Some banks acquire particular product-differentiating skills analogous to those found in some goods-producing industries; they can explain banks' foreign investments in less-developed countries and in countries with large populations of migrants from the source country. Also, national banking markets commonly appear somewhat noncompetitive because of cartelization or regulation or both, and foreign banks are well-equipped potential entrants. The Eurocurrency markets' rise can be largely explained on this basis. The traits of foreign banks' operations in the United States affirm these propositions. . . .

The prominence of transaction-specific assets as a factor driving foreign investment is apparently matched in other service industries such as advertising agencies, accounting, and consulting firms. Studies of other multinational service industries, however, bring out different factors. . . .

2. VERTICALLY INTEGRATED MNEs

The vertically integrated MNE is readily regarded as a vertically integrated firm whose production units lie in different nations. Theoretical models that explain vertical integration should therefore be directly applicable. Again, we assume that production units are dispersed in different countries due to conventional locational pressures — the bauxite mine where the bauxite is, bauxite converted to alumina at the mine because the process is strongly weight-losing, and the smelter that converts alumina into aluminum near a source of low-cost electric power. The question is, why do they come under common administrative control? The proprietary-assets model is not necessary, because neither upstream nor downstream production unit need bring any distinctive qualification to the parties' vertical consolidation. Some proprietary advantage of course *could* explain which producer operating at one stage undertakes an international forward or backward vertical integration.

Models of Vertical Integration

Until the rise of transaction-cost economics the economic theory of vertical integration contained a large but unsatisfying inventory of special-case models. Some dealt with the physical integration of production processes: If you make structural shapes out of the metal ingot before it cools, you need not incur the cost of reheating it. Such gains from physical integration explain why sequential processes are grouped in a single plant, but they neither preclude two firms sharing that plant nor explain the common ownership of far-flung plants. Another group of traditional models regard vertical integration as preferable to a stalemate between a monopolistic seller and a monopolistic buyer, or to an arm's-length relation between a monopolistic seller and competitive buyers whose activities are distorted due to paying the monopolist's marked-up price for their input. Some models explain vertical integration as a way around monopolistic distortions, while others explain it as a way to profit by fostering such distortions.

The theory of vertical integration has been much enriched by the same transaction-cost approach that serves to explain horizontal MNEs. Vertical integration occurs, the argument goes, because the parties prefer it to the ex ante contracting costs and ex post monitoring and haggling costs that would mar the alternative state of arm's-length transactions. The vertically integrated firm internalizes a market for an intermediate product, just as the horizontal MNE internalizes markets for proprietary assets. Suppose that there were pure competition in each intermediate-product market, with large numbers of buyers and sellers, the product homogeneous (or its qualities costlessly evaluated by the parties), information about prices and availability in easy access to all parties in the market. Neither seller nor buyer would then have reason to transact repeatedly with any particular party on the other side of the market. When these assumptions do not hold, however, both buyers and sellers acquire motives to make long-term alliances. The two can benefit mutually from investments that each makes suited to special attributes of the other party. Each then incurs a substantial fixed cost upon shifting from one transaction partner to another. Each seller's product could be somewhat different, and the buyer incurs significant costs of testing or adapting to new varieties, or merely learning the requirements and organizational routines of new partners. The buyer and seller gain an incentive to enter into some kind of long-term arrangement.

If transaction-specific assets deter anonymous spot-market transactions, they leave open the choice between long-term contracts and vertical integration. Contracts, however, encounter the costs of negotiation and of monitoring and haggling previously mentioned. These ex ante and ex post costs trade off against one another — a comprehensive contract can reduce subsequent haggling — but the overall cost remains. The problem is compounded because, even in a market with many participants, unattached alternative transaction partners tend to be few *at any particular time* when a party might wish to recontract. Fewness compounds the problems of governance in arm's-length vertical relationships.

One special case of the transaction-cost theory of vertical integration holds promise for explaining MNEs involved in processing natural resources. Vertical integration can occur because of failings in markets for information, as analyzed earlier in the context of proprietary assets. A processing firm must plan its capacity on some assumption about the future price and availability of its key raw material. The producers of that raw material have the cheapest access (perhaps exclusive) to that information. But they have an incentive to overstate availability to the prospective customer: The more capacity customers build, the higher they are likely to bid in the future for any given quantity of the raw material. Therefore, vertical integration could occur in order to evade problems of impacted information.

To summarize, intermediate-product markets can be organized in a spectrum of ways stretching from anonymous spot-market transactions through a variety of long-term contractual arrangements at arm's length to vertical integration. Switching costs and durable, specialized assets discourage spot transactions and favor one of the other modes. If, in addition, the costs of negotiating and monitoring arm's-length contracts are high, the choice falls on vertical integration. These empirical predictions address both where vertical MNEs will appear and how they will trade off against contractual relationships.

Empirical Evidence

Far fewer statistical studies address these hypotheses than the ones concerned with horizontal MNEs. . . .

A great deal of information exists on individual extractive industries in which MNEs operate on a worldwide basis, and this case-study evidence merits a glance in lieu of more systematic findings. For example, Stuckey found the international aluminum industry to contain not only MNEs integrated from the mining of bauxite through the fabrication of aluminum projects but also a network of long-term contracts and joint ventures. Market participants are particularly unwilling to settle for spot transactions in bauxite (the raw ore) and alumina (output of the first processing stage). The problem is not so much the small number of market participants worldwide as the extremely high switching costs. Alumina refining facilities need to be located physically close to bauxite mines (to minimize transportation costs), and they are constructed to deal with the properties of specific ores. Likewise, for technical and transportation-cost reasons, aluminum smelters are somewhat tied to particular sources of alumina. Therefore, arm's-length markets tend to be poisoned by the problems of small numbers and switching costs. And the very large specific and durable investments in facilities also invoke the problems of long-term contracts that were identified earlier. Finally, Stuckey gave some weight to Arrow's model of vertical integration as a route to securing information: Nobody knows more about future bauxite supplies and exploration than an existing bauxite producer.

A good deal of evidence also appears on vertical integration in the oil industry. The ambitious investigations have addressed the U.S. segment of the industry, but there appears to be no strong difference between the forces traditionally affecting vertical integration in national and international oil companies. These studies give considerable emphasis to the costs of supply disruption faced by any noninte-grated firm in petroleum extraction or refining. Refineries normally operate at capacity and require a constant flow of crude-oil inputs. Storing large inventories of input is quite costly, and so backward integration that reduces uncertainty about crude supplies can save the refiner a large investment in storage capacity. It also reduces risks in times of "shortages" and "rationing," when constraints some-where in the integrated system (crude-oil supplies are only the most familiar con-straint) can leave the unintegrated firm out in the cold. The hazard of disrupted flows translates into a financial risk, as vertically integrated firms have been found to be able to borrow long-term funds more cheaply than those with exposure to risk.

Country-based studies of the foreign-investment process have also underlined vertical MNEs as the outcome of failed arm's-length market transactions. Japanese companies became involved with extractive foreign investments only after the experience of having arm's-length suppliers renege on long-term con-tracts, and they also experimented with low-interest loans to independent foreign suppliers as a way to establish commitment.

Vertical Integration: Other Manifestations

The identification of vertically integrated foreign investment with extractive activ-ities is traditional and no doubt faithful to the pattern accounting for the bulk of MNE assets. However, it gives too narrow an impression of the role of vertically subdivided transactions in MNEs.

First of all, it neglects a form of backward integration that depends not on nat-ural resources but on subdividing production processes and placing abroad those that are both labor-intensive and footloose. For example, semiconductors are pro-duced by capital-intensive processes and assembled into electronic equipment by similarly mechanized processes, both undertaken in the industrial countries. But, in between, wires must be soldered to the semiconductors by means of a labor-intensive technology. Because shipping costs for the devices are low relative to their value, it pays to carry out the labor-intensive stage in a low-wage country. The relationship of the enterprises performing these functions in the United States and abroad must obviously be a close one, involving either detailed contractual arrangements or common ownership. This subdivision of production processes should occur through foreign investment to an extent that depends again on the transactional bases for vertical integration.

Writers on offshore procurement and the associated international trade always refer to the role of foreign investment in transplanting the necessary know-how and managerial coordination explored statistically both the structural determinants of this type of trade and the role of MNEs in carrying it out. [The] data pertain to imports under a provision of the U.S. tariff whereby components exported from the United States for additional fabrication abroad can be reimported with duty paid only on the value-added abroad. [S]tatistical analysis explains how these activities vary both among U.S. industries and among countries taking part in this trade. [The] results confirm the expected properties of the industries that make use of vertically disintegrated production: Their outputs have high value per unit of weight, possess reasonably mature technology (so are out of the experimental stage), are produced in the United States under conditions giving rise to high labor costs, and are easily subject to decentralized production. Among overseas countries, U.S. offshore procurement favors those not too far distant (transportation costs) and with low wages and favorable working conditions. With these factors controlled, the component flows increase with the extent of U.S. foreign investment, both among industries and among foreign countries.

A considerable amount of vertical integration is also involved in the "horizontal" foreign investments described earlier in this chapter, and the behavior of horizontal MNEs cannot be fully understood without recognizing the complementary vertical aspects of their domestic and foreign operations. Many foreign subsidiaries do not just produce their parents' goods for the local market; they process semifinished units of that good, or package or assemble them according to local specifications. Pharmaceuticals, for example, are prepared in the locally desired formulations using basic preparations imported from the parent. The subsidiary organizes a distribution system in the host-country market, distributing partly its own production, but with its line of goods filled out with imports from its parent or other affiliates. Or the subsidiary integrates forward to provide local servicing facilities. These activities are bound up with the development and maintenance of the enterprise's goodwill asset, as described earlier, through a commitment of resources to the local market. The firm can thereby assure local customers, who are likely to incur fixed investments of their own in shifting their purchases to the MNE, that the company's presence is not transitory. This consideration helps explain foreign investment in some producer-goods industries for which the proprietary-assets hypothesis otherwise seems rather dubious. All of these activities represent types of forward integration by the MNE, whether into final-stage processing of its goods or into ancillary services.

The evidence of this confluence of vertical and horizontal foreign investments mainly takes the form of case studies rather than systematic data. . . . It is implied by the extent of intracorporate trade among MNE affiliates — flows that would be incompatible with purely horizontal forms of intracorporate relationships. Imports of finished goods by Dutch subsidiaries from their U.S. parents are high (as percentages of the affiliates' total sales) in just those sectors where imports might complement local production for filling out a sales line — chemicals (24.9 percent), electrical equipment (35.4 percent), and transportation equipment (65.5 percent). The prevalence of intracorporate trade in engineering industries also suggests the importance of components shipments. . . .

Statistical evidence on U.S. exports and imports passing between corporate affiliates sheds light on this mixture of vertical and horizontal foreign investment. Lall analyzed the factors determining the extent of U.S. MNEs' exports to their affiliates (normalized either by their total exports or by their affiliates' total production). He could not discriminate between two hypotheses that together have significant force: (1) That trade is internalized where highly innovative and specialized goods are involved, and (2) that trade is internalized where the ultimate sales to final buyers must be attended by extensive customer engineering and after-sales services. Jarrett confirmed these hypotheses with respect to the importance in U.S. imports of interaffiliate trade, which in his data includes exports by foreign MNEs to their manufacturing and marketing subsidiaries in the United States as well as imports by U.S. MNEs from their overseas affiliates. Jarrett also found evidence that interaffiliate trade in manufactures reflects several conventional forms of vertical integration: More of it occurs in industries populated (in the United States) by large plants and companies, capable of meeting the scale-economy problems that arise in the international disintegration of production, and in industries that carry out extensive multiplant operations in the United States. . . .

3. PORTFOLIO DIVERSIFICATION AND THE DIVERSIFIED MNE

This section completes the roster of international multiplant firms by accounting for those whose international plants have no evident horizontal or vertical relationship. An obvious explanation of this type of MNE (though not the only one, it turns out) lies in the spreading of business risks. Going multinational in any form brings some diversification gains to the enterprise, and these reach their maximum when the firm diversifies across "product space" as well as geographical space. . . .

Now we consider empirical evidence on diversification as a motive for the MNE. Within a national economy, many shocks affect all firms rather similarly — recessions, major changes in macroeconomic policy. Between countries, such disturbances are more nearly uncorrelated. Also, changes in exchange rates and terms of trade tend to favor business profits in one country while worsening them elsewhere. Statistical evidence confirms that MNEs enjoy gains from diversification: The larger the share of foreign operations in total sales, the lower the variability of the firm's rate of return on equity capital. MNEs also enjoy lower levels of risk in the sense relevant to the stock market — financial risk (beta). . . . In general, this evidence supports the hypothesis that the MNE attains appreciable international diversification. However, the diversification might result from investments that were propelled by other motives. . . .

4. SUMMARY

The existence of the MNE is best explained by identifying it as a multiplant firm that sprawls across national boundaries, then applying the transaction-cost approach to explain why dispersed plants should fall under common ownership and control rather than simply trade with each other (and with other agents) on the open market. This approach is readily applied to the horizontal MNE (its national branches produce largely the same products), because the economies of multi-plant operation can be identified with use of the firm's proprietary assets, which suffer many infirmities for trade at arm's length. This hypothesis receives strong support in statistical studies, with regard both to intangible assets and to capabilities possessed by the firm.

A second major type of MNE is the vertically integrated firm, and several economic models of vertical integration stand ready to explain its existence. Once again, the transaction-cost approach holds a good deal of power, because vertical MNEs in the natural-resources sector seem to respond to the difficulties of working out arm's-length contracts in small-numbers situations where each party has a transaction-specific investment at stake. Evading problems of impacted information also seems to explain some vertical foreign investment. The approach also works well to explain the rapid growth of offshore procurement by firms in industrial countries, which involves carrying out labor-intensive stages of production at foreign locations with low labor costs. Although procurement occurs through arm's-length contracts as well as foreign investment, the role of foreign investment is clearly large. Finally, numerous vertical transactions flow between the units of apparently horizontal MNEs as the foreign subsidiary undertakes final fabrication, fills out its line with imports from its corporate affiliates, or provides ancillary services that complement these imports.

Diversified foreign investments, which have grown rapidly in recent decades, suggest that foreign investment serves as a means of spreading risks to the firm. Foreign investment, whether diversified from the parent's domestic product line or not, apparently does offer some diversification value. Diversified foreign investments can be explained in part by the parent's efforts to utilize its diverse R&D discoveries, and certain other influences as well. However, other diversified investments appear specifically aimed at spreading risks through international diversification, especially among geographic markets.

10

Third World Governments and Multinational Corporations: Dynamics of Host's Bargaining Power

SHAH M. TARZI

Shah M. Tarzi examines the bargaining relationship between Third World host governments and multinational corporations (MNCs). While host governments seek to encourage firms to locate within their countries on the best terms possible, MNCs want to minimize the conditions and restrictions the host government is able to impose on their operations. Tarzi identifies several factors that affect the bargaining power of the host government. He distinguishes between factors that influence the potential power of the state, such as its managerial skills, and those that affect the ability of the state to exercise its bargaining power. Actual power, as he terms it, is determined by societal pressures the host government faces, the strategy of the MNC, and the international pressures from the MNC's home government.

INTRODUCTION

In their economic relationships with multinational corporations, Third World countries would seem to have the critical advantage, inasmuch as they control access to their own territory. That access includes internal markets, the local labour supplies, investment opportunities, sources of raw materials, and other resources that multinational firms need or desire. In practical terms, however, this apparent bargaining advantage on the part of the host nation, in most instances, is greatly surpassed by the superior advantages of the multinationals. Multinational corporations possess the required capital, technology, managerial skills, access to world markets, and other resources that governments in the Third World need or wish to obtain for purposes of economic development.

In addition to firm-specific assets — technology, managerial skills, capital and access to markets — the economic power of the multinationals grows out of a combination of additional factors. First, foreign investment accounts for large percentages of the total stock of local investment, local production and sales. Secondly, multinationals tend to dominate key sectors of the economy that are critical to the host states' economic development. Thirdly, multinationals usually prevail in the highly concentrated industries in the Third World — petroleum, aluminum, chemicals, transportation, food products and machinery. This economic concentration in single industries gives the multinational firms oligopoly power, allowing them to monopolize and control supply and price in a way that does not occur in more competitive industries.

In the first decade and a half after World War II, the multinational corporations were so powerful that they could essentially prevent any challenges to their dominance from host governments. The unique position they held as the sole source of capital, technology and managerial expertise for the Third World states gave them special negotiating advantages. Third World governments in their developing state could not easily duplicate the skills of the corporations, and when they did attempt to bypass the assistance of the multinationals, the cost to them in reduced efficiency was extremely high. Furthermore, the exposure of individual corporations was low, except for corporations in natural resources, plantations and utilities. In Latin America and the Middle East, where most of direct foreign investment in raw materials was concentrated, long-term concession contracts protected companies from immediate risk exposure. Host countries could neither remove nor replace them without sustaining enormous costs to their economies. Thus, the multinationals were usually able to exercise de facto sovereign power over the pricing and marketing of output.

Nevertheless, despite the colossal power of the multinational corporations, the historic trend has been one of increasing ascendance of Third World host states. By the 1960s the multinationals were facing pressure from the host states to make substantial contributions to the long-term goals of economic development. Regarding foreign investment in natural resources, for example, ownership and control over raw material production was transferred to OPEC members. In the process, the Seven Sisters (the major oil companies) were relegated from their positions of independence and dominance to the role of junior partners of host governments in the Middle East. Similarly, in manufacturing there is a visible trend toward a sharing of ownership and control in foreign manufacturing ventures.

Several factors help to explain the relative ascendancy or improved position of some Third World host states with respect to their relationships with multinationals. A number of changes have increased the bargaining power of the Third World countries. And in addition to favourable changes in their bargaining power, other constraining factors in both domestic and international environments of the host countries have been eased, improving the ability of the hosts to exact better terms from the multinational corporations.

THIRD WORLD GOVERNMENTS:
DYNAMICS OF POTENTIAL BARGAINING POWER

In order to examine the extent to which host states in the Third World can in-fluence the behaviour of multinational corporations, we call attention to the dis-tinction between potential power and actual power (the power to exercise or implement).

Potential power connotes the relative bargaining power of the host state which is dependent upon: (1) the level of the host government's expertise, (2) the degree of competition among multinationals, (3) the type of direct foreign investment, and (4) the degree or extent of prevailing economic uncertainty.

Actual power, on the other hand, may be defined as the ability and willingness of host governments to exercise their bargaining power in order to extract more favourable terms from foreign firms. Domestic factors, including host country politics, along with international factors, such as foreign political and economic coercion, constrain Third World host states in their efforts to translate potential bargaining power into power that engenders favourable outcomes with foreign investors. These domestic and international factors act as a wedge between poten-tial and actual power. The dynamics of potential bargaining power for the Third World governments is examined below.

Level of Host's Expertise

Most host states have antiquated government structures and inadequate laws for collecting taxes and controlling foreign business. These institutional weaknesses impair the ability of host states in their negotiations with multinational corpora-tions. Shortages of competent, trained, and independent administrators exacerbate these institutional problems and make it difficult for host states to manage multi-nationals and monitor their behaviour. . . .

The trend, however, has been toward tougher laws in the host countries. Frequently, the host countries become dependent upon the revenue generated by foreign investors in order to finance government services and meet domestic requirements for employment. In turn, the desire for economic growth produces certain incentives within host states to strengthen their administrative expertise in international tax law, corporate accounting and industrial analysis. Thus, the development of economic and financial skills in host states is facilitated by the need to monitor multinational corporations and negotiate with them more effec-tively. Over time, therefore, host countries have developed or acquired many of the managerial skills which had long been employed by the multinationals as bar-gaining tools. By improving their expertise and capacity to monitor the corpora-tions more closely, some host states were able to renegotiate terms when conditions permitted. The development of producer cartels also created a strong impetus for improving expertise within host countries to manage multinationals better. . . . Multinational corporations can be expected to regain their bargaining advantage vis-à-vis a Third World government, however, when certain conditions arise: (1) the rate of change in technological complexity of the foreign investment regime grows faster relative to the host country's capabilities and rate of innovations; and/or (2) if the optimum scale of the investment regime expands so as to make it extremely difficult for the host government to manage it, in spite of initial strides in managerial expertise.

Both technological and managerial complexity for developing products or extracting resources correlate positively with bargaining power for the multinational corporations. Nevertheless, during the last two decades, the cumulative effect of improvement in the host countries' expertise has resulted in a relative tightening of terms with respect to direct foreign investment. This phenomenon has resulted in a relative improvement in Third World governments' bargaining positions.

Level of Competition for Investment Opportunities

Competition among multinational corporations for investment opportunities in a Third World country also affects the bargaining power of host countries. Essentially, a lack of competition among multinationals predicts a weak bargaining position for the host country. Conversely, increased competition is likely to improve the bargaining power of the host government. Competition among multinationals is likely to be greater where a host country provides a cheap source of needed labour and also functions as an "export platform" when the purpose of the investment project is to serve external markets. Competition for investment projects is likely to be limited, however, when projects are both capital intensive and designed to serve only local markets.

During the 1950s and 1960s, the absence of competition for investment opportunities served to diminish the bargaining power of host states in the Third World. The availability of alternative sources of raw materials and the existence of cheap labour elsewhere also work together to weaken the bargaining power of any individual country. In the last two decades, the spread of multinational corporations of diverse national origins (American, Japanese, European) has provided host countries with alternatives. In the international oil industry, for example, host countries have successfully used competition among multinationals to increase revenues from oil production. As a case in point, J. Paul Getty's Pacific Western Oil Company upset the stability of other corporations' agreements when it acquired an oil concession in Saudi Arabia by offering larger tax payments than the established oil companies were then willing to pay.

The option of choice from several willing foreign investors is extremely important to a host country. The ability to choose allows a host state to avoid the concentration of investment from one traditionally dominant Western country. Thus, for instance, Japanese multinationals have emerged as an alternative to U.S. firms in Latin America, and American firms have, in turn, emerged as an alternative to French firms in Africa.

If competition were to intensify among the multinational corporations for the resources of Third World countries and host governments' ability to manage and monitor multinationals were to improve, it is likely that host nations would pay less than before for services provided by the corporations.

Economic Uncertainty and the Obsolescing Bargain

Uncertainty about the success of a particular foreign investment project, its final cost, and the desire of a host country to attract investment create a marked asymmetry of power favouring the multinational corporations. During this initial phase, the host country must pursue permissive investment policies with the corporations. But as uncertainty decreases and the investment projects become successful, the multinational's initial bargaining advantage begins to erode. Invested fixed capital becomes "sunk," a hostage to and a source of the host country's bargaining strength as it acquires jurisdiction over valuable foreign assets. The foreign firm's financial commitment to assets located in host nations weakens the bargaining advantage it enjoyed at the beginning of the investment cycle. Consequently, when the bargaining advantage begins to shift to the host state, the initial agreements that favoured the multinationals are renegotiated.

In manufacturing, high technology, and services ventures, the probability of obsolescence is extremely low. Multinational corporations in natural resources, on the other hand, are most vulnerable. . . .

This paradigm interprets the interaction between multinational corporations and host countries as a dynamic process. Furthermore, given the level of economic uncertainty for both parties, the interests of host countries and foreign investors are likely to diverge. The two parties then become antagonists. Gradually, a change in the bargaining advantages on the side of the multinational shift to that of the host country. The developments that follow may result in the renegotiation by the government of the initial concession agreement.

Characteristics of the Foreign Investment Project

As noted earlier, the probability of obsolescence is, to a large extent, a function of the foreign investment assets. Thus, the bargaining power or negotiating ability of a host country substantially depends on the type of direct foreign investment that is involved. Characteristics of the foreign investment project affecting the outcome of the bargaining process are: (1) absolute size of fixed investment; (2) ratio of fixed to variable costs; (3) the level of technological complexity of the foreign investment regime; and (4) the degree of marketing complexity.

Those foreign investment projects which do not require high fixed investments have a low fixed-to-relative cost ratio. Based on changeable technology and marketing complexity, they are less vulnerable to the dynamics of obsolescing bargaining than are foreign investment projects having high fixed costs, slowly changing technology and undifferentiated project lines. Investment projects in natural resources, plantation agriculture and utilities fall into this group. Once the investment is sunk and the project becomes profitable, foreign firms may be exposed to the threat of nationalization or, more likely, the renegotiation of the original terms of investment.

Knowing these economic and political risks, multinational corporations would not commit large sums of money unless they were likely to get extremely generous terms. These "over-generous" terms to which the host country initially agrees often become a major source of national discontent and resentment against the foreign firm.

In manufacturing, where marketing skills are complex and products differentiated, foreign corporations have considerable flexibility in their response to the host country's demands. In order to counter the demands of the host government, these firms can diversify product lines, move to a new activity such as export, incorporate additional technology, or threaten to withdraw their operation altogether.

Corporations in the vanguard of scientific and technological development such as computers or electronics have only recently begun to penetrate Third World economies. This group is especially immune to the obsolescing bargain. The pace and complexity of research and development (R&D) in computers and electronics is, for the most part, beyond the capability and geographic reach of any of the host governments in the Third World.

Constraints on the Exercise of Power: Implementation

The literature on bargaining provides a prevailing conceptual framework of bilateral monopoly to describe Third World–multinational corporation interaction. According to this model, the distribution of benefits between multinationals and Third World countries is a function of relative power. It is assumed that power is a function of the demand of each party for resources that the other possesses. This model is essentially static, however, because it does not deal with political and economic constraints on the exercise of power arising from the international environment. Similarly, it fails to account for constraints that are posed by the multinational's economic power. More importantly, it ignores the constraints posed by the host country's domestic politics. Specifically, the bilateral monopoly model does not distinguish between potential bargaining power and its implementation. Domestic politics within a host country, as well as international political and economic pressures from multinationals (or their home governments), may hinder host countries in their efforts to exploit the bargaining advantage once gained from the relative demand for its resources.

In order to fill this theoretical gap in the literature, we identify and analyse various constraining factors in both the domestic and international environments. The objective is to illuminate the extent to which a host government is able or willing to translate its bargaining advantage into actual power, to exercise this power in order to extract favourable terms from foreign investors. These relationships are presented below.

Domestic Constraints on the Exercise of Power

Key determinants in translating potential power into actual power are the attitudes and beliefs of the ruling elite regarding foreign investment, and their willingness and ability to discount international economic and political pressure in their confrontation with multinational corporations. During the 1950s and 1960s, Third World governments provided stability to foreign investments by working to preserve the status quo, despite changes that improved their bargaining power. At least two reasons can be given for the leadership of these countries to favour the status quo. One possibility is that their ideological predisposition was such that they saw multinationals as a benevolent force for economic development. Another possibility is that they may have feared that the international political and economic costs of seeking change would outweigh the benefits. There were also, of course, those instances where individual leaders in host countries were known to accept private payments in exchange for their efforts to preserve the status quo. In other instances, changes in the host country's leadership led to classic confrontations. The new elite, having divergent ideological and policy priorities, attempted to persuade the foreign investment regimes to become more responsive to domestic economic priorities. When Mossadeq became the prime minister of Iran in the early 1950s, for example, in efforts to finance Iran's First Development Plan he attempted to nationalize the British-owned Anglo-Iranian Oil company. Similarly, the Kinshasa government's struggle to use earnings from the copper mines of Katanga to pay for post-independence development of the Congo led to a major confrontation. The ultimate result was the nationalization of foreign assets.

Since the mid-1960s there has been a change in attitude among most Third World leaders with respect to foreign investment. Exposés of political intervention by multinational corporations in the domestic politics of host states, the IT&T scandal in Chile in particular, contributed to this change. Unlike IT&T's interference in Chilean politics, most multinationals do not pursue such ruthless politics of intervention. Nevertheless, the degree to which multinationals can influence, by legal or illegal means, the domestic political process can reduce the host country's ability to change corporate behaviour and to make it cater to domestic needs.

A major force for change has been the emergence of new diverse groups which have become involved in the host country's political processes. Students, labour, business, intelligentsia, middle echelon government technocrats and even farmers' associations have greater political clout than ever before. Mobilized by the processes of industrialization and urbanization, and facilitated by global technology, these groups came to place intense pressure on their governments for improving the domestic economy; providing welfare, housing, transportation; and creating jobs. The extractive sector in particular, dominated by foreign firms, became a focus for nationalistic demands of an intensity that could not be ignored by the leadership of Third World states. Among the above groups, business and labour are especially noteworthy. The lack of a strong labour movement, however, remains a major source of institutional weakness in underdeveloped countries. . . .

In a similar vein, the lack of competition from local businesses creates another source of institutional weakness. Too often local businesses, for whom multinational corporations might mean intense competition, are unable to compete with the giant corporations because the latter have access to cheaper sources of capital, better terms from suppliers, and marketing and distribution advantages. The absence of countervailing power via a competitive indigenous business sector helps to explain why the global corporations are able to continue to exert dominant power in underdeveloped countries. A similar and more prevalent situation is one wherein local business owners find that by cooperating with global firms, they too can benefit.

There often exists a strong alliance between the foreign corporation and various powerful home state groups such as landowners, or other pro-business conservative groups. All these groups tend to share the multinationals' distaste for radical social change. This alliance serves as a major constraint on the ability of host countries to translate their bargaining power into favourable outcomes. The effect is the perpetuation of the status quo.

International Constraints: Non-State Actors

We can distinguish between two types of constraints in the international environment. First, there are constraints posed by non-state actors. Second, constraints often emerge as a result of home governmental actions on behalf of the multinational corporations. Constraints posed by non-state actors include the level of global integration of multinationals, local political risk and transnational risk management strategies.

Global integration includes the flow of raw materials, components and final products as well as flows of technology, capital and managerial expertise between the units and subsidiaries of a global corporation. In essence, it is a complex system of a globally integrated production network, at the disposal of the corporation. This complex transnational system is augmented by global logistical and information networks, global advertising and sometimes global product differentiation. The host government's desire to acquire access to this global network and the dependence of host states on the foreign firms who created it produce a constraint on the former's bargaining power.

Global integration, therefore, is an important determinant of multinational strategy. Increasingly, multinational corporations have developed globally based systems of integrated production, marketing and distribution networks in order to reduce costs and enhance their global outreach. A host country that engages in joint ventures with highly integrated and sophisticated foreign firms invariably becomes dependent on the multinationals' controlled globally integrated networks.

Global integration is usually found in companies having very complex technology. There is little that the host country can do to influence integration, and consequently the host country may be severely constrained in its bargaining position. The majority of research and development is undertaken by highly integrated firms and is located in the industrialized home countries. As a result technological developments are beyond the reach or control of developing host countries. Royalties charged by highly integrated firms on the use of their technologies further increase the relative vulnerability of host states. International Business Machines, for instance, continues to maintain an unconditional 10 per cent royalty for the use of its technology despite the efforts of host countries to reduce it.

Another constraint on a host government's ability to exercise power arises from the use of political risk management strategies by multinational corporations. In order to diminish or control better their political risks, multinationals often establish transnational alliances that dramatically increase the cost to the host state of changing the foreign investment regime in their favour. The experience of Third World governments with the pharmaceutical and automobile industries demonstrates how a web of alliances built by the global corporations can seriously impair their exercise of governmental power.

One tactic used by the multinationals is to spread the equity in the foreign investment project over a number of companies from other developed countries. This strategy increases the legal, political and economic obstacles to unilateral alterations in contracts with host states. Another tactic is to raise debt capital for the foreign investment project from banks of different countries (United States, Japan, Germany). Multinationals structure the financing in such a way that banks are paid only if the project is profitable. Host governments' retaliatory actions against the corporations could, therefore, alienate these powerful global banks which have bankrolled the investment project. In view of the significant role of some of the largest global banks involved in the Third World debt problem, this particular risk management strategy may act as a powerful constraint on the host state's ability to turn its potential bargaining power into actual power. Another tactic that multinationals use for protection is to involve the World Bank, IMF and Inter-American Development Banks. The formidable power and prestige of these institutions and their ability to deny financing to host governments' development projects can also deter the host governments from taking actions against multinational corporations.

These and other transnational risk management strategies tend to support the general proposition that multinationals can structure the international economic system and respond to their own financial needs to the detriment of host states in the Third World.

International Constraint: Home Government of Multinational Corporations

The extent to which multinational corporations can mobilize the support of their home government, and the ability (or inability) of the Third World government to withstand retaliation from the powerful governments of the United States and Western Europe on behalf of multinationals can also affect the bargaining equation. For example, between 1945 and 1960 the bargaining power of the multinationals was strengthened by the actions of the United States, which was home to most of the corporations. The American government prevented the emergence of multilateral lending institutions that might have provided alternative capital sources to multinationals. It promoted instead direct foreign investment in the Third World as a major aspect of its foreign assistance program. It also provided diplomatic support to protect the assets of American multinationals. In a few instances, the American government used covert operations and force to protect economic and strategic interests and, in the process, promoted corporate interests.

The home government may support multinational corporations for a variety of national security reasons, to maintain access to cheap sources of foreign raw materials, to improve its balance of payments position or to use the corporations to transfer aid to pro-Western governments in the Third World. In addition, global corporations are powerful domestic political actors in their own right. They can (and do) take advantage of the fragmentation and decentralization of the democratic political process in Western countries in order to influence government policy. Since business groups are likely to be the best organized and best financed groups, with a persistent interest in the outcome of U.S. policy, they could bias the "pluralism" of the political process in the Western countries. For example, in the United States, the Hickenlooper Amendment and the Gonzalez Amendment were the result of corporate lobbying, and both tied American foreign economic interests to the preservation of corporate interests in the Third World.

To be sure, there is no systematic relationship between the home government's interests and corporate interests that might automatically trigger home government support for multinational corporations vis-à-vis Third World governments. In the first place, if there is a conflict between the strategic interests of the nation and narrow corporate interests, the former is likely to prevail. An example of this is American support for Israel in the Arab-Israeli conflict. Secondly, there often exist sharp divisions among multinationals so that they cannot articulate a unified view of their interests. Finally, the result of American extraterritorial diplomatic support on behalf of established corporations — Alcoa, Reynolds, Anaconda, Exxon — in Latin America did not result in favourable outcomes for the corporations. As a result, corporations are becoming more reluctant to seek the support of their home government.

In spite of the above reasons, the potential for conflict with the U.S. government weighs heavily in Third World governments' decisions to confront foreign firms. Since investment in the Third World tends to be highly concentrated according to the interests of the multinationals' home country (often raw materials are key to national security), and because multinationals are highly influential political actors in the politics of their home country, Third World governments' fears of the U.S. superpower are well-founded. Thus, the host government's willingness (or lack of it) to discount the corporation's home government's potential retaliation (in the form of economic, political or military pressure) may crucially alter both decision-making processes and potential bargaining advantages.

SUMMARY AND CONCLUSION

... [T]he model presented in this paper predicts that multinational corporation/ Third World country interaction will tend to be unstable over time and that the interests of the two actors are likely to diverge increasingly as the relative bargaining position of the host country improves.

In order to model the bargaining power of Third World countries with respect to multinational corporations, we have made a distinction between potential and actual power. The former is the capability, as yet unrealized, of a host Third World country to alter or influence the behaviour of multinationals. The latter connotes the ability or willingness of the host government to exercise this power in order to extract favourable terms from foreign firms. Potential power is a function of four variables: (1) the level of the host country's expertise, (2) the degree of competition among multinationals, (3) economic uncertainty, and (4) the type of direct foreign investment.

This discussion leads to policy implications for host governments. Obviously, they need to build national capabilities that would help them to regulate better the multinationals. More importantly, in order for them to be effective, national policies need to be revised to conform more closely to the stage of foreign investment cycle. This article's principal thesis is that, despite their apparent bargaining advantage, the dependence of Third World countries which are host to multinational corporations on the international economic system severely limits the ability of host countries to exercise their potential power.

11

"A New Imperial System"? The Role of the Multinational Corporations Reconsidered

DAVID FIELDHOUSE

David Fieldhouse discusses the impact of multinational corporations (MNCs) on the development experiences of Third World
states. He starts with the "dependency" school's view that MNCs
reinforce the underdevelopment of the Third World, and then
reviews the potential costs and benefits to developing countries
of multinational production. He concludes that the impact of the
MNC depends on the host government's ability to manage its
relations with the firm. Many factors might affect the state's position in regard to foreign firms, especially the advantages of a host
state in the bargaining relationship. Fieldhouse concludes that
without looking at specific cases it is generally impossible to
know whether an MNC will benefit or harm a host country.

A multinational company (alias multinational corporation, transnational enterprise and many other synonyms, but hereafter referred to as MNC) can be defined
as a firm which owns or controls income-generating assets in more than one country. The substance has existed for more than a century, but it was only twenty-five
years ago that it was given a special name within the framework of foreign direct
investment (FDI) and so became a defined concept. . . .

. . . [O]nce it was christened, the MNC assumed an autonomous existence as a
special category of capitalist organization and was seized on by intellectuals and
publicists of many types as a convenient pole on which to raise their particular
flags. In this, of course, the MNC resembled "imperialism," once the word came
into vogue in the later nineteenth century, though with this difference. It might be
possible to house all books of any significance written on the theory of imperialism since, say, 1900 on one short shelf. The literature on MNCs is now so large
that books are published as guides to the bibliography. An historian of European
overseas expansion can hope only to know a selection of those works that he can
understand (that is, not in the shorthand of the mathematical economists) and
which bear on the questions the historian thinks important.

There are many such questions, but this chapter concentrates on one only: is
the MNC an affront to the sovereignty of the Third World, a form of imperialism

after empire and a cause of "underdevelopment"? I do not claim to answer it, merely to summarize the issues and to suggest a broad line of approach.

THE MULTINATIONAL AS "A NEW IMPERIAL SYSTEM" IN THE THIRD WORLD

The most important question concerning the modern MNC is why its character and activities should be regarded as a special problem. At one level, of course, the MNC is liable to the same criticism as any capitalist enterprise: that it exists to extract surplus value and thus exploit the proletariat. Its two special features are that, in common with all forms of FDI, it operates across national frontiers and that control is retained by one global centre. It might, therefore, have been expected that the first and main attack on MNCs would have come from Marxists; yet this was one dog that did not bark until there was a chorus into which it could join. It is always difficult to explain why something did not happen. The probable explanation is that . . . Lenin and later Marxist-Leninists chose not to distinguish between different forms of capitalist enterprise that collectively constituted what they called "imperialism." Thus it was not until 1968 that those two stalwart New England Marxists, Baran and Sweezy, included in their book *Monopoly Capital,* a direct Marxist appreciation of MNCs. Ironically, this stemmed from their reading an article in the Wall Street journal, *Business Week,* for 20 April 1963. Following *Business Week* . . . they took Standard Oil (NJ) as their model of an MNC, noting with surprise that it really was a world-wide enterprise and that, far from exporting capital in the way finance capital was supposed to do, its post-1945 expansion had been financed almost entirely by its overseas earnings. Moreover, they realized that since 1945 sales and profits of American overseas subsidiaries had been rising faster than those in the United States. Clearly, the MNC needed special analysis; but this led Baran and Sweezy only to the somewhat naïve conclusion that the main reason why the United States opposed the growth of socialism in the Third World was that this would restrict further opportunities for expanding FDI, despite the fact that socialist states, being industrialized, were the best trading partners.

Baran and Sweezy did not, then, pursue the matter further. They were, in fact, merely getting on to a bandwagon that had been set in motion the previous year by J.-J. Servan-Schreiber, a Frenchman whose *American Challenge* is conventionally taken to have been the first widely noticed rationalization of the impact of American industrial investment on post-1945 Europe. His central argument was that American corporations had seen the opportunity presented first by postwar reconstruction and the shortage of dollars which inhibited normal imports, then by the integration of the market following the Treaty of Rome in 1958. They had moved into Europe on a very large scale, concentrating mainly in the more technologically advanced industries, in which they now had a commanding lead, using the products of their research and development facilities (R&D) at home to make money abroad. Paradoxically, 90 per cent of this "investment" had been raised by loans and government grants within Europe. But the most important fact was that Europe stood in danger of becoming dependent on the United States not only for its most sophisticated industries but, more serious, for the technology that made them possible. Europe would thus be condemned to remain in perpetuity on the second rung of a five-rung ladder, as an "advanced industrial" economy below the . . . "post-industrial" states — the United States, Canada, Japan and Sweden. The solution was not to exclude American investment but for Europe to compete more effectively through a genuine federation, including Britain, state support for R&D, specialization by major European corporations in advanced products and improved technical education.

Servan-Schreiber's book aroused much interest and may have helped to trigger off widespread investigation into the character of MNCs (a term, incidentally, which he did not use). Probably his most influential concept was that of an emerging "hierarchy" of countries in different stages of technological development which might, because of the unprecedented advantage then possessed by American companies, become ossified. This challenged the then conventional assumption that all economies were on the same escalator which would bear them from poverty to affluence. It is uncertain whether this idea was his own creation; but there is no doubt that within a year or two this became the key element in two quite different strands of radical thinking on MNCs and Third World development. On the one hand, some of the Latin American dependency theorists who, as a group, had hitherto shown no great interest in MNCs, now quickly built them into their existing concept of "underdevelopment." This was frankly derivative and is not worth discussing here. Much more important and influential was the work of S.H. Hymer whose seminal ideas, published between 1970 and 1972, are central to the modern debate over the role of the MNC in less developed countries.

Hymer accurately reflects the way in which assessments of the MNC became increasingly hostile after about 1960. His PhD dissertation, completed at MIT in 1960 but not published until 1976, was widely read in typescript and seems to have been the origin of the argument that the primary function of FDI was to exploit control of overseas investment to obtain a monopoly rent. Yet in 1960 Hymer was not an unqualified critic of MNCs; his position was that of a conventional North American liberal (he was a Canadian) who believed in an anti-trust approach to large enterprises of all types in order to counter monopoly and promote competition within a competitive economy. By the later 1960s, however, he had become a Marxist; and it was from this standpoint that he developed a more radical critique of the MNC in a series of articles which were subsequently collected and published after his accidental death (1974) in 1979.

Hymer's central message was that, although MNCs might increase the world's wealth through their efficient use of resources, the benefits would go mainly to the countries in which the MNCs were based, while the rest of the world paid the price of their monopoly profits. The result would be an hierarchical world order as corporations developed a complex division of labour within individual firms and throughout the international economy. . . .

These ideas form the starting point of most recent assessments of the impact of the MNC on host countries in which it has subsidiaries under its effective control. The essence of Hymer's concept of an international hierarchy was that the interests of its lower echelons must be subordinated to those of the highest level: that is, subsidiaries exist only to serve the shareholders in the parent company at the top of the pyramid; so that, when a conflict of interest arises, the interests of the base will necessarily be sacrificed to those of the apex. Without this assumption the debate over the role of the MNC would be merely technical, concerned with its motivation, organization and profitability. By contrast, most of the literature since about 1970 has turned on two different issues. First, whether there is a necessary conflict of interest between MNCs and host countries. Secondly, whether the specific methods adopted by MNCs in particular countries are to the disadvantage of their hosts, even if the MNC performed a generally useful role; and if so, what measures the host should adopt to minimize or reduce these disadvantages.

It is important to recognize that these issues are not necessarily related. That is, we could take the view that FDI may, in principle, be in the best interests of host countries, while accepting that particular corporations, types of enterprise, or the way in which they operate may be disadvantageous to the host. I propose very briefly to outline the standard arguments on both these issues. To simplify, I shall concentrate on two of the four generally accepted types of MNC: those that manufacture in host countries for international markets ("off-shore" enterprises) and those that manufacture for the host market. That is not to ignore the importance of enterprises which specialize in the extraction of minerals and petroleum or in production of agricultural commodities. These are central to the debate over the MNC and will be considered in the conclusion. But most of the modern literature tends to assume, rightly, that these are now historic phenomena, rapidly losing their importance as host countries nationalize oil supplies, mines and plantations. The central issue in the debate over the MNC turns on its industrial investments, now the largest single element in FDI and its dynamic sector. Let us consider first the general theoretical arguments for and against direct investment in manufacturing from the standpoint of host countries, then some evidence of their actual effects.

It is conventional to discuss the effects of MNCs under two heads: the "direct" economic effect on the host country and "externalities" or side effects. The direct economic effect of establishing a manufacturing subsidiary of an MNC should consist of an increase in the real income of the host country resulting from the import of capital, skills and technology which would otherwise not be available. Provided the total increase of the income of the host government (through taxes) and of the society (through higher incomes or cheaper goods) exceeds the amount accruing to the owners of the MNC as profits, we would expect the direct economic effect to be favourable. Only if the profits made by the MNC are, in effect, provided by the host government in the form of subsidies (direct, by remission of taxes or through public investment in the infrastructure made solely to attract or facilitate the MNC's operations); or, alternatively, if the level of effective protection is so high that the subsidiary adds no value (because the goods it makes could be bought more cheaply on world markets) should there fail to be a net direct benefit to the host economy.

The list of actual or potential indirect benefits is much longer and can, in fact, be cut to taste. Let us take the relatively simple example of FDI in a developed economy. In his pioneering survey of American direct investment in Britain, published in 1958, J.H. Dunning singled out the following indirect benefits. The general effect on British industrial development was good because of the diffusion of imported skills and the creation of close links with the more dynamic American economy. The impact of this imported efficiency was both vertical (affecting British suppliers of American firms "upstream" and consumers of American products "downstream" of the subsidiary), and horizontal, affecting many other parts of the British economy. American firms set higher standards of pay and conditions, which had a valuable demonstration effect on British labour and employers. Some American factories were set up in development areas. Although these caused some strain on the supply of skilled labour, this was not a general or serious problem. Finally, American firms had a directly measurable effect on the British balance of payments. Partly because they were geared to exporting to established markets for their products, American firms had an excellent export record and, in 1954, accounted for 12 per cent of total British manufacturing exports. In that year the net balance of payments effect was plus £231 million. In addition, Britain was saved an unmeasurable quantity of dollars through the import-substituting effect of American industries in Britain.

Dunning therefore sums up the direct and indirect benefits of American FDI to Britain before 1958 in terms of the law of comparative costs. Just as, under Ricardo's law of comparative advantage, and in a free trade world, any two countries could trade to their mutual advantage provided each concentrated on those products in which it had a relative (though not necessarily absolute) advantage, so in the modern age of protection and economic management, American FDI in Britain enabled each country to use its respective assets more effectively than either could have done in isolation. . . .

There could be no clearer statement of both the theoretical and actual benefits of FDI in a developed country: Servan-Schreiber's clarion call nine years later was a false alarm, since the Continent had benefited as much as Britain, and in much the same ways, from the activities of American MNCs. Moreover, the United States had long since lost the monopoly of advanced technology it had briefly held in the 1940s and was no longer the only large-scale foreign investor: by 1978 Western Europe's accumulated stock of FDI had almost caught up with that of the United States. Clearly, what had been sauce for the goose was now sauce for the gander. Europe had nothing to fear from the United States because it could play the same game.

The question that is central to the study of the multinational in the Third World is whether the same holds true there as in developed countries. On any principle of comparative costs or comparative advantage it ought, of course, to do so. The main reason for wondering whether it does is that for less developed countries (LDCs) FDI is a one-way, not a two-way process: they are almost entirely recipients of foreign investment, not investors. Defined as "underdeveloped" countries, they do not, for the most part, possess the technology, capital, or know-how which might enable them to reverse roles. Their governments may not have the sophistication (or, perhaps, as dependency theorists commonly argue, the patriotism and concern for public welfare) which is expected of Western governments and which might enable them to judge whether the cost of providing conditions attractive to

MNCs will outweigh the "direct" economic benefits their countries might obtain. Above all, the indirect effects may be very different because the host country may not be able to respond to the stimulus of foreign enterprise in the way expected in developed countries. Thus, even if Dunning's law of comparative costs holds good at a purely economic level, there may be other non-economic considerations specific to LDCs which outweigh the direct benefits provided by MNCs.

This, indeed, is the basic assertion made by a large number of critics of MNCs who do not seriously question their utility in the developed world but argue, from very diverse standpoints, that they are of dubious benefit to LDCs. To adopt Sanjay Lall's typology, there are three common ways of looking at the deficiencies of the MNC in poor countries: that of the "nationalists," who accept the potential benefits of FDI but have reservations about certain aspects of it; the *dependencia* approach, which (according to Lall) cannot be incorporated into any formal economic analysis; and that of some Marxists, who deny all possibility that an MNC can convey any benefits on host countries. All three are interesting; but, since most criticism of MNCs falls under the first head, let us consider the reservations made by Lall himself and Paul Streeten from a "nationalist" standpoint.

Their starting-point is the dual proposition that the proper criterion for assessing the role of MNCs in LDCs must be social welfare in the broadest sense; but also that there is no possibility of making a final objective judgement on their welfare implications. The reasons are limited information on many aspects of MNC activities, unmeasurable "externalities," different economic theories of development, differing value judgements on "welfare" and wide contrasts in defining "alternative situations." Nevertheless, conventional assessments of the costs and benefits of MNCs which use these difficulties as a ground for mere agnosticism are vulnerable to the accusation of circularity. Thus, if we accept the neo-classical Paretian welfare paradigm, which assumes a basic harmony of interests in society, the ability of individuals to know and pursue their own interests and the neutrality of the state, which pursues a "national" interest, then MNCs are bound to be in the best interests of a host country because they satisfy individual preferences in the market and provide technology, marketing, management skills and other externalities. Adverse effects can simply be blamed on the policies of the host government: transfer prices within MNCs alone lie to some extent beyond state control. Thus, to obtain any grip on the subject, we must look for limitations in this basic welfare critique.

Lall and Streeten point to four possible defects in welfare theory as it relates to MNCs. It makes no distinction between "wants" on ethical or social grounds: that is, consumer preference may not be the ultimate criterion of welfare. Wants may not be genuine but learnt. Income distribution is excluded. The state may not be neutral, rather reflecting class or group control of state power in its own interests. . . .

This means that we have to go beyond the actual activities of MNCs into a normative assessment of "desirable" forms of social and economic development in LDCs. Or, to put it bluntly, the standard of assessment must be what conduces most to the sort of society the critic would like to see. For Lall and Streeten, as for most "nationalist" critics of MNCs, this would seem to be one in which the needs of the poor majority take precedence over the wants of the relatively affluent minority, so that the character and distribution of the benefits provided by MNCs are more important as a measure of their contribution to "growth" than undifferentiated figures of per capita or national income, which conceal the distribution of advantages.

Once this is conceded, it is possible to construct a quite different critique of the desirability of MNCs, in which the test is whether some alternative source of a desired good would make a greater contribution to social welfare, as defined above. Lall and Streeten therefore survey the various benefits conventionally ascribed to MNCs under three main heads, in each case emphasizing concomitant costs and alternative policies.

(1) Capital

MNCs have preferential access to the capital market and their investment may stimulate further aid from foreign governments. But, in fact, MNCs bring in very little capital, which might benefit the host's foreign-exchange position, instead reinvesting local profits and raising funds in the host country. This is desirable in so far as the MNC raises equity capital, since it reduces the "rent" and the foreign-exchange costs of servicing the investment; but less good if it uses local loan capital, since this diverts local savings from other activities. Thus the main capital import consists of machinery, know-how, patents, and so on; and here the danger is that these things, coming as part of a "package," may be overpriced. Thus the role of MNCs as a source of capital is far from simple. Each case must stand alone and there may be better ways for an LDC to acquire these capital assets than through an MNC.

(2) Organization and Management

In this field the superiority of an MNC is undoubted, both as an efficient user of resources and as a demonstrator of sound business methods in countries where corporate "management" is a novelty. Yet, once again, there may be hidden costs, seen from a "nationalist" or "welfare" position.

First, as Hymer argued, the price of accepting an MNC may be subordination as a "branch-plant" in an hierarchical world system, which means dependence.

Secondly, there is transfer-pricing within MNCs, which Lall and Streeten define as follows.

The problem arises from the fact that transfer prices, being under the control of the firm concerned, can be put at levels which differ from prices which would obtain in "arms-length" transactions, and so can be manipulated to shift profits clandestinely from one area of operations to another. If the different units of an MNC behaved like independent firms, clearly the problem would not arise. However, given the growing extent of intra-firm trade, it is the *centralization of authority* and the growth of a *global business strategy* that creates fears on the part of governments (both host and home) that they are losing legitimate tax revenue.[1]

Obviously the host government can and should attempt to monitor such trans-actions so as to ensure that profits declared reflect actual profits made. But there are technical difficulties in doing so, particularly for LDCs with comparatively weak bureaucracies; and transfer-pricing remains one of the most suspect aspects of MNCs.

Thirdly, the very efficiency of an MNC may have an adverse effect on domestic entrepreneurship in the host country. If all the dynamic and technically advanced sectors of the LDC's economy pass into the hands of foreign firms, this may check economic development by reducing the rate of capital accumulation. But this, in fact, is very unlikely. It would happen only in any of three hypothetical cases: first, if the MNC made no higher profits than local men and repatriated a proportion of these profits, by contrast with local capitalists, if these are assumed to reinvest all their retained profits at home; secondly, if subsidiaries were made to pay more for technology than local entrepreneurs could have paid for the same thing on an open market; and, thirdly, if the MNCs created an oligopolistic market structure, as contrasted with an assumed competitive market if local capitalists had it entirely to themselves.

These are potentially disadvantageous economic consequences of the organi-zational superiority of the MNC. But other, non-economic, costs may also have weight in a nationalistic welfare balance sheet. National ownership of the means of production may be intrinsically desirable. MNCs may adversely affect social, cultural and political values. Patterns of development may be distorted, local élites reinforced and the road to "socialist" change blocked. The inclusion of such crite-ria in almost any "nationalist" or "radical" critique of the MNC is significant. However valid, they are necessarily subjective and incompatible with economic assessment of the value of MNCs to developing countries.

(3) Technology

. . . Technology, rather than capital, is now usually taken to be the main contribu-tion made by MNCs to LDCs and . . . two questions have to be asked in each case. First, could the same benefits have been obtained by the LDC except through the medium of a multinational so that some of the associated costs could have been avoided: for example, by licensing indigenous producers? Secondly, and charac-teristic of the "radical" critique, are the technologies imported by MNCs "appro-priate" to the circumstances of LDCs? For example, are they excessively capital-intensive and do they serve the desires of an élite rather than the "basic needs" of the masses? Such questions, of course, reflect normative assumptions: there are "optimal" patterns of production which are "appropriate" to the special circumstances of LDCs and should therefore be preferred on welfare criteria. The same applies to another MNC specialty, marketing skills. However valuable these may be in stimulating an internal market and domestic production, MNC advertising may create "unsuitable" tastes, inducing the starving to spend their money on Coca Cola rather than on milk.

To sum up, the common denominator of such reservations is that the apparent economic benefits of the types of industrial activity normally associated with MNCs may be outweighed for LDCs either by the economic costs included in the "package" in which they are imported or, alternatively, by the fact that they are "inappropriate" by other, non-economic criteria. In either case, the standard answer is that it is up to the host government to decide and to control. But on this also most radical critics of MNCs tend to question whether the state in most LDCs can match up to its assigned role. If not, if it is too weak or class-dominated, if its officials are too ignorant or corrupt to promote "suitable" policies, then sovereignty becomes no defence against the MNC. So, ultimately, our assessment of the probable and potential impact of MNCs on host countries must turn on how effectively the host state performs its role as maker of policy and defender of the "national interest." Let us, therefore, finally consider the capacity of the nation-state to use and control the potential of the MNC and whether the multinational constitutes a form of economic imperialism after the end of formal empire.

STATE SOVEREIGNTY AND THE MULTINATIONAL

It is only when one poses these questions that the fundamental difficulty of studying MNCs becomes fully evident. Unless one is an unqualified believer in dependency theory, or a neo-Marxist of the sort denounced by Warren and Emmanuel — both of whom reject the possibility that a nonsocialist state could wish, let alone be competent, to subordinate class or sectoral interests to those of the society as a whole — there is no possibility of providing a definite answer. This is not to be evasive: there are two sound reasons for agnosticism.

First, there is very little hard information on the operations of MNCs. Their operations can be studied at two levels: the general and the specific. Most published information is general, based on surveys of a very large number of firms and their activities in host countries. So far as it goes, such information is valuable as the basis for making general statements concerning both the source and distribution of FDI by country of origin and investment and as between the several hundred largest MNCs. It also throws light on methods of entry into host countries, the extent of local equity holding, output, profitability according to published accounts, receipts from royalties and fees, expenditure on R&D and on the contribution to export earnings. Such information makes possible broad statements indicating the importance of the economic role of the MNC in the modern world economy; but it has two obvious limitations. It gives no insight into the motivation and internal operations of individual corporations or the attitudes and policies of host governments; and, consequently, it cannot provide the evidence by which we might assess the "welfare" implications of FDI as we have defined it. The first need can only be met by detailed research on particular corporations with deliberate emphasis on the issues raised by theorists.

But even if the flow of specific information increases greatly (and both large corporations and host governments are commonly very reluctant to allow their inner secrets to be revealed) there is a second reason why no comprehensive answer could be given on the compatibility of the MNC and the welfare of host countries. Each corporation and each country is a special case. Individual examples can neither prove nor disprove general propositions. Thus no general theory of the MNC and its relationship with the sovereign state can be drawn up. At most I can suggest some broad propositions that seem to be reasonably consistent with the facts of the case in the 1980s. Let me, therefore, attempt a broad answer to the main question posed in this chapter: what is the role of the MNC in the world economy? Is it a key weapon in the armoury of a new informal imperialism?

The fundamental point is that while the public image of the MNC in the Third World has remained virtually static for over two decades, the reality has changed, and is changing very fast. In the 1950s, when the alarm bells started to ring, the common assumption was that most MNCs were American-owned, expressing the United States' postwar economic and political hegemony throughout the world; and that most of these enterprises extracted oil or minerals, or ran plantations. Neither assumption was valid then, and they have become almost entirely untrue three decades later. Western Europe has now achieved rough parity with the United States as the source of FDI; and in the Third World the focus of MNC activity has shifted decisively from "exploitation" of "irreplaceable" reserves of oil and minerals or growing tropical crops to investment in manufacturing for reexport or for local consumption. This structural change is reflected in the critical literature: where once Standard Oil and United Fruit were the villains, now it is the multitude of industrial companies who are accused of debauching indigenous tastes and extracting Baran's "surplus" through excessive profits and the abuse of transfer prices, royalty payments, and so on. My argument is that the change in the functions of the multinational has significantly affected its relationship with the sovereign state in which it operates; and that, even if accusations of "imperialism" might have been to some extent justified in a Third World context in the past, they are much less relevant in the present.

The most legitimate criticism of MNCs has always been that their very function was to make competition imperfect, distorting the economic process and obtaining a "monopoly rent" by internalizing the market. This makes them agents of a new mercantilism, which has historically tended towards some form of imperialism. Is this, indeed, their common aim and, if so, why can private firms frustrate market forces in this way?

First, the question of intention. There are a number of alternative theoretical explanations of why large business firms should wish to establish overseas subsidiaries, and all assume that they do so to obtain a higher overall profit by "internalizing" their total operations than they might do by using some alternative strategy. Their reasons, however, vary according to the nature of their activities and the environment in which they operate; and the main contrast is between the extractive and utility companies, on the one hand, and those which manufacture in host countries on the other.

The salient fact about the utility, oil, mineral and agricultural corporations is that, by and large, they grew in a more or less free-trade environment: that is, the things they dealt in were seldom subject to protective duties, quantity controls (except in wartime), or tariffs. These firms engaged in production and trade in commodities for many reasons, but most did so either to achieve vertical integration within a single firm, or to sell to third parties on the international market. In both cases, however, and also in that of public utilities, one of their primary aims was to erect some form of monopoly as a defence against the risks of a competitive free-trade market. Oil companies, primarily concerned with refining and marketing, nevertheless bought leases of oil deposits so that they could control the price of their raw material and balance supplies from low- and high-cost areas within their global operations. Mineral firms and agricultural producers were both notorious for using monopoly, monopsony, cartels, rings, and so on, to force down the price paid to host governments, peasant producers, and so on, and conversely to force up the price they could charge to consumers.

Thus MNCs of this type attempted to create some form of monopoly in a free-trade environment as their best means of maximizing profits. As an important by-product, they tended also to be "imperialistic." Because their activities commonly depended on concessions (for oil, mines, plantations) or, if they were engaged in trade, on satisfactory access to the producers of their commodity, relations with host governments were of crucial importance. And because much of their business was done with the relatively weak states of Latin America and the Middle East and with the early post-colonial states of Africa and Asia, they commonly achieved a position approaching dominance over their hosts: hence the concept of United Fruit's "banana republics" and the near-sovereignty of Standard Oil or Anglo-Iranian in some parts of the Middle East. In this sense it was characteristic of MNCs engaged in the commodity trade, and some in public utilities (ITT, for example) that they established "informal empires" as a response to the need to establish monopoly as the basis of profitability in a competitive environment.

Exactly the opposite is generally true of the modern manufacturing multinationals. They are, by their nature, interested in freedom of trade outside their protected home base. They do not need physical control over their markets. Above all, they normally engage in manufacture in other countries as a direct response to some form of obstruction in the market, which either threatens an established export trade or offers opportunities for higher profit through some form and degree of monopoly in a previously competitive market. The chronology of FDI in manufacturing shows this to be universally true. The timing of the great spate of direct industrial investment, which started in the 1920s in Britain after the McKenna duties of the First World War, and from the 1950s in most LDCs as they adopted severe protectionism along with their new independence constitutions, shows that (with probably the sole exception of post-1950 American "off-shore" industries in South-East Asia) the manufacturing multinational was conjured up by protectionist governments. The effect was a double distortion of the market. "Effective protection" raised domestic prices above international prices, so creating for the first time a market that might be profitable for modern industry, despite the restricted demand and high production costs of the Third World countries. For their part, the multinationals, compelled or tempted by protectionism to jump the tariff wall, further distorted the market by exploiting the opportunities provided by their monopoly of technology and know-how. Thus, as Hymer argued as early as 1960, it was indeed imperfections in the market that attracted MNCs to undertake overseas manufacturing; but in the Third World these imperfections were created by the protectionist state.

If, then, the power held by the MNCs in the Third World is in any sense "a New Imperial System" (or perhaps a "third colonial occupation") then it must be said that the gates were opened from the inside. But we must not beg this question. Empire means the imposition of external authority, the transfer of the power to make final decisions to a central metropolis. Hymer's concept of a world hierarchy assumed that senior corporate executives in Manhattan could determine what happened in Manchester, Bombay, or Nairobi; that the power of the great corporations was greater than that of small or even middling states. Is this really so, or is his New Imperial System merely a fable?

Paradoxically, there was more substance in Hymer's vision in the past than when he saw it and there is still less in the 1980s. His prototypes were the big utility and extractive corporations. These, as we have seen, were a special case. They needed power to achieve their objectives and were able to hold it because of the weakness of many of the states (including some colonies) in which they operated. They were, indeed, states within states, largely autonomous, latter-day feudal barons, able to bargain, even dictate, because of the importance of their activities to the host states. It was precisely because they were so powerful that the new sovereign states found it essential, whenever they had the power, to destroy them: in many countries effective decolonization consisted in the nationalization of telecommunications, oil wells and copper mines.

It is entirely different with the modern, manufacturing multinational. Its very presence in the host country reflects local policy decisions: it is a genie summoned to serve protectionism. It depends for its profit on the continuance of that policy. It has little power because, in most cases, the only sanction it could impose on a hostile state would be to stop production; and, since this is seldom for export, the economic consequences for the host would be negligible. Physically, moreover, a factory bears no resemblance to a large mine or plantation. It is in no sense autonomous or remote; not a city-state. It is easy to starve out by simply refusing licenses for essential inputs. Indeed, virtually the only threat the modern manufacturing multinational can make to its host government is that unreasonable treatment may inhibit further foreign investment or technological transfer. The threat is real but seldom compelling. A determined state will normally act as it wishes and risk the consequences.

My conclusion, therefore, is that in so far as there is a latent tension between the power of the MNC and that of the sovereign host state, it is the state that now holds most of the cards and can determine the rules of the game. At the macroeconomic level it can adjust its policies in such a way that it is no longer possible for MNCs to make "excessive" profits or attractive for them to import factors of production. At the administrative level, it is always possible to use anti-trust laws against excessive concentration; to impose quotas, limit prices; above all to insist on a minimal level of local participation in the equity and of nationals in employment. Nationalization is a rare last resort simply because experience shows that very large foreign corporations will normally accept the bid from the very small states.

Yet we must end on a note of caution. I have argued that the modern multinational chief executive in Hymer's allegorical skyscraper is not the ruler of an informal overseas empire. The humblest LDC is in no danger from the power of a multinational which is engaged in manufacturing and technology transfer. But there are other, more subtle dangers. The main danger of the modern MNC to the LDC lies not in its power, but in two much less dramatic qualities: its superior cunning and its apparent harmlessness. The cunning of an MNC is one aspect of its managerial efficiency and its ability to take a global view of its interests. Without it an MNC could not operate successfully in Third World states with their jungle of regulations. The problem is to draw the line between cunning and dishonesty as, for example, represented by abuse of transfer-pricing; and much of the substance in criticisms made by "nationalist" and "radical" critics of MNC behaviour amounts to the accusation that this line has been crossed. Lall's study of the pharmaceutical industry supports the general prejudice that this is commonly the most guilty type of multinational. Yet, while such practices may cause loss to LDCs, they are unlikely to cause disaster. The real danger lies rather in the seductiveness of the industrial MNC. The benefits a foreign corporation can offer to a poor, non-industrial state are extremely attractive: an instant, advanced factory at little or no immediate cost with payments due only when, and if, the subsidiary flourishes. It is not surprising that during the optimistic "development" decades before the mid-1970s so many LDCs welcomed manufacturing corporations with open arms and failed to see the long-term risks they were running.

The analogy with much of the borrowing in which many Latin American and Islamic states in the Mediterranean indulged during the nineteenth century is obvious and the dangers equally great: on the economic side, a growing and ultimately intolerable strain on foreign-exchange earnings to pay for imported inputs and to meet the cost of repatriated profits, and so on; more generally, a host of social and political problems at home as the alien presence makes itself felt. In the later twentieth century the result will not be the formal imperialism of a Dual Control or a protectorate; but a number of LDCs have now learnt that excessive foreign investment, if coupled with inappropriate economic and social management, may lead to virtual bankruptcy, dictation by the World Bank or the IMF and possibly domestic revolution. Sovereignty, in fact, may be proof against the multinational, but it carries no guarantee against lack of wisdom; and the essential message of the "national" or "radical" critic of the MNC to developing countries should be *caveat emptor*. . . .

NOTE

1. S. Lall and P. Streeten, *Foreign Investment, Transnationals, and Developing Countries* (London, 1977), 59; italics in original.

12

Strategic Trade and Investment Policies: Implications for the Study of International Political Economy

JEFFREY A. HART AND ASEEM PRAKASH

Governments have long used trade policies to protect national producers. In recent years, policymakers and others have begun to champion new approaches that intervene in both international trade and international investment flows. Such policies have been especially prominent in the high-technology sectors, which many believe are essential to national economic prowess. Jeffrey Hart and Aseem Prakash assess such policies, especially those that attempt to encourage the development of high-technology industries. They analyze the economics and politics of strategic trade and investment policies and then outline their potential impact on the international political economy.

1. INTRODUCTION

Business gurus point out that successful firms often carefully strategise about what to sell, where to sell, how to sell, and how and where to manufacture their goods and services. Suppose a country, drawing inspiration from such firms, were to formulate a set of economic policies to become globally competitive in leading economic sectors. How specific or encompassing would such policies be and what might be the justifications for them? Even though the theory and practicality of such policies — the strategic trade and industrial policies (STIPs) — is contested, they retain their appeal for politicians and policymakers. In this paper we discuss how and why STIPs have created a new agenda for the study of international political economy.

State intervention to directly guide industrial activity is called industrial policy and to guide foreign trade is called trade policy. Industrial policies differ from macroeconomic policies in that they target only a subset of the economy. Whereas macroeconomic policies (such as tax rates, level of deficit spending and interest-rate policies) generally do not discriminate among types of firms or industries, industrial policies (such as R&D subsidies, tax subsidies, preferential loans and credit allocations) are targeted at specific firms or industries.

Industrial and trade policies are often compartmentalised as reflected in the administrative institutions of various states, where trade policies are handled by the commerce ministry and industrial policies by the industry ministry. However, trade and industrial policies may overlap if trade policies affect the international competitiveness of domestic firms or industrial policies deny domestic markets and technologies to foreign firms.

Industrial policies have a long history. Nationalists of the late 18th and early 19th centuries, such as List and Hamilton, sought state interventions to promote domestic manufacturing in the face of British manufacturing dominance. The infant-industry argument of the German Historical School suggested that new industries took a while to get established because of startup problems, or because a particular country or region was somehow initially disadvantaged and needed to insulate itself temporarily from competition. The infant-industry argument was resurrected after World War II for justifying state interventions for the industrialisation of the developing countries of Asia, Africa, and South America.

Debates on trade policy also have a long history — particularly, arguments over the proposition that free trade benefits all countries, as Smith and Ricardo asserted, as opposed to the idea that some countries may benefit more than others, especially if they engage in certain forms of state intervention. A recent example of this ongoing debate centres on the work of the strategic trade theorists. Neoclassical trade theorists assume declining or constant returns to scale (growth of output can never grow faster than the growth of inputs), perfect competition in product and factor markets (many producers and very few barriers to entry for new producers), and no information or transactions costs connected with technology flows. Strategic trade theorists relax these assumptions and deduce that domestic firms can benefit asymmetrically from international trade if the state intervenes on their behalf. By doing so, the state can shift not only profits, but also jobs, from one country to another. Therefore, states are tempted to do this.

Industrial policies may or may not be justified in terms of strategic trade theory. For example, some scholars justify industrial policies as being necessary to reduce adjustment costs connected with changes in international markets so as to prevent the creation of protectionist coalitions without reference to strategic trade. Others, stressing the differences in national economic institutions which create barriers to technology flows, argue that R&D subsidies are necessary to compensate for these impeded flows.

In this paper we focus on policies arising due to the overlap between industrial and strategic trade policies. This overlap has become critical since, with increasing globalisation, economic actors are treating the whole globe as the relevant unit for securing inputs, processing them, manufacturing, as well as selling the final product. Traditionally, foreign direct investment (FDI) and exports have been treated as mutually exclusive. However, since FDI flows are now acknowledged to encourage exports, and the intra-firm trade exceeds the arm's-length trade, impediments to FDI (via industrial policy) are equivalent to trade barriers (trade policy). Hence, strategic trade and investment policies (STIPs) need to be seen as two synergistic pillars of state interventions to support domestic firms in the global economy. Though economic globalisation, technologisation of traded goods and the increasing economic salience of multinational corporations (MNCs) constrain contemporary governments, they also create incentives and new rationales for state interventions in the form of STIPs.

We have organised this paper in six sections, including the introduction. In Section 2, we discuss the three categories of industrial policy theories. We focus on the 'technological trajectory' version since it provides a rationale for state interventions in high-technology industries. In Section 3, we review the main theories of international trade: Smith's absolute advantage, Ricardo's comparative advantage and the neoclassical Heckscher-Ohlin theory. We then discuss the infant-industry argument, import-substitution policies and strategic trade theory. In Section 4, we present STIPs as an Intervention Game to highlight the incentives for states to intervene in the economy. We then discuss the criticisms of STIPs. In Section 5, we discuss how STIPs create a new agenda for the study of international political economy, particularly by challenging the post–World War II order based on 'embedded liberalism.' In Section 6, we present our conclusions.

2. INDUSTRIAL POLICY THEORIES

Industrial policies refer to domestic interventions to encourage specific industries. Such interventions have many rationales and we identify three broad categories of industrial policy theories:

    a. the technological-trajectory theory;
    b. the structuralist theory; and
    c. the institutionalist theory.

Though these categories overlap, they provide different rationales for industrial policies. The technological-trajectory theorists argue that technological flows across national boundaries are imperfect even when capital is highly mobile. State intervention is needed to secure 'first-mover advantages' for domestic firms in industries where learning curves are steep and supply infrastructures are difficult to reproduce. A good example is the integrated circuit (IC) industry, where average costs decline sharply with cumulative production because of the ability of producers to learn over time how to make the same devices more reliably and using less silicon. IC product and production technologies are often difficult to license from the original producer and sometimes are also difficult to reverse-engineer. First-movers, such as Intel in microprocessors and Toshiba in dynamic random access memory (DRAM) devices, have experienced rapid growth and high profit levels. . . .

The structuralists emphasise the differences in the relative positions of countries in the international system, particularly the distribution of economic power across countries. The hegemon, usually the country with the largest GNP, has a

self-interest in providing international public goods, such as free trade and investment regimes, a stable monetary order, etc., since it corners the bulk of the benefits. For example, if trade is denominated in U.S. dollars — the reserve currency
for trade — then the U.S. benefits from monetary seigniorage.

Non-hegemons free ride the liberal trade and monetary institutions by promoting exports and capital to the rest of the world while protecting their domestic
economy from international competition. If they can do this along with increasing
the international competitiveness of their domestic firms (not an easy task, of
course), then over time they advance their relative standing in the world economy,
leading to the relative economic decline of the hegemon. Structuralists argue, in
short, that industrial policies are one way that non-hegemons can challenge the
power of the hegemon.

Another structuralist argument is that when hegemons face a relative economic
decline, they begin to act in a predatory manner by copying the industrial and
trade policies of their principal competitors. By doing so, they undermine the liberal economic regimes that they established earlier. Thus, structuralists explain
the implementation of industrial policies by both non-hegemons and declining
hegemons as part of a larger process of economic competition among countries.

Institutionalists focus on the historically-rooted differences in state-societal
arrangements and their impact on the competitiveness of domestic firms. They
highlight how some institutional configurations systematically create barriers to
imports and inward investments, and thereby shelter domestic firms from international competition. In particular, they contrast the relatively open U.S. system
with the relatively closed Japanese system, with its incestuous forms of busi-
ness/government collaboration and its industrial combines *(keiretsu),* and how
such differences create advantages for Japanese firms to compete in international
markets.

In this paper we focus on the technological-trajectory version since it provides
a rationale for state intervention in high-technology industries. The twin hall-
marks of economic globalisation are mobile capital (fixed as well as portfolio) and
the technologisation of trade — the increasing salience of high-technology products in global trade. High-technology could be embodied in the final product or be
used in the production process. Technologisation creates incentives for state interventions to develop domestic architectures-of-supplies in critical technologies,
enabling firms located in the country to have adequate and timely access to such
technologies. Such architectures-of-supplies therefore become a major 'pull-
factor' for attracting FDI from multinational corporations, and thereby furthering
the economic agenda of the politicians and policymakers.

3. TRADE THEORIES

Smith made a case for free trade based on absolute advantage. If country A has an
absolute advantage or lower costs in producing cars, and country B has an
absolute advantage in producing bicycles, then both A and B can gain by trading
with each other — A by exporting cars and B by exporting bicycles. The Ricardian

trade theory, also known as the classical trade theory, argued for trade based on comparative and not absolute advantage. Ricardo emphasised that for trade to take place, countries need not have absolute advantages for producing different goods. To use Ricardo's example, consider two countries — Portugal and Britain, and two sectors — agriculture and manufacturing. For trade to benefit both countries, Portugal can be more productive than Britain in agriculture as well as manufacturing, as long as it is not more productive than Britain by the same percentage in both. For example, suppose Portugal's agricultural productivity is higher by 50 per cent versus Britain's. As long as Portugal's manufacturing productivity is less than or greater than 50 per cent versus Britain's, both can gain from trade.

The neoclassical trade theory, pioneered by Heckscher and Ohlin, also identifies comparative advantage as the basis of international trade. Among the main assumptions of the simpler Heckscher-Ohlin models are that: (i) though the factors of production are mobile within the country, they are not mobile across national boundaries; (ii) product markets, both domestically and internationally, are perfectly competitive and there are no super-normal profits; (iii) there are constant returns to scale in production of all goods (or production functions are homogeneous of the first degree) and firms cannot acquire a monopoly position through 'learning curve' advantages; (iv) since there are no transaction costs for technology acquisition, access to technology is not a source of comparative advantage; and (v) since goods have different factor intensities, a labour-rich country exports labour-intensive goods and a capital-rich country exports capital-intensive goods. Note that this specialisation results not from access to a superior technology (technology is assumed to be the same everywhere), but from differences in factor endowments.

A. Strategic Trade Theories

Though comparative advantage creates gains from trade and specialisation, such gains may be distributed unequally across countries. Strategic trade theorists suggest that certain types of state intervention can shift such gains, in special circumstances, from foreign to domestic firms.

Brander and Spencer suggest that in industries with imperfect competition and super-normal profits, subsidies can shift global profits to domestic firms such that the increase in their profits exceeds the subsidies. Hence, on the aggregate, there is a net increase in national welfare. Krugman (1994) gives a hypothetical example of the application of strategic trade theory. Imagine that there is some good that could be developed either by an American or a European firm. If either firm developed the product alone, it could earn large profits; however, the development costs are large enough that if both firms tried to enter the market, both would lose money. Which firm will actually enter? If European governments subsidise their firm, or make it clear that it will have a protected domestic market, they may ensure that their firm enters while deterring the U.S. firm — and thereby also ensure that Europe, not America, gets the monopoly profits. . . .

Strategic trade policies are not the same as governmental interventions in strategic sectors. A strategic sector may generate externalities only for the domestic economy and does not necessarily have international linkages. A good example of this would be a governmental subsidy to promote the construction of fibre-optic networks. If such a network does not enhance the global competitiveness of domestic firms, then the subsidy is not a strategic trade policy.

Strategic trade theories, in conjunction with the technological-trajectory theory of the industrial policies, provide the rationale for STIPs. A case can be made for state support of high-technology industries through a combination of trade and industrial policies, with an objective that the country retains thriving domestic architectures-of-supply in critical industries, thereby enabling domestic firms to be competitive in global markets characterised by super-normal profits and creating incentives for foreign firms in those same industries to invest directly in the country. Tyson (1992) defends STIPs in the United States as preferable to the incoherence and ineffectiveness of the military-oriented industrial policies of the past. In the Cold-War era, the U.S. government intervened in militarily sensitive sectors. Such interventions, however, were not designed to maximise 'spin-offs' to civilian sectors, but rather to assure local sources of supply for key military components and systems. Tyson's message is clear: since states need to intervene anyway, they should do it in a way which maximises economic welfare, which means that they should do it in a manner consistent with strategic trade and industrial policy theories.

4. THE LOGIC OF STIPs

Do STIPs have any historical validity, and will they be equally efficacious across political systems? Some scholars see STIPs as being the key to the rapid industrialisation of Japan and the Newly Industrialised Countries (NICs). It is suggested that Japan followed a phased process of industrial development. During the first phase, the Japanese firms were disadvantaged in both development and production costs. To shelter these firms against international competition, the domestic market was closed with a combination of import barriers and inward investment restrictions. Without inward investment restrictions, foreign firms would have been tempted to jump the import barriers by establishing local subsidiaries. This would have impeded the development of local architectures-of-supply. In contrast to the import substitution models in operation in other regions of the world, fierce domestic competition ensured that domestic firms did not become complacent rent-seekers.

In the second phase, Japanese and other Asian firms borrowed technology from abroad to bridge the technology gap. The state therefore relaxed import restrictions while maintaining inward investment restrictions. The state also encouraged firms to export by linking state support, such as concessional credits, to export performance. Hence, the domestic firms, having established themselves in the home market, were gradually exposed to foreign competition.

The close networking of *keiretsu* firms in Japan allowed them to compete domestically without fear of hostile takeovers. The role of the Japanese Ministry of International Trade and Industry (MITI) as 'gate-keeper' and dispenser of subsidies to specific firms and industries was also important since it created hurdles for foreign firms to sell and invest in Japan. As a result of increased U.S. awareness of the implications of the *keiretsu* system, a major U.S. demand during the Structural Impediment Initiative talks with Japan in 1989–90 was the reform of that system. Since neoclassical explanations of industrial performance denied the importance of institutions like the Japanese *keiretsu,* they were unable to explain the impact of such "relational structures" on business performance.

In the third phase, Asian producers began to build world market positions without fearing foreign competition. They now tapped foreign markets through exports as well as through foreign direct investment. The international expansion of Japanese and other Asian multinational corporations was now perceived to be impeding the development of architectures-of-supply in other regions, as Asian component manufacturers followed the main manufacturing companies to foreign countries. Since the main research and development competencies remained in Asia, especially in Japan, the non-Asian firms chafed over their limited access to critical Japanese technologies.

Japan's policies have changed the contemporary game of economic rivalry by creating an enormous temptation for other states to copy them. This situation can be conceptualised as a form of prisoner's dilemma game. Suppose state A is debating whether to intervene or not to intervene in a particular strategic industry. It faces the following payoff structure, as discussed in Table 1.

We assume that: (1) $e > c$ and $e > d$; (2) a, b, c, d, and $e > 0$; and (3) $c > a$ and $d > b$. For B, "intervene" (defect) is the dominant strategy no matter whether A intervenes ($a > 0$) or not ($e > c$). Similarly, for A, the dominant strategy is to intervene irrespective of whether B intervenes ($b > 0$) or not. Thus, both countries intervene and the Nash equilibrium (a, b) is pareto inefficient because the highest joint payoffs occur when both refrain from intervening ($c > a$ and $b > d$).

. . . The prisoner's dilemma payoff structure of the intervention-game creates incentives for . . . the widespread adoption of STIPs. This suggests that new or modified international institutions are needed to change incentives, which make STIPs less attractive to politicians and policymakers. We elaborate on this in the next section.

TABLE 1. The Intervention Game

		Country A	
		Intervene	Not Intervene
Country B	**Intervene**	Rents Shared between A & B (a, b)	All Rents to B (e, 0)
	Not Intervene	All Rents to A (0, e)	Rents Shared between A & B (c, d)

Source: Adapted from Richardson (1986, p. 271).

A. Criticisms of STIPs

The efficacy of STIPs in promoting economic development is disputed. While some scholars attribute the recent economic successes of Japan and the newly industrialised countries (NICs) of Asia largely to STIPs, others attribute it to low wage and inflation rates, rapid copying of the product and process technologies of competitors, high domestic savings rates (enabling low interest and high invest-ment rates) and undervalued currency exchange-rates, just to name a few of the possible alternative explanations.

STIPs are also criticised for normative, positive, as well as theoretical reasons. The normative critics focus on the dangers of giving too much power to the state. Classical liberals and neoclassical economists argue that the state should be restrained from asserting its authority in new terrains unless there is no other way to resolve market failures. Critics question particularly the need for strategic inter-vention to increase aggregate economic welfare. Consider a situation where a state identifies a set of strategic industries and provides them with an export sub-sidy. Suppose that such strategic industries compete for the same scarce factors. In this case, state support drives up the prices of the scarce factor (a pecuniary exter-nality) and no industry benefits. Further, if equity is also an objective of state pol-icy, then such interventions will skew the income distribution in favour of the scarce factor.

Critics also point out that STIPs can advance the interests of a particular coun-try only if others do not retaliate by providing matching supports to their domestic firms and industries. If such retaliation occurs, then the relative gains promised by STIPs may not materialise.

It is also suggested that special interests will abuse the willingness of govern-ments to intervene. Firms, as rational actors, have incentives to externalise their problems to avoid painful internal restructuring. Such firms can therefore be expected to lobby for state support. It will therefore be difficult to separate strate-gic interventions from non-strategic interventions.

Many scholars question the implementability of STIPs. They consider STIPs to be similar to infant-industry and import-substitution policies, encouraging rent-seeking and leading to misallocation of resources. One of their concerns is that it is difficult, *ex ante,* to specify which industries are strategic. This is, in part, related to the difficulties in measuring externalities. In the absence of reliable and objective measures of externalities, political rather than economic criteria may dominate the choice of strategic industries. . . .

Strategic interventions have to be focused on industries with super-normal profits and states often have only limited ability to identify such industries. Further, it is difficult to determine whether a particular level of profit is super-normal. Imperfect competition also does not *per se* signal super-normal profits since competition among a few rival firms can be fierce enough to drive the prices down to competitive levels.

STIPs require that the national firms be clearly distinguished from foreign firms and that policies be targeted to benefit national firms only. However, in a globalised economy it is often difficult to distinguish between national firms (us) and foreign firms (them).

We have suggested that STIPs help to create domestic architectures-of-supplies, a source of competitive advantage if technology is not mobile across national boundaries. However, . . . technology flows across national boundaries are growing with the help of innovative institutional arrangements such as joint research ventures, technology exchange agreements, customer-supplier relationships, etc.

Critics argue that STIPs cannot explain how domestic firms became R&D leaders in the absence of government assistance, or how state-assisted industries failed in the face of massive assistance. Hence, they argue, STIPs can at best be only a facilitating condition for the success of domestic firms.

Scholars also point out that there are different forms of capitalism and that only some forms are consistent with strategic interventions. An important research question is whether some countries are more willing and capable of using STIPs than others. The U.S. has rarely engaged in strategic interventions in the past, partly because of the ideational and institutional grip of neoclassical economics. On the other hand, since neoclassical ideas are less influential in Japan, the Japanese state faces less opposition to its interventionist role. . . .

STIPs do not show instantaneous results since their effects are usually visible after considerable time lags, sometimes longer than the electoral cycles. The successful implementation of STIPs requires that firms believe that state support will continue, irrespective of political changes. Can every state make such credible commitments? Johnson (1982) identifies two kinds of states: regulatory and developmental. Regulatory states have minimal capabilities for strategic economic interventions, and their policies seek to ensure an unfettered working of markets and a correction of market failures wherever they arise. The developmental states, in contrast, are capable of adopting, and willing to stick with STIPs even in the face of temporary difficulties.

The nature of domestic socio-political institutions such as the relative autonomy of the state from domestic interests groups, the transparency of domestic decision making, and social and political cohesiveness critically shape firms' perceptions of state commitments. For example, if political power is dispersed domestically, then it may be difficult for the government to make credible commitments. In a relatively decentralised federal system, the executive may face strong opposition from provincial governments, as well as from the national legislature and competing bureaucracies, and therefore may not be able to sustain its interventionist policies. Thus, one would expect countries with more centralised and bureaucratic (and therefore relatively autonomous) political regimes to be more likely to adopt and sustain STIPs. . . .

5. IMPLICATIONS FOR THE STUDY OF
INTERNATIONAL POLITICAL ECONOMY

. . . If STIPs are politically attractive and may get implemented, then what are the implications for international political economy? STIP theories help in explaining the increased activity to form regional economic alliances, particularly the ones in high-technology industries. For example, the Single European Act of 1987 as well as the Maastricht Treaty were preceded by a series of programmes to promote high-technology industries in the region to ensure that Europe does not fall behind Japan and the United States in key technologies and industries. Esprit, Eureka, JESSI and the Airbus Consortium are examples of such programmes.

Similarly in the U.S., the Sematech consortium for R&D in semiconductor technologies is co-funded by the federal government and industry. Sematech was motivated largely by the success of the Japanese VLSI (very large-scale integrated circuits) Programme co-sponsored by the Japanese government and Japanese industry. The VLSI Programme subsidised the imports of U.S. semiconductor manufacturing equipment as well as their reverse engineering.

Another U.S. STIP project, the National Flat Panel Display Initiative, has created an umbrella for R&D funding for commercialisation of new flat panel display technologies by U.S. firms. This initiative was the U.S. government's answer to the large lead of Japanese electronics firms in the production of active matrix liquid crystal displays, mostly for laptop computers.

Recent work on high-technology industries suggests that the traditional emphasis on spin-offs from military to civilian technology needs to be supplemented with consideration of spin-ons from civilian to military. An example of this is the use of computer displays and microelectronic circuits developed for commercial products in military avionics systems. Political arguments over this question have fuelled a debate within the national security community over dual-use technologies which have both civilian and military applications. Advocates of strategic trade theory support strategic interventions to promote dual-use technologies, while critics of the theory argue that such policies should be avoided because it is impossible to accurately assess the degree of technological interdependence of civilian and military technologies, and that such interventions may simply encourage domestic rent-seeking behaviour. In short, STIPs pose important questions about what kinds of R&D the state should subsidise.

A. STIPs and 'Embedded-Liberalism'

STIPs undermine the postwar Bretton Woods order based on "embedded-liberalism," and underline the need for developing new international institutions to meet the challenges of a globalised world economy. Ruggie's notion of embedded-liberalism links the rise of the welfare state (which generally combines a variety of social insurance schemes with Keynesian demand management) to an agreement among the major industrialised nations to keep the global trading system as open as possible. In many major trading nations, as long as there was some faith in the efficacy of Keynesian demand-management policies to smooth out economic cycles, the free-traders were able to make side-payments to supporters of social welfare policies in order to secure their acceptance or the liberal trade regime. Within the domestic economy, embedded-liberalism combined macroeconomic state intervention with non-intervention in micro markets.

Challenges to embedded-liberalism posed by STIPs create pressures for changing the liberal international economic regimes established after World War

II. In particular, the World Trade Organisation, the main guarantor of an open trading system, will have to adapt to the proliferation of STIPs by a growing number of states. Free-traders, in particular, will have to identify new domestic and transnational coalitions to support non-intervention of the state at both macro and micro levels, and the preservation of an open trading system. The putting together of such alliances is increasingly challenged by the progressive dismantling of the welfare state. The welfare state permitted governments to promise assistance to those elements of society most badly hurt by adjustments to changes in the world economy. It permitted governments to compensate the losers with some of the gains extracted from the winners in international economic competition, to maintain support for free trade policies abroad and the regulatory state at home. As that padding is removed, governments find themselves less and less able to defend free trade and investment policies against the forces of protectionism.

6. CONCLUSIONS

In an increasingly globalised world economy, trade and industrial policies need to be viewed as two complementary aspects of state interventions in market processes. Globalisation is marked by the increasing salience of high-technology products and services in world trade. STIPs are designed to create: (1) domestic architectures-of-supply in critical technologies, enabling domestic firms to compete in international markets; and (2) incentives for multinational corporations to invest in the country. Hence, STIPs are attractive to politicians and policymakers.

STIPs differ from infant-industry and import-substitution policies in that state interventions are not designed to encourage manufacturing by raising barriers to imports. However, STIPs, like infant-industry and import-substitution policies, are inconsistent with classical and neoclassical theories of international trade, since any action by the state to promote specific industries will lead to allocative inefficiencies. Further, critics argue that it will be difficult to unambiguously identify strategic industries.

We have discussed the positive, normative and theoretical criticism of STIPs. The positive critiques include the inability of governments to identify strategic industries *ex ante* due to difficulties in measuring externalities, problems in differentiating normal from super-normal profits and domestic from foreign firms, and the dangers of public officials and/or private interest groups using STIPs for rent-seeking. Since such problems are more significant in regulatory states than in developmental states, the implementation of STIPs becomes critically dependent on state-societal relationships, transparency in policy-making processes and the credibility that changes in governments will not lead to withdrawal of state support.

Even though STIPs are challenged on theoretical as well as practical grounds, they remain attractive for politicians and policymakers. The intuitive appeal of STIPs should not be underestimated. Ideas influence policies by providing roadmaps to cause and effect relationships about contemporary societal problems. STIPs provide such roadmaps of why certain economies are on a relative decline and what policies need to be adopted to ensure competitiveness of domestic firms in the global economy. However, STIPs as intervention games . . . highlight the need for developing new international institutions to prevent costly and senseless competitive interventions. . . .

Thus the controversy over STIPs, on the one hand, is provoking new domestic debates on how to modify the relationships between states and markets to enhance the economic well-being of a country's population, and, on the other, highlights the dangers of widespread adoption of such policies.

REFERENCES

Brander, J.A., and B.J. Spencer (1985). "Export Subsidies and International Market Share Rivalry," *Journal of International Economics* 18, 85–100.

Johnson, C. (1982). *MITI and the Japanese Miracle.* Stanford, CA: Stanford University Press.

Krugman, P.R. (1994). *Peddling Prosperity: Economic Sense and Nonsense in the Age of Diminished Expectations.* New York: Norton.

Richardson, J.D. (1986). "The New Political Economy of Trade Policy," in P.R. Krugman (ed.), *Stategic Trade Policy and the New International Economics.* Cambridge, MA: The MIT Press.

Ruggie, J.G. (1982). "International Regimes, Transactions and Change: Embedded Liberalism in the Postwar Economic Order." *International Organization* 36, 379–415.

Tyson, L.D. (1992). *Who's Bashing Whom? Trade Conflict in High Technology Industries.* Washington, DC: Institute of International Economics.

IV

MONEY AND FINANCE

The international economy, like domestic economies, requires a common monetary standard to function smoothly. For individuals and firms to buy and sell and to save and invest, they need some generally acceptable and predictable unit of account against which other goods can be measured, a medium of exchange with which transactions can be carried out, and a store of value in which wealth can be held. National currencies serve this purpose within countries: for example, Americans buy, sell, save, and invest in dollars. In international trade and payments, a variety of possible common measures can be imagined; in practice, however, the two pure cases are a commodity standard and an international currency standard. Economic actors could use a widely traded commodity, such as gold or pork bellies, against which to measure other goods; or they might arrive at some fictitious unit in which goods could be priced. The former approximates the classical gold standard; the latter, present-day special drawing rights, which are a sort of "paper gold" issued by the International Monetary Fund and equal to a mix of national currencies. Because reaching agreement on a fictitious international currency is difficult, such national currencies as the dollar or the pound sterling have often been used as the basis for international payments.

If the international monetary system provides the measures needed to conduct world trade and payments, the international financial system provides the means to carry out trade and payments. For many hundreds of years, financial institutions — especially banks — have financed trade among clients in different nations, sold and bought foreign currencies, transferred money from one country to another, and lent capital for overseas investment. If, as is often averred, the international monetary system is the "Great Wheel" that enables goods to move in international trade, the international financial system is the grease that allows the wheel itself to turn.

In the modern era (since 1820 or so), there have been, essentially, four well-functioning international monetary systems; each has had corresponding international financial characteristics. From about 1820 until World War I, the world was on or near the classical gold standard, in which many major national currencies were tied to gold at a legally fixed rate. In principle, as Lawrence Broz and Barry Eichengreen explain (in Readings 13 and 14, respectively) the gold standard was self-regulating; should any national currency (and economy) move out of balance, it would be forced back into equilibrium by the very operation of the system. In practice, the pre–World War I system was actually a gold-sterling standard; the

British pound sterling, backed by a strong government and the world's leading financial center, was "as good as gold," and most international trade and payments were carried out in sterling.

The world financial system in the century before World War I was indeed dominated by British banks, which financed much of world trade and channeled enormous amounts of investment capital to such rapidly developing countries as the United States, Australia, Argentina, and South Africa. As time wore on, the financial institutions of other European powers, especially France and Germany, also began to expand abroad. The result was a highly integrated system of international monetary and financial interactions under the Pax Britannica. In Reading 13, Lawrence Broz argues that this relatively smoothly functioning system was due largely to the concerns of the dominant private interests in the world's monetary and financial leaders.

Even before World War I, however, strains and rivalries were beginning to test the system. Once the war started, in 1914, international trade and payments collapsed: of all the world's major financial markets, only New York stayed open for the duration of the conflict. Indeed, by the time World War I ended, the center of international finance had shifted from London to New York, and Wall Street remained the world's principal lender until the Great Depression of the 1930s.

As might be expected, given the reduced economic might of Great Britain, the prewar gold sterling standard could not be rebuilt. Yet neither was the United States, which was beset by the isolationist-internationalist conflict at home, willing to simply replace Great Britain at the apex of the world monetary system. What emerged was the so-called gold exchange standard, whereby most countries went back to tying their currencies to gold but no single national currency came to dominate the others. Dollars, sterling, and French francs were all widely used in world trade and payments, yet, given the lack of lasting international monetary cooperation in the period, the arrangement was quite unstable and short-lived. Normal international economic conditions were not restored until 1924, and within a few years the Depression had brought the system crashing down. With the collapse of the gold exchange standard and the onset of the Depression and World War II, the international monetary and financial systems remained in disarray until after 1945.

As World War II came to an end, the Allied powers, led by the United States, began reconstructing an international monetary system under the Bretton Woods agreement. This system was based, in the monetary sphere, on an American dollar tied to gold at the rate of thirty-five dollars an ounce; other Western currencies were, in turn, tied to the dollar. This was a modified version of the pre-1914 gold standard, with the dollar at its center rather than sterling. As in the Pax Britannica, massive flows of capital from the leading nation — Great Britain, in the first instance; the United States, in the second — were crucial to the proper functioning of the mechanism. Whereas in the British case these capital flows were primarily private loans, from 1945 to 1965 they were essentially government or multilateral loans and foreign direct investment. After 1965, private international finance once again become significant, rapidly reaching historically unprecedented proportions and developing new characteristics.

Even as the new international financial system, generally known as the Euro-market, was gathering steam, the Bretton Woods monetary system was beginning to weaken. In particular, it was becoming more and more difficult to maintain the dollar's price of thirty-five dollars an ounce. As pressure built on the dollar and attempts at reform stagnated, the Richard Nixon administration finally decided that the system was unsustainable. In August 1971, President Nixon "closed the gold window," ending the dollar's free convertibility into gold. The dollar was soon devalued, and by 1975, the gold-dollar standard had been replaced by the current floating-rate system. In Reading 14, Barry Eichengreen evaluates the ability of an international political explanation — the so-called theory of hegemonic stability — to explain the evolution of international monetary relations across these historical systems.

Under the current system of floating exchange rates, the value of most currencies is set, more or less freely, by private traders in world currency markets. Thus, the values of the dollar, the yen, the pound, and so on fluctuate on international currency markets. This has led to frequent and rapid changes in the relative prices of major currencies, as well as to frequent complaints about the unplanned nature of the new system. Because of the central role of the U.S. dollar, even in today's floating-rate system, changes in American economic policy can drive the dollar up and down dramatically, in ways that have important effects on the economy of the United States and of the rest of the world.

The "unholy trinity" of a fixed exchange rate, capital mobility, and autonomous monetary policy — and the necessary trade-offs engendered by the pursuit of these three goals — is central to understanding the current floating-rate system and the potential for cooperation among the world's leading nations in international monetary affairs. This problem is examined by Benjamin J. Cohen (Reading 15). In Reading 16, Jeffry A. Frieden discusses the domestic societal implications of the trade-offs involved, arguing that interest groups will vary in their views on the desirability of one exchange-rate policy or another.

In the 1970s, as American inflation rates rose, the dollar's value dropped relative to other major currencies. From 1979 to 1985, American monetary policy concentrated on fighting inflation while fiscal policy was expansionary, leading to a dramatic rise in the dollar's value. Although inflation was brought down, the strong dollar wreaked havoc with the ability of many American industries to compete internationally. In the mid-1980s the dollar dropped back down to its lowest levels in nearly forty years, and in the 1990s it has gone up and down continually.

Through all these fluctuations, there was dissatisfaction in many quarters about the underlying uncertainty concerning international monetary and financial trends. Today currencies fluctuate widely, many of the world's major nations are experiencing unprecedented trade surpluses or deficits, and capital flows across borders in enormous quantities.

Monetary uncertainty has led some nations to seek security in a variety of alternative institutions. Some countries and observers support the development of a new international money, of which special drawing rights might be a precursor. Others desire a return to the gold standard and the monetary discipline that this system implied. The principal strategy has been to seek stability through cooperative regional agreements.

The most important of these regional monetary agreements is Europe's Economic and Monetary Union (EMU). In 1999 the members of the EMU introduced a single currency, the euro, which has quickly gained a place as one of the world's three leading currencies. Charles Wyplosz, in Reading 17, describes and analyzes the complex process by which most of the members of the European Union gave up their national moneys in favor of a common currency. It is widely believed that the EMU is simply part of a broader process in which the world will tend to form itself into currency blocs around the dollar, the euro, and, perhaps, the Japanese yen.

In international finance, the period since 1965 has been extraordinarily eventful. The Euromarket has grown to several trillion dollars, and international banking has become one of the great growth industries in the world economy. The recent explosion of international finance is unprecedented. Net international bond and bank lending amounted to $865 billion in 1997, having risen from just $245 billion five years earlier. Capital outflows from the thirteen leading industrialized economies averaged $677 billion in 1995, in contrast to $52 billion in the late 1970s; moreover, today almost two-thirds of such outflows consist of portfolio investment while only one-third is foreign direct investment, the reverse of twenty years ago. Indeed, in the late 1970s, total global outflows of portfolio capital averaged $15 billion a year, whereas between 1992 and 1995, they averaged $420 billion a year, a nearly thirtyfold increase.

To put these annual flows in perspective, capital outflows were equivalent to 7 percent of world merchandise trade in the late 1970s but averaged 15 percent in the 1990s. Likewise, in 1980, cross-border transactions in stocks and bonds were equal to less than 10 percent of the gross domestic product (GDP) of all major industrial countries, whereas today they are equivalent to more than twice the GDP of the United States and Germany, and to three times the GDP of France and Canada.

In addition, recent changes in regulations and technology have made it possible for money to move across borders almost instantly, giving rise to massive, short-term international financial transactions. By 1997, for instance, the total amount outstanding of such short-financial "derivatives," including those traded both over the counter and on exchanges, was more than $40 trillion. Foreign exchange trading in the world's financial centers averaged more than $2 trillion a day, equivalent to $2 billion per minute and to a hundred times the amount of world trade each day.[1]

John B. Goodman and Louis W. Pauly (Reading 18) examine how recent changes in international financial markets have made national capital controls obsolete and produced among countries a remarkable convergence toward more liberal international financial policies. In their view, based on the predominance of international economic factors, increased capital mobility has overwhelmed the kinds of national and group differences emphasized by domestic societal scholarship.

Postwar monetary and financial affairs have given rise to both academic and political polemics. Developing countries especially have argued that the existing systems of international monetary relations and international banking work to their detriment, and they have proposed sweeping reforms. However, most developed nations believe that the current arrangements, imperfect as they may be, are the best available and that reform schemes are simply unrealistic.

Among scholars, the nature of international monetary and financial relations raises important analytical issues. As in other arenas, the very rapid development of globe-straddling international financial markets has led some to believe that the rise of supranational financial actors has eroded the power of national states. In this view, international monetary relations essentially serve increasingly to enrich global international investors and their allies in such international institutions as the International Monetary Fund (IMF). Other analysts believe that national governments are still the primary determinants of international monetary and financial trends. The specific policies of major states toward their own banks and currencies are, in this view, set in line with national interests; banks and currency movements are instruments of national policy, and not the other way around. The tension between a monetary and financial system that is, in a sense, beyond the reach of individual states and currencies and banks that clearly have home countries gives rise to a fundamental tension in world politics and in the study of the international political economy.

NOTE

. 1. These figures are from the International Monetary Fund's *Balance of Payments Yearbook and International Financial Statistics;* from the Bank for International Settlements, *Sixty-third Annual Report* (Basel: Bank for International Settlements [BIS], 1993) and *Sixty-eighth Annual Report* (Basel: BIS, 1998); and from Jeffry A. Frieden, "Invested Interests: The Politics of National Economic Policies in a World of Global Finance," *International Organization* 45, 4 (1991): 428.

13

The Domestic Politics of International Monetary Order: The Gold Standard

LAWRENCE BROZ

In the late nineteenth and early twentieth centuries, the world's principal economies were tied together by the classical gold standard. The stability of this international monetary system depended on the accommodating policies of the major financial powers. Lawrence Broz argues that these policies, in turn, rested on domestic societal foundations. He surveys the British, French, and German experiences, showing the domestic coalitional bases of support for their contributions to the operation of the gold standard.

An international monetary regime is a set of clearly defined principles, rules, and conventions that regulate and harmonize the economic policies of member nations. From the perspective of international political economy, such a regime is something of an international public good. When a sufficient number of governments commit credibly to a set of international monetary rules, the result is that goods, services, and capital can flow across borders relatively unimpeded by currency concerns, creating joint-welfare gains and promoting technical efficiency. From a perspective of comparative politics, however, a smoothly functioning monetary regime is far from a natural state of affairs. Adherence to a common set of monetary rules and conventions requires a certain degree of macroeconomic-policy cooperation among member governments, despite potentially vast differences in the domestic constraints confronting policy makers. The overriding political obstacle in the way of establishing and maintaining a multilateral commitment to a common set of exchange-rate rules is that national politicians face heterogeneous *domestic* electorates and organized constituencies, not homogenous global ones. According to this view, the paradox is not the difficulty of designing a stable international monetary regime in a world of opportunistic but like-minded national governments, but that such systems, composed of an extremely diverse group of nation-states, have ever existed, let alone operated relatively smoothly for extended periods of time.

The literature on international political economy offers several solutions. One focuses on the existence of a dominant economic power in the world economy, a "hegemon," that either unilaterally provides the international public good or leads the coordination effort that produces adherence to the rules of the game. The internal logic of the argument is simple: only a state large enough to appropriate a significant share of the benefits of producing a public good like international monetary stability would have the incentive to perform the functions necessary to assure such stability. Empirical work, however, finds this hegemonic-stability thesis a weak predictor of the level of international monetary cooperation: hegemony is associated with elements of both stability and extreme instability. Logical flaws have also been uncovered. Most problematic is the supposition that the strongest incentives and constraints that states face originate at the international level, which trivializes the role of domestic political conditions in shaping the macroeconomic choices of states. Likewise, functional theories of international regimes, which predict cooperation in the absence of hegemony, also give analytical primacy to problems of international-level collective action. Here, cooperation leading to greatly expanded joint welfare gains (assuming shared preferences) can occur in the presence of international institutions because such institutions reduce information, communication, and enforcement costs.

A final possibility . . . is that, at both the international and domestic levels, a stable regime has dynamic effects that create a kind of "virtuous circle" in support of the system. At the international level, the increased trade and investment the regime engenders encourages nations to commit to the regime by offering improvements in national economic welfare. At the domestic level, the existence of exchange-rate predictability in one part of the world economy gives internationally oriented interest groups (for instance, international banks, multinational investors and corporations, and major exporters) in as yet unaffiliated areas a stronger incentive to encourage their governments to associate with the regime. . . .

Despite obvious differences, these approaches see the essential problem as one of coordinating the behavior of national governments who have, in one way or another, come to regard a certain exchange-rate regime as a common national objective. That is, regardless of the processes by which international monetary regimes are created and maintained, these perspectives treat all members of a regime as having homogenous preferences in regard to currency issues. As a result, the analytical problem becomes how a group of like-minded national governments resolve the international collective-action problems (for instance, free riding, ex-post opportunism) that normally constrain the production of international public goods to suboptimal levels.

The approach of this chapter turns the public-goods puzzle "outside-in." The underlying premise that all parties to an exchange-rate regime share the same objectives in the same order of priority is treated as problematic. This supposition is grounded in the logic of comparative political economy: that the preferences and constraints influencing policy formation diverge markedly across countries. Nations differ in their political, economic, and institutional characteristics, and these differences make it highly improbable that national policy preferences will converge sufficiently to make international agreements on currency values simply a matter of establishing credible commitments and effective enforcement mechanisms to prevent defections of the "beggar-thy-neighbor" sort.

The argument advanced in this chapter allows for the possibility of stable international monetary regimes in conjunction with *heterogeneous* national policy preferences. Participants of a regime can have different — even conflicting — national preferences on exchange-rate policy if regime stability entails a *specialization of tasks* among members of the system, whereby members of different preference and power perform different regime-stabilizing functions. The analytical point of departure is still [the] extension of public-goods theory to the international arena. However, there is no theoretical reason requiring any one nation-state to provide all of these functions. Instead a division of responsibility may arise due to *asymmetries of interest* among states (which is a function of domestic politics) regarding the importance of these goods, and due to *asymmetries of power* among states (which is a function of the relative international positions of nation-states) in the global system.

The place to begin is with comparative politics. Nations differ with respect to their social, economic, and political characteristics; so we can expect that they will attach different values to the fundamental trade-offs entailed in adhering to alternative international monetary regimes. The primary efficiency advantage of stable exchange rates is that international trade and investment can be conducted with minimal risk of capital losses due to currency fluctuations. The well-known trade-off is that stable (fixed) exchange rates require the subordination of domestic monetary policy to currency and balance-of-payments considerations. . . . [A]ctors deeply involved in international trade and payments (export-oriented producers of tradable goods, international merchants, global investors) favor stability in exchange rates, while actors whose economic activity is confined primarily to the domestic economy (import-competing producers of tradable goods, producers of non-tradables) favor the domestic-monetary flexibility that comes with variable exchange rates. From this base it is a relatively small step to move to the comparative level: the dissimilar composition of nations in terms of their "production profiles" suggests the likelihood of *uncommon* national objectives with respect to the issue of exchange-rate variability.

The fundamental point is that national governments pursue international monetary policies for domestic political reasons having to do with the policy interests of important social groups and coalitions. But the processes of policy formation cannot be considered in a national vacuum. Exchange rates are, after all, relational. More importantly, the actions of at least the major states in the system inevitably affect the international monetary system, and thus their own domestic economies. As a result, analysis must also consider how the policy choices of major states affect the operation and stability of the international monetary system and, in so doing, feed back upon the domestic processes of exchange rate policy making.

Domestic groups and coalitions lobby government because they know that policy has direct effects on their welfare through its national impact. Domestic groups and coalitions in major "price-maker" countries, however, are also aware that government policy has indirect effects on their welfare by way of its impact on the international monetary order. Awareness of this second-order international impact suggests that groups and coalitions at least partially internalize the international externalities of their governments' actions. Full internalization does not occur because groups in other countries absorb some of the benefits or bear some of the costs of the externalities as well. And because *the international spillovers of domestic policy choices may be positive as well as negative,* a stable international monetary regime can exist even when the preferences of major states vary widely.

In essence, this is the "joint product" model applied to the workings of international monetary systems. States produce and consume two goods: a private good (happiness of the domestic dominant coalition) and a public good (international monetary stability). As long as the production of joint products involves a supply technology in which the private outputs cannot feasibly be separated from the associated collective outputs, then a convergence can arise between the private (national) and social (international) costs of public goods provision. Hence, for states large enough in economic terms to produce systemic effects, there can be incentives to absorb the overall costs of producing systemic benefits, if the private goods they seek cannot be produced without generating the associated public goods. Nevertheless, it is the excludable private benefits that drive the micro-processes of international monetary order: domestic politics are primary, while the international consequences of domestic policy choices are viewed largely as by-products. . . .

Consider the following example. There are two major nation-states in the world, state A and state B. State A prefers stable currency while state B is inclined toward domestic monetary independence. These heterogeneous preferences reflect differences in domestic political situations: the dominant political coalition in state A prefers that its government maintain stable currency over competing macroeconomic goals; the dominant coalition in state B prefers domestic macro-economic policy flexibility over stable currency values. If we assume that state A is a large state in global economic terms, its preference for stable currency can be expected to have important and beneficial global spillovers: its strong commit-ment to sound money means, for example, that its national currency is well posi-tioned to serve internationally as a medium of exchange and a reliable store of value. State B, however, can also be expected to take on a system-sustaining role — if only as a means of advancing its preference for domestic macroeco-nomic autonomy. Because disruptions to the flow of capital in the international economy can threaten state B's domestically oriented macroeconomic agenda (including, for instance, stable interest rates, a steady rate of economic growth, low unemployment), state B may find it advantageous to play a stabilizing role alongside state A — by acting as the system's emergency source of liquidity, for example. Since its dominant preference is to remain as free as possible to run the domestic macroeconomic policies it chooses, undertaking the role of systemic lender of last resort can serve this end by forestalling sudden and destabilizing capital flows. A *division of labor* results in the provision of the regime's sustaining functions: state A provides the international system with a key currency while state B serves as the system's lender of last resort. In both cases these are the pos-itive international externalities of disunited, domestically determined preferences. They are externalities because the governments that actually run system-sustaining policies have no special desire to help stabilize the international system. Instead, governments are driven by domestic imperatives, to satisfy the dominant coalition. The result is a state of international relations in which unilateral actions taken for domestic reasons generate positive spillover effects for other nations.

This argument suggests that a stable international monetary order need not require implicit or explicit agreement among member states about the characteristics and requirements of membership; policy divergence and systemic stability are not logically incompatible. Nor is it necessary that a hegemon exist to provide the requisite stabilizing functions. While stability does seem to require the existence of the equilibrating functions identified by Kindleberger, member states can have divergent objectives if the international externalities of their national-policy choices are strongly positive. International stability does not mean that all states adopt identical policies, but policies that through their external effects largely complement or offset one another.

This chapter, in short, addresses the paradox of how international public goods are provided when countries are allowed to have different or conflicting policy preferences. Just as a true application of collective-goods theory undermines the hegemonic-stability thesis — privileged groups need not be limited to a single state — so, too, does the logic of the positive-externalities framework. The logic that says international economic stability results when countries with homogenous preferences solve the free-rider problem is undone when heterogeneity of preferences is allowed to enhance the probability of stability. In its place comes the logic of international stability derived from the sum of the (positive) externalities produced by major states advancing their *uncommon,* national interests. . . . [T]he systemic characteristic of stability can be the consequence of the individual actions of major states, taken for domestic political reasons. Thus international stability can arise even if national preferences vary significantly and even if no dominant stabilizer sets out to produce this result, if the externalities of individual state behavior are allowed to be positive as well as negative.

The following section applies this logic to the archetypal case of international monetary order: the era of the classical gold standard. The evidence supports two main predictions. First, the degree to which individual nations accepted the principles of the gold standard varied dramatically. These differences, in turn, are shown to have resulted from the fact that members did not share the same political and economic objectives — a function of distinct domestic socioeconomic conditions. The comparative portion of this chapter is devoted to identifying the monetary preferences of major states in the system — Great Britain, France, Germany after unification — and linking these policy preferences to each nation's unique social, economic, and political structures. Second, the evidence conforms to the expectation that the pursuit of national interests can have beneficial global spillovers; that nations pushing their self-interests can have strongly positive externalities that facilitate the production of international public goods. Here, the focus is on the global effects of each nation's policy choices. Overall the evidence supports the dual claims that national (individual) as opposed to international (collective) interests motivated state behavior during the era of the gold standard and that the global result was a fixed exchange-rate regime that operated smoothly for several decades. This chapter's conclusion summarizes the findings and briefly extends the argument to the Bretton Woods system and the European Monetary System.

THE CLASSICAL GOLD STANDARD

Like other international monetary orders, an international gold standard is supposed to consist of a group of sovereign countries bound together by a common commitment to certain fundamental *principles* of monetary organization and *rules* of monetary behavior. In a true gold standard, there are two basic principles. First, a country must commit its monetary authorities to freely exchange (buy and sell) the domestic currency for gold at a fixed rate without limitation or condition. Second, monetary officials must pledge to allow residents and nonresidents the absolute freedom to export and import gold in whatever quantities they desire. When a group of countries bind themselves to the first principle, fixed exchange rates are established; when they commit to respect the free flow of gold, a pure fixed-exchange-rate mechanism of balance-of-payments adjustment comes into being. Thus a stylized international gold standard is a system of states linked together by two general monetary principles (to uphold the gold convertibility of their national currencies at par; to allow gold to cross national borders unimpeded) and two basic rules of behavior governing international monetary policy (to deflate in the event of a gold drain; to inflate in the event of an inflow). As an economic model, this describes an efficient, self-sustaining system for reducing the transactions costs of international exchange and investment and providing a nearly automatic mechanism for reconciling international imbalances. As an approximation of late nineteenth- and early twentieth-century reality, however, the model is quite inappropriate.

As the following comparison will illustrate, there were sharp national differences in the degree to which countries maintained a commitment to the underlying principles and operational rules of the gold standard. Among the European countries, England stayed most consistently on the gold standard, meaning both that the pound sterling was convertible into gold on demand at the legally defined rate and that individuals had complete freedom to export or import gold. On the continent, in contrast, free and unlimited convertibility was by no means guaranteed, especially if gold was sought for export purposes, and monetary officials often placed administrative barriers on the free flow of gold. As for the rules of the game, the received wisdom today is that all gold-standard countries engaged at times in practices that were in "violation" of the regime's rules. Although this conclusion is certainly valid in general, it masks significant national differences.

Great Britain paid only occasional attention to internal conditions while on the continent internal targets loomed much larger. In England, discount-rate policy was the main instrument of international monetary policy, and the Bank of England looked to the size of its gold reserve in setting its discount rate. Because its reserve ratio was affected primarily by movements of gold, the Bank's operating principle was that a reduction in its reserve due to a foreign drain was to be met with a hike in "Bank Rate" — a policy that implied acceptance to at least half of the gold standard's rules. At no time did the Bank of England hold its discount rate steady in the face of a serious foreign drain. The same cannot be said of the continental central banks, which relied far less extensively on discount-rate policy as the basis for their international monetary policies. To avoid the internal consequences of gold losses or frequent variations in interest rates, the central banks developed other techniques for dealing with gold drains. Although no country perfectly subordinated considerations of internal balance to external balance, England came the closest to this principle.

Yet in spite of such national differences, the international gold standard functioned smoothly for several decades. This paradox is explained by the positive systemic externalities that the major countries' policies produced. On the one hand, England's stronger commitment to gold-standard orthodoxy gave the world a medium of exchange and a store of value of unquestioned credibility. No other currency could match sterling's supremacy as a medium for reserves and transactions, so long as gold convertibility and free gold movements were conditional elsewhere. As a result the world was provided with a currency eminently suitable for international transaction and reserve purposes — one of the necessary system-sustaining functions identified by Kindleberger. On the other hand, France (and to a lesser extent Germany) came to provide the system with lender-of-last-resort facilities for balance-of-payments financing by reason of the dominant sociopolitical interest the French had in limiting the extent to which external economic forces restricted domestic macroeconomic flexibility. In order to maintain domestic macroeconomic flexibility, France built up a very large gold reserve and made it a point of policy to lend abroad from this fund to stem speculative pressures against the franc. The goal was to prevent large and sudden movements of reserves and gold from undermining domestic macroeconomic goals. Together, the nationally based and self-interested policies of Great Britain and France meshed compatibly to provide the public goods . . . the international monetary system needed for smooth operation. England alone did not manage the gold standard. Instead, management was a collective endeavor that derived from differences in national preferences. These differences in turn were rooted in the domestic political economies of the major states.

DOMESTIC SOURCES OF ENGLAND'S GOLD STANDARD POLICIES

It was during the first decades of the nineteenth century that a powerful circle of societal interests — land, the City's merchant banks and acceptance houses, and creditors of the government — congealed in England around the internationalist and deflationary monetary framework of the gold standard. The coalition demonstrated its political power by institutionalizing the gold standard first in Peel's Act of 1819 and then more strongly in the Bank Charter Act of 1844. In the second half of the century, the financial sector reaped the international advantages of the country's domestic monetary arrangements. On the strength of the commitment to gold, London flourished as a worldwide financial center, and sterling became the premier international currency. This commitment ensured sterling's place in the international financial system and thereby generated rents for the banking sector; it also brought to the international system a medium of reserve and payment of unquestioned reliability — a systemic public good.

The Napoleonic Wars set the stage for the formal institutionalization of the gold standard in England, which was suspended due to the war effort from 1797 to 1821. Suspension brought inflation and the depreciation of sterling against other currencies, which had distinct and predictable effects: a redistribution of wealth from *all* creditors and producers of nontradable goods to *all* debtors and producers of tradables. By violating the contract to redeem notes on demand for a fixed weight of gold, suspension usurped the property rights of all persons whose wealth consisted of money (creditors). In addition, depreciation worked to the advantage of tradables producers by raising the prices of traded goods relative to nontradables. This redistribution set the stage for a broad, intersectoral battle over the terms of the postwar monetary settlement.

The key beneficiaries of suspension — and hence the advocates of "soft money" rules — were farmers and manufacturers. Tenant farmers in particular found strong incentives to support the existing state of monetary affairs. . . . The price of wheat, for example, jumped from 6s. 9d. per bushel in 1797 to 16s. in 1800, while rents on agricultural land remained fixed at pre-inflation levels by long-term leases. . . . Debtors of all classes gained by the long period of suspension as they made interest and principal payments in a currency worth about 17 percent less in gold than when their debts were contracted.

In addition, the monetary attitude of manufacturers and industrial labor tended to correspond with that of the farmer, as industrial demand, prices, and wages all rose as a result of the depreciation of sterling and the general stimulus of war. The expansion, however, brought habits attuned to price, profit, and wage levels that were difficult to sustain after the final defeat of Napoleon. With war's end, demand dropped off, import competition increased (as blockades were lifted), and prices dropped dramatically. Domestic manufacturers, represented most vocally by organized Birmingham industrialists, sided with farmers in seeking monetary relief from the deflation/appreciation. . . . The coalition's anti-gold-standard platform alternatively called for the continuation of suspension, or a return to gold convertibility at a rate substantially lower than the pre-war level. . . .

In contrast to the views of farmers and manufacturers, depreciation was injurious to England's powerful creditor, rentier, and saver groups, who coalesced around the gold standard. . . . The position of the landed aristocracy is instructive. From the late seventeenth century on, this group built larger and larger estates and rented their acres to tenant farmers in larger units on long leases. . . . During the inflationary war years, landlords found that they were receiving only about two-thirds of their rent in real terms. Unable to raise rents in line with the upward trend in commodity prices, rentier lords became strong supporters of deflation and an early return to the gold standard. In this they found ready allies in the rapidly internationalizing financial sector.

London emerged from the Napoleonic Wars as the greatest financial center in the world. Just as World War I helped shift the locus of world finance from London to New York, the years of war from 1793 to 1815 helped cement London's position by disrupting established patterns of continental finance, especially those based in Amsterdam. Émigré financiers, fleeing the tide of Napoleon's invasions and attracted by England's political stability and the prospect of financing the country's burgeoning worldwide trading relations, played a key role in this transition. Nathan Rothschild, for example, arrived in London in 1798 and the Dutch banking house of Hope and Company set up shop in the City and strengthened its ties to Baring Brothers during the war period.

The wars acted as a major stimulus to the international lending activities of these bankers. In the area of short-term foreign lending, the wars displaced Dutch participation in not only British trade credits but also in the financial arrangements behind a large and growing body of trade transactions between other countries. As a result, foreign traders, already familiar with the names and reputations of the international banking houses that had recently settled in London, began to look to these institutions for facilities to effect the international transmission of remittances.

The internationalization of the London money market was paralleled by similar developments in the London capital market. In fact, several of the same private banks that financed bilateral and multilateral trade became the channel through which foreign governments and other large borrowers approached the British capital market. By virtue of their extensive foreign connections and their knowledge of the mercantile world gained in the course of financing trade, these firms were well placed for the handling of loans to foreign governments and corporations.

The depreciation and general instability of sterling during the period of suspended gold payments constrained the foreign expansion of British finance. The City's international short-term lending business in its nascent form was harmed in two ways. First, and most obviously, instability in the exchange rate posed the risk of exchange losses to bankers long accustomed to fixed exchange rates. With the prospect of debt repayment in depreciated currency, the banks and acceptance houses involved in financing trade had strong reasons for advocating a return to the gold standard before they extended their external activities. Second, foreigners who received payment for their goods in sterling bills or held sterling assets as working balances had to be confident in the stability of the pound because they too could suffer losses from exchange instability. Indeed, for sterling to gain usage internationally as a secure means of financing trade and making payments, and for the London financial community to earn the "denomination rents" that accrue specifically to the banking sector of nations whose currency serves as international currency, foreigners had to have complete confidence in sterling's gold value. If nonresidents were to utilize sterling as an international medium of exchange and as a reserve asset, England had to produce a protracted record of low inflation and inflation variability, which in turn depended upon stable and consistent government policies, particularly monetary policy. For Britain's international banking firms, the key to sterling's status as a global currency, and the key to London's position at the hub of short-term international finance, was gold convertibility.

International investment banking operations also depended, but to a lesser degree, upon the restoration of monetary predictability. Since the fall in the value of sterling meant losses for holders of long-term foreign securities that bore a fixed rate of interest, private bankers supported the return to the gold standard. Their objective was to distribute foreign securities to English savers; the reduction of exchange risk would facilitate the sale of issues contracted in sterling.

The international segment of the financial sector was joined in its quest for sound currency by a powerful new economic group that emerged as a result of the wars. This group was composed of the owners of British government bonds (Consols) that had been issued in vast quantities to finance the wars at a time of high prices and interest rates. There were roughly 17,000 of these "fundholders." . . . Depreciation was decidedly costly to the fundholders, because it reduced the purchasing power of the Consols' dividends and, through the rise in interest rates, reduced their capital value as well. If the inflationary trend could be reversed, the fundholders — who had bought into the national debt with depreciated currency — would receive repayment in a currency with much greater purchasing power. In effect, deflation — the requisite of the return to gold payments — would produce a large bonus for fundholders as the real value of the war loans and interest payments rose. Indeed, interest on the war debt came to absorb over half the government's total revenue by 1827, redistributing wealth from taxpayers to investors.

The gold standard thus had a formidable political constituency behind it. It was supported by the established center of wealth and power in England (the landed aristocracy) and the economy's most dynamic advancing sectors (international banking and finance). With the addition of the country's "first investing public" (the fundholders) it is not surprising that England returned to gold at the prewar parity as soon as the war emergency permitted. . . .

INTERNATIONAL EFFECTS OF ENGLAND'S MONETARY PRIORITIES

An important international consequence of England's early and unfaltering commitment to the principles of the gold standard was the full globalization of the London money market. The immutable commitment to pay in gold and to let market forces determine gold flows meant that sterling was as "good as gold" for all international purposes. Systemic factors, in turn, provided the demand for sterling facilities. England's position as the world greatest trading nation meant that foreigners were continually earning incomes in Britain or in countries making payments there, and also continually making payments to Britain or to countries earning incomes there. Sterling was thus attractive both as a unit of account and as a medium of international exchange, and London was positioned to serve as the world's great settling center for commercial contracts — huge sterling balances were built up in a system committed to the gold convertibility of sterling. In addition, England's head start in industrialization combined with the policy of free trade to generate a huge stock of wealth and savings available for loan and investment abroad. With the gold standard firmly in place English bankers, financiers, and investors were no longer deterred by the possibility that unfavorable exchange rate movements might cut deeply into profits. The great expansion in foreign short- and long-term lending that followed further internationalized the London money market. With London operating both as the "clearinghouse" for the world's commodity and product markets and as its primary source of capital, foreigners were obliged to keep working balances in London to meet their short-term obligations and to service British overseas portfolio investments. Finally, Britain's pledge of convertibility at a fixed rate and on unqualified terms meant that sterling was also a secure store of value. This led not just foreign individuals and banks to make short-term investments in London but foreign governments and central banks themselves to hold reserves in sterling assets and bank deposits. In short, the English commitment to the gold standard served as the primary institutional underpinning of sterling's central position in the world economy. . . .

England thus provided the world with a currency eminently suitable for international purposes — an international public good. However, to attribute other system-sustaining functions to Britain, as the international political economy literature frequently does, misinterprets the facts. First, the Bank of England definitely did not serve as the classical gold standard's lender of last resort. . . . The real "hegemon" in regard to this function was the Bank of France, as discussed below. Second, there is scant evidence confirming the view that England consciously managed the international monetary system in non-crises times, with an eye toward coordinating national macroeconomic policies so as to mitigate global inflation and business cycles. . . .

. . . [W]hile other aspects of British "hegemony" remain in doubt, the international public good that English policy *unambiguously* provided was a currency appropriate for international use. Sterling was acceptable as a private and official international money because it was convertible into gold upon demand. British authorities attached clear priority to the defense of gold convertibility and demonstrated this commitment repeatedly in the face of adverse domestic conditions. The London financial market, in turn, possessed the necessary characteristics of breadth, depth, and resilience that ensured nonresidents of the liquidity of the working balances they held there. This commitment to gold reflected the enduring dominance of the gold standard coalition: the alliance of the City of London, landlords, bondholders, and international-competitive industry. When gold flowed out or in, the Bank of England took actions on interest rates consistent with the coalition members' interest in maintaining the gold value of the currency, whether or not these actions accorded with the needs of the domestic economy. Domestic economic activity — and all those interests that were tied to it — were thus subject to frequent variations in interest rates. To internationalists and creditors, it was simply more essential that the value of the currency remain constant in terms of foreign currencies than that the Bank rate and general interest rates remain stationary and/or low.

The victory of gold at home produced a monetary orientation that was beneficial to the functioning of the international gold standard. But this public good of a key currency was not provided by Britain out of conscious concern for sustaining the international economic order. Instead, it was a spillover — a positive externality — of Britain's individual preference for monetary orthodoxy in a world in which Britain was the most powerful financial and trading nation. The externality was partially internalized, however. As City bankers and acceptance houses earned rents from the increasing internationalization of sterling, the intensity of their preference for orthodoxy increased. Nevertheless, the English preference for monetary orthodoxy reflected the hierarchy of social interests *within* Britain. That the Bank of England's policies had beneficial global effects was a by-product of this structure and of the central position of London in the global system.

The political conditions that produced this spillover were for the most part evident only in England. In other countries, deflationist and internationalist groups were generally weaker than their domestically oriented rivals, and this was reflected in monetary institutions and practices. The commitment to the gold standard's principles and rules was far more conditional and uncertain on the continent than in England. In France, our next case, the tendency to insulate the domestic economy from external influences resulted primarily from the inward orientation of land, industry, and banking but came at the expense of Paris's role as an international financial center. Yet ironically, by reason of its predominant interest in domestic objectives, France came to act globally as the system's lender of last resort during the relatively infrequent emergencies that arose, thus providing the gold-standard regime with another of its stabilizing functions.

FRENCH DOMESTIC AND INTERNATIONAL MONETARY POLICY

Nominally, France maintained a bimetallic standard throughout the nineteenth century, but silver constituted the greater part of the coinage before 1850. The Bank of France usually cashed its notes in silver; when gold coin was wanted for export in bulk, it generally commanded a premium. In the early 1870s, when a glut of silver on world markets threatened to drive gold entirely from circulation, France and the other bimetallic countries of the Latin Monetary Union responded by suspending the free coinage of silver. The French, however, did not adopt a full gold standard. Instead, from 1878 until 1914, they operated a "limping gold standard," which gave monetary authorities greater flexibility in accommodating external pressures to domestic macroeconomic priorities. The convertibility of banknotes into gold was not guaranteed by law but was left to the central bank's discretion: in effect, capital controls were imposed in order to maintain monetary sovereignty.

Under the limping standard the Bank of France could legally redeem its notes in either French gold coin or in five-franc silver pieces at its own discretion. Having the right to make any payments in silver rather than in gold, the Bank could protect its gold reserve from the pressure of foreign drains. In practice, whenever the Bank wished to limit gold exports, it refused to redeem its notes in gold at the mint par rate of exchange and developed the policy of making gold payments at a premium. In other words, instead of refusing to maintain the gold convertibility of the franc, the Bank elected to charge a premium for gold — a mini-devaluation — to check external drains.

. . . While the policy had the effect of discouraging gold exports, its main disadvantage was that it impaired the credibility of the French gold standard and thereby limited the expansion of French international banking and the development of the franc as an international currency.

Indeed, the Bank of France's occasional insistence on attaching a premium to redemption of its notes in gold meant a virtual abandonment of the gold standard.

The uncertainty surrounding redemption of the currency in gold at the legal parity made foreigners less eager to utilize franc exchange for international purposes or to buy bills of exchange or securities issued in francs. As long as the policy was in practice, therefore, Paris could never challenge London's position. . . .

The policy also affected the reserve-currency role of the franc. The Reichsbank and the Austro-Hungarian Bank, for example, both held large portfolios of foreign bills yet had few bills drawn on Paris because of the uncertainty of obtaining gold there. Only Russia held substantial franc assets. These holdings, however, were not based on the calculation that the franc was absolutely secure. Instead, they were closely linked to Russian access to the French capital market: the Russian State Bank, in order to insure continued access to long-term loans, kept large sums on deposit in the French banks that distributed Russian bonds to French investors. Without the connection between the deposits and long-term loans — and the special economic and political relationships between France and Russia — it is unlikely that the Russian central bank would have preferred francs as the basis of its foreign currency reserves.

After 1900, the Bank of France began to lessen its dependence on the gold premium policy. To do so, it began to accumulate and hold a much larger gold reserve so that even a substantial drain could be accommodated without threatening gold convertibility. By 1900, the bank had amassed a gold reserve of $409 million. By 1908 the figure had increased to $593 million, well over three times the reserve held by the Bank of England. The Bank of England could maintain convertibility on such a "thin film of gold" by the adroit manipulation of interest rates; the French preference was to keep interest rates low and stable by amassing a reserve large enough to accommodate even severe foreign drains. . . .

The result of this policy (and the occasional use of the gold premium policy) was that the Bank of France was able to keep its discount rate extraordinarily stable, in line with the nation's preference for domestic monetary independence. While the Bank of England changed its discount rate about six times per year on average between 1880 and 1913, it was not uncommon for the Bank of France to go for stretches of five years or more without a change from its traditional 3 percent rate. . . .

INTERNATIONAL EFFECTS OF FRENCH MONETARY PRIORITIES

The Bank of France also had another weapon in its arsenal to defend against the contractionary effects of gold outflows and discount-rate hikes. The policy was to come to the aid of foreign countries — especially England — experiencing financial distress in order to prevent the crises from reverberating back upon France. In effect, the Bank of France used its huge gold reserves as an instrument of international stabilization. When some major disturbance caused the Bank of England to contemplate imposing an especially high rate of discount, the Bank of France released gold to England, typically by discounting sterling bills. By lending the Bank of England a portion of its gold reserves, the Bank of France helped alleviate the pressures that threatened to force the Bank of England to raise its discount rate to higher levels. Because a crisis in London necessarily produced a backlash in France in the form of gold outflows, coming to the assistance of the Bank of England allowed the Bank of France to maintain a more stable structure of domestic interest rates.

France's role as lender of last resort to England can be credited with relieving the most severe crises of the era (the Barings Crisis of 1890; the American crises of 1906 and 1907). The picture of the classical gold standard as managed by the Bank of England alone is thus far from complete. In fact, it was Bank of France officials who thought of themselves as the "monetary physicians of the world," and allocating a portion of the Bank's immense gold holdings anywhere it was needed became an explicit component of French monetary policy. It is important to stress that there was nothing cosmopolitan about this policy. The goal was always to prevent foreign crises from destabilizing the French economy and forcing an upward adjustment in interest rates. . . .

The Bank of England, often regaled as the "manager" of the classical gold standard, never made such bold statements of its international role nor consciously acted in ways consistent with the role. In fact, the Bank of England was so dependent on the French bank in times of crisis that the latter became known as the Bank of England's "second gold reserve." It is therefore difficult to substantiate the view that attributes the durability of the classical gold standard to management by a single financial center. If the Bank of England served to protect the value of sterling so essential to its role as international money, in periods of extraordinary stress, France was the international lender of last resort.

The French commitment to protect the domestic market from foreign influences was also reflected in its longer and more avid use of "gold devices." Before 1900, the Bank of France frequently charged more for gold bars or foreign gold coins to discourage the export of gold in these forms. It was also quite common for the bank to induce gold imports by raising its purchase price for gold bullion above the mint rate. In later years the same policy of buying gold at a loss was pursued from time to time with the essential purpose of imposing upon the Bank the costs of protecting convertibility instead of imposing them upon the business community by an advance in the rate of discount. Lastly, the Bank also regularly granted interest-free advances to gold importers and on occasion bought gold at its border branches to reduce shipping and insurance fees.

Taken as a whole, French monetary institutions and policies were far less consistent with the principles and operational rules of the gold standard than England's. Indeed, even considering France a gold-standard country stretches the definition of the concept because the central bank's commitment to redeem its notes in gold was always conditional and discretionary, and the market for gold was in no sense free. Moreover, since the Bank used an array of methods to avoid adjusting domestic macroeconomic conditions in line with gold flows — which, of course, eliminated any positive equilibrating role for monetary policy — it avoided playing by the rules of the game. In contrast to England, the French monetary system was designed and operated to insulate the domestic economy as much as possible from external pressures. Domestic targets took precedence over international ones, and one important consequence of this was that Paris could not develop as an international money market. However, regarding the stability of the international gold standard, the French practice of assisting Britain in time of crisis certainly played a role. These actions as lender of last resort were not based on the desire to provide the system with this public good but to insulate the French economy from the untoward effects of British policies, to which it was vulnerable.

DOMESTIC POLITICS OF FRENCH MONETARY POLICY

The political sources of French monetary institutions and policies were deeply ingrained in the structure of French society. Unlike England, France did not develop an alliance of land, finance and bondholder in favor of gold-standard orthodoxy. Although these groups played a crucial role in the formation of the country's monetary institutions and policies, their specific situations vis-à-vis the domestic and international economies produced monetary outlooks that were quite different from those of their English counterparts. The French landed sector is a case in point.

In terms of land tenure, one of the consequences of the revolutionary period in France was that there was no precise equivalent of the English landed aristocracy. In contrast to the British landlord, who made his living by renting his land on long leases to tenant farmers, land was widely distributed in France and worked in small, inefficient units by owner-operators for subsistence needs or for the domestic market. This fundamental difference in land-tenure systems was of considerable importance to national monetary preferences. Whereas the small group of well-placed English landlords sought stable or falling prices to preserve the purchasing power of their rental incomes, the multitudes of small farmers in France preferred rising prices for their crops. For this reason, land was consistently in the nationalist camp in France, seeking a policy to insulate the domestic economy from the deflationary aspects of the gold standard. Moreover, the landed sector was politically powerful in France but for a reason different from that in England. While English lords could obtain a favorable hearing by virtue of their positions in Parliament, the rural constituencies in France were empowered by revolutionary era political structures that gave effective voice to their numbers.

The structure of French industry also tended to mitigate against the development of a strong pro-gold lobby among manufacturers. Staple French exports (other than wines and spirits) were mainly the manufactured textile specialties of silk, wool, or cotton usually produced in traditional small workshops and sold in the high-income urban areas of the world. These were not the inexpensive, standardized goods produced for mass foreign markets, such as those in which the British excelled. Even the most modern sectors of French industry (iron and steel, for example) were not competitive on world markets. Overall, exports played a much smaller role in industrial activity than in England. As a consequence, France did not possess a strong segment of the manufacturing class that stood behind a gold standard and fixed-exchange-rate regime. . . .

Without a powerful rentier landed elite and an externally oriented manufacturing segment to support it, the fate of the gold standard rested upon the position and influence of the French financial community. French finance, however, developed along lines quite distinct from the trajectory in Britain and, consequently, there were few enthusiasts among its ranks for committing to a full gold standard. . . .

French finance was primarily a domestic business until the final third of the nineteenth century, when foreign-portfolio lending blossomed under the encouragement and political guidance of the state. Other than its role in distributing foreign bonds to small investors — who were protected from the vagaries of the limping standard by gold clauses in the loan contracts — French finance was decidedly parochial. The market for foreign short loans was limited, the international significance of the Paris money market small, and the use of the franc as a reserve currency largely confined to Russia for political reasons. In short, there was little internationalization to give money-market participants an interest in encouraging a stronger commitment to the gold standard. Without a key-currency position comparable to sterling and lacking an overwhelming stake in international finance, the banking sector realized no significant benefit in striving for gold-standard orthodoxy. Their business consisted in discounting domestic bills for French firms and merchants, a business that benefited from the French bank's low and non-fluctuating interest rate. For this reason, there were few calls from the financial sector for altering the existing state of affairs along British lines.

In summary, political conditions within France precluded the development of solid gold standard institutions. The prevalence of small holding gave agriculture a decidedly "easy money" orientation. The relative underdevelopment of industry left few manufacturing firms competitive enough to encourage or endure the harshness of British-style adjustment mechanisms. Finance, despite its substantial involvement in distributing foreign bonds, remained domestically bound in terms of the money market and showed little interest in pursuing the short-term international business dominated by English firms. Instead, all three sectors preferred to devote their political energies to keeping the structure of domestic interest rates stable and low, even if that put at risk confidence in the franc. Nevertheless, France came to play a crucial role in stabilizing the gold standard. Its lender-of-last-resort policies, however, were first and foremost attempts to advance national as opposed to international objectives. Though Germany did not share the obsession with interest rate stability, monetary authorities there were nearly as reticent to allow a free market in gold and to maintain gold convertibility under all conditions. As with Paris, Berlin's international standing suffered, but Germany also stood in as lender of last resort for the global economy in times of distress.

GERMAN DOMESTIC AND INTERNATIONAL MONETARY POLICY

Although the German case differs from the French in terms of monetary institutions and policy choices, there was one important similarity: at no time after the formal adoption of the gold standard in 1873 did German monetary authorities fully adhere to the principles of the gold standard. As in France, the monetary standard was jeopardized for domestic political reasons.

In 1871, one of the most pressing issues facing the newly established German Empire was monetary reform. The nascent political union needed a common coinage sufficient for national circulation. The silver standard was no longer considered advantageous as Germany's major trading partners in Eastern Europe (Russia and Austria-Hungary) had been forced by inflation off silver onto inconvertible paper. With the help of the large gold indemnity paid by France for losing the Franco-Prussian War, Germany was able to adopt the gold standard in 1873. The gold mark became the new monetary unit, and the free and unlimited coinage of silver was discontinued.

Formally, the new German standard was not a limping standard of the French variety but a full gold standard along textbook lines. In practice, however, the gold convertibility of the mark was not automatic but discretionary, and the German gold market was frequently subject to official manipulation. As in France, monetary policy was geared to restrict convertibility and gold flows whenever the well-being of the domestic economy was threatened.

Although Reichsbank officials claimed that discount-rate policy was their primary tool for increasing or protecting the gold reserve, they employed several other techniques that were outside the norms of the gold standard. Several of these were of the "gold device" variety. For example, when the Reichsbank wanted to draw gold to Germany, it often paid a premium or granted interest-free loans to importers, a policy that was given unqualified praise by German bankers and economists. To discourage gold drains, the Reichsbank also offered foreign coin for export that was as light as legally possible.

The Reichsbank also added some new twists to the manipulation of the gold market. For example, it sometimes made use of the option to redeem its notes only at its head office in Berlin rather than at its branches near the borders, with the effect that the gold export point could be raised minutely. That is, by forcing the exporter to pay the added freight and insurance costs of sending gold from Berlin to the port, the Bank initiated a small advance in the gold export point. Though small, the action could influence the foreign exchanges in Germany's favor. In addition, the Reichsbank developed what was perhaps its most powerful weapon to restrict convertibility and undesirable gold movements — a policy of quiet, yet effective, "moral suasion."

To prevent bankers from exporting gold at times when it was profitable to do so, the Reichsbank let it be known that it would look with disfavor upon gold taken for export. . . . German monetary authorities never codified or openly admitted this subtle policy; yet money-market participants understood the policy very well. It was effective in stemming foreign drains because bankers dared not risk the vengeance of the Reichsbank; to do so could mean years of discrimination or worse — the outright loss of privileges with the central bank. . . .

As a consequence of its reluctance to allow a free market in gold, international bills of exchange drawn in the German market did not have the same definite gold value as those drawn in London, and this uncertainty limited Berlin's role as an international center. . . .

What political forces steered Germany away from monetary orthodoxy? On the surface, this is a perplexing question because major segments of German industry and finance, lifted by their stunning successes in international markets after 1890, would have benefited from currency stability and ready gold convertibility. Yet German monetary policy remained focused on internal targets. The paradox is explained by the opposition and political power of Prussian landowners, the Junkers.

Banking and industry developed in Germany quite differently from how they developed in Britain. British banks had few connections with industry (which tended to be self-financed) and thus developed a completely different orientation to the international economy. Rising to prominence financing international trade, foreign governments, and overseas infrastructure, British banks championed monetary internationalism in opposition to the nationalism of the fading manufacturing sector. In Germany, however, the interests of industry and finance tended to move together because there were strong and durable links between the two sectors. German joint-stock banks were originally established to provide manufacturing with the large amounts of long-term capital it needed to initiate and sustain "late" development. Indeed, the four "D-Banks" (Deutsche Bank, Disconto-Gesellschaft, Dresdener Bank, and Darmsteder Bank) provided much of the capital, entrepreneurship, and management of the German industrial revolution. The relevant point is that these interrelations made the banks vitally concerned with the well-being of their industrial progeny. As German industry sought export markets, German banks aggressively established branches abroad to provide foreign purchasers of German goods with short-term financing and floated foreign bonds in Germany that stood to improve the market position of German businesses. Yet despite the growing internationalism of German industry, banking, and finance, monetary policy remained geared toward the needs of the domestic economy.

Part of the explanation is that the Berlin money market, like the Paris market, was still far less dependent on the confidence of foreigners than the London market. The bread and butter of German banking was channeling funds to industry, not issuing, accepting, and discounting international bills of exchange. The interests of German bankers were, thus, not as tied up with the willingness of foreign bankers, traders, and investors to deal in the home currency and in the national money market as they were in London. Since maintaining international confidence in the currency could require restrictive monetary policy inimical to industry, German banks were at best tepid supporters of gold-standard orthodoxy. The political consequence was that the financial sector's support for a full gold standard was weaker than in England.

Yet to understand fully the sources of Germany's "conditional" gold standard requires a look at the preferences and enduring political power of the German landed elite. After unification, Germany was by and large a country of free landholding peasants and power-cultivating squires — the Junkers. The Junkers, like the British landed elite, were powerful beyond their numbers in the German political system. Their monetary interests, however, tended to be more in line with tenant and small holding farmers than with the British aristocracy. This was because Junkers were not primarily rentiers. Instead, they managed great agricultural estates organized along the lines of the Spanish system of latifundia. As agricultural producers, the Junkers preferred a monetary system capable of enhancing the price of the low-quality grains they raised, not a system that put protecting the value of the currency above all else.

Without the support of the powerful Junkers, represented at the pinnacle of the German political system by Bismark himself, it is understandable why Germany did not adhere strictly to the principles of the gold standard. That Germany also lacked an equivalent of the City of London's internationally focused money market to champion orthodoxy was another constraint on the development of the German gold standard. The result was a distinct bias in monetary policy toward domestic objectives, as revealed by the Reichsbank's frequent resort to moral pressure and gold devices when external pressures were strong.

INTERNATIONAL EFFECTS OF
GERMAN MONETARY PRIORITIES

Like France, Germany also recognized how domestic priorities could be advanced by releasing gold abroad in times of international stress. This policy as lender of last resort resulted from the fact that the effectiveness of Reichsbank attempts to moderate external pressures, through the techniques outlined above, had obvious limits. If, for example, the Bank of England chose to raise Bank rate to whatever height was necessary to attract capital and gold flows from the Continent, German macroeconomic independence would be threatened. Hence, Germany had a *domestic* interest in joining France in providing the gold standard system with the services of the lender of last resort. The Reichsbank was willing to open its reserves to the Bank of England because the policy offered the possibility of smaller, and certainly more predictable, gold outflows. . . .

Germany was thus more like France than England in terms of the way it resolved the age-old dilemma between the internal and external objectives of monetary policy. Neither country subordinated domestic credit conditions and economic growth to the international objective of maintaining confidence in the strength of the national currency so thoroughly or for so long as did England. Yet Germany came to share with France the role of international lender of last resort, smoothing out shocks to the payments systems that threatened the independence of domestic macroeconomic policy making. Both the source of the national concern for internal targets and the Reichsbank's regime stabilizing policies at the international level were rooted in German domestic politics. Unable to perfectly insulate the German financial system from external pressures in line with the interests of Germany's dominant coalition, monetary authorities found it advantageous to release gold to the source of the shock, via the Bank of England. The action, however, was not based on any cosmopolitan commitment to stabilizing the international gold standard on the part of German monetary authorities. Instead, the German element of "central bank cooperation" can be interpreted as an international spillover of German national preferences, which again were far from orthodox.

CONCLUSION

Although international monetary stability may require the provision of Kindle-berger's equilibrating mechanisms, states can have different objectives and diver-gent policy preferences if the international spillovers of their national policy choices are solidly positive. Thus, agreement among member states about the rules and requirements of membership is not a necessary condition for global monetary stability. Nor is it necessary that a hegemon exist to provide the requisite stabilizing functions. An international "social order," like the classical gold stan-dard, can be maintained when states advance their internally determined private national interests in ways that generate nonexcludable systemic benefits, accord-ing to the logic of the joint-products model.

Historical evidence tends to support these claims. Not only did major gold standard countries have different (private) preferences regarding the basic trade-offs implicit in adhering to a fixed exchange-rate regime but the aggregate (public) result of their individual national choices was a modicum of international stability. The British leaned more consistently toward gold-standard orthodoxy — mone-tary authorities advanced external priorities over internal concerns. This was a function of the political dominance of those economic groups that found advan-tages in the internationalist and deflationary agenda of the gold standard: the bankers of the City of London, rentier landlords, and bondholders. For these groups, maintaining the purchasing power of the currency took precedent over domestic targets when these objectives clashed.

In conjunction with London's central position in world trade and payments, this commitment spilled over into the international arena in the form of the eleva-tion of sterling to the status of international currency. The commitment to gold, meant that the pound sterling became almost universally accepted as a transaction and reserve currency, and England therefore became the main source of liquidity for international payments. The two continental powers, in contrast, did not wel-come their loss of independence in forming monetary policy that the gold stan-dard required. They preferred instead to give monetary policy a decidedly domestic slant. They did so by artificially restricting the free flow of gold and restricting the gold convertibility of their currencies when necessary. Yet France and Germany came to share the position of international lender of last resort. Their concern for internal targets and for their policies of international lender of last resort had a common source — domestic politics and priorities. Unable to perfectly insulate their domestic economics from external pressures in line with the interests of their dominant coalitions, monetary authorities in France and Germany found it necessary to release gold from their reserves to the Bank of En-gland, which then channeled it abroad to the source of the shock. The French and Germans, however, did not provide this stabilizing function for the international gold-standard system out of a commitment to global welfare or regime stability. Instead, the central bank's support operations under the gold standard were a means by which weaker members of the regime — members who were not fully committed to gold — sought to drive a wedge between gold standard discipline and domestic macroeconomic policy making. Paradoxically, it was because

France and Germany did *not* share England's commitment to the gold standard that the regime was able to accommodate the handful of shocks that it experienced.

The international externalities of heterogeneous national preferences can, of course, be negative as well as positive. The collapse of the gold standard in the interwar period, the breakup of the Bretton Woods system in the early 1970s, and the 1992 crisis in the EMS can all be interpreted as the result of large negative externalities produced by the policy choices of the major states, in response to domestic political forces. Although we still lack general propositions about the conditions in which national interests sustain (or fail to sustain) an international regime, the research presented here is a necessary first step toward understanding international monetary relations. The value of the framework, and the measure against which it should be judged, is primarily empirical. The quality of the externalities produced by national policy choices determines the stability of the international monetary system. The facts of the nineteenth-century case of the gold standard are more consistent with this view than with models derived from existing international relations theory — hegemonic stability theory and regime theory. Although future theoretical work must specify the precise conditions under which heterogeneous national social orders will or will not generate the systemic public goods by which international social orders are maintained, this chapter has demonstrated the benefit of shifting the focus from international to domestic social order.

14

Hegemonic Stability
Theories of the International
Monetary System
BARRY EICHENGREEN

Barry Eichengreen evaluates the applicability of hegemonic stability theory (see Krasner, Reading 1, and Lake, Reading 8) to
international monetary relations. He examines the argument that
the existence of a single dominant power in the international
arena is necessary for the establishment and maintenance of
stable monetary systems. Eichengreen examines three monetary systems — the classical gold standard, the interwar gold-
exchange system, and the Bretton Woods system — to see
whether the presence or absence of a hegemon was the primary
cause of their development and maintenance. He finds that while
hegemons may contribute to the smooth operation of international monetary regimes, international cooperation has been
equally important to their design and functioning.

An international monetary system is a set of rules or conventions governing the
economic policies of nations. From a narrowly national perspective, it is an unnat-
ural state of affairs. Adherence to a common set of rules or conventions requires a
certain harmonization of monetary and fiscal policies, even though the preferences and constraints influencing policy formulation diverge markedly across
countries. Governments are expected to forswear policies that redistribute economic welfare from foreigners to domestic residents and to contribute voluntarily
to providing the international public good of global monetary stability. In effect,
they are expected to solve the defection problem that plagues cartels and —
equivalently in this context — the free-rider problem hindering public good provision. Since they are likely to succeed incompletely, the public good of international monetary stability tends to be underproduced. From this perspective, the
paradox of international monetary affairs is not the difficulty of designing a stable
international monetary system, but the fact that such systems have actually persisted for decades.

Specialists in international relations have offered the notion that dominance by
one country — a hegemonic power — is needed to ensure the smooth functioning

of an international regime. The concentration of economic power is seen as a way of internalizing the externalities associated with systemic stability and of ensuring its adequate provision. The application of this "theory of hegemonic stability" to international monetary affairs is straightforward. The maintenance of the Bretton Woods system for a quarter century is ascribed to the singular power of the United States in the postwar world, much as the persistence of the classical gold standard is ascribed to Britain's dominance of international financial affairs in the second half of the nineteenth century. . . . By contrast, the instability of the interwar gold exchange standard is attributed to the absence of a hegemonic power, due to Britain's inability to play the dominant role and America's unwillingness to accept it.

The appeal of this notion lies in its resonance with the public good and cartel analogies for international monetary affairs, through what might be called the carrot and stick variants of hegemonic stability theory. In the carrot variant, the hegemon, like a dominant firm in an oligopolistic market, maintains the cohesion of the cartel by making the equivalent of side payments to members of the fringe. In the stick variant, the hegemon, like a dominant firm, deters defection from the international monetary cartel by using its economic policies to threaten retaliation against renegades. In strong versions of the theory . . . all participants are rendered better off by the intervention of the dominant power. In weak versions . . . either because systemic stability is not a purely public good or because its costs are shunted onto smaller states, the benefits of stability accrue disproportionately or even exclusively to the hegemon.

Three problems bedevil attempts to apply hegemonic stability theory to international monetary affairs. First is the ambiguity surrounding three concepts central to the theory: *hegemony,* the *power* the hegemon is assumed to possess, and the *regime* whose stability is ostensibly enhanced by the exercise of hegemonic power. Rather than adopting general definitions offered previously and devoting this paper to their criticism, I adopt specialized definitions tailored to my concern with the international monetary system. I employ the economist's definition of economic — or market — power: sufficient size in the relevant market to influence prices and quantities. I define a hegemon analogously to a dominant firm: as a country whose market power, understood in this sense, significantly exceeds that of all rivals. Finally, I avoid defining the concept of regime around which much debate has revolved by posing the question narrowly: whether hegemony is conducive to the stability of the international monetary system (where the system is defined as those explicit rules and procedures governing international monetary affairs), rather than whether it is conducive to the stability of the international regime, however defined.

The second problem plaguing attempts to apply hegemonic stability theory to international monetary affairs is ambiguity about the instruments with which the hegemon makes its influence felt. This is the distinction between what are characterized above as the carrot and stick variants of the theory. Does the hegemon alter its monetary, fiscal, or commercial policies to discipline countries that refuse to play by its rules, as "basic force" models of international relations would suggest?

Does it link international economic policy to other issue areas and impose military or diplomatic sanctions on uncooperative nations? Or does it stabilize the system through the use of "positive sanctions," financing the public good of international monetary stability by acting as lender of last resort even when the probability of repayment is slim and forsaking beggar-thy-neighbor policies even when used to advantage by other countries?

The third problem is ambiguity about the scope of hegemonic stability theories. In principle, such theories could be applied equally to the design, the operation, or the decline of the international monetary system. Yet in practice, hegemonic stability theories may shed light on the success of efforts to design or reform the international monetary system but not on its day-to-day operation or eventual decline. Other combinations are equally plausible a priori. Only analysis of individual cases can throw light on the theory's range of applicability.

In this paper, I structure an analysis of hegemonic stability theories of the international monetary system around the dual problems of range of applicability and mode of implementation. I consider separately the genesis of international monetary systems, their operation in normal periods and times of crisis, and their disintegration. In each context, I draw evidence from three modern incarnations of the international monetary system: the classical gold standard, the interwar gold exchange standard, and Bretton Woods. These three episodes in the history of the international monetary system are typically thought to offer two examples of hegemonic stability — Britain before 1914, the United States after 1944 — and one episode — the interwar years — destabilized by the absence of hegemony. I do not attempt to document Britain's dominance of international markets before 1914 or the dominance of the United States after 1944; I simply ask whether the market power they possessed was causally connected to the stability of the international monetary system.

The historical analysis indicates that the relationship between the market power of the leading economy and the stability of the international monetary system is considerably more complex than suggested by simple variants of hegemonic stability theory. While one cannot simply reject the hypothesis that on more than one occasion the stabilizing capacity of a dominant economic power has contributed to the smooth functioning of the international monetary system, neither can one reconcile much of the evidence, notably on the central role of international negotiation and collaboration even in periods of hegemonic dominance, with simple versions of the theory. Although both the appeal and limitations of hegemonic stability theories are apparent when one takes a static view of the international monetary system, those limitations are most evident when one considers the evolution of an international monetary system over time. An international monetary system whose smooth operation at one point is predicated on the dominance of one powerful country may in fact be dynamically unstable. Historical experience suggests that the hegemon's willingness to act in a stabilizing capacity at a single point tends to undermine its continued capacity to do so over time. . . .

THE GENESIS OF MONETARY SYSTEMS
AND THE THEORY OF HEGEMONIC STABILITY

My analysis begins with an examination of the genesis of three different monetary systems: the classical gold standard, the interwar gold exchange standard, and the Bretton Woods system.

The Classical Gold Standard

Of the three episodes considered here, the origins of the classical gold standard are the most difficult to assess, for in the nineteenth century there were no centralized discussions, like those in Genoa in 1922 or Bretton Woods in 1944, concerned with the design of the international monetary system. There was general agreement that currencies should have a metallic basis and that payments imbalances should be settled by international shipments of specie. But there was no consensus about which precious metals should serve as the basis for money supplies or how free international specie movements should be.

Only Britain maintained a full-fledged gold standard for anything approaching the century preceding 1913. Although gold coins had circulated alongside silver since the fourteenth century, Britain had been on a de facto gold standard since 1717, when Sir Isaac Newton, as master of the mint, set too high a silver price of gold and drove full-bodied silver coins from circulation. In 1798 silver coinage was suspended, and after 1819 silver was no longer accepted to redeem paper currency. But for half a century following its official adoption of the gold standard in 1821, Britain essentially remained alone. Other countries that retained bimetallic standards were buffeted by alternating gold and silver discoveries. The United States and France, for example, were officially bimetallic, but their internal circulations were placed on a silver basis by growing Mexican and South American silver production in the early decades of the nineteenth century. The market price of silver was thus depressed relative to the mint price, which encouraged silver to be imported for coinage and gold to be shipped abroad where its price was higher. Then, starting in 1848, gold discoveries in Russia, Australia, and California depressed the market price of gold below the mint price, all but driving silver from circulation and placing bimetallic currencies on a gold basis. Finally, silver discoveries in Nevada and other mining territories starting in the 1870s dramatically inflated the silver price of gold and forced the bimetallic currencies back onto a silver basis.

The last of these disturbances led nearly all bimetallic countries to adopt the gold standard, starting with Germany in 1871. Why, after taking no comparable action in response to previous disturbances, did countries respond to post-1870 fluctuations in the price of silver by abandoning bimetallism and adopting gold? What role, if any, did Britain, the hegemonic financial power, play in their decisions?

One reason for the decision to adopt gold was the desire to prevent the inflation that would result from continued silver convertibility and coinage. Hence the plausible explanation for the contrast between the 1870s and earlier years is the danger of exceptionally rapid inflation due to the magnitude of post-1870 silver discoveries. Between 1814 and 1870, the sterling price of silver, of which so much was written, remained within 2 percentage points of its 1814 value, alternatively driving gold or silver from circulation in bimetallic countries but fluctuating insufficiently to raise the specter of significant price level changes. Then between 1871 and 1881 the London price of silver fell by 15 percent, and by 1891 the cumulative fall had reached 25 percent. Gold convertibility was the only alternative to continued silver coinage that was judged both respectable and viable. The only significant resistance to the adoption of gold convertibility emanated from silver-mining regions and from agricultural areas like the American West, populated by proprietors of encumbered land who might benefit from inflation.

Seen from this perspective, the impetus for adopting the gold standard existed independently of Britain's rapid industrialization, dominance of international finance, and preeminence in trade. Still, the British example surely provided encouragement to follow the path ultimately chosen. The experience of the Latin Monetary Union impressed upon contemporaries the advantages of a common monetary standard in minimizing transactions costs. The scope of that common standard would be greatest for countries that linked their currencies to sterling. The gold standard was also attractive to domestic interests concerned with promoting economic growth. Industrialization required foreign capital, and attracting foreign capital required monetary stability. For Britain, the principal source of foreign capital, monetary stability was measured in terms of sterling and best ensured by joining Britain on gold. Moreover, London's near monopoly of trade credit was of concern to other governments, which hoped that they might reduce their dependence on the London discount market by establishing gold parities and central banks. Aware that Britain monopolized trade in newly mined gold and was the home of the world's largest organized commodity markets, other governments hoped that by emulating Britain's gold standard and financial system they might secure a share of this business.

Britain's prominence in foreign commerce, overseas investment, and trade credit forcefully conditioned the evolution of the gold standard system mainly through central banks' practice of holding key currency balances abroad, especially in London. This practice probably would not have developed so quickly if foreign countries had not grown accustomed to transacting in the London market. It would probably not have become so widespread if there had not been such strong confidence in the stability and liquidity of sterling deposits. And such a large share of foreign deposits would not have gravitated to a single center if Britain had not possessed such a highly articulated set of financial markets.

But neither Britain's dominance of international transactions nor the desire to emulate Bank of England practice prevented countries from tailoring the gold standard to their own needs. Germany and France continued to allow large internal gold circulation, while other nations limited gold coin circulation to low levels. The central banks of France, Belgium, and Switzerland retained the right to redeem their notes in silver, and the French did not hesitate to charge a premium for gold. The Reichsbank could at its option issue fiduciary notes upon the payment of a tax. In no sense did British example or suggestion dictate the form of the monetary system.

The Interwar Gold Exchange Standard

The interwar gold exchange standard offers a radically different picture: on the one hand, there was no single dominant power like nineteenth century Britain or mid-twentieth century America; on the other, there were conscious efforts by rivals to shape the international monetary order to their national advantage.

Contemporary views of the design of the interwar monetary system were aired at a series of international meetings, the most important of which was the Genoa Economic and Financial Conference convened in April 1922. Although the United States declined to send an official delegation to Genoa, proceedings there reflected the differing economic objectives of Britain and the United States. British officials were aware that the war had burdened domestic industry with adjustment problems, had disrupted trade, and had accentuated financial rivalry between London and New York. Their objectives were to prevent worldwide deflation (which was sure to exacerbate the problems of structural adjustment), to promote the expansion of international trade (to which the nation's prosperity was inextricably linked), and to recapture the financial business diverted to New York as a result of the war. To prevent deflation, they advocated that countries economize on the use of gold by adopting the gold exchange standard along lines practiced by members of the British Empire. Presuming London to be a reserve center, British officials hoped that these measures would restore the City to its traditional prominence in international finance. Stable exchange rates would stimulate international trade, particularly if the United States forgave its war debt claims, which would permit reparations to be reduced and encourage creditor countries to extend loans to Central Europe.

The United States, in contrast, was less dependent for its prosperity on the rapid expansion of trade. It was less reliant on income from financial and insurance services and perceived as less urgent the need to encourage the deposit of foreign balances in New York. Influential American officials, notably Benjamin Strong of the Federal Reserve Bank of New York, opposed any extension of the gold exchange standard. Above all, American officials were hesitant to participate in a conference whose success appeared to hinge on unilateral concessions regarding war debts.

In the absence of an American delegation, Britain's proposals formed the basis for the resolutions of the Financial Committee of the Genoa Conference. . . . Participating countries would fix their exchange rates against one another, and any that failed to do so would lose the right to hold the reserve balances of the others. The principal creditor nations were encouraged to take immediate steps to restore convertibility in order to become "gold centers" where the bulk of foreign exchange reserves would be held. Following earlier recommendations by the Cunliffe committee, governments were urged to economize on gold by eliminating gold coin from circulation and concentrating reserves at central banks. Countries with significantly depreciated currencies were urged to stabilize at current exchange rates rather than attempting to restore prewar parities through drastic deflation, which would only delay stabilization.

To implement this convention, the Bank of England was instructed to call an early meeting of central banks, including the Federal Reserve. But efforts to arrange this meeting, which bogged down in the dispute over war debts and reparations, proved unavailing. Still, if the official convention advocated by the Financial Committee failed to materialize, the Genoa resolutions were not without influence. Many of the innovations suggested there were adopted by individual countries on a unilateral basis and comprised the distinguishing features differentiating the prewar and interwar monetary standards.

The first effect of Genoa was to encourage the adoption of statutes permitting central banks to back notes and sight deposits with foreign exchange as well as gold. New regulations broadening the definition of eligible assets and specifying minimum proportions of total reserves to be held in gold were widely implemented in succeeding years. The second effect was to encourage the adoption of gold economy measures, including the withdrawal of gold coin from circulation and provision of bullion for export only by the authorities. The third effect was to provide subtle encouragement to countries experiencing ongoing inflation to stabilize at depreciated rates. Thus Genoa deserves partial credit for transforming the international monetary system from a gold to a gold exchange standard, from a gold coin to a gold bullion standard, and from a fixed-rate system to one in which central banks were vested with some discretion over the choice of parities.

Given its dominance of the proceedings at Genoa, Britain's imprint on the interwar gold exchange standard was as apparent as its influence over the structure of the prewar system. That British policymakers achieved this despite a pronounced decline in Britain's position in the world economy and the opposition of influential American officials suggests that planning and effort were substitutes, to some extent, for economic power.

The Bretton Woods System

Of the three cases considered here, U.S. dominance of the Bretton Woods negotiations is most clearly supportive of hegemonic stability theories about the genesis of the international monetary system. U.S. dominance of the postwar world economy is unmistakable. Yet despite the trappings of hegemony and American dominance of the proceedings at Bretton Woods, a less influential power — Great Britain — was able to secure surprisingly extensive concessions in the design of the international monetary system.

American and British officials offered different plans for postwar monetary reconstruction both because they had different views of the problem of international economic adjustment and because they represented economies with different strengths and weaknesses. British officials were preoccupied by two weaknesses of their economic position. First was the specter of widespread unemployment. Between 1920 and 1938, unemployment in Britain had scarcely dipped below double-digit levels, and British policymakers feared its recurrence. Second was the problem of sterling balances. Britain had concentrated its wartime purchases within the sterling bloc and, because they were allies and sterling was a reserve currency, members of the bloc had accepted settlement in sterling, now held in London. Since these sterling balances were large relative to Britain's hard currency reserves, the mere possibility that they might be presented for conversion threatened plans for the restoration of convertibility.

U.S. officials, in contrast, were confident that the competitive position of American industry was strong and were little concerned about the threat of unemployment. The concentration of gold reserves in the United States, combined with the economy's international creditor position, freed them from worry that speculative capital flows or foreign government policies might undermine the dollar's stability. U.S. concerns centered on the growth of preferential trading systems from which its exports were excluded, notably the sterling bloc.

The British view of international economic adjustment was dominated by concern about inadequate liquidity and asymmetrical adjustment. A central lesson drawn by British policymakers from the experience of the 1920s was the difficulty of operating an international monetary system in which liquidity or reserves were scarce. Given how slowly the global supply of monetary gold responded to fluctuations in its relative price and how sensitive its international distribution had proven to be to the economic policies of individual states, they considered it foolhardy to base the international monetary system on a reserve base composed exclusively of gold. Given the perceived inelasticity of global gold supplies, a gold-based system threatened to impart a deflationary bias to the world economy and to worsen unemployment. This preoccupation with unemployment due to external constraints was reinforced by another lesson drawn from the 1920s: the costs of asymmetries in the operation of the adjustment mechanism. If the experience of the 1920s was repeated, surplus countries, in response to external imbalances, would need only to sterilize reserve inflows, while deficit countries would be forced to initiate monetary contraction to prevent the depletion of reserves. Monetary contraction, according to Keynes, whose views heavily influenced those of the British delegation, facilitated adjustment by causing unemployment. To prevent unemployment, symmetry had to be restored to the adjustment mechanism through the incorporation of sanctions compelling surplus countries to revalue their currencies or stimulate demand.

From the American perspective, the principal lessons of the interwar experience were not the costs of asymmetries and inadequate liquidity, but the instability of floating rates and the disruptive effects of exchange rate and trade protection. U.S. officials were concerned about ensuring order and stability in the foreign exchange market and preventing the development of preferential trading systems cultivated through expedients such as exchange control.

The Keynes and White plans, which formed each side's basis for negotiations, require only a brief summary. Exchange control and the centralized provision of liquidity ("bancor") were two central elements of Keynes's plan for an international clearing union. . . . Exchange control would insulate pegged exchange rates from the sudden liquidation of short-term balances. Symmetry would be ensured by a charge on creditor balances held with the clearing bank.

The White plan acknowledged the validity of the British concern with liquidity, but was intended to prevent both inflation and deflation rather than to exert an expansionary influence. It limited the Stabilization Fund's total resources to $5 billion, compared with $26 billion under the Keynes plan. It was patterned on the principles of American bank lending, under which decisionmaking power rested ultimately with the bank; the Keynes plan resembled the British overdraft system, in which the overdraft was at the borrower's discretion. The fundamental difference, however, was that the White plan limited the total U.S. obligation to its $2 billion contribution, while the Keynes plan limited the value of unrequited U.S. exports that might be financed by bancor to the total drawing rights of other countries ($23 billion).

It is typically argued that the Bretton Woods agreement reflected America's dominant position, presumably on the grounds that the International Monetary Fund charter specified quotas of $8.8 billion (closer to the White plan's $5 billion than to the Keynes plan's $26 billion) and a maximum U.S. obligation of $2.75 billion (much closer to $2 billion under the White plan than to $23 billion under the Keynes plan). Yet, relative to the implications of simple versions of hegemonic stability theory, a surprising number of British priorities were incorporated. One was the priority Britain attached to exchange rate flexibility. The United States initially had wished to invest the IMF with veto power over a country's decision to change its exchange rate. Subsequently it proposed that 80 percent of IMF members be required to approve any change in parity. But the Articles of Agreement permitted devaluation without fund objection when needed to eliminate fundamental disequilibrium. Lacking any definition of this term, there was scope for devaluation by countries other than the United States to reconcile internal and external balance. Only once did the fund treat an exchange rate change as unauthorized. If countries hesitated to devalue, they did so as much for domestic reasons as for reasons related to the structure of the international monetary system.

Another British priority incorporated into the agreement was tolerance of exchange control. Originally, the White plan obliged members to abandon all exchange restrictions within six months of ceasing hostilities or joining the IMF, whichever came first. A subsequent U.S. proposal would have required a country to eliminate all exchange controls within a year of joining the fund. But Britain succeeded in incorporating into the Articles of Agreement a distinction between controls for capital transactions, which were permitted, from controls on current transactions, which were not. In practice, even nondiscriminatory exchange controls on current transactions were sometimes authorized under IMF Article VIII. As a result of this compromise, the United States protected itself from efforts to divert sterling bloc trade toward the British market, while Britain protected itself from destabilization by overseas sterling balances.

In comparison with these concessions, British efforts to restore symmetry to the international adjustment mechanism proved unavailing. With abandonment of the overdraft principle, the British embraced White's "scarce currency" proposal, under which the fund was empowered to ration its supply of a scarce currency and members were authorized to impose limitations on freedom of exchange operations in that currency. Thus a country running payments surpluses sufficiently large to threaten the fund's ability to supply its currency might face restrictions on foreign customers' ability to purchase its exports. But the scarce currency clause had been drafted by the United States not with the principle of symmetry in mind, but in order to deal with problems of immediate postwar adjustment — specifically, the prospective dollar shortage. With the development of the Marshall Plan, the dollar shortage never achieved the severity anticipated by the authors of the scarce currency clause, and the provision was never invoked.

If the "Joint Statement by Experts on the Establishment of an International Monetary Fund," made public in April 1944, bore the imprint of the U.S. delegation to Bretton Woods, to a surprising extent it also embodied important elements of the British negotiating position. It is curious from the perspective of hegemonic stability theory that a war-battered economy — Britain — heavily dependent on the dominant economic power — America — for capital goods, financial capital, and export markets was able to extract significant concessions in the design of the international monetary system. Britain was ably represented in the negotiations. But even more important, the United States also required an international agreement and wished to secure it even while hostilities in Europe prevented enemy nations from taking part in negotiations and minimized the involvement of the allies on whose territory the war was fought. The United States therefore had little opportunity to play off countries against one another or to brand as renegades any that disputed the advisability of its design. As the Western world's second largest economy, Britain symbolized, if it did not actually represent, the other nations of the world and was able to advance their case more effectively than if they had attempted more actively to do so themselves.

What conclusions regarding the applicability of hegemonic stability theory to the genesis of international monetary systems follow from the evidence of these three cases? In the two clearest instances of hegemony — the United Kingdom in the second half of the nineteenth century and the United States following World War II — the leading economic power significantly influenced the form of the international monetary system, by example in the first instance and by negotiation in the second. But the evidence also underscores the fact that the hegemon has been incapable of dictating the form of the monetary system. In the first instance, British example did nothing to prevent significant modifications in the form of the gold standard adopted abroad. In the second, the exceptional dominance of the U.S. economy was unable to eliminate the need to compromise with other countries in the design of the monetary system.

THE OPERATION OF MONETARY SYSTEMS AND THE THEORY OF HEGEMONIC STABILITY

It is necessary to consider not only the genesis of monetary systems, but also how the theory of hegemonic stability applies to the operation of such systems. I consider adjustment, liquidity, and the lender-of-last-resort function in turn.

Adjustment

Adjustment under the classical gold standard has frequently been characterized in terms compatible with hegemonic stability theory. The gold standard is portrayed as a managed system whose preservation and smooth operation were ensured through its regulation by a hegemonic power, Great Britain, and its agent, the Bank of England. . . .

Before 1914, London was indisputably the world's leading financial center. A large proportion of world trade — 60 percent by one estimate — was settled through payment in sterling bills, with London functioning as a clearinghouse for importers and exporters of other nations. British discount houses bought bills from abroad, either directly or through the London agencies of foreign banks. Foreigners maintained balances in London to meet commitments on bills outstanding and to service British portfolio investments overseas. Foreign governments and central banks held deposits in London as interest-earning alternatives to gold reserves. Although the pound was not the only reserve currency of the pre 1914 era, sterling reserves matched the combined value of reserves denominated in other currencies. At the same time, Britain possessed perhaps £350 million of short-term capital overseas. Though it is unclear whether Britain was a net short-term debtor or creditor before the war, it is certain that a large volume of short-term funds was responsive to changes in domestic interest rates.

Such changes in interest rates might be instigated by the Bank of England. By altering the rates at which it discounted for its customers and rediscounted for the discount houses, the bank could affect rates prevailing in the discount market. But the effect of Bank rate was not limited to the bill market. While in part this reflected the exceptional integration characteristic of British financial markets, it was reinforced by institutionalization. In London, banks automatically fixed their deposit rates half a percentage point above Bank rate. Loan rates were similarly indexed to Bank rate but at a higher level. Though there were exceptions to these rules, changes in Bank rate were immediately reflected in a broad range of British interest rates.

An increase in Bank rate, by raising the general level of British interest rates, induced foreign investors to accumulate additional funds in London and to delay the repatriation or transfer of existing balances to other centers. British balances abroad were repatriated to earn the higher rate of return. Drawings of finance bills, which represented half of total bills in 1913, were similarly sensitive to changes in interest rates. Higher interest rates spread to the security market and delayed the flotation of new issues for overseas borrowers. In this way the Bank of England was able to insulate its gold reserve from disturbances in the external accounts. . . .

But why did the Bank of England's exceptional leverage not threaten convertibility abroad? The answer commonly offered is that Britain's unrivaled market power led to a de facto harmonization of national policies. . . . As Keynes wrote in the *Treatise on Money,* "During the latter half of the nineteenth century the influence of London on credit conditions throughout the world was so predominant that the Bank of England could almost have claimed to be the conductor of the international orchestra."

Since fiscal harmonization requires no discussion in an era of balanced budgets, the stability of the classical gold standard can be explained by the desire and ability of central banks to harmonize their monetary policies in the interest of external balance. External balance, or maintaining gold reserves adequate to defend the established gold parity, was the foremost target of monetary policy in the period preceding World War I. In the absence of a coherent theory of unemployment, much less a consensus on its relation to monetary policy, there was relatively little pressure for central banks to accommodate domestic needs. External balance was not the sole target of policy, but when internal and external balance came into conflict, the latter took precedence. Viewed from an international perspective, British leadership played a role in this process of harmonization insofar as the market power and prominence of the Bank of England served as a focal point for policy coordination.

But if the Bank of England could be sure of defeating its European counterparts when they engaged in a tug of war over short-term capital, mere harmonization of central bank policies, in the face of external disturbances, would have been insufficient to prevent convertibility crises on the Continent. The explanation for the absence of such crises would appear to be the greater market power of European countries compared with their non-European counterparts. Some observers have distinguished the market power of capital-exporting countries from the inability of capital importers to influence the direction of financial flows. Others have suggested the existence of a hierarchical structure of financial markets: below the London market were the less active markets of Berlin, Paris, Vienna, Amsterdam, Brussels, Zurich, and New York; followed by the still less active markets of the Scandinavian countries; and finally the nascent markets of Latin America and other parts of the non-European world. When Bank rate was raised in London, thus redistributing reserves to Britain from other regions, compensatory discount rate increases on the Continent drew funds from the non-European world or curtailed capital outflows. Developing countries, due to either the thinness of markets or the absence of relevant institutions, were unable to prevent these events. In times of crisis, therefore, convertibility was threatened primarily outside Europe and North America. . . .

Thus, insofar as hegemony played some role in the efficiency of the adjustment mechanism, it was not the British hegemony of which so much has been written but the collective hegemony of the European center relative to the non-European periphery. Not only does this case challenge the conception of the hegemon, therefore, but because the stability of the classical gold standard was enjoyed exclusively by the countries of the center, it supports only the weak form of hegemonic stability theory — that the benefits of stability accrued exclusively to the powerful.

The relation between hegemonic power and the need for policy harmonization is equally relevant to the case of the interwar gold exchange standard. One interpretation . . . is that in the absence of a hegemon there was no focal point for policy, which interfered with efforts at coordination. But more important than a declining ability to harmonize policies may have been a diminished desire to do so. Although the advent of explicit stabilization policy was not to occur until the

1930s and 1940s, during the 1920s central banks placed increasing weight on internal conditions when formulating monetary policy. The rise of socialism and the example of the Bolshevik revolution in particular provided a counterweight to central bankers' instinctive wish to base policy solely on external conditions. External adjustment was rendered difficult by policymakers' increasing hesitancy to sacrifice other objectives on the altar of external balance. Britain's balance-of-payments problems, for example, cannot be attributed to "the existence of more than one policy" in the world economy without considering also a domestic unemployment problem that placed pressure on the Bank of England to resist restrictive measures that might strengthen the external accounts at the expense of industry and trade.

Under Bretton Woods, the problem of adjustment was exacerbated by the difficulty of using exchange rate changes to restore external balance. Hesitancy to change their exchange rates posed few problems for countries in surplus. However, those in deficit had to choose between aggravating unemployment and tolerating external deficits; the latter was infeasible in the long run and promoted an increase in the volume of short-term capital that moved in response to anticipations of devaluation. Although the IMF charter did not encourage devaluation, the hesitancy of deficit countries to employ this option is easier to ascribe to the governments' tendency to attach their prestige to the stability of established exchange rates than to U.S. hegemony, however defined. Where the singular role of the United States was important was in precluding a dollar devaluation. A possible solution to the problem of U.S. deficits, one that would not have threatened other countries' ability to accumulate reserves, was an increase in the dollar price of gold, that is, a dollar devaluation. It is sometimes argued that the United States was incapable of adjusting through exchange rate changes since other countries would have devalued in response to prevent any change in bilateral rates against the dollar. However, raising the dollar price of gold would have increased the dollar value of monetary gold, reducing the global excess demand for reserves and encouraging other countries to increase domestic demand and cut back on their balance-of-payments surpluses. But while a rise in the price of gold might have alleviated central banks' immediate dependence on dollars, it would have done nothing to prevent the problem from recurring. It would also have promoted skepticism about the U.S. government's commitment to the new gold price, thereby encouraging other countries to increase their demands for gold and advancing the date of future difficulties.

Does this evidence on adjustment support hegemonic theories of international monetary stability? The contrast between the apparently smooth adjustment under the classical gold standard and Bretton Woods and the adjustment difficulties of the interwar years suggests that a dominant power's policies served as a fixed target that was easier to hit than a moving one. . . . [W]hat mattered was not so much the particular stance of monetary policy but that the leading players settled on the same stance. The argument . . . is that a dominant player is best placed to signal the other players the nature of the most probable stance. The effectiveness of the adjustment mechanism under the two regimes reflected not just British and American market power but also the existence of an international consensus on the objectives and formulation of monetary policy that permitted central bank policies to be harmonized. The essential role of Britain before 1914 and the United States after 1944 was not so much to force other countries to alter their policies as to provide a focal point for policy harmonization.

Liquidity

Under the classical gold standard, the principal source of liquidity was newly mined gold. It is hard to see how British dominance of international markets could have much influenced the changes in the world price level and mining technology upon which these supplies depended. As argued above, where Britain's prominence mattered was in facilitating the provision of supplementary liquidity in the form of sterling reserves, which grew at an accelerating rate starting in the 1890s. It is conceivable, therefore, that in the absence of British hegemony a reserve shortage would have developed and the classical gold standard would have exhibited a deflationary bias.

Liquidity was an issue of more concern under the interwar gold exchange standard. Between 1915 and 1925, prices rose worldwide due to the inflation associated with wartime finance and postwar reconstruction; these rising prices combined with economic growth to increase the transactions demand for money. Yet under a system of convertible currencies, world money supply was constrained by the availability of reserves. Statutory restrictions required central banks to back their money supplies with eligible reserves, while recent experience with inflation deterred politicians from liberalizing the statutes. The output of newly mined gold had been depressed since the beginning of World War I, and experts offered pessimistic forecasts of future supplies. Increasing the real value of world gold reserves by forcing a reduction in the world price level would only add to the difficulties of an already troubled world economy. Countries were encouraged, therefore, to stabilize on a gold exchange basis to prevent the development of a gold shortage.

There are difficulties with this explanation of interwar liquidity problems, which emphasizes a shortage of gold. For one, the danger of a gold shortage's constraining the volume of transactions was alleviated by the all but complete withdrawal of gold coin from circulation during the war. As a result, the percentage of short-term liabilities of all central banks backed by gold was little different in 1928 from its level in 1913, while the volume of the liabilities backed by that gold stock was considerably increased. It is hard to see why a gold shortage, after having exhibited only weak effects in previous years, should have had such a dramatic impact starting in 1929. It is even less clear how the absence of a hegemon contributed to the purported gold shortage. The obvious linkages between hegemony and the provision of liquidity work in the wrong direction. The straightforward way of increasing the monetary value of reserves was a round of currency devaluation, which would revalue gold reserves and, by raising the real price of gold, increase the output of the mining industry. As demonstrated in 1931, when the pound's depreciation set off a round of competitive devaluations, sterling remained the linchpin of the international currency system; the only way a round of currency devaluation could have taken place, therefore, was if Britain had stabilized in 1925 at a lower level. But had her dominance of the international economy not eroded over the first quarter of the twentieth century, the political pressure on Britain to return to gold at the prewar parity would have increased rather than being reduced. It seems unlikely, therefore, that a more successful maintenance of British hegemony, ceteris paribus, would have alleviated any gold shortage.

An alternative and more appealing explanation for interwar liquidity problems emphasizes mismanagement of gold reserves rather than their overall insufficiency. It blames France and the United States for absorbing disproportionate shares of global gold supplies and for imposing deflation on the rest of the world. Between 1928 and 1932, French gold reserves rose from $1.25 billion to $3.26 billion of constant gold content, or from 13 to 28 percent of the world total. Meanwhile, the United States, which had released gold between 1924 and 1928, facilitating the reestablishment of convertibility in other countries, reversed its position and imported $1.49 billion of gold between 1928 and 1930. By the end of 1932 the United States and France together possessed nearly 63 percent of the world's central monetary gold. . . .

The maldistribution of reserves can be understood by focusing on the systematic interaction of central banks. This approach builds on the literature that characterizes the interwar gold standard as a competitive struggle for gold between countries that viewed the size of their gold reserve as a measure of national prestige and as insurance against financial instability. France and the United States in particular, but gold standard countries generally, repeatedly raised their discount rates relative to one another in efforts to attract gold from abroad. By leading to the accumulation of excess reserves, these restrictive policies exacerbated the problem of inadequate liquidity, but by offsetting one another they also failed to achieve their objective of attracting gold from abroad. . . .

The origins of this competitive struggle for gold are popularly attributed to the absence of a hegemon. The competing financial centers — London, Paris, and New York — worked at cross-purposes because, in contrast to the preceding period, no one central bank was sufficiently powerful to call the tune. Before the war, the Bank of England had been sufficiently dominant to act as a leader, setting its discount rate with the reaction of other central banks in mind, while other central banks responded in the manner of a competitive fringe. By using this power to defend the gold parity of sterling despite the maintenance of slender reserves, the bank prevented the development of a competitive scramble for gold. But after World War I, with the United States unwilling to accept responsibility for leadership, no one central bank formulated its monetary policy with foreign reactions and global conditions in mind, and the noncooperative struggle for gold was the result. In this interpretation of the interwar liquidity problem, hegemony — or, more precisely, its absence — plays a critical role.

In discussing the provision of liquidity under Bretton Woods, it is critical to distinguish the decade ending in 1958 — when the convertibility of European currencies was restored and before U.S. dominance of international trade, foreign lending, and industrial production was unrivaled — from the decade that followed. In the first period, the most important source of incremental liquidity was dollar reserves. Between 1949 and 1958, when global reserves rose by 29 percent, less than one-third of the increment took the form of gold and one-fifteenth was in quotas at the IMF. The role of sterling as a reserve currency was limited almost exclusively to Commonwealth members and former British colonies that had traditionally held reserves in London and traded heavily with Britain. Consequently, the accumulation of dollar balances accounted for roughly half of incremental liquidity in the first decade of Bretton Woods.

In one sense, U.S. dominance of international markets facilitated the provision of liquidity. At the end of World War II, the United States had amassed 60 percent of the world's gold stock; at $35 an ounce, this was worth six times the value of the official dollar claims accumulated by foreign governments by 1949. There was little immediate question, given U.S. dominance of global gold reserves, of the stability of the gold price of the dollar and hence little hesitation to accumulate incremental liquidity in the form of dollar claims. But in another sense, U.S. international economic power in the immediate postwar years impeded the supply of liquidity to the world economy. Wartime destruction of industry in Europe and Japan left U.S.-manufactured exports highly competitive in world markets and rendered Europe dependent on U.S. capital goods for industrial reconstruction. The persistent excess demand for U.S. goods tended to push the U.S. balance of payments into surplus, creating the famous "dollar shortage" of the immediate postwar years. While U.S. hegemony left other countries willing to hold dollar claims, it rendered them extremely difficult to obtain.

Various policies were initiated in response to the dollar shortage, including discrimination against dollar area exports, special incentives for European and Japanese exports to the United States, and a round of European currency devaluations starting in September 1949. Ultimately the solution took the form of two sharply contrasting actions by the hegemon: Marshall Plan grants of $11.6 billion between mid-1948 and mid-1952, and Korean War expenditures. Largely as a result of these two factors, U.S. trade surpluses shrank from $10.1 billion in 1947 to $2.6 billion in 1952; more important, U.S. government grants and private capital outflows exceeded the surplus on current account. By 1950 the U.S. balance of payments was in deficit and, after moving back into surplus in 1951–52, deficits returned to stay. Insofar as its singular economic power encouraged the United States to undertake both the Marshall Plan and the Korean War, hegemony played a significant role in both the form and adequacy of the liquidity provided in the first decade of Bretton Woods.

Between 1958 and 1969, global reserves grew more rapidly, by 51 percent, than they had in the first decade of Bretton Woods. Again, gold was a minor share of the increment, about one-twentieth, and IMF quotas were one-eighth. While foreign exchange reserves again provided roughly half, Eurodollars and other foreign currencies grew in importance: their contribution actually exceeded that of official claims on the United States. In part these trends reflected rapid growth in Europe and Japan. More important, they reflected the fact that starting in 1965 the value of foreign government claims on the United States exceeded U.S. gold reserves. Prudence dictated that foreign governments diversify their reserve positions out of dollars.

The role of U.S. hegemony in the provision of liquidity during this second decade has been much debated. The growth of liquidity reflected both supply and demand pressures: both demands by other countries for additional reserves, which translated into balance-of-payments surpluses, and the capacity of the United States to consume more than it produced by running balance-of-payments deficits financed by the willingness of other countries to accumulate dollar reserves. The United States was criticized sharply, mainly by the French, for exporting inflation and for financing purchases of foreign companies and pursuit of the Vietnam War through the balance of payments. Although these complaints cannot be dismissed, it is incorrect to conclude that the dollar's singular position in the Bretton Woods system permitted the United States to run whatever balance-of-payments deficit it wished. Moreover, it is difficult to envisage an alternative scenario in which the U.S. balance of payments was zero but the world was not starved of liquidity. Owing to the sheer size of the American economy, new claims on the United States continued to exceed vastly the contribution of new claims on any other nation. Moreover, U.S. economic, military, and diplomatic influence did much to encourage if not compel other countries to maintain their holdings of dollar claims. Thus U.S. dominance of international markets played a critical role in resolving the liquidity crisis of the 1960s.

The distinguishing feature of Bretton Woods is not that other countries continued to hold dollar reserves in the face of exchange rate uncertainty and economic growth abroad, for neither development has deterred them from holding dollars under the flexible exchange rate regime of the 1970s and 1980s. Rather, it is that they continued to hold dollar reserves in the face of a one-way bet resulting from dollar convertibility at a fixed price when the dollar price of gold seemed poised to rise. In part, the importance of American foreign investments and the size of the U.S. market for European exports caused other countries to hesitate before cashing in their chips. Yet foreign governments also saw dollar convertibility as essential to the defense of the gold-dollar system and viewed the fixed exchange rates of that system as an international public good worthy of defense. Not until 1965 did the French government decide to convert into gold some $300 million of its dollar holdings and subsequently to step up its monthly gold purchases from the United States. But when pressure on U.S. gold reserves mounted following the 1967 devaluation of sterling, other countries, including France, sold gold instead of capitalizing on the one-way bet. They joined the United States in the formation of a gold pool whose purpose was to sell a sufficient quantity of gold to defend the official price. Between sterling's devaluation in 1967 and closure of the gold market on March 15, 1968, the pool sold $3 billion of gold, of which U.S. sales were $2.2 billion. France purchased no gold in 1967 or 1968, presumably due in part to foreign pressure. U.S. leverage undoubtedly contributed to their decisions. But a plausible interpretation of these events is that foreign governments, rather than simply being coerced into support of the dollar by U.S. economic power, were willing to take limited steps to defend the international public good of a fixed exchange rate system defined in terms of the dollar price of gold.

What does this discussion imply for the role of hegemony in the provision of international liquidity? The strongest evidence for the importance of a hegemon is negative evidence from the interwar years, when the absence of a hegemon and the failure of competing financial centers to coordinate their policies effectively contributed greatly to the liquidity shortage. In other periods, when a dominant economic power was present, it is difficult to credit that power with sole responsibility for ensuring the adequate provision of liquidity. Under the gold standard, the principal source of incremental liquidity was newly mined gold; Britain contributed to the provision of liquidity only insofar as its financial stature encouraged other countries to augment their specie holdings with sterling reserves. After World War II, U.S. economic power similarly rendered dollars a desirable form in which to acquire liquid reserves, but the same factors that made dollars desirable also rendered them difficult to obtain.

The Lender of Last Resort

If adjustment were always accomplished smoothly and liquidity were consistently adequate, there would be no need for an international lender of last resort to stabilize the international monetary system. Yet countries' capacity to adjust and the system's ability to provide liquidity may be inadequate to accommodate disturbances to confidence. Like domestic banking systems, an international financial system based on convertibility is vulnerable to problems of confidence that threaten to ignite speculative runs. Like depositors who rush to close their accounts upon receiving the news of a neighboring bank failure, exchange market participants, upon hearing of a convertibility crisis abroad, may rush to liquidate their foreign exchange balances because of incomplete information about the liabilities and intentions of particular governments. This analogy leads Charles Kindleberger, for example, to adopt from the domestic central banking literature the notion that a lender of last resort is needed to discount in times of crisis, provide countercyclical long-term lending, and maintain an open market for distress goods, and to suggest that, in the absence of a supranational institution, only a hegemonic power can carry out this international lender-of-last-resort function on the requisite scale.

Of the episodes considered here, the early Bretton Woods era provides the clearest illustration of the benefits of an international lender of last resort. The large amount of credit provided Europe in the form of grants and long-term loans and the willingness of the United States to accept European and Japanese exports even when these had been promoted by the extension of special incentives illustrate two of the lender-of-last-resort functions identified by Kindleberger: countercyclical lending and provision of an open market for distress goods. Many histories of the Marshall Plan characterize it in terms consistent with the benevolent strand of hegemonic stability theory: the United States was mainly interested in European prosperity and stood to benefit only insofar as that prosperity promoted geopolitical stability. Revisionist histories have more in common with the coercive strand of hegemonic stability theory: they suggest that the United States used Marshall aid to exact concessions from Europe in the form of most-favored-nation status for Germany, IMF exchange rate oversight, and Swiss links with the Organization for European Economic Cooperation. While it is certain that the European countries could not have moved so quickly to relax capital controls and quantitative trade restrictions without these forms of U.S. assistance, it is not clear how far the argument can be generalized. The Marshall Plan coincided with a very special era in the history of the international monetary system, in which convertibility outside the United States had not yet been restored. Hence there was little role for the central function of the lender of last resort: discounting freely when a convertibility crisis threatens. When convertibility was threatened in the 1960s, rescue operations were mounted not by the United States but cooperatively by the Group of Ten.

Kindleberger has argued that the 1929–31 financial crisis might have been avoided by the intervention of an international lender of last resort. The unwillingness of Britain and the United States to engage in countercyclical long-term lending and to provide an open market for distress goods surely exacerbated convertibility crises in the non-European world. Both the curtailment of overseas lending and the imposition of restrictive trade policies contributed greatly to the balance-of-payments difficulties that led to the suspension of convertibility by primary producers as early as 1929. Gold movements from the periphery to London and New York in 1930 heightened the problem and hastened its spread to Central Europe.

But it is not obvious that additional U.S. loans to Britain and other European countries attempting to fend off threats to convertibility would have succeeded in altering significantly the course of the 1931 financial crisis. Heading off the crisis would have required a successful defense of the pound sterling, whose depreciation was followed almost immediately by purposeful devaluation in some two dozen other countries. Britain did succeed in obtaining a substantial amount of short-term credit abroad in support of the pound, raising $650 million in New York and Paris after only minimal delay. Total short-term lending to countries under pressure amounted to approximately $1 billion, or roughly 10 percent of total international short-term indebtedness and 5 percent of world imports (more than the ratio of total IMF quotas to world imports in the mid-1970s). It is noteworthy that these credits were obtained not from a dominant power but from a coalition of creditor countries.

Could additional short-term credits from an international lender of last resort have prevented Britain's suspension of convertibility? If the run on sterling reflected merely a temporary loss of confidence in the stability of fixed parities, then additional loans from an international lender of last resort — like central bank loans to temporarily illiquid banks — might have permitted the crisis to be surmounted. But if the loss of confidence had a basis in economic fundamentals, no amount of short-term lending would have done more than delay the crisis in the absence of measures to eliminate the underlying imbalance. The existence of an international lender of last resort could have affected the timing but not the fact of collapse.

The fundamental disequilibrium that undermined confidence in sterling is typically sought in the government budget. The argument is that by stimulating absorption, Britain's budget deficit, in conjunction with the collapse of foreign demand for British exports, weakened the balance of trade. Although the second Labour government fell in 1931 precisely because of its failure to agree on measures to reduce the size of the budget deficit, historians disagree over whether the budget contributed significantly to the balance-of-payments deficit. The trade balance, after all, was only one component of the balance of payments. The effect on the balance of payments of shocks to the trade balance appears to have been small compared with the Bank of England's capacity to attract short-term capital. If this is correct and the 1931 financial crisis in Britain reflected mainly a temporary loss of confidence in sterling rather than a fundamental disequilibrium, then additional short-term loans from the United States or a group of creditor countries might have succeeded in tiding Britain over the crisis. But the loans required would have been extremely large by the standards of either the pre-1914 period of British hegemony or the post-1944 period of U.S. dominance.

The international lender-of-last-resort argument is more difficult to apply to the classical gold standard. . . . In 1873, as in 1890 and 1907, the hegemonic monetary authority, the Bank of England, would have been the "borrower of last resort" rather than the lender. [This fact] might be reconciled with the theory of hegemonic stability if the lender, Paris, is elevated to the status of a hegemonic financial center — a possibility to which Kindleberger is led by his analysis of late nineteenth century financial crises. But elevating Paris to parity with London would do much to undermine the view of the classical gold standard that attributes its durability to management by a single financial center.

What does this historical analysis of the lender-of-last-resort function imply for the validity of hegemonic theories of international monetary stability? It confirms that there have been instances, notably the aftermath of World War II, when the economic power of the leading country so greatly surpassed that of all rivals that it succeeded in ensuring the system's stability in times of crisis by discounting freely, providing countercyclical lending, and maintaining an open market. It suggests, at the same time, that such instances are rare. For a leading economic power to effectively act as lender of last resort, not only must its market power exceed that of all rivals, but it must do so by a very substantial margin. British economic power in the 1870s and U.S. economic power in the 1960s were inadequate in this regard, and other economic powers — France in the first instance, the Group of Ten in the second — were needed to cooperate in providing lender-of-last-resort facilities.

THE DYNAMICS OF HEGEMONIC DECLINE

Might an international monetary system that depends for its smooth operation on the dominance of a hegemonic power be dynamically unstable? There are two channels through which dynamic instability might operate: the system itself might evolve in directions that attenuate the hegemon's stabilizing capacity; or the system might remain the same, but its operation might influence relative rates of economic growth in such a way as to progressively reduce the economic power and, by implication, the stabilizing capacity of the hegemon.

The hypothesis that the Bretton Woods system was dynamically unstable was mooted by Robert Triffin as early as 1947. Triffin focused on what he saw as inevitable changes in the composition of reserves, arguing that the system's viability hinged on the willingness of foreign governments to accumulate dollars, which depended in turn on confidence in the maintenance of dollar convertibility. Although gold dominated the dollar as a source of international liquidity (in 1958 the value of gold reserves was four times the value of dollar reserves when all countries were considered, two times when the United States was excluded), dollars were the main source of liquidity on the margin. Yet the willingness of foreign governments to accumulate dollars at the required pace and hence the stability of the gold-dollar system were predicated on America's commitment and capacity to maintain the convertibility of dollars into gold at $35 an ounce. The threat to its ability to do so was that, under a system in which reserves could take the form of either dollars or gold (a scarce natural resource whose supply was insufficiently elastic to keep pace with the demand for liquidity), the share of dollars in total reserves could only increase. An ever-growing volume of foreign dollar liabilities was based on a fixed or even shrinking U.S. gold reserve. Thus the very structure of Bretton Woods — specifically, the monetary role for gold — progressively undermined the hegemon's capacity to ensure the system's smooth operation through the provision of adequate liquidity.

Dynamic instability also could have operated through the effect of the international monetary system on the relative rates of growth of the U.S. and foreign economies. If the dollar was systematically overvalued for a significant portion of the Bretton Woods era, this could have reduced the competitiveness of U.S. exports and stimulated foreign penetration of U.S. markets. If the dollar was overvalued due to some combination of European devaluations at the beginning of the 1950s, subsequent devaluations by developing countries, and the inability of the United States to respond to competitive difficulties by altering its exchange rate, how might this have depressed the relative rate of growth of the U.S. economy, leading to hegemonic decline? One can think of two arguments: one that proceeds along Heckscher-Ohlin lines, another that draws on dynamic theories of international trade.

The Heckscher-Ohlin hypothesis builds on the observation that the United States was relatively abundant in human and physical capital. Since, under Heckscher-Ohlin assumptions, U.S. exports were capital intensive, any measure that depressed exports would have reduced its rate of return. Reducing the rate of return would have discouraged investment, depressing the rate of economic growth and accelerating the U.S. economy's relative decline.

The dynamic trade theory hypothesis builds on the existence of learning curves in the production of traded goods. If production costs fall with cumulative output and the benefits of learning are external to the firm but internal to domestic industry, then exchange rate overvaluation, by depressing the competitiveness of exports, will inhibit their production and reduce the benefits of learning. If overvaluation is sufficiently large and persistent, it will shift comparative advantage in production to foreign competitors. The weakness of this hypothesis is that it is predicated on the unsubstantiated assumption that learning effects are more important in the production of traded goods than nontraded goods. Its strength lies in the extent to which it conforms with informal characterizations of recent trends.

Precisely the same arguments have been applied to the downfall of the interwar gold exchange standard. The interwar system, which depended for liquidity on gold, dollars, and sterling, was if anything even more susceptible than its post–World War II analog to destabilization by the operation of Gresham's law. As noted above, the legacy of the Genoa conference encouraged central banks to accumulate foreign exchange. Promoting the use of exchange reserves while attempting to maintain gold convertibility threatened the system's stability for the same reasons as under Bretton Woods. But because foreign exchange reserves were not then concentrated in a single currency to the same extent as after World War II, it was even easier under the interwar system for central banks to liquidate foreign balances in response to any event that undermined confidence in sterling or the dollar. Instead of initiating the relatively costly and complex process of acquiring gold from foreign monetary authorities in the face of at least moral suasion to refrain, central banks needed only to swap one reserve currency for the other on the open market. Gresham's law operated even more powerfully when gold coexisted with two reserve currencies than with one.

This instability manifested itself when the 1931 financial crisis, by undermining faith in sterling convertibility, induced a large-scale shift out of London balances. Once Britain was forced to devalue, faith in the stability of the other major reserve currency was shaken, and speculative pressure shifted to the dollar. The National Bank of Belgium, which had lost 25 percent of the value of its sterling reserve as a result of Britain's devaluation, moved to liquidate its dollar balances. The Eastern European countries, including Poland, Czechoslovakia, and Bulgaria, then liquidated their deposits in New York. Between the end of 1930 and the end of 1931, the share of foreign exchange in the reserve portfolios of twenty-three European countries fell from 35 to 19 percent, signaling the demise of the exchange portion of the gold exchange standard.

The argument that structuring the international monetary system around a reserve asset provided by the leading economic power led eventually to that country's loss of preeminence has been applied even more frequently to Britain after World War I than to the United States after World War II. Because the gold exchange standard created a foreign demand for sterling balances, Britain was able to run larger trade balance deficits than would have been permitted otherwise. In a sense, Britain's reserve currency status was one of the factors that facilitated the restoration of sterling prewar parity. Despite an enormous literature predicated on the view that the pound was overvalued at $4.86, there remains skepticism that the extent of overvaluation was great or the effect on the macroeconomy was significant. While it is not possible to resolve this debate here, the point relevant to the theory of hegemonic stability is that evidence of reserve currency overvaluation is as substantial in the earlier period, when hegemony was threatened, as in the later period, when it was triumphant.

Of the three monetary systems considered here, the classical gold standard is the most difficult to analyze in terms of the dynamics of hegemonic decline. It might be argued that the pound was overvalued for at least a decade before 1913 and that Britain's failure to devalue resulted in sluggish growth, which accelerated the economy's hegemonic decline. The competitive difficulties of older British industries, notably iron and steel, and the decelerating rate of economic growth in the first decade of the twentieth century are consistent with this view. The deceleration in the rate of British economic growth has been ascribed to both a decline in productivity growth and a fall in the rate of domestic capital formation. This fall in the rate of domestic capital formation, especially after 1900, reflected, not a decline in British savings rates, but a surge of foreign investment. Thus, if Britain's hegemonic position in the international economy is to have caused its relative decline, this hegemony would have had to be responsible for the country's exceptionally high propensity to export capital. The volume of British capital exports in the decades preceding World War I has been attributed, alternatively, to the spread of industrialization and associated investment opportunities to other countries and continents and to imperfections in the structure of British capital markets that resulted in a bias toward investment overseas. It is impossible to resolve this debate here. But the version of the market imperfections argument that attributes the London capital market's lack of interest in domestic investment to Britain's relatively early and labor-intensive form of industrialization implies that the same factors responsible for Britain's mid-nineteenth-century hegemony (the industrial revolution occurred there first) may also have been responsible for the capital market biases that accelerated its hegemonic decline.

Although the classical gold standard experienced a number of serious disruptions, such as the 1907 panic, when a financial crisis threatened to undermine its European core; the prewar system survived these disturbances intact. Eventually, however, the same forces that led to the downfall of the interwar gold exchange standard would have undermined the stability of the prewar system. As the rate of economic growth continued to outstrip the rate of growth of gold (the supply of which was limited by the availability of ore), countries would have grown increasingly dependent on foreign exchange reserves as a source of incremental liquidity. As in the 1960s, growing reliance on exchange reserves in the face of relatively inelastic gold supplies would have eventually proven incompatible with the reserve center's ability to maintain gold convertibility.

De Cecco argues that the situation was already beginning to unravel in the first decade of the twentieth century — that the Boer War signaled the end of the long peace of the nineteenth century, thereby undermining the willingness of potential belligerents to hold their reserves as deposits in foreign countries. . . . More important for our purposes, he suggests that the system was destabilized by the growth of U.S. economic power relative to that of Great Britain. Given the experimental nature of U.S. Treasury efforts to accommodate seasonal variations in money demand, the United States relied heavily on gold imports whenever economic conditions required an increase in money supply, notably during harvest and planting seasons. When the demand for money increased, the United States imported gold, mainly from the Bank of England, which was charged with pegging the sterling price of gold on the London market with a gold reserve of only £30 million. As the American economy grew, both its average demand for gold from London and that demand's seasonal fluctuation increased relative to the Bank of England's primary reserve and its capacity to attract supplementary funds from other centers. To rephrase de Cecco's argument in terms of hegemonic stability theory, the growth of the United States relative to that of Britain undermined Britain's capacity to stabilize international financial markets: specifically, its ability to serve simultaneously as the world's only free gold market, providing however much gold was required by other countries, and to maintain the stability of sterling, the reference point for the global system of fixed exchange rates. In a sense, de Cecco sees indications of the interwar stalemate — a Britain incapable of stabilizing the international system and a United States unwilling to do so — emerging in the first decade of the twentieth century. From this perspective, the process of hegemonic decline that culminated in the international monetary difficulties of the interwar years was at most accelerated by World War I. Even before the war, the processes that led to the downfall of established monetary arrangements were already under way.

CONCLUSION

Much of the international relations literature concerned with prospects for international monetary reform can be read as a search for an alternative to hegemony as a basis for international monetary stability. Great play is given to the contrast between earlier periods of hegemonic dominance, notably 1890–1914 and 1945–1971, and the nature of the task presently confronting aspiring architects of international monetary institutions in an increasingly multipolar world. In this paper I suggest that hegemonic stability theories are helpful for understanding the relatively smooth operation of the classical gold standard and the early Bretton Woods system, as well as some of the difficulties of the interwar years. At the same time, much of the evidence is difficult to reconcile with the hegemonic stability view. Even when individual countries occupied positions of exceptional prominence in the world economy and that prominence was reflected in the form and functioning of the international monetary system, that system was still fundamentally predicated on international collaboration. Keohane's notion of "hegemonic cooperation" — that cooperation is required for systemic stability even in periods of hegemonic dominance, although the presence of a hegemon may encourage cooperative behavior — seems directly applicable to international monetary relations. The importance of collaboration is equally apparent in the design of the international monetary system, its operation under normal circumstances, and the management of crises. Despite the usefulness of hegemonic stability theory when applied to short periods and well-defined aspects of international monetary relations, the international monetary system has always been "after hegemony" in the sense that more than a dominant economic power was required to ensure the provision and maintenance of international monetary stability. Moreover, it was precisely when important economic power most forcefully conditioned the form of the international system that the potential for instability, in a dynamic sense, was greatest. Above all, historical experience demonstrates the speed and pervasiveness of changes in national economic power; since hegemony is transitory, so must be any international monetary system that takes hegemony as its basis. Given the costs of international monetary reform, it would seem unwise to predicate a new system on such a transient basis.

15

The Triad and the Unholy Trinity: Problems of International Monetary Cooperation

BENJAMIN J. COHEN

In this essay, Benjamin J. Cohen explores the attractions and diffi-culties of cooperation among nations concerning international monetary matters and emphasizes how international political realities constrain interactions among independent nation-states. Monetary policy coordination has some potential benefits, but there are many uncertainties that countries face in engaging in cooperative behavior. The primary dilemma is that governments cannot simultaneously achieve the objectives of exchange-rate stability, capital mobility, and monetary policy autonomy. As governments are forced to make trade-offs among these goals, they will abandon the goal of exchange-rate stability — and thus monetary cooperation — if it is too costly relative to the other policy objectives. The cyclical and episodic qualities of monetary cooperation are linked to governments' changing incentives to pursue stable exchange rates. Cohen's argument highlights the difficulty of sustaining cooperative arrangements when states' national interests diverge.

... Among the G-7 [Group of Seven] countries (the United States, Britain, Canada, France, Germany, Italy and Japan), procedures for monetary cooperation have been gradually intensified since the celebrated Plaza Agreement of September 1985, which formally pledged participants to a coordinated realign-ment of exchange rates. Ostensibly the aim of these evolving procedures is to jointly manage currency relations and macroeconomic conditions across Europe, North America and Japan — the area referred to by many simply as the Triad. Finance ministers from the G-7 countries now meet regularly to discuss the cur-rent and prospective performance of their economies; policy objectives and instru-ments are evaluated for possible linkages and repercussions; the principle of mutual adjustment in the common interest is repeatedly reaffirmed in official communiqués. ... Yet for all their promises to curb unilateralist impulses, the governments involved frequently honour the process more in word than deed. In fact, if there has been one constant in the collaborative efforts of the Triad, it has been their lack of constancy. Commitments in practice have tended to ebb and flow cyclically like the tides. In its essence, G-7 monetary cooperation has had a distinctly episodic quality to it.

The main premise of this chapter is that international monetary cooperation, like passionate love, is a good thing but difficult to sustain. The reason, I argue, is systematic and has to do with the intrinsic incompatibility of three key desiderata of governments: exchange-rate stability, capital mobility, and national policy autonomy. Together these three values form a kind of "Unholy Trinity" that operates regularly to erode collective commitments to monetary collaboration. The impact of the Unholy Trinity has been evident in the experience of the G-7. The principal implication . . . is that the conditions necessary for a serious and sustained commitment to monetary cooperation are not easy to satisfy and, without major effort, appear unlikely to be attained any time soon. The irony is that even without such a commitment most . . . governments will find their policy autonomy increasingly eroded in the coming decade — in a manner, moreover, that may seem even less appealing to them than formal cooperation.

The organisation of this chapter is as follows. Following a brief evaluation in Part 1 of the basic case for monetary cooperation, Part 2 reviews the experience of the G-7 countries since 1985 noting, in particular, a distinctly cyclical pattern in the Triad's collective commitment to policy coordination. Reasons for the episodic quality of monetary cooperation with emphasis on the central role of the Unholy Trinity are explored in Part 3, and the question of what might be done about the resulting inconstancy of policy commitments is addressed in Part 4. . . .

1. THE CASE FOR POLICY COOPERATION

Conceptually, international cooperation may take many forms, ranging from simple consultation among governments, or occasional crisis management, to partial or even full collaboration in the formulation and implementation of policy. In this chapter, following the lead of standard scholarship on international political economy, cooperation will be identified with a mutual adjustment of national-policy behaviour in a particular issue-area, achieved through an implicit or explicit process of inter-state bargaining. Related terms such as "coordination" and "joint" or "collective decision-making" will, for our purposes, be treated as essentially synonymous in meaning.

In the issue-area of international monetary relations, the theoretical case for policy cooperation is quite straightforward. It begins with the undeniable fact of intensified interdependence across much of the world economy. In recent decades, states have become increasingly linked through the integration of markets for goods, services and capital. Structurally, the greater openness of economies tends to erode each country's insulation from commercial or financial developments elsewhere. In policy terms it means that any one government's actions will generate a variety of "spillover" effects — foreign repercussions and feedbacks — that can significantly influence its own ability, as well as the ability of others, to achieve preferred macroeconomic or exchange-rate objectives. (Technically, the size, and possibly even the sign, of policy multipliers is altered both at home and abroad.) Such "externalities" imply that policies chosen unilaterally, even if seemingly optimal from an individual country's point of view, will almost certainly turn out to be sub-optimal in a global context. The basic rationale for monetary cooperation is that it can *internalise* these externalities by giving each government partial control over the actions of others, thus relieving the shortage of instruments that prevents each one separately from reaching its chosen targets on its own.

At least two sets of goals may be pursued through policy coordination. At one level, cooperation may be treated simply as a vehicle by which countries together move closer to their individual policy targets. (In the formal language of game theory favoured by many analysts, utility or welfare-seeking governments bargain their way from the suboptimality of a so-called Nash equilibrium to something closer to a Pareto optimum.) Peter Kenen calls this the *policy-optimising* approach to cooperation. At a second level, mutual adjustments can also be made in pursuit of broader collective goals, such as defence of existing international arrangements or institutions against the threat of economic or political shocks. Kenen calls this the *regime-preserving* or *public-goods* approach to cooperation. Both approaches derive from the same facts of structural and policy interdependence. Few scholars question the basic logic of either one.

What is accepted in theory, of course, need not be favoured in practice — however persuasive the logic. . . .

In recent years there has been a virtual avalanche of formal literature citing various qualifications to the basic case for monetary cooperation and casting doubt on its practical benefits. The irony is evident: even as policy coordination since the mid-1980s has ostensibly become fashionable again among governments, it seems to have gone out of style with many analysts. At least five major issues have been raised for discussion by economists working in this area.

First is the question of the *magnitude of the gains* to be expected. Although in theory the move from a Nash equilibrium to Pareto optimality may seem dramatic, in practice much depends on the size of the spillovers involved. If externalities are small, so too will be the potential benefits of cooperation.

Many analysts cite a pioneering study by Oudiz and Sachs designed to measure the effects of monetary and fiscal policy coordination by Germany, Japan and the United States, using data from the mid-1970s. Estimated gains were disappointingly meagre, amounting to no more than half of one per cent of GNP in each country as compared with the best noncooperative outcomes. Although some subsequent studies have detected moderately greater income increases from coordination, most tend to confirm the impression that on balance very large gains should not be expected.

Second is the other side of the ledger: the question of the *magnitude of the costs* to be expected. Theoretical models typically abstract from the costs of coordination. In reality, however, considerable time and effort are needed to evaluate performance, negotiate agreements, and monitor compliance among sovereign governments. Moreover, the greater the number of countries or issues involved, the more complex are the policy adjustments that are likely to be required of each.

All this demands expenditure of resources that may loom large when compared with the possibly meagre scale of anticipated benefits. For some analysts, this suggests that the game may simply not be worth the candle. For others, it implies the need for a more explicit framework for cooperation — some formally agreed set of rules — that could substitute for repeated negotiations over individual issues. . . . The advantage of an articulated rule-based regime is that it would presumably be more cost-effective than endless *ad hoc* bargaining. The disadvantage is that it would require a greater surrender of policy autonomy than many governments now seem prepared to tolerate (a point to which I shall return below).

Third is the so-called *time-inconsistency* problem: the risk that agreements, once negotiated, will later be violated by maverick governments tempted to renege on policy commitments that turn out to be inconvenient. The risk, in principle, is a real one. In relations between sovereign states, where enforcement mechanisms are weak or nonexistent, there is always a threat that bargains may be, at some point, broken. But whether the possibility of unilateral defection constitutes much of a threat in practice is hotly debated among specialists, many of whom stress the role of reputation and credibility as deterrents to cheating by individual governments. In the language of game theory, much depends on the details of how the strategic interactions are structured, for example, the number of players in the game, whether and how often the game is iterated, and how many other related games are being played simultaneously. Much depends as well on the historical and institutional context, and how the preferences of decision-makers are formed — matters about which it is inherently difficult to generalise. In the absence of more general specifications, few definitive judgements seem possible *a priori*.

Fourth is the possible *distortion of incentives* that might be generated by efforts at policy coordination. In an early and influential article, Kenneth Rogoff argued that international cooperation could actually prove to be counterproductive — welfare-decreasing rather than Pareto-improving — if the coordination process were to encourage governments collectively to choose policies that are more politically convenient than economically sound. Formal coordination of monetary policies, for example, could simply lead to higher global inflation if governments were all to agree to expand their money supplies together, thus evading the balance-of-payments constraint that would discipline any country attempting to inflate on its own. More generally, there is always the chance that ruling élites might exploit the process to promote particularist or even personal interests at the expense of broader collective goals. This risk too is widely regarded as realistic in principle and is hotly debated for its possible importance in practice. And here too few definitive judgements seem possible *a priori* in the absence of more general specifications.

Finally, there is the issue of *model uncertainty:* the risks that policy-makers simply are badly informed and do not really understand how their economies operate and interact. Frankel and Rockett in a widely cited study demonstrated that when governments do differ in their analytical views of policy impacts, coordination could well cause welfare losses rather than gains for at least some of the countries involved. For some analysts, this is more than enough reason to prefer a return to uncoordinated pursuit of national self-interest. For others, however, it suggests instead the value of consultation and exchanges of information to avoid misunderstandings about transmission mechanisms and the size and sign of relevant policy multipliers. . . .

Where, then, does all this discussion come out? None of the five issues that have been so thoroughly aired in the literature is unimportant; sceptics have been right to raise and emphasize them. But neither do any of these qualifications appear to deal a decisive blow to the underlying case for cooperation, which retains its essential appeal. For this reason most analysts, myself among them, still remain disposed to view policy cooperation, for all its imperfections, in much the same light as virtue or motherhood — an inherently good thing. Net gains may be small; motivations may get distorted; outcomes may not always fulfill expectations. Nonetheless, despite all the risks the effort does seem justified. . . .

2. THE EBB AND FLOW OF POLICY COMMITMENTS

A problem remains, however. To be effective, the collective commitment to cooperation must appear credible; and to be credible, that commitment must above all be *sustained.* Individual governments may play the maverick on occasion (the time-inconsistency problem); a little cheating at the margins is after all hardly unexpected, or even unusual, in international relations. But the commitment of the collectivity must be seen to be enduring: there can be no room for doubt about the continuing relevance, the *seriousness,* of the process as such. Otherwise incentives will indeed be distorted for state and non-state actors alike, and outcomes could well turn out to be every bit as counterproductive as many analysts fear. As Peter Kenen has warned, "Sporadic management may be worse than no management at all." Yet, as noted at the outset, that is precisely the pattern that policy coordination has tended to display in practice. The history of international monetary cooperation is one long lesson in the fickleness of policy fashion.

During the early inter-war period, for example, the central banks of the major industrial nations publicly committed themselves to a cooperative attempt to restore something like the pre–World War I gold standard, only to end up in the 1930s energetically battling one another through futile rounds of competitive devaluations and escalating capital controls. And similarly during the Bretton Woods era, early efforts at cooperative institution-building and joint consultations ultimately terminated in mutual recriminations and the demise of the par-value system. In the middle 1970s, endeavours to revive some kind of rule-based exchange-rate regime were overwhelmed by policy disagreements between the Carter administration in the United States and its counterparts in Europe and Japan, leading to a record depreciation of the U.S. dollar. At the turn of the decade renewed attempts at joint stabilization were cut short by the go-it-alone policies of the new Reagan administration, leading to the record appreciation of the dollar which, in turn, set the stage for the Plaza Agreement of 1985. The broad picture of monetary relations in the twentieth century is clearly one of considerable ebbs and flows in the collective commitment to policy cooperation.

Moreover, the big picture — much in the manner of Mandelbrot fractals — tends broadly to be replicated in the small. (A fractal is an object or phenomenon that is self-similar across different scales.) Often superimposed on longer waves of enthusiasm or disillusionment with policy cooperation have been briefer "stop-go" cycles of commitment and retreat, such as the short-lived attempts of the London Monetary Conference and later Tripartite Agreement to restore some measure of monetary stability in the 1930s. In the 1960s and early 1970s, even as the Bretton Woods system was heading for breakdown, the major financial powers cooperated at one point to create a new international reserve asset, the Special Drawing Right (SDR), and then at another to temporarily realign and stabilise exchange rates in the Smithsonian Agreement of December 1971. And even before the Plaza Agreement in 1985 there were already regular meetings of finance ministers and central bankers to discuss mutual policy linkages, as well as of lower-level officials in such settings as the Organisation for Economic Cooperation and Development (OECD) and the Bank for International Settlements (BIS). The now-fashionable process of multilateral surveillance was, in fact, first mandated by the leaders of the G-7 countries at the Versailles summit in 1982.

Most significantly, the same cyclical pattern has been evident even . . . since the announcement of the Plaza Agreement. The appetite for mutual accommodation in the Triad continues to wax and wane episodically; inconstancy remains the rule. Formally the G-7 governments are now fully committed to the multilateral-surveillance process. In actual practice, despite regular meetings and repeated reaffirmations of principle, policy behaviour continues to betray a certain degree of recurrent recidivism. . . .

This is not to suggest that the multilateral-surveillance process has been utterly without redeeming social value. On the contrary, one can reasonably argue that for all its episodic quality the effort has on balance been beneficial, both in terms of what has in fact been accomplished and in terms of what has been avoided. Anecdotal evidence seems to suggest that policy-makers have had their consciousness genuinely raised regarding the foreign externalities of their domestic actions; in any event, the regularity of the schedule of ministerial meetings now clearly compels officials to integrate the international dimension much more fully than ever before into their own national decision processes. At the same time potentially severe challenges to regime stability have been successfully averted, including in particular the rising wave of U.S. protectionism in 1985 and the stock market crash of 1987.

Collective initiatives have been designed cautiously to avoid the pitfalls of model uncertainty and have not typically been chosen simply for their political convenience. Overall, gains do appear to have outweighed costs.

The gains might have been larger, however. One can also reasonably argue that the positive impact of the process might have been considerably greater than it was had there been less inconstancy of behaviour. That is perhaps the chief lesson to be learned from this brief recitation of recent monetary history. Governmental credibility has undoubtedly been strained by the cyclical ebb and flow of commitments since 1985. With each retreat to unilateralism market scepticism grows, requiring ever more dramatic *démarches* when, once again, joint initiatives seem warranted. *Net* benefits, as a result, tend to be diminished over time. Multilateral surveillance may have redeeming social value, but its stop-go pattern makes it more costly than it might otherwise be. In a real sense we all pay for the fickleness of policy fashion.

3. THE INFLUENCE OF THE UNHOLY TRINITY

Why is international monetary cooperation so episodic? To answer that question it is necessary to go back to first principles. Blame cannot be fobbed off on "karma," accidental exogenous "shocks," or even that vague epithet "politics." Consideration of the underlying political economy of the issue suggests that the dilemma is, in fact, systematic — endogenous to the policy process — and not easily avoided in relations between sovereign national governments.

The central analytical issue, which has been well understood at least since the pioneering theoretical work of economist Robert Mundell is the intrinsic incompatibility of three key desiderata of governments: exchange-rate stability, private-capital mobility, and monetary-policy autonomy. As I wrote in the introduction to this chapter my own label for this is the "Unholy Trinity." The problem of the Unholy Trinity, simply stated, is that in an environment of formally or informally pegged rates and effective integration of financial markets, any attempt to pursue independent monetary objectives is almost certain, sooner or later, to result in significant balance-of-payments disequilibrium, and hence provoke potentially destabilising flows of speculative capital. To preserve exchange-rate stability, governments will then be compelled to limit either the movement of capital (via restrictions or taxes) or their own policy autonomy (via some form of multilateral surveillance or joint decision-making). If they are unwilling or unable to sacrifice either one, then the objective of exchange-rate stability itself may eventually have to be compromised. Over time, except by chance, the three goals cannot be attained simultaneously.

In the real world, of course, governments might be quite willing to limit the movement of capital in such circumstances — if they could. Policymakers may say they value the efficiency gains of free and integrated financial markets. If polled "off the record" for their private preferences, however, most would probably admit to prizing exchange-rate stability and policy autonomy even more. The problem, from their point of view, is that capital mobility is notoriously difficult to control. Restrictions merely invite more and more sophisticated forms of evasion, as governments from Europe to South Asia to Latin America have learned to their regret. . . .

In practice, therefore, this means that in most instances the Unholy Trinity reduces to a direct trade-off between exchange-rate stability and policy autonomy. Conceptually, choices can be visualised along a continuum representing varying degrees of monetary-policy cooperation. At one extreme lies the polar alternative of a common currency or its equivalent — full monetary integration — where individual governments sacrifice policy autonomy completely for the presumed benefits of a permanent stabilisation of exchange rates. Most importantly, these benefits include the possible improvement in the usefulness of money in each of its principal functions: as a medium of exchange (owing to a reduction of transaction costs as the number of required currency conversions is decreased), store of value (owing to a reduced element of exchange risk as the number of currencies is decreased), and unit of account (owing to an information saving as the number of required price quotations is decreased). Additional gains may also accrue from the possibility of economies of scale in monetary and exchange-rate management as well as a potential saving of international reserves due to an internalisation through credit of what would otherwise be external trade and payments. Any saving of reserves through pooling in effect amounts to a form of seigniorage for each participating country.

At the other extreme lies the polar alternative of absolute monetary independence, where individual governments sacrifice any hope of long-term exchange-rate stability for the presumed benefits of policy autonomy. Most importantly, as Mundell demonstrated as early as 1961, these benefits include the possible improvement in the effectiveness of monetary policy as an instrument to attain national macroeconomic objectives. Today, of course, it is understood that much depends on whether any trade-off can be assumed to exist between inflation and unemployment over a time horizon relevant to policy-makers — technically, whether there is any slope to the Phillips curve in the short-term. In a strict monetarist model of the sort popular in the 1970s, incorporating the classical neutrality assumption ("purely monetary changes have no real effects"), such a trade-off was excluded by definition. The Phillips curve was said to be vertical at the so-called "natural" (or "non-inflation-accelerating") unemployment rate, determined exclusively by microeconomic phenomena on the supply side of the economy. More recently, however, most theorists have tended to take a more pragmatic approach, allowing that for valid institutional and psychological reasons Phillips-curve trade-offs may well persist for significant periods of time — certainly for periods long enough to make the preservation of monetary independence appear worthwhile to policy-makers. From this perspective, any movement along the continuum in the direction of a common currency will be perceived as a real cost by individual governments.

The key question is how this cost compares with the overall benefit of exchange-rate stabilisation. Here we begin to approach the nub of the issue at hand. My hypothesis is that for each participating country both cost and benefit vary systematically with the degree of policy cooperation, and that it is through the interaction of these costs and benefits that we get the episodic quality of the cooperation process we observe in practice.

Assume absolute monetary independence to start with. Most gains from exchange-rate stabilisation, I would argue, can be expected to accrue "up front" and then decline at the margin for successively higher degrees of policy cooperation. That is because the greatest disadvantage of exchange-rate instability is the damage done to the usefulness of money in its various functions. Any move at all by governments to reduce uncertainty about currency values is bound to have a disproportionate impact on market expectations and, hence, transaction costs in foreign exchange; further steps in the same direction may add to the credibility of the collective commitment but will yield only smaller and smaller savings to participants. Most of the cost of stabilisation, on the other hand, can be expected to be "back-loaded" in the perceptions of the relevant policy-makers. That is because governments have an understandable tendency to discount the disadvantages of foreign agreements until they find themselves really constrained in seeking to attain their domestic objectives — at which point disproportionate importance comes to be attached to the compromises of interests involved. Where initial moves towards coordinated decision-making may be treated as virtually costless, further steps in the same direction tend to be seen as increasingly threatening. Thus, the marginal cost of policy cooperation for each country tends to rise systematically even as the marginal benefit may be assumed to fall. . . .

4. CAN COOPERATION BE "LOCKED IN"?

The dilemma posed by the Unholy Trinity thus helps us to understand why international monetary cooperation is so episodic. The question remains: what, if anything, can be done about it?

One answer can be ruled out from the start: the proposition that the observed inconstancy of policy behaviour could be overcome if only governments could be educated to comprehend their own best interests. If my hypothesis is correct, governments are already acting in their own best interests and behaving in a manner consistent with a rational calculus of their own costs and benefits. The issue is not myopia: policy-makers surely are not unaware of the impacts of their behaviour on market expectations . . . and would stick to their commitments if that seemed desirable. Rather, it is a question of how policy incentives change over time as a result of the shifting tide of events. Fundamentally, my reasoning may be understood as a variant of the logic of collective action first elucidated by Mancur Olson more than a quarter of a century ago. A common interest is evident to all, yet individually rational behaviour can, at least part of the time, lead to distinctly suboptimal outcomes. This is true whether the common interest is understood in terms of policy optimisation or regime preservation.

Moreover, my hypothesis has the advantage of being consistent with a wide range of alternative paradigms that have been employed in the standard international political-economy literature. It is certainly compatible with traditional realist or structuralist approaches in which the sovereign state, for reasons of analytical parsimony, is automatically assumed to behave like a rational unitary actor with its own set of well-defined national interests. It is also consistent with more pluralist models of policy-making, in which conceptions of interest are distilled from the interplay of differing combinations of domestic political and institutional forces; and even with models drawn from public-choice theory, in which policy behaviour is assumed to reflect first and foremost the personal interests of policy-makers (the principal-agent problem). For the purposes of my hypothesis, it really does not matter where the policy preferences of governments come from. It only matters that they act systematically on them.

Assuming education is not the answer, the crux of the issue becomes whether any collective commitment to cooperation once made can be "locked in" in some way. If the problem is that governments find it difficult to sustain their enthusiasm for the process, can a solution be found that will effectively prevent them from retreating?

One obvious possibility is the extreme of a common currency, where individual autonomy is — in principle — permanently surrendered by each participating country. In practice, of course, not even full currency unions have proved indissoluble, as we saw in the case of the East African shilling in the 1970s or as evidently we are about to see in the case of the (former) Soviet Union today. But cases like these usually stem from associations that were something less than voluntary to begin with. When undertaken by consenting sovereign states, full monetary unification generally tends to be irreversible — which is precisely the reason why it is seen so seldomly in the real world. During the *laissez-faire* nineteenth century, when monetary autonomy meant less to governments than it does now, two fairly prominent currency unions were successfully established among formally independent nations — the Latin Monetary Union, dating from 1865, and the Scandinavian Monetary Union created in 1873 — each built on a single, standardised monetary unit (respectively, the franc and the krone). Both groupings, however, were effectively terminated with the outbreak of World War I. In the twentieth century, the only comparable arrangement has been the Belgium-Luxembourg Economic Union, established in 1921. (Other contemporary currency unions, such as the CFA franc zone and the East Caribbean dollar area, had their origins in colonial relationships.) The recent difficulties experienced by the European Community (EC) in negotiating the details of a formal Economic and Monetary Union (EMU) illustrate just how tough it is to persuade governments even as closely allied as these to make the irrevocable commitment required by a common currency.

Short of the extreme of a common currency, an effective solution would require participating governments to voluntarily pre-commit to some form of external authority over their individual policy behaviour. The authority might be supplied by an international agency armed with collectively agreed decision-making powers — corresponding to what I have elsewhere called the organising principle of supra-nationality. It might also be supplied by one single dominant country with acknowledged leadership responsibilities (the principle of hegemony). Or it might be supplied by a self-disciplining regime of norms and rules accepted as binding on all participants (the principle of automaticity). Unfortunately, neither experience nor the underlying logic of political sovereignty offers a great deal of hope in the practical potential of any of these alternatives. Supra-nationality and automaticity, for example, have always tended to be heavily qualified in international monetary relations. In the G-7 multilateral-surveillance process, the International Monetary Fund (in the person of its managing director) has been given a role, but limited only to the provision of essential data and objective analytical support, and public articulation of any sort of binding rules (regarding, for example, exchange-rate targets) has been strenuously resisted by most governments. Hegemony, in the meantime, may be tolerated where it is unavoidable, as in the sterling area during the 1930s or the Bretton Woods system immediately after World War II. But as both these historical episodes illustrate, dominance also tends to breed considerable resentment and a determined eagerness by most countries to assert individual autonomy as soon as circumstances permit.

The principal exception in recent years has been the joint currency float (the "snake") of the European Community, first implemented in the 1970s by a cluster of smaller countries effectively aligned with West Germany's Deutschemark, and later extended and formalised under the European Monetary System (EMS), starting in 1979. Under the rules of the EC's joint float, national monetary discretion for most members has been distinctly constrained, despite relatively frequent realignments of mutual exchange rates and, until the end of the 1980s, the persistence of significant capital controls in some countries. German policy, on the other hand, has not only remained largely autonomous but has effectively dominated monetary relations within the group. In effect, therefore, the snake has successfully locked in a collective commitment to cooperation through a combination of automaticity and hegemony. Yet not only has the arrangement proved tolerable to its members, over time it has gradually attracted new participants; and now, despite the difficulties of gaining irrevocable commitments to a common currency, may be about to be extended again in the form of EMU.

The reasons for this success quite obviously are unique and have to do most with the distinctive character of the institutional ties that have developed among EC members. Over time, as Robert Keohane and Stanley Hoffmann have recently noted, the EC has gradually built up a highly complex process of policy-making in which formal and informal arrangements are intricately linked across a wide range of issues. Decisions in one sector are closely affected by what is happening elsewhere and often lead to the sort of inter-sectoral "spillover" effects that were first emphasised in early neo-functional theory. (Note that these effects are quite different from those featured in the theoretical case for policy cooperation, which stresses spillovers in a single sector or issue-area.) More generally, member governments have come to fully accept a style of political behaviour in which individual interests are jointly realised through an incremental, albeit fragmented, pooling of national sovereignty — what Keohane and Hoffmann call a "network" form of organisation, "in which individual units are defined not by themselves but in relation to other units." And this, in turn, has been made possible only because of the existence of a real sense of commitment and attachment — of *community* — among all the countries involved. In this sense, the EC truly is the exception that proves the rule. Among states less intimately connected, resistance to any form of external authority over individual policy behaviour is bound to be correspondingly more stubborn and determined.

Does this mean then that nothing can be done about the episodic quality of monetary cooperation? Not at all. In principle, any number of technical innovations can be imagined to moderate underlying tendencies towards recidivism by cooperating governments. As in the G-7 process, for example, meetings could be put on a regular schedule and based on an agreed analytical framework to help ensure greater continuity of policy behaviour. Much the same impact might also be attained by giving more precision as well as greater publicity to policy guidelines and commitments. And there might also be some benefit to be had from establishing a permanent, independent secretariat to provide an institutional memory and ongoing objective analysis of priorities and issues. The issue, however, is not administrative creativity but political acceptability. Each such innovation makes it just that much more difficult for policy-makers to change their minds when circumstances might seem to warrant it. Is the underlying relationship among the states involved sufficiently close to make them willing to take such a risk? This is not a question that can be answered *a priori,* as the exceptional case of the EC demonstrates, it is certainly not a question of monetary relations alone. Ultimately prospects for sustaining any cooperative effort in this crucial area of public policy will depend on how much basic affinity governments feel in other areas as well — in effect, on the extent to which they feel they share a common destiny across the full spectrum of economic and political issues.

16

Exchange Rate Politics
JEFFRY A. FRIEDEN

Government policies toward national currencies can be controversial. Commitments to a fixed exchange rate, devaluation, or
real appreciation can all lead to political conflict. Jeffry Frieden
argues that currency policy is more likely to excite controversy in
those economies that are more open. He then provides an interpretation of the domestic societal divisions over exchange rates.
Internationally oriented economic actors are more likely to
desire a fixed exchange rate than are domestically oriented ones.
By the same token, tradables producers are more likely to want a
weak (relatively depreciated) currency than are nontradables producers. This leads to expectations about domestic societal cleavages in debates over national currency policies.

For 20 years currency values have been a growing concern of policy makers, analysts, and investors. Exchange rates have also been a topic of increasing domestic
and international political debate, and it is widely recognized that they involve an
inseparable mix of politics and economics. . . .

This essay has two related purposes. The first is to explain changes in the political importance of exchange rates. Here my principal argument is that the distributional impact of exchange rate movements increases as economies become more
open on capital and current account, and that the politicization of currency policy
is an inevitable result of higher levels of international trade and payments.

My second purpose is to explain the patterns of political division and debate
that arise over exchange rates. Here I project which groups in society will be more
and less favorable to fixed or floating exchange rates, and to relatively appreciated
or depreciated exchange rates. For illustrative purposes, I discuss several historical and contemporary episodes: American exchange rate politics in the late 19th
and early 20th century, and current developments in European monetary integration.

THE POLITICS OF EXCHANGE RATES: GENERAL PRINCIPLES

My first task is to explain the degree to which the exchange rate becomes a target
of important political conflict. The second is to explain the sorts of political divisions that develop when exchange rates become a topic of political debate.

To understand the reasons for variation in the political significance of currency issues, we can start with a basic principle of macroeconomic policy, that no country can have more than two of the following three conditions: a fixed exchange rate, an independent monetary policy, and capital mobility. The reasoning is simple. If capital is mobile across borders, interest rates cannot vary across countries. Given capital mobility, monetary policy operates primarily via the exchange rate: money growth faster than the rest of the world leads to depreciation, which (generally) causes economic expansion.

This implies that capital mobility leads to a trade-off between exchange rate stability and monetary independence: a government can only ensure its currency's stability by giving up its principal instrument of monetary policy. The development of such a trade-off where none was previously present constrains monetary policy in purely economic terms; but it also has a political economy impact, that is, it affects the activity of socioeconomic groups in the political arena.

In a financially closed economy, a monetary stimulus raises the nominal price level, reduces real interest rates, lowers borrowing costs and encourages both investment and credit-financed consumer spending. Closed-economy monetary policy affects the nominal price level but not relative prices among most goods and services. It has broad but diffuse effects on growth, and more targeted effects on those with nominal contracts, such as debtors and creditors. Political divisions can be expected between borrowers and savers. A few specific industries — especially housing construction and major consumer durables — are sensitive to interest rates, as their products are typically purchased on credit; the financial sector generally supports higher interest rates. But the principal impact is on such broad macroeconomic aggregates as growth and unemployment.

For these reasons, it is reasonable to expect the politics of monetary policy in a closed economy to be subdued, and the divisions to be relatively broad-gauged. Those principally concerned are either relatively small groups — the housing construction industry, the financial sector — or broad masses of borrowers and savers, as well as workers and consumers affected by general macroeconomic trends.

However, in a financially open economy, in which monetary policy primarily affects the exchange rate, it operates not by way of its impact on the nominal price level but rather by changing the relative price of tradable and non-tradable goods and services. Monetary expansion, for example, drives the currency's value down, makes locally produced goods cheaper in comparison to imports, and stimulates demand for domestically produced tradable goods. Exchange rate movements therefore, unlike interest rate movements, have an immediate impact on a wide range of relative prices. They affect those exposed to international trade and payments, such as exporters, import-competers, international banks, and multinational corporations. They also have a second-order impact on producers of non-tradable goods and services. Policies that implicate the exchange rate therefore call into play well-defined economic interests.

In a financially open economy in which monetary policy runs through the exchange rate, relative price effects are immediate and significant for specific interests, so that political pressures from concentrated groups can be expected. Currency movements affect relative prices more directly and for more concentrated interests than overall movements in the nominal price level. This implies that financial integration heightens political debates over monetary policy, even as it shifts their focus toward the relative prices affected by exchange rate movements.

Monetary politics is affected in an analogous way by commercial openness. While integration of financial markets changes monetary policy trade-offs, trade openness increases the intensity with which these trade-offs are felt by economic actors. Greater exposure to world trade swells the ranks of those sensitive to the exchange rate. Tradables producers are especially sensitive to the exchange rate; as more goods become tradable, more producers are more concerned about currency values. Even non-tradables producers care more about exchange rates as the economy is opened to trade, for the import component of their inputs rises, as does the effect on them of the expenditure-switching caused by exchange rate movements. Increased trade intensifies the interest of producers in policies that move exchange rates in their favor.

All of this serves to explain that increasing political attention to exchange rates is a predictable result of goods and capital market integration. The more closely linked financial markets are, the more national monetary policies are forced to operate by way of the exchange rate. The more closely linked markets for goods and capital are, the more economic agents care about exchange rate movements. This leads to my second problem, the exchange rate policy preferences I expect in an open economy.

Two policy issues are relevant. First, governments need to decide whether to have an independent monetary policy, which requires a flexible exchange rate, or to forgo an autonomous monetary policy in the interests of having a stable and predictable exchange rate. Second, and presuming they take action to affect the exchange rate, governments need to decide on the desired level of the currency. Let me take these in turn.

Different economic agents can be expected to have different views of the trade-off between exchange rate stability and national ability to affect domestic monetary conditions. Those whose business is fully domestic, for whom foreign trade and payments — thus the exchange rate — are insignificant, will prefer national policy independence to the stability of a price that matters little to them. This group includes producers of nontradable goods and services, and producers of traded goods that find their market primarily at home. Their fortunes are dependent upon domestic business conditions, and the government's ability to affect national monetary conditions requires a flexible exchange rate.

On the other hand, those heavily involved in international trade and investment care deeply about the predictability of the exchange rate, which has a major impact on their economic performance. Indeed, inasmuch as they can move production or sales easily from home to foreign markets, they care less about domestic conditions than about the predictability of currency values. This range of variation is represented on the vertical axis of Figure 1, in which monetary independence and exchange rate flexibility co-vary as we assume an open economy.

| | | Preferred Level of the Exchange Rate | |
		High	Low
Preferred Degree of Exchange-Rate Flexibility/ National Monetary Independence	**Low**	International traders and investors	Export-competing traded goods producers
	High	Non-tradables producers	Import-competing traded goods producers

FIGURE 1. Exchange Rate Policy Preferences, Given Capital Mobility

Note: As regards the level of the exchange rate, "high" refers to a more appreciated exchange rate and "low" to a more depreciated exchange rate. As regards the degree of exchange rate flexibility, "low" implies a fixed rate such as the gold standard, while "high" implies freely floating rates. Given capital mobility, this variation also implies variation from the absence of national monetary independence to effective and nationally autonomous monetary policy. These are, of course, only rough approximations, and variation is along a continuum rather than dichotomous.

Economic agents also care about the level of the currency's value. Typically, producers of tradable goods favor a relatively lower (more depreciated) exchange rate, which makes their products cheaper relative to foreign goods. Producers of non-tradable goods and services favor a relatively higher (more appreciated) exchange rate, which raises the price of their products relative to tradable goods in the home market. International investors tend to favor a strong currency, which allows them to purchase overseas assets more cheaply. These preferences are reflected on the horizontal axis of Figure 1.

None of these assertions about the distributional effects of exchange rate movements is unqualified. Preferences over the level of the exchange rate may well vary in intensity. Producers of standardized goods are probably most sensitive to exchange rate movements: they compete on price alone, and small movements in currency values can mean the difference between profitability and bankruptcy. Those whose products are tradable but compete largely on quality and other non-price variables are likely to be less concerned. Put differently, the sensitivity of tradables producers to exchange rate movements is a function of the price elasticities of demand for their products.

Another point is that generally the influence of exchange rate movements on non-tradable goods and services is less direct than on tradables. While an appreciation raises the price of non-tradables relative to tradables, the process can be gradual (as in the United States in the early and mid-1980s). And whatever positive impact price increases may have on relative prices has to be measured against the negative effects of higher prices on demand and the entry of new competitors. Non-tradables producers especially have to worry about the relative importance of income and substitution effects — whether a real appreciation might reduce total spending enough to counterbalance the positive impact of the increased price of non-tradables. Overseas investors care both about asset prices and about returns: a strong currency makes assets relatively cheaper in home-currency terms, but also makes the income stream less valuable.

Another complication is that the two issues, exchange rate flexibility and currency value (the horizontal and vertical axes of Fig. 1) are often elided. Currency values are frequently linked to the overarching regime of exchange rate determination. This is most obvious in the case of a fixed rate regime such as the gold standard or the European Monetary System, in which it is difficult to devalue without damaging the credibility of sustaining the fixed rate.

Where policy toward the level of the exchange rate and its variability are linked and actors' interests cut in different directions, they must decide which matters more to them. Exporters weigh the relative importance of the increased competitiveness given by a devaluation against the uncertainty that devaluations introduce. For some — especially with long-term contracts where hedging is difficult — variable exchange rates may lead to substantial loss of business. For others, the added competitive edge dominates. To take another example, international investors may care less about the level of the exchange rate than about its variability. Firms with globally diversified production may be insensitive to particular levels of the exchange rate — the negative impact of a strong franc on French operations is presumably counterbalanced by the positive impact of the mirror-image weakness of other currencies on non-French operations — but their ability to formulate investment plans may be very sensitive to exchange rate instability.

All of these nuances are important to the detailed evaluation of political debates over monetary and exchange rate policy. However, my purpose is only to indicate the broad trends involved in such evaluation, and for this purpose the general tendencies discussed above hold.

In summary, increased levels of financial and commercial integration drive monetary policy toward the exchange rate, make the exchange rate more distributionally divisive, and lead to a more politicized context for the making of macroeconomic policy. In such an open economy, clear differences arise among economic agents over both the desired level of the exchange rate and the desired degree to which it will be fixed. All else equal, domestically oriented producers prefer a flexible exchange rate, internationally oriented ones a fixed exchange rate. Tradables producers prefer a weak (depreciated) currency, non-tradables producers and overseas investors a strong (appreciated) one. In this context, I now turn to some illustrative examples drawn largely from the American past and contemporary Europe.

HISTORICAL PATTERNS IN MONETARY POLITICS

If my first argument is correct, the political prominence of exchange rates should vary with the openness of a country to international trade and financial flows. This should hold both over time and across countries: as the world becomes more (less) integrated on current and capital account, the exchange rate should become more (less) politicized; at any given point in time, more open economies should have more political debate over exchange rates.

Both historical and contemporary evidence supports these propositions. From about 1870 until the First World War, and again in the 1920s and early 1930s, world trade and payments were at extremely high levels. Indeed, there is strong evidence that capital markets were closely linked in the late 19th and early 20th century. From the 1930s until about 1975, however, capital was not particularly mobile among developed countries. Virtually all of them had capital controls of varied effectiveness, most capital movements took the form of direct investment by multinational corporations. Countries could, at least in the short and medium run, sustain both independent monetary policies and fixed exchange rates.

As expected, monetary policy was extremely hotly contested in the 60 years before 1930. In most of the world's countries it was, typically along with the tariff, the principal economic issue. This was true in developed and developing, primary producing and industrial countries alike. But from the 1930s until the early 1970s, exchange rate issues, and indeed monetary policy more generally, were typically relegated to a subordinate place on national political agendas. The Money Question, as it had been known before, became the precinct of a few lonely academics, market operators, and monetary policy makers.

However, over the course of the 1970s and 1980s, capital became far more mobile. Capital controls were removed, and the offshore financial markets grew to enormous size. Today, markets for short-term financial assets are highly integrated within the OECD, far more integrated than they were between the 1930s and the 1970s. Under these conditions, monetary policy has come to operate primarily through the exchange rate.

Change in the economic environment, toward a higher level of capital mobility, thus gave the exchange rate great prominence. As countries attempted to pursue autonomous monetary policies, exchange rates fluctuated substantially. At the same time, the continual increase in trade and investment among developed economies made more and more economic agents sensitive to the effects of exchange rate fluctuations. Whether as traders and exporters or as foreign investors and borrowers, there are many more for whom the exchange rate is a crucial component of the economic environment.

This has led to prominent political debates over exchange rates all over the world. This is most obvious in the European Community and countries on its periphery, for which monetary and exchange rate problems have been central since the early 1980s. It is certainly the case in Japan, where the value of the yen is a topic of constant policy and political debate. It is true in the newly industrializing countries of East Asia and Latin America, in a wide variety of ways. . . . And even in the United States, as the dollar rose in the early and mid-1980s the exchange rate became a central economic policy issue for the first time in 50 years.

Variation in the political prominence of the exchange rate does track financial and commercial integration. We can also turn to the historical and contemporary evidence to see if the political divisions I expect are indeed observed in reality. To do so I focus first on the American experience in the late 19th and early 20th centuries, then on the more recent European experience.

Exchange Rate Politics in the United States, 1870–1935

Monetary policy was, along with the tariff, the great national issue in American politics from the Civil War until the 1930s. If the analytical propositions advanced above are correct, we should observe the sorts of divisions presented in Figure 1 over the course of these American debates.

International trade and payments affected relatively small portions of the United States economy in the late 19th century. However, business groups tied to the foreign sector were powerful, especially Northeastern financial and commercial interests. So too were exports important to very large numbers of American producers, especially primary producers. In the 1880s one-fifth of the country's farm output was exported, and in 1879 exports were 30 per cent of American wheat and 60 per cent of cotton production. American financial markets were quite closely linked with those abroad, especially in London.

As projected above, those directly involved in international trade and payments wanted stability in the international value of the dollar, while those who sold primarily to the domestic market cared little about the exchange rate. By the same token, tradables producers, both import-competing manufacturers and export-oriented farmers, were adamant in their support for a currency depreciation that would raise the relative price of their products.

Preferences about fixing the exchange rate often became elided with views on whether to devalue the dollar. Inasmuch as dollar devaluation implied going off gold, those who wanted a weaker currency opposed the gold standard — even where they might have been indifferent or favorable to it in principle.

Interest groups divided into two broad camps over the course of the decades. "Hard money" interests wanted unshakable commitment to gold, with no devaluation; support for hard money came from Northeastern traders, bankers, and investors, and some export-oriented manufacturers more concerned about stability than price competitiveness. "Soft money," devaluation and going off gold, was preferred by farmers and manufacturers from the interior, whose markets were domestic and who worried primarily about the low domestic prices of their products. The division persisted throughout decades of conflict.

The Money Question in America reached its peak with three episodes: Greenback populism (1865–79), silver populism (1888–96), and price stability (1920–35). The first episode stemmed from the fact that the dollar was taken off gold in 1862 amidst wartime inflation. After the Civil War, two broad groups developed. "Soft money" meant staying on the depreciated paper currency (greenbacks) introduced during the war. "Hard money" advocates wanted to put the country back on gold at the prewar parity, which implied a substantial real appreciation.

The strongest original proponents of greenback populism were iron and steel manufacturers, who regarded a depreciated dollar as a complement to the trade protection they desired. Along with them were the railroad industry and associated non-tradables producers, who appreciated the reflationary government policies that a floating currency allowed.

After 1873 two important groups joined the greenback camp. Farmers flocked to the movement as agricultural prices dropped, recognizing that a depreciated currency meant higher dollar prices for their exportable crops. Silver miners similarly joined as silver prices fell. The silver connection is complicated. Over the course of the 1870s, the greenback movement modified its position to favor the free coinage of silver at a 16:1 ratio against gold. This would have kept the country off gold and on a depreciated silver standard. The economic implications were similar to those of a depreciated paper currency, except for the direct subsidy to silver producers (the government would have been obligated to purchase silver at above the market rate). The motivation for this turn was that silver miners had great influence in the sparsely populated Rocky Mountain West and thereby controlled many Senate seats.

Congress was favorable to greenback and silver ideas, as was almost certainly the country as a whole. The return to gold was only effected by President Ulysses Grant manipulating a lame-duck Congress in January 1875. The Resumption Act so passed was repealed by Congress repeatedly after that, but the two-thirds majority to override the presidential veto was not forthcoming. The country returned to gold on 1 January 1879.

Anti-gold sentiment erupted again with the agricultural depression that began in 1888. Farmers were well aware that reflation and devaluation under the silverite banner would raise agricultural prices. The silver miners, for obvious reasons, continued to support silver monetization. The Populists thus called for a paper money-silver standard, with the dollar fluctuating against gold. The treasury would have been directed to regulate the money supply to avoid deflation. Gold clauses, tying contracts to the value of gold as a hedge against devaluation, would have been made illegal.

Northeastern commercial and financial interests remained at the core of the hard-money camp. The bankers' position had if anything hardened: Wall Street hoped to become an international financial center, for which ironclad commitment to gold was a prerequisite. Manufacturers were less committed to soft money than they had been in the 1870s, for three reasons. First, declining prices of manufactured products were more than compensated by rapid productivity increases, so that few manufacturers felt substantially disadvantaged by the real appreciation. Second, by the 1890s some of American industry had become internationally oriented: manufactured exports had expanded and foreign direct investment was increasing. Third, import-competing manufacturers' interest in the money question was secondary to their concern to defend high tariffs, which were under attack from agricultural interests. They were willing to forgo support for silver if tariff protection were continued.

After nearly a decade of agitation, the issue came to a head in the 1896 presidential election, which was fought largely over the gold standard. Democrats and Populists jointly fielded William Jennings Bryan, who ran against the "cross of gold" upon which, Bryan thundered, the country was being crucified. The Republicans, in response, cobbled together a hard money–high tariff coalition. Presidential candidate William McKinley had impeccable protectionist credentials, having designed the tariff of 1890; despite long-standing support for silver, he switched to gold in 1896. The McKinley coalition of hard-money international trading and financial interests and high-tariff manufacturers narrowly defeated Bryan's farmer-miner coalition.

The third episode stretched from soon after the end of the First World War until the middle 1930s. The distributional cleavages carried on the prewar pattern. Most prominent were demands by farmers and many manufacturers for "price stability," government policy to reverse postwar deflation. They blamed much of the relative decline of tradables prices on the new Federal Reserve's commitment to gold and hard money, and argued that the Fed should change course. As before, support for orthodox monetary policies came from international financial, commercial, and industrial interests. These were the core of the "internationalist" foreign policy bloc more generally, for whom the international role of the dollar was important.

These debates involved both the content of monetary policy and the structure of the Federal Reserve. Dozens of bills were introduced to force more reflationary monetary policy, devaluation, and Congressional control of the Fed. All of the bills were blocked by the Executive and the Senate, which was dominated by financial conservative Carter Glass of the Senate Banking and Commerce Committee.

Conflict over monetary policy increased during the Depression. The hardest-hit victims of price trends in the early Depression were producers of traded goods. Between 1929 and 1933, as GNP fell 46 per cent in nominal terms, output of durable goods fell 67 per cent and that of farm products 53 per cent; services output fell 28 per cent. Meanwhile, the Fed was torn between domestic and international demands. Interest rate increases to defend the dollar exacerbated the domestic downturn, and provoked domestic protests.

Congress made repeated attempts to force reflation and devaluation, and in May 1932 the House overwhelmingly passed a Price Stabilization Bill, which mandated inflation and going off gold. Still, easy-money proposals were blocked by the Senate and the Hoover administration until the Democrats swept the presidency and the Senate in the 1932 elections.

Hard-money sentiment also softened as the Depression dragged on, especially after the British went off gold in 1931. The world economy was collapsing, and in the interest of domestic recovery many hard-money men were willing to go off gold, at least for a time. So while the strongest support for devaluation continued to come from tradables producers, many paragons of gold-standard orthodoxy had by early 1933 come to regard easier money as a temporarily necessary evil.

Faced with overwhelming support within the House and Senate for devaluation, in April 1933 President Roosevelt took the dollar off gold. From October 1933 until January 1934 the Administration reduced the gold value of the dollar, depreciating it 44 per cent from its March 1933 level against the pound.

This brief survey of the American experience between the Civil War and the 1930s indicates that the political divisions postulated in Figure 1 were, in fact, observed in practice. There are some amendments worth noting. First, the two dimensions in Figure 1 were typically reduced to one in the political debates. Supporters of gold were primarily concerned about exchange rate stability; opponents were primarily interested in a devaluation. Inasmuch as a devaluation could only be obtained by going off gold, the pro-devaluation groups were anti-gold. Inasmuch as exchange rate stability could only be defended if a devaluation were avoided, pro-gold groups were anti-devaluation. Those groups in, so to speak, the off-diagonals, were relatively less important to the debates. That is, non-tradables producers might have preferred a floating appreciated rate; and many exporters might have preferred a fixed depreciated rate; but these policy possibilities were not on the political agenda.

Second, for import-competing tradables producers a tariff can be an effective substitute for a depreciation. This was indeed the case for Midwestern American manufacturers, for whom prohibitive tariffs essentially made the Money Question moot. Most farmers, who sold into foreign markets, could not have recourse to tariffs so easily, but for at least some former devaluationists, a tariff was as good as going off gold. This implies that such economic actors may evaluate the relative difficulty of obtaining a tariff against the difficulty of obtaining a devaluation, and act accordingly. . . .

It might be objected that the American political divisions were anomalous. However, throughout the world during the late 19th and early 20th centuries similar conflicts, and similar political line-ups, could be observed. In Germany grain-producing Junkers, like American wheat farmers, were strong supporters of silver, and only turned toward trade protection after they had lost the battle against the gold standard. In Argentina, the country's dominant wheat producers were able to force the peso off gold while world wheat prices declined, only to tie the peso back onto gold at a severely depreciated rate once world wheat prices began rising again. Similar divisions, pitting internationally oriented supporters of gold against import-competing or exporting supporters of depreciations, were to be found in virtually every country.

Exchange Rate Politics in Europe since 1970

Without presenting more historical evidence, I now turn to suggestive illustrations drawn from a contemporary problem in international monetary policy, European monetary integration. The members of the European Union (EU) have, along with several states on the periphery of the union, been pursuing attempts to stabilize exchange rates among themselves for over 20 years. Such attempts began just as the Bretton Woods system collapsed between 1971 and 1973, and have continued apace up to the present.

In 1979, EU members created the European Monetary System (EMS), whose exchange rate mechanism (ERM) linked member currencies to each other in a narrow band of fluctuation. The EMS experienced many realignments of currency values between 1979 and 1985, then stabilized with no major realignments between 1987 and late 1992. In the flush of this success, in the late 1980s EMS members undertook to move toward full currency union.

Plans for monetary union were sideswiped by the economic dislocations associated with German unification after 1989. In September 1992 Italy, a charter ERM member, and the United Kingdom, which had joined in October 1990, left the ERM. Eventually, the currencies of Spain, Portugal, and Ireland were devalued within the mechanism. Exchange market pressure continued through summer 1993, leading the remaining ERM members to widen the permitted fluctuation bands to 15 per cent (except for the Dutch guilder, which remained at 2.25 per cent).

Both aspects of the argument presented above should be relevant to European monetary integration. First, political attention to monetary issues should be related to the level of commercial and financial integration within the union. This should be true both over time and across countries. That is, as the union became more economically integrated, the prominence of discussions of monetary union (or some related form of monetary and exchange rate arrangements) should have grown. In addition, those countries most strongly integrated into the union should have been those most interested in such movement toward monetary integration.

Second, EU members' support for and opposition to monetary integration, inasmuch as this meant fixing exchange rates, should follow the principles evinced above and applied in the American case. That is, import-competing tradables producers should be the strongest supporters of maintaining the option of a national devaluation; and internationally (or, in this instance, regionally) oriented banks and corporations should be the strongest supporters of currency stabilization.

Both these hypotheses appear consistent with the evidence from recent European monetary events. . . . [E]ven a casual examination of recent history indicates that interest in monetary integration grew in tandem with the level of financial and commercial integration in the union. It was, in fact, the removal or prospective removal of capital controls and residual trade barriers among the members of the EU that quickened the pace of monetary integration over the course of the 1980s. The higher levels of international goods and capital market integration within the EU raised the probability that divergent macroeconomic policies would lead to countervailing trends on capital and currency markets. This is simply another illustration that high levels of capital mobility make independent monetary policy inconsistent with a fixed exchange rate — although, of course, this is true only for countries other than Germany, which became the *de facto* determiner of EMS monetary policy. Greater integration of financial markets within Europe tended to quicken the rate at which divergent national monetary policies led to substantial capital flows and eventually currency crises. Financial integration made the resolution of the conflict between national monetary autonomy and exchange rate stability pressing.

Similarly, the countries most enthusiastic about monetary integration have indeed been the small, open economies of the Union (and even some outside it). Support for monetary integration (including, in some cases, monetary union) has been relatively strong from Belgium and Luxembourg, the Netherlands, Denmark, Ireland, Spain, and Portugal; and from Austria, Norway, Finland, and Sweden outside the EU. The larger EU members less integrated into Union trade and finance — prominently the UK and Italy — have been far less enthusiastic.

On the second dimension, higher levels of economic integration within Europe affected the interests of domestic economic actors. As trade and capital flows within the EU grew, ever larger segments of EU business communities developed more important markets and investments in other EU nations. The growth of intra-EU trade and investment, therefore, increased the real or potential support base for economic policies that would facilitate and defend such economic activities. Stabilizing exchange rates within the EU was a prominent example of a policy that benefited the growing ranks of economic actors with cross-border intra-EU economic interests, whether these were export markets or investment sites. By the same token, import-competing tradables producers — especially those in traditionally high-inflation countries — faced the prospect that fixing their exchange rate would lead to a real appreciation of the currency that would harm them in important ways.

There is in fact substantial anecdotal evidence that much of the private sector's support for monetary integration came precisely from internationally oriented firms in the EU. Perhaps more striking is evidence that principal opposition to fixing exchange rates came from import-competing producers in relatively high-inflation countries that anticipated (correctly, as it turned out) that fixed exchange rates meant real appreciations. . . .

In Europe in the 1980s as in the United States in the late 19th and early 20th century, then, political attention to international monetary issues grew as levels of economic integration rose. And in both instances, tradables producers were the principal supporters of currency devaluations, while internationally oriented banks and corporations were the principal supporters of fixed exchange rates. Similar patterns can be observed both historically and today.

CONCLUSIONS: LESSONS FROM THE DISTANT AND RECENT PAST

This essay has identified a set of factors expected to affect the political prominence of international monetary policies, and the sorts of political cleavages to be expected in this area. As such, it is relevant to contemporary problems.

The first implication of the analysis and evidence presented here is that political debates over exchange rates can be expected to grow as the world becomes more financially and commercially integrated. It is also the case that the more financially and commercially open a country is, the more politically important currency issues are likely to be.

This implies that as the international economy becomes more integrated, controversies over economic policy will be more oriented toward issues that directly or indirectly implicate exchange rates. In this sense, while history will certainly not repeat itself, some of the flavor of gold standard-era mass politics concerning monetary policy may recur. It is certainly already the case that since 1980 in some developing countries, and some European countries, exchange rates and monetary policy have moved toward the top of the political agenda.

The second implication concerns the political cleavages that can be expected over exchange rate policy in a world in which goods and capital markets are closely integrated. Those observed in the American case, as indicated in Figure 1, reflect general economic regularities, and analogous divisions exist today in most countries. This means that I expect domestically oriented economic agents to be unenthusiastic about fixing the exchange rate, and tradables producers to want a lower exchange rate. On the other hand, the international financial and commercial sectors, along with multinational corporations and some exporters, will be supportive of a fixed rate.

Inasmuch as exchange rates become more politicized, and the divisions over exchange rates are as I anticipate, this implies a relatively new set of political cleavages and potential alliances. Divisions between tradables and non-tradables sectors were not particularly important in closed economies, in which other class or sectoral divisions predominated. Such divisions appear to be increasing in many of the world's nations, and may presage a reformulation of both politics and political institutions as they solidify.

None of this says very much directly about the *outcomes* of the policy debates in question. These outcomes will largely be the consequence of a wide range of socioeconomic, political, institutional, and historical factors that vary in important ways from country to country. However, understanding the conditions under which exchange rates are likely to be a major issue, and the sorts of socioeconomic divisions likely to arise as they are debated, is a first step on the road to analyzing international and domestic monetary policy. In a world increasingly tied together by trade and investment, this set of issues is likely to be ever more important — and understanding it ever more crucial.

17

EMU: Why and How
It Might Happen
CHARLES WYPLOSZ

One of the more striking events of recent international monetary history is the adoption of a single currency, the euro, by
member states of the European Union. French economist Charles
Wyplosz traces this complex process from the 1950s to the com-
pletion of the Economic and Monetary Union (EMU). He describes
the economic and political sources of the movement to a single
currency. He also analyzes some of the problems that have arisen
along the way and others that may develop as EMU continues to
move forward.

The adoption of a single currency has long been a Holy Grail for Europe. Since
the late 1950s, various plans had been devised and shelved. . . . But in a few sharp
steps between 1988 and 1991, bewildered Europeans saw their governments agree
to what is now known as the Maastricht Treaty.

The story begins auspiciously in 1986. The European Community emerges
from a decade-long period of little institutional progress, high inflation and rising
unemployment following the oil shocks. This is the year when three new countries
(Greece, Spain and Portugal) join the European Community and when the Single
European Act (frequently dubbed "1992," the year when it came into effect) is
adopted as an extension of the founding Treaty of Rome. The aim of the Single
Act is to plug the loopholes which limited the full mobility of people, goods and
capital within Europe. In the process, all restrictions to capital movements were
eliminated.

This last innocuous-seeming step made a move to monetary union unavoidable. The reason is a straightforward implication of the Mundell-Fleming textbook model of an open economy, known in Europe as the "impossible trilogy"
principle. This principle asserts that only two of the three following features are
mutually compatible: full capital mobility, independence of monetary policy, and
a fixed exchange rate. The problem arises because, under full capital mobility, a
nation's domestic interest rate is tied to the world interest rate (at least for a country too small to influence worldwide financial conditions). More precisely, any
difference between the domestic and world interest rate is equal to the expected
rate of depreciation of the exchange rate; that is, if interest rates are 5 percent in
the domestic market and 3 percent in global markets, this must reflect that global

currency markets expect the currency to depreciate by 2 percent this year. This is known as the interest parity condition: it implies that integrated financial markets equalize expected asset returns, and so assets denominated in a currency expected to depreciate must offer an exactly compensating higher yield.

A country that wants to conduct an independent monetary policy, raising or lowering interest rates for the purpose of its domestic economy, must allow its exchange rate to fluctuate in the market. Conversely, a country confronted with full capital mobility that wants to fix its exchange rate must set its domestic interest rate to be exactly equal to the rate in the country to which it pegs its currency; since monetary policy is now determined abroad, the country has effectively lost monetary policy independence. The alternative option of letting exchange rates float was never acceptable to Europeans. The perception is that markets are too integrated to allow for sizable relative price changes. The exchange rate and trade wars from before World War II are still remembered as an example of a jack that must absolutely be kept in the box.

By the time it was decided to free capital flows, the European Monetary System (EMS) had been in place for nearly ten years. Most European Community members had agreed in early 1979 to set up a system of fixed bilateral exchange rates with fluctuation bands of ±2.25 percent around the declared central parity (±6 percent for Italy and, briefly, the United Kingdom). Member central banks were committed to intervene jointly to defend the parities, in principle with no limit. When it was felt that existing parities had to be changed, the decision had to be taken by consensus. By the late 1980s, the EMS was commonly hailed as a major success, credited with the relative stability of intra-European real exchange rates during the turbulent post–Bretton Woods period. . . .

Perhaps blinded by the success of the EMS, leading European policymakers did not perceive that the freeing of capital flows meant the end of monetary policy independence in all but one EMS country. By the late 1980s it had become obvious that the Bundesbank, Germany's central bank, was setting monetary policy for Europe as a whole. One reason for this evolution was relative economic size (further increased by unification following the fall of the Berlin Wall in late 1989). In addition, the Bundesbank had acquired a strong reputation for fighting inflation and keeping its currency strong. For countries where inflation was the number one target, adopting tough monetary conditions under the Bundesbank leadership was in fact welcomed. Small countries, like the Netherlands, had already given up monetary independence. Among the larger ones, the United Kingdom was outside the fixed exchange rate mechanism and therefore could retain monetary policy independence.

However, other larger European nations like France, Italy, and Spain, gradually realized that they had lost control of their domestic monetary policy. They concluded that the only way through which they could regain some influence over their monetary policies was to create a broader European monetary institution which would supersede the Bundesbank, and in which they would have a voice. Naturally, since Germany was being asked to sacrifice one of its most valued institutions for the sake of Europe, it was going to ask a lot in return. In particular,

Germany was bound to require that this new European monetary institution offer strong guarantees of price stability. From the very beginning, Europe's future currency would have to be as strong as the deutsche mark. This would mean explicit institutional safeguards and exacting startup conditions. The negotiations leading to the Maastricht Treaty would bear the birthmark of this situation: what Germany asks, Germany gets, provided that it gives up the Bundesbank.

THE MAASTRICHT TREATY

The Maastricht Treaty updates and incorporates the 1957 Treaty of Rome, the founding act of the European Community, and incorporates the Single European Act implemented in 1992 (free movement of goods, people, and capital). The treaty has been formally ratified by all member countries. With the Maastricht Treaty, Europe ceases to be called the European Economic Community and becomes instead the European Union or EU, which involves both economic and political union. The economic component of the treaty mainly involves the adoption of a single currency. The political component has been left rather vague, hinting at an evolution towards joint defense and foreign affairs. . . .

IS EUROPE AN OPTIMAL CURRENCY AREA?

The decision to adopt a single currency is the outcome of constrained optimization. The constraint is the impossible trilogy: given the freedom of capital flows, the choice is between freely floating exchange rates and monetary union. The assessment is that monetary union dominates a free float. This assessment is based on the experience with floating exchange rates since 1973: wide and long-lasting fluctuations (20 to 50 percent over three to five years) are just not compatible with fully open markets and the complete removal of border posts. While that assessment is open to debate (but seldom challenged so far), the discussion on the intrinsic desirability of the monetary union is moot as long as it ignores the constraint.

Yet, it is probably unavoidable that the question be asked whether EMU is welfare-increasing *per se*. . . .

The (unconstrained) optimum currency area literature establishes the conditions under which two or more countries could share the same currency without seriously adverse consequences. It assumes that the nominal exchange rate has real effects; otherwise, there is no cost in a nation's giving up its own currency. In particular, the exchange rate is a policy instrument which can affect relative prices such as the real wage paid by producers, the ratio of traded to nontraded goods prices, or the ratio of export to import goods prices. As one example of where this tool could be useful, consider the case where some exogenous shock requires that relative domestic to foreign prices change. Such an adjustment can plausibly be made easier and faster through the exchange rate, rather than by changing nominal prices throughout the economy or through migration of the factors of production from one sector to another.

The three criteria proposed in the literature are those features which make adjustment through exchange rates less effective or less compelling. One criterion is openness to mutual trade; greater openness means that most prices are being determined on markets at the area level, which reduces the ability of the exchange rate to alter significant relative prices. A second criterion is diversification of individual economies; a more diversified economy is less likely to suffer country-specific shocks, which makes its own exchange rate a less useful tool. Finally, the third criterion is mobility of inputs across the area, especially labor. Greater mobility allows an economy to deal with asymmetric shocks through migration, lessening the need for adjustment through exchange rate changes.

On the openness criterion, Europe scores rather well. Measuring openness by looking at exports as a share of GDP, the United States and Japan score 11 percent and 9 percent, respectively. Larger European economies, like Germany, Italy, France, and the United Kingdom, all have export/GDP ratios above 20 percent, and smaller EU economies, like Ireland and Belgium, have export/GDP ratios above 70 percent. It makes sense that the smallest European countries are traditionally warm supporters of monetary union. Because of their extreme openness to foreign trade, relative prices in their economy are set on world markets, and the exchange rate is a less useful policy tool.

As to the second criterion, European economies are found usually to be well-diversified. Countries with important endowments in natural resources, like the Netherlands and the United Kingdom with their oil and gas resources, stand apart, but only slightly so. A wide body of research looks at the risk of country-specific (asymmetric) shocks. One set of studies investigates co-movements of key macroeconomic variables like GDP, unemployment, inflation, or the current account balance across European countries. Other studies compare shocks across regions with shocks across countries. The general message is that there is more co-movement in macroeconomic variables among European countries than between individual European countries and the United States or Japan. Further studies attempt to separate out domestic from external shocks, and demand from supply shocks. The underlying argument is that demand shocks are at least partly due to divergence in monetary policy which will be less prevalent in EMU — so attention should focus on supply shocks. . . .

Work on the labor mobility criterion clearly suggests that Europe is not an optimum currency area. . . . Two caveats are in order, however. First, the evidence is that the lack of labor mobility is not a national but a regional phenomenon in Europe. It affects regions within existing nations of Europe, and there is no reason why monetary union would make things worse. Second, both the occurrence of shocks and labor mobility may change as economic integration proceeds. . . . It then comes as no surprise that the United States, which has shared the same currency for a century, appears better suited for a single currency than does Europe.

In the end, we need not be impressed by the result that Europe is not as much an (unconstrained) optimum currency area as the United States. The choice is not between EMU and heaven. It is between EMU and freely-floating exchange rates, with possibly poorly coordinated monetary policies, within an area gradually becoming as tightly integrated as the United States. Would the United States have passed the currency area tests a century ago? And had it failed, all things considered, was it a mistake for the country to adopt a single currency?

CONVERGENCE: WILL TOUGH CRITERIA BACKFIRE?

One striking feature of the Maastricht Treaty is that it anticipates a long eight-year phase from the passage of the treaty in 1991 to the deadline for a single currency by 1999. This long phase-in was the result of a conflict between two competing views.

One view argued that monetary union would be sustainable only if those countries that joined had first achieved a low level of inflation and had resolved fiscal imbalances. This position is commonly referred to as the "economist's view," although it does not seem to have been fully articulated in the professional literature. However, it was popular among the monetary authorities; for example, the Bundesbank championed it under the name of "coronation approach," seeing the shift to monetary union as the last step of successful efforts to eradicate inflationary behavior. Economic and monetary union was to be born in a land dedicated to a culture of price stability.

The opposing view, generally referred to as the "monetarists' view," had the favor of most academic economists. Their argument was that the creation of a new currency with its own independent central bank would radically alter the wage and price mechanisms, inflation trends, and the incentives of national governments when they decide on fiscal policies. In this view, . . . pre–monetary union behavior of both the public and private sectors is a bad predictor of their behavior once the single central bank is in place. Instead, what is needed in the monetarist view are solid institutions, chiefly central bank independence. Other convergence criteria create pain with no assured gain.

Predictably, the "economist" view favored by central bankers won out over the "monetarist" views of academic economists. It is impossible to say what would have happened if EMU had started fairly promptly after ratification of the Maastricht Treaty in 1991. However, what is known is that the period dedicated to convergence has been especially agitated. Even before the Maastricht Treaty could be ratified, a series of exchange rate crises forced Italy and the United Kingdom out of the EMS. . . .

Of the criteria set in Maastricht, those mandating inflation convergence have proven relatively easy to achieve. However, the budgetary criteria — that the debt/GDP must not be above 60 percent nor the deficit/GDP exceed 3 percent — are more challenging. . . . Why after such a long period of convergence are the budget criteria still some way off? Part of the problem is that the tight monetary policies aimed at meeting the inflation criteria have helped create a slow-growth climate for Europe in the 1990s, with double-digit unemployment rates and no net job creation since the beginning of the decade. While this effort has made it possible to achieve inflation convergence, it has also reduced tax revenues, causing deficits that will not go away and forcing governments to adopt further policies of fiscal contraction. This vicious cycle is jeopardizing monetary union both by making the fiscal targets more difficult to achieve and by undermining public support.

The situation is now a gamble: either a country reaches EMU and is able to relax after having indeed put its fiscal house in order, or it fails entry (or EMU does not take place at all) because excessively restrictive economic policies have deepened the budget deficit.

MONETARY UNION AND FISCAL DISCIPLINE

The inclusion of restrictions on fiscal policy in a treaty which, after all, aims at monetary union, is a source of considerable debate. Before the Maastricht Treaty, most academic analyses emphasized that national fiscal policy would have to become more active to compensate for the loss of the exchange rate instrument. The opposite approach, that monetary union requires fiscal policy restraint, is grounded in the view that excessive budget deficits may lead to eventual monetization of the debt. Monetary authorities were clearly concerned by high debts in some countries, especially in Italy, whose public debt represents some 18 percent of Europe's GDP. They feared that an explicit or implicit lender-of-last-resort function might force the European Central Bank to step in and indirectly monetize a country's public debt if banks faced a financial crisis in the wake of a default. This concern is reflected in the budgetary criteria for EMU membership and in the "excessive deficit" procedures designed to enforce fiscal rectitude once in the monetary union.

While it is difficult to disagree with the view that fiscal policy ought not to jeopardize monetary and financial stability, how to provide the incentives for appropriate fiscal policy is open to debate. The debate implicitly revolves around one's view of the ability of fiscal policy to play a macroeconomic stabilizing role. It also hinges on the ability to define at the time a deficit is enacted that it is "excessive." In principle, the proper answer must be in terms of "sustainability," since by definition, unsustainable debt buildup will eventually have to be reversed. Fiscal policy sustainability is often associated with stationarity of the debt, usually defined as a stable debt/GDP ratio. In fact, the proper definition of sustainability would hold only that the state will remain solvent, a definition that emphasizes the future behavior of fiscal authorities. By emphasizing future behavior, this view of sustainability also implies that information from the past does not reveal what a country will do after it is inside EMU, and that rules for fiscal rectitude must affect future fiscal policies. A workable definition of sustainability along these lines is a tall order.

The Maastricht approach, relying on arbitrary quantitative limits, is quite unsophisticated. The 3 percent annual debt/GDP rule corresponds to what is called the "golden rule" in Germany: governments may only borrow to pay for investment spending, and it turns out that governments usually dedicate about 3 percent of GDP to such spending. Even if one ignores doubts about the 3 percent estimate itself, the rule is naive at best; it ignores socially productive spending like education which is classified as consumption, while it may include ill-designed investment spending. The 60 percent debt/GDP rule was chosen because it was the average of EU countries when the Maastricht Treaty was being negotiated, with not even the pretense of any deeper economic justification.

Yet Europe is not alone in adopting quantitative limits for fiscal policy. How does it work elsewhere, where a unique central bank coexists along with several fiscal authorities? In the United States, for example, states must operate under balanced budgets, borrowing money only by issuing bonds for explicit capital projects. But the comparison must be handled quite carefully. In true federations, the central government is as large as the lower-level governments, and is in charge of macroeconomic stabilization. In Europe, in contrast, the equivalent of a central government is the European Commission, which is not allowed to run deficits and whose spending represents a mere 2 percent of the Europe Union's gross domestic product.

The size and role of a powerful central government matters for two main reasons. First, several studies have shown that in federal states, the center smooths out income fluctuations through redistribution from regions in good economic shape to regions undergoing a recession. This function operates automatically through the federal budget, the result of a combination of welfare support and income taxes. In this setup, it can make sense to limit the stabilization role of sub-central authorities. Second, quantitative fiscal restraints at some levels of government can actually encourage the buildup of debts at other levels. . . . The problem occurs when fiscally irresponsible lower-level governments refuse to borrow and can bait the federal authorities into rescuing them. In Europe, a central government with powerful redistribution and stabilization authority is not likely within the foreseeable future. Consequently, Europe needs national-level stabilization policies much more than individual U.S. states do, and there is no risk that national governments will conduct irresponsible fiscal policies in an attempt to extract transfers from a penniless center.

Are there less coarse methods than quantitative limits of providing governments with effective incentives against fiscal irresponsibility? One attractive approach would be to rely on financial markets to impose discipline. In a single currency area, interest rates no longer reflect a country's sovereign risk. Instead, they reflect the risk category of borrowers, be they fiscal authorities (a municipality in the United States, a province in Canada, or a government in Europe) or private borrowers. To the extent that markets price risk correctly, the demand for public debt of various governments could act as both a barometer and a constraint. If a country lets its debt grow and there is an enhanced risk of default, markets should react by downgrading their evaluation and by increasing the interest rate at which new debt is being financed, until fiscal authorities see it to be in their best interest to curtail the deficit.

However, history suggests skepticism about the ability of markets to impose discipline in this way. For one, markets tend to throw good money after bad for a time. When markets do react, it is often too late and too violently. They abruptly cut financing, making it impossible for the government to borrow further and bankrupting large bondholders, among them commercial banks and other financial institutions. This leads to a scenario where central banks may feel compelled to monetize (part of) the debt.

This is presumably why the Maastricht Treaty includes a no-bailout clause which explicitly forbids the rescue of one government either by its fellow members or by community institutions, including the European Central Bank. In this way, fiscal misbehavior becomes a strictly national issue with no union-wide implication and fiscal restraint is unnecessary. Yet Germany has argued that the no-bailout clause cannot be fully credible, that any rule can always be circumvented.

In the end, the explicit fiscal restraints embodied in the excessive deficit procedure can be seen as insurance against a remote risk that European institutions would be compelled to monetize some nation's out-of-control debts. This insurance scheme may turn out to be very costly in terms of the ability to run countercyclical policies.

EMU AND THE REST OF THE WORLD

The potential for the euro to replace the U.S. dollar as the world's premier currency is one of the understated motivations of EMU. In part, the desire is a symbolic one. . . . In part, it is a hope to reap seigniorage, although U.S. benefits from seigniorage are worth only about 0.2 percent of GDP. The usual criteria for becoming the world's lead currency are measures like size (GDP or the share of world trade). By these measures, the prospects for the euro to challenge the dollar are favorable but not overwhelming. For example, Europe's international trade with non-European nations will not exceed by much Germany's current level of foreign trade — once intra-European trade is netted out. Also, history teaches that it takes time for a reserve currency to change. To overcome its handicap relative to the incumbent U.S. dollar, the euro must discover some absolute advantage.

One potential advantage is likely to be greater price stability. As a currency expected to follow a long-run trend of appreciation, the euro will be a currency that stores value better than the alternatives. This prediction derives from the constitution of the European Central Bank, which makes it more independent and more focused on price stability than the U.S. Federal Reserve. If anything, the constitution is even stricter than that of the Bundesbank, so that Europe's economy will be more stable than Germany's. A counterargument is based on politico-economic considerations. The board of the European Central Bank will be composed of representatives of all member countries. With the one-man, one-vote principle, Germany's weight will be no larger than that of Belgium or Italy. The constituencies of the European Central Bank will not share the German allergy to even moderate inflation. In theory, the outcome may differ from the wishes of the median European voter, and the bias can go in either direction. Ultimately, this counterargument is not fully convincing.

A second potential advantage for the euro could be the depth and cost-efficiency of financial markets. The market for the euro and euro-denominated assets could be the world's largest, depending on whether the city of London shifts to the euro. Yet the location and prominence of markets relies increasingly less on regional considerations and more on the regulatory environment. Europe will have to fight its own heavy-handed approach and powerful lobbies if it wants the euro to become the world's currency.

Thus, the best bet is that, for a long while at least, the dollar's supremacy will remain. Still, the creation of the euro is bound to affect international monetary relations. Will it lead to more or less instability on exchange markets? Two arguments suggest more instability. First, if the U.S. dollar has been acting as a market leader on exchange rate markets, the shift to a situation of bargaining between more equal partners is likely to create greater volatility. Second, while the fairly open economies of Europe are now keenly interested in stabilizing world currencies, a euro zone would join the United States and Japan as giant economies less inclined to give up domestic policy objectives for the sake of exchange rate coordination. However, the opposite view is that moving from G-7 to G-3 should make it easier to negotiate methods for reducing volatility in exchange rates. In the end, little should change when the European Central Bank steps in the shoes of the Bundesbank as the master of the EMS exchange rate.

Finally, what will be the impact of economic and monetary union on the International Monetary Fund? One view is: nothing much. Each country will retain its existing role. In its annual review exercise, the IMF will have to take account of the fact that monetary policy is no longer a national responsibility, but that is already the case for other monetary unions in Africa and the Caribbean. However, a more entertaining scenario, if unlikely, envisions EMU countries merging as a single IMF member. Not only would Europe cast the largest number of votes and challenge U.S. dominance, but it could invoke the agreements' article that states "the principal office of the Fund shall be in the territory of the member having the largest quota" and request that the IMF move from Washington to Madrid, Frankfurt, Paris, or Amsterdam. . . .

CONCLUSION

Currencies and nations normally coincide. Europe is set to attempt an original experiment. . . .

The Maastricht Treaty is the fundamental act on which Europe rests. It is an international treaty, formally ratified by all European Union countries, and it supersedes national legislation. Giving up EMU would throw up more than just monetary union. It would create a situation of deep political crisis with unpredictable consequences. For that reason alone, the bet is that EMU will be on, on time.

Is the logic behind monetary union only political? Quite the contrary. The political aim of a single currency has been pursued relentlessly by its advocates since the late 1950s; several explicit attempts failed because economic conditions were not ripe. The Maastricht Treaty only came about because the lifting of capital controls had reduced the alternate options to just two unpalatable extremes: either allow exchange rates to float freely or accept the complete domination of Germany's Bundesbank over Europe's monetary policy.

Freely floating exchange rates are not compatible with a completely borderless economic area. They carry the germs of protectionist pressure and financial instability which threaten economic integration. As for dominance by the Bundesbank, it has been largely beneficial over the last decade, chiefly because inflation has been eliminated. Yet there have been costs: lasting double-digit unemployment, major policy mistakes that led to the currency crises of 1992–93, and continuing disagreements over the objectives of the Bundesbank. The current situation is not sustainable because it entails a fundamental contradiction. On one hand, the Bundesbank derives its leadership from a reputation of undeterred commitment to price stability in Germany. On the other hand, long-lasting leadership requires that all of Europe's economic conditions be taken into account, which is against the Bundesbank's constitutional duty to Germany. Tinkering with the Bundesbank's constitution is not only politically impossible, but doing so would also undermine its credibility and its ability to lead. In this setting, EMU emerges as the best possible economic solution.

Assessing the costs and benefits of monetary union quantitatively is both frustrating and useless. It is frustrating because, frankly, as economists we are unable to compute them with any precision, and we owe it to the profession to admit so in public. Our understanding of monetary and exchange rate policy is regrettably limited, and the lack of a precedent leaves us with more conjectures than certainties. Moreover, quantitative estimates are useless unless they are sized up against the costs and benefits of the relevant alternatives, which is equally beyond our current ability. The best that can be done in this situation is to gain an understanding of where the costs and benefits are likely to reside.

The direct benefits come in the form of reduced transaction costs and reduced uncertainty, possibly including additional transparency in competition. Such effects are likely to be small, but not trivial. Direct benefits also include lower real interest rates for countries where a sizable currency risk premium exists. Indirect benefits come from the institutional arrangements that accompany EMU. The broadening of central bank independence from political control would not have happened without EMU, and with it comes the realization that international competition is not achieved through lobbying for exchange rate manipulation.

More ambiguous is the role of the fiscal restraints, both the entry conditions and the excess deficit procedure. In most countries, these restraints have promoted long-needed efforts at coming to grip with unsustainable deficits. At the same time, the insistence on price stability along with the adoption of rigid and arbitrary criteria of fiscal rectitude have already played a role in deepening and lengthening Europe's phase of slow growth, with huge costs in terms of unemployment and social suffering. The risk now is of more of the same in the early EMU years. As already noted, these costs are the consequence of EMU's parenthood: Germany could not be expected to give up its famed deutsche mark without extensive guarantees. These demands could not be turned down and have probably become excessive. However, once monetary union exists, many arrangements can be changed. Right now, Europeans are biting the bullet and looking beyond the 1999 horizon.

REFERENCES

Bayoumi, Tamim. "A Formal Model of Optimum Currency Areas," *International Monetary Fund Staff Papers* 41 (December 1994), pp. 537–54.

Ricci, Luca. "A Model of an Optimum Currency Area." Working Paper 97/76. Washington, DC: International Monetary Fund, 1997.

18

The Obsolescence of Capital Controls? Economic Management in an Age of Global Markets
JOHN B. GOODMAN
AND LOUIS W. PAULY

John Goodman and Louis Pauly explain why countries reduced controls on capital flows from the late 1970s to the early 1990s and why various countries did so at different times during this period. Focusing on the international economy as the fundamental cause of changes in government policy, Goodman and Pauly argue that transformations in the structure of global production and international financial markets made it both possible and desirable for firms to successfully evade government controls. This made government attempts to control capital movements more costly and less effective, and governments eventually abandoned them. Examining the cases of France, Germany, Japan, and Italy, Goodman and Pauly conclude that the exact timing of the abandonment of controls was a function of whether states were experiencing capital inflows or outflows and, consequently, of the costs of abandonment.

The movement of capital across national borders has long raised sensitive political questions. Whatever the benefits, international investment complicates national economic management. Most research on this subject has focused on the causes and consequences of foreign direct investment. Less studied, but no less important, are short-term capital flows — those arising from the purchase or sale of financial instruments with maturities of less than one year. In contrast to investments in plant and equipment, short-term flows are highly sensitive to interest rate differentials and exchange rate expectations. Indeed, the mere announcement of a change in economic policy can trigger massive capital inflows or outflows, undermining the anticipated benefits of the new policy. For this reason, most governments regularly resorted to various types of controls on short-term capital movements in the decades following World War II.

In recent years, however, the world has witnessed a remarkable shift away from the use of capital controls. In country after country, governments have abolished controls and dismantled the bureaucratic machinery used to administer them. And in the rare instances where governments have fallen back on controls, their tempo-rary nature has usually been emphasized. This general trend toward liberalization has stimulated a growing body of research on the political and economic conse-quences of capital mobility. In this article, our principal aim is to address two prior puzzles: First, why did policies of capital decontrol converge across a rising num-ber of industrial states between the late 1970s and the early 1990s? Second, why did some states move to eliminate controls more rapidly than others? We argue that the movement away from controls on short-term capital flows did not result, as regime or epistemic community theories might predict, from the emergence of a common normative framework or widespread belief in the benefits of unfettered capital mobility. Nor has it simply reflected the overarching power of a liberal state. Instead, we contend that it has been driven by fundamental changes in the structures of international production and financial intermediation, which made it easier and more urgent for private firms — specifically, corporations and financial institutions whose aspirations had become increasingly global — effectively to pursue strategies of evasion and exit. For governments, the utility of controls declined as their perceived cost thereby increased.

Still, not all governments abandoned capital controls at the same pace. In order to examine both the process through which these pressures impinged on policy at the national level and variations in the timing of policy reform, we analyze policy developments in four advanced industrial states that relied extensively on capital controls — Japan, Germany, France, and Italy. The first two moved decisively away from capital controls in 1980 and 1981; the latter two, at the end of the decade. These differences can be traced to the interaction between generic types of external pressure and remaining distinctions in domestic structures. Specifi-cally, governments facing capital inflows liberalized sooner than governments facing capital outflows — a conclusion that is not obvious, since capital inflows can be as threatening to national policy-making autonomy as capital outflows. Our analysis at the national level highlights the mechanisms by which such systemic economic pressures were transmitted to unique domestic political arenas. But it also provides a clue as to the increasingly common constraints governments would now have to overcome if they wanted to move back to policies designed to influence and control short-term capital flows.

In theoretical terms, our argument and evidence address a central question in international political economy regarding the relative importance of, and relation-ship between, international and domestic variables. In the crucial area of capital flows, the two interact in a clear pattern: global financial structures affect the dynamics of national policy-making by changing and privileging the interests and actions of certain types of firms. Once those interests have been embedded in pol-icy, movement back is not necessarily precluded but is certainly rendered much more difficult.

The rest of this article is divided into four sections. The first section examines the debate over capital controls in the postwar period and shows that the nor-mative conclusion of this debate remained remarkably consistent throughout subsequent decades. The second section analyzes how changes in international financial markets influenced firm behavior and reframed the issue of capital controls for governments. The third section compares the way in which such changes affected government decisions to eliminate controls in Japan and Germany, which confronted problems associated with chronic capital inflows, and in France and Italy, which faced problems associated with capital outflows. Finally, the fourth section explores the conditions under which a retreat from liberal capital policies could occur and speculates on the normative implications of policy convergence witnessed thus far.

CAPITAL CONTROLS IN THE POSTWAR MONETARY ORDER

Following World War II, capital controls were an accepted part of the international monetary system. Despite pressure from the United States to allow investment as well as goods to cross borders without governmental interference, the 1944 Bretton Woods agreement intentionally legitimated the imposition of controls on capital movements that were not directly linked to trade flows. The agreement gave the International Monetary Fund (IMF) a mandate to discourage exchange restrictions and other financial impediments to trade but pointedly did not give it jurisdiction over capital controls. Most industrial countries accepted the logic of restoring currency convertibility but jealously guarded their right to control short-term capital flows. . . .

Facing persistent payments imbalances and problematic exchange rate rigidities in the 1960s, virtually all leading industrial states resorted to some type of control on capital movements. Even the United States adopted controls to prevent "disequilibrating" outflows. Similar controls were put in place by other states with external deficits, while states with external surpluses adopted measures to ward off unwelcome capital inflows. Ironically, these controls gave a boost to incipient "offshore" financial markets in Europe and elsewhere. The subsequent growth of Euro-currency banking, bond, and equity markets reflected a number of factors — including the unwillingness of governments to coordinate their associated regulatory and tax policies and the development of new technologies. . . .

The disintegration in the early 1970s of the Bretton Woods system of pegged exchange rates potentially opened the door for a new normative framework to coordinate efforts to influence international capital flows. An intergovernmental forum on international monetary reform, the Committee of Twenty of the IMF board of governors was established in 1972, and a group of technical experts was appointed by the committee to examine the problem of disequilibrating capital flows. They concluded that controls should not become a permanent feature of a reformed system because of their potentially negative impact on trade and investment flows. But since capital flows could continue to disrupt even a more flexible exchange rate arrangement, they recommended the adoption of a code of conduct monitored by the IMF to govern the future use of controls. In the end, however, their recommendation was not pursued by the committee.

When the IMF Articles of Agreement were finally amended in 1976 to accommodate floating exchange rates, the normative framework guiding international capital movements originally articulated at Bretton Woods remained intact. States retained the right to resort to controls at their own discretion. In sum, at the official level, neither the beliefs concerning capital controls nor the rules governing them changed significantly over the postwar period. The forces behind the wave of policy liberalization that was about to occur were located elsewhere.

GLOBAL FINANCE AND FIRM BEHAVIOR

Between the late 1970s and the early 1990s, the development of truly international financial markets and the globalization of production undercut the rationale for capital controls. To analyze how these changes affected policies designed to limit capital mobility, it is useful to begin by looking at why such policies were deemed necessary in the first place. In the early 1960s strong theoretical support for the use of capital controls was provided by J. Marcus Fleming and Robert Mundell, who demonstrated that a government could achieve at most two of the following three conditions: capital mobility, monetary autonomy, and a fixed exchange rate. Consider what happens when a government decides to tighten monetary policy and maintain a constant exchange rate. Without capital mobility, the rise in interest rates will simply reduce aggregate demand. With capital mobility, such autonomy is lost, as funds attracted from abroad drive interest rates back down to world levels. A decision to loosen monetary policy would have the opposite effect. Of course, few countries have ever sought to insulate themselves completely from capital inflows or outflows. But throughout the postwar period, many did seek to limit the volume of those flows and thus preserve a degree of autonomy.

During the 1960s a growing number of economists argued that a preferable way to preserve national monetary autonomy was to abandon fixed exchange rates. With flexible exchange rates, a decision to tighten monetary policy might still attract capital, but its principal effect would be on the value of the national currency, not domestic interest rates. . . .

In practice, the shift to flexible exchange rates in the 1970s did not provide the desired panacea. The Mundell-Fleming analysis . . . ignored feedback effects between exchange rates and domestic prices. As predicted, a country that sought to stimulate production by lowering interest rates suffered a depreciation of its currency. This depreciation, in turn, raised the price of its imports. If the country could not reduce imports quickly, higher import costs translated into higher prices for domestic production, thereby reducing the anticipated increase in output. Despite the shift to floating rates, many countries therefore still considered capital controls necessary to carve out as much autonomy as possible for their monetary policies.

In the 1970s and 1980s, however, two developments dramatically reduced the usefulness of capital controls. The first was the transformation and rapid growth of international financial markets. Between 1972 and 1985, for example, the size of the international banking market increased at a compound growth rate of 21.4 percent, compared with compound annual growth rates of 10.9 percent for world gross domestic product and 12.7 percent for world trade. Moreover, just as this pool of funds increased in size, technological changes reduced the time it took to transfer funds across borders. Since the early 1970s the daily turnover on the world's exchange markets has risen tremendously. In the midst of the currency crisis in March 1973, $3 billion were converted into European currencies in one day. In the late 1970s, daily turnover around the world was estimated at $100 billion; a decade later, that figure had reached $650 billion.

Just as these changes were occurring, a related development was taking place — an increasing number of businesses were moving toward a global configuration. Multinational enterprises (MNEs) were, of course, not new. What was new was the growth in their number, from just a few hundred in the early 1970s to well over a thousand in 1990. Moreover, for more and more MNEs, the home base was outside the United States. Globalization was also evident in the rapid growth of foreign direct investment. During the latter half of the 1980s, for example, flows of new FDI rose at an annual rate of 29 percent. According to one recent study, more than $3.5 trillion of business assets came under "foreign control" in the 1980s.

These twin changes had dramatic consequences for the use of capital controls. Most importantly, the expansion of financial markets made it progressively easier for private firms whose operations had become increasingly global to adopt strategies of exit and evasion. Evasion had obviously taken place for decades, but the means by which it could be conducted were now multiplied. Multinational structures enabled firms to evade capital controls by changing transfer prices or the timing of payments to or from foreign subsidiaries. The deepening of financial markets meant that firms could use subsidiaries to raise or lend funds on foreign markets. If controls in a country became too onerous, MNEs could also attempt to escape them altogether by transferring activities abroad, that is, by exercising the exit option.

This possibility, in turn, constrained the choices available to governments. Assume that a government maintains a more expansionary monetary policy than the rest of the world in order to stimulate growth and create jobs. Assume further that it recognizes that higher interest rates abroad are likely to attract domestic savings needed to finance domestic investment, and it therefore imposes controls on capital outflows. If MNEs react to these controls by moving certain operations offshore, the domestic savings base essentially shrinks. In this instance, the country finds itself in a worse position than when it started. Clearly, if a government can anticipate this effect, credible threats of exit would deter the imposition of capital controls. To the extent that such threats are indeed credible, they highlight the deepening interrelationship between short-term and long-term investment flows. A government that is truly serious about restricting short-term capital movements would also have to be prepared to restrict offshore direct investments by domestic firms. It would then have to balance the losses (in terms of efficiency) borne by those firms and the national economy against the anticipated benefits of capital controls.

From the perspective of firms, however, neither evasion nor exit is a costless option. Firms surely prefer to avoid capital controls or to have them removed, rather than having to consider either option. Thus, MNEs and financial institutions might be expected to mobilize against controls and promote policies encouraging international capital mobility. Governments concerned with the issue of national competitiveness might be expected to be especially responsive to such entreaties. They might also be expected to press other governments to liberalize.

Government decisions to abandon capital controls during the 1980s reflected fundamental changes in the markets through which capital could flow. In our examination of specific decisions in the cases of Japan, Germany, France, and Italy, we provide examples of how these changes affected decision-making processes. Not surprisingly, indisputable evidence of evasion and exit on the part of firms is difficult to find — the former because firms have little interest in making apparent their use of loopholes; the latter because it involves, in essence, a kind of structural power. It need not be exercised to have effect. What comes out clearly, however, is the perception by national policymakers that capital controls had become less useful and more costly.

Although similar pressures affected all advanced industrial countries, the speed with which specific governments responded depended upon whether they were experiencing capital inflows or outflows. The four countries we examine in the next section provide examples of each. Japan and Germany, typically recording surpluses in their current accounts and experiencing capital inflows, liberalized in 1980–81. France and Italy, typically recording external deficits and experiencing capital outflows, did not abandon capital controls until the end of the decade. This difference in timing should not be exaggerated, but neither should it be overlooked, for it helps to clarify the way in which the pressures discussed above shaped the development of particular national policies.

Countries that sought to control capital inflows faced different incentives from those facing countries that sought to control capital outflows. The reason lies mainly in the asymmetric impact of capital movements on foreign exchange reserves. Current account deficits, capital outflows, weakening exchange rates, and depleting reserves often go together; when they do, governments must either adjust their policies or adopt controls before the loss of reserves is complete. In contrast, governments facing the obverse situation find it easier to abandon controls since their reserve position is not threatened. This asymmetry can be enhanced for deficit countries committed to maintaining a fixed exchange rate, as was the case for France and Italy in the context of the European Monetary System (EMS).

THE FOUR CASES

Germany

Development of Controls   In the early years of the Federal Republic, current account deficits and a dearth of foreign exchange reserves led to a strict prohibition on all exports of capital by residents. The legal basis for these controls was provided in the foreign exchange regulations of the Allied Occupation. By the early 1950s, however, West Germany's current account turned to surplus and the country's war-related external debts were finally settled. Restrictions on foreign direct investment abroad began to be liberalized in 1952, and residents were allowed to purchase foreign securities in 1956. By 1957 export of capital by residents was generally permitted without authorization. The relaxation of controls on outflows was effectively completed following restoration of currency convertibility in 1958, a policy stance legally enshrined in the Foreign Trade and Payments Act of 1961.

Owing largely to structural pressures on the deutsche mark in the Bretton Woods system of pegged exchange rates, however, this liberalization was not matched by similar progress on capital inflows. These pressures first emerged in the mid-1950s, when West Germany's low inflation rate and growing current account surplus increased the attractiveness of the mark relative to other currencies, notably the dollar. Under the Bretton Woods rules, the Bundesbank was required to enter the foreign exchange market and sell marks whenever the intervention point with the dollar was reached. But, of course, such obligatory purchases served to increase liquidity in the banking system and expand the money supply, thus creating inflation. Capital inflows therefore quickly came to be seen as significant threats to the Bundesbank's goal of maintaining price stability. Periodic expectations of revaluation and the resulting increase in speculative capital inflows dramatically underlined the dilemma.

In this situation, Germany essentially had two options as it struggled to maintain control over its domestic money supply. It could either revalue its currency or impose capital controls. Given the strong opposition of export interests to revaluation, transmitted in the subtle interplay between the government (which had responsibility for exchange rate policy) and the Bundesbank, the central bank's inclination tended in the latter direction. In June 1960, for example, the purchase of domestic money market paper by nonresidents was subjected to an authorization requirement. Simultaneously, a ban was imposed on interest payments on bank deposits held by nonresidents. These restrictions remained in place after the mark was revalued in 1961 and were not removed until the second revaluation in October 1969. Controls were reintroduced, however, when pressure once again mounted against the mark in 1971. The following year, the Bundesbank required 40 percent of all loans raised abroad to be placed in non-interest-bearing accounts. It also extended authorization requirements to the purchase of domestic bonds by nonresidents. Capital nevertheless continued to pour into Germany and ultimately necessitated two revaluations. Faced with massive speculative pressures in early 1973, the mark was finally allowed to float.

The transition to floating initially eased many of the pressures on the currency; the Bundesbank therefore began loosening some of its earlier restrictions but not dismantling its control apparatus altogether. Indeed, when confidence in the dollar began to decline in 1977, the Bundesbank again tightened existing capital controls and raised minimum reserve requirements on nonresidents' bank deposits to prevent what it considered an excessive appreciation of the mark. These measures were eased somewhat in 1978, when a shift in U.S. economic policy reduced inflows from abroad.

In the wake of the second oil shock, the German current account moved sharply into an uncharacteristic deficit position. A surplus of DM 17.5 billion in

1978 became a deficit of DM 10.5 billion in 1979. Capital inflows suddenly dried up; indeed, capital began exiting the country. The value of the mark slid, and the Bundesbank was forced to finance the deficit first by borrowing and then by dipping into its reserves, which fell by DM 8 billion in 1980 alone. Faced with the novel need to attract rather than ward off capital, the Bundesbank lifted remaining controls on capital flows in 1981.

Reasons for Liberalization   The sudden lifting of controls in 1981 was certainly triggered by a shift in Germany's external accounts. What is striking, however, is that the Bundesbank did not consider it necessary to reimpose capital controls when the current account returned to surplus in 1982 or when the mark once again began to appreciate after the Plaza Agreement in 1985. The reasons for this policy turnaround are several.

Official views on the deutsche mark clearly underwent a dramatic change in the early 1980s. Throughout the 1960s and 1970s, the Bundesbank had, in effect, sought to prevent the mark from becoming a reserve currency largely to protect its ability to conduct an autonomous monetary policy and to deflect pressures for revaluation. Yet by 1983 the Bundesbank had reluctantly accepted the mark's increasing role in the world economy. Financial openness was seen to promise benefits. . . .

The rapid transformation in the Bundesbank's perspective reflected the changing interests of German banks. By the early 1980s, the large West German banks had become extensively involved in external markets. Their international assets (loans), for example, rose from $6.7 billion in 1973 to $73.3 billion in 1980 and $191 billion in 1985. With such rapidly rising international assets subject to world interest rates, banks became concerned about retaining a similar flexibility on the deposit side. In other words, changes on one side of bank balance sheets required similar changes on the other. Henceforth, the ability of German banks to compete abroad would depend increasingly upon the free movement of capital.

Deregulatory developments in Britain deepened such concerns; so too did policy changes further afield. In 1984, for example, the United States and Japan concluded a bilateral agreement aimed at facilitating the access of American financial firms to the Tokyo markets. West German banks feared that this agreement would forever lock them out of Japan unless their government stopped waiting for multilateral liberalization and began to negotiate a similar bilateral deal. The reciprocity provision built into the subsequent German-Japanese discussions of the management of securities issues in one another's markets underlined the new complexities that would have to be addressed if a unilateral movement toward closure were ever again contemplated.

More subtle pressures on official policies also emanated from changing corporate strategies. In the 1970s and 1980s German companies became increasingly multinational and directed larger volumes of their investment overseas. Reflecting this evolution, German foreign direct investment in foreign markets rose from DM 3.2 billion in 1970 to DM 7.6 billion in 1980 and DM 14.1 billion in 1985. The growing internationalization of German business strengthened resistance to the reimposition of capital controls.

In the same vein, financial institutions, which had adapted well to the restrictiveness of the German capital market in the early years of the Federal Republic, gradually became willing to threaten the exit option. The decision, for example, by the Deutsche Bank to buy 5 percent of Morgan Grenfell and move its international capital market operations to London provided the West German authorities with a clear signal that something had to be done to prevent international business from gravitating away from Frankfurt to London. The Deutsche Bank, after all, was not just any bank. It dominated the German capital market, led nearly half of all new mark-denominated Eurobond issues, underwrote 90 percent of new West German equity issues, and accounted for nearly one-quarter of all trading in German securities. More generally, since the strength of the major German banks had long been viewed by policymakers as critical to the health of the country's leading industries — for which they served as lenders, shareholders, and advisers — the liberalization of their domestic base quickly became an important goal of policy. The subsequent renewal of integration efforts in the European Community, including adoption of the 1992 program and initial planning for monetary union, accelerated policy efforts to expand "Finanzplatz Deutschland."

By the opening of the 1990s, the desire to see Frankfurt more deeply integrated into global financial markets had overwhelmed residual concerns about the implications of capital decontrol. The perennial issue of enhancing the competitiveness of German industry would be advanced by other means, including the expansion of production facilities outside the Federal Republic. The massive financial challenges posed by unification only reinforced the policy movement away from controls. The inflows that had proved so problematic in earlier decades were now deliberately encouraged.

Japan

Development of Controls   As in Germany, the priority of economic reconstruction in Japan during the immediate years after World War II entailed tight official controls over both inflows and outflows of short-term capital. The policy was put into place during the early days of the occupation and eventually drew its legal justification from the Foreign Exchange and Foreign Trade Control Law of 1949. In principle, all cross-border flows were forbidden unless specifically authorized by administrative decree. Only in the early 1960s did these arrangements begin to loosen, and then only for certain flows closely related to trade transactions. By 1964 this limited liberalization was enough to qualify Japan for Article VIII status in the IMF and for entry into the OECD.

Notwithstanding the first tentative moves toward financial openness, much publicized at the time, an extremely tight regime of controls over most capital movements remained. To be sure, certain inflows of hard currency, mainly U.S. dollars in the form of portfolio investment and foreign currency loans from American banks, were welcomed, but outflows and direct investment inflows were rigorously discouraged. The rationale for this policy stance was obvious. Even twenty years after the war, the country had no foreign currency reserves and was pursuing an ambitious strategy of indigenous industrial development. In effect, the policy amounted to husbanding and rationing scarce national resources. With an export-oriented economic growth strategy in place, the direct beneficiaries of the policy were leading industries selling their products in external markets. Financing was channeled to them mainly through highly regulated banks. Capital controls were key elements in a complex, but bureaucratically organized and directed financial system. In view of its own overarching foreign policy interests, the United States, the only possible challenger to this arrangement, willingly acquiesced.

A string of current account surpluses began to generate increasing volumes of reserves in the early 1970s, and corporate as well as official interest began to shift in the face of impending resource scarcities, domestic environmental problems, and the rise of trade barriers in several foreign markets. Restraints on capital outflows consequently started to loosen, but short-term capital inflows continued to be discouraged through a variety of measures. Strict new limitations, for example, were placed on new foreign currency loans. The goal was to counter the need for an upward revaluation of the yen and thereby to protect the competitiveness of the export sector.

With the international monetary crisis of 1971, the subsequent pressure on the yen, and the first oil shock in 1973, the policy environment turned upside down. For three years, Japan registered deficits in its current account. Controls were quickly eased on short-term inflows and tightened on outflows, particularly those occurring through the overseas networks of Japanese banks. When the situation improved in 1976, and current account surpluses returned, the controls on outflows gradually came off again, but several new controls on short-term inflows were put in place for the familiar purpose of countering upward pressure on the yen. In 1979 a second oil price shock reversed the current account balance, this time for two years. But new controls on outflows were now surprisingly limited. By then, Japanese money markets had become more deeply integrated with international markets, and stabilizing inflows more than matched outflows. Instead of being concerned that the new crisis would hurt the value of their investments in Japan, international investors, including OPEC governments, now focused on the underlying strength of the economy, and funds poured into the country.

Reasons for Liberalization   Having contributed to tensions in its economic relations with the United States and Western Europe in the early 1970s and again in 1976, exchange rate issues were in the background in 1979 when the Ministry of Finance announced its intention to initiate a major liberalization program to cover inward as well as outward capital movements. The relative ease with which the economy was adjusting to the second oil crisis provided a permissive policy context for this shift. In 1980 it was codified in a new Foreign Exchange and Foreign Trade Control Law, which replaced the concept of capital flow interdiction with the concept of automaticity-in-principle.

It is no coincidence that such a regime was put into place at a time when remarkable changes were under way in the international direct investment strategies of Japanese firms. After decades of slight involvement abroad, Japanese FDI went into a period of explosive growth. Comparable to volumes recorded throughout the late 1960s and early 1970s, net long-term capital movements from Japan totaled U.S. $3.1 billion in 1977. In 1978 that number jumped to $12.4 billion, or

1.5 percent of Japan's GNP. By 1986 it had reached $132.1 billion, or 6.7 percent of GNP. In the face of these flows, and the options of evasion and exit that they implied for externally oriented Japanese firms, the control regime originally enshrined in law in 1949 had outlived its usefulness.

Although the new law did not limit the government's formal capacity to intervene in Japanese financial markets, in practice a policy of decontrol was aggressively pursued. The apparatus for controlling capital movements was dismantled, a policy reinforced by parallel moves to free up gradually the operations of both domestic and foreign financial intermediaries. Although external pressures from private markets and foreign governments may have hastened the overt pace of change in each area, it is worth noting that foreign financial interests were far from unanimous in welcoming this shift. Foreign banks long established in Japan, for example, benefited materially from the earlier regime.

It is clear, however, that well-positioned Japanese intermediaries had the most to gain from the deepening of domestic capital markets promised by the twin policies of decontrol and deregulation, while Japanese manufacturing and financial firms overseas benefited to the extent that such policies defended their positions in foreign markets. In the mid-1960s Japan's cross-border banking business was mainly related to trade flows, and the Bank of Tokyo, the officially designated international bank, accounted for most of the fifty Japanese branches abroad. Twenty years later all of the major banks, as well as many smaller intermediaries, maintained physical networks overseas, comprising over two hundred branches and subsidiaries and three hundred representative offices. Japanese securities companies and insurance vendors followed the banks in major international expansions. Japanese intermediaries and some of their foreign rivals formed the institutional infrastructure for Euro-yen markets, whose development received a boost from the so-called yen-dollar negotiations that the United States and Japan concluded in 1984. Thereafter, it would become much more difficult to prevent the yen from evolving into a major international reserve currency.

By the early 1980s Japan was on the way to becoming the world's largest creditor. In practical terms, this meant that Japanese financial institutions began to play an increasingly important role in overseas capital markets — a development that expanded the range of arbitrage (or "exit") opportunities for Japanese investors and borrowers and complicated the problem of economic management for the Japanese government. After Sumitomo Bank purchased a majority interest in the Swiss universal bank Banco del Gottardo, for example, it became exceptionally difficult for the Ministry of Finance to keep the Eurobond market separate from the Japanese domestic market, since major Sumitomo clients could henceforth raise funds more easily in either market.

The private pressure for increased openness thereby generated was matched during much of the 1980s by the effects of rising public sector indebtedness, which further encouraged the deepening of domestic debt markets. Even without the added pressure coming from foreign governmental demands for decontrol, by 1990 high volumes of inward as well as outward capital flows translated into a broadening domestic political base for progressive financial liberalization and capital decontrol. Although countervailing domestic pressures emerged as inward flows pushed up the exchange value of the yen, the authorities now attempted to manage them more generally through the medium of interest rates and more directly through selective policies of compensation.

At the firm level, foreign direct investment was an obvious and increasingly used method for coping with a rising yen [¥]. Indeed, such a consideration has been widely cited as an explanation for the rapid pace of growth in Japanese FDI in the 1980s. From a base of U.S. $2.4 billion in 1980, direct investment outflows from Japan increased to $6 billion in 1984, $14.4 billion in 1986, and $34.1 billion in 1988. During the latter years of the 1980s, Japanese FDI grew at an average rate of 35.5 percent per year. For Japanese companies, the progressive internationalization of their production facilities was matched by the increasing global diversification of their financing. In 1975 they raised ¥2.8 billion on domestic capital markets and ¥.5 billion on overseas markets. In 1989 the comparable figures were ¥17.2 billion on domestic markets and ¥11.1 billion overseas.

Despite extreme financial turbulence in the 1990s, including a collapse in stock and real estate prices and an associated pullback of Japanese financial intermediaries from foreign markets, few observers expected a movement back to capital controls. The internationalization of Japanese business and the international integration of Japanese financial markets had proceeded far enough to make such an option much less feasible than it had been even a decade earlier. For leading Japanese firms, in particular, strategies of evasion and exit were now embedded in their very structures. That reality gave them significant new leverage over Japan's capital policies.

France

Development of Controls   Controls on foreign exchange transactions in France, although first introduced in 1915, became firmly established only after the Second World War. Like most other European countries, France initially used capital controls to ensure that its limited foreign exchange be used for domestic reconstruction and development. In later years, controls on capital outflows were kept in place because of persistent current account deficits. In these circumstances, controls were deemed necessary to insulate domestic interest rates from world markets. In 1966 a new law gave the government the right to control all foreign exchange transactions between France and the rest of the world, oversee the liquidation of foreign funds in France and French funds abroad, and prescribe conditions for the repatriation of all income earned abroad.

These new controls on capital movements added to France's already impressive array of administrative measures designed to direct the flow of savings and investment. The Treasury, for example, channeled funds directly from the government budget to industry. It also controlled the country's parapublic banks — such as the Banque Française du Commerce Extérieur and the Crédit National — which had been created to provide favored sectors with access to credit at subsidized rates. And finally, it guided the trajectory of financial flows through its use of controls over domestic interest rates and bank lending (the famous *encadrement du crédit*).

The importance of both capital and credit controls increased with France's decision in 1979 to join the EMS. Although French authorities had never allowed the franc to float freely, the EMS fixed the value of the franc more rigidly. Yet between 1979 and 1984, no government, whether of the Right or the Left, was willing to raise interest rates high enough to maintain the value of the franc in the EMS. Capital controls enabled the government to keep interest rates lower than would otherwise have been required.

The use of capital controls intensified following the 1981 election of François Mitterrand, the first socialist president of the Fifth Republic. Mitterrand inherited a currency that had become substantially overvalued, and his government's commitment to fiscal expansion and income redistribution soon triggered a run on the franc. In the midst of this crisis, Mitterrand and his advisers refused to sacrifice the goal of exchange rate stability. . . . Nor was the government willing to sacrifice monetary autonomy; despite the fact that France's major trading partners were in recession, the government continued with its plans to stimulate the economy. With these options ruled out, the government therefore tightened controls on the foreign exchange positions of French companies, on the overseas accounts of individuals, and on borrowing by nonresidents in France.

These controls provided the government with some breathing space, but the combination of growth at home and recession abroad soon caused France's trade and current accounts to fall deeply into the red. Even with more restrictive capital controls and tighter credit ceilings, however, the socialist government was unable to eliminate pressure against the franc and was therefore forced to devalue on three occasions during its first two years in office. In the aftermath of the third devaluation, the government decided to reverse course and replace its earlier expansion plans with deflationary monetary and fiscal policies. In addition, it adopted draconian capital controls: foreign equities and bonds could only be traded by French citizens among themselves. Importers faced strict limits on their ability to cover their foreign exchange risk, while exporters were forced to repatriate foreign-currency earnings almost immediately. French nationals could only keep a foreign bank account while they resided abroad. French tourists could take only a small amount of foreign exchange outside the country and were deprived of the use of their credit cards.

For the socialists as for their conservative predecessors, heavy reliance on capital controls thus resulted primarily from a desire to keep domestic interest rates lower than those generally prevailing in the rest of the world without abandoning the objective of exchange rate stability. Lower interest rates reduced demand for franc-denominated assets and stimulated domestic demand for imports. Together, these two effects increased net capital outflows and placed pressure on the franc. To avoid a precipitous decline of the franc (even if France left the EMS), tighter capital controls were deemed necessary. As the socialist government discovered, however, such controls had to be continuously tightened if they were to be effective. The controls of 1983 placed the French economy in the tightest corset since World War II.

Reasons for Liberalization   In November 1984 Prime Minister Laurent Fabius announced a dramatic new plan to reform the entire financial system. The government planned not only to eliminate credit ceilings and capital controls, but also to create new money, bond, and futures markets. Such wholesale reform had not been expected. Unlike France's decision to remain in the EMS, pressure from its EC partners was not part of the policy calculation; indeed, the announcement of its financial reform package *preceded* the commission's June 1985 white paper on European financial integration. . . .

What drove this new program of financial liberalization? Evasion strategies on the part of individuals and firms were certainly in the background; the famous stories about suitcases filled with foreign currency being carried into Switzerland come to mind. More subtle and ultimately more decisive pressures emanated, however, from the boardrooms of large French firms and financial intermediaries. In the French case, direct threats of exit were muted by the fact that virtually all of these firms were owned or controlled by the state. In this environment, such an option was transmuted into the rising concerns of government officials regarding the competitiveness of those firms relative to their foreign rivals. Jobs and investment that were promised by growth in the service sector, for example, were seen to be leaving France and migrating to less-restricted markets. In a very real sense, especially in financial services, Paris was increasingly seen to be in direct competition with London and Frankfurt. . . .

By 1984 the situation had become severe, and French policymakers recognized the pressing need to change course. When international capital markets were rapidly developing elsewhere, the competitiveness of both French industry and finance was now seen to be seriously undermined by capital controls. In 1985 the elimination of credit ceilings began, and new money, bond, and futures markets were created. The phaseout of capital controls followed, with major steps taking place in 1986 and 1989; in January 1990 controls disappeared completely with the lifting of the ban on the holding of foreign deposits by French nationals.

The shift in favor of capital mobility eventually tied in directly with plans for European Monetary Union (EMU), and France became a key promoter of the idea. The freedom of capital movements across the member states of the prospective union, indeed, was a prerequisite. But the planning for EMU followed the new commitment to restore and enhance the competitiveness of French industrial firms and financial intermediaries. The Delors Committee report on EMU came in 1988, three years after decontrol became the thrust of financial policy within France. That policy remained consistent despite the election of a conservative government in 1986 and the return of the socialists in 1988. In effect, as international financial integration outside France accelerated, French policymakers came to the conclusion that their preference for national monetary autonomy was unrealistic. The decision to initiate capital decontrol followed and accelerated as the country's external accounts improved.

Italy

Development of Controls   Restrictions on capital movements were initially put in place in Italy during the First World War. They were refined and tightened by Mussolini during the following two decades. Controls were relaxed in the late

1950s, a period of current account surpluses and currency stability. The "hot autumn" of 1969, however, dramatically altered Italy's economic trajectory. Facing increased labor militancy, the government put into place an expansionary fiscal policy to spur growth and ensure social peace. By 1973 this policy resulted in fiscal imbalances and current account deficits. The lira soon came under speculative attack. Rather than reverse its economic policy and risk unrest, the government responded by tightening capital controls.

Italian economic policy after the 1973 oil shock followed a classic stop-and-go cycle that made capital controls even more necessary. The oil shock caught Italy in a difficult position — with both a booming economy and a significant current account deficit. With the backing of the IMF, macroeconomic policy shifted to a decidedly more restrictive course in 1974, and by 1975 the Italian economy had fallen into its deepest recession since the 1950s. A shift to easier monetary and fiscal policy in early 1975, however, brought an exceptionally rapid recovery. Booming imports created downward pressure on the lira, and fears of a communist electoral victory accelerated capital flight. Despite heavy intervention in the foreign exchange markets, which left Italy with only $500 million in reserves, the lira depreciated by 20 percent in the first four months of 1976.

The Italian authorities responded by tightening monetary policy, fiscal policy, and capital controls. The most draconian measures were embedded in Law 159 of 1976, which essentially decreed that every foreign exchange transaction was illegal unless specifically authorized. In particular, the law made it a criminal offense either to send or to hold more than 5 million lire abroad without permission. Moreover, Italians owning residential property abroad were required to sell it and bring the proceeds back to Italy. A year later, these controls were eased somewhat after the communists were finally included in the governing majority, after the trade unions agreed to make wage concessions, and after a standby arrangement was negotiated with the IMF.

Still, government officials viewed capital controls as a means of avoiding hard choices. By the mid-1980s the annual budget deficit had topped 11 percent of GDP and cumulative debt approached 100 percent of GDP. To finance these deficits, the government had long relied on a large domestic savings pool. Household savings in Italy amounted to 20 percent of personal disposable income — the second highest savings rate in the world after Japan. Doing away with capital controls in the face of such deficits meant that domestic savers would be able to purchase foreign assets, forcing the government to offer a higher rate of interest on its own debt. . . .

Italy's decision to join the EMS in 1979 made matters even more difficult. With an economic policy more expansionary than that of its neighbors, exchange markets would not long find credible the country's commitment to maintain a fixed exchange rate. Here, too, capital controls were seen as a way of avoiding hard choices. Controls were eased and then reimposed each time the lira came under attack in exchange markets.

Reasons for Liberalization   The elimination of capital controls in Italy did not begin until 1987 and was not completed until 1992. Given the difficulties faced by

Italian policymakers, the source of this policy change is particularly interesting. Of the major EC countries, Italy was the only one whose decision was affected by pressure from its partners, particularly Germany, to comply with the EC directive on capital movements. In July 1986, for example, the European Court of Justice ruled that Italy had to give up insisting that every Italian citizen who held securities abroad had to keep 25 percent of their value in a non-interest-bearing account with the central bank. (In this instance, the Italian government responded by reducing the deposit to 15 percent.)

Still, it would be a mistake to attribute Italy's policy shift primarily to such external pressure, for in Italy — as in Germany, Japan, and France — private pressure for liberalization had become pervasive. Evasion of capital controls, of course, was a national sport, practiced by business executives, government ministers, and even church officials.

More important for the shift in policy, however, was the increasingly assertive position taken by private firms. Financial institutions, for example, had become concerned about the effect of controls on their ability to compete. It was perhaps not surprising that foreign companies opposed capital controls. . . . Yet domestic institutions also believed they were being disadvantaged. . . .

Manufacturing firms, like Olivetti and Fiat, also favored an end to controls. As the power of organized labor diminished in the 1980s, these firms became more profitable and competitive in foreign markets. They were therefore also more directly hampered by restrictions on capital movements and concerned about the prospect of not being able to take full advantage of the expanding EC market. Moreover, throughout the 1980s, many corporate groups — including Fiat, Montedison, and Ferruzi — had entered the financial sector, both individually and in concert with Italian banks. With diversification, these corporations developed new interest in the further development of domestic capital markets, as well as the extension of access to external markets. Capital controls impeded this prospect. So too did the never-ending rise in public borrowing. Accordingly, corporate leaders pushed for the elimination of controls in the hope of forcing greater discipline upon the government. In 1987, in a political environment significantly reshaped by changing corporate structures and preferences, the Italian government began stripping away existing controls on capital movements — a move completed in 1992 — and pushed through legislation limiting its own power to reimpose new controls during times of currency crisis.

CONCLUSION

In the early years of the postwar period, governments relied on controls over short-term capital movements for one fundamental purpose — to provide their economies with the maximum feasible degree of policy-making autonomy without sacrificing the benefits of economic interdependence. Controls were a shield that helped deflect the blows of international competition and ameliorate its domestic political effects. In the Bretton Woods system of pegged exchange rates, controls promised to provide both the space needed for the design of distinct national economic policies and the time needed for gradual economic adjustment to a changing external environment. To the surprise of some, they remained essential for many governments even when that system was replaced by managed floating.

Between the late 1970s and the early 1990s, a broad movement away from capital controls was evident across the industrialized world. The rapid growth of liquid international funds and the increasing globalization of production drove this process. Offshore markets eroded national financial barriers, not least by providing ever-widening sources of funding for multinational firms engaged in the process of globalizing their production facilities. In so doing, they enhanced the capability of firms to develop evasion and exit strategies. Governments thus first found that controls had to be tightened continuously to remain useful and then discovered that the resulting or potential economic costs of such tightening soon exceeded the benefits.

To be sure, governments encouraged or at least acquiesced in both the growth of offshore money markets and the international expansion of firms. Yet as our case histories show, governments continued to impose capital controls long after such developments became salient. In this sense, the diminishing utility of capital controls can be considered the unintended consequence of other and earlier policy decisions.

Strategies of evasion and exit on the part of firms, we have argued, threatened to reduce the volume of domestic savings and investment, the promotion of which often constituted the original rationale for controls. Of course, firms could use direct methods for pushing the decontrol agenda, as we saw in the French case where state ownership was a significant factor. But their ultimate influence on policy came from the pressure to evade controls or exit from their national jurisdictions if they were to remain competitive. In the German case, for example, by making moves offshore, the Deutsche Bank effectively made the case that capital controls were inconsistent with the goal of building a strong national financial center.

Other factors have influenced the elimination of capital controls, but our cases suggest that such factors played a secondary role. The principle of international capital mobility, for example, had long been enshrined in the OECD Code on Capital Movements, but until the 1980s virtually every major signatory country had at some point honored that principle in the breach. Similarly, a common European capital market was a key objective of the 1992 program, but the success of this effort was preceded (and made possible) by national programs of capital decontrol in both France and Germany. Fundamental changes at the domestic level also underpinned the apparent success of direct political pressure by other governments. In the Japanese case, for example, American pressure appeared at most to reinforce firm-level pressures associated with the rapid expansion of Japanese financial intermediaries and companies in overseas markets.

Notwithstanding the general movement in the direction of capital liberalization across the advanced industrial world, our cases point to important differences in the timing of actual decisions to decontrol. It was easier for countries facing capital inflows (Japan and Germany) to lift capital controls, than it was for countries facing capital outflows (France and Italy). The difference in timing — roughly a decade — underlines the mechanism by which systemic forces were translated into national decisions. Our cases do not enable us to reach definitive conclusions in this regard, but it seems likely that these differences in timing are correlated with broader variations in domestic political structures. Whether a country is facing chronic capital inflows or outflows may depend upon the structure of the state and the relative strength of domestic interest groups. But the fundamental convergence in the direction of capital mobility noted in all of our cases suggests that systemic forces are now dominant in the financial area and have dramatically reduced the ability of governments to set autonomous economic policies.

Our argument and evidence do not suggest, however, that a movement back toward capital controls or analogous policies to influence the flow of capital is impossible, only that such a movement would be more costly from a national point of view. Indeed, the restoration of controls is not just a theoretical possibility. In the midst of the European currency crisis in September 1992, for example, Spain and Ireland imposed new controls on banks' foreign exchange transactions. Despite the fact that such "temporary" measures did not contravene the letter of a prior agreement to eliminate impediments to capital mobility throughout the European Community, they surely conflicted with its spirit. More generally, continuing instability in global currency markets did subsequently lead the G-7, at the urging of American treasury secretary Nicholas Brady, to commission a new study to explore multilateral approaches to dealing with the consequences of international capital mobility.

If our argument is correct, two theoretical as well as policy implications bear underlining. First, if pressures for capital decontrol are now deeply embedded in firm structure and strategy, any efforts to understand or deal with the political effects of short-term capital mobility would seem to entail dealing with the politics of foreign direct investment. The two issues have long been related, but have also long been viewed as distinguishable for conceptual as well as for policy purposes. The distinction has broken down. The adoption of policies to influence short-term capital flows would now have a clearer impact on long-term investment decisions. Further research on this deepening connection is warranted.

Second, if policy convergence on the issue of capital controls is intimately linked to the development of international financial markets, attempts to understand and manage the effects of short-term capital mobility cannot be divorced from efforts to enhance the cross-national coordination of financial policies. As the negotiators at Bretton Woods recognized in 1944, open and stable markets ultimately depend upon a modicum of shared behavioral norms. Despite deepening interdependence across contemporary financial markets, states retain the right to change their policies on capital movements, either individually or on a regional basis. What remains unclear is their obligation to take into account the consequences of such policies for other states and for the world community. Thus, the time may now be ripe to begin considering new international arrangements to define and demarcate national responsibilities in an age of global markets.

V

TRADE

The international trade regime constructed under American leadership after World War II and now embodied in the World Trade Organization (WTO) has facilitated the emergence of the most open international economy in modern history. After World War II, political leaders in the United States and many other advanced industrialized countries believed, on the basis of their experience during the Great Depression of the 1930s, that protectionism contributes to depressions, depressions magnify political instability, and protectionism, therefore, leads to war. Drawing on these beliefs, the United States led the postwar fight for a new trade regime, to be based on the economic principle of comparative advantage. Tariffs were to be lowered, and each country would specialize in those goods that it produced best and trade for the products of other countries, as appropriate. To the extent this goal was achieved, American decisionmakers and others believed that all countries would be better off and prosperity would be reinforced.

The American vision for the postwar trade regime was originally outlined in a plan for an International Trade Organization (ITO), which was intended to complement the International Monetary Fund. As presented in 1945, the American plan offered rules for all aspects of international trade relations. The Havana Charter, which created the ITO, was finally completed in 1947. A product of many international compromises, the Havana Charter was the subject of considerable opposition within the United States. Republican protectionists opposed the treaty because they felt it went too far in the direction of free trade, while free-trade groups failed to support it because it did not go far enough. President Harry Truman, knowing that it faced almost certain defeat, never submitted the Havana Charter to Congress for ratification. In the absence of American support, the nascent ITO died a quick and quiet death. The General Agreement on Tariffs and Trade (GATT) was drawn up in 1947 to provide a basis for the trade negotiations then underway in Geneva. Intended merely as a temporary agreement to last only until the Havana Charter was fully implemented, the GATT became, by default, the principal basis for the international trade regime. The GATT was finally replaced by the WTO in 1995.[1]

Despite its supposedly temporary origins, the GATT was, for decades, the most important international institution in the trade area. Trade negotiations within the GATT — and now, the WTO — proceed in "rounds," typically initiated by new grants of negotiating authority delegated from the United States Congress to the president. Since 1947, there have been eight rounds of negotiations, each resulting in a new treaty, which was subsequently ratified by member states under their individual constitutional provisions.

The WTO is based on three primary norms. First, all members agree to extend unconditional most-favored-nation (MFN) status to one another. Under this agreement, no country receives any preferential treatment not accorded to all other MFN countries. Additionally, any benefits acquired by one country are automatically extended to all MFN partners. The only exceptions to this rule are customs unions, such as the European Union.

Second, the WTO is based on the norm of reciprocity — the concept that any country that benefits from another's tariff reduction should reciprocate to an equivalent extent. This norm ensures fair and equitable tariff reductions by all countries. In conjunction with the MFN (or nondiscrimination) norm, it also serves to reinforce the downward spiral of tariffs initiated by the actions of any one country.

Third, "safeguards," or loopholes and exceptions to other norms, are recognized as acceptable if they are temporary and imposed for short-term balance-of-payments reasons. Exceptions are also allowed for countries experiencing severe market disruptions from increased imports.

The GATT and WTO have been extremely successful in obtaining the declared goal of freer trade and lower tariffs. By the end of the Kennedy Round of the GATT in 1967 (initiated by President John F. Kennedy in 1962), tariffs on dutiable nonagricultural items had declined to approximately 10 percent in the advanced industrialized countries. In the Tokyo Round, concluded in 1979, tariffs in these same countries were reduced to approximately 5 percent, and member countries pledged to reduce their remaining tariffs by a further 40 percent in the Uruguay Round, concluded in late 1993. These significant reductions initiated an era of unprecedented growth in international trade, which continues today. The two most rapidly increasing areas are the overlapping realms of trade between advanced industrialized countries and intrafirm trade (the exchange of goods within, rather than between, corporations).

The WTO continues to be an active force for liberalization. In the late 1980s and early 1990s, the Uruguay Round focused on the thorny issues of services and agricultural trade — two areas that had been excluded from earlier negotiations. Governments have long regulated many of their domestic service industries, such as insurance, banking, and financial services. Often differing dramatically from country to country, these regulations have become politically contentious barriers to trade. Likewise, governments in most developed countries subsidize their agricultural sectors, leading to reduced imports and increasing surpluses that can only be managed through substantial sales abroad. Nearly all analysts agree that national and global welfare could be enhanced by reducing agricultural subsidies and returning to trade based on the principle of comparative advantage; yet as the prolonged negotiations of the Uruguay Round demonstrated, politicians have found it difficult to resist demands from farmers for continued government intervention. Here, as in other areas, the tension between national wealth and the self-seeking demands of domestic interest groups has created a difficult diplomatic issue — but one that, after years of comparative neglect, finally made it onto the trade liberalization agenda. The Uruguay Round did make substantial progress on many fronts, including services and agricultural trade; the primary exception, from the American point of view, was entertainment products, such as films, which were excluded from the final agreement at the insistence of the European Union.

While tariffs have been declining and trade increasing, however, new threats have emerged to the free-trade regime. With the success of trade liberalization, more and more industries have been exposed to increased international competition. Industry demands for some form of protection have multiplied in nearly all countries, and increasingly, governments have sought to satisfy these demands for protection through nontariff barriers to trade (NTBs). The most important of these NTBs are voluntary export restraints, in which exporters agree to restrain or limit their sales in the importer's market. Current estimates suggest that almost 20 percent of all goods imported into the European Union, for instance, enter under some type of NTB.[2] Although the Uruguay Round agreement has helped to bring their growth under control and even produced reductions in some areas, NTBs remain an important threat to free trade and a source of concern to observers of the international economy.

The readings in this section address the causes and implications of trade policy. Cletus C. Coughlin, K. Alec Chrystal, and Geoffrey E. Wood (Reading 19) review the classic economic argument for free trade and survey explanations for protection. The remaining articles use economic insights to address the politics of international trade. Ronald Rogowski (Reading 20) examines how changing exposure to international trade influences political cleavages within states. In this international economic perspective, political coalitions are a product of a country's position within the international division of labor and of exogenous changes in the costs of trade. Building on the insights offered by Rogowski and then extending their analysis to other models of trade policy, James E. Alt and Michael Gilligan (Reading 21) synthesize domestic societal and domestic institutional theories into a broad explanation of trade policy.

Richard B. Freeman (Reading 22) then examines what is sometimes referred to as the "trade and wages" debate. In theory, less skilled labor in the United States and Europe should have been harmed by increasing international trade, and real wages have fallen for such workers. Nonetheless, identifying the independent effects of international trade remains quite difficult, and as Freeman concludes, trade probably accounts for only a fraction of the decline. Edward D. Mansfield and Marc L. Busch (Reading 23) explain the cross-national pattern of nontariff barriers to trade through a combination of domestic societal and "statist" variables, with the latter covering both international political factors related to relative size and domestic political institutions. Finally, regional trade agreements have proliferated in recent years. The North American Free Trade Agreement (NAFTA) is perhaps the best known, but similar trade pacts have grown, both within and between, developed and developing country regions. Again illustrating the importance of domestic societal factors, Ronald W. Cox (Reading 24) explains business support for such agreements.

NOTES

1. The GATT continues to exist as a legal entity related to the WTO. Nonetheless, the GATT secretariat and director-general were transferred to the WTO, and the latter organization is expected to subsume, and fully replace, its predecessor over time. Except where specifically referring to the GATT, we refer to the international trade regime as the WTO.

2. Based on import coverage ratio from Organization for Economic Co-operation and Development (OECD), *Indicators of Tariff and Non-Tariff Trade Barriers* (Paris: OECD 1997), p. 53.

19

Protectionist Trade Policies: A Survey of Theory, Evidence, and Rationale

CLETUS C. COUGHLIN, K. ALEC CHRYSTAL, AND GEOFFREY E. WOOD

In this selection, three economists review traditional arguments in favor of free trade in light of new theories and evidence. Beginning with an exposition of the principle of comparative advantage, Cletus Coughlin, Alec Chrystal, and Geoffrey Wood examine modern forms of protection, the costs of trade protection in the United States and the world, and contemporary arguments for restricting trade and conclude that free trade remains the optimal policy for all countries. To explain why countries nonetheless adopt protection, the authors emphasize societal theories focusing on the distributional effects of trade policy and the incentives for specific groups to seek governmentally imposed trade restrictions.

Protectionist pressures have been mounting worldwide during the 1980s. These pressures are due to various economic problems including the large and persistent balance of trade deficit in the United States, the hard times experienced by several industries, and the slow growth of many foreign countries. Proponents of protectionist trade policies argue that international trade has contributed substantially to these problems and that protectionist trade policies will lead to improved results. Professional economists in the United States, however, generally agree that trade restrictions such as tariffs and quotas substantially reduce a nation's economic well-being.

This article surveys the theory, evidence and rationale concerning protectionist trade policies. The first section illustrates the gains from free trade using the concept of comparative advantage. Recent developments in international trade theory that emphasize other reasons for gains from trade are also reviewed. The theoretical discussion is followed by an examination of recent empirical studies that demonstrate the large costs of protectionist trade policies. Then, the rationale for restricting trade is presented. The concluding section summarizes the paper's main arguments.

THE GAINS FROM FREE TRADE

The most famous demonstration of the gains from trade appeared in 1817 in David Ricardo's *Principles of Political Economy and Taxation*. We use his example involving trade between England and Portugal to demonstrate how both countries can gain from trade. The two countries produce the same two goods, wine and cloth, and the only production costs are labor costs. The figures below list the amount of labor (e.g., worker-days) required in each country to produce one bottle of wine or one bolt of cloth.

	Wine	Cloth
England	3	7
Portugal	1	5

Since both goods are more costly to produce in England than in Portugal, England is absolutely less efficient at producing both goods than its prospective trading partner. Portugal has an absolute advantage in both wine and cloth. At first glance, this appears to rule out mutual gains from trade; however, as we demonstrate below, absolute advantage is irrelevant in discerning whether trade can benefit both countries.

The ratio of the production costs for the two goods is different in the two countries. In England, a bottle of wine will exchange for ³⁄₇ of a bolt of cloth because the labor content of the wine is ³⁄₇ that for cloth. In Portugal, a bottle of wine will exchange for ⅕ of a bolt of cloth. Thus, wine is relatively cheaper in Portugal than in England and, conversely, cloth is relatively cheaper in England than in Portugal. The example indicates that Portugal has a comparative advantage in wine production and England has a comparative advantage in cloth production.

The different relative prices provide the basis for both countries to gain from international trade. The gains arise from both exchange and specialization.

The gains from *exchange* can be highlighted in the following manner. If a Portuguese wine producer sells five bottles of wine at home, he receives one bolt of cloth. If he trades in England, he receives more than two bolts of cloth. Hence, he can gain by exporting his wine to England. English cloth producers are willing to trade in Portugal; for every ³⁄₇ of a bolt of cloth they sell there, they get just over two bottles of wine. The English gain from exporting cloth to (and importing wine from) Portugal, and the Portuguese gain from exporting wine to (and importing cloth from) England. Each country gains by exporting the good in which it has a comparative advantage and by importing the good in which it has a comparative disadvantage.

Gains from *specialization* can be demonstrated in the following manner. Initially, each country is producing some of both goods. Suppose that, as a result of trade, 21 units of labor are shifted from wine to cloth production in England, while in Portugal, 10 units of labor are shifted from cloth to wine production. This reallocation of labor does not alter the total amount of labor used in the two countries; however, it causes the production changes listed below.

	Bottles of wine	Bolts of cloth
England	− 7	+ 3
Portugal	+ 10	− 2
Net	+ 3	+ 1

The shift of 21 units of labor to the English cloth industry raises cloth production by three bolts, while reducing wine production by seven bottles. In Portugal, the shift of 10 units of labor from cloth to wine raises wine production by 10 bottles, while reducing cloth production by two bolts. This reallocation of labor increases the total production of both goods: wine by three bottles and cloth by one bolt. This increased output will be shared by the two countries. Thus, the consumption of both goods and the wealth of both countries are increased by the specialization brought about by trade based on comparative advantage.

TRADE THEORY SINCE RICARDO

Since 1817, numerous analyses have generated insights concerning the gains from trade. They chiefly examine the consequences of relaxing the assumptions used in the preceding example. For example, labor was the only resource used to produce the two goods in the example above; yet, labor is really only one of many resources used to produce goods. The example also assumed that the costs of producing additional units of the goods are constant. For example, in England, three units of labor are used to produce one bottle of wine regardless of the level of wine production. In reality, unit production costs could either increase or decrease as more is produced. A third assumption was that the goods are produced in perfectly competitive markets. In other words, an individual firm has no effect on the price of the good that it produces. Some industries, however, are dominated by a small number of firms, each of which can affect the market price of the good by altering its production decision. . . .

These theoretical developments generally have strengthened the case for an open trading system. They suggest three sources of gains from trade. First, as the market potentially served by firms expands from a national to a world market, there are gains associated with declining per unit production costs. A second source of gains results from the reduction in the monopoly power of domestic firms. Domestic firms, facing more pressure from foreign competitors, are forced to produce the output demanded by consumers at the lowest possible cost. Third is the gain to consumers from increased product variety and lower prices. Generally speaking, the gains from trade result from the increase in competitive pressures as the domestic economy becomes less insulated from the world economy.

FORMS OF PROTECTIONISM

Protection may be implemented in numerous ways. All forms of protection are intended to improve the position of a domestic relative to foreign producer. This can be done by policies that increase the home market price of the foreign product, decrease the costs of domestic producers or restrict the access of foreign producers to the home market in some other way.

Tariffs

Tariffs, which are simply taxes imposed on goods entering a country from abroad, result in higher prices and have been the most common form of protection for domestic producers. Tariffs have been popular with governments because it appears that the tax is being paid by the foreigner who wishes to sell his goods in the home economy and because the tariff revenue can be used to finance government services or reduce other taxes.

In the 20th century, U.S. tariff rates peaked as a result of the Smoot-Hawley Tariff of 1930. For example, in 1932, tariff revenue as a percentage of total imports was 19.6 percent. An identical calculation for 1985 yields a figure of 3.8 percent. The decline was due primarily to two reasons. First, since many of the tariffs under Smoot-Hawley were set as specific dollar amounts, the rising price level in the United States eroded the effective tariff rate. Second, since World War II, numerous tariff reductions have been negotiated under the General Agreement on Tariffs and Trade.

On the other hand, various other forms of protection, frequently termed nontariff barriers, have become increasingly important. A few of the more frequently used devices are discussed below.

Quotas

A quota seems like a sensible alternative to a tariff when the intention is to restrict foreign producers' access to the domestic market. Importers typically are limited to a maximum number of products that they can sell in the home market over specific periods. A quota, similar to a tariff, causes prices to increase in the home market. This induces domestic producers to increase production and consumers to reduce consumption. One difference between a tariff and a quota is that the tariff generates revenue for the government, while the quota generates a revenue gain to the owner of import licenses. Consequently, foreign producers might capture some of this revenue.

In recent years, a slightly different version of quotas, called either orderly marketing agreements or voluntary export restraints, has been used. In an orderly marketing agreement, the domestic government asks the foreign government to restrict the quantity of exports of a good to the domestic country. The request can be viewed as a demand, like the U.S.-Japan automobile agreement in the 1980s, because the domestic country makes it clear that more restrictive actions are likely unless the foreign government "voluntarily" complies. In effect, the orderly marketing agreement is a mutually agreed upon quota.

Regulatory Barriers

There are many other ways of restricting foreigners' access to domestic markets. . . . The 1983 *Tariff Schedules of the United States Annotated* consists of 792 pages, plus a 78-page appendix. Over 200 tariff rates pertain to watches and clocks. Simply ascertaining the appropriate tariff classification, which requires legal assistance and can be subject to differences of opinion, is a deterrent.

Product standards are another common regulatory barrier. These standards appear in various forms and are used for many purposes. The standards can be used to service the public interest by ensuring that imported food products are processed according to acceptable sanitary standards and that drugs have been screened before their introduction in the United States. In other cases, the standards, sometimes intentionally, protect domestic producers. An example of unintended restrictions may be the imposition of safety or pollution standards that were not previously being met by foreign cars.

Subsidies

An alternative to restricting the terms under which foreigners can compete in the home market is to subsidize domestic producers. Subsidies may be focused upon an industry in general or upon the export activities of the industry. An example of the former . . . is the combination of credit programs, special tax incentives and direct subsidy payments that benefit the U.S. shipbuilding industry. An example of the latter is the financial assistance to increase exports provided by the U.S. Export-Import Bank through direct loans, loan guarantees and insurance, and discount loans. In either case, production will expand.

An important difference between subsidies and tariffs involves the revenue implications for government. The former involves the government in paying out money, whereas tariffs generate income for the government. The effect on domestic production and welfare, however, can be the same under subsidies as under tariffs and quotas. In all cases, the protected industry is being subsidized by the rest of the economy.

Exchange Controls

All of the above relate directly to the flow of goods. A final class of restrictions works by restricting access to the foreign money required to buy foreign goods. For example, a government that wishes to protect its exporting and import competing industries may try to hold its exchange rate artificially low. As a result, foreign goods would appear expensive in the home market while home goods would be cheap overseas. Home producers implicitly are subsidized and home consumers implicitly are taxed. This policy is normally hard to sustain. The central bank, in holding the exchange rate down, has to buy foreign exchange with domestic currency. This newly issued domestic currency increases the domestic money stock and eventually causes inflation. Inflationary policies are not normally regarded as a sensible way of protecting domestic industry.

There is another aspect to exchange controls. The justification is that preventing home residents from investing overseas benefits domestic growth as it leads to greater domestic real investment. In reality, it could do exactly the opposite. Restricting access to foreign assets may raise the variance and lower the return to owners of domestic wealth. In the short run, it also may appreciate the domestic exchange rate and, thereby, make domestic producers less competitive.

COSTS OF TRADE PROTECTIONISM

The specific goal of protectionist trade policies is to expand domestic production in the protected industries, benefiting the owners, workers and suppliers of resources to the protected industry. The government imposing protectionist trade policies may also benefit, for example, in the form of tariff revenue.

The expansion of domestic production in protected industries is not costless; it requires additional resources from other industries. Consequently, output in other domestic industries is reduced. These industries also might be made less competitive because of higher prices for imported inputs. Since protectionist policies frequently increase the price of the protected good, domestic consumers are harmed. They lose in two ways. First, their consumption of the protected good is reduced because of the associated rise in its price. Second, they consume less of other goods, as their output declines and prices rise.

The preceding discussion highlights the domestic winners and losers due to protectionist trade policies. Domestic producers of the protected good and the government (if tariffs are imposed) gain; domestic consumers and other domestic producers lose. Foreign interests are also affected by trade restrictions. The protection of domestic producers will harm some foreign producers; oddly enough, other foreign producers may benefit. For example, if quotas are placed on imports, some foreign producers may receive higher prices for their exports to the protected market.

There have been numerous studies of the costs of protectionism. We begin by examining three recent studies of protectionism in the United States, then proceed to studies examining developed and, finally, developing countries.

Costs of Protectionism in the United States

Recent studies by Tarr and Morkre (1984), Hickok (1985), and Hufbauer et al. (1986) estimated the costs of protectionism in the United States. These studies use different estimation procedures, examine different protectionist policies and cover different time periods. Nonetheless, they provide consistent results.

Tarr and Morkre (1984) estimate annual costs to the U.S. economy of $12.7 billion (1983 dollars) from all tariffs and from quotas on automobiles, textiles, steel and sugar. Their cost estimate is a net measure in which the losses of consumers are offset partially by the gains of domestic producers and the U.S. government.

Estimates by Hickok (1985) indicate that trade restrictions on only three goods — clothing, sugar, and automobiles — caused increased consumer expenditures of $14 billion in 1984. Hickok also shows that low-income families are affected more than high-income families. The import restraints on clothing, sugar and automobiles are calculated to be equivalent to a 23 percent income tax surcharge (that is, an additional tax added to the normal income tax) for families with incomes less than $10,000 in 1984 and a 3 percent income tax surcharge for families with incomes exceeding $60,000.

Hufbauer et al. (1986) examined 31 cases in which trade volumes exceeded $100 million and the United States imposed protectionist trade restrictions. They generated estimates of the welfare consequences for each major group affected. [Their] figures indicate that annual consumer losses exceed $100 million in all but six of the cases. The largest losses, $27 billion per year, come from protecting the textile and apparel industry. There also are large consumer losses associated with protection in carbon steel ($6.8 billion), automobiles ($5.8 billion) and dairy products ($5.5 billion).

The purpose of protectionism is to protect jobs in specific industries. A useful approach to gain some perspective on consumer losses is to express these losses on a per-job-saved basis. In 18 of the 31 cases, the cost per-job-saved is $100,000 or more per year; the consumer losses per-job-saved in benzenoid chemicals, carbon steel (two separate periods), specialty steel, and bolts, nuts, and screws exceeded $500,000 per year.

[This study] also reveals that domestic producers were the primary beneficiaries of protectionist policies; however, there are some noteworthy cases where foreign producers realized relatively large gains. For the U.S.-Japanese voluntary export agreement in automobiles, foreign producers gained 38 percent of what domestic consumers lost, while a similar computation for the latest phase of protection for carbon steel was 29 percent.

Finally, [the study] indicates that the efficiency losses are small in comparison to the total losses borne by consumers. These efficiency losses . . . result from the excess domestic production and the reduction in consumption caused by protectionist trade policies. In large cases such as textiles and apparel, petroleum, dairy products, and the maritime industries, these losses equal or exceed $1 billion. It is likely that these estimates understate the actual costs because they do not capture the secondary effects that occur as production and consumption changes in one industry affect other industries. In addition, restrictive trade policies generate additional costs because of bureaucratic enforcement costs and efforts by the private sector to influence these policies for their own gain as well as simply comply with administrative regulations.

Costs of Protectionism throughout the World

In 1982, the Organization for Economic Cooperation and Development (OECD) began a project to analyze the costs and benefits of protectionist policies in manufacturing in OECD countries. The OECD (1985) highlighted a number of ways that protectionist policies have generated costs far in excess of benefits. Since protectionist policies increase prices, the report concludes that the attainment of sustained noninflationary growth is hindered by such price-increasing effects. Moreover, economic growth is potentially reduced if the uncertainty created by varying trade policies depresses investment.

... [The] OECD study stresses the fact that a reduction in imports via trade restrictions does not cause greater employment. A reduction in the value of imports results in a similar reduction in the value of exports. One rationale for this finding is that a reduction in the purchases of foreign goods reduces foreign incomes and, in turn, causes reduced foreign purchases of domestic goods.

While the reduction in imports increases employment in industries that produce products similar to the previously imported goods, the reduction in exports decreases employment in the export industries. In other words, while some jobs are saved, others are lost; however, this economic reality may not be obvious to businessmen, labor union leaders, politicians and others. . . . [The] jobs saved by protectionist legislation are more readily observed than the jobs lost due to protectionist legislation. In other words, the jobs that are protected in, say, the textile industry by U.S. import restrictions on foreign textiles are more readily apparent (and publicized) than the jobs in agriculture and high technology industries that do not materialize because of the import restrictions. These employment effects will net to approximately zero. . . .

ARGUMENTS FOR RESTRICTING TRADE

If protectionism is so costly, why is protectionism so pervasive? This section reviews the major arguments for restricting trade and provides explanations for the existence of protectionist trade policies.

National Defense

The national defense argument says that import barriers are necessary to ensure the capacity to produce crucial goods in a national emergency. While this argument is especially appealing for weapons during a war, there will likely be demands from other industries that deem themselves essential. For example, the footwear industry will demand protection because military personnel need combat boots.

The national defense argument ignores the possibility of purchases from friendly countries during the emergency. The possibilities of storage and depletion raise additional doubts about the general applicability of the argument. If crucial goods can be stored, for example, the least costly way to prepare for an emergency might be to buy the goods from foreigners at the low world price before an emergency and store them. If the crucial goods are depletable mineral resources, such as oil, then the restriction of oil imports before an emergency will cause a more rapid depletion of domestic reserves. Once again, stockpiling might be a far less costly alternative.

Income Redistribution

Since protectionist trade policies affect the distribution of income, a trade restriction might be defended on the grounds that it favors some disadvantaged group. It is unlikely, however, that trade policy is the best tool for dealing with the perceived evils of income inequality, because of its bluntness and adverse effects on the efficient allocation of resources. Attempting to equalize incomes directly by tax and transfer payments is likely less costly than using trade policy. In addition, as Hickok's (1985) study indicates, trade restrictions on many items increase rather than decrease income inequality.

Optimum Tariff Argument

The optimum tariff argument applies to situations in which a country has the economic power to alter world prices. This power exists because the country (or a group of countries acting in consort like the Organization of Petroleum Exporting Countries) is such a large producer or consumer of a good that a change in its production or consumption patterns influences world prices. For example, by imposing a tariff, the country can make foreign goods cheaper. Since a tariff reduces the demand for foreign goods, if the tariff-imposing country has some market power, the world price for the good will fall. The tariff-imposing country will gain because the price per unit of its imports will have decreased.

There are a number of obstacles that preclude the widespread application of this argument. Few countries possess the necessary market power and, when they do, only a small number of goods is covered. Secondly, in a world of shifting supply and demand, calculating the optimum tariff and adjusting the rate to changing situations is difficult. Finally, the possibility of foreign retaliation to an act of economic warfare is likely. Such retaliation could leave both countries worse off than they would have been in a free trade environment.

Balancing the Balance of Trade

Many countries enact protectionist trade policies in the hope of eliminating a balance of trade deficit or increasing a balance of trade surplus. The desire to increase a balance of trade surplus follows from the mercantilist view that larger trade surpluses are beneficial from a national perspective.

This argument is suspect on a number of grounds. First, there is nothing inherently undesirable about a trade deficit or desirable about a surplus. For example, faster economic growth in the United States than in the rest of the world would tend to cause a trade deficit. In this case, the trade deficit is a sign of a healthy economy. Second, protectionist policies that reduce imports will cause exports to decrease by a comparable amount. Hence, an attempt to increase exports permanently relative to imports will fail. It is doubtful that the trade deficit will be reduced even temporarily because import quantities do not decline quickly in response to the higher import prices and the revenues of foreign producers might rise.

Protection of Jobs — Public Choice

The protection of jobs argument is closely related to the balance of trade argument. Since a reduction in imports via trade restrictions will result in a similar reduction in imports via trade restrictions will result in a similar reduction in exports, the overall employment effects, as found in the OECD (1985) study and many others, are negligible. While the *overall* effects are negligible, workers (and resource owners) in specific industries are affected differently.

A domestic industry faced with increased imports from its foreign competition is under pressure to reduce production and lower costs. Productive resources must move from this industry to other domestic industries. Workers must change jobs and, in some cases, relocate to other cities. Since this change is forced upon these workers, these workers bear real costs that they are likely to resist. A similar statement can be made about the owners of capital in the affected industry.

Workers and other resource owners will likely resist these changes by lobbying for trade restrictions. The previously cited studies on the costs of protectionism demonstrated that trade restrictions entail substantial real costs as well. These costs likely exceed the adjustment costs because the adjustment costs are one-time costs, while the costs of protectionism continue as long as trade restrictions are maintained.

An obvious question is why politicians supply the protectionist legislation demanded by workers and other resource owners. A branch of economics called public choice, which focuses on the interplay between individual preferences and political outcomes, provides an answer. The public choice literature views the politician as an individual who offers voters a bundle of governmentally supplied goods in order to vote in elections. Many argue that politicians gain by providing protectionist legislation. Even though the national economic costs exceed the benefits, the politician faces different costs and benefits.

Those harmed by a protectionist trade policy for a domestic industry, especially household consumers, will incur a small individual cost that is difficult to identify. For example, a consumer is unlikely to ponder how much extra a shirt costs because of protectionist legislation for the textiles and apparel industry.

Even though the aggregate effect is large, the harm to each consumer may be small. This small cost, of which an individual may not even be aware, and the costs of organizing consumers deter the formation of a lobby against the legislation.

On the other hand, workers and other resource owners are very concerned about protectionist legislation for their industry. Their benefits tend to be large individually and easy to identify. Their voting and campaign contributions assist politicians who support their positions and penalize those who do not. Thus, politicians are likely to respond to their demands for protectionist legislation.

Infant Industries

The preceding argument is couched in terms of protecting a domestic industry. A slightly different argument, the so-called infant industry case, is couched in terms of *promoting* a domestic industry. Suppose an industry, already established in other countries, is being established in a specific country. The country might not be able to realize its comparative advantage in this industry because of the existing cost and other advantages of foreign firms. Initially, owners of the fledgling firm must be willing to suffer losses until the firm develops its market and lowers its production costs to the level of its foreign rivals. In order to assist this entrant, tariff protection can be used to shield the firm from some foreign competition.

After this temporary period of protection, free trade should be restored; however, the removal of tariff protection frequently is resisted. As the industry develops, its political power to thwart opposing legislation also increases.

Another problem with the infant industry argument is that a tariff is not the best way to intervene. A production subsidy is superior to a tariff if the goal is to expand production. A subsidy will do this directly, while a tariff has the undesirable side effect of reducing consumption.

In many cases, intervention might not be appropriate at all. If the infant industry is a good candidate for being competitive internationally, borrowing from the private capital markets can finance the expansion. Investors are willing to absorb losses *temporarily* if the prospects for future profits are sufficiently good.

Spillover Effects

The justification for protecting an industry, infant or otherwise, frequently entails a suggestion that the industry generates spillover benefits for other industries or individuals for which the industry is not compensated. Despite patent laws, one common suggestion is that certain industries are not fully compensated for their research and development expenditures. This argument is frequently directed toward technologically progressive industries where some firms can capture the results of other firms' research and development simply by dismantling a product to see how it works.

The application of this argument, however, engenders a number of problems. Spillovers of knowledge are difficult to measure. Since spillovers are not market transactions, they do not leave an obvious trail to identify their beneficiaries. The lack of market transactions also complicates an assessment of the value of these spillovers. To determine the appropriate subsidy, one must be able to place a dollar value on the spillovers generated by a given research and development expenditure. Actually, the calculation requires much more than the already difficult task of reconstructing the past. It requires complex estimates of the spillovers' future worth as well. Since resources are moved from other industries to the targeted industry, the government must understand the functioning of the entire economy.

Finally, there are political problems. An aggressive application of this argument might lead to retaliation and a mutually destructive trade war. In addition, as interest groups compete for the governmental assistance, there is no guarantee that the right groups will be assisted or that they will use the assistance efficiently.

Strategic Trade Policy

Recently theoretical developments have identified cases in which so-called strategic trade policy is superior to free trade. As we discussed earlier, decreasing unit production costs and market structures that contain monopoly elements are common in industries involved in international trade. Market imperfections immediately suggest the potential benefits of governmental intervention. In the strategic trade policy argument, governmental policy can alter the terms of competition to favor domestic over foreign firms and shift the excess returns in monopolistic markets from foreign to domestic firms.

Krugman (1987) illustrates an example of the argument. Assume that there is only one firm in the United States, Boeing, and one multinational firm in Europe, Airbus, capable of producing a 150-seat passenger aircraft. Assume also that the aircraft is produced only for export, so that the returns to the firm can be identified with the national interest. This export market is profitable for either firm if it is the only producer; however, it is unprofitable for both firms to produce the plane. Finally, assume the following payoffs are associated with the four combinations of production: (1) if both Boeing and Airbus produce the aircraft, each firm loses $5 million; (2) if neither Boeing nor Airbus produces the aircraft, profits are zero; (3) if Boeing produces the aircraft and Airbus does not, Boeing profits by $100 million and Airbus has zero profits; and (4) if Airbus produces the aircraft and Boeing does not, Airbus profits by $100 million and Boeing has zero profits.

Which firm(s) will produce the aircraft? The example does not yield a unique outcome. A unique outcome can be generated if one firm, say Boeing, has a head start and begins production before Airbus. In this case, Boeing will reap profits of $100 million and will have deterred Airbus from entering the market because Airbus will lose $5 million if it enters after Boeing.

Strategic trade policy, however, suggests that judicious governmental intervention can alter the outcome. If the European governments agree to subsidize Airbus' production with $10 million no matter what Boeing does, then Airbus will produce the plane. Production by Airbus will yield more profits than not producing, no matter what Boeing does. At the same time, Boeing will be deterred from producing because it would lose money. Thus, Airbus will capture the entire market and reap profits of $110 million, $100 million of which can be viewed as a transfer of profits from the United States.

The criticisms of a strategic trade policy are similar to the criticisms against protecting a technologically progressive industry that generates spillover benefits. There are major informational problems in applying a strategic trade policy. The government must estimate the potential payoff of each course of action. Economic knowledge about the behavior of industries that have monopoly elements is limited. Firms may behave competitively or cooperatively and may compete by setting prices or output. The behavior of rival governments also must be anticipated. Foreign retaliation must be viewed as likely where substantial profits are at stake. In addition, many interest groups will compete for the governmental assistance. Though only a small number of sectors can be considered potentially strategic, many industries will make a case for assistance.

Reciprocity and the "Level Playing Field"

. . . U.S. trade policy discussions in recent years have frequently stressed the importance of "fair trade." The concept of fair trade, which is technically referred to as reciprocity, means different things to different people.

Under the General Agreement on Tariffs and Trade, negotiations to reduce trade barriers focus upon matching concessions. This form of reciprocity, known as first-difference reciprocity, attempts to reduce trade barriers by requiring a country to provide a tariff reduction of value comparable to one provided by the other country. In this case, reciprocity is defined in terms of matching changes.

Recent U.S. demands, exemplified by the Gephardt amendment to the current trade legislation, reveal an approach that is called full reciprocity. This approach seeks reciprocity in terms of the level of protection bilaterally and over a specific range of goods. Reciprocity requires equal access and this access can be determined by bilateral trade balances. A trade deficit with a trading partner is claimed to be *prima facie* evidence of unequal access. Examples abound. For example, U.S. construction firms have not had a major contract in Japan since 1965, while Japanese construction firms did $1.8 billion worth of business in the United States in 1985 alone. Recent legislation bars Japanese participation in U.S. public works projects until the Japanese offer reciprocal privileges.

As the name suggests, the fundamental argument for fair trade is one of equity. Domestic producers in a free trade country argue that foreign trade barriers are unfair because they place them at a competitive disadvantage. In an extreme version, it is asserted that this unfair competition will virtually eliminate U.S. manufacturing, leaving only jobs that consist primarily of flipping hamburgers at fast food restaurants or . . . rolling rice cakes at Japanese owned sushi bars. While domestic producers *are* relatively disadvantaged, the wisdom of a protectionist response is doubtful. Again, the costs of protectionism exceed substantially the benefits from a national perspective.

In an attempt to reinforce the argument for fair trade, proponents also argue that retaliatory threats, combined with changes in tariffs and non-tariff barriers, allow for the simultaneous protection of domestic industries against unequal competition and induce more open foreign markets. This more flexible approach is viewed as superior to a "one-sided" free trade policy. The suggestion that a fair trade policy produces a trading environment with fewer trade restrictions allows proponents to assert that such a policy serves to promote both equity and efficiency. In other words, not only will domestic and foreign producers in the same industry be treated equally, but the gains associated with a freer trading environment will be realized.

On the other hand, critics of a fair trade policy argue that such a policy is simply disguised protectionism — it simply achieves the goals of specific interest groups at the expense of the nation at large. In many cases, fair traders focus on a specific practice that can be portrayed as protectionist while ignoring the entire package of policies that are affecting a nation's competitive position. In these cases, the foreign country is more likely either not to respond or retaliate by increasing rather than reducing their trade barriers. In the latter case, the escalation of trade barriers causes losses for both nations, which is exactly opposite to the alleged effects of an activist fair trade policy.

Critics of fair trade proposals are especially bothered by the use of bilateral trade deficits as evidence of unfair trade. In a world of many trading countries, the trade between two countries need not be balanced for the trade of each to be in global balance. Differing demands and productive capabilities across countries will cause a specific country to have trade deficits with some countries and surpluses with other countries. These bilateral imbalances are a normal result of countries trading on the basis of comparative advantage. Thus, the focus on the bilateral trade deficit can produce inappropriate conclusions about fairness and, more importantly, policies attempting to eliminate bilateral trade deficits are likely to be very costly because they eliminate the gains from a multilateral trading system.

CONCLUSION

The proliferation of protectionist trade policies in recent years provides an impetus to reconsider their worth. In the world of traditional trade theory, characterized by perfect competition, a definitive recommendation in favor of free trade can be made. The gains from international trade result from a reallocation of production resources toward goods that can be produced less costly at home than abroad and the exchange of some of these goods for goods that can be produced at less cost abroad than at home.

Recent developments in international trade theory have examined the consequences of international trade in markets where there are market imperfections, such as monopoly and technological spillovers. Do these imperfections justify protectionist trade policies? The answer continues to be no. While protectionist trade policies may offset monopoly power overseas or advantageously use domestic monopoly power, trade restrictions tend to reduce the competition faced by domestic producers, protecting domestic producers at the expense of domestic consumers.

The empirical evidence is clear-cut. The costs of protectionist trade policies far exceed the benefits. The losses suffered by consumers exceed the gains reaped by domestic producers and government. Low-income consumers are relatively more adversely affected than high-income consumers. Not only are there inefficiencies associated with excessive domestic production and restricted consumption, but there are costs associated with the enforcement of the protectionist legislation and attempts to influence trade policy.

The primary reason for these costly protectionist policies relies on a public choice argument. The desire to influence trade policy arises from the fact that trade policy changes benefit some groups, while harming others. Consumers are harmed by protectionist legislation; however, ignorance, small individual costs, and the high costs of organizing consumers prevent the consumers from being an effective force. On the other hand, workers and other resource owners in an industry are more likely to be effective politically because of their relative ease of organizing and their individually large and easy-to-identify benefits. Politicians interested in reelection will most likely respond to the demands for protectionist legislation of such an interest group.

The empirical evidence also suggests that the adverse consumer effects of protectionist trade policies are not short-lived. These policies generate lower economic growth rates than the rates associated with free trade policies. In turn, slow growth contributes to additional protectionist pressures.

Interest group pressures from industries experiencing difficulty and the general appeal of a "level playing field" combine to make the reduction of trade barriers especially difficult at the present time in the United States. Nonetheless, national interests will be served best by such an admittedly difficult political course. In light of the current Uruguay Round negotiations under the General Agreement on Tariffs and Trade, as well as numerous bilateral discussions, this fact is especially timely.

REFERENCES

Hickok, Susan. "The Consumer Cost of U.S. Trade Restraints," Federal Reserve Bank of New York *Quarterly Review* (Summer 1985), pp. 1–12.

Hufbauer, Gary Clyde, Diane T. Berliner, and Kimberly Ann Elliott. *Trade Protectionism in the United States: 31 Case Studies,* Institute for International Economics (1986).

Krugman, Paul R. "Is Free Trade Passé?" *Journal of Economic Perspectives* (Fall 1987), pp. 131–144.

Organization for Economic Cooperation and Development (OECD). *Costs and Benefits of Protection* (1985).

Tarr, David G., and Morris E. Morkre. *Aggregate Costs to the United States of Tariffs and Quotas on Imports: General Tariff Cuts and Removal of Quotas on Automobiles, Steel, Sugar, and Textiles,* Bureau of Economics Staff Report to the Federal Trade Commission (December 1984).

World Bank. *World Development Report 1987,* Oxford University Press (1987).

20

Commerce and Coalitions: How Trade Affects Domestic Political Alignments

RONALD ROGOWSKI

According to the Stolper-Samuelson theorem, free trade benefits locally abundant factors of production — such as land, labor, or capital — and harms locally scarce factors of production. Building on this insight, Ronald Rogowski offers a compelling theoretical and empirical account of political cleavages within countries. He extends the Stolper-Samuelson theorem to reason that increasing exposure to trade — say, because of falling transportation costs — will increase the political power of locally abundant factors, whereas decreasing exposure to trade will hurt these factors. Although not seeking to explain trade policy outcomes (such as the level of protection within a country), Rogowski provides a powerful explanation of the political coalitions and the politics surrounding trade policy. This essay shows how international economic forces can exert a profound effect on domestic politics.

THE STOLPER-SAMUELSON THEOREM

In 1941, Wolfgang Stolper and Paul Samuelson solved conclusively the old riddle of gains and losses from protection (or, for that matter, from free trade). In almost any society, they showed, protection benefits (and liberalization of trade harms) owners of factors in which, relative to the rest of the world, that society is *poorly* endowed, as well as producers who use that scarce factor intensively. Conversely, protection harms (and liberalization benefits) those factors that — again, relative to the rest of the world — the given society holds *abundantly,* and the producers who use those locally abundant factors intensively. Thus, in a society rich in labor but poor in capital, protection benefits capital and harms labor; and liberalization of trade benefits labor and harms capital.

So far, the theorem is what it is usually perceived to be, merely a statement, albeit an important and sweeping one, about the effects of tariff policy. The picture is altered, however, when one realizes that *exogenous* changes can have exactly the same effects as increases or decreases in protection. A cheapening of transport costs, for example, is indistinguishable in its act from an across-the-board decrease in every affected state's tariffs; so is any change in the international regime that decreases the risks or the transaction costs of trade. The converse is of course equally true: when a nation's external transport becomes dearer or its trade less secure, it is affected exactly as if it had imposed a higher tariff.

The point is of more than academic interest because we know, historically, that major changes in the risks and costs of international trade have occurred: notoriously, the railroads and steamships of the nineteenth century brought drastically cheaper transportation; so, in their day, did the improvements in shipbuilding and navigation of the fifteenth and sixteenth centuries; and so, in our own generation, have supertankers, cheap oil, and containerization. According to the familiar argument, . . . international hegemony decreases both the risks and the transaction costs of international trade; and the decline of hegemonic power makes trade more expensive, perhaps — as, some have argued, in the 1930s — prohibitively so. . . .

Global changes of these kinds, it follows, should have had global consequences. The "transportation revolutions" of the sixteenth, the nineteenth, and scarcely less of the mid-twentieth century must have benefited in each affected country owners and intensive employers of locally abundant factors and must have harmed owners and intensive employers of locally scarce factors. The events of the 1930s should have had exactly the opposite effect. What, however, will have been the *political* consequences of those shifts of wealth and income? To answer that question, we require a rudimentary model of the political process and a somewhat more definite one of the economy.

SIMPLE MODELS OF THE POLITY AND THE ECONOMY

Concerning domestic political processes, I shall make only three assumptions: that the beneficiaries of a change will try to continue and accelerate it, while the victims of the same change will endeavor to retard or halt it; that those who enjoy a sudden increase in wealth and income will thereby be enabled to expand their political influence as well; and that, as the desire and the means for a particular political preference increase, the likelihood grows that political entrepreneurs will devise mechanisms that can surmount the obstacles to collective action.

For our present concerns, the first assumption implies that the beneficiaries of safer or cheaper trade will support yet greater openness, while gainers from dearer or riskier trade will pursue even greater self-sufficiency. Conversely, those who are harmed by easier trade will demand protection or imperialism; and the victims of exogenously induced constrictions of trade will seek offsetting reductions in barriers. More important, the second assumption implies that the beneficiaries, potential or actual, of any such exogenous change will be strengthened politically (although they may still lose); the economic losers will be weakened politically as well. The third assumption gives us reason to think that the resultant pressures will not remain invisible but will actually be brought to bear in the political arena.

The issue of potential benefits is an important one, and a familiar example may help to illuminate it. In both great wars of this century, belligerent governments have faced an intensified demand for industrial labor and, because of the military's need for manpower, a reduced supply. That situation has positioned workers — and, in the U.S. case, such traditionally disadvantaged workers as blacks and women — to demand greatly increased compensation: these groups, in short, have had large *potential* gains. Naturally, governments and employers have endeavored to deny them those gains; but in many cases — Germany in World War I, the United States in World War II, Britain in both world wars — the lure of sharing in the potential gains has induced trade on leaders, and workers themselves, to organize and demand more. Similarly, when transportation costs fall, governments may at first partially offset the effect by imposing protection. Owners of abundant factors nonetheless still have substantial *potential* gains from trade, which they may mortgage, or on which others may speculate, to pressure policy toward lower levels of protection.

So much for politics. As regards the economic aspect, I propose to adopt with minor refinements the traditional three-factor model — land, labor, and capital — and to assume . . . that the land-labor ratio informs us fully about any country's endowment of those two factors. . . . No country, in other words, can be rich in both land and labor: a high land-labor ratio implies abundance of land and scarcity of labor; a low ratio signifies the opposite. Finally, I shall simply define an *advanced* economy as one in which capital is abundant.

This model of factor endowments . . . permits us in theory to place any country's economy into one of four cells (see Figure 1), according to whether it is advanced or backward and whether its land-labor ratio is high or low. We recognize, in other words, only economies that are: (1) capital rich, land rich, and labor poor; (2) capital rich, land poor, and labor rich; (3) capital poor, land rich, and labor poor; or (4) capital poor, land poor, and labor rich.

	Land-Labor Ratio	
	High	**Low**
Economy Advanced	ABUNDANT: Capital Land SCARCE: Labor	ABUNDANT: Capital Labor SCARCE: Land
Economy Backward	ABUNDANT: Land SCARCE: Capital Labor	ABUNDANT: Labor SCARCE: Capital Land

FIGURE 1. Four Main Types of Factor Endowments

POLITICAL EFFECTS OF EXPANDING TRADE

The Stolper-Samuelson theorem, applied to our simple model, implies that increasing exposure to trade must result in *urban-rural conflict* in two kinds of economies, and in *class conflict* in the two others. Consider first the upper right-hand cell of Figure 1: the advanced (therefore capital-rich) economy endowed abundant in labor but poorly in land. Expanding trade must benefit both capitalists and workers; it harms only landowners and the pastoral and agricultural enterprises that use land intensively. Both capitalists and workers — which is to say, almost the entire urban sector — should favor free trade; agriculture should on the whole be protectionist. Moreover, we expect the capitalists and the workers to try, very likely in concert, to expand their political influence. Depending on preexisting circumstances, they may seek concretely an extension of the franchise, a reapportionment of seats, a diminution in the powers of an upper house or of a gentry-based political elite, or a violent "bourgeois" revolution.

Urban-rural conflict should also rise in backward, land-rich economies (the lower left-hand cell of Figure 1) when trade expands, albeit with a complete reversal of fronts. In such "frontier" societies, both capital and labor are scarce; hence both are harmed by expanding trade and, normally, will seek protection. Only land is abundant, and therefore only agriculture will gain from free trade. Farmers and pastoralists will try to expand their influence in some movement of a "populist" and antiurban stripe.

Conversely, in backward economies with low land-labor ratios (the lower right-hand cell of Figure 1), land and capital are scarce and labor is abundant. The model therefore predicts *class conflict:* labor will pursue free trade and expanded political power (including, in some circumstances, a workers' revolution); landowners, capitalists, and capital-intensive industrialists will unite to support protection, imperialism, and a politics of continued exclusion.

The reverse form of class conflict is expected to arise in the final case, that of the advanced but land-rich economy (the upper left-hand cell of Figure 1) under increasing exposure to trade. Because both capital and land are abundant, capitalists, capital-intensive industries, and agriculture will all benefit from, and will endorse, free trade; labor being scarce, workers and labor-intensive industries will resist, normally embracing protection and (if need be) imperialism. The benefited sectors will seek to expand their political power, if not by disfranchisement then by curtailment of workers' economic prerogatives and suppression of their organizations.

These implications of the theory of international trade (summarized in Figure 2) seem clear, but do they in any way describe reality? . . . [I]t is worth observing how closely the experience of three major countries — Germany, Britain, and the United States — conforms to this analysis in the period of rapidly expanding trade in the last third of the nineteenth century; and how far it can go to explain otherwise puzzling disparities in those states' patterns of political evolution.

Germany and the United States were both relatively backward (i.e., capital-poor) societies: both imported considerable amounts of capital in this period, and neither had until late in the century anything like the per capita industrial capacity

Land-Labor Ratio

	High	Low
Economy Advanced	CLASS CLEAVAGE: Land and Capital free-trading, assertive; Labor defensive, protectionist	URBAN-RURAL CLEAVAGE: Capital and Labor free-trading, assertive; Land defensive, protectionist Radicalism
Economy Backward	URBAN-RURAL CLEAVAGE: Land free-trading, assertive; Labor and Capital defensive, protectionist U.S. Populism	CLASS CLEAVAGE: Labor free-trading, assertive; Labor and Capital defensive, protectionist Socialism

FIGURE 2. Predicted Effects of Expanding Exposure to Trade

of the United Kingdom or Belgium. Germany, however, was rich in labor and poor in land; the United States, of course, was in exactly the opposite position. (Again, we observe that the United States imported, and Germany exported — not least to the United States — workers, which is not surprising since, at midcentury, Prussia's labor-land ratio was fifteen times that of the United States.)

The theory predicts class conflict in Germany, with labor the "revolutionary" and free-trading element, and with land and capital united in support of protection and imperialism. Surely this description will not ring false to any student of German socialism or of Germany's infamous "marriage of iron and rye!" For the United States, conversely, the theory predicts — quite accurately, I submit — urban-rural conflict, with the agrarians now assuming the "revolutionary" and free-trading role; capital and labor unite in a protectionist and imperialist coalition. . . .

Britain, on the other hand, was already an advanced economy in the nineteenth century. Its per capita industrial output far exceeded that of any other nation, and it exported capital in vast quantities. That it was also rich in labor is suggested by its extensive exports of that factor to the United States, Canada, Australia, New Zealand, and Africa; in fact, Britain's labor-land ratio then exceeded Japan's by 50 percent and was over thirty times that of the United States. Britain therefore falls into the upper right-hand quadrant of Figure 1 and is predicted to exhibit a rural-urban cleavage whose fronts are opposite those found in the United States: capital-ists and labor unite in support of free trade and in demands for expanded political power, while landowners and agriculture support protection and imperialism.

Although this picture surely obscures important nuances, it illuminates crucial differences — between, for example, British and German political development in this period. In Britain, capitalists and labor united in the Liberal party and forced an expanded suffrage and curtailment of (still principally land-owning) aristocratic power. In Germany, liberalism shattered, the suffrage at the crucial level of the individual states was actually contracted, and — far from eroding aristocratic power — the bourgeoisie grew more and more *verjunkert* in style and aspirations.

POLITICAL EFFECTS OF DECLINING TRADE

When rising costs or declining security substantially increases the risks or costs of external trade, the gainers and losers in each situation are simply the reverse of those under increasing exposure to trade. Let us first consider the situation of the highly developed (and therefore by definition capital-rich) economies.

In an advanced economy with a high land-labor ratio (the upper left-hand cell of Figure 1), we should expect intense *class conflict* precipitated by a newly aggressive working class. Land and capital are both abundant in such an economy; hence, under declining trade owners of both factors (and producers who use either factor intensively) lose. Moreover, they can resort to no such simple remedy as protection or imperialism. Labor being the only scarce resource, workers and labor-intensive industries are well positioned to reap a significant windfall from the "protection" that dearer or riskier trade affords; and, according to our earlier assumption, like any other benefited class they will soon endeavor to parlay their greater economic power into greater political power. Capitalists and landowners, even if they were previously at odds, will unite to oppose labor's demands.

Quite to the contrary, declining trade in an advanced economy that is labor rich and land poor (the upper right-hand cell of Figure 1) will entail renewed *urban-rural* conflict. Capital and labor are both abundant, and both are harmed by the contraction of external trade. Agriculture, as the intense exploiter of the only scarce factor, gains significantly and quickly tries to translate its gain into greater political control.

Urban-rural conflict is also predicted for backward, land-rich countries under declining trade; but here agriculture is on the defensive. Labor and capital being both scarce, both benefit from the contraction of trade; land, as the only locally abundant factor, is threatened. The urban sectors unite, in a parallel to the "radical" coalition of labor-rich developed countries under expanding trade discussed previously, to demand an increased voice in the state.

Finally, in backward economies rich in labor rather than land, class conflict resumes, with labor this time on the defensive. Capital and land, as the locally scarce factors, gain from declining trade; labor, locally abundant, suffers economic reverses and is soon threatened politically.

Observe again, as a first test of the plausibility of these results — summarized in Figure 3 — how they appear to account for some prominent disparities of political response to the last precipitous decline of international trade, the depression of the 1930s. The U.S. New Deal represented a sharp turn to the left and occasioned a significant increase in organized labor's political power. In Germany, a depression of similar depth (gauged by unemployment rates and declines in industrial production) brought to power first Hindenburg's and then Hitler's dictatorship. Landowners exercised markedly greater influence than they had under Weimar; and indeed a credible case can be made that the rural sector was the principal early

Land-Labor Ratio

	High	Low
Economy Advanced	CLASS CLEAVAGE: Labor assertive, Land and Capital defensive, U.S. New Deal	URBAN-RURAL CLEAVAGE: Land assertive, Labor and Capital defensive, West European Fascism
Economy Backward	URBAN-RURAL CLEAVAGE: Labor and Capital assertive, Land defensive, South American Populism	CLASS CLEAVAGE: Land and Capital assertive, Labor defensive, Asian and East European Fascism

FIGURE 3. Predicted Effects of Declining Exposure to Trade

beneficiary of the early Nazi regime. Yet this is exactly the broad difference that the model would lead us to anticipate, if we accept that by 1930 both countries were economically advanced — although Germany, after physical reparations and cessions of industrial regions, was surely less rich in capital than the United States — but the United States held land abundantly, which in Germany was scarce (respectively, the left- and right-hand cells of the upper half of Figure 3). Only an obtuse observer would claim that such factors as cultural inheritance and recent defeat in war played no role; but surely it is also important to recognize the sectoral impact of declining trade in the two societies.

As regards the less developed economies of the time, it may be profitable to contrast the depression's impact on such South American cases as Argentina and Brazil with its effects in the leading Asian country, Japan. In Argentina and Brazil, it is usually asserted, the depression gave rise to, or at the least strengthened, "populist" coalitions that united labor and the urban middle classes in opposition to traditional, landowning elites. In Japan, growing military influence suppressed representative institutions and nascent workers' organizations, ruling in the immediate interest — if hardly under the domination — of landowners and capitalists. Similar suppressions of labor occurred in China and Vietnam. In considering these contrasting responses, should we not take into account that Argentina and Brazil were rich in land and poor in labor, while in Japan (and, with local exceptions, in Asia generally) labor was abundant and land was scarce? . . .

POSSIBLE OBJECTIONS

Several objections can plausibly be raised to the whole line of analysis that I have advanced here. . . .

[1.] It may be argued that the effects sketched out here will not obtain in countries that depend only slightly on trade. A Belgium, where external trade (taken as the sum of exports and imports) roughly equals gross domestic product (GDP), can indeed be affected profoundly by changes in the risks or costs of international commerce; but a state like the United States in the 1960s, where trade amounted to scarcely a tenth of GDP, will have remained largely immune.

This view, while superficially plausible, is incorrect. The Stolper-Samuelson result obtains at any margin; and in fact, holders of scarce factors have been quite as devastated by expanding trade in almost autarkic economics — one need think only of the weavers of India or of Silesia, exposed in the nineteenth century to the competition of Lancashire mills — as in ones previously more dependent on trade.

[2.] Given that comparative advantage always assures gains from trade, it may be objected that the cleavages described here need not arise at all: the gainers from trade can always compensate the losers and have something left over; trade remains the Pareto-superior outcome. As Stolper and Samuelson readily conceded in their original essay, this is perfectly true. To the student of politics, however, and with even greater urgency to those who are losing from trade in concrete historical situations, it remains unobvious that such compensation will in fact occur. Rather, the natural tendency is for gainers to husband their winnings and to stop their ears to the cries of the afflicted. Perhaps only unusually strong and trustworthy states, or political cultures that especially value compassion and honesty, can credibly assure the requisite compensation . . . and even in those cases, substantial conflict over the nature and level of compensation will usually precede the ultimate agreement.

[3.] Equally, one can ask why the cleavages indicated here should persist. In a world of perfectly mobile factors and rational behavior, people would quickly disinvest from losing factors and enterprises (e.g., farming in Britain after 1880) and move to sectors whose auspices were more favorable. Markets should swiftly clear; and a new, if different, political equilibrium should be achieved.

To this two answers may be given. First, in some cases trade expands or contracts so rapidly and surprisingly as to frustrate rational expectations. Especially in countries that experience a steady series of such exogenous shocks — the case in Europe, I would contend, from 1840 to the present day — divisions based on factor endowments (which ordinarily change only gradually) will be repeatedly revived. Second, not infrequently some factors' privileged access to political influence makes the extraction of rents and subsidies seem cheaper than adaptation: Prussian *Junkers,* familiarly, sought (and easily won) protection rather than adjustment. In such circumstances, adaptation may be long delayed, sometimes with ultimately disastrous consequences.

At the same time, it should be conceded that, as improved technology makes factors more mobile . . . and anticipation easier, the theory advanced here will likely apply less well. Indeed, this entire analysis may be a historically conditioned one, whose usefulness will be found to have entered a rapid decline sometime after 1960. . . .

[4.] This analysis, some may contend, reifies such categories as "capital," "labor," and "land," assuming a unanimity of preference that most countries' evidence belies. In fact, a kind of shorthand and a testable hypothesis are involved: a term like "capital" is the convenient abbreviation of "those who draw their income principally from investments, plus the most capital-intensive producers"; and I indeed hypothesize that individuals' political positions will vary with their derivation of income — or, more precisely, of present value of all anticipated future income — from particular factors.

A worker, for example, who derives 90 percent of her income from wages and 10 percent from investments will conform more to the theory's expectation of "labor"'s political behavior than one who depends half on investments and half on wages. An extremely labor-intensive manufacturer will behave less like a "capitalist" than a more capital-intensive one. And a peasant (as noted previously) who depends chiefly on inputs of his own labor will resemble a "worker," whereas a more land-intensive neighbor will behave as a "landowner."

[5.] Finally, it may be objected that I have said nothing about the outcome of these conflicts. I have not done so for the simple reason that I cannot: history makes it all too plain, as in the cases of nineteenth-century Germany and America, that the economic losers from trade may win politically over more than the short run. What I have advanced here is a speculation about *cleavages,* not about outcomes. I have asserted only that those who gain from fluctuations in trade will be strengthened and emboldened politically; nothing guarantees that they will win. Victory or defeat depends, so far as I can see, both on the relative size of the various groups and on those institutional and cultural factors that this perspective so resolutely ignores.

CONCLUSION

It is essential to recall what I am *not* claiming to do. . . . I do not contend that changes in countries' exposure to trade explain all, or even most, of their varying patterns of political cleavage. It would be foolish to ignore the importance of ancient cultural and religious loyalties, of wars and migrations, or of such historical memories as the French Revolution and the *Kulturkampf.* Other cleavages antedate, and persist through, the ones I discuss here, shaping, crosscutting, complicating, and indeed sometimes dominating their political resolution. . . .

In the main, I am presenting here a theoretical puzzle, a kind of social-scientific "thought experiment" in Hempel's original sense: a teasing out of unexpected, and sometimes counterintuitive, implications of theories already widely accepted. For the Stolper-Samuelson theorem *is* generally, indeed almost universally, embraced; yet, coupled with a stark and unexceptionable model of the political realm, it plainly implies that changes in exposure to trade must profoundly affect nations' internal political cleavages. Do they do so? If they do not, what conclusions shall we draw, either about our theories of international trade, or about our understanding of politics?

21

The Political Economy of Trading States: Factor Specificity, Collective Action Problems, and Domestic Political Institutions

JAMES E. ALT AND MICHAEL GILLIGAN

In this essay, James Alt and Michael Gilligan contrast Rogowski's factor-based approach to political coalitions (see Reading 20) with a sectoral approach drawn from the Ricardo-Viner, or "specific factors," model of international trade. They explain under what circumstances political coalitions will take the form of broad classes, as predicted by Rogowski, and under what circumstances they will organize along the lines of specific industries. The authors then examine how collective action costs (the costs incurred by groups in organizing for political action) and domestic political institutions influence the formation of political coalitions, and they conclude that these constraints may exert a more important effect than strictly economic considerations. Alt and Gilligan provide a broad survey of the most important theoretical concepts used by contemporary analysts and develop a synthetic approach to the domestic politics of international trade.

I. INTRODUCTION

The fundamental problem that international trade poses for states is this. Trade typically offers cheaper goods, with more choice for consumers and the greatest economic output for society as a whole. But at the same time, it is also very disruptive to individuals' lives, tying their incomes to the vagaries of international markets. In so doing, trade affects the distribution of wealth *within* the domestic economy, raising questions of who gets relatively more or less, and what they can do about it politically. Trade also has important effects, naturally, on aggregate domestic economic welfare and on the distributions of wealth and power among national societies. Anyone theorizing about "trading states" (states of trading societies) should consider the state's problem of how to weigh the aggregate, external effects against the internal, distributional effects — and indeed against the costs or disturbances that those internal redistributions may bring.

All too often, however, theories of states and trade neglect the domestic political dimension. The purpose of this article is to present a manual (or perhaps a map) explicating what is required to understand the domestic consequences of a society's "choosing to trade." It discusses considerations fundamental to answering a range of questions, from "Can a state enhance aggregate welfare by intervening in a trading economy?" to "What consequences would/should an increase in trade have for the design of state institutions?"

In domestic politics the conflict over these distributional consequences will reflect the trade policy coalitions that form around shared interests in liberalization as opposed to protection. Whether trade policies are taken to be chosen democratically or imposed from above, whether those coalitions are engaged in vote mobilization or protest, the balance between the opposed coalitions favoring freer trade and those favoring protection creates the "demand" by society for liberalization or protection. At one level, our central concern is with explaining how and why these coalitions take the form they do. In these terms, the essential problem for the state of a trading economy (or indeed for any government which seeks to stay in office) may become weighing the good of the many, which is often served by relatively free trade, against the good of the powerful few which may be served by restricting trade. At other times and places, however, the battle may be between two groups of the few or between two groups of the many. . . .

II. COLLECTIVE ACTION FROM PARETO TO THE PRESENT

Let us first consider the problem as one purely of collective action. Seventy years ago the Italian economist Vilfredo Pareto argued:

> In order to understand how those who champion protection make themselves heard so easily it is necessary to add the consideration which applies to social movements generally. . . . If a certain measure A is the cause of a loss of one franc to each of a thousand persons, and of a one thousand franc gain to one individual, the latter will expend a great deal of energy, whereas the former will resist weakly; and it is likely that, in the end, the person who is attempting to secure the thousand francs via A will be successful.
>
> A protectionist measure provides large benefits to a small number of people, and causes a very great number of consumers a slight loss. This circumstance makes it easier to put a protection measure in practice.[1]

Similarly, in his classic study of the Smoot-Hawley Act of 1930 Schattschneider explained the costly increase in protection by arguing, "Benefits are concentrated while costs are distributed."[2] It is vital to note that Pareto's and Schattschneider's statements are empirical observations, not general theoretical points. In what follows we will discuss the conditions under which we would expect to observe what they describe. . . . Collective action problems continue to be a major component of explanations in trade policy today, particularly in the endogenous tariff literature in economics.

There are really two interactive problems of organizing or taking collective political action: one is "excludability" and the other is the cost of organizing a group. The problem of excludability stems from the fact that collective political action is a public good: all members of a group benefit from acting in favor of their preferred trade policy whether they contribute to that effort or not, so each has an incentive to free ride. . . .

. . . Since each member can consume the lobbying supplied by all the other members of the group, they receive less benefit from the lobbying that they actually pay for and consequently buy less than they would if they could not consume the lobbying of others. This is essentially where the free rider problem comes from. . . .

Even though the problem of free-riding is less in smaller groups, . . . they should not always be expected to win. We are still left with Pareto and Schattschneider's empirical puzzle: how policies which benefit a small minority of the population are enacted. Two answers to the puzzle are possible. First, there may be *per person* transaction costs in organizing groups. Second, if policy outcomes are probabilistic, members of large groups with small per person stakes and contributions may suppose that their own contributions will be insignificant to the political outcome and therefore not make them. On the other hand, members of smaller groups, with their larger stakes and contributions per person, may see that their contribution has a non-negligible impact on the likelihood that a policy will be enacted, and therefore they will make their contributions. . . .

First, if transaction costs are fixed per person, larger groups will find it costlier to organize than smaller groups. These per person transaction costs may be paid by the organization (for instance the costs of soliciting contributions door to door or through the mail) or they may be borne by the members of the group (through the costs of learning which groups are active on an issue and how a new member can help). . . .

A second reason why smaller groups may have an advantage over larger groups is that outcomes of political action are uncertain. Members of each group will only be concerned with the probability that their contribution will decide the political outcome. . . . [I]n smaller groups individuals' contributions will be larger, and as a result their probabilities of deciding the outcome will be larger. In very large groups like consumer groups, on the other hand, individual contributions will be quite small, and as a result individual probabilities of deciding outcomes will be small as well — so small, perhaps, as to make the expected benefits of a contribution negligible.

In other words, expected benefits will outweigh expected costs only at fairly high contributions, because only high contributions have a non-negligible chance of deciding the outcome. Furthermore, these contributions will only be made by individuals with fairly high individual stakes, which is to say, people in the smaller group. So because the members of the smaller group make larger contributions per person, they also have a larger effect on the probability of changing the outcome and therefore benefits can outweigh costs. On the other hand, members of large groups have very small stakes per person in the issue: their contributions are small, and therefore so too are their chances of changing the outcome also small. Consequently, the expected benefits are too small to outweigh even the small cost of a contribution. To bring it down to earth, a one million dollar lobbying contribution from GM will likely have a large effect on trade policy. A ten dollar contribution from an individual auto consumer will have virtually no effect. Thus even though the cost of the auto consumer's contribution is negligible, the expected benefits are even more negligible.

III. A BRIEF PRIMER OF THE STOLPER-SAMUELSON AND RICARDO-VINER MODELS

The expected costs facing organizers of potential collective political actions are a feature of the domestic political and economic environment, affected by but also largely independent of the variables we discuss (namely, political institutions, and factor abundance and mobility). But these economic variables cannot be ignored if one is to understand the demand for political outcomes, independently of the costs of collective action. These variables, in short, determine the "stakes," which we held constant in the last section. We need to understand their role in determining individual-level preferences, reflected in the incentives to form coalitions and demand political redress, in who goes with whom and at what cost. To illustrate this for the case of international trade, we organize our discussion around two models, the Stolper-Samuelson or "mobile factors" approach (central in Rogowski's work; see Reading 20) and the Ricardo-Viner or "specific factors" model. . . .

A. The Stolper-Samuelson Model

In 1944 Wolfgang Stolper and Paul Samuelson seemingly settled a long debate within economics about the effects of a change in the price of a product on the real incomes of the owners of factors (such as labor and capital) that produce that product and other products in the economy. The Stolper-Samuelson theorem, as it was later called, argued that a change in the price of a product — for the sake of argument, let us say an increase — would *more than proportionally* increase the return to the factor that is used intensively in the production of that good. Therefore the real incomes of owners of that intensively used factor will unambiguously rise, giving them, in our terms, a stake in bringing about that change in prices. So, for example, an increase in the price of the labor-intensive good leads to an increase in the real wage rate of labor throughout the economy and an increase in the real incomes of laborers. Furthermore, if there are only two factors of production, the theorem shows that the real incomes of the owners of the factor that is used less intensively will fall.

It takes a few steps to establish this overall result. First, protection of an industry will raise the price of the good produced by that industry. That is where the change in relative prices comes from. Protection increases the returns to the owners of the factors that are used most intensively in the protected (import-competing) industry and less intensively in the unprotected (export) industry; and it reduces the returns to those factors that are used less intensively in the protected industry and more intensively in the unprotected industry. The big consequence from our point of view is that, because factors are assumed to be mobile between sectors, owners of the same factor have the same change to its returns, *regardless of whether it is actually employed in the protected industry* or in the unprotected industry. Therefore the conflict is between the factors of production, regardless of the industry in which they work.

Second, let us reground the prediction of which groups within a country will be relatively more disposed to favor protection or free trade. Instead of basing that prediction, as before, on intensity of use let us instead base it a point prior to that: the country's actual endowments. To do this, combine the Stolper-Samuelson theorem's predictions about factor price changes and income changes with the Hecksher-Ohlin theorem. This theorem states that a country will export the good which intensively uses whichever factor of production is relatively abundant in that country. Therefore, according to the Hecksher-Ohlin theorem, if there are two factors of production (say, capital and labor) a country which is relatively abundant in capital will export capital-intensive products and import labor-intensive products, while a country that is relatively abundant in labor will export labor-intensive products and import capital-intensive products. Combining this prediction with the Stolper-Samuelson theorem yields the usual conclusion that, other things being equal, in a relatively capital-abundant country labor will favor protection because it cannot be intensively used in exports, while capital will favor relatively free trade. Conversely, in a relatively labor-abundant country capital will favor protection and labor will favor relatively free trade. These were Rogowski's main arguments.

Finally, to predict individual preferences over policy outcomes we need to add one further consideration. The "magnification effect" allows us to translate "returns to factors" into real incomes and thus establish the Stolper-Samuelson theorem's central point, which is that trade policy can more than proportionally increase the real incomes of owners of the factor that is used intensively in making that product. The mechanism through which the Stolper-Samuelson theorem works is known as the "Rybczynski theorem." Suppose that in a capital-rich country (which imports labor-intensive products) some shock increases imports, thus producing lower relative prices for the imported (that is to say, labor-intensive) good and higher relative prices for the exported (that is to say, capital-intensive) good. This reduction in the relative price of the imported good leads to reduced production in the labor-intensive industry, while the increase in the relative price of the exported good leads to an increase in production in the export industry. To accommodate these changes in production in each of the two industries, labor and capital are freed up in the labor-intensive industry, and the need for labor and capital is increased in the capital-intensive industry. Since it is after all a capital-intensive industry, in order to increase production that industry needs relatively *less* labor and relatively *more* capital than would a labor-intensive industry. Meanwhile, as it reduces production the labor-intensive industry sheds relatively *more* labor and relatively *less* capital (it is after all a labor-intensive industry).

Therefore, there is excess labor on the market, and the relative price of labor falls to bring the market back into equilibrium. Meanwhile, there is excess demand for capital, so the price for capital is bid up to bring the market back into equilibrium.

Precisely because relatively more labor is freed up from the labor-intensive industry and it is needed less by the capital-intensive industry, the wage falls proportionally more than the relative price of the import-competing good. Similarly, precisely because relatively less capital is freed up from the labor-intensive industry while it is needed more by the capital-intensive industry, the price of capital increases by relatively more than the increase in relative price for the capital-intensive good. This magnification effect of changes in relative prices of goods on the rewards to the factors that produce them is the heart of the Stolper-Samuelson theorem. The logic may be somewhat involved, but the bottom line is not: in this example of a capital-abundant country, labor loses and capital wins from freer trade.

B. The Ricardo-Viner (Specific Factors) Model

The assumption that factors are mobile between sectors of the economy is crucial to the derivation of the Stolper-Samuelson theorem. It is only because capital can flow from the import-competing (labor-intensive industry) to the capital-intensive industry that it is able to enjoy the effect of the increased production of the capital-intensive good. But what if the capital used in the labor-intensive industry is different from the capital used in the capital-intensive industry? To bring the example back down to earth, what if knitting machines cannot be used to make microchips? Indeed, in many real world situations it seems intuitively likely that this will be the case: capital (or certain kinds of labor, for that matter) will not be able to flow easily from a declining sector to a rising sector. A different set of assumptions is needed for this contingency. According to the assumptions of the Ricardo-Viner model (or "specific factors" model as it is often called) factors of production are "specific" to a particular industry, and when that industry declines they cannot move to the rising industry.

"Cannot move" is a matter of degree. Specificity corresponds to the loss of value in moving an asset from its current to its next-best use. Specificity relates to ways in which investments are tied to particular production relationships: it can involve location, human capital (expertise) and many other forms in which assets may be dedicated to a particular use. What specific assets have in common is that, apart from their present use, they just do not have any very good alternate uses. Various social characteristics can increase the general level of specific assets in an economy. *Economic development,* to the extent that it involves increasingly taking advantage of differentiation and specialization, probably increases the frequency of specific factors. Any general increase in *transaction costs,* even if narrowly construed to involve only monitoring and policing, probably increases specificity throughout an economy. Such disparate factors as *geographical separation* and *ethnic rivalries* can reduce the ability of labor to move freely. In fact, all sorts of *entry barriers* increase specificity: insofar as entry to one sector involves exit from another, specificity just reflects costs of exit. In this sense, specificity is probably very high in *centrally planned* economies, where factor owners would not think of moving without asking the permission of bureaucrats.

In this situation, what are the effects of the relative price changes following an increase in imports? Let us assume for exposition that there are two industries, the export industry and the import industry, and that each industry has a factor that is specific to it. Let us further assume that there is also a mobile factor, which we will call labor, that is needed by both industries and that can move easily between them. To continue now with the example from the previous section, as the price of the import-competing good decreases as a result of the increased competition from imports, production will also decrease in that industry; and the mobile factor, labor, will flow out of that sector, just as before. However, the factor that is specific to that industry must obviously remain in that industry. The specific factors remaining in that industry still need labor to produce their product. But as labor flows out of the import-competing industry, they find it increasingly hard to get it and become less productive in consequence. Because of this productivity decline, the income of the specific factor in the import-competing industry will fall with respect to the price of both the export good and the imported good. Meanwhile, labor will flow into the export industry, since the relative price of the export good will increase as a result of the falling price of the import-competing good. Factors of production that are specific to the export industry will become more productive (because of the extra labor that they can now use), and as a result the return to that factor will increase relative to the price of both the export good and the imported good.

In the Ricardo-Viner model, the effect on the real income of the mobile factor is ambiguous. It depends, not only on intensities of use (which work much as described in the previous part), but also on consumption patterns. Since the labor-intensive industry is in our running example the one in decline, wages have to fall. . . . The second part of the effect, the consumption effect, is however more complicated. First, the nominal wage paid to the mobile factor will fall, but by less than the reduction in the price of the imported good: thus owners of the mobile factor enjoy an increase in their wage, relative to the price of the imported good. Second, however, the price of the exported good remains the same, so the wage rate falls relative to it. The net effect on each owner of the mobile factor of the price changes and the change in the return to the mobile factor therefore depends on (a) the size of the nominal reduction in the wage rate and (b) the share of each of the two products in each person's budget. If workers consume a great deal of the import good, their real incomes are more likely to rise because their wages have risen relative to the price of the import good. If they consume a great deal of the export good, their incomes are likely to fall because their real incomes have fallen relative to the export good. . . .

What changes in moving from the Stolper-Samuelson to the Ricardo-Viner model? First, we lose the simple derivation, working through relative intensity of use, of economic interest from factor abundance. In the specific factors model there is a zero-sum conflict of interest between exporting and import-competing sectors: their interests are diametrically opposed; whatever one side gains the other loses, rather than gains and losses being distributed according to factor ownership within both sectors. However, the interests of one of these groups of factor owners will in general be aligned with the interests of the owners of the mobile factor(s). It seems probable that the stakes of the mobile factor owners will be smaller than those of the specific factor owners. Supposing however that the mobile factor could be more or less scarce and supposing that scarcer factors mean fewer owners of that factor, the per capita stakes will be the larger. This opens up intriguing possibilities for coalition formation even in a specific factors model.

IV. TRADE POLICY COALITIONS: FACTOR SPECIFICITY, COLLECTIVE ACTION AND DOMESTIC INSTITUTIONS

From these economic models, we can thus infer individuals' preferences from the stakes facing them in potential situations of collective action. Let us now, reflecting on the collective action literature, consider how people might respond. In so doing we shall initially set aside, and then reintroduce, the effects of institutional context.

A. From Preferences to Trade Policy Coalitions

The implication for politics of the "mobile factors" approach is just this: the scarce factor (labor, in the above example) will favor restricting trade, and the abundant factor (capital, in the above example) will have incentives to favor liberalizing trade, no matter where in the economy those factors are employed. Let us further assume, for the moment, that there are no barriers to collective action (or that any that exist are easily surmounted) and that one or another coalition can actually get what it wants. (These are not always good assumptions about politics, as we will argue below, but for now let us make them in order to highlight the effects of economic variables on trade policy coalitions.) It then follows from the "mobile factors" model that owners of the abundant factor will favor liberalization while the scarce factor will favor protection. . . .

The predictions about trade policy coalitions flowing from the Ricardo-Viner model are somewhat more complicated. We proceed in two steps, continuing throughout to focus on the case where labor is the mobile factor. First, were we to assume away the interests of the mobile factor . . . the coalitions predicted by the Ricardo-Viner model would be simply the specific factors used in the export industry versus the specific factors used in the import industry. As argued above, the former unambiguously gains from the relative price reduction of the imported good, while the latter unambiguously loses. As the mobile factor flows out of the import-competing industry and into the export industry, the specific factor in the import-competing industry becomes less productive and its real return falls. Meanwhile the real return to the specific factor in the export industry rises, as that factor becomes more productive due to the larger pool of the mobile factor available to it. As Figure 1 shows, pro-liberalization (protectionist) groups will always

Stolper-Samuelson			Ricardo-Viner	
			Export Industry Relatively Labor-Intensive	Import Industry Relatively Labor-Intensive
Pro-trade	**Abundant Factor**	Consumption of Imported Good High	Export Industry Specific Factor and Labor	Export Industry Specific Factor Labor "Biddable"
		Low	Export Industry Specific Factor Labor "Biddable"	Export Industry Specific Factor
			Export Industry Relatively Labor-Intensive	Import Industry Relatively Labor-Intensive
Protectionist	**Scarce Factor**	Consumption of Imported Good High	Import-Competing Specific Factor	Import-Competing Specific Factor Labor "Biddable"
		Low	Import-Competing Specific Factor Labor "Biddable"	Import-Competing Specific Factor and Labor

FIGURE 1. Trade Policy Coalitions under the Stolper-Samuelson and Ricardo-Viner Assumptions

include the specific factor in the export (import-competing) industry. But where will the mobile factor, labor, be allied?

. . . [W]here the export industry is labor-intensive and labor consumes relatively much of (spends a disproportionate share of its consumption budget on) the imported good, labor has an interest in liberalization; so too, naturally, does the owner of the specific factor in the export industry. Set against this pro-liberalization coalition is the specific factor in the import-competing industry alone. Change the relative labor intensities of the two industries, and switch labor's consumption of imports to "relatively low," and we move to [a situation where] the owners of the export industry's specific factor stand alone in wanting liberalization, other things equal. . . . The underlying logic is simply this: the factor that is politically *advantaged* is that which is specific to the good that *uses labor intensely,* labor does not disproportionately consume that as well.

But what if the direct effect of relative price changes on the mobile factor is ambiguous? Even then, each of the two specific factors may want to pull the mobile factor into its coalition. To do so, they may be willing to offer side payments to labor to bring it into their coalition. In these cases, which coalition labor allies with (or at least is bought by more cheaply) will depend on whether the effects of the consumption bundle or of factor intensity are stronger.

In any case, it would be wrong to assume that, in the Ricardo-Viner model, the mobile factor will not take sides in the trade policy coalitions. This is particularly true in political systems where "numbers matter" — that is, where a majority or at least fairly large numbers must be behind a particular policy for it to be enacted. In such political systems the mobile factor holds a very powerful political position. If the changes in its income resulting from a change in relative prices are smaller than the changes in the income of the specific factors involved, the mobile factor is in a sense the median group between the two specific factors. If so, it commands what is sometimes important political turf, and it might therefore be courted by the two specific factors. This consideration is our link to the role of institutions.

B. The Relationship Between Factor Mobility, Institutions, and Collective Action Costs

What, then, determines the policy outcomes? Partly the distribution of benefits, as described before: that is the demand side. But neither the Stolper-Samuelson nor the Ricardo-Viner models are by themselves sufficient to understand coalition formation on trade policy issues. The severity of collective action problems — the difficulty of mobilizing or organizing resources in order to secure a favorable political decision — also has a role in the maintenance and extension of protection. Let us, purely for the sake of analytic convenience, disaggregate "collective action problems" into three parts: (1) those which relate systematically to factor mobility or specificity, (2) those which relate directly to the nature of domestic political institutions and (3) all the rest. Much more might be said about this last category, but for our purposes it will serve merely as a residual category reflecting the effects of ease of communication, geographical concentration and preexisting collective organizations, all of which reduce the cost of collective action in any particular case.

Factor mobility has obvious effects on possibilities for collective action. Mobility automatically disperses the benefits of any trade policy across all the owners of a particular factor, regardless of which industry employs them. This produces non-excludability, which in turn opens up the possibility of free-riding. Collective action is easier the more any non-participant can be excluded from the benefits: factor mobility, conversely, makes collective action harder. With perfect factor mobility, the scarce factor in the economy will benefit from protection (and from the lobbying that secures it) wherever it is employed. Contrast that with the case in which, when protection is granted to one industry, the benefits of that protection flow only to the specific factors employed in that industry (and possibly the mobile factor): there, the benefits of protection would be more excludable, mitigating the free-rider problem. With mobile factors, however, the benefits are more broadly dispersed, and thus the result should be that they are less excludable.

Ignore now, for a moment, factor mobility. Focus instead on political institutions, and where the jurisdiction for taking decisive actions on trade policy lies. Many possibilities exist. One is that action is taken directly by majoritarian voting, as in a referendum. Here, to obtain a favorable outcome one needs (relatively) large numbers of supporters. The Stolper-Samuelson model, in which one's "interest" depends on how large a share of one's income is derived from each of the factors of production, interacts with such majoritarian politics in a straightforward way: if, for example, the great mass of the population derives most of its income from labor then there will be a standing majority ready to vote the interest of labor. Another possibility, not quite so extreme, is that policy is made in a legislature by party bloc voting. Large numbers of supporters are once again involved, although the possibilities for using organizational channels facilitate some collective action that might be too costly if everyone affected had to be mobilized individually.

Where numbers count most, outcomes depend on the distribution of income, which can be used as shorthand for distribution of factor ownership. This, combined with the level of development of an economy (which is to say, whether capital is scarce or abundant), determines trade policy outcomes. A capital-rich country in which capital is highly concentrated in a few hands (strictly speaking, a country in which a large majority have little capital or derive little of their income from capital) should adopt trade restrictions, because the majority of the population would benefit from them. The more equitable the distribution of income (again, technically, the greater the extent to which a majority of the population derive most of their income from capital) the lower trade barriers should be, since a larger share of the population would own capital and would be hurt by trade barriers.

At the other end of the scale, imagine decision-making institutions completely insulated from majoritarian pressures. All one has to do to get protection, say, is to convince a bureaucrat (perhaps just a regional administrator) in a centrally planned economy. Or maybe it is one or a small group of legislators, whose interest in maintaining office requires pleasing only a relatively small, sector-specific, geographically differentiated constituency. Or maybe the outcome can be achieved by bargaining between ministers or even within ministries. In cases such as these, support from large segments of the population is not necessary for a policy to be enacted. Much more important for a group's success is its ability to access and to influence the decision-making system. There is then no need for an interest group to make sure that its preferred policy benefits a large share of the population — to do so would only lower the per-person benefits within the group and increase the organizational costs of political action. The point is that majoritarian institutions force groups to disperse benefits more broadly than do non-majoritarian systems. For any aggregate amount of benefit that would flow from some trade policy change, the less majoritarian the institution the fewer who will share in the benefit, either directly or indirectly (through compensatory payments).

This effect of political institutions is not the same as the effect of factor mobility, however. Benefits can, in principle be as excludable as you like in a majoritarian politics model. Majoritarianism affects the number of supporters that must be brought within a winning coalition, and thus the dispersion of benefits across members of that coalition. In majoritarian political systems the benefits must be spread across a large number of individuals to make the policy politically viable. Non-excludability, on the other hand, means that the benefits of a trade policy will flow to many regardless of whether or not they participate in the winning coalition, which will be more of a problem in a Stolper-Samuelson world because the benefits of a particular trade policy accrue to a particular factor regardless of where in the economy it is employed. The effect of these two variables — factor mobility and political institutions — is in another sense the same, however. Other things being equal, majoritarian political systems and factor mobility will both mean that benefits will be more disperse and, therefore, that it will be harder to organize a successful interest group. . . .

It is not only the case that factor mobility and majoritarian institutions produce their effects in different ways. They also vary independently of each other to some extent. That is not to say that the two do not affect each other. The existence of non-majoritarian institutions probably does make it easier for the owners of specific factors to invest in securing policies which in fact make factors more specific, and even to seek institutional changes which make it easier to achieve such policies. But deciding to make trade policy by referendum would not by itself make all factors of production mobile, nor would inventing legislative subcommittees necessarily make factors sticky. Neither does the mobility of factors by itself generate complementary political institutions. There may be some effects in each direction. But when considering costs of collective action facing a possible interest group in securing trade policy outcomes, factor mobility and political institutions are independent variables.

C. Collective Action Costs and Trade Policy Coalitions

What coalitions, then, are we actually likely to observe? To see how the effects of the costs of collective action work, let us first hold the institutional variable constant. Then the implications of collective action costs and factor mobility for trade policy coalitions are as summarized in Figure 2. The horizontal axis specifies the severity of collective action costs, net of institutions and factor mobility — that is, how costly it is to organize an interest group, holding constant the problems of non-excludability and dispersion of benefits that may arise due to factor mobility or political institutions. The vertical axis specifies whether the Stolper-Samuelson or the Ricardo-Viner model is appropriate for the degree of factor mobility between industrial sectors.

The northeast quadrant contains the assumptions underlying Rogowski's book (excerpted in Reading 20). The absence of collective action problems and the complete mobility of labor and capital (and perhaps land) between sectors of the economy imply a cleavage between scarce and abundant factors, which Rogowski interpreted (depending on which was the scarce factor) as class and urban-rural conflict. Notice that the assumptions of both perfect mobility and small collective action costs are necessary for his argument. With less than perfect factor mobility, the costs of increased international trade would be concentrated primarily on the factor specific to production of the particular traded good in question (and perhaps the perfectly mobile factor). Therefore, other factors in the economy would have no reason to oppose freer trade of that good; indeed, they should support it, and the broad coalitions Rogowski speaks of would not form.

Collective Action Costs

	High	Low
Factors Mobile	Rampant free riding No trade policy coalitions	Rogowski
Factors Specific	Standard trade policy models (Pareto, Olson, etc.)	Many interest groups, Consumers active, Coalitions between the specific and mobile factors

FIGURE 2. Coalition Possibilities: The Effects of Factor Mobility and Collective Action Costs

Furthermore, even if factors were perfectly mobile, high costs of collective action might mean that many of the factor owners would have little incentive to take costly political action to affect trade policy, free-riding instead on the political action of others. Then, as in the northwest quadrant of the Figure 2, it is likely that there would be no coalitions over trade issues (except perhaps in some cases where capital is the scarce factor). In a capital-rich country, for instance, labor in one industry would let labor in other industries lobby for protection, and as a result very little lobbying would be done. Depending on how far you push the assumption of mobility, it could even be that exit — in the form of moving to another employment, emigration or capital flight — would be a far more common response than lobbying.

Let us now revert to the assumption of easy collective action, but assume factors are specific. The southeast corner describes just such a political economy, where individual industries seeking protection for their products are opposed by the consumers of those products. Assuming no collective action problems in this domestic political economy, however, *any* consumers might participate in trade politics, however small their stake in the issue; they would not free ride, relying on their fellow consumers to do the lobbying for them. An industry interested in protection could only really win, then, if it banded together with other industries interested in protection and lobbied for protection for all of them. The coalition that would emerge in such a situation would pit import competers against non-tradeable producers and exporters. The problem with this coalition is that all the protected industries might be worse off from this "universalistic logroll" than if they simply accepted free trade, since the costs to them of the protection to all the other industries might very well be higher than their gains from protection of their own industry. Therefore, such a coalition is inherently unstable. The existence of collective action problems is, thus, essential to the Ricardo-Viner explanation of trade policy coalitions generating protection for individual industries, as this quadrant serves to show.

The southwest quadrant contains the ideal type of trade policy "coalition" described by Pareto, Schattschneider, Olson, and the endogenous tariff literature. In that ideal type, collective action problems exclude most of the public from participating in trade politics. In fact, there really are no coalitions at all: there are simply individual industries requesting, and often receiving, protection for their particular products. They may be opposed, in that request, by the consumers of that product if those consumers are sufficiently concentrated (if, for example, they are industrial consumers who need the product for their production); but otherwise trade policy will be dominated by special interests seeking protection.

D. The Effect of Institutions

Of course, domestic political institutions also affect the severity of collective action problems and, through them, trade policy coalitions as well. To illustrate this, we transform Figure 2 into Figure 3 adding a further distinction between majoritarian and non-majoritarian institutions. Collective action costs still vary across the horizontal axis. The vertical axis reflects the individual's share of a given aggregate gain, allowing for the effects of both dispersion and nonexcludability, with per capita benefits being lowest at the top and highest at the bottom (although the two middle rows on the vertical axis could actually be in either order).

The two polar "ideal types" are still present, in opposite corners. The Rogowski model is in the upper right: factor mobility means that benefits are relatively nonexcludable, and thus the numbers (and hence coalitions) of those affected will be larger; majoritarian institutions mean that large numbers are needed to win, and costs of collective action must (other things being equal) be small enough to allow such large organizations to develop. Clearly, as you increase costs of collective action (moving leftward in the first row of Figure 3 exit once again becomes more

	Collective Action Costs	
	High	**Low**
Factors Mobile **Majoritarian Inst.**	Rampant free riding No trade policy coalitions Exit (?)	Rogowski
Factors Mobile **Non-maj. Inst.**	Rampant free riding Trade policy coalitions Exit (?)	Class-based coalitions possible, but not necessary for victory
Factors Specific **Majoritarian Inst.**	Individual interest groups unable to affect trade policy Consumer groups inactive Universalistic logroll (?)	Cross sector coalitions (logrolling) or coalitions with labor Consumer groups active
Factors Specific **Non-maj. Inst.**	Standard trade policy Model (Pareto, Olson, etc.) Lobbying for protection Consumer groups inactive	Cross sector coalitions (logrolling) or coalitions with labor possible, but not necessary for victory Consumer groups active

FIGURE 3. Coalition Possibilities: The Effects of Factor Mobility, Collective Action Costs, and Domestic Political Institutions

appealing: thus, there really seems to be a natural affinity between the Stolper-Samuelson model and majoritarian politics.

In the second row, given any significant costs of collective action, factor mobility would mean that free-riding should be rampant, inhibiting collective action. If conversely the cost of collective action goes to zero, any coalition should form. These should be large because the costs of collective action are low and benefits are non-excludable. There would be little incentive to build large coalitions, however, because size would not guarantee victory in this case: the political institutions are non-majoritarian. This cell seems to yield few interesting predictions.

Where factors are specific a number of different cases arise, surrounding the "classic" case of interest-group lobbying in the lower left corner. Protectionism is the likely outcome in this cell. There, costs of collective action are high, thus excluding consumers (who are, after all, a very large group with non-excludable benefits) from trade politics. The benefits of trade policy are concentrated on particular industries, due to factor specificity. Thus, these industries have an incentive to pay the collective action costs, even though they are high, in order to gain their favored trade policy.

In the penultimate row, where factors are specific but majorities are needed to win, exit is costly (because factors are specific) but high costs of collective action mean that groups must be small or benefits concentrated to form. In such situations, the universal logroll mentioned above would be a possibility. In this case, as costs of collective action decrease and large groups are needed to gain victory, alliances between a specific factor and the mobile factor become more likely, as do alliances between various specific factors. The numbers of the mobile factor group are large enough to make it worthwhile for specific factor groups to try to bring them into a coalition, provided the stake can be made large enough to motivate their participation.

Finally, in the lower-right corner (where factors are specific and institutions non-majoritarian, but costs of collective action are low) even dispersed losers can organize because costs are low. Any group could win, however, because the size of a group is not important to political victory. This cell, too, appears to yield few interesting predictions.

As should be clear from Figure 3, the two major models of international trade policy coalitions carry with them hidden assumptions — one about the severity of costs of collective action, the other about the domestic political institutions which make trade policy. In any case the models presume ideal types of political organization which may not exist. Without considering political variables, economic explanations are biased, and vice versa.

V. CONCLUSIONS

The narrowest purpose of this paper has been to review the determinants of trade policy coalitions. Although recent studies have stressed economic factors such as abundance and mobility of factors of production, we have argued that other more political factors (collective action costs, political institutions) are likely to be just as important. Furthermore, we have argued that these effects are interactive, the effects of some of these variables depending on the levels of others. The Stolper-Samuelson model really requires that collective action costs be low for Rogowski's broad trade policy coalitions to emerge: if there are collective action problems and factors are perfectly mobile, trade policy coalitions will not necessarily form along class lines and in fact may not form at all, due to familiar collective action problems. The Ricardo-Viner model, in contrast, is much more amenable to the incorporation of varying degrees of collective action costs. We made a related argument regarding domestic political institutions, suggesting that the Stolper-Samuelson theorem is more consistent with a majoritarian mode of policy making, while the Ricardo-Viner model is more consistent with a non-majoritarian or interest group politics model. In all these ways the paper raises broader issues about the interplay of politics and economics, while laying out a calculus of preferences, effects and likely actions and outcome which anyone contemplating the domestic effects of trade needs to consider. . . .

NOTES

1. Pareto (1927), p. 379.
2. Schattschneider (1935), pp. 127–128.

REFERENCES

Pareto, Vilfredo. 1927. *Manual of Political Economy.* New York: A.M. Kelley.
Schattschnieder, E.E. 1935. *Politics, Pressures and the Tariff.* New York: Prentice-Hall.

22

Are Your Wages Set in Beijing?
RICHARD B. FREEMAN

During the 1990s, the wages of unskilled workers in the United States have fallen in real (inflation-adjusted) terms. In Europe, in an analogous trend, real wages have remained stable but unemployment levels for unskilled workers have dramatically increased. Economist Richard B. Freeman surveys the growing literature on the effect of trade on wages and employment. Drawing on the theories used to understand the political economy of trade in earlier articles (Rogowski, Reading 20; Alt and Gilligan, Reading 21), Freeman argues that there are good economic reasons for expecting trade to lead to the "immiseration" of low-skilled workers in developed or capital-abundant states. Factor prices, including wages, in different national markets that are open to trade should tend to converge.

Freeman then examines the empirical evidence and finds the picture more mixed. The consensus opinion is that trade may have contributed to a fall in real wages for low-skilled workers, but it cannot itself account for the scope of the existing problem. Estimates of the future effects of trade are even more uncertain. Freeman has analyzed an important trend within the international economy. Whether the effects of trade are real or partly exaggerated, his analysis helps explain why in many developed countries labor is moving into the protectionist camp.

In the 1980s and 1990s, the demand for less-skilled workers fell in advanced countries. In the United States, this showed up primarily in falling real wages for less-educated men, although hours worked by these men also declined. In OECD-Europe, it took the form of increased unemployment for the less skilled. Over the same period, manufacturing imports from third world countries to the United States and OECD-Europe increased greatly. In 1991, the bilateral U.S. merchandise trade deficit with China was second only to its deficit with Japan.

The rough concordance of falling demand for less-skilled workers with increased imports of manufacturing goods from third world countries has created a lively debate about the economic consequences of trade between advanced and developing countries. This debate differs strikingly from the debate over the benefits and costs of trade in the last few decades. In the 1960s and 1970s, many in the third world feared that trade would impoverish them or push them to the periphery of the world economy; virtually no one in advanced countries was concerned about competition from less-developed countries. In the 1980s and 1990s, by contrast, most of the third world has embraced the global economy; whereas many in the advanced world worry over the possible adverse economic effects of trade. The new debate focuses on one issue: whether in a global economy, the wages or employment of low-skill workers in advanced countries have been (or will be) determined by the global supply of less-skilled labor, rather than by domestic labor market conditions. Put crudely, to what extent has, or will, the pay of low-skilled Americans or French or Germans be set in Beijing, Delhi, and Djakkarta rather than in New York, Paris or Frankfurt?

On one side of the new debate are those who believe in factor price equalization — that in a global economy, the wages of workers in advanced countries cannot remain above those of comparable workers in less-developed countries. They fear that the wages or employment of the less skilled in advanced countries will be driven down due to competition from low-wage workers overseas. On the other side of the debate are those who reject the notion that the traded goods sector can determine labor outcomes in an entire economy or who stress that the deleterious effects of trade on demand for the less skilled are sufficiently modest to be offset readily through redistributive social policies funded by the gains from trade. They fear that neoprotectionists will use arguments about the effect of trade on labor demand to raise trade barriers and reduce global productivity. . . .

This paper provides a viewer's guide to the debate. I review the two facts that motivate the debate: the immiseration of less-skilled workers in advanced countries and the increase in manufacturing imports from less-developed countries. Then I summarize the arguments and evidence brought to bear on them and give my scorecard on the debate. I conclude by examining the fear that, whatever trade with less-developed countries did in the past, it will impoverish less-skilled Americans and western Europeans in the future, as China, India, Indonesia and others make greater waves in the world economy.

THE IMMISERATION OF LOW-SKILL WORKERS IN THE UNITED STATES AND EUROPE

An economic disaster has befallen low-skilled Americans, especially young men. Researchers using several data sources — including household survey data from the Current Population Survey, other household surveys, and establishment surveys — have documented that wage inequality and skill differentials in earnings and employment increased sharply in the United States from the mid-1970s through the 1980s and into the 1990s. The drop in the relative position of the less skilled shows up in a number of ways: greater earnings differentials between those with more and less education; greater earnings differentials between older and younger workers; greater differentials between high-skilled and low-skilled occupations; in a wider earnings distribution overall and within demographic and skill groups; and in less time worked by low-skill and low-paid workers.

If the increase in earnings inequality had coincided with rapidly growing real earnings, so that the living standards of low-skill workers increased or fell a trifle, no one would ring alarm bells. But in the past decade or two, real earnings have grown sluggishly at best, and fallen for men on average. The economic position of low-skill men has fallen by staggering amounts. For instance, the real hourly wages of males with 12 years of schooling dropped by some 20 percent from 1979 to 1993; for entry-level men with 12 years, the drop has been 30 percent! The real hourly earnings of all men in the bottom decile of the earnings distribution fell similarly since the early or mid-1970s, while that of men in the upper decile has risen modestly — producing a huge increase in inequality.

Similar economic forces have led to somewhat different problems in Europe. For most of the period since World War II, OECD-Europe had lower unemployment rates than the United States. For example, in 1973, the rate of unemployment was 2.9 percent for OECD-Europe compared to 4.8 percent for the United States, and the ratio of employment to population was as high in Europe as in the United States. This changed in the 1980s. From 1983 to 1991 unemployment averaged 9.3 percent in OECD-Europe compared to 6.7 percent in the United States. Unemployment in OECD-Europe seems destined to remain above American levels throughout the '90s decade. The ratio of employment to the population of working age and the hours worked per employee has also fallen in Europe relative to the United States, adding to the U.S.-Europe gap in the utilization of labor. In addition, unemployment has been highly concentrated in Europe: in OECD-Europe, nearly half of unemployed workers are without jobs for over a year, compared to less than 10 percent of unemployed workers in the United States. . . .

If wage inequality had risen in Europe as much as in the United States, or was near U.S. levels, or if the real wages of low-skill Europeans had fallen, high joblessness would be a devastating indictment of European reliance on institutional forces to determine labor market outcomes. In effect, Europe would be suffering unemployment with no gain in equality. But in general, Europe has avoided an American level of inequality or changes in inequality, and wages at the bottom of the distribution rose rather than fell. By the early 1990s, workers in the bottom tiers of the wage distribution in Europe had higher compensation than did workers in the bottom tiers in the United States. Western Europe's problem was one of jobs, not of wages: the workers whose wages have fallen through the floor in the United States — the less skilled and (except in Germany) the young — were especially likely to be jobless in Europe.

The rise in joblessness in Europe is thus the flip side of the rise in earnings inequality in the U.S. The two outcomes reflect the same phenomenon — a relative decline in the demand against the less skilled that has overwhelmed the long-term trend decline in the relative supply of less-skilled workers. In the United States, where wages are highly flexible, the change in the supply-demand balance lowered the wages of the less skilled. In Europe, where institutions buttress the bottom parts of the wage distribution, the change produced unemployment. The question then is not simply why the United States and Europe experienced different labor market problems in the 1980s and 1990s, but what factors depressed the relative demand for low-skill, labor in both economies?

TRADE BETWEEN THE UNITED STATES
AND EUROPE WITH THE THIRD WORLD

One thing that distinguishes the 1980s and 1990s from earlier decades following World War II is the growth of the global economy, which in practical terms can be seen in reduced trade barriers, increased trade, highly mobile capital, and rapid transmission of technology across national lines. Multinationals, who locate plants and hire workers almost anywhere in the world, have replaced national companies as the cutting edge capitalist organization. The most commonly used indicator of globalization is the ratio of exports plus imports to gross domestic product. In the United States, this ratio rose from 0.12 in 1970 to 0.22 in 1990. Trade ratios rose substantially throughout the OECD. Although most trade is among advanced countries, trade with less-developed countries increased greatly. By 1990, 35 percent of U.S. imports were from less-developed countries, compared with 14 percent in 1970. In the European Community, 12 percent of imports were from less-developed countries, compared with 5 percent in 1970. (The less-developed country portion of European trade is lower largely because trade among U.S. states doesn't count as imports and exports, while trade among European countries does, thus inflating the overall total of intra-Europe trade.) In 1992, 58 percent of less-developed country exports to the western industrialized nations consisted of (light) manufacturing goods, compared with 5 percent in 1955.

The increase in manufacturing imports from less-developed countries presumably reflects the conjoint working of several forces. Reductions in trade barriers must have contributed: why else the huge international effort to cut tariff and non-tariff barriers embodied in GATT, NAFTA, WTO and other agreements? The shift in development strategies of less-developed countries, from import substitution to export promotion, must also have played a part. Perhaps World Bank and IMF pressures on less-developed countries to export as a way of paying off their debts contributed as well. Advanced country investments in manufacturing in less-developed countries also presumably increased their ability to compete in the world market.

Changes in the labor markets of less-developed countries have also contributed to the increased role of those countries in world markets. The less-developed country share of the world workforce increased from 69 percent in 1965 to 75 percent in 1990; and the mean years of schooling in the less-developed country world rose from 2.4 years in 1960 to 5.3 years in 1986. The less-developed country share of world manufacturing employment grew from 40 percent in 1960 to 53 percent in 1986. Finally, diffusion of technology through multinational firms has arguably put less-developed countries and advanced countries on roughly similar production frontiers. Skills, capital infrastructure, and political stability — rather than pure technology — have become the comparative advantage of advanced countries.

Given these two facts, it is natural to pose the question: to what extent might trade with less-developed countries be reducing demand for less-skilled labor in the advanced countries?

ECONOMIC THEORY: FACTOR PRICE EQUALIZATION

At the conceptual heart of the debate over the effects of trade on the labor market is the strength of forces for factor price equalization. Consider a world where producers have the same technology; where trade flows are determined by factor endowments, so that advanced countries with many skilled workers compared to unskilled workers import commodities made by less-skilled workers in developing countries, while developing countries with more unskilled labor import commodities made by skilled labor in advanced countries; and where trade establishes a single world price for a good. Trade makes less-skilled labor in advanced countries and skilled labor in developing countries less scarce and can thus be expected to reduce their wages. By contrast, trade will increase the production of goods made by skilled labor in advanced countries and by less-skilled labor in developing countries and can thus be expected to raise their wages. In equilibrium, under specified conditions, the long-term outcome is that factor prices are equalized throughout the world: the less-skilled worker in the advanced country is paid the same as his or her competitor in a developing country; and similarly for the more-skilled workers.

But does factor price equalization . . . capture economic reality? For years, many trade economists rejected factor price equalization as a description of the world. The wide, and in some cases increasing, variation in pay levels among countries seemed to make it a textbook proposition of little relevance. . . .

To labor economists, the observation that trade with less-developed countries places some economic pressures on low-skill westerners is a valuable reminder that one cannot treat national labor markets in isolation. If the West can import children's toys produced by low-paid Chinese workers at bargain basement prices, surely low-skilled westerners, who produce those toys at wages 10 times those of the Chinese, will face a difficult time in the job market. It isn't even necessary that the West import the toys. The threat to import them or to move plants to less-developed countries to produce the toys may suffice to force low-skilled westerners to take a cut in pay to maintain employment. In this situation, the open economy can cause lower pay for low-skilled westerners even without trade; to save my job, I accept Chinese-level pay, and that prevents imports. The invisible hand would have done its job, with proper invisibility.

For the factor price equalization argument to carry weight, advanced countries should export commodities to less-developed countries made with relatively skilled labor and import commodities from less-developed countries produced by unskilled labor. U.S. trade operates in just this way. American exports are skill intensive: our net exports are positive for such goods as scientific instruments, airplanes, and in intellectual property, including software. Imports make less intensive use of skilled labor: our net imports are positive for toys, footwear and clothing. Europe also imports low-skill intensive goods from less-developed countries and exports high-skill, intensive goods. While factors other than labor skills affect trade — natural resource endowments, infrastructure capital, perhaps capital overall, technological changes that diffuse slowly — the flows of goods between advanced countries and less-developed countries seems to fit the Hecksher-Ohlin model well enough to raise the specter of factor price equalization for low-skilled westerners.

The argument for complete factor price equalization is, to be sure, an extreme one. It implies that in an economy fully integrated in the world trading system, domestic market developments have *no* effect on wages. Instead, there is a single global labor market that sets the factor prices for inputs, even if trade is only a small part of the economy. Whether 5 percent or 95 percent of less-skilled workers are employed in import-competing activities, their pay is determined in Beijing. Transportation costs, immediacy of delivery, and such factors are assumed to be irrelevant in differentiating the location of production. If unskilled labor can readily switch from traded goods to nontraded goods, it would be a single factor, so that the pay of even those working in nontraded goods or services would be set in the global market. Only when *all* less-skilled workers are employed in nontraded activities or if those in nontraded activities have sector-specific skills that make them "different" from workers in traded activities (for some period) will their pay depend on domestic market considerations.

These predictions run counter to a wide body of evidence that domestic developments do affect wages: for instance, that the baby boom affected the pay of young workers; that the relative number of college graduates altered the premium paid for education; that sectoral developments affect pay in certain industries; that your wages are likely to be higher if your firm does well than if it is doing poorly. In the United States, wage differences among states and localities have persisted for decades despite free trade, migration, and capital flows. Among countries, wage differences between workers with seemingly similar skills have also persisted for decades, albeit exaggerated by the divergence between purchasing power parities and exchange rates, and by differences in skills that are hard to measure.

Given these considerations, factor price equalization should not be viewed as the Holy Grail giving the answer of economic science as to why demand fell for low-skill western workers in the 1980s and 1990s. Instead, the theory is a flag alerting us to the possibility that increased linkages with less-developed countries *may have* contributed to the immiseration of the less skilled, and pointing to some routes through which such linkages *may have* worked. The gap between "may have" contributed and "has" contributed is large — bridgeable only by empirical analysis, with all of its compromises and difficulties.

EMPIRICAL WORK

The effort to see whether or not trade has contributed to the growing immiseration of low-skill workers in developed economies has taken two forms. One set of studies exploits data on the "factor content" of import and export industries to estimate the implicit change in factor endowments in advanced countries due to trade. A second set of studies exploits price data to see if increased imports from less-developed countries have induced sizable drops in the prices of goods produced by low-skilled westerners, which would reduce demand for their labor and lower their pay or disemploy them. The debate has drawn attention to problems with both sets of calculations.

Factor Content Analysis: Can the Tail Wag the Dog?

In factor content studies, analysts estimate the impact of trade on the demand for labor at given wages or, alternatively, on the nation's "effective" factor endowments, that is, the domestic *and* foreign labor inputs used to produce society's consumption bundle. Since the U.S. imports goods that make heavy use of low-skilled labor, and exports goods that make heavy use of high-skilled labor, trade with developing countries reduces the relative demand for less-skilled labor in the United States, or, if you prefer, increases the relative supply of less-skilled labor. Given estimates of the labor skills used in various sectors, one can estimate how changes in imports and exports altered the demand-supply balance for high- and low-skilled labor at given relative wages and prices. To see how the changed supply-demand balance for labor skills affected relative wages (the variable of interest in the United States), analysts transform the calculated shifts in quantities into changes in wages using estimates of the effect of changes in supply and demand on relative pay from other studies (for instance, studies of how the increase in the relative supply of college graduates on the domestic labor market affects their relative pay).

For example, if the United States imported 10 additional children's toys, which could be produced by five American workers, the effective supply of unskilled workers would increase by five (or alternatively, domestic demand for such workers would fall by five), compared with the alternative in which those 10 toys were produced domestically. This five-worker shift in the supply-demand balance would put pressure on unskilled wages to fall, causing those wages to fall in accord with the relevant elasticity. Any trade-balancing flow of exports would, contrarily, reduce the effective endowment of skilled workers (raise their demand) and thus increase their pay. . . .

[Several recent] studies find that changes in actual trade flows have not displaced all low-skilled workers from manufacturing (taken as the major traded goods sector) for one basic reason: that only a moderate proportion of workers now work in manufacturing. In 1993, roughly 15 percent of American workers were employed in manufacturing. The vast majority of unskilled workers were in nontraded goods, such as retail trade and various services. In such a world it is hard to see how pressures on wages emanating from traded goods can determine wages economy-wide. To be sure, the strong version of factor price equalization argues that the wage of low-skilled labor is set in a global market, affecting workers in both traded goods and untraded services. But this seems implausible. Compare two situations: in the first, 50 percent of the nation's unskilled workers are in import-competing industries, and increased trade with less-developed countries displaces one in 10 of them; in the second, only 1 percent of unskilled workers are in import-competing industries, and trade displaces one in 10 of them. To argue that trade would have the same effect in both cases seems far-fetched, dependent on the simplifying assumptions of the trade model (notably that elasticities of supply are infinite, with no variation in products produced in developed and less-developed countries).

However, Adrian Wood's (1994) factor content study . . . reaches a different conclusion. Wood argues that standard factor content analyses understate the effect of trade on employment. Once the proper corrections are made, he argues, trade becomes the root cause of the fall in demand for less-skilled workers in advanced countries.

Wood begins by arguing that estimated changes in effective labor endowments, based on existing labor input coefficients in advanced countries, are biased against finding a big disemployment effect. The reason is that less-developed countries export different and noncompeting goods within sectors than the goods produced by advanced countries; for example, the United States might make high-tech toys, while the Chinese make low-tech toys. The typical factor content analysis would observe the import of low-tech Chinese toys and then multiply that by the quantity of labor, of various skills, used in the U.S. manufacture of high-tech toys. But if the low-tech toys were made in the United States, manufacturers would in fact use more less-skilled labor than in producing high-tech toys. To correct for this possible bias, Wood uses the labor input coefficients for developing countries, adjusted for labor demand responses to higher western wages, rather than those for the advanced countries. With this procedure, he estimates that labor demand due to imports of manufactures fell by "ten times the conventional ones" (Wood, 1994, p. 10).

The problem of differing mixes of products within industries is real. Ideally, one would like the change in labor input coefficients associated with the actual change in goods produced domestically as a result of imports. My guess is that the conventional factor content approach does underestimate the effect of trade on demand for low-skilled labor, but I also suspect that Wood's upward adjustment is probably excessive.

Wood (1994) also asserts that trade with less-developed countries induced substantial labor-saving innovation in the traded goods sector. This further reduces demand for unskilled labor. Although there is no reason to expect innovation to respond to import competition any more or less than to any other form of competition, the problem of induced technical change is a real one, and Wood's adjustment is potentially in the right direction. But he may be claiming too much for this factor. . . . As the evidence stands, the claim that trade induces large labor-saving technological change in low-skill industries is not especially strong.

Standard factor content analysis studies indicate that trade can account for 10–20 percent of the overall fall in demand for unskilled labor needed to explain rising wage differentials in the United States or rising joblessness in Europe. If one accepts Wood's (1994) adjusted factor content analysis for traded goods and his estimate of induced technological change, then trade accounts for about half of the requisite fall in demand for labor. Where can we find the other half?

As a final step, Wood assumes that trade-induced labor-saving technological changes spill over to nontraded sectors, where most nonskilled workers are employed. This final assumption leads him to conclude that increased trade with less-developed countries accounts for all of the rise of inequality in the United States and all of the increase in unskilled unemployment in Europe.

If one is going to use a factor content approach to attribute immiseration of the less skilled in the West to globalization, Wood's clear and careful approach shows the way. But as he is fully aware, some of the steps along the way are arguable or problematic. . . .

Price Effects Studies and Other Evidence

Two additional bodies of evidence have been brought to bear on this debate: price data on the goods produced by low-skill labor; and data on changes in the employment of skilled and less-skilled workers in industries that produce traded and non-traded goods. In the trade model, price declines in import-competing sectors should lower the relative wages of unskilled labor, which those sectors use intensely, and ultimately the prices of all goods and services produced by those workers. The lower relative pay of the less skilled ought further to lead firms to substitute them for more expensive skilled labor throughout the economy.

Two studies have looked for evidence that the prices of sectors that extensively use unskilled labor have fallen greatly. Lawrence and Slaughter (1993) correlate changes in import prices with the share of production workers across industries and find that when prices are adjusted for changes in total factor productivity, the prices of less skill intensive goods fell only slightly. Sachs and Shatz (1994) examine output prices for all of manufacturing, not just imports, which provides a larger sample of industries. After adjusting for productivity changes that should independently affect prices, they find a modest negative relation between the production worker share of employment and changes in industry prices. They also find that prices fell faster in sectors that make more intensive use of low-skilled workers in the 1980s than in previous decades compared with sectors that use fewer low-skilled workers. They conclude that relative prices exerted some pressure on the pay of the less skilled, but not by enough to account for a significant widening of wage inequality. . . .

Like the factor content studies, price studies provide a clue to how trade could affect relative wages — the greater the estimated import-induced reduction in the prices of goods produced by low-skill labor, the greater the likely trade effect on wages and employment—but they also are far from the final word. . . .

CONCLUSION

The debate over whether increased trade with less-developed countries is the main cause of the immiseration of the less-skilled has raised numerous conceptual and empirical issues, as well as some hackles. Adherents of one side in the debate, or of one approach to the problem, have found it easy to criticize the other. Most criticisms have at least an element of truth, making scoring the debate a bit of a judgment call. Largely because neither the factor content nor the price analysis comes up with a smoking gun, and because demand for the less skilled has fallen even in nontraded goods sectors, my scorecard reads: trade matters, but it is neither all that matters nor the primary cause of observed changes.

That we lack compelling evidence that trade underlies the problems of the less skilled in the past does not, of course, rule out the possibility that trade will dominate labor market outcomes in the future. Indeed, it is commonplace in the trade-immiseration debate for those who reject trade as *the* explanation of the past decline in the demand for the less skilled to hedge their conclusion by noting that there is a good chance that in the future, pressures for factor price equalization will grow. Maybe your wages were not set in Beijing yesterday or today, but tomorrow they will be.

I have problems with this prognostication. Economists do not have a good record as soothsayers, and neither trade nor labor economists are exceptions. Trade economists once worried about the perpetual dollar shortage; believed that flexible exchange rates would be more stable than fixed exchange rates; and saw the Common Market as the cure-all to European problems. Labor economists declared unions were dead just before the formation of the CIO; worried about the falling return to skills and were as shocked as anyone else by the increased inequality of the 1980s; did not expect the Civil Rights Act to raise the demand for black workers; and so on. For what it is worth, I am not convinced that continued expansion of trade with less-developed countries spells doom for low-skill westerners. As more and more low-skilled western workers find employment in the nontraded goods service sector, the potential for imports from less-developed countries to reduce their employment or wages should lessen. In the standard trade model, a factor used exclusively in nontraded goods has its pay determined by the domestic economy. The closer Western economies get to this situation, the smaller should be the trade-induced pressures on low-skilled workers. Wildly heralded trade agreements such as the U.S.-Canadian agreement, the Common Market, and NAFTA have not dominated our wages and employment in the ways their advocates or opponents forecast.

In the past, other factors have been more important than trade in the well-being of the less skilled: technological changes that occur independent of trade; unexpected political developments, such as German reunification and instability in various regions of the world; policies to educate and train workers; union activities; the compensation policies of firms; and welfare state and related social policies. In the future, I expect that these factors will continue to be more important. I could, of course, be utterly wrong. The best we can do is probe and poke at the evidence and arguments, and present our analyses and prognostications with appropriate humility.

REFERENCES

Lawrence, Robert, and Matthew Slaughter, "Trade and U.S. Wages: Great Sucking Sound or Small Hiccup?" In *Brookings Papers Economic Activity, Microeconomics.* Vol. 2. Washington, DC: Brookings Institution, 1993.

Sachs, Jeff, and Howard Shatz, "Trade and Jobs in U.S. Manufacturing." *Brookings Papers on Economic Activity.* Vol. 1. Washington, DC: Brookings Institution, 1994, pp. 1–84.

Wood, Adrian, *North-South Trade, Employment and Inequality.* Oxford: Clarendon Press, 1994.

23

The Political Economy of Nontariff Barriers: A Cross-national Analysis

EDWARD D. MANSFIELD
AND MARC L. BUSCH

Since the 1970s, nontariff barriers (NTBs) have emerged as one of the primary impediments to international trade. As tariffs were negotiated away over the successive rounds of the General Agreement on Tariffs and Trade, previous NTBs were exposed and new NTBs were created to insulate uncompetitive industries from the consequences of liberalization. In this essay, Edward Mansfield and Marc Busch synthesize domestic societal and domestic institutional arguments and find that NTBs are most pervasive when deteriorating macroeconomic conditions prompt industries to make new demands for protection, when countries are sufficiently large to give policymakers incentives to impose protection, and when domestic institutions permit groups to influence policymakers. In short, NTBs appear to be most pervasive in cases where the incentives of pressure groups and policymakers converge.

Much research on the determinants of trade policy has focused on the efficacy of societal and statist approaches. Societal theories typically attribute patterns of protection to variations in demands made by pressure groups, whereas statist theories emphasize the effects of the "national interest" and domestic institutions in determining the level of protection. While both approaches have gained considerable currency, debates concerning their relative merits have been heated and long-standing. Yet very little quantitative evidence has been brought to bear on this topic.

In this article, we provide some of the first results of this sort. Our findings indicate that although societal and statist approaches often are considered mutually exclusive, it is more fruitful to view them as complementary. Moreover, the interaction between factors that give rise to demands for protection and those that regulate the provision of protection by policymakers has not been treated adequately in the literature on foreign economic policy. This gap in the literature is fundamentally important, since our results indicate that the interaction between these factors is a central determinant of trade policy. Thus, analyses of commercial policy that fail to consider both societal and statist variables and the interaction between them are likely to be inadequate.

Our analysis centers on explaining cross-national patterns of nontariff barriers (NTBs). Scholars have conducted little cross-national research on trade policy and virtually none with a focus on NTBs. Instead, single-country studies of tariffs comprise much of the existing literature on the political economy of commercial policy. Yet the usefulness of societal and statist theories of foreign economic policy hinges on the ability of these theories to explain variations in protection across states, and NTBs have become increasingly pervasive among the advanced industrial countries. Because the General Agreement on Tariffs and Trade (GATT) and the World Trade Organization (WTO) limit the ability of contracting parties to impose tariffs, policymakers who view protection as an attractive means by which to meet the demands of pressure groups or advance state interests are likely to rely primarily on NTBs. Many observers have suggested that this is occurring with increasing regularity and that the recent proliferation of NTBs has done much to offset the gains in liberalization made during successive rounds of the GATT. A fuller understanding is therefore needed of the factors that account for variations in NTBs across states.

SOCIETAL APPROACHES TO TRADE POLICY

Societal (or pluralist) approaches to the study of foreign economic policy focus primarily on the effects of demands for protection by pressure groups. Societal explanations consider trade policy to be the product of competition among pressure groups and other nonstate actors that are affected by commerce. The impact of these groups on policy depends largely on their ability to organize for the purpose of articulating their demands and on the amount of electoral influence they possess. Societal approaches attribute little importance to policymakers and political institutions for the purposes of explaining trade policy. . . .

Societal approaches to the study of trade policy characterize much of the literature on endogenous protection. Empirical studies of this sort infer the demands for protection based on macroeconomic and/or sectoral fluctuations. Most analyses of endogenous protection conducted by political scientists have been cast at the sectoral level. A large and growing body of literature, however, centers on the macroeconomic determinants of protection. Much of this research supports the view advanced by certain societal theories that macroeconomic fluctuations strongly influence pressures for protection. Therefore we focus our societal analysis of NTBs on macroeconomic factors.

Chief among the macroeconomic variables that these studies emphasize are unemployment and the real exchange rate. It is widely accepted by analysts of trade policy that high levels of unemployment contribute to demands for protection. . . . Widespread unemployment increases the stress to workers of adjusting to rising import levels. Workers who are displaced by imports will find it progressively more difficult to obtain alternative employment, and when they do, downward pressure will be placed on their wages. Together these factors promote pressures to restrict the flow of imports.

In addition to unemployment, variations in the exchange rate are expected to give rise to protectionist pressures. . . .

Central to the effects of the exchange rate on demands for protection is the influence of the price of a state's currency on the competitiveness of its exports and its import-competing products. An appreciated currency, by increasing the price of domestically produced goods, threatens to undermine both exports and import-competing sectors of the economy. . . .

Public officials in liberal democracies are expected to meet demands for protection that arise due to high levels of unemployment and an appreciated currency because these variables influence the voting behavior of constituents. There is evidence that voters cast ballots on the basis of their personal economic circumstances, especially if they are recently unemployed. However, substantial evidence also indicates that voters cast ballots on the basis of macroeconomic conditions, regardless of whether they are directly affected by these conditions. In fact, some studies have concluded that macroeconomic factors are more salient determinants of voting behavior than are personal economic circumstances. Other survey research further suggests that public support for protection increases during downturns in the economy and when domestic industries are under severe pressure from foreign competition. As a result, public officials seeking to enhance their electoral fortunes have incentives to impose protection during periods of high unemployment and currency appreciation because such measures are likely to be popular and may blunt the short-term effects of macroeconomic pressures. These analyses therefore lead us to expect a direct relationship to exist between both the level of unemployment and the real exchange rate, on the one hand, and the incidence of NTBs, on the other hand.

STATIST APPROACHES TO TRADE POLICY

While societal approaches have been especially influential in the field of political economy, they also have been criticized on a number of grounds. Especially important is the charge leveled by statists and others that societal approaches systematically underestimate the effects of two factors that regulate the provision of protection: state interests with respect to trade policy and domestic institutions. Analyses that emphasize state interests generally focus on the roles of politicians and policymakers in the formation of trade policy, holding constant societal pressures. . . .

Many statists conclude that the ability of policymakers to advance the national interest depends in large measure on the extent to which domestic political institutions render them susceptible to demands by pressure groups and other nonstate actors. Policymakers who are poorly insulated from, and lack autonomy with respect to, pressure groups will face difficulty advancing the national interest unless (as discussed further below) it converges with the preferences of societal groups. Thus, one hypothesis we will test is that institutional factors that foster the insulation and autonomy of public officials bolster the ability of states to pursue trade policy consistent with the national interest.

Relative Size

Clearly, the national interest with respect to trade is likely to vary across states; and it is not possible to assess adequately the influence of institutional factors on trade policy from a statist perspective unless each state's interest can be specified. On this score, many analysts have argued that a state's economic size governs its national interest with respect to trade policy.

There is ample reason to expect that larger states will display a more pronounced interest in protection than their smaller counterparts. First, international trade theory suggests that this should be the case. By virtue of their size, large states are likely to be vested with disproportionate market power. They can exploit their monopoly power through the use of tariffs, as well as quotas and other NTBs that duplicate a tariffs effect. If the imposition of an optimal quota elicits retaliation, the welfare of both parties will suffer. This, however, only limits the incentives for a large state to impose NTBs against a state of similar size, since only states with some monopoly power have an incentive to retaliate in response to the imposition of protection. Large states retain an incentive to target small states, since the latter have no incentive to retaliate. In contrast, small states are unlikely to possess the market power necessary to benefit from optimal protection and face the prospect of retaliation by trade partners (thereby reducing foreign commerce on which they tend to be highly dependent) if they impose NTBs. Hence, on average, we expect larger states to display a greater preference for NTBs than their smaller counterparts.

Second, state size is likely to be directly related to patterns of protection due to the time period analyzed in this article. As discussed further below, the empirical analysis conducted in this study is based on the mid-1980s. In the opinion of many scholars, this was a period characterized by a moderately skewed distribution of power among a few relatively large nonhegemonic states. A number of studies have concluded that systems of this sort — as well as ones in which hegemony is declining — provide incentives for the dominant states to behave in a commercially predatory manner. Based on these considerations, we expect that economic size will be directly related to the incidence of NTBs. . . .

Domestic Institutions

From a statist viewpoint, NTBs should be most prevalent in large states characterized by high degrees of institutional insulation and autonomy, since these conditions provide policymakers with an economic incentive to impose NTBs and vest them with the capacity to advance those interests.

Our analysis of institutions draws heavily on an important study by Rogowski. He argues that "insulation from regional and sectoral pressure in a democracy . . .

is most easily achieved with large electoral districts. . . . [This argument is] easily defended, in part because institutional theorists have almost universally accepted it . . . , but more because it is almost self-evident. When automakers or dairy farmers entirely dominate twenty small constituencies and are a powerful minority in fifty more, their voice will be heard in a nation's councils. When they constitute but one or two percent of an enormous district's electorate, representatives may defy them more freely."[1] . . .

[S]mall electoral districts encourage patronage and pork-barrel politics. Since legislators representing small districts are likely to be beholden to a few influential pressure groups, they are likely to attempt to provide those groups with benefits, including trade policies that reflect their preferences. Yet in polities composed of many small constituencies, no single legislator has the capacity to provide these benefits. . . . The logrolling to which this situation gives rise is likely to yield trade policy that covers more types of goods and services than would be the case in a country characterized by large electoral districts and less influential interest groups.

In addition to the number of parliamentary constituencies, another important institutional feature of democracies concerns whether a list-system proportional representation (PR) or a winner-take-all system exists. Rogowski maintains that the autonomy of public officials in democratic states is bolstered by both large constituencies and the existence of a list-system PR regime. As he notes: "Pressure groups are restrained where campaign resources or the legal control of nominations are centralized in the hands of party leaders. Of course, such control is achieved quite effectively in rigid list-system PR."[2] . . .

EFFECTS OF THE INTERACTION BETWEEN SOCIETAL AND STATIST FACTORS ON TRADE POLICY

. . . We focus on two related issues concerning the interaction between societal and statist factors. As noted above, some statists argue that the policies of states in which policymakers are poorly insulated from societal pressures tend to reflect the interests of societal groups rather than the national interest. There is also reason to expect increases in societal demands for protection during cyclical downturns in the economy and when macroeconomic conditions undermine the competitiveness of a state's goods. Thus, one hypothesis we will examine is that the incidence of NTBs tends to be greatest in states characterized by (1) high levels of unemployment and appreciated currencies and (2) domestic institutions that undermine the insulation and autonomy of public officials with respect to pressure groups.

A second hypothesis we will test is that the incidence of NTBs is greatest in cases where both state and societal actors display a preference for protection. . . . If such a convergence is an important determinant of NTBs, then their incidence should be greatest in large states characterized by (1) high levels of unemployment and appreciated currencies and (2) political institutions that bolster the insulation and autonomy of public officials with respect to pressure groups. As noted above, deteriorating macroeconomic conditions elicit demands for protection, and public officials who fail to respond to these demands may suffer accordingly in subsequent elections. Further, in contrast to small states, large states often have an incentive to impose protection; and public officials that are well-insulated and vested with considerable autonomy will be in a position to act on those incentives, and would be expected to do so.

A high degree of institutional insulation and autonomy is essential in this regard. Although we expect high levels of unemployment and appreciated currencies to yield widespread demands for protection, some societal groups are likely to retain an interest in lower trade barriers. These groups include multinational corporations, industries that depend on or are highly sensitive to the price of imports, and industries that depend on exports and fear either that increases in protection by their government will elicit retaliation by foreign governments or that protection will reduce foreign exports and hence the ability of foreign consumers to purchase their imports. . . . Their influence, like that of other societal groups, depends on the structure of domestic institutions. Thus, large states characterized by high levels of unemployment and appreciated currencies should experience a higher incidence of NTBs when institutions insulate policymakers from those groups that prefer lower trade barriers than when porous institutions enhance the influence of these groups on trade policy.

THE RELATIONSHIP BETWEEN TARIFFS AND NTBs

In addition to the hypotheses described above, we also examine the effects of pre-existing tariff levels on NTBs. Doing so is important because preexisting tariff levels may influence both the strength of societal demands for NTBs and the willingness of public officials to meet these demands. Groups already well protected by tariffs may bring less pressure for new NTBs and face more governmental resistance to their demands than less well protected groups. This suggests that tariffs and NTBs are substitutes, which is consistent with the view expressed by some economists that NTBs are often used to protect industries that have lost tariff protection due to successive rounds of the GATT. . . .

In contrast to this view, another prominent position holds that tariffs and NTBs are complements. Those who advance this argument maintain that NTBs are often used to protect those industries that are also the beneficiaries of high tariffs, while states avoid using NTBs to shield industries that receive little tariff protection. . . . [A] direct relationship between tariffs and NTBs might suggest that NTBs are used to counter new foreign challenges to important sectors that are already the beneficiaries of tariff protection. Indeed, the results of a number of single-country analyses seem to support this position. . . .

A related reason to include tariffs in our model is that they might account for any observed relationship between societal and statist variables, on the one hand, and the incidence of NTBs, on the other hand. Various studies have found that the unemployment rate, the exchange rate, economic size, and institutional factors are related to patterns of tariffs; and the research discussed in this section links tariffs to patterns of NTBs. It is therefore important to determine whether tariffs influence the effects of macroeconomic and institutional factors on NTBs.

A MODEL OF NONTARIFF BARRIERS TO TRADE

Our initial model then, is:

$$NTB_{t+1} = A + B_1 SIZE_t + B_2(\log CONST)_t + B_3(SIZE \cdot \log CONST)_t \quad (1)$$
$$+ B_4 UNEM_t + B_5(UNEM \cdot \log CONST)_t + B_6(UNEM \cdot$$
$$SIZE \cdot \log CONST)_t + B_7 REER_t + B_8(REER \cdot \log CONST)_t$$
$$+ B_9(REER \cdot SIZE \cdot \log CONST)_t + B_{10} TARIFF_t + e_t.$$

The dependent variable, NTB_{t+1}, is the proportion of imports subject to NTBs in each state in year $t + 1$ based on the United Nations Conference on Trade and Development's (UNCTAD) "inventory list" of NTBs. As Sam Laird and Alexander Yeats observe, this list includes "Variable import levies and product specific charges (excluding tariff quotas); Quotas; Prohibitions (including seasonal prohibitions); non-automatic import authorisations including restrictive import licensing requirements; quantitative 'voluntary' export restraints; and trade restraints under the Multifibre Arrangement."[3] . . .

[W]e examine the incidence of NTBs. This measure is chosen because the UNCTAD trade coverage ratios are viewed by many experts as the most reliable estimates of NTBs across states and because it is the most appropriate variable with which to test our theory. For example, polities characterized by many (and therefore small) parliamentary constituencies may be especially prone to pork-barrel politics. Under these conditions, logrolling is likely to be pervasive and the preferences of many different interest groups are therefore likely to be reflected in trade policy. Since the extent and variety of interest-group demands reflected in trade policy bear directly on the incidence of protection, we focus on explaining the incidence of NTBs. The coverage ratios that we analyze measure the proportion of a state's imports that are subject to NTBs.

Turning to the independent variables, $SIZE_t$ is the economic size of each state in year t. . . . In addition, $\log CONST_t$ is the natural logarithm of the number of parliamentary constituencies in each state in year t based on Rogowski's data; $UNEM_t$ is the unemployment rate in each state in year t; $REER_t$ is an index of the real exchange rate in each state in year t; $TARIFF_t$ is the average national post–Tokyo Round offer rate for each state; and e_t is an error term. The remaining variables are included in order to determine whether, as we hypothesized above, the interaction between factors that regulate the provision of protection ($SIZE \cdot \log CONST$), and the interaction between factors that govern demands for protection and those that regulate its supply, are important determinants of cross-national patterns of NTBs.

Data limitations led us to focus on explaining NTBs in 1983 and 1986. UNCTAD provides data on NTBs for fourteen advanced industrial states in these years. The fourteen states are: Belgium-Luxembourg, Denmark, Finland, France, Greece, Ireland, Italy, Japan, the Netherlands, Norway, Switzerland, the United Kingdom, the United States, and West Germany. Although UNCTAD also provides NTB data for New Zealand, our results indicated that this country was a statistical outlier. We therefore excluded New Zealand and focus on the aforementioned fourteen states in the following analysis. Because NTBs are measured in 1983 and

1986 (years $t + 1$), the independent variables in equation (1) (except for *TARIFF*) are measured in 1982 and 1985 (years t). The observations for 1983 and 1986 are initially pooled; however, the extent to which the incidence of NTBs varied between 1983 and 1986 is also examined below.

It should be noted at the outset that all of the states analyzed in this study are advanced industrial countries. This precludes, for example, an assessment of whether our findings vary depending on a state's level of economic development. It is also clear that caution must be exercised when offering generalizations based on an analysis of such a limited time period. But since the tendency for advanced industrial countries to rely on NTBs became increasingly pervasive during the 1980s and virtually no quantitative cross-national research has been conducted on the issues addressed here, our results should provide a useful first cut at the hypotheses presented above.

Estimates of the Parameters

. . . [Our] findings indicate that our model explains about 80 percent of the variation in NTBs. They also indicate that unemployment, the real exchange rate, economic size, and domestic institutions each exert a strong effect on the incidence of NTBs. . . .

[Our] results . . . bear out the statist hypotheses discussed above. First, there is evidence that economic size is directly related to the incidence of NTBs. . . . Second, our results indicate that the number of parliamentary constituencies exerts a strong influence on the incidence of NTBs. . . .

Third, in addition to their individual effects, the interaction between the number of constituencies and economic size helps to shape patterns of NTBs. . . . These results indicate that NTBs are most pervasive in economically large states characterized by a small number of (and, hence, large) constituencies. . . .

[Our] results also provide support for the societal hypothesis that high rates of unemployment and appreciated currencies are strongly linked to a high incidence of NTBs. . . .

Further, our findings yield substantial evidence that the interaction between factors related to demands for and the provision of protection is a centrally important influence on NTBs. . . .

The results based on equation (1) demonstrate that the highest (lowest) values of *NTB* obtain when: (1) states are largest (smallest); (2) policymakers are well (poorly) insulated from societal pressures and most (least) autonomous; and (3) domestic pressures for protection are most (least) pronounced. . . . These findings are therefore consistent with the hypothesis that the incidence of *NTB* is greatest when state and societal interests converge regarding the desirability of protection and policymakers are vested with the institutional capacity to advance these interests.

The strength of our results depends fundamentally on the inclusion of factors concerning demands for and the provision of protection, as well as the interaction between them. . . . [Models without interaction effects] explain between 1 and 50 percent of the variation in NTBs, depending on whether or not both societal and statist variables are included and the particular measure of economic size that is used. Thus, our model of NTBs is considerably more powerful than a societal model, a statist model, or a model that includes both types of factors but neglects the interaction between them.

Another purpose of this study is to assess the impact of tariffs on NTBs. The results . . . provide considerable evidence of an inverse relationship between tariffs and NTB. . . . Moreover, tariffs exert a large quantitative effect on NTBs: for every 1 percent reduction in tariffs, the share of imports subject to NTBs rises by about 1.4 percent, holding constant the remaining variables in the model. Thus, tariffs and NTBs seem to be substitutes.

Proportional Representation and NTBs

In addition to the number of parliamentary constituencies, whether the state is PR or not also influences the autonomy of public officials. In order to analyze the effects of PR systems on NTBs, we include in equation (1) a dummy variable that takes on a value of 1 if the state in question was classified by Rogowski as a PR regime and 0 otherwise. Further, because it has been argued that the autonomy of public officials is bolstered in PR systems characterized by large average-sized parliamentary constituencies, we also include a variable designed to capture the interaction between these institutional factors ($PR \cdot \log CONST$) in our model. . . .

Our extended model . . . explains about 90 percent of the variation in the incidence of NTBs across the states considered here. Further, in addition to the factors discussed above, whether or not a PR system exists is an important influence on the incidence of NTBs. . . .

[T]hese results continue to support the hypothesis that the incidence of NTBs is greatest when the imposition of protection is in both the national interest and the interest of many pressure groups, and when public officials possess the institutional means necessary to advance those interests. . . .

SOME ILLUSTRATIONS OF THE STATISTICAL FINDINGS

Having tested our model, it is useful to illustrate how the societal and statist variables on which we focused affected trade policy in the countries considered here. While detailed case studies are beyond the scope of this article, anecdotal evidence suggests that these variables were salient influences on commercial policy during the 1980s.

Consider, for example, the role that the exchange rate played in United States trade policy. Between 1983 and 1986, the incidence of U.S. NTBs rose by over 25 percent. Much of this rise seems to be due to a significant appreciation in the dollar. While the values of the other independent variables in our model changed relatively little from 1982 to 1985 in the case of the United States, the value of *REER* increased dramatically. The societal view that this appreciation should precipitate an increase in demands for protection accords with a number of accounts of exchange-rate politics in the United States during this period. . . . [B]y the early 1980s, many sectors of U.S. industry had concluded that the dollar's strength was degrading their competitiveness. By 1985, their opposition to the dollar's strength reached a peak. Imports were flooding into the United States at a rate unprecedented during the post–World War II era. . . . U.S. industry and labor petitioned the Reagan administration and Congress to remedy the dollar appreciation. . . . It is also noteworthy that the period from 1982 to 1985 witnessed a rapid surge in the number of petitions for trade-policy relief by U.S. industry and a turn toward managed-trade policies by the United States. These developments both led directly to an increase in the incidence of NTBs and . . . were largely attributable to the dollar's appreciation.

The effects of unemployment on NTBs are illustrated by the case of West Germany during the 1980s. From 1983 to 1986 the incidence of West German NTBs rose by approximately 15 percent; and from 1982 to 1985, the level of West German unemployment rose by about 25 percent, while the remaining independent variables in our model experienced only very modest fluctuations. . . . By 1983, the West German economy had deteriorated to the point where unemployment had reached its highest level since the end of World War II. Of particular importance for present purposes was the structural nature of West German unemployment. In 1983, over a quarter of those West Germans without jobs had been unemployed for more than one year. . . . Labor problems reached a peak in 1984 with the metal workers' strike, which was designed in part to reduce unemployment. It is interesting that the Organization for Economic Cooperation and Development reported in 1986 that West German NTBs were most pervasive in those sectors where tariffs had been reduced and that among these were sectors in which metal workers were employed in large numbers (such as steel). This suggests that the government responded to mounting unemployment by increasing the incidence of NTBs in 1986. Given the political strength of organized labor, the traditional unwillingness of the government to enact macroeconomic policies to counter unemployment at the risk of undermining monetary stability, and Germany's mounting unemployment problems, West Germany's course of action is not surprising.

Further, it is interesting to compare the effects of institutional variations between Japan and the United States on their respective propensities to impose NTBs. It is often argued that Japan is a "strong" state in which policymakers are extremely well-insulated and autonomous with respect to interest groups. The United States, on the other hand, is often portrayed as a "weak" state in which policymakers lack both insulation and autonomy. Yet both of these countries are characterized by a relatively large number of parliamentary constituencies based on our sample of states. This suggests that public officials in both countries are likely to be susceptible to societal pressures (although not necessarily to the same extent); and it jibes with the view expressed in a number of recent studies that Japanese policymakers are far less autonomous and less insulated from interest groups than is implied by those who characterize it as a strong state. . . . A primary foreign policy interest of these groups is the prevention of the loss of domestic markets to imports, and this has led them to form alliances with politicians and bureaucrats that are likely to undermine the insulation and autonomy of these state actors.

Going a step further, it is useful to consider the results presented [here] in light of this discussion of Japanese and U.S. institutions. In 1986, for example, Japan and the United States were the two largest states in our sample, both countries had appreciated currencies and relatively little unemployment, and neither state's electoral system was PR. From the standpoint of our model, the primary difference between them was that the United States had noticeably more constituencies than did Japan. As a result, it would be expected on the basis of this model that Japanese policymakers would be somewhat better insulated and more autonomous than their American counterparts, and that this institutional feature would better enable them to pursue the national interest. It, therefore, is not surprising that the incidence of NTBs was greater in Japan than in the United States during 1986. At the same time, however, both Japanese and U.S. NTBs were relatively high in 1986 based on the sample of countries considered here. This is consistent with the view described above that, while Japanese policymakers are vested with greater institutional capacity (and therefore are better able to advance the national interest as they see it) than their American counterparts, the institutional characteristics of Japan and the United States are more similar than is often recognized.

Clearly, the cases presented in this section can be taken as no more than suggestive of the ways in which societal and statist factors influence trade policy. Yet these examples do illustrate why the variables emphasized in our model are so strongly related to cross-national patterns of NTBs.

IMPLICATIONS AND CONCLUSIONS

Our results have a number of implications for studies of the political economy of trade policy. In recent years, one of the most persistent sources of debate among both economists and political scientists has centered on the relative merits of societal and statist explanations of foreign-economic policy. Our findings lend support for the societal argument that macroeconomic fluctuations contribute to demands for protection, which are in turn central determinants of trade policy. Consistent with societal theories, high levels of unemployment and appreciated currencies are strongly related to a high incidence of NTBs. In addition to their effects on NTBs, both of these macroeconomic factors also have been linked to cross-national patterns of tariffs. What is often referred to as the "new" protection (i.e., NTBs) may therefore be newer in form than in cause: it appears to be the product of many of the same factors that explain the "old" protection (i.e., tariffs).

While factors emphasized by societal approaches are strongly related to cross-national patterns of NTBs, factors highlighted by statist approaches also are centrally important in this regard. As statist analyses predict, economic size (which, in the opinion of many statists, helps to shape the preferences of policymakers with respect to trade policy) is strongly related to the incidence of NTBs. Large states have a greater incentive to impose protection than their smaller counterparts, and our findings indicate that they do in fact impose NTBs more widely than small states. It is curious that, despite the clear importance of this factor, it has been considered so rarely in empirical research on trade policy. Our results indicate that this omission is likely to yield incomplete and potentially misleading conclusions regarding the determinants of commercial policy.

So, too, is the failure to consider cross-national variations in domestic institutions in analyses of trade policy. Even though studies of political economy increasingly emphasize the need to understand the effects of institutions, few attempts have been made to assess the quantitative impact of institutions on trade policy. Further, no previous study has attempted to link cross-national variations in domestic institutions to patterns of NTBs. We find considerable evidence that institutions help to shape differences in NTBs. Particularly important in this regard is their effect on the relationships between macroeconomic variables and size, respectively, and NTBs.

Our findings bear out the position that the provision of NTBs is at least partially governed by economic size, domestic institutions, and the interaction between these factors. More specifically, NTBs are highest in large states that are characterized by high levels of institutional insulation and autonomy. Thus, states are most likely to impose NTBs when economic incentives to do so exist and when strong domestic institutions insulate policymakers from interest-group pressures, thereby allowing them to advance the national interest unencumbered by those pressure groups that display preferences for freer trade.

In addition to the interaction between variables that regulate the provision of NTBs, the interaction between these variables and those related to domestic pressures for protection also exerts a significant influence on trade policy. A number of political scientists and economists have argued that this should be the case, but little empirical evidence bearing on this fundamental topic has been accumulated. Our results indicate that an understanding of the interaction between these factors is crucial for the purposes of explaining cross-national patterns of NTBs. All other things being equal, the incidence of NTBs is greatest when deteriorating macroeconomic conditions generate widespread demands for protection, a state is sufficiently large to give policymakers incentives to impose protection, and public officials are vested with the institutional capacity necessary to act on these preferences and resist pressures exerted by groups with an interest in lower trade barriers.

These findings stand in stark contrast to predictions based on either societal or statist models of foreign economic policy alone. Societal models — including most endogenous models of protection — emphasize factors related to societal demands for protection, but systematically neglect the factors that regulate the provision of trade barriers. Statist models place considerable emphasis on factors that account for the provision of protection, but often fail to address adequately the influence of pressure groups on trade policy. Each of these approaches correctly emphasizes one type of factor, while giving short shrift to the other type. Rather than considering these approaches as mutually exclusive, it is more fruitful to view them as complementary.

Many studies of foreign economic policy imply that protection is likely to be most pervasive in states characterized by vehement demands for protection articulated by well-organized groups and state institutions that fail to insulate policymakers from the brunt of these demands. This is particularly prevalent in the "state-society" literature that has been the topic of much heated controversy among scholars of foreign economic policy. Our findings indicate that these debates have been miscast. Rather than viewing protection as an outcome whereby pressure groups run roughshod over public officials who are inherently liberal with respect to trade, NTBs are greatest when the interests of state and societal actors converge. Similarly, much of the recent disagreement among analysts of foreign economic policy has centered on whether societal demands for protection or domestic institutions that regulate the provision of protection should be emphasized. This debate has served to create a false dichotomy. The issue is not which factor should be emphasized, since both are centrally important determinants of NTBs. Rather, the central issue is how to integrate both factors in a comprehensive manner. Although it is obvious that our results should be taken as tentative, their strength is striking. These findings strongly indicate that it would be fruitful to further integrate societal models — especially models of endogenous protection — and statist models, and that this research strategy is likely to generate new and important insights concerning the determinants of trade policy.

Finally, our results yield substantial evidence that tariffs are strongly related to the incidence of NTBs, and that these forms of protection are substitutes. This finding is consistent with the law of constant protection. Among the states considered here, new tariffs could not easily have been imposed due to GATT restrictions. States with low tariff levels that wish to augment their trade barriers therefore have had reason to rely on NTBs for this purpose. Further, states characterized by high tariff levels are likely to be sufficiently well-protected that they need not supplement tariffs with NTBs. Our findings suggest the possibility that many of the tariff reductions made by the GATT during the Tokyo Round may not have had the intended effect of reducing protection. Instead, these cuts seem to have produced countervailing increases in the incidence of NTBs. . . .

NOTES

1. Ronald Rogowski, "Trade and the Variety of Democratic Institutions," *International Organization* 41 (Spring 1987), p. 200.

2. Rogowski, "Trade and the Variety of Democratic Institutions," p. 209.

3. Sam Laird and Alexander Yeats, *Quantitative Methods for Trade-Barrier Analysis* (New York: New York University Press, 1990), p. 90.

24

Explaining Business Support for Regional Trade Agreements
RONALD W. COX

> One of the most important developments in the international trading system has been the recent proliferation of regional trade agreements (RTAs), like the European Union's single market, the North American Free Trade Agreement (NAFTA), or the Caribbean Basin Initiative (CBI). Ronald W. Cox offers a domestic societal explanation for the growth of these arrangements and argues that business interests — in the United States, at least — are divided into two communities, both of which support regional agreements, but for different reasons. Although they often back RTAs as stepping stones to greater liberalization, "multilateralists" prefer the comprehensive trade negotiations of the World Trade Organization. "Regionalists," on the other hand, prefer more limited RTAs because they give firms preferential access to both low-wage export platforms and rich country markets, and thus, important advantages relative to their foreign competitors. Cox examines the economic preferences and political strategies of the American automotive and consumer electronics industries (both of which are strong regionalists) in the cases of the CBI and NAFTA.

. . . [O]ne of the primary roles of the U.S. executive branch in foreign economic policy has been to facilitate the accumulation of capital on a global scale by working to promote the conditions for profitable trade and investment for U.S.-based transnational corporations. In the area of U.S. trade policy, the degree to which the state performs this task is dependent in part on the political mobilization of sectors of business that articulate their demands to influential state actors. In addition, divisions among diverse business sectors often will be reflected in policy debates, with business internationalists joining with the White House, State Department, and Treasury to advocate measures to facilitate increased trade and foreign direct investment and business nationalists and labor groups joining with congressional representatives to promote protectionist measures. Throughout much of the post–World War II period, a dominant liberal-internationalist coalition of business groups, political elites, and intellectuals advocated a U.S. commitment to the policies of multilateralism embodied in the GATT agreements.

Since the mid-1970s, the collapse of the Bretton Woods system has been accompanied by increased divisions among business internationalists previously committed to multilateralism. U.S. foreign direct investors in automobiles and electronics have moved both economically and politically to restructure their operations in order to better compete with Japanese and Western European firms for the triad markets of Japan, Western Europe, and the United States. At one level, firms involved in such restructuring have integrated their North American operations by dividing production of component parts to take advantage of cheap labor and low-cost access to the U.S. market. The project of industrial restructuring represents an ongoing effort by some U.S. transnational corporations to counteract the dual trends of excess capacity and dwindling market share that characterized the late 1970s and early 1980s.

Politically, U.S. foreign direct investors in Mexico, Canada, and the Caribbean Basin have formed coalitions since the mid-1980s to pressure and assist U.S. officials to pursue regional trade agreements that will give them greater protection against foreign competition for the U.S. market. These investors are part of a broad coalition of business groups that have come together in support of CBI [Caribbean Basin Initiative] and NAFTA as alternatives to the multilateralism of GATT.

For foreign direct investors facing declining rates of profit and increased foreign competition, regional trade agreements promise numerous advantages. First, they allow U.S.-based multinationals to increase the exploitation of workers by relocating and reorganizing production to low-wage areas. Second, regional operations backed up by regional trade agreements allow U.S. firms proximity to the U.S. market to better compete with foreign rivals. Third, as we will see, regional trade agreements discriminate in several ways against foreign competitors by extending preferential treatment to regionally based firms.

However, it is important to note that not all corporate supporters of CBI and NAFTA view the agreements as a preferable alternative to the multilateralism of GATT. Some firms see these regional agreements as a necessary transition to the renewed promotion of multilateralism on a global scale. For the purposes of brevity and precision, the corporate coalitions behind CBI and NAFTA can be divided into two categories, each of which supports the agreements for different reasons.

The first group can be labeled "multilateralists" or "anti-protectionist" due to their political propensity to support free trade in a variety of different contexts. This group includes retailing, banking and service industries, pharmaceutical companies, and agricultural exporters (especially of grains and oilseeds). Many of the leading Fortune 500 firms in these sectors are heavily dependent on international transactions for their profitability and tend to be highly competitive in global markets. They have been frustrated with the slow progress of GATT and see regional trade agreements as a short-term route to securing important export markets. However, they do not see the regional trade agreements as a substitute for multilateralism. They view the agreements as a first step toward rebuilding the multilateral trading system, and they see CBI and NAFTA as compatible with pursuing free trade agreements through GATT.

The second group can be labeled "regionalists" due to their preference for discriminatory regional trade agreements and their recent opposition to multilateralism. Led by U.S. auto and electronics firms, this group has tended to support nontariff barriers against Japan and Western Europe, while supporting regional trade agreements perceived to give them greater leverage against foreign competition. This group is dominated by foreign direct investors who have struggled to maintain a competitive advantage against European and Japanese companies in the triad markets of Western Europe, Japan, and the United States. These firms see NAFTA as a way to continue the reorganization and rationalization of production necessary to compete with Japanese and European firms who have penetrated the U.S. market.

An example of this regionalist strategy involves U.S. auto firms that successfully won a provision in the U.S.-Canada free trade agreement that has allowed them to continue to bring parts and vehicles into Canada duty-free from any country (including Brazil, Korea, Mexico, Taiwan, and Thailand). Conversely, Japanese firms, including Honda, Hyundai, and Toyota, still have to pay duties on any imports from outside the United States. U.S. auto and electronics firms have insisted on maintaining preferential treatment for North American firms in the trade agreement with Mexico, which places them at a further advantage relative to their Japanese and Western European counterparts. In this sense, these regionalist firms see NAFTA as leverage against foreign competition and advocate restrictive measures that some analysts believe are incompatible with the multilateralism of GATT.

In addition, regionalist firms, especially consumer and industrial electronics, were among the leading advocates of the Caribbean Basin Initiative, which brought together direct foreign investors and export-import interests with a stake in improving the terms of trade with the Caribbean Basin. Like the case of NAFTA, CBI represented a significant departure from GATT in its discriminatory treatment of foreign companies. Regionalists applauded the initiative for giving greater leverage to U.S. firms engaged in global economic competition with their Japanese and European rivals.

The following analysis will focus on regionalist U.S. firms, especially automobiles and electronics, in attempting to explain the appeal of NAFTA. In addition, a focus on regionalist firms will be useful in highlighting the implications of the global restructuring of the world economy for political trade coalitions in the United States. I argue that regionalist firms that supported NAFTA are likely to maintain their opposition to multilateralism, given the current realities of the world economy.

I will attempt to expand upon these general observations by performing three tasks: (1) locating the process of industrial restructuring within the larger context of global competition for production advantage in the U.S. market; (2) connecting the economic process of industrial restructuring to the development of a U.S.-based political coalition supporting CBI and NAFTA; and (3) drawing lessons from these agreements regarding the future prospects for multilateralism, regionalism, and protectionism on a global scale.

INDUSTRIAL RESTRUCTURING AND REGIONAL TRADE

The trend of relocating partial production of a product to the less-developed world for reexport to the home market has been occurring to various degrees since the early to mid-1960s. This approach was feasible only for companies with access to appropriate capital, marketing, administration, or technology that made relocation less costly than producing the entire product within the domestic market. Multinationals able to take advantage of this approach found partial production abroad to be preferable to other options for maintaining their competitive position within the domestic market. . . .

[F]irms often chose to relocate their labor-intensive operations to low-cost areas abroad as a strategy to maintain their competitive position against foreign firms that had penetrated the U.S. market. As other analysts have noted, this process was facilitated in the case of U.S. firms by tariff codes 806.30 and 807, which permit the "duty-free entry of U.S. components sent abroad for processing or assembly." In addition, U.S. foreign direct investors lobbied heavily for regional trade agreements with Canada, Mexico, and the Caribbean Basin, which allowed them to further integrate their production strategies for the U.S. market. As we will see, the regional agreements also have given (or promise to give) U.S. firms preferential treatment versus their most important international rivals. U.S. foreign direct investors facing declining profitability and increased competition in the U.S. market saw the regional trade agreements as an important political extension of their ongoing efforts to restructure their global operations against increasing foreign competition.

As part of this process, multinational corporations in electronics and automobiles have increasingly viewed Mexico as an ideal location to cut costs and bolster their competitive positions. Since the late 1960s, U.S.-based firms in these industries have used locations in Mexico for production of component parts for export to the U.S. market.

Since the mid-1980s, export production from Mexico has been increasingly important for U.S. firms due to two primary factors. First, U.S.-based firms in electronics and automobiles faced domestic obstacles to lowering the costs of production in the U.S. market. These included relatively high wages and capital costs, which made it difficult to compete with foreign rivals. For electronics industries, the Caribbean Basin and Mexico allowed for the division of production between capital-intensive production in the U.S. and labor-intensive production in cheap labor regions, continuing a trend well established in Asia. For U.S. auto companies, Mexico provided an increasingly important platform for the assembly of component parts and vehicles destined for the U.S. market.

Secondly, these U.S.-based firms faced an internationalization of the U.S. economy that involved increases in foreign direct investment in the U.S. market by Japanese and European competitors. The reaction to such competition was the increased sourcing of component parts to Mexico and (in the case of electronics firms) to the Caribbean Basin, a strategy designed to lower costs of production and maintain profitability in the face of growing competition for the U.S. market.

The internationalization of the U.S. market meant that efforts by electronics and automobile firms to limit imports (through voluntary export restraints) had minimal effects on impeding their international rivals, which merely relocated to the U.S. market to avoid voluntary export restraints and other trade barriers. Also, the strategy of reinvesting in new technology and equipment in the U.S. market proved to be too costly in the short term.

Thus the preferred option was to locate production of component parts in areas characterized by cheap labor and proximity to the U.S. market. Some electronics firms moved their operations from Asia to Mexico and the Caribbean Basin to lower their transportation costs in exporting to the U.S. market. Auto firms increasingly used Mexico to source component parts for the U.S. market. Furthermore, the beginning of the 1990s [saw] auto companies expand their Mexican operations to include production of finished vehicles, including state-of-the-art autos that were previously produced only in the advanced markets of the United States and Europe.

Apparel producers have also used foreign locations for low-cost advantage in producing component parts for the U.S. market. U.S. apparel firms typically subcontract with garment producers in the Caribbean Basin and Mexico for the production of clothing or textiles for export to the U.S. market. As a result, some of the leading U.S. apparel firms have joined other U.S. industries, such as electronics, automobiles, and electrical equipment, to push for CBI and NAFTA. However, as I discuss in detail later, other apparel firms tied to the U.S. market have mounted successful opposition against tariff reductions proposed by their international counterparts in lobbying for CBI.

These foreign direct investors and subcontractors form part of a powerful political coalition lobbying for NAFTA and CBI, often against nationalist firms. The next section of this paper locates the emergence of this coalition in the context of the internationalization of the U.S. market, especially the dramatic increases in foreign direct investment by Japanese companies. . . .

THE INTERNATIONALIZATION OF THE U.S. MARKET: THE CASES OF AUTOMOBILES AND CONSUMER ELECTRONICS

U.S. auto and electronics firms faced vigorous competition from their Japanese counterparts in the 1980s, which provided the major impetus for industrial restructuring. Prior to 1982, Japanese auto firms did not have a single production plant outside Japan. Instead, Japanese firms, led by Toyota, relied on a "lean production" strategy that emphasized exports to the developed market economies as a method for increasing market share. Innovations in Japanese production provided formidable challenges to U.S. car manufacturers, who had been late in shifting from "mass production" methods to a more flexible production system. . . .

The production strategy employed by Japanese firms involved a number of interrelated changes designed to increase output at considerably lower costs. They included the introduction of sophisticated computer technology to facilitate the designing and engineering phases of production, the relatively low parts inventory achieved by reliance on close functional relationships between customers and suppliers, the multiple tasks performed by Japanese autoworkers to enhance productivity and inhibit the formation of independent unions, and protection from the Japanese government, which limits access to foreign firms and practices discriminatory intervention in favor of domestic producers. Prior to 1982, this productive system was combined with an emphasis on export promotion to successfully penetrate the developed market economies.

Such import penetration posed a considerable challenge to U.S. auto firms, which saw their competitive advantage eroding in the U.S. market. In response, U.S. auto firms most severely affected by Japanese imports joined the United Automobile Workers Union to pressure the government to negotiate voluntary export restraints with Japan. U.S. manufacturers and labor union officials hoped these restraints would help to create a level playing field in the U.S. market by encouraging Japanese companies to reduce exports in favor of foreign direct investment. In this regard, it was hoped that Japanese direct investors would then have to operate under the same conditions as did U.S. companies.

Japanese companies' newfound interest in direct foreign investment went well beyond the expectations of U.S. business and government elites, however. From 1982 to 1989, Japanese auto firms began establishing production plants in the U.S. market that provided further challenges to U.S. companies. . . .

In addition, Japanese firms in consumer electronics were increasing their direct foreign investment in the United States, although this trend began in the 1970s with the television industry (where it had its greatest impact) and continued in the 1980s with the videotape recorder industry. . . .

Historically, the Japanese consumer electronics companies, like their automobile counterparts, [exported] to European and U.S. markets. However, the proliferation of voluntary export restraints, coupled with the development of new technology, made it necessary and profitable to engage in direct foreign investments in the United States and Europe. The 1970s saw a wave of Japanese companies invest in television manufacturing plants in the United States. . . . Consequently, only Zenith remained as an indigenous U.S. manufacturer by the end of the 1970s. By the 1980s, Japanese firms were repeating this wave of foreign investment in the area of videotape recorders. . . .

U.S. firms began to shift protection strategies in an effort to withstand the Japanese competitive threat. . . . U.S. producers sought to rely increasingly on supply and production networks in Canada and Mexico in an effort to gain a competitive advantage in the U.S. market.

Thus, U.S. auto and electronics firms were solidly behind the free trade agreements with Mexico and Canada, which they saw as essential regional locations for improving their production system in the U.S. market. The recent investments by U.S. auto firms in Canada and Mexico represent an effort to integrate production for the U.S. market via the expansion of low-cost supply networks and production facilities. Thus, regional trade agreements are seen as preferable to GATT in meeting the competitive challenges of global competition. Meanwhile, electronics firms have lobbied heavily for both CBI and NAFTA, reflecting their global production strategies in the face of the internationalization of the U.S. market in the 1980s. . . .

ELECTRONICS FIRMS AND THE CARIBBEAN BASIN INITIATIVE

Beginning in 1979, the Caribbean/Central American Action (CCAA) lobby, representing the interests of 90 percent of the Fortune 500 firms with investments in the Caribbean Basin, formed to lobby U.S. governmental officials to ease trade restrictions on products imported from Caribbean Basin countries. The formation of the CCAA anticipated and supported the efforts of the Reagan administration to promote CBI, which lowered tariffs on selected manufactured goods exported from Caribbean Basin countries that qualified. . . .

U.S. electronics firms viewed CBI as a means to discriminate against foreign competitors for the U.S. market. The agreement allowed producers of integrated circuits and metal oxide semiconductors to export partially produced products from the region duty-free. These provisions complemented the duty-free provisions already established in Caribbean Basin free trade zones. In addition, CBI implemented a low and flexible local content requirement that gave preferential treatment to U.S. firms. Eligibility for duty-free treatment was contingent on 35 percent of the product being produced in the Caribbean Basin, of which 15 percent could be accounted for by U.S. materials.

U.S.-based electronics firms joined with pharmaceutical firms and producers of baseball gloves, belts, fabricated metals, and food processors to lobby for CBI. Electronics firms saw the agreement as a way to regionalize their operations by relying on low-cost, partial production in the Caribbean Basin to compete for the U.S. market. U.S. controlled and/or operated firms accounted for five of the top ten imports from the region eligible for duty-free treatment. . . .

The battle over CBI reflected the diverse business interests involved in trade legislation. First, there were the regionalist firms represented by electronics companies that saw the agreement as leverage against foreign competition for the U.S. market. Spokespersons for AVX, Dataram, and other U.S. electronics firms testified before Congress that CBI would give them a necessary competitive advantage in competing against Japanese and European firms for access to the U.S. market. These firms saw CBI as further institutionalizing an ongoing trend of corporate relocation and restructuring necessary to reverse declining profitability and intensified global competition. As a result, U.S.-based electronics firms lobbied for local content laws that would give preferential treatment to U.S. firms.

The second group of firms in favor of CBI were the multilateralists in pharmaceuticals, services, and banking. These firms were more competitive in global markets and did not seek the restrictive local content laws preferred by electronics firms. Instead, they saw the regional trade agreement as complementary to broader efforts to revitalize the multilateralism of GATT on a global scale. They valued the agreement because it allowed for a further reduction in U.S. tariff barriers, which in turn furthered free trade goals.

Reagan administration officials supported CBI mainly because it complemented broader security goals in the region. The administration insisted that the largest percentage of CBI money should go to El Salvador, where the administration was actively engaged in bolstering the military regime against rebel insurgents. As such, much of the aid attached to CBI reflected the Reagan administration's policy of bolstering a Salvadoran government that was facing an economic and political crisis.

Opponents of the regional trade agreement included domestic firms that stood to lose the most from reducing tariff barriers, especially the domestic textile and clothing industries tied to the national market. An examination of congressional debates over the content of CBI reveals that business nationalists also had some influence on the final legislation. The American Textile Manufacturers Institute and the American Apparel Manufacturers Association joined with the American Clothing and Textile Workers Union and the International Ladies Garment Workers Union to lobby Congress, especially the Subcommittee on Trade of the House Ways and Means Committee, to maintain import restrictions. These business nationalists and their labor counterparts succeeded in excluding all textile and apparel products from the duty-free provisions of CBI. . . .

AUTO FIRMS AND THE NORTH AMERICAN
FREE TRADE AGREEMENT

The U.S. automobile industry has developed a corporate production strategy that seeks to combat the effects of increased global competition. An important pillar of the strategy is regionalization of production along continental lines. This regionalization has proceeded along three general dimensions, involving: (1) moving phases of the production process (including the fabrication of engines and transmissions) from the United States to lower-wage sites in Mexico, Brazil, and Argentina, with Mexico becoming a preferred location since the 1980s; (2) developing a North American production scheme characterized by knowledge-based or lean production in order to better compete with Japanese rivals for the U.S. market; and (3) lobbying for a NAFTA agreement that extends preferential treatment to North American producers in Mexico. . . .

By the late 1980s, U.S. firms increasingly looked to Mexico as a preferred site for relocation of motor vehicle production for the U.S. market, including the production of auto parts, engines and transmissions, and finished motor vehicles. A number of factors converged to make Mexico especially attractive to U.S. producers. First, the Mexican government implemented a series of trade liberalization measures that facilitated and encouraged U.S. transnationals to export more finished motor vehicles and auto parts. Second, the Mexican state implemented neoliberal reforms that have resulted in a devaluation of the peso and a reduction in wages in the auto industry and elsewhere, making Mexico more attractive to foreign investors. Finally, U.S.-based auto firms have been able to take advantage of Mexico's proximity to the United States, which has given them a cost edge over European and Japanese competitors in the production of parts and finished vehicles for the U.S. market.

This combination of Mexican incentives and corporate interests has already resulted in dramatic increases in U.S. foreign direct investment in auto parts and assembly in Mexico. . . .

At the same time, U.S. firms have asked for dual rules of origin requirements that extend preferential treatment to U.S. firms and discriminate against new entrants into the North American market. In free trade agreements, rules of origin requirements are used to determine what goods were actually produced in the member countries and therefore qualify for preferential treatment. In negotiations over NAFTA, U.S. auto firms have insisted on 50 percent rules of origin agreements, which gives preferential treatment to firms already established in North America.

The discriminatory measures embedded in regional trade agreements contrast with the multilateralism advocated by GATT. . . . To the extent that NAFTA institutionalizes preferential treatment for U.S. firms and discriminates against foreign competitors, it can hardly be seen as compatible with the broad principles of GATT. . . .

In fact, NAFTA brought together a coalition of corporate supporters advocating both discriminatory treatment against foreign investors and reduced tariff barriers. On the one hand, foreign direct investors in autos and electronics advocated tough rules of origin requirements that privileged existing market players and penalized late entrants. . . . On the other hand, multilateralists represented by banks, U.S. exporters, and retailers supported NAFTA for its liberalized trade provisions.

These corporate coalitions came together to lobby for NAFTA against import-competing industries who stood to lose market share if trade was liberalized. Opponents of NAFTA included labor-intensive industries producing footwear, glassware, luggage, brooms, and ceramics, and agricultural producers of asparagus, avocados, canned tomatoes, citrus, sugar and sugar beets. Other powerful critics of NAFTA included labor unions, religious organizations, and consumer and environmental interest groups that feared the consequences of liberalized trade and investment for U.S. labor, Mexican workers, and the environment.

The battle over NAFTA suggested that multilateralists faced stiff opposition in securing a regional trade agreement that was compatible with the multilateralism of GATT. This was true for two reasons. First, corporate supporters of NAFTA included an uneasy alliance of foreign direct investors, multinational banks, and exporters, each of which supported the agreement for different reasons. These interests came together to lobby for NAFTA, but they have often been on opposing sides of the free trade debate in other, nonregional contexts. Second, NAFTA became a lightning rod for popular discontent, influenced by the legacy of corporate-labor battles of the 1980s that resulted in considerable union concessions in autos, steel, and textiles. The concessions were often won as a result of corporate flight or threats to close down plants in lieu of reduced wages and/or benefits.

MULTILATERALISM, REGIONALISM, AND PROTECTIONISM IN THE WAKE OF THE NORTH AMERICAN FREE TRADE AGREEMENT

There are several noticeable trends that have affected trade politics from the late 1970s to the present. The first has been a defection of some multinational firms from the free trade coalition that previously dominated U.S. trade policy. Firms were more likely to defect if they faced the following conditions: increased import competition leading to loss of market share in the United States and elsewhere, reliance on foreign direct investment geared toward regional markets, and low levels of trade relative to direct foreign investment. U.S.-based firms in electronics and autos have geared production around regional markets via foreign direct investment in North America, the EEC (European Economic Community) and Asia. The international character of these firms has not meant continued support for multilateralism but, instead, has resulted in support for regional trading blocs designed to increase protection against foreign competitors. In addition, electronics and auto firms supported nontariff barriers to trade throughout the late 1970s and 1980s, including voluntary export restraints.

Does this mean an end to the multilateralism of GATT in favor of regional trading blocs? Not necessarily. Another trend in trade politics has been the emergence of antiprotectionist political organizations based among exporters, business and industrial import users, retailers and other trade-related services, and foreign governments of exporting countries. In general, the degree to which firms are dependent on exports as a percentage of overall production is a determining factor in their commitment to antiprotectionism. One well-documented trend in the late 1970s and 1980s was the fact that the U.S. economy as a whole saw substantial increases in trade dependence as a percentage of GNP. This trend meant that certain U.S. firms in selective industries developed a greater interest in antiprotectionist activity.

Since the mid-1970s, groups with a high export dependence, including the National Association of Wheat Growers and the American Soybean Association, have increased their antiprotectionist lobbying efforts. However, these efforts tend to selectively lobby against trade restrictions involving particular foreign customers and do not usually involve a defense of multilateralism as a general principle. In addition, certain export-dependent groups, such as cotton growers, have joined the American Textile Manufacturers in lobbying for textile protection. Cotton growers identify their interests with domestic textile producers who would be hurt by free trade measures. Other industries that were export dependent, such as aircraft, included firms with an interest in opposing trade restrictions with steel-producing countries, since these countries constituted 21 percent of all aircraft exports and 8 percent of aircraft production. However, aircraft firms had less interest in opposing trade restrictions on countries producing shoes, since only 2 percent of industrial output went to these countries.

The selective nature of antiprotection interests indicates significant limits in the development of an aggressive political coalition advocating multilateralism. However, other political interests have developed since the 1990s with a more widespread interest in antiprotectionist legislation. These groups tend to be concentrated in retailing and service firms with a stake in importing automobiles, textiles and footwear, all targets of protectionist efforts in the 1970s and 1980s. In fact, retailers formed several antiprotectionist coalitions in the 1980s designed to lobby against trade restrictions on textiles, automobiles, and footwear. . . .

[Nonetheless] one has to search elsewhere to find stable political coalitions or interests that advocate a generalized commitment to multilateralism. The leading proponents of multilateralism are difficult to readily identify, since they often eschew overt lobbying efforts used by the previous antiprotection groups. Instead, multilateralists often work with the executive branch in promoting multilateralism in specific institutional contexts, such as the GATT talks, U.S. bilateral negotiations with foreign governments, and multilateral organizations such as the World Bank and the IMF (International Monetary Fund). The most notable multilateralists include banking and service firms that have numerous financial and trade interests connected to open markets.

The top Fortune 500 U.S.-based banks dramatically expanded their overseas lending throughout the 1970s and 1980s to both foreign governments and firms. Bankers have been consistent proponents of multilateralist policies in negotiations with less-developed countries over terms of debt repayment. In addition, bankers have promoted U.S. policies toward Europe designed to maximize trade and foreign investment. Bankers are not as subject to the limitations of sectoral politics as are other firms, since their capital is more fluid and their interests are tied to a wide range of investments in foreign governments and private firms. As a result, bankers have consistently advocated a commitment to multilateralism consistent with their varied interests in collecting government debts and reaping a return on investments in foreign and U.S.-based multinationals.

With those general observations as a starting point, it must be said that not all bankers will be vigorous proponents of multilateralism. Bankers will be more likely to support multilateralism if they exhibit the following characteristics: (1) commercial banks that are thoroughly multinational in character, with loans dispersed around the world to both foreign governments and foreign firms; (2) investment banks linked to multinational firms heavily dependent on foreign trade relative to foreign investment; and (3) bankers ideologically committed to multilateralism as a means to facilitate debt repayment from governments in the less-developed world.

The fact that not all bankers will be committed to multilateralism weakens the potential free trade coalition. In fact, a striking development that may illuminate future trade patterns is the extent to which multilateralists in the banking community have been increasingly isolated from other multinational firms in recent decades, as support for multilateralism has steadily eroded. The only context in which a wide range of multinational firms have been able to coalesce around a trade agreement has been the case of NAFTA, where such diffuse organizations as the Chambers of Commerce, the National Association of Manufacturers, and the Business Advisory Council have taken strong positions in favor of the agreement.

However, as I have argued, the extent of interest group agreement around NAFTA is a product of the regional nature of the agreement, which attracts different multinationals for different reasons. While multilateralists see it as an important step for reinvigorating GATT, regionalists view it as additional leverage against foreign competition. The likelihood of such a powerful free trade coalition emerging in another, nonregional context is minimal at best. What is equally interesting is that, even with such a high degree of unity in the corporate community over NAFTA, the agreement is politically divisive, with nationalists being led by the unlikely bedfellows of organized labor and Ross Perot in opposing the accord. If, in fact, multilateralism is, in part, the product of interest group pressure, then the future for the global trading regime looks increasingly shaky in the 1990s.

VI

ECONOMIES IN DEVELOPMENT AND TRANSITION

The liberal international economy created after 1945 and the increase in international finance and trade (discussed in previous sections) have helped produce unprecedented levels of national and global growth. Within this broad pattern of economic success, however, there are important variations. While some countries and people enjoy the highest standards of living in human history, many more remain mired in poverty.

Indeed, the gap between the richest and the poorest people on earth not only is large but also is growing wider every year. The richest one-fifth of the world's population currently enjoys 86.0 percent of global consumption expenditures, while the world's poorest one-fifth accounts for only 1.3 percent. And while the ratio between the income of the richest 20 percent and the poorest 20 percent of the world's population was 30:1 in 1960, it grew to 45:1 in 1980 and then to 82:1 in 1995.

This pattern is replicated at the level of individual countries as well. Where all developing countries have seen their GNP per capita rise from 5.0 percent of the industrialized countries in 1960 to 7.0 percent in 1995, the "least" developed countries (those with a GNP per capita of $300 or less) fell from 3.5 percent to 1.8 percent. These income trends are repeated in the areas of trade, savings, and investment.[1] While economic growth has increased over the post-1945 period, raising the average standard of living around the globe, the gaps between the world's wealthiest and poorest societies have increased even faster. As Jeffrey A. Williamson points out in Reading 28, the comparisons between current trends — in income differentials both among countries and within them — and those of the nineteenth and early twentieth centuries is illuminating and potentially worrisome.

For decades, scholars and practitioners have debated the sources of economic growth and the best strategies for producing rapid increases in standards of living. Many analysts argue that development, at least in its initial stages, requires that the country insulate itself from more established economic powers and stimulate key industries at home through trade protection and government subsidies. Indeed, Alexander Hamilton, the first secretary of the treasury of the United States, argued for just such a policy in his famous *Report on Manufactures,* which he presented to the House of Representatives in 1791.

Starting in the 1930s with the collapse of the international economy in the Great Depression, many so-called developing countries began de facto strategies of import-substituting industrialization (ISI) in order to increase domestic production to fill the gap created by the decrease in foreign trade. After World War II, especially in Latin America but elsewhere as well, this de facto strategy was institutionalized de jure in high tariffs and explicit governmental policies of industrial promotion. Behind protective walls, countries sought to substitute domestic manufactures for foreign imports, first in light manufactures, such as textiles, apparel, and food processing, and later in intermediate and capital goods production.

Beginning in the 1960s, however, ISI started to come under increasing criticism. Government incentives for manufacturing benefited industry at the expense of agriculture — increasing rural-to-urban migration and often worsening income distribution — and produced many distortions and inefficiencies in the economy. The later stages of ISI, which focused on intermediate and capital goods production and were often more dependent on technology and economies of scale in production, also had the paradoxical effect of increasing national dependence on foreign firms and capital. Yet despite these criticisms, virtually all countries that have industrialized successfully have also adopted ISI for at least a brief period. While many economists argue that success occurs in spite of trade protection and government policies of industrial promotion, historical experience suggests that some degree of import substitution may be a necessary prerequisite for economic development.

In the 1980s, ISI generally gave way to policies of export-led growth. Many developing countries came to recognize the economic inefficiencies introduced by protectionist policies. The debt crisis of the early 1980s and the subsequent decline in new foreign lending increased the importance of exports as a means of earning foreign exchange. Rapid technological changes made "self-reliance" less attractive. There were also important political pressures to abandon ISI. The World Bank and International Monetary Fund (IMF), important sources of capital for developing countries, pressed vigorously for more liberal international economic policies. Proclaiming the "magic of the marketplace," the United States also pushed for more liberal economic policies in the developing world.

Particularly important in reorienting development policy was the success of the newly industrializing countries (NICs) of East Asia: South Korea, Taiwan, Hong Kong, and Singapore. All these states achieved impressive rates of economic growth and industrialization through strategies of aggressive export promotion. While they all adopted ISI during their initial stages of development, the NICs generally sought to work with, rather than against, international market forces. With well-educated labor forces but limited raw materials, the NICs exploited their comparative advantage in light manufactures and, over time, diversified into more capital-intensive production. Today, the NICs are among the most rapidly growing countries in the world, and they have achieved this result with relatively egalitarian income distributions.

The sources of this success remain controversial. Some analysts, especially neoclassical economists, point to the market-oriented policies of the NICs. This view is represented in the article by Joseph E. Stiglitz and Lyn Squire, two prominent officials of the World Bank (Reading 25). Others argue, however, that unique domestic political factors were important prerequisites for successful policies of export-led growth — in particular, weak labor movements and leftist parties; strong, developmentally oriented bureaucracies; and, to varying degrees, authoritarian political regimes. These conditions, it is averred, facilitated market-oriented policies that are not feasible politically in other circumstances. Relatedly, critics of export-led growth have suggested that the success enjoyed by the NICs cannot be repeated. The number of countries that can, at any moment in time, specialize profitably in labor-intensive manufacturing is limited, and the industrial states have consistently protected their domestic markets when threatened with "too much" competition from the NICs, thus creating a barrier to further upward movements in the international division of labor. As a result, they argue, the path blazed by the NICs is no longer open to other developing countries. This critical perspective is developed in the essay by Robin Broad, John Cavanagh, and Walden Bello (Reading 26).

Macroeconomic policy in developing countries is central to both perspectives on development. For proponents of export-led growth, successful stabilization policies are a cornerstone of economic advancement; high inflation and rapidly changing fiscal and monetary policies undermine incentives for private investment. For skeptics, such policies are merely an artifact of underlying political factors; the same conditions that allow export-led growth also facilitate stable macroeconomic policies. The problems and politics of inflation and stabilization are addressed by Stephan Haggard (Reading 28).

The former centrally planned economies — most notably the former Soviet Union and its allies in Eastern and Central Europe, and China — are something of a special case in the political economy of development. With the collapse of communist rule in Eastern Europe and the former Soviet Union and with rapid economic reforms in China and Vietnam, the former "socialist bloc" has ceased to represent a recognizable and distinct economic order. Almost all its members have abandoned central planning, state ownership of productive assets, and economic insularity and have sought to join the liberal international economy; most have moved to join the IMF and the WTO. However, these attempts have had varying success.

Most of the former centrally planned economies have gone in one of two directions. Some of the more advanced nations, especially in Central Europe and the Baltic, have been very successful at turning toward the market. They are on-track for membership in the European Union at some point in the next twenty years and, more generally, appear to be converging on existing European economic and political patterns. The Czech Republic and Slovenia, for example, are probably most usefully compared to Portugal or Greece for the purposes of political economy. They have largely eliminated the vestiges of central planning, and the problems they face today are similar to those faced by other relatively poor industrial nations — especially those of determining how to move into the ranks of the most developed states.

Most of the other former centrally planned economies, however, look quite different from the rapidly advancing nations of Central Europe. This group includes most of the former Soviet Union, China, Vietnam, and the Balkans. This group possesses one or two characteristics, and sometimes both. First, the societies in question started at a relatively low level of socioeconomic development, and second, the transition from central planning to the market has been less successful. China and Vietnam suffer from the first problem, which is a starting point of general underdevelopment; Russia and Ukraine are especially plagued by the second problem — a troubled transition; and Central Asia and the Balkans have both problems.

It is not too much of an exaggeration to say that by now, these formerly socialist economies have simply joined the ranks of the so-called developing world. To be sure, they continue to have some features that differentiate them from the other less developed countries (LDCs), but their problems are very similar to those of other nations in Africa, Asia, and Latin America. While many achieved high rates of industrialization under communist rule, their economies are not competitive in current international markets; indeed, the system of centralized planning and intrabloc trade that arose under the old regimes can be understood as an extreme case of ISI, with all the problems that strategy entails. In addition, state ownership of most of the productive assets and the absence of effective internal markets created further economic distortions. Today, the former centrally planned economies must compete with other developing countries on international markets, even as they attempt to put their economies on sounder foundations.

The difficult process of political and economic reform that both the developing and the former communist states have undertaken is virtually unprecedented. This is especially true for the countries moving away from central planning. While similar to Western Europe's transition from mercantilism to liberalism in the eighteenth and, especially, nineteenth centuries (see Kindleberger, Reading 5), the jump from a command to a market economy is farther, and states have attempted to traverse this chasm more quickly than ever before. This transition, and the problem of development more generally, raises questions central to the study of international political economy. How, and under what circumstances, should countries seek to integrate themselves into the international market? How can the international economy be structured so as to fulfill the needs of separate nation-states? How does the international economy affect politics within states?

An examination of the historical and contemporary international political economy can shed important light on these questions and produce essential insights into the future of the economies in development and transition. Nonetheless, the final outcome of this process will not be known for many years and depends fundamentally on the weight of decades of past developments. As Karl Marx wrote in 1852: "Men make their own history, but they do not make it just as they please; they do not make it under circumstances chosen by themselves, but under circumstances directly encountered, given and transmitted from the past."[2]

NOTES

1. These figures are from United Nations Development Programme (UNDP), *Human Development Report 1992* (New York: Oxford University Press, 1992), pp. 35, 141; and UNDP, *Human Development Report 1998* (New York: Oxford University Press, 1998), pp. 2, 29–30, 206.

2. Karl Marx, *The Eighteenth Brumaire of Louis Napoleon,* 1852.

25

International Development: Is It Possible?

JOSEPH E. STIGLITZ AND LYN SQUIRE

The economic growth patterns of developing countries have varied widely since 1970. There have been some impressive success
stories, as well as some depressing failures. Government policies,
too, have varied widely among developing nations. According to
World Bank economists Joseph Stiglitz and Lyn Squire, experience demonstrates that certain government policies have proven
more conducive than others to successful growth and development. Especially important, they argue, are government credibility, an orientation toward the market, and the effective provision
of essential public goods and services. While many questions
remain, they believe that the essential components of developmental success are relatively well known.

Is development possible? Yes. Despite continuing concerns arising from the currency crisis in East Asia, the evidence of the last 25 years is unequivocal: the
developing world has made dramatic advances on many fronts. Two examples
illustrate this progress. One benefit of being born in the developing world in 1995
rather than 1970 is 10 years of extra life. Another is that per capita annual incomes
are 50 percent higher. Thus, even with conservative assumptions about future
growth, someone born in 1995 can expect to enjoy four times the lifetime income
of someone born in 1970.

Of course, averages for the entire developing world hide marked regional differences. Per capita annual income in sub-Saharan Africa actually fell during the
25 years following 1970. . . . In contrast, the people of East Asia saw theirs rocket,
with an increase of almost 400 percent. These huge differences support the claim
that development — indeed, rapid development — is possible. They also show
that growth does not simply occur with the passage of time.

Many of the grand theories of development originated in the 1950s and 1960s,
when information about the development process was scarce. We now know more
about the mechanics of development, by which we mean the broad relationships
between growth, inequality, and poverty, and the relationship between these economic variables and other dimensions of development such as life expectancy and
literacy. We are also in a better position to identify key policy lessons by analyzing
the broad strategies and policies that lie behind recent success stories. Finally, we

can identify the remaining gaps in knowledge that reflect the need to seek deeper insights into three areas: particular markets, especially complex and critical ones such as the financial market; particular policies such as an industrial policy that favors one sector over another — an idea that remains controversial; and particular issues such as pollution.

THE MECHANICS OF DEVELOPMENT

Almost everyone agrees that development cannot be equated solely with reductionist economic measures such as GDP. Nevertheless, higher output and hence higher incomes are important because they expand the choices available to individuals, families, and societies. Where higher incomes are used for military aggression, the enrichment of a small ruling class, or the oppression of the population at large, growth is clearly seen as socially harmful. Strategies that exhibit these characteristics usually contain the seeds of their own destruction — witness recent events in Congo. But where parents choose to use higher incomes to clothe their children and improve their nutrition, or governments use higher revenues to provide primary health-care and expand educational opportunities, most observers acknowledge the social value of economic growth — witness Chile. The fact of the matter is that the record of the last quarter century demonstrates two points: Aggregate economic growth benefits most of the people most of the time; and it is usually associated with progress in other, social dimensions of development.

Growth, Inequality, and the Poor

One of the most famous propositions in development economics, the Kuznets Hypothesis — named after Simon Kuznets, the 1971 Nobel Prize laureate in economics — claimed that in the early stages of development, increases in income would be associated with increases in inequality. Although it was based on just a few observations of three industrialized countries (West Germany, Great Britain, and the United States), the hypothesis attracted much attention and led to concerns that growth in GDP might actually impoverish the poor. Related work — for example, Arthur Lewis' model of a dual economy, in which growth in a small modern sector was gradually supposed to help lift a larger traditional sector — provided a theoretical underpinning for the view that growth could take a long time to "trickle down" to the poor. Worse yet, models by Nicholas Kaldor and others concluded that high inequality was not just a consequence of development but a necessary condition. Savings adequate to finance the investment necessary to generate rapid growth would only be forthcoming if a small part of the population controlled a large part of national income.

None of these views is consistent with the evidence now available:

- We now know that aggregate growth usually benefits the poor. Indonesia is a classic case where GDP per capita increased by more than 170 percent in only 20 years (between 1975 and 1995), and the share of the population in poverty declined from 64 to 11 percent — a dramatic reduction in less than a generation. A recent compilation of cross-country evidence confirms the point. In 88 decade-long spells of growth drawn from across the world, the poorest fifth of the population benefited in 77 of the cases.

- We also know why growth benefits the poor. Changes in inequality are modest and not systematically related to growth as the early theorists suggested. Thus, for the same 88 growth spells, inequality worsened in about half the cases and improved in the other half, but in most cases the changes were small. Consequently, even when inequality worsened, the beneficial impact of overall growth usually dominated. As a crude rule of thumb, per capita growth in excess of 2 percent almost invariably benefits the poor.
- Finally, we know that egalitarian societies can generate high levels of saving and investment. Indeed, some of the most successful economies in East Asia — Indonesia and Japan, for example — had relatively low levels of inequality but generated high savings and investment rates and, until recently, enjoyed rapid growth for more than 25 years.

Growth and Other Dimensions of Well-Being

In the 1970s, a different set of concerns arose regarding the "quality" of development. Growth, it was argued, need not translate into improvements in nonincome measures of well-being such as life expectancy and literacy; in fact, even low-income countries could achieve substantial progress on these fronts. Thus, it was claimed, growth in income was neither sufficient nor necessary for improvements in nonincome measures of development. Well-known examples provide support for this view: Today, less than one-quarter of females are literate in Pakistan, despite a growth rate of almost 6 percent between 1975 and 1990. And although Sri Lanka had a modest GNP per capita of only $280, by 1980 it had achieved one of the highest life expectancies — 68 years — in the developing world. This way of thinking led to a call for approaches that played down the role of growth and emphasized the direct provision of "basic needs" to the poor.

The evidence shows that although there is no automatic link between income and other measures of development, there is a strong association. Using the World Bank classification of countries, low-income countries have a life expectancy of 63 years and an adult literacy rate of 66 percent. The corresponding figures for middle-income countries are 68 years and 82 percent, and for high-income countries 77 years and over 95 percent. Moreover, and more important, countries such as South Korea have made progress on both income and nonincome measures of development. Indeed, the two are complementary and mutually reinforcing: "Investment" in people stimulates growth, which in turn provides the resources for people-focused investment. In the two examples cited above, Sri Lanka has not seen a return — in terms of income growth — from its investment in human capital, and Pakistan has chosen not to translate its income growth into improvements in literacy and life expectancy.

WHAT HAVE WE LEARNED?

If we accept that aggregate economic growth benefits most people most of the time and provides the means to achieve many of society's goals, then we should question how some countries have managed to grow much more quickly than others. An obvious answer is that countries that invest more will grow faster. This answer is only partially correct. Both East Asia and the former Soviet Union have achieved high rates of investment, but only East Asia has managed to translate this into increasing levels of income. Although investment may be necessary for growth, it is not sufficient.

What caused the difference in these outcomes? In an almost tautological sense, the answer is that in one case funds were invested at far higher returns than in the other. The question is why. The clear, negative lesson from this comparison and other evidence is that highly centralized state planning has failed as a development strategy. Indeed, it led to many well-known failures and not just in the communist countries. Early development theorists and practitioners, especially in the former colonies, embraced a strategy of heavy state involvement in industrialization, in particular, and the economy, in general. In Tanzania in the 1980s, subsidies to state-owned enterprises were one and a half times public spending on health. State planners cannot process the information required to make millions of decisions involved in producing and distributing goods and services. The market may not be perfect in dealing with all informational requirements, but it has clearly demonstrated its superiority over central planning.

The alternative to state-directed investment is greater reliance on the decentralized decisions of private entrepreneurs through the marketplace. The positive message emerging from the experience of the successful East Asian countries is that we now know the broad package of policies that lead to high rates of private investment and enhance the likelihood that investment is well used. The empirical evidence is, in fact, nothing more than a corroboration of common sense. Three conditions are critical: a stable and credible policy environment, an open and competitive economy, and a focused public sector.

Credibility

Entrepreneurs will not invest in countries where the policy regime is unstable — investors require a degree of certainty. Countries that do not manage the fundamentals of macroeconomic policy well will inevitably become unstable. Thus, basic fiscal and monetary discipline, including a properly managed exchange rate, helps establish the credibility of economic policy that gives entrepreneurs the confidence to invest. Two statistics illustrate the point: Almost 40 percent of Africa's wealth is held abroad, evidence that, in this case, investing overseas is safer and more profitable than investing at home. Worldwide, 80 percent of total foreign direct investment has gone to just 12 developing countries in the period 1990–95, countries that, at least until recently, have been well managed and highly stable.

Credibility is also served by a transparent and effective legal and judicial system. If there is no accepted recourse in the event of failure to honor a contract, business relationships will remain confined to family members and close acquaintances, resulting in lower levels of investment and less efficient allocation. A recent study, prepared for the International Finance Corporation, compares the quantitative impact of various sources of uncertainty on investment in 58 countries for the period 1974–89. It finds that high levels of corruption, volatility in real exchange rate distortions, and a lack of rule of law are the most detrimental to investment. One example from the study shows that if the level of corruption in Nigeria could be reduced to that prevailing in Hong Kong, Nigeria's yearly investment rate would increase by more than five percentage points, which, given the right policies, could increase the country's growth rate by as much as one percentage point.

Competition

Entrepreneurs are interested in making profits. If market circumstances (absence of competition either from domestic or foreign sources) allow them to benefit at the expense of consumers, they will do so. In the 1950s and 1960s, many development experts, especially Latin American scholars such as Raúl Prebisch, thought that industrialization could only be achieved if domestic manufacturing was protected from foreign competition while it grew from infancy to maturity. Given the small size of Latin American domestic markets, this strategy of import substitution often resulted in monopoly profits for those lucky or persuasive enough to capture the rights to produce.

We now know that competition is a powerful force for ensuring that investment is well directed and yields the greatest possible benefits. Competition among domestic producers helps, but for many countries domestic markets may not be large enough to support many firms, so competition with foreign producers is also important. On almost any measure of openness — share of trade in GDP or average levels of tariffs — the successful East Asian countries have been much more open than the slow-growing economies of Latin America, South Asia, and sub-Saharan Africa. But openness — trade and foreign investment liberalization — is not enough to ensure a competitive economy. In some cases, monopoly importers have used the opportunity of lower tariffs simply to garner higher profits for themselves, with consumers benefiting little.

Openness serves another purpose. Acquiring knowledge and adapting it for local use is generally seen as an important part of the East Asian experience. Not only did the East Asian countries invest a lot and well, they also benefited from closing the "knowledge gap." True, it is difficult to establish empirically how much of growth is due to new technology, because measurement of the contributions of other factors — physical and human capital — is subject to a host of problems, and because new technology itself provides the impetus for additional investment. But fortunately, the best mechanisms for closing the knowledge gap — competing in foreign markets and attracting foreign investment — are encouraged by the same policies of openness mentioned above. Indeed, the East Asian countries have consistently promoted exports in sharp contrast to the strategy of import substitution pursued by many other countries. This strategy, combined with limited domestic competition, impeded both efficiency and the transfer of advances in global technology that are so critical to the emergence of a modern industrial sector.

Public Sector Focus

The failure of extensive state production of goods and services in the former Soviet Union and elsewhere, and the success of private investment in East Asia, provide a clear message for the public sector: It should focus its efforts on those areas where the private sector fails. Macroeconomic policy is one example where government involvement is pivotal. Stable macroeconomic policy has been a key ingredient of past East Asian success. Defense, redistribution, the legal and judicial system, regulation of financial markets, and protection of the environment are all areas in which the public sector has to play the central role.

The public sector has also traditionally been a supplier of goods and services in such areas as health, education, infrastructure, power, water, and telecommunications. Each of these sectors has characteristics that have led to public provision. Some — telecommunications, for example — were regarded as natural monopolies; others — health and education — were thought to generate social benefits that the private sector would not be interested in supplying. Indeed, public provision of these services has been a critical aspect of East Asia's success. For example, thanks to almost universal public education at the primary level, more than 95 percent of the population was literate in South Korea in 1995.

But the principle of focus also applies to telecommunications, power, and even education and health. Recent experience suggests that private provision of these goods and services may be feasible and in some instances desirable. Where one draws the line, however, remains an open question when social objectives are not fully reflected in market prices.

LESSONS FOR THE FUTURE

We have learned much in the last 25 years about the mechanics of development and about the broad strategies and policies that support rapid and equitable growth. But there is still more to learn about the particulars of development. We need a much deeper understanding of how certain key markets function; why some policies work in some situations and not in others; and how to deal with new issues generated by the process of development.

Markets

The failure of state enterprises and the success of market economies have led to strong efforts to privatize and liberalize markets. But sometimes these efforts are motivated more by ideology than economic analysis and may proceed too far, too fast. When that happens, the economy may suffer. Privatizing a natural monopoly before an effective regulatory framework is in place may lead to higher, not lower, prices and may establish a vested interest resistant to regulations that encourage competition. Striking the right balance between unfettered markets and state regulation is difficult and requires a thorough understanding of how markets work. Nowhere has this become more apparent than in the current crisis in East Asian financial markets.

Financial markets are key to the success of a market economy, yet in virtually every successful economy, financial markets remain highly regulated. Regulations are required to ensure fair competition, protect consumers, provide for the safety and soundness of financial institutions, and ensure that underserved groups have access to capital. Attempts at unregulated or weakly regulated banking systems in Chile, Indonesia, Thailand, and Venezuela have universally ended in disaster. Investors lose confidence in insufficiently regulated capital markets that fail to serve their roles in raising capital and spreading risk. Thus, Thailand's relaxation of restrictions on lending to the real estate sector in the early 1990s contributed to overextension and to the current collapse of not only the Thai market but of other markets in East Asia as well.

Interpreting this evidence requires an understanding of the critical ways in which financial markets differ from other markets. There are substantial informational requirements arising from the fact that what is exchanged is money today for a promise to pay tomorrow, a promise which may or may not be fulfilled. Bank management may choose a risky asset portfolio because they benefit from high profits if the gamble succeeds, but their depositors or insurers bear the costs if the gamble fails. Liberalization exacerbates this situation because it increases competition, erodes profits, and reduces franchise values, thereby reducing incentives to make good loans.

Thus, both evidence and theory suggest that mild financial restraint, which increases the franchise value of banks, will lead to better risk decisions and a more stable financial system. But identifying the best location on the continuum between highly regulated and completely free is difficult. A better understanding of the specifics of individual financial markets is required before moving too quickly down the path of liberalization.

Policies

Understanding which policies work is complicated by the significant role that implementation plays in their success or failure. For example, industrial policy — the provision of special incentives to particular industries or firms — has been an unquestionable failure in Latin America, South Asia, and sub-Saharan Africa. It has led to inefficient manufacturing as well as the establishment of vested interests sufficiently powerful to prevent the abandonment of these policies once introduced. Not so in East Asia: There, industrial policies led to a rapidly growing and competitive industrial sector. Indeed, some of the most successful steel mills and shipyards anywhere in the world were established in East Asia as government enterprises.

The close links that developed between key ministries and major industries as part of East Asia's industrial policy were seen as a way to overcome difficult problems of coordination. Moreover, where the incentives failed to achieve the desired outcomes, East Asian countries, especially Japan and South Korea, had the capacity to withdraw them.

The close collaboration between government and business inevitably risked collusion and corruption. While there were always allegations, the economic benefits, as evidenced by rapid growth, seemed to outweigh the problems. Although the current financial crisis in East Asia is often attributed to this "cronyism" (witness the allegations in Indonesia), the real source seems to lie elsewhere — real estate lending in Thailand and high indebtedness in Korea, for example. While government intervention cannot be blamed for the former — if there is blame, it is insufficient regulation and misguided foreign exchange policies — questions have been raised about the extent to which high debt-equity ratios in the Korean chaebol were a result of government pressure on banks.

Industrial policy offers one of the clearest examples of how implementation can be as important as the policy itself. But the point extends well beyond industrial policy. Understanding the structure of incentives that govern the implementation of public policy, the delivery of public services, and public management in general will be key to future development.

Unresolved Issues

The successes of East Asia over the past three decades are not a house of cards, no matter what critics may say in the midst of the current currency turmoil. However, the East Asian experience raises four sets of issues:

- To what extent are its lessons replicable? How can we achieve comparable levels of savings elsewhere? How can we ensure that such high levels of savings can be well invested? How do we close the knowledge gap with such rapidity? How do we minimize the potential for collusion and corruption that seems endemic in the collaboration between government and business, which is sometimes described as the hallmark of the success of East Asia?
- To what extent are the lessons drawn from East Asia's "miracle" relevant to the globalized economy of the twenty-first century? Do the problems these countries face today reflect a fundamental flaw in their strategy to deal with the demands of globalized capital markets, or do they arise from a too rapid departure from the principles of sound economic management that had long contributed to their success?
- While the East Asian countries addressed major lacunae of earlier development efforts — in particular, they succeeded in achieving equitable growth — their environmental record has been less than stellar. Some of the major cities in East Asia have severe levels of urban pollution that are much higher than those found elsewhere and sufficient to cause serious health problems. . . . Massive forest fires in Indonesia not only present a health hazard but have taken a major toll on the country's natural resource base. What are

the strategies that are most effective in achieving sustainable development — development that protects the environment as it raises living standards?

• By the same token, can we combine rapid growth with a more rapid transition to democracy? Moreover, how can we construct more effective governments that feature greater transparency and less corruption? South Korea seemed to have made a successful transition to democratic government; were it not for the currency turmoil, South Korea's peaceful change of government with the election of President Kim Dae Jung in December 1997 would have been hailed as a major victory. But citizens in these countries had to wait for decades to achieve democracy. And as recent government revelations about South Korea's economic travails show, only now is it beginning to embrace the standards of openness and transparency necessary for a healthy political and economic system.

HOW FAR HAVE WE COME?

There has been considerable progress in our knowledge and understanding of development. Some of the grand debates of the past have been resolved. In particular, the evidence reveals that growth in national income can ultimately benefit all members of society and is strongly associated with progress on many other measures of well-being, including health, nutrition, and education. The great experiment with central planning has decidedly failed. Markets are not perfect and cannot be left completely uncontrolled, but they are an essential ingredient of a modern economy.

We have broadened the development agenda to include democratic, equitable, sustainable development that raises living standards on a broad basis, and we have brought to bear a wider set of instruments — not just sound macroeconomic policies and trade liberalization, but also strong financial markets, enhanced competition, and improved public services. There have been major advances in our understanding of development.

But some words of caution seem in order. Simple ideologies will not suffice; indeed, they are likely to be dangerous. Neither of the extremes advocated — state-run development or unfettered markets — will likely lead to success. Developing nations must aim for a balance, with governments and markets working together as partners. The solutions to Latin America's macroeconomic crises, characterized by high inflation, large public deficits, and high levels of public indebtedness, may not work in East Asia, with its low inflation, low public deficits (or actual surpluses) and, at least in some cases, low public indebtedness. Where Mexico and other Latin American and African countries faced a crisis in public debt, East Asia's crisis was primarily a problem of private indebtedness.

The need to tailor our thinking about development strategies and our policy recommendations to the distinctive problems of each country, coupled with the continuing evolution of the global economy, requires that we keep learning and adapting our views. Otherwise, yesterday's truths may well become tomorrow's mistakes.

26

Development:
The Market Is Not Enough

ROBIN BROAD,
JOHN CAVANAGH, AND
WALDEN BELLO

This essay challenges the viability of development models based on free-market principles. The authors argue that the newly industrializing countries of East Asia are not models of successful development, as evidenced by their recent labor unrest and ecological destruction; that the socialist command economies' failure was not due primarily to their eschewal of market mechanisms; and that policies of "structural adjustment" have not set the stage for sustained development in the 1990s. Instead, the authors advocate development strategies that promote broadly representative government, equitable income distribution, and ecologically sound policies. In their view, such models will better foster environmentally sustainable and equitable growth and enhance political stability and democracy in developing countries.

As the 1990s begin, the development debate has all but disappeared in the West. Monumental changes in Eastern Europe and Latin America are widely interpreted as proof of the superiority of development models that are led by the private sector and oriented toward exports. Free-market capitalism is said to have prevailed because only it promises growth and democracy for the battered economies of Africa, Asia, and Latin America. World Bank President Barber Conable summed up this prevailing view in remarks made in February 1990: "If I were to characterize the past decade, the most remarkable thing was the generation of a global consensus that market forces and economic efficiency were the best way to achieve the kind of growth which is the best antidote to poverty."

Ample evidence exists, however, to suggest caution in the face of triumphalism. Warning signs are surfacing in South Korea and Taiwan, the miracle models of capitalist development. After decades of systematic exploitation, the South Korean labor force erupted in thousands of strikes during the late 1980s, undermining the very basis of that country's export success. Meanwhile, decades of uncontrolled industrial development have left large parts of Taiwan's landscape with poisoned soil and toxic water.

Additional evidence reveals extensive suffering throughout Africa, parts of Asia, and Latin America, where privatized adjustment has been practiced for more than a decade in a world economy of slower growth. As the United Nations Children's Fund noted in its 1990 annual report, "Over the course of the 1980s, average incomes have fallen by 10 per cent in most of Latin America and by over 20 per cent in sub-Saharan Africa. . . . In many urban areas, real minimum wages have declined by as much as 50 per cent." The World Bank estimates that as many as 950 million of the world's 5.2 billion people are "chronically malnourished" — more than twice as many hungry people as a decade ago.

In Latin America, people are talking about a lost decade, even a lost generation. In Rio de Janeiro, the lack of meaningful futures has given birth to a new sport: train surfing. Brazilian street children stand atop trains beside a 3,300 volt cable that sends trains hurtling at speeds of 120 kilometers per hour. During an 18-month period in 1987–88, train surfing in Rio produced some 200 deaths and 500 gruesome injuries. "It's a form of suicide," said the father of a *surfista* who was killed. "Brazilian youth is suffering so much, they see no reason to live."

This generalized failure of development in the 1980s is producing a very different kind of consensus among people the development establishment rarely contacts and whose voices are seldom heard. A new wave of democratic movements across Africa, Asia, and Latin America is demanding another kind of development. Through citizens' organizations millions of environmentalists, farmers, women, and workers are saying they want to define and control their own futures. They are beginning to lay the groundwork for a new type of development in the 1990s — one that emphasizes ecological sustainability, equity, and participation, in addition to raising material living standards.

The false impression that the free-market model has triumphed in development is rooted in three misconceptions about the past decade:

- that the newly industrializing countries (NICs) of East Asia were exceptions to the "lost decade" and continue to represent models of successful development;
- that socialist command economies in Eastern Europe or the developing world failed principally because they did not use market mechanisms;
- that the export-oriented structural adjustment reforms that were put in place in much of the developing world have laid the groundwork for sustained growth in the 1990s.

The NICs did achieve the fastest growth rates among developing countries over the last three decades. But as the Berlin Wall was dismantled, the costs of high-speed, export-oriented industrialization were beginning to catch up with South Korea and Taiwan. The foundations of these supposed miracles of capitalist development were cracking.

In South Korea centralized authoritarian development has created a virtual time bomb. From afar, South Korea's spectacular growth may seem to have justified so-called transitional costs like severe labor repression. But many South

Korean workers feel differently. Taking advantage of a small democratic opening between 1987 and 1989, more than 7,200 labor disputes broke out, compared with only 1,026 from 1981 through 1986. No major industry was spared; over the 1987–88 period the number of unions increased two and a half times. In perhaps the best-known confrontation, 14,000 policemen stormed the Hyundai shipyard in March 1989 to put down a 109-day strike.

The priority of many South Korean workers is not the maintenance of Korea's export competitiveness but rather acquiring what they regard as their overdue share of the fruits from three decades of growth. Indeed, the 45 per cent rise in average Korean wages over the last three years constitutes a central factor behind the erosion of Korea's export competitiveness. As export growth falls, the country is likely to experience its first trade deficit in years in 1990.

While a resentful labor movement threatens South Korea's traditional growth model by demanding greater equity and participation, a powerful environmental movement in Taiwan is challenging the island's fragile social consensus on export-oriented growth. This decentralized multi-class movement comprises consumers, farmers, influential intellectuals, residents of polluted areas, and workers. Although less-publicized than Eastern Europe's environmental devastation, Taiwan's is also severe and results from the same technocratic assumption that "some" environmental damage is the necessary price of economic growth. As it turned out, "some" damage included at least 20 per cent of the country's farmland, now polluted by industrial waste. Dumping of industrial and human waste (only 1 per cent of the latter receives even primary treatment) has been unregulated. Uncontrolled air pollution has also contributed to a quadrupling of asthma cases among Taiwanese children in the last decade.

A growing awareness of these environmental realities has led some Taiwanese to fight back. Citizen actions have halted work on a Dupont chemical plant, shut down an Imperial Chemical Industries petrochemical factory, stopped expansion of the naphtha cracker industry, and prevented construction of a fourth nuclear power plant on the island, thus thwarting the government's plan to build 20 nuclear plants by the end of the century. Large segments of the populations of Korea and Taiwan now reject the path to growth long touted as a model for the Third World. According to one 1985 survey, 59 per cent of Taiwanese favor environmental protection over economic growth.

These points do not mean that South Korea and Taiwan are about to become basket cases. Nor does the argument deny that they experienced periods of economic growth greater than that of most other developing countries. Instead, the evidence demonstrates that both countries can no longer practice a growth strategy based on repression of workers and abuse of the environment. It is now clear that each would have been better off trading some economic growth for more democracy and more ecological sensitivity from the start. Korea and Taiwan hardly serve as exemplary models for development.

While the cracks in the NIC model of development have been largely ignored in the West, the failure of socialism as an agent of development has been overplayed. There is no disputing this model's collapse; one cannot argue with the millions who have taken to the streets across Eastern Europe. Yet an overlay of the NICs experience with that of Eastern Europe suggests a less facile explanation for the failure of socialism than blaming it solely on the suppression of market mechanisms.

During the 1960s in Eastern Europe, the government-led "command" economies achieved growth rates higher than those of the capitalist world, according to a 1984 United Nations Conference on Trade and Development report, while building the infrastructure for further industrial advance. Only the Japanese, who seem less blinded by free-market ideology and more appreciative of the role of a centralized state, have reconciled the two models in a more insightful lesson. . . .

The authoritarian regime in South Korea also achieved spectacular growth rates by practicing command economics. This fact flies in the face of conventional development dogma. Government incentives, subsidies, and coercion fueled the drive for heavy industry in such areas as iron and steel that market forces would have rendered uncompetitive in the early stages. These sectors then built up the infrastructure South Korea needed to become a world-class exporter of such higher value-added goods as cars and VCRs.

South Korea's technocrats enlarged the application of market principles in the early 1980s, whereas the East European economies failed to do so. The South Korean economy's resumption of growth after a brief period of stagnation at the onset of the 1980s and Eastern Europe's slowdown after rapid growth in the 1960s confirm a more complex truth than that purveyed by free-market ideologues: Command economies may propel societies through the first stages of development, but further growth into a more sophisticated economy necessitates a greater role for market mechanisms.

At the same time, there should be no illusions about the adverse consequences of market mechanisms on equity. Both China and Vietnam, for example, have increased agricultural output by freeing market forces. Yet both countries have experienced growing inequalities. While some farmers are getting richer, some consumers are going hungry in the face of rising food prices. Post-1978 economic reforms in China have increased income inequalities in both urban and rural areas.

Other lessons emerge from Eastern Europe and the socialist developing world. While some of these countries did perform redistributive reforms, providing significant health and education services, they, like the NICs, have failed in the realms of ecological sustainability and political participation. Indeed, proponents of the free market fail to address a common demand coming from the citizens of China, Eastern Europe, South Korea, and Taiwan: Free markets are not a panacea; the average citizen must participate in decision making that affects his or her life.

Most developing countries, however, fall neither into the category of the NICs nor into the socialist world. For the development establishment, the lesson drawn from the experience of the NICs and the socialist countries is that developing countries' only hope rests with exporting their way to NIC status through the purgatory of structural adjustment. Dozens of countries across Africa, Asia, and Latin America have been force-fed this harsh prescription.

Supervised by the World Bank and the International Monetary Fund (IMF), these adjustment packages mandate severely cutting government spending to balance budgets, eliminating trade barriers and social subsidies, encouraging exports, tightening money policies, devaluing currencies, and dismantling nationalist barriers to foreign investment.

Part of the West's sense of triumph flows from a feeling that a worldwide consensus has developed about the necessity of these reforms. But many Western development authorities ignore that this "consensus" has been pushed on developing-country governments with a heavy hand. After borrowing sprees in the 1970s most developing countries ran into debt-servicing difficulties in the 1980s. Creditor banks, using the World Bank and IMF as enforcers, conditioned debt rescheduling on acceptance of export-oriented structural adjustment packages. In fact, many least-developed countries (LDCs) faced serious external constraints on export opportunities — from growing protectionism in developed-country markets to increased substitution for raw-material exports.

THE FAILURES OF STRUCTURAL ADJUSTMENT

The strategy urged on the LDCs suffers from other shortcomings as well. Structural adjustment in practice has damaged environments, worsened structural inequities, failed even in the very narrow goal of pulling economies forward, and bypassed popular participation. Now many of the democratic movements expanding across the globe are rejecting the profoundly undemocratic approach of structural adjustment.

Ecological sustainability has been undermined in country after country. In their frenzy to export, countries often resort to the easiest short-term approach: unsustainable exploitation of natural resources. The stories of ecological disasters lurking behind export successes have become common: Timber exporting has denuded mountains, causing soil erosion and drying critical watersheds. Cash crop exports have depended on polluting pesticides and fertilizers. Large fishing boats have destroyed the coral reefs in which fish breed and live. Tailings from mines have polluted rivers and bays.

One example is the production of prawns in the Philippines. Prawns were one of the fastest growing Philippine exports during the 1980s and are heavily promoted throughout Asia by some UN and other development agencies. By 1988, Philippine prawn exports had reached $250 million, ranking them fifth among the country's exports. The government's Department of Trade and Industry is seeking to boost that figure to $1 billion by 1993.

Prawn farming requires a careful mixture of fresh and salt water in coastal ponds. Vast quantities of fresh water are pumped into the ponds and mixed with salt water drawn from the sea. But some rice farmers in the Philippines' biggest prawn area fear that as salt water seeps into their nearby lands, their crop yields will fall as they have in Taiwan. Other farmers complain that not enough fresh water remains for their crops. In one town in the heart of prawn country, the water supply has already dropped 30 per cent: Potable water is being rationed. Like many cash crops, prawns do little to increase equity. Invariably, they make the rich richer and the poor poorer, weakening the prospect for mass participation in development. In one typical Philippine province, the substantial initial investment of approximately $50,000 per hectare limited potential prawn-pond owners to the wealthiest 30 or 40 families, including the province's vice governor, the ex-governor, and several mayors. Moreover, as the wealthy renovated old milkfish ponds into high-tech prawn ponds, the supply of milkfish, a staple of the poor, fell and its price rose.

Structural adjustment hurts the poor in other ways, too. As government spending is reduced, social programs are decimated. One May 1989 World Bank working paper concluded that a byproduct of the "sharply deteriorating social indicators" that accompany contractionary adjustment packages is that "people below the poverty line will probably suffer irreparable damage in health, nutrition, and education." Another World Bank working paper, published in September 1989, on Costa Rica, El Salvador, and Haiti suggested that the concentration of land in the hands of a few, along with population growth, was a major cause of environmental degradation. Skewed land distribution, it argued, pushed marginalized peasants onto fragile ecosystems. However, as the report noted, the adjustment programs in these countries failed to address distributional issues, focusing instead on correcting "distorted prices." In this regard, Taiwan and South Korea offer historical precedents: Their economic success rested on an initial redistribution of the land. Although some recent agricultural policies have been biased against the peasantry, extensive land reforms in the 1950s helped create the internal market that sustained the early stages of industrialization.

The failures of structural adjustment in the areas of environment and equity might appear less serious if the adjustment packages were scoring economic successes. They are not. The first World Bank structural adjustment loans were given to Kenya, the Philippines, and Turkey a decade ago; none can be rated a success story today. A new UN Economic Commission for Africa study has highlighted the World Bank's own findings that after structural adjustment programs, 15 African countries were worse off in a number of economic categories.

None of these examples is meant to deny that developing countries need substantial reforms, that some governments consistently overspend, or that markets have an important role to play. Rather, the lesson of the 1980s teaches that there are no shortcuts to development. Development strategies will not succeed and endure unless they incorporate ecological sustainability, equity, and participation, as well as effectiveness in raising material living standards.

Countries focusing on any of these principles to the exclusion of others will probably fall short in the long run, if they have not already. The World Bank and the IMF, either by ignoring these first three principles in their structural adjustment reforms or, at best, by treating them as afterthoughts, have adjusted economies to the short-term benefit of narrow elite interests. Their fixation on high gross national product growth rates ensures that the costs in terms of people and resources will mount and overwhelm an economy at a later date, much as they have in South Korea and Taiwan.

PEOPLE POWER

While governmental approaches to development are failing across Africa, Asia, and Latin America, development initiatives are flourishing among citizens' organizations. Indeed, a natural relationship exists between the two levels. The failure of governments in development has given birth to many citizens' initiatives.

Popular organizations are taking on ecological destruction, inequitable control over resources and land, and governments' inability to advance the quality of life. And often the people are struggling in the face of government and military repression. Many citizens' groups are pushing for a central role in development — a concept they do not measure solely in terms of economic growth. At the core of almost all these movements lies an emphasis on participation of members in initiating and implementing plans, and in exercising control over their own lives. Hence, democracy becomes the central theme.

In the Philippines some 5 million people participate in citizens' groups. Alan Durning of the Worldwatch Institute estimated in the Fall 1989 issue of *Foreign Policy* that across the developing world more than 100 million people belong to hundreds of thousands of these organizations. Official development organizations have difficulty taking these groups seriously and to date act as though they have little bearing on national development strategies. Our research suggests the opposite: The programs and experience of these grassroots groups will form the basis for new development strategies of the 1990s.

During the past decade, many of the most vibrant organizations have been born in battles over the destruction of natural resources. The Philippines clearly illustrates this phenomenon as various citizens' groups raise ecological issues as a key measure of sustainable development. By some estimates, the destruction of forests and other natural resources in the Philippines has been among the most rapid in the world. The Philippines loses more than 140,000 hectares of forest a year, leaving only 22 per cent of the country covered with trees — versus the 54 per cent estimated as necessary for a stable ecosystem in that country.

But out of the Philippines' devastation dozens of environmental groups have sprung up, with farming and fishing communities at their core. The largest and most influential is *Haribon* (from the Filipino words "king of birds," a reference to the endangered Philippine eagle). *Haribon* matured in a battle to save Palawan, an island that contains the country's most extensive tropical rain forests. A local citizens' group evolved into a *Haribon* chapter and took on the wealthy logger whose forest concessions control 61 per cent of Palawan's productive forests. Among other strategies, *Haribon* launched a nationwide campaign to gather a million signatures to save Palawan's forest. In 1989 *Haribon* also joined with other Philippine organizations (more than 500 by April 1990) to launch a "Green Forum" that is defining what equitable and sustainable development would involve at both the project and national levels.

By the end of the 1980s, the thousands of organizations across the developing world were campaigning against timber companies, unsustainable agriculture, industrial pollution, nuclear power plants, and the giant projects that many governments equate with development. In 1989, 60,000 tribal people, landless laborers, and peasants gathered in a small town in India to protest a series of dams in the Narmada Valley to which the World Bank has committed $450 million. On the other side of the world, Brazilian Indians from 40 tribal nations gathered that year to oppose construction of several hydroelectric dams planned for the Xingu River. Soon thereafter, Indians, rubber tappers, nut gatherers, and river people formed the Alliance of the Peoples of the Forest to save the Amazon.

In struggles over the control of resources, many also have ended up challenging powerful entrenched interests and inequitable structures. It is in this context that the president of *Haribon,* Maximo Kalaw, summed up the struggle over Philippine forest resources: "In the past fifteen years we have had only 470 logging concessionaires who own all the resources of the forests. The process created poverty for 17 million people around the forest areas."

In addition to ecology and equity, people's organizations have acted on the inability of governments to meet the most basic human needs and rights outlined in the UN's International Covenant on Economic, Social and Cultural Rights: the rights to "adequate food, clothing and housing." All over the world, informal economic institutions have sprung up to fill the economic void left by cuts in government spending. Development analysts Sheldon Annis and Peter Hakim have filled a book, *Direct to the Poor* (1988), with examples of successful worker-owned businesses, transportation collectives, peasant leagues, micro-enterprise credit associations, and other citizen initiatives across Latin America. Africa specialist Fantu Cheru, in his 1989 book *The Silent Revolution in Africa,* refers to such groups in Africa as participants in a "silent revolution."

Will this decade see coalitions of citizens' organizations drawing on mass participation create governments with sustainable development agendas in Brazil, the Philippines, South Africa, and elsewhere — much as they ushered new governments into Eastern Europe in 1989? Even where citizens' coalitions do not take over the reins of state power, will these new, innovative groups be able to build links to segments of bureaucracies and even militaries that express openness to the sustainable development agenda?

Our research has uncovered positive signs in many countries. But a caveat is important: In order to gauge the success of these initiatives, one must shift away from exclusive interest in aggregate growth figures toward the more meaningful indicators of ecological sustainability, participation, equity, and quality of life for the poorer majority.

Beyond the sheer number of citizen initiatives that advance these indicators, a further measure of success revolves around the ability of local groups to form countrywide associations that address national issues. Over the past half-decade in the Philippines, for example, a coalition of dozens of peasant organizations representing 1.5 million members has gathered tens of thousands of signatures for a comprehensive and technically feasible national "People's Agrarian Reform Code." The code could become the centerpiece of a national development strategy in this predominantly agrarian country that suffers from an awful land-tenure situation. The Philippine land distribution problem is also seen in the loophole- and scandal-ridden 1988 land-reform bill passed by President Corazon Aquino's Congress. According to land-reform expert Roy Prosterman, it is "likely to redistribute barely 1 per cent of the Philippines' cultivated land." By contrast, the peasant groups' code would cover all lands, abolish rampant absentee landownership, and offer support services to peasants acquiring land.

As the peasant supporters of the People's Agrarian Reform Code lobby Congress for passage of their code, they are simultaneously taking steps to implement portions of the desperately needed reform on their own. A 1989 report documented

14 representative cases around the country: actions by thousands of poor families to occupy 800 hectares of idle or abandoned lands, the seizure of idle fishponds, boycott of rent payments on land, spread of organic farming techniques, revival of traditional rice varieties, and the reforestation of mangroves in coastal areas. In other African, Asian, and Latin American countries, coalitions of peasants, workers, women, and small entrepreneurs are banding together to craft policy alternatives.

Ultimately, the greatest successes in sustainable development will come when citizens' groups seat their representatives in government. Governments that are more representative can help transform sustainable development initiatives into reality. Such governments can help build up an economic infrastructure and an internal market, create a network of social services, and set rules for a country's integration into the world economy. These three tenets do not represent another universal model to replace those of free marketeers, Marxist-Leninists, or the World Bank; the past four decades are littered with the failures of universal models. However, the outlines of a more positive government role in development can be sketched using the principles of ecological sustainability, equity, participation, and effectiveness.

South Korea and Taiwan offer positive lessons for the ideal governmental role in the economy. The main lesson is not that the government should be taken out of the economy. Instead, the NICs' experiences suggest that success depends on governments standing above vested interests to help create the social and political infrastructure for economic growth. Indeed, though it may sound paradoxical, one needs an effective government to create the market.

The problem in many developing countries is not too much government, but a government that is too tangled in the web of narrow interest groups. The Philippine government, for example, serves as the private preserve of special economic interests. In South Korea, on the other hand, the weakness of the landed and business elite allowed the government to set the direction for development in the 1960s and 1970s. Without an assertive government that often acted against the wishes of international agencies and big business, South Korea would never have gained the foundation of heavy and high-technology industries that enabled it to become a world-class exporter of high value-added commodities.

Placing governments above the control of economic interest groups presents no easy task in countries where a small number of powerful families control much of the land and resources. To increase the chances of success, strong citizens' groups must put their representatives in government, continue to closely monitor government actions, and press for redistributive reforms that weaken the power of special interests.

While independent governments can help push economies through the early stages of development, progress to more mature economies seems to require more market mechanisms to achieve effective production and distribution. For market mechanisms to work, however, there must first be a market. And for the majority of the developing world, creating a market with consumers possessing effective demand requires eliminating the severe inequalities that depress the purchasing power of workers and peasants. The "how to" list necessitates such steps as land reform, progressive taxation, and advancement of workers' rights.

Pragmatism is also essential for the integration of developing countries into the world economy. The choice facing these countries should not be viewed as an ideological one between import substitution and export-oriented growth, neither of which alone has generated sustainable development. Basing development on exports that prove to be ecologically damaging not only ignores sustainability, it fails to ask the more fundamental question of whom development should benefit. But building an export base on top of a strong internal market does make sense. In this scheme, foreign exchange receipts would shift from primary commodities to processed commodities, manufactures, and environmentally sensitive tourism. China, India, South Korea, and Taiwan all based their early industrial development on slowly raising the real incomes of their domestic populations. Each opened up to varying degrees to the world market and to foreign capital only after substantial domestic markets had been developed and nurtured.

Concerted citizen action can bring about more participatory, equitable, and ecologically sustainable development. At least one historical precedent can be cited, albeit on a subnational level: the postwar experience of Kerala, traditionally one of India's poorest states. With a population of 27 million, Kerala has more people than most developing countries. A long history of large movements by people of the lower castes culminated in the election of progressive state governments beginning in 1957. Constant pressure by India's most active agricultural labor unions and other peasant organizations forced these governments to abolish tenancy in what was one of the most sweeping agrarian reforms in South and Southeast Asia and place a high priority on health and literacy. In periods when conservative governments were voted into power in Kerala, the nongovernmental citizens' organizations remained strong enough to win reforms and ensure enforcement of existing laws. Today, despite income levels below the Indian average, Kerala boasts the highest life expectancy and literacy rates among Indian states, as well as the lowest infant mortality and birth rates.

Kerala also highlights an important caveat: New, more accountable governments should not be seen as a panacea. Even popular governments cannot provide the answer to the wide array of development problems. No matter who wields state power, strong independent citizens' groups will continue to be central to sustainable development. Perhaps South Korea and Taiwan would be more successful societies if they had combined their early land reforms and thoughtful state intervention with a prolonged commitment to ecology, equity, and participation.

Democratic participation in the formulation and implementation of development plans forms the central factor in determining their medium- and long-term viability. This, however, is a controversial premise. Indeed, such a pronounced emphasis on democracy flies in the face of political scientist Samuel Huntington's claim in the 1960s that order must precede democracy in the early stages of development. Many still believe authoritarian governments in Eastern Europe, South Korea, and Taiwan served as the catalysts for industrialization that in turn created the conditions for advancing democracy.

Experiences of the last two decades suggest otherwise. Africa, home to dozens of one-party authoritarian states, remains a development disaster. Argentina, Brazil, the Philippines, and other Asian and Latin American countries ruled by authoritarian governments have suffered similar fates. As political scientist Atul

Kohli has documented, the economies of the relatively democratic regimes in Costa Rica, India, Malaysia, Sri Lanka, and Venezuela have "grown at moderate but steady rates" since the 1960s and income inequalities have "either remained stable or even narrowed."

Moreover, in South Korea and Taiwan, authoritarian characteristics of the government were not responsible for industrialization and growth. Far-reaching land reforms and each state's ability to rise above factions in civil society deserve credit for sparking growth. The only "positive" growth impact of repression by these governments was to hold down wage levels, thereby making exports more competitive. Yet heavy dependence on exports no longer serves as an option in today's increasingly protectionist global markets. The percentage of imports into the major developed countries that were affected by nontariff barriers to trade rose more than 20 per cent during the 1980s, a trend that is likely to continue. In this hostile global economic climate, respect for workers' rights can lead to the creation of local markets by increasing domestic buying power. Democratic development therefore implies shifting emphasis from foreign to domestic (or, for small countries, to regional) markets. This shift meets more needs of local people and takes into account the difficult world market of the 1980s and 1990s.

The portrait painted at the outset — of a global development crisis masked by triumphant Western development orthodoxy — was a decidedly gloomy one. Why then should citizens' movements pushing for more equitable, sustainable, and participatory development stand a chance in the 1990s? Much of the answer lies in the extraordinary possibilities of the current historical moment.

DEVELOPMENT AFTER THE COLD WAR

For four decades, the Cold War has steered almost all development discussions toward ideological arguments over capitalism versus communism, market versus planning. It has also diverted public attention away from nonideological global concerns (such as environment, health, and economic decay) and toward the Soviet Union as the source of problems. Hence, the dramatic winding down of the Cold War opens great opportunities for development.

At the very minimum, real debate should now become possible, getting beyond sharply drawn ideological categories in order to discuss development in more pragmatic terms. What are the proper roles of government and market? If one values both effectiveness and equity, what kind of checks should be placed on the market? What do the experiences of Japan, South Korea, and Taiwan offer to this discussion?

The 1990s provide other opportunities to cut across Cold War polarities. Paranoid Cold War governments often saw communists lurking behind popular organizations fighting for a better society. But citizens' movements played a central role in the recent transformation of Eastern Europe. A greater openness should emerge from this phenomenon. Not only should governments and development experts treat such nongovernmental organizations with the respect they deserve, but they should realize that these groups have vital roles to play beyond the reach of governments and individuals.

Beyond the Cold War, global economic shifts also offer new possibilities for the sustainable development agenda. While much attention has been focused on the relative decline of the United States, this shift offers potentially positive openings. A decade of unprecedented U.S. military spending, for example, has bequeathed fiscal deficits that preclude significant increases in foreign aid. This situation adds impetus to proposals that the United States give less but better aid. That can be accomplished by slashing military aid that in areas like Latin America has often been used to suppress citizens' movements, and by redirecting development assistance away from unaccountable governments and toward citizens' organizations.

Likewise, persistent trade deficits are pushing the U.S. government to restrict imports that enter the domestic market with the assistance of unfair trade practices. The United States could assist developing-country movements for equity and workers' rights by implementing existing legislation that classifies systematic repression of worker rights as an unfair trading practice. Finally, the failure of the Baker and Brady plans to halt the pileup of debt should reopen the door for substantial debt plans that shift payments toward sustainable development initiatives.

Japan's displacement of the United States as the world's most dynamic large economy and biggest aid-giver provides perhaps more intriguing questions about development efforts in the next decade. Japan stands at a juncture fraught with both danger and opportunity. It can take the easy road and mimic what the United States did: ally with local elites and subordinate development policy to security policy. Or Japan can practice enlightened leadership by divorcing the two policies and opening up the possibility for a qualitative change in North-South ties. Will Japan seize the opportunities? During the Marshall Plan years, the United States bestowed substantial decision-making power on the recipient governments. Can Japan, using that experience as a starting point, broaden the decision-making group to include nongovernmental organizations? In fact, voices within Japan are calling for the Japanese government to redirect its aid flows to include citizens' organizations. . . .

The question also remains whether Japan will follow the U.S. example of using the World Bank and IMF as extensions of its aid, commercial, and trade policies, further eroding the credibility of these institutions in the Third World. Perhaps Japan's ascension will encourage these institutions to delve more objectively into the development lessons of Japan, South Korea, and Taiwan, thus adding realism to their prescriptions.

Finally, both Japan and the United States will have to face the need to respect the emerging citizens' movements as the groups reach out internationally to work with one another. The realization that governments suffer from severe limits in the development field should not be seen as negative. Rather, this understanding opens a variety of possibilities for new forms of government-citizen initiatives. In February 1990, for instance, African nongovernmental organizations, governments, and the UN Economic Commission for Africa jointly planned and participated in a conference that adopted a strong declaration affirming popular participation in development. NGOs may also enjoy an enhanced role at the 1992 UN Conference on Environment and Development in Brazil as the realization spreads that governments alone can do little to stop forest destruction and other activities that contribute to the emission of greenhouse gases.

In the face of such opportunities, the seeming death of the development debate in the industrial world represents an enormous travesty. Rekindling that debate, however, requires listening to new approaches from the rest of the world. Excessive confidence in free-market approaches melts when one examines the mounting crises in the supposed success stories of South Korea and Taiwan. Exciting alternatives to the dominant development paradigms are emerging in the hundreds of thousands of citizens' groups that flourish amid adversity and repression in Africa, Asia, and Latin America. These voices must be heard in the development establishments of Washington, Tokyo, and Bonn.

27

Globalization and Inequality, Past and Present

JEFFREY A. WILLIAMSON

The gap between the rich and the poor is a source of much political strife, both within countries and among them. Economic historian Jeffrey Williamson analyzes the experience of the past 150 years with an eye to the impact of globalization on inequality and finds that international economic integration before World War I exacerbated inequality in many developing countries, especially those with relatively abundant natural resources. This increased inequality may have contributed to a backlash against the international economy in the interwar period. Inasmuch as there is evidence of similar trends in income inequality in the past thirty years, Williamson's historical analysis suggests that we may see similar political conflict over the global economy in the future.

Economic growth after 1850 in the countries that now belong to the Organization for Economic Cooperation and Development (OECD) can be divided into three periods: the late nineteenth century belle epoque, the dark middle years between 1914 and 1950, and the late twentieth century renaissance. The first and last epochs were characterized by rapid growth; economic convergence as poor countries caught up with rich ones; and globalization, marked by trade booms, mass migrations, and huge capital flows. The years from 1914 to 1950 are associated with slow growth, a retreat from globalization, and economic divergence. Thus history offers an unambiguous positive correlation between globalization and convergence. When the pre–World War I years are examined in detail, the correlation turns out to be causal: globalization was *the* critical factor promoting economic convergence.

Because contemporary economists are now debating the impact of the forces of globalization on wage inequality in the OECD countries, the newly liberalized Latin American regimes, and the East Asian "tigers," it is time to ask whether the same distributional forces were at work during the late nineteenth century. A body of literature almost a century old argues that immigration hurt American labor and accounted for much of the rise in income inequality from the 1890s to World War I. The decision by a labor-sympathetic Congress to enact immigration quotas shows how important the issue was to the electorate. An even older literature argues that cheap grain exported from the New World eroded land rents in Europe so sharply that landowner-dominated continental parliaments raised tariffs to protect domestic growers from the impact of globalization. But nowhere in this historical literature had anyone constructed data to test three contentious hypotheses with important policy implications:

> *Hypothesis 1:* Inequality rose in resource-rich, labor-scarce countries such as Argentina, Australia, Canada, and the United States. Inequality fell in resource-poor, labor-abundant agrarian economies such as Ireland, Italy, Portugal, Scandinavia, and Spain. Inequality was more stable among the European industrial leaders, including Britain, France, Germany, and the Lowland countries, all of whom fell in between the rich New World and poor Old World.
> *Hypothesis 2:* If the first hypothesis is true, a second follows: these inequality patterns can be explained largely by globalization.
> *Hypothesis 3:* If this second hypothesis holds, then these globalization-induced inequality trends help explain the retreat from globalization between 1913 and 1950.

This article reviews the historical debate about the first globalization boom in the late nineteenth century and attempts to tie it to the current debate about the globalization boom in the late twentieth century. The two debates are strikingly similar. They also share a shortcoming in the empirical analysis: nobody has yet explored this issue with late nineteenth century panel data across poor and rich countries, and, with the important exception of Wood (1994), few have done so for the late-twentieth-century debate either. Indeed, until very recently, most economists had focused solely on the American experience. The central contribution of this paper is to explore a database for the late nineteenth century that includes both rich and poor countries or, in the modern vernacular, North and South.

It appears that globalization did contribute to the implosion, deglobalization, and autarkic policies that dominated between 1913 and 1950. Indeed, during these years of trade suppression and binding migration quotas, the connection between globalization and inequality completely disappeared. It took the globalization renaissance of the early 1970s to renew this old debate.

GLOBALIZATION AND INEQUALITY
IN THE LATE TWENTIETH CENTURY

From 1973 through the 1980s, real wages of unskilled workers in the United States fell as a result of declining productivity growth and an increasing disparity in wages paid to workers with different skills. This difference was manifested primarily by higher wages for workers with advanced schooling and age-related skills. The same trends were apparent elsewhere in the OECD in the 1980s, but the increase in wage gaps was typically far smaller. The widening of wage inequalities coincided with the forces of globalization, both in the form of rising trade and increased immigration, the latter characterized by a decline in the skill levels of migrants. Trade as a share of gross national product in the United States increased from 12 percent in 1970 to 25 percent in 1990 (Lawrence and Slaughter 1993), while exports from low-income countries rose from 8 percent of total output in 1965 to 18 percent in 1990. These developments coincided with a shift in spending patterns that resulted in large trade deficits in the United States.

The standard Heckscher-Ohlin trade model makes unambiguous predictions: every country exports those products that use abundant and cheap factors of production. Thus a trade boom induced by a drop in tariffs or in transport costs will cause exports and the demand for the cheap factor to boom as well. Globalization in poor countries should favor unskilled labor; globalization in rich countries should favor skilled labor. . . .

Thus far the discussion has focused mainly on the United States, perhaps because rising inequality and immigration have been greatest there. But the question is not simply why the demand for unskilled labor in the United States and even Europe was depressed in the 1980s and 1990s, but whether the same factors were *stimulating* the relative demand for low-skill labor in developing countries. This is where Adrian Wood (1994, ch. 6) enters the debate. Wood was one of the first economists to systematically examine inequality trends across industrial and developing countries.

Wood distinguishes three skill types: uneducated workers, those with a basic education, and the highly educated. The poor South has an abundance of uneducated labor, but the supply of workers with basic skills is growing rapidly. The rich North, of course, is well endowed with highly educated workers; its supply of labor with basic skills is growing slowly. Wood assumes that capital is fairly mobile and that technology is freely available. As trade barriers fall and the South improves its skills through the expansion of basic education, it produces more goods that require only basic skills, while the North produces more high-skill goods. It follows that the ratio of the unskilled to the skilled wage should rise in the South and fall in the North. The tendency toward the relative convergence of factor prices raises the relative wage of workers with a basic education in the South and lowers it in the North, producing rising inequality in the North and falling inequality in the South.

Wood concludes that the decline in the relative wages of less-skilled northern workers is caused by the elimination of trade barriers and the increasing abundance of southern workers with a basic education. . . .

Wood's research has met with stiff critical resistance. Since his book appeared in 1994, more has been learned about the link between inequality and globalization in developing countries. . . . [A] study of seven countries in Latin America and East Asia shows that wage inequality typically did not fall after trade liberalization but rather *rose*. This apparent anomaly has been strengthened by other studies, some of which have been rediscovered since Wood's book appeared. . . . None of these studies is very attentive to the simultaneous role of emigration from these countries, however, leaving the debate far from resolved.

GLOBALIZATION AND INEQUALITY
IN THE LATE NINETEENTH CENTURY

The spread between real wages from 1854 to 1913 in fifteen countries is shown in Figure 1. The downward trend confirms what new-growth theorists call convergence, that is, a narrowing in the economic distance between rich and poor countries. The convergence is more dramatic when America and Canada — which were richer — or when Portugal and Spain — who failed to play the globalization

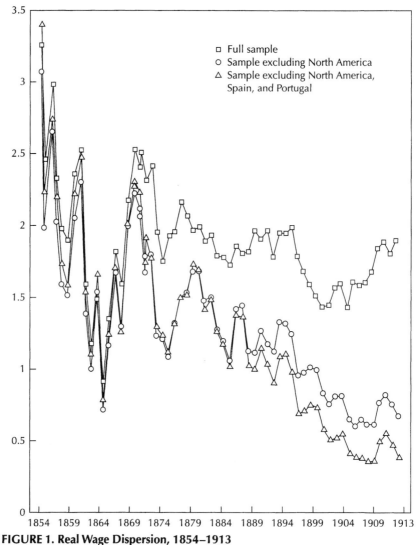

Coefficient of variation

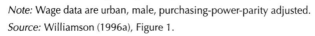

FIGURE 1. Real Wage Dispersion, 1854–1913

Note: Wage data are urban, male, purchasing-power-parity adjusted.

Source: Williamson (1996a), Figure 1.

game — are excluded. . . . Most of this convergence was the combined result of the trade boom and the prequota mass migrations.

Trade Issues

The late nineteenth century was a period of dramatic integration of commodity markets: railways and steamships lowered transport costs, and Europe moved toward free trade in the wake of the 1860 Cobden-Chevalier treaty. These developments implied large trade-induced price shocks that affected every European participant. The drop in grain prices was the canonical case: wheat prices in Liverpool were 60 percent higher than those in Chicago in 1870, for example, but they were less than 15 percent higher in 1912, a decline of forty-five percentage points. The commodity price differential declined by even more when the spread is measured from wheat-growing regions outside of Chicago. Furthermore, prices of all tradables, not just grain, were affected. . . .

The standard trade model argues that, as countries everywhere expand the production and export of goods that use their abundant (and cheap) factors relatively intensively, the resultant market integration would lead to an international convergence of factor prices. Under this theory, then, the late-nineteenth century trade boom accounted for 10 to 20 percent of the convergence in GDP per worker hour and in the real wage. It also had distributional implications for poor countries: it meant rising wages for unskilled workers relative to land rents and skilled wages. For rich countries, it meant that unskilled wages fell relative to land rents and skilled wages.

Migration Issues

The correlation between real wages or GDP per worker hour and migration rates is positive and highly significant. The poorest Old World countries tended to have the highest emigration rates, while the richest New World countries tended to have the highest immigration rates. The correlation is not perfect since potential emigrants from poor countries often found the cost of the move too high, and some New World countries restricted inflows of such migrants. But the correlation is still very strong. Furthermore, the effect on the labor force was very important, augmenting the New World labor force by almost 37 percent and reducing the Old World labor force by 18 percent (at least among the emigrant countries around the European periphery), much larger than U.S. experience in the 1980s. One estimate suggests that mass migrations explain about 70 percent of the real wage convergence in the late nineteenth century. This estimate, in contrast with the contemporary debate about immigration in the 1980s, which focuses only on immigration into Europe and the United States, includes the total impact on rich receiving countries *and* poor sending countries.

Because the migrants tended to be unskilled, and increasingly so toward the end of the century, they flooded the receiving countries' labor markets at the bottom of the skill ladder. Thus immigration must have lowered unskilled wages relative to those of skilled artisans and educated white-collar workers and relative to land rents. These immigration-induced trends implied increased inequality in rich countries, while emigration-induced trends must have moved in the opposite direction and reduced inequality in poor countries.

So much for plausible assertions. What were the facts?

Establishing the Facts, 1870–1913

How did the typical unskilled worker near the bottom of the distribution do relative to the typical landowner or capitalist near the top, or even relative to the skilled blue-collar worker and educated white-collar employee near the middle? The debate over inequality in the late twentieth century has fixed on wage inequality, but a century earlier, land and landed interests were far more important sources of income, so they need to be added to the inquiry. (I believe this is true throughout the developing world, certainly its poorer parts.) In any case, two kinds of evidence are available to document nineteenth century inequality trends so defined: the ratio of unskilled wages to farm rents per acre, and the ratio of the unskilled wage to GDP per worker hour. Everyone knows that farm land was abundant and cheap in the New World, while scarce and expensive in the Old World. And labor was scarce and expensive in the New World, while abundant and cheap in the Old World. Thus, the ratio of wage rates to farm rents was high in the New World and low in the Old. What everyone *really* wants to know, however, is how the gap evolved over time: Are the trends consistent with the predictions of the globalization and inequality literature? Was there, in Wood's language, relative factor price convergence in the late-nineteenth century, implying rising inequality in rich countries and declining inequality in poor countries? Figure 2 supplies some affirmative answers.

In the New World the ratio of wage rates to farm rents plunged. By 1913 it had fallen in Australia to a quarter of its 1870 level; in Argentina to a fifth of its mid-1880 level; and in the United States to less than half of its 1870 level. In the Old World the reverse occurred, especially where free trade policies were pursued. In Great Britain the ratio in 1910 had increased by a factor of 2.7 over its 1870 level, while the Irish ratio had increased even more, by a factor of 5.5. The Swedish and Danish ratios had both increased by a factor of 2.3. The surge was less pronounced in protectionist countries, increasing by a factor of 1.8 in France, 1.4 in Germany, and not at all in Spain.

Because landowners tended to be near the top of the income distribution pyramid, this evidence confirms Hypothesis 1: inequality rose in the rich, labor scarce New World and fell in the poor, labor-abundant Old World. There is also some evidence that globalization mattered: countries that were open to trade absorbed the biggest distributional changes; those that retreated behind tariff walls sustained the smallest distributional changes. . . .

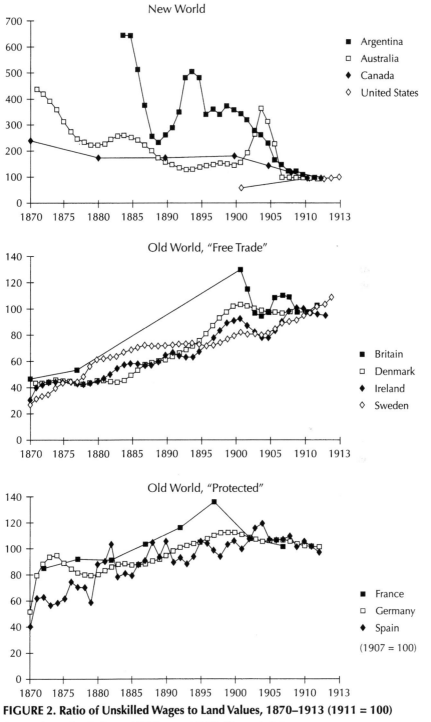

FIGURE 2. Ratio of Unskilled Wages to Land Values, 1870–1913 (1911 = 100)

Source: O'Rourke, Taylor, and Williamson (1996), Figures 1, 2, 3.

THE IMPACT OF GLOBALIZATION
ON INEQUALITY TRENDS, 1870–1913

Theory suggests that globalization can account for this key stylized fact: In an age of unrestricted international migration, poor countries should have the highest emigration rates and rich countries should have the highest immigration rates; in an age of liberal trade policy, poor countries should export labor-intensive products and rich countries should import labor-intensive products. Theory is one thing: fact is another. What evidence on trade and migration in the late nineteenth century supports this (apparently plausible) globalization hypothesis?

I start with trade effects. There was a retreat from trade liberalism after 1880, and the retreat included France, Germany, Italy, Portugal, and Spain. In the absence of globalization forces, poor labor-abundant countries that protect domestic industry should raise the returns to scarce factors (such as land) relative to abundant factors (such as unskilled labor). In the face of globalization forces, the same countries should at least mute the rise in the relative scarcity of unskilled labor and thus stem the fall in inequality. The evidence seems to be roughly consistent with these predictions. That is, the correlation between rising inequality and initial labor scarcity turns out to be better for 1870–1890 — an environment of shared liberal trade policies — than for 1890–1913 — an environment of rising protection on the Continent.

I turn next to the impact of mass migration. As indicated above, the impact of mass migration on labor supplies in sending and receiving countries between 1870 and 1910 ranged from 37 percent for three New World destination countries (Canada at 44 percent absorbing the largest supply of immigrant labor) to –18 percent for six poor European sending countries (Italy at –39 percent losing the largest share of its labor supply). Migration's impact on the receiving country's labor force is also known to be highly correlated with an initial scarcity of labor, although not perfectly. Migration is therefore a prime candidate in accounting for the distribution trends. Figure 3 plots the result: where immigration increased the receiving country's labor supply, inequality rose sharply; where emigration reduced the sending country's labor supply, inequality declined.

Unfortunately it is impossible to decompose globalization effects into trade and migration using this information because the correlation between migration's impact and initial labor scarcity is so high. Yet an effort has been made by constructing a trade-globalization-impact variable as the interaction of initial labor scarcity and "openness." The result is that the impact of migration is still powerful, significant, and of the right sign: when immigration rates were small, inegalitarian trends were weak; when emigration rates were big, egalitarian trends were strong; when countries had to accommodate heavy immigration, inegalitarian trends were strong. In the Old World periphery, where labor was most abundant, the more open economies had more egalitarian trends, just as the Heckscher-Ohlin trade model would have predicted. It appears that the open economy tigers of that time enjoyed benign egalitarian effects, while those among them opting for autarky did not. In the Old World industrial core, this effect was far less powerful. It appears that open economy effects on income distribution were ambiguous

Average annual percentage change in inequality index

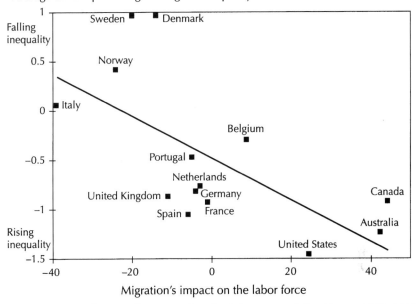

FIGURE 3. Inequality Trends versus Migration's Impact on Labor Force, 1870–1913
Source: Williamson (1996b).

among the land-scarce industrial leaders in Europe where the farm sector was relatively small. Heckscher and Ohlin would have predicted this result too. In the
labor scarce New World, however, the more open economies also had more egalitarian trends, which is certainly *not* what Heckscher and Ohlin would have predicted. The result is not significant, however.

Overall, I read this evidence as strong support for the impact of mass migration
on income distribution and as weak support for the role of trade. This empirical
exercise explains about two-thirds of the variance in distributional trends across
the late nineteenth century. What forces could possibly account for the remaining
third, forces that were also highly correlated with initial labor scarcity and GDP
per worker-hour? Late twentieth century critics of the globalization thesis have
argued that the answer lies with technological change. Lawrence and Slaughter
(1993) contend that a skill-using bias in the United States has driven rising
inequality. Wood (1994) counters that it cannot be so because inequality in the
United States and the other OECD countries was on the rise just when the slowdown in productivity was in full swing. Whichever view the reader believes, it is
important to remember that we are searching for an explanation that can account
simultaneously for falling inequality in the South, rising inequality in the North,
and some mixture among the newly industrializing countries in the middle. But is
there any reason to believe that technological change should be unskilled labor-
saving in rich countries and unskilled labor-using in poor countries?

This issue has been explored at length (O'Rourke, Taylor, and Williamson,
1996) using the data on the ratio of wages to land rent shown in Figure 2. Almost

by definition, industrial revolutions embody productivity growth that favors industry. Because industrial output makes little use of farmland, industrialization instead raises the relative demands for labor and capital. Industrial revolutions tend, therefore, to raise wages relative to land rents. According to this prediction, more rapid industrialization in Europe than in the New World should also have raised the wage-rental ratio by more in Europe. Such events should have contributed to a convergence in the prices of factors of production, including a rise in real wages in Europe relative to those in the New World. This prediction would be reinforced if productivity advance in the late nineteenth century New World was labor-saving and land-using, as the above hypothesis suggests and as economic historians generally believe. The prediction would be further reinforced if productivity advance in the Old World was land-saving and labor-using, as economic historians generally believe.

O'Rourke, Taylor, and Williamson's results (1996, Table 4) are striking. The combination of changes in land-labor ratios and capital deepening accounted for about 26 percent of the fall in the wage-rental ratio in the New World, but for none of its rise in the Old World. Commodity price convergence and Heckscher-Ohlin effects accounted for about 30 percent of the fall in the New World wage-rental ratio and for about 23 percent of its rise in the Old World. Advances in productivity, as predicted, were labor-saving in the labor-scarce New World and labor-using in the labor-abundant Old World. Labor-saving technologies appear to have accounted for about 39 percent of the drop in the wage-rental ratio in the New World, while labor-intensive technologies accounted for about 51 percent of its rise in the Old World, powerful technological forces indeed. Globalization accounted for more than half of the rising inequality in rich countries and for a little more than a quarter of the falling inequality in poor ones. Technology accounted for about 40 percent of the rising inequality in rich countries in the forty years before World War I, and about 50 percent of the decline in inequality in poor countries.

ESTABLISHING THE INEQUALITY FACTS, 1921–1938

What happened after World War I, when quotas were imposed in immigrating countries, capital markets collapsed, and trade barriers rose?

First, wage differentials between countries widened. Some of the differences were war-related, and some were due to the Depression, but even in the 1920s the trend was clear. Second, the connection between inequality and the forces of globalization was broken (see Figure 4). Inequality rose more sharply in poorer countries than in richer countries, where in four cases, it actually declined.

SOME THINGS NEVER CHANGE

At least two events distinguish the late nineteenth century period of globalization from that of the late twentieth century. First, a decline in inequality seems to

Average annual percentage change in inequality index

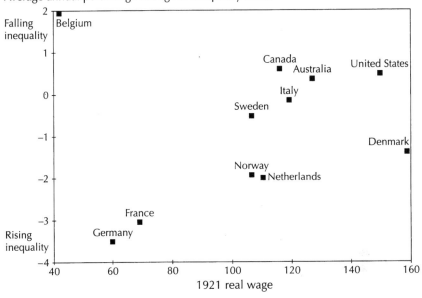

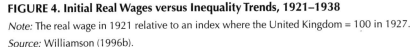

FIGURE 4. Initial Real Wages versus Inequality Trends, 1921–1938

Note: The real wage in 1921 relative to an index where the United Kingdom = 100 in 1927.

Source: Williamson (1996b).

have been significant and pervasive in the poor, industrial latecomers in the late nineteenth century sample. This move toward equality has not been universally true of the Latin American and East Asian countries recently studied by other researchers. Second, mass migration appears to have had a more important effect than trade on inequality in the late nineteenth century. Except for the United States, and perhaps West Germany, this phenomenon does not seem to have been true of the late twentieth century, although it should be noted that no economist has assessed the impact of emigration on wages and inequality in Turkey, Mexico, the Philippines, or other developing countries in which net outmigration has been significant over the past quarter century or so.

Some things never change, and that fact implies a warning. Globalization and convergence ceased between 1913 and 1950. It appears that rising inequality in rich countries induced by globalization was responsible, at least in part, for the interwar retreat from globalization. The connection between globalization and inequality was also broken between World War I and 1950. Rising inequality in the rich countries stopped exactly when immigration was choked off by quotas, global capital markets collapsed, and the international community retreated behind high trade barriers. Are these interwar correlations spurious? The pre–World War I experience suggests not.

Is there a lesson from this history? Will the world economy soon retreat from its commitment to globalization just as it did almost a century ago?

REFERENCES

Lawrence, Robert Z., and Matthew J. Slaughter. 1993. "International Trade and American Wages in the 1980s: Giant Sucking Sound or Small Hiccup?" *Brookings Papers on Economic Activity, Microeconomics* 2:161–226.

O'Rourke, Kevin H., Alan M. Taylor, and Jeffrey G. Williamson. 1996. "Factor Price Convergence in the Late 19th Century." *International Economic Review* 37(3):499–530.

Williamson, Jeffrey G. 1996a. "Globalization, Convergence and History." *Journal of Economic History* 56 (June): 277–306.

———. 1996b. "Globalization and Inequality, Past and Present." Appendixes 1, 2. Harvard University, Department of Economics, Cambridge, Mass. Processed.

Wood, Adrian. 1994. *North-South Trade, Employment, and Inequality: Changing Fortunes in a Skill-Driven World.* Oxford: Clarendon Press.

28

Inflation and Stabilization
STEPHAN HAGGARD

In this selection, Stephan Haggard seeks to explain why some developing countries have been more successful than others in promoting stable macroeconomic policies. Blending domestic societal and state-centered approaches, he argues that both the density and composition of social groups and how they express their interests through state institutions shape policy outcomes. Haggard's analysis of middle-income Latin American and East Asian countries suggests that a combination of interest-group pressure and the nature and design of particular institutions determines the incentives faced by state leaders to pursue stable macroeconomic policies. The developing countries with the highest inflation, he finds, have been those featuring urban labor movements mobilized into populist parties within relatively polarized party systems.

Why have some middle-income developing countries had histories of high inflation over the past two decades, while others have pursued stable macroeconomic policies? Among countries experiencing inflation, why do some governments move to stabilize with alacrity, while others postpone the adjustment decision, often with disastrous costs? Once the decision to stabilize is taken, why are some countries capable of sustaining stabilization policies while others falter and reverse course?

A wide array of economic factors is important in understanding particular national experiences with inflation, including the severity of exogenous shocks. Nonetheless, inflation often has political roots, and whatever its causes, stabilization poses profound political dilemmas.

This chapter reviews some current thinking about the political economy of fiscal policy and advances some hypotheses about differences in inflation and stabilization efforts among middle-income developing countries. The rent- and revenue-seeking approach of the new political economy is useful for understanding the political incentives to government spending and explains why subsidies and state-owned enterprises become politically entrenched. This approach, however, does not explain cross-national *differences* in fiscal performance and inflation. Such variation can be accounted for in part by pressures for government spending that result from interest group and partisan conflict. The organization of urban labor and its incorporation into the party system appear to be important factors. The developing countries with histories of high inflation, mostly in Latin America, have been those in which urban "popular sector" and labor groups have been mobilized into populist parties within relatively polarized party systems. Such high-conflict countries also had the greatest difficulties stabilizing in the 1980s, particularly where stabilization episodes overlapped with transitions to democratic rule. It is difficult to disentangle lines of causality because the size of external shocks and initial disequilibria posed greater difficulties for the large Latin American debtors, but the vulnerability to external shocks was itself partly the result of previous policy choices.

The structure of interest groups and the nature of the political regime are, of course, not easily changed. Other political factors affecting fiscal outcomes may offer greater scope for reform, though. The political difficulties of macroeconomic adjustment appear to be less severe where decision making is relatively centralized within the government and insulated from rent-seeking pressures. This suggests the importance of institutional reform for sustaining credible macroeconomic policy.

THE POLITICAL ECONOMY OF INFLATION AND STABILIZATION

Albert Hirschman has pointed out that "the explanation of inflation in terms of social conflict between groups, each aspiring to a greater share of the social product, has become the sociologist's monotonous equivalent of the economist's untiring stress on the undue expansion of the money supply." To construct a political theory of inflation and stabilization demands an explication of the precise mechanisms through which political variables contribute to increases in the price level and difficulties in stabilization.

In studies of the advanced industrial states, cross-national variations in inflation have been traced to differences in wage-setting institutions and relations among business, organized labor, and government. Wage policy has played a role in efforts to control inflation in the developing world, but a growing body of evidence suggests that fiscal policy is a more appropriate focus for an examination of the political economy of inflation in developing countries. Since developing country governments generally have limited scope for domestic borrowing, financing fiscal deficits usually involves recourse to foreign borrowing and the inflation tax. There appear to be few cases of severe and prolonged inflation in the developing world that were not associated with fiscal deficits financed by money creation.

Fiscal policy also helps explain the accumulation of debt and the subsequent vulnerability of debtor countries to external shocks. When net capital inflows ceased abruptly in the early 1980s, debtors were unable to cut expenditures and raise revenues quickly. They thus relied on instruments that constituted implicit taxes on financial intermediation, with adverse consequences for investment.

Not surprisingly, fiscal policy has been central to stabilization efforts. International Monetary Fund stabilization programs invariably target some monetary indicator as the key performance criterion, but the focus on monetary policy reflects the availability of data and the political problems of appearing to interfere in sensitive allocational decisions rather than a belief in the primacy of monetary measures. The actions required to meet monetary targets are usually fiscal: some combination of increased taxes or nontax revenues and cuts in expenditures. The principal political dilemma is that no matter how beneficial these measures may be in the long run for the country as a whole, they entail the imposition of short-term costs and have distributional implications for particular groups.

CONTRIBUTIONS AND LIMITS
OF THE NEW POLITICAL ECONOMY

The new, or neoclassical, political economy relies heavily on interest group models that seek to explain policy, including taxation and expenditure, as the result of political exchanges between welfare-maximizing constituents and support-maximizing politicians. On the demand side of the political market are constituents, conceptualized as individual voters, interest groups, or even bureaucratic groups within the state itself. The political process consists of spending by these constituents to influence the size and direction of fiscal redistribution. Rational constituents will expend resources — on lobbying, political contributions, demonstrations, and so forth — until the marginal cost of their influence efforts equals the expected marginal return from securing their desired policy outcome. Where rival constituencies have conflicting interests, groups expending the most on the influence attempt will prevail.

Politicians constitute the supply side of the market, though the real "suppliers" are those groups from whom income and wealth transfers are ultimately sought. The key insight of the new political economy into fiscal policy is that politicians view expenditures to their constituents not as costs, but as benefits. They will thus seek to increase expenditures to constituents to the point at which the political return is offset by the economic and political costs, including the inflationary consequences of high budget deficits. The lure of deficits is strengthened by fundamental asymmetries between spending and taxing decisions: the means of financing deficits — inflation and borrowing — are less visible than taxation, spread more widely across the population (inflation), or pushed onto future generations (borrowing).

The new political economy underlines the incentives facing politicians to spend and explains puzzles such as the bias against least-cost alternatives and the tendency for projects to assume unnecessary scale. Ultimately, however, this rent-seeking approach cannot predict whether central government accounts will be in surplus, balance, or deficit. Put differently, there is a problem in getting from the microlevel of a particular expenditure or tax to the macrolevel of aggregate fiscal outcomes.

Discussions of subsidies and state-owned enterprises that draw on rent-seeking models illustrate this difficulty. Subsidies give politicians an instrument for building electoral or clientele support. Because they can grow into virtually open-ended government commitments and are seen as entitlements by their recipients, subsidies have been a major factor contributing to fiscal deficits in a number of middle-income countries. Their reduction or elimination has been a central component of most stabilization plans and is one of the most difficult to carry through because of the vulnerability of most governments to urban consumer groups. Yet not all governments have fallen into the subsidy trap, and some have managed to reduce subsidies.

A related example is provided by the growing literature on state-owned enterprises (SOEs). SOEs played a major role in contributing to fiscal deficits and external borrowing in a number of developing countries over the 1970s and 1980s. Some of this expenditure was no doubt for legitimate purposes; viewed politically, however, SOEs represent powerful constituencies within the government because of the resources under their control and their importance in generating employment. In many cases, SOEs are more powerful than the ministries that presumably oversee their activities; state-owned oil enterprises, such as Mexico's PEMEX, are important examples. Governments have also been politically vulnerable to pressures from customers, contractors, and suppliers to maintain purchases of goods and services, limit price increases, raise wages, and retain employees. Again, the puzzle for the new political economy is in explaining variance. In some countries, SOEs have mushroomed and been a major drain on national treasuries, while in others their role has been limited or subject to effective control.

One way of bridging the gap between the micro- and macrolevels of political analysis is through the political business cycle. This literature argues that regardless of the party in power, economic policy will change over the electoral cycle as politicians seek to manipulate the short-run Phillips curve (showing the trade-off between unemployment and inflation) to electoral advantage. The evidence for a political business cycle remains weak for the advanced industrial states. The model assumes short voter memory concerning past performance and myopia concerning future inflation, or, as Brian Barry has put it, "a collection of rogues competing for the favors of a larger collection of dupes."

Many of the political and institutional characteristics that mitigate political business cycles in the advanced industrial states are absent, however, in the developing countries. These include, among other things, informed publics; independent media coverage of economic policy; institutionalized forms of consultation between business, government, and labor; and welfare systems that cushion the costs of unemployment. Given lower levels of income, extensive poverty, and the insecurity of political tenure in a number of polities, it is plausible that politicians' time horizons in the developing world are oriented toward the delivery of short-term benefits for electoral gain.

A second way of joining the micro- and macrolevels is through models emphasizing partisan conflict. In one such model, the economy is divided into two groups, "workers" and "capitalists," each with its own political party. The party in power seeks to redistribute income in favor of its constituency: right-wing governments pursue policies that favor profits; left-wing governments, those that favor wages. In designing fiscal policy, each party will seek to tax its opponents to the maximum feasible extent, while redistributing to its own constituency. Governments in power have a strong incentive to borrow, knowing that the full cost of servicing current obligations will be borne by political successors.

Two hypotheses result from this line of inquiry. First, a high level of political instability, measured by frequent changes of government, is likely to generate higher fiscal deficits, since politicians will have particularly short time horizons. Second, a polarized political system in which the objectives of the competing parties are highly incompatible will generate higher fiscal deficits than those systems in which the objectives of the competing parties overlap and are less zero-sum in nature.

BRINGING INSTITUTIONS BACK IN

Economists who have branched into political economy tend to think of the polity in terms of economic cleavages. Workers have different interests than capitalists; holders of financial assets have different inflation preferences than debtors; urban consumers have different preferences regarding agricultural prices than rural producers. As the partisan-conflict model suggests, economists assume a close "mapping" between economic cleavages and political organization, and see the state and politicians as relatively passive registers of social demands. With this approach, every policy that has a distributional consequence could be explained on the grounds that it favored some group. The more demanding task is to explain why some polities are riddled with revenue seeking, while others have developed mechanisms of fiscal control.

Answering such questions requires greater attention to organizational and institutional factors. First, different types of economic activity may be more or less amenable to political organization and collective action. The agricultural sector may loom large in the economy, but peasants are difficult to organize and rural influence on policy can easily be offset by smaller, but better organized urban forces. It is therefore important to have information not only on economic cleavages, which provides good clues about policy preferences, but also on which social groups are in fact capable of effective organization.

Second, party organization can aggregate interests in different ways. In some polities, the party system reinforces societal and economic cleavages and conflicts, for example, pitting populist or labor parties against conservative and middle-class parties, or urban-based parties against rural-based ones. In other countries, broad, catchall parties cut across class or economic divisions and tend to mute them. These organizational differences can have profound influence on the political appeals parties make, on the demands on public finance, and consequently on the conduct of macroeconomic policy. Macroeconomic stability is more likely in two-party systems with broad, catchall parties than in those that pit class-based parties against one another or in multiparty systems that foster more ideological parties.

It is not enough to know how groups are organized for political action; equally, if not more, important is the question of how social demands are represented in the decision-making process. The new political economy has focused its attention on the advanced industrial states, and thus assumed the existence of political processes such as general elections. Elections are not relevant for policy making in authoritarian regimes, and may not be relevant for policy making in some arenas even under democratic conditions. For example, monetary policy and the details of budgeting may have more to do with internal bureaucratic politics or the independence of the central bank, than with electoral or party constraints.

The absence of democratic processes in the developing world may help explain the attraction of lobbying and rent-seeking models, which can presumably be applied to both democratic and authoritarian regimes. Democracy may not be ubiquitous, but lobbying is. Yet interest group pressures constrain authoritarian rulers less than they do democratic rulers. It is thus plausible that the political regime can be an important factor in explaining the ability to impose stabilization costs.

These observations suggest the importance of combining interest group and partisan explanations with an analysis of the overall institutional context: the nature of the party system, the budget process, and the type of regime. This analysis can be illustrated, though not definitively tested, by examining some hypotheses about the variation in inflation and stabilization efforts among the middle-income countries.

POLITICS AND INFLATION IN MIDDLE-INCOME COUNTRIES

Although the debt crisis of the 1980s has had global implications, its effects have been felt quite differently in various geographic regions. Among the middle-income countries, Latin America has been the hardest hit. Twelve of the seventeen countries designated by the World Bank as the most heavily indebted are in the Western Hemisphere. The most severe problems with inflation are found in that region as well. By contrast, the middle-income countries of East and Southeast Asia — South Korea, Taiwan, Indonesia, Thailand, Malaysia, and the Philippines — have largely been immune from devastating inflations.

. . . [D]ifferences in inflation are not simply the result of recent events. Before the onset of the debt crisis, Latin America consistently had higher levels of inflation than other developing countries, though there are important contrasts within regions. Brazil, Chile, and Uruguay all have histories of comparatively high inflation. The current hyperinflations in Brazil and Argentina are outside the range of those countries' historical experience, but both have experienced severe inflations before. Other Latin American countries, including Colombia, Venezuela, and Mexico, have not had chronically high levels of inflation, though all have suffered increasing inflationary pressures in recent times. Peru, historically a low-inflation country compared with the Southern Cone nations (Argentina, Chile, and Uruguay), is now veering toward hyperinflation.

In Asia, Thailand, Taiwan, and Malaysia have had histories of low inflation and all largely escaped the debt crisis of the 1980s. Indonesia had a near hyperinflation in the mid-1960s, but its fiscal and monetary policy have been conservative since. South Korea has had high levels of debt and inflation by Asian standards but adjusted relatively smoothly in the early 1980s. The Philippines, by contrast, had painful problems of adjustment in 1984, though by comparison to the Latin American debtors, that country's difficulties appear relatively mild.

Recognizing that economic circumstances vary across cases as well, what political factors help account for these long-term patterns? The new political economy would suggest that differences in the density and composition of interest group organization should be a starting point. Through most of the postwar period, the Latin American countries can be differentiated from the Asian cases in terms of the size and organization of urban-industrial interest groups, including the so-called popular sector, which has played a crucial role in Latin American politics.

Mexico, Brazil, and particularly the countries of the Southern Cone had longer histories of industrialization, larger urban-industrial populations, and comparatively small agrarian sectors at the outset of the borrowing boom of the 1970s than the East and Southeast Asian countries. These conditions have implied denser and more established networks of unions, white-collar associations, and manufacturers' groups linked to the import-substituting industrialization (ISI) process in Latin America.

This density of urban-industrial groups, in turn, had two implications for economic policy. The first concerns overall economic strategy. There have been important economic barriers to shifting the pattern of incentives toward export-oriented strategies in Latin America, including the problem of setting exchange rates where there is a strong comparative advantage in natural resource export. The number and extent of groups linked to import-substituting industrialization have also been significant factors. Even authoritarian governments with preferences for market-oriented policies, such as Brazil after 1964, faced constraints from groups linked to the ISI process. The well-known balance of payments problems associated with ISI were, in turn, one factor in the expansion of foreign borrowing during the 1970s and the subsequent macroeconomic policy problems.

In South Korea and Taiwan, by contrast, industrialization, and particularly ISI, were of shorter duration, and there were consequently fewer interests opposed to the crucial exchange rate and trade reforms that launched export-led growth. Elite concern with rural incomes may also have had some effect on policy, constituting a political counterweight to ISI forces. This constellation of interest groups may help explain the ability of the Philippines, Thailand, Malaysia, and Indonesia to maintain realistic exchange rates and to shift, though to varying degrees, toward the promotion of manufactured exports.

The second consequence of the density of urban-industrial groups relates more immediately to macroeconomic policy. The political mobilization of urban groups and unions, particularly in a context of high income inequality, is an important factor in explaining the appeal of populist economic ideologies in Latin America. . . . [T]here is a remarkable similarity in populist economic programs across countries. Their main political objective is to reverse the loss in real income to urban groups that results from traditional stabilization policies or simply from the business cycle.

Populist prescriptions include fiscal expansion; a redistribution of income through real wage increases; and a program of structural reform designed to relieve productive bottlenecks and economize on foreign exchange. Populists reject the claim that deficit financing is inflationary, arguing that the mobilization of unused spare capacity, declining costs, and, if necessary, controls, will moderate inflation.

Populist experiments go through a typical cycle, usually triggered by orthodox stabilization efforts:

Phase 1. Policy makers enjoy a honeymoon as their prescriptions appear to be vindicated. Output grows and real wages and employment improve. Direct controls are used to manage inflation. The easing of the balance of payments constraint and the buildup of reserves under the previous orthodox program provide the populists a crucial cushion for meeting import demand.

Phase 2. Strong domestic demand starts to generate a foreign exchange constraint, but devaluation is rejected as inflationary and detrimental to maintaining real wage growth. External controls are instituted. The budget deficit widens because of the growth of subsidies on wage goods and on foreign exchange.

Phase 3. Growing disparity between official and black market exchange rates and general lack of confidence lead to capital flight. The budget deficit deteriorates because of continuing high levels of expenditure and lagging tax collections. Inflation soars.

Phase 4. Stabilization becomes a political priority, and the principal political debate concerns whether to pursue a more "orthodox" or "heterodox" policy mix.

Why do such cycles appear in one political setting and not in another? Stop-and-go macroeconomic policies themselves are partly to blame, since they carry particular costs for urban workers. One determinant of such populist cycles is the way urban political forces are initially organized — in other words whether historical partisan alignments mute or reinforce sectoral and class cleavages.

In Argentina, Peru, Chile, and Brazil, antioligarchical parties of the center and the left recurrently sought the support of urban workers and small manufacturers by appealing to class and sectoral interests. These appeals produced the kind of political polarization and macroeconomic policy outcomes predicted by the partisan-conflict model outlined above. In Colombia and Venezuela, by contrast, such conflicts were discouraged by the electoral dominance of broadly based patronage parties. In Uruguay, the traditional Colorado and Blanco parties also tended to discourage class and sectoral conflicts that lead to expansionary macroeconomic policies, though by the mid-1960s, the influence of these parties had come under challenge from a coalition of center-left parties with strong bases of support in Montevideo.

Mexico provides an important example of the significance of institutions in determining the ability of new urban-industrial groups to formulate effective demands on the state. Under the leadership of President Lázaro Cárdenas in the 1930s, the ruling Partido Revolucionario Institucional (PRI) encompassed peasant, middle-class, and working-class organizations. Mexico experienced structural changes comparable to those in Brazil and Argentina in the 1950s and 1960s, but under stable macroeconomic policies. This regime of "stabilizing development" was achieved following a painful devaluation in 1954. The government was able to withstand short-term protests to this crucial reform because of the special relationship it enjoyed with state-sanctioned unions. Not until the early 1970s did deepening social problems and the populist political strategy of President Luis Echeverría combine to break the pattern of stable monetary and fiscal policies. Nonetheless, Mexico still managed to pursue more "orthodox" stabilization policies in the 1980s under Presidents Miguel de la Madrid and Carlos Salinas than either of the other two large Latin American countries, Brazil and Argentina. This is due in large part to the PRI's continuing ability to engineer political compromises and exercise discipline over urban workers.

Even when populist forces surfaced in East and Southeast Asian countries, they never succeeded in gaining a political foothold. A larger proportion of the population remained outside the framework of urban interest group politics altogether than in Latin America, and patterns of political organization also differed. Broad, anticolonial movements muted class and sectoral conflicts. Generally, the most serious political challenges came not from the urban areas, but from rural insurgencies. When and where urban working-class politics did emerge, it was either assimilated into corporatist structures or suppressed.

In the Philippines, two diffuse political machines dominated the electoral system before the announcement of martial law by Ferdinand Marcos in 1972. Pork-barrel conflicts were more important than programmatic differences, but elite domination of the political system resulted in extremely low levels of taxation. Beginning in the late 1960s, urban-based leftist organizations grew, but they were crushed following the declaration of martial law. Even when political liberalization provided new opportunities for the left to organize, its influence was counterbalanced by that of the old political machines and the new middle-class democratic political movement, headed finally by Corazon Aquino, which owed little to the left.

In Malaysia, politics was dominated by a single nationalist party and its minor coalition partners, but class and sectoral conflicts were secondary to ethnic rivalries. Indonesia remains a single-party system, with very limited pluralism. Thailand, despite periodic democratic openings, has shown a continuity in economic policy thanks to the central role of the bureaucracy and the continuing influence of the military.

South Korea and Taiwan once again provide sharp contrasts to the Latin American cases. Until the transition toward more pluralist politics in the two countries in the mid-1980s, both South Korea and Taiwan (beginning in 1972 and 1949, respectively) were ruled by strong, anticommunist, authoritarian regimes that limited the possibilities for interest group organization. Taiwan's one-party system effectively organized and controlled the unions and disallowed opposition parties. The South Korean government combined informal penetration of the unions and periodic repression to keep labor and urban-based opposition forces in check. The recurrence of urban-based opposition among students and workers may explain the Korean government's greater tolerance for an expansionist macroeconomic policy, but the opportunity for open political organization and populist appeals was severely limited. Both countries showed a continuity in government unparalleled in any of the Latin American governments except Chile.

This discussion suggests that the middle-income countries of Latin America and East and Southeast Asia can be arrayed on a continuum from very high to low levels of group and party conflict. Argentina, Chile, Brazil, Uruguay, and Peru appear at one extreme, with relatively large popular sectors and with political movements and party structures that historically tended to reinforce sectoral and class conflicts; these countries have historically also had higher levels of inflation. At the other pole are Indonesia, Taiwan, and Thailand, where the popular sectors were smaller and both political alliances and party structures less conducive to the emergence of populist movements; these countries have also generally had lower levels of inflation. The other Latin American and Asian countries fall between these two polar types, with varying degrees of urban and working-class mobilization and organization.

THE POLITICS OF STABILIZATION

These stylized patterns of political conflict also help explain variations in the political management of stabilization over time. Stabilization efforts have encountered the greatest difficulties in those countries where intense group conflicts and persistently high levels of inflation have fed on each other over long periods of time. In these circumstances, the capacity to impose stabilization has in the past been linked to the nature of the political regime, suggesting once again the importance of institutional variables in explaining policy outcomes.

There are examples of populist military governments: Bolivia in 1970–1971, the Peruvian experiment in the early 1970s, and the first year of South Korea's military rule in 1961–1962. Typically, however, militaries have seized power in the midst of political-economic crises characteristic of the later stages of the populist cycle outlined above. They have initially pursued policies designed to impose discipline and rationalize the economic system, in part by limiting the demands of leftist, populist, and labor groups. This general pattern was followed, with varying constraints, in Brazil (1964), Argentina (1966, 1976), Indonesia (1965), Chile (1973), Uruguay (1973), and arguably South Korea (1980–1981).

As the initial crisis is brought under control, military regimes begin to face new problems of consolidation or transition. Old political forces resurface, and regimes face pressure to build support and moderate the militancy of the opposition. Brazil provides an example. The government's decision to pursue high-growth policies during the oil shocks coincided closely with the military's decisions concerning the opening of the political system.

The transition to democratic rule in such systems is likely to pose particular problems for stabilization efforts. The transition opens the way for well-organized and long-standing popular sector groups to reenter politics, groups that had been controlled or repressed under military rule. High inflation and erratic growth make the distributional and political costs of fiscal restraint appear particularly formidable, but these costs are compounded by the uncertainties associated with the transition itself. New political leaders are necessarily preoccupied with securing the transition, and thus have relatively short time horizons. Those political forces that have been in opposition, or simply suppressed, are eager to press new demands on the government. As political leaders attempt to accommodate these strongly conflicting demands, it becomes difficult to maintain macroeconomic stability.

It could be argued, however, that the transition process is less important in explaining macroeconomic policy than the nature of the economic problems these governments inherited from their authoritarian predecessors. First, in countries with chronically high inflation, both authoritarian and democratic governments have accommodated conflicts over income shares through indexing. Indexing itself generates inertial inflation and complicates the conduct of monetary and fiscal policy. Second, the severity and speed of external shocks, particularly the withdrawal of external lending, severely narrowed the range of economic policy choice. Economic legacies, rather than political constraints, matter; Argentina simply inherited greater difficulties than the Philippines or South Korea.

Yet in the transitional democracies that faced high inflations, political constraints do appear to be significant in the making of macroeconomic policy. The three experiments with heterodox adjustment strategies — Argentina, Brazil, and Peru — occurred in systems with a high level of popular sector mobilization. Brazil under José Sarney and Peru under Alán García responded to high inflation with heterodox policies in the mid-1980s that included wage-price controls and currency reforms. In contrast to Mexico, however, neither new democratic government placed a high priority on containing wage pressures, reducing subsidies, or controlling spending, and both experiments ran into difficulties. Raúl Alfonsín's middle-class government in Argentina also pursued a heterodox shock policy to manage high inflation, but initially placed greater emphasis on negotiating wage restraint and bringing deficits under control. Nonetheless, fiscal policy remained a source of inflationary pressure, stabilization efforts faltered, and political competition with the Peronists and the anticipation of a change of government ultimately undermined the coherence of macroeconomic policy.

The interesting exception is Uruguay, one of the most economically successful of the new Latin American democracies. The return to constitutionalism in Uruguay restored the dominance of the two, broad-based centrist parties that had dominated political life until the coup in 1973, providing a framework for elite negotiation and accord much like that in more established democratic systems such as Colombia and Venezuela. Negotiations between the Blanco and Colorado parties led to an economic policy agreement in early 1985 that emphasized controlling budget deficits and inflation, promoting exports, and undertaking structural reforms.

The transition to democracy has played a less important role in explaining macroeconomic policy in countries with a lower level of popular sector mobilization and a greater institutional continuity in political and decision-making structures. Not coincidentally, these countries also faced less daunting economic problems, and it can once again be argued that economic circumstance rather than political factors account for the variance. It nonetheless appears plausible that politics had at least an intervening effect on policy choices and outcomes.

In Thailand, the new political order ushered in by parliamentary elections in 1979 might be labeled semidemocratic. In 1980, General Kriangsak was forced to resign over economic mismanagement in the face of rising protest and pressure from within the military. Another general, Prem Tinsulanon, was elected by a large majority in both houses to replace him. Prem moved to incorporate opposition parties into a broad-based coalition, yet to Thailand's "bureaucratic polity," power continued to reside in the army and bureaucracy. There were no fundamental discontinuities in business-government relations and technocrats even gained in influence.

In South Korea, General Chun Doo-hwan's handpicked successor, Roh Tae-woo, was forced to widen the scope of political liberalization and constitutional reforms in the wake of widespread urban protests in 1986 and 1987 that included students, workers, and middle-class elements. Running against a split opposition, Roh captured the presidency with just over one-third of the popular vote. Though the conservative ruling party subsequently lost control of the National Assembly and has been forced to make a number of economic concessions, including those to labor and farmers, the executive and bureaucracy maintain comparatively tight control over fiscal policy.

In the Philippines, Aquino was brought to power by massive middle-class demonstrations against fraudulent elections in February 1986. The "revolution" did not rest on popular sector mobilization; indeed, the left made the tactical error of not supporting Aquino's presidential candidacy. Subsequent development planning focused greater attention on rural problems in an effort to counteract the insurgency, and the government pursued a mild Keynesian stimulus through a public works program. But Aquino also moved quickly to cement ties with those portions of the private sector disadvantaged by Marcos' cronyism and Aquino's economic cabinet was dominated by businessmen-turned-technocrats. The reconvening of Congress in 1987 provided new opportunities for pork-barrel politics, but as in Thailand and Korea, fundamental political and institutional continuities limited political pressures on macroeconomic policy.

More generally, in those countries where underlying class and sectoral cleavages are less intense, or where class and sectoral cleavages have been muted by integrative forms of party organization, the political stakes of stabilization appear lower. This has two further implications. First, the capacity to carry out stabilization programs in these cases is not closely influenced by the type of regime. Democratic governments in Venezuela and Colombia have done as well or better at maintaining fiscal discipline as systems dominated by one party such as Mexico.

Second, where the parties are less polarized and the process of political succession is institutionalized, changes of government should not be expected to produce major shifts in policy. In such crises, unlike in high-conflict societies, newly elected governments do not usually represent previously excluded groups that expect immediate material payoffs. The time horizons of political leaders are therefore likely to be longer.

Democratic governments of this sort may be subject to political business cycles, but they are also in a better position to capitalize on the honeymoon effect by imposing stabilization programs early in their terms. This, too, is related to the time horizons of politicians in more institutionalized systems. With greater expectations that they will be able to reap the political benefits of stable policies, politicians will be less tempted toward unsustainable expansionist policies. . . .

VII

CURRENT PROBLEMS IN INTERNATIONAL POLITICAL ECONOMY

At the dawn of the new millennium, the international economy is ever more global in scope and orientation. In the 1970s, analysts worried that America's economic decline would lead to a new bout of protectionism and economic closure. In the 1980s, scholars trumpeted the Japanese model of state-led economic growth and feared the consequences of the international debt crisis. Today, policy makers and analysts alike are concerned with the consequences of a global market. Although less fearful that the international economy will collapse into a new round of beggar-thy-neighbor policies, analysts and individual citizens today worry more about untrammeled markets degrading the environment, displacing the nation-state as the primary locus of political activity and undermining the social welfare state, which had been the foundation of the postwar international economic order in the developed world.

As we become increasingly aware of the effects of environmental degrada-tion — both globally, as with ozone depletion, and locally, as with species preser-vation — pressures build for the imposition of greater governmental regulations to control pollution and manage scarce natural resources. But these pressures have increased at different rates in different countries, creating difficult problems of international policy coordination. Alison Butler (Reading 29) surveys the eco-nomics of environmental degradation, examines how efforts to protect the envi-ronment affect trade, and explores how countries with different preferences and policies on the environment can best manage their relations and influence environ-mental quality without damaging trade relations.

As the international political economy becomes more "globalized," many observers predict that the nation-state will be forced to cede political authority upward, to supranational entities (like the European Union); downward, to sub-national regions (as reflected in the growth of regionalist movements in Spain, the United Kingdom, and elsewhere); or sideways, to nongovernmental organiza-tions (NGOs) (such as Greenpeace or Amnesty International). Even if Charles Kindleberger's pronouncement that the "nation-state is just about through as an economic unit" proved premature when first issued in 1969, many expect it to become increasingly relevant in the near future.[1] Addressing this debate, Philip G. Cerny (Reading 30) argues that states and markets are diverging under the pressures of the "complex, globalizing world of the third industrial revolution." He predicts the development of an increasingly heterogeneous, multilayered system of political authority in which different economic activities are regulated by varying sets of institutions functioning above, below, and alongside the sovereign territorial state.

Dani Rodrik (Reading 31) counters the common view that globalization is significantly reducing the policy autonomy of states. To date, globalization has rested on resilient social safety nets in the industrialized countries; Rodrik finds a strong relationship between openness to trade and national spending on various forms of social protection. The real danger, he argues, is that globalization depresses the wages of the lowest-skilled workers in developed economies and is beginning to erode the safety nets. If present trends continue unchecked, he concludes, political support for policies of international economic openness may erode as well.

NOTE

1. Charles P. Kindleberger, *American Business Abroad* (New Haven: Yale University Press, 1969), p. 207.

29

Environmental Protection and Free Trade: Are They Mutually Exclusive?

ALISON BUTLER

In this essay, Alison Butler surveys the complex relationship between environmental protection and trade. Beginning with an economic analysis of pollution and environmental protection, Butler identifies the primary effects of environmental regulation on international trade. Environmental regulation typically reduces the supply of a controlled good in a regulated country; therefore, producers in other states increase production of that good and export it to the regulated state. Whether such a shift in production and trade will improve welfare, Butler argues, depends on national preferences for environmental quality. The selection concludes by examining transboundary pollution issues and current international regulations on the environment and trade.

Having to compete in the United States in a totally free market atmosphere with companies and countries who have yet to develop such environmental standards is inherently unfair. It puts us into a game where the unevenness of the rules almost assures that we cannot win or even hold our own.

— James E. Hermesdorf, *Testimony to Senate Finance Committee on Trade and the Environment,* October 25, 1991

Comments like the one cited above are being heard with increasing frequency. In fact, protecting the environment has always had implications for international trade. In 1906, for example, the United States barred the importation of insects that could harm crops or forests. Similarly, the Alaska Fisheries Act of 1926 established federal regulation of nets and other fishing gear and made it illegal to import salmon from waters outside U.S. jurisdiction that violated these regulations. More recently, a U.S. law restricting the method of harvesting tuna to protect dolphins has been the subject of a trade dispute between the United States and Mexico.

In recent years, as global warming and other environmental concerns have multiplied, environmental issues have played an increasing role in trade negotiations, further complicating what are generally difficult negotiations. Negotiating environmental regulations multilaterally is especially problematic because of differences in preferences and income levels across countries. What's more, scientific evidence is not always conclusive on the effects of certain types of environmental degradation. Finally, environmental considerations can be used to disguise protectionist policies.

This paper examines the different ways environmental policy can have international ramifications and their implications for international trade and international trade agreements. A general introduction to environmental economics is given, followed by an analysis of the relationship between environmental policy and international trade. The paper concludes with a discussion of the status of environmental considerations in multilateral trade agreements.

AN ECONOMIC RATIONALE FOR ENVIRONMENTAL POLICY

The environment is used primarily in three ways: as a consumption good, a supplier of resources and a receptacle of wastes. These three uses may conflict with one another. For example, using a river as a receptacle of wastes can conflict with its use as a supplier of resources and as a consumption good. When either the production or consumption of a good causes a cost that is not reflected in a market price, market failures that are termed "externalities" may exist. Such market failures frequently involve the environment.

A.C. Pigou, in *The Economics of Welfare* (originally published in 1920), presented one of the classic examples of an externality. In the early 1900s, many towns in Great Britain were heavily polluted by smoke coming from factory chimneys. Laundered clothes hung outside to dry were dirtied by the smoke. A study done in the heavily polluted city of Manchester in 1918 compared the cost of household washing in that city with that of the relatively cleaner city of Harrogate. According to the Manchester Air Pollution Advisory Board:

> The total loss for the whole city, taking the extra cost of fuel and washing materials alone, disregarding the extra labour involved, and assuming no greater loss for middle-class than for working-class households (a considerable understatement), works out at over £290,000 a year for a population of three quarters of a million.

Thus, a by-product of production — smoke — unintentionally had a negative effect on another economic activity — clothes-washing.

Why Do Externalities Occur?

Externalities exist when the *social cost* of an activity differs from the *private cost* because of the absence of property rights. In the preceding example, because no one "owns" the air, the factory does not take into account the extra washing costs it imposes on the citizens of the town. As a result, more pollution than is socially optimal will occur because the private cost of the smoke emissions to the firm (zero) is lower than the social cost (£290,000 a year). In general, if nothing is done about negative externalities, environmental damage will result as ecologically harmful products are overproduced and the environment is overused.

To eliminate externalities, the divergence between the social and private costs must be eliminated, either by assigning private property rights (that is, ownership rights) or by direct government regulation. The approach taken often depends on whether property rights can be assigned. The advantage of assigning property rights to an externality is that it creates a market for that product and allows the price mechanism to reflect the value of the externality.

Example of Assigning Property Rights

Suppose a chemical factory locates upstream from a small town and emits waste into the river as part of its production process. Suppose further that the town uses the river as its primary source of water. As a result of these emissions, the town must process the water before use. Clearly there is an externality associated with the firm's use of the water — it is no longer usable to the town without cost. If property rights to the river could be assigned to either the town or the firm, then the two parties could bargain for the most efficient level of pollutants in the water.

If property rights are assigned to the firm, the town pays the firm to reduce its pollution. The town's willingness to pay for reduced levels of pollution depends on the benefits it receives from cleaner water. Generally speaking, as the water becomes more pure, the additional (marginal) benefits to the town likely decrease. On the other hand, the firm's willingness to reduce pollution depends on the costs it incurs to reduce pollution by, for example, changing to a more costly production or waste-disposal method. Generally speaking, as the firm pollutes less, the additional (marginal) costs to the firm increase. The amount of pollution agreed upon will be such that the added benefits to the town of a further reduction in pollution are less than the added costs to the firm of the further reduction.

If property rights are assigned to the town, on the other hand, the firm pays the town [for the right] to pollute. The firm's willingness to pay for the right to pollute depends on the benefits it receives from polluting. These benefits are directly related to the costs it incurs from using a more costly production or waste-disposal method. Similarly, the town's willingness to sell pollution rights depends on the costs it incurs from additional pollution. The amount of pollution agreed upon is where the additional benefits to the firm of increasing pollution are less than the additional costs to the town of additional pollution.

The Coase theorem proves that the equilibrium level of pollution is the same in the preceding cases. Furthermore, such an outcome is efficient. Thus, when property rights are clearly defined and there is an explicitly designated polluter and victim, the efficient outcome is independent of how the property rights are assigned.

Limitations of the Coase Theorem

The key result of the Coase theorem, that the allocation of property rights does not affect the efficient amount of pollution, has limited application. If there are multiple polluters and/or many parties affected by the pollution, the outcome *can* depend on how property rights are assigned. Similarly, if there are significant transactions costs, such as measurement and enforcement costs, the Coase theorem may not hold.

Assume, for example, that two towns are affected by the factory's emissions, one further downstream than the other. Suppose that the town further away from the chemical plant has lower costs associated with cleaning the water. In this case, the amount of compensation the towns would be willing to pay to reduce emissions by any given amount would differ. Thus, the allocation of property rights among the firm and the two towns would affect the outcome of their bargaining.

Suppose, instead, that more than one firm is polluting. Determining how much pollution is coming from each firm, along with ensuring that each firm lives up to any agreement, may be difficult and costly. If monitoring costs are high, the Coase theorem may not hold and the allocation of property rights again affects the choice of optimal emissions.

The lack of general applicability of the Coase theorem is not an indictment of using market-oriented incentives (which usually requires assigning property rights). Most economists believe that market-oriented solutions will lead to the most efficient use of resources because, rather than having the government attempt to estimate preferences, it allows the market mechanism to reveal them.

Government Regulation

Property rights are not always assigned because many uses of the environment are considered public goods. A pure public good is one that has two qualities: First, it is impossible or extremely costly to exclude people from the benefits or costs of the good (non-excludability). For example, even if a person does not contribute to cleaning the air, she still cannot be excluded from breathing the cleaner air. Second, the consumption of the good by one person does not diminish the amount of that good available to someone else (non-rivalry). For example, the fact that one person is breathing clean air does not reduce the amount of clean air others breathe. In this case, property rights cannot be assigned because rationing is impossible.

While few uses of the environment are pure public goods like air, many have enough features of non-excludability and non-rivalry to make assigning property rights virtually impossible. The functions of the environment that are public goods, such as breathable air and clean water, are summarized by the term *environmental quality*.

Regulating environmental quality is difficult because the government first needs to determine the public's demand for environmental quality before deciding the efficient level of pollution. The *free-rider* problem that occurs with public goods makes this determination especially difficult. When people cannot be excluded from use, they have an incentive to understate their willingness to pay for environmental quality because they can gamble that others will be willing to pay. Similarly, if they are asked their preferences and know they will not have to pay, people have an incentive to overstate their desire for a given public good. The degree to which free-riding is a problem depends on the size of the non-rival group affected. The larger the group, the greater the free-rider problem.

For the purposes of this paper, we will assume that to determine the "true" value of public goods, the government measures the costs of pollution reduction and the benefits of pollution abatement accurately. Using a cost-benefit approach, the optimal outcome is where the marginal cost of pollution reduction equals the marginal benefit of pollution abatement.

It is important to recognize that the socially optimal level of pollution is generally not zero. Achieving zero pollution would require an extremely low level of production or an extremely high cost of pollution control. In determining the optimal amount of pollution, both the costs to individuals and industry need to be taken into account.

Example of Government Regulation of the Environment: An Emissions Tax

Recall the previous example of a firm emitting pollutants into a river. Suppose the government decides to regulate the industry because there are too many polluting firms on the river to define property rights adequately. After determining the socially optimal level of pollution, the government imposes a per-unit tax on emissions to reduce pollution to the optimal level.

What happens to production? Figure 1 shows the supply and demand curves for the industry's output. The effect of the tax is to shift the supply curve the

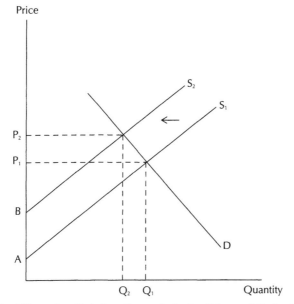

FIGURE 1. The Effect of an Emissions Tax on Industry Price and Output

distance AB (the additional per-unit cost of output given the new tax). The price rises from P_1 to P_2, and the quantity of output falls from Q_1 to Q_2, which is the output level associated with the efficient emission level. Emissions are reduced and environmental quality improves.

THE TRADE-RELATED ASPECTS OF ENVIRONMENTAL QUALITY

Pollution can have international effects in two ways. First, it might be localized within national boundaries but, through the impact of environmental policy, affect a country's international trade. On the other hand, pollution may be transported across borders without the consent of the countries affected (so-called transfrontier pollution). These two types of environmental damage have different effects on international trade and, therefore, are discussed separately.

Why Do Countries Trade?

Countries trade because of differences in comparative advantage. The idea of comparative advantage suggests that, given demand, countries should export products that they can produce relatively cheaply and import products for which they have a relative cost disadvantage. Traditional international trade models ignore externalities such as non-priced uses of the environment.

By not explicitly including the environment as a factor of production, the costs associated with using the environment are ignored. More recent economic models have extended the definition of factors to include *assimilative capacity,* that is, the capacity of the environment to reduce pollutants by natural processes. The degree to which the environment will be affected by its use or by the production of ecologically harmful products depends on its assimilative capacity. The higher the assimilative capacity, the less the environmental damage caused by the emission of a given amount of pollutants. Assimilative capacity can differ across regions and countries and thus is an important factor in determining the effects of environmental use on trade.

Traditional trade models also ignore the non-priced use of the environment as a consumption good. This underestimates the value consumers may place on the environment and therefore the cost of using the environment for other functions. These two factors can be significant in determining a country's comparative advantage.

Why Would Countries Choose Different Levels of Environmental Quality?

Assimilative capacity is one of the principal factors affecting a country's choice of environmental quality. In general, assimilative capacity is lower in industrialized countries because of the effects of past pollution. Less-industrialized countries often have greater assimilative capacities and thus can tolerate a higher level of emissions without increasing pollution levels. Population density and geography also affect a country's assimilative capacity. For example, the introduction of a polluting industry in a sparsely populated area, all else equal, will likely not affect the assimilative capacity of that area as much as it would in a densely populated area.

Other factors can also affect a country's willingness to accept environmental degradation. For example, poor countries may put a higher priority on the benefits of production (such as higher employment and income) relative to the benefits of environmental quality than wealthy countries. As income levels increase, however, demand for environmental quality also rises. Thus, countries with similar assimilative capacities might choose different levels of environmental quality. As the example below demonstrates, environmental policies that result from differences in countries' preferences and income levels can have significant trade effects.

Environmental Policy When Pollution Is within National Boundaries

How does environmental policy affect trade? Recall that, in the emissions tax example, the higher production costs that resulted from the tax caused the price of the industry's output to increase and the quantity produced to fall. Assume there is a chemical industry in another country producing the same product with the same level of emissions. For simplicity, assume that prior to the implementation of environmental controls, each industry produced just enough to meet its home demand, and the price was the same in both countries. As a result, trade did not occur. Suppose, because of different preferences, income levels or assimilative capacity, it is optimal to impose environmental controls in one country but not in the other. What happens to price, output, and environmental quality in the two countries?

The answer depends in part on whether the two countries can trade. If trade does not occur, the effect is the same as in the previous example. As Figure 1 shows, in the country where pollution controls were imposed, the price will rise to P_2 and the quantity of output will fall to Q_2, while in the other country nothing changes. Figure 2 shows the effect of an emissions tax on price and output in the two countries when trade occurs. The reduction in supply of the chemical in the taxed country (Tax) will reduce the world supply of that product, causing the world supply curve to shift upward to the left. At the new world equilibrium, D, the price, P_3, is lower than the autarkic (no trade) equilibrium price in Tax (P_2), but higher than the autarkic equilibrium price in the other country, Notax (P_1). At P_3, consumers in Notax demand Q_4, but firms are willing to supply Q_5. The distance X_2 is exactly equal to the distance X_1, which measures the difference between what firms in Tax are willing to supply at P_3 (Q_4) and what consumers demand at that price (Q_5). As a result, Notax exports the quantity X_2 of the chemical to Tax.

What is the effect on other economic variables? Consumption of the chemical falls in Notax, even though output rises. In general, because of the increased production in Notax, there will be an increase in pollution emissions in that country. How much the pollution *level* actually increases in Notax (if at all) depends on the assimilative capacity and the method of production used in that country. Whether

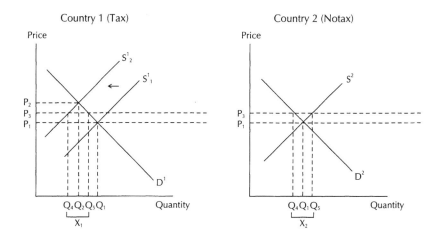

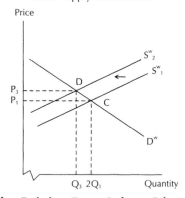

FIGURE 2. The Effect of an Emissions Tax on Industry Price and Output in a Two-Country World

the people in Notax are better off at the potentially higher level of pollution that resulted from increased production depends on that country's willingness to accept higher pollution for higher income.

Pollution declines in Tax. If the assimilative capacity is higher in Notax, world pollution will likely be lower after environmental controls are implemented. The effect on world employment is ambiguous and depends on certain country-specific variables. The terms of trade will deteriorate for the country with the emissions tax.

If the new level of emissions in each country is optimal given preferences and income, both countries are better off by trade. The taxed country is able to consume more at a lower price than in the autarkic case, while the value of total output rises in Notax. If measures of national income or wealth accurately reflected environmental damage, they would increase in both countries.

Does Environmental Protection Distort Trade?

One concern is that environmental regulation unfairly discriminates against domestic firms when they compete with firms in a country that has lower environmental standards. In the example discussed above, an externality existed in Tax but, by assumption, not in Notax. As a result, introducing environmental controls eliminated a distortion that previously existed. This changed the flow of trade, but caused all the costs of using the environment, both as inputs in production and as consumption items, to be reflected in market prices. Thus, assuming that environmental quality was not socially optimal before protections were enacted, pollution-intensive sectors in Tax were actually receiving an implicit subsidy from those who had been incurring the external costs of pollution.

The difficulties in trying to determine the optimal amount of environmental quality within a country, as discussed above, are substantial. The optimal level of environmental quality in one country is unlikely to be optimal in another, particularly if the two countries have significantly different income levels. Attempting to impose one country's environmental standards on another by using import restrictions does not allow countries to capitalize fully on their comparative advantage. As discussed later, it is also illegal under current international trading rules.

Environmental Policy When Pollution Crosses National Boundaries

The previous section discussed the international effects of environmental policy when environmental damage is contained within national borders. Many other uses of the environment cause environmental damage across borders, such as acid rain, which results from sulphur dioxide emissions or worldwide, such as ozone depletion, which results primarily from chlorofluorocarbons (CFCs). Transfrontier pollution may occur in essentially four ways:

1. A firm's production takes place in one country, but pollutes *only* in another.
2. Both countries have firms whose production processes pollute, but each country's pollution is experienced *only* in the other country.
3. Pollution occurs as a result of production in one country but the effects are felt in *both* countries.
4. Both countries pollute, and the pollution generated by each is felt in *both* countries.

If pollution is of form 1 or 2, in the absence of an international agreement, the polluting country has no incentive to curtail its polluting activities by implementing an environmental policy. If, instead, pollution is of form 3 or 4, pollution may be regulated domestically. Without taking into account the pollution in the other country, however, these controls will not likely be optimal internationally. In the absence of a globally optimal international agreement, domestic policymakers have less incentive to take into account the costs imposed on a foreign country than if the costs were borne domestically. Thus, from a global perspective there will be excessive use of the environment.

International Policy in the Presence of Transfrontier Pollution

Suppose, as in case 1, the river being polluted by the chemical firm runs directly into another country and all the towns affected are in the foreign country. How is an appropriate policy determined? Previously, we assumed that a country weighed the costs and benefits of pollution, given its preferences for environmental quality, its income level and its assimilative capacity. Unfortunately, in the case of transfrontier pollution, this is no longer sufficient. In this case, domestic policymakers will be less concerned with the costs imposed on a foreign country than those borne domestically. In addition, the desired level of pollution could differ significantly between the two countries because of their preferences and income levels. Other issues contribute to the difficulties in negotiating an international agreement on pollution control. For example, should the polluter pay to reduce emissions or should the residents of the country affected by the pollution pay to induce the firm to reduce emissions?

In the early 1970s, countries belonging to the Organization for Economic Cooperation and Development (OECD), the multilateral organization of the industrialized countries, adopted the Polluter Pays Principle (PPP) to deal with purely domestic pollution. This principle requires that the polluter bear the cost of pollution-reducing measures. This approach, however, provides no guidance about how to determine environmental damage or what to make the polluter responsible to pay for. For example, should a polluter be responsible for damage that has already occurred, or should it be required only to pay to reduce current emission levels? In addition, PPP offers no instruction regarding transfers between governments to resolve problems of transfrontier pollution.

As a result of an OECD conference on transfrontier pollution, it was suggested that the OECD adopt the so-called "mutual compensation principle." This proposal requires the polluting country to provide an estimate of the costs of pollution abatement for various levels of pollution, while the polluted country similarly provides an estimate of the costs of treating the damages. An independent agency determines the optimal level of pollution with these two cost functions. Given the level of pollution set by the agency and the cost functions provided by the two countries, the polluting (polluted) country pays a pollution (treatment) tax based on the cost of the cleanup (control) estimated by the other country and is also required to pay for the cost of pollution abatement (cleanup) in their own country. The advantage of this approach is that it induces countries to reveal their "true" value of the environment. Unfortunately, because of the problems inherent in determining the optimal level of pollution as well as negotiating and implementing such a proposal, the mutual compensation principle has never been used.

There are other impediments to reaching international agreements on environmental use. For certain types of environmental degradation, there is debate about how much damage is actually being done to the environment. An obvious example of this is global warming. Many environmentalists and governments are concerned that excessive emissions of carbon dioxide, nitrogen oxide and methane gas from energy use are irreversibly warming the planet. Many others, including the U.S. government, however, feel that the evidence is insufficient at this point and are unwilling to significantly alter their environmental policy. Scientific evidence on global warming is inconclusive. An August 31, 1991, survey on energy and the environment in *The Economist* pointed out one of the difficulties with transfrontier environmental damage such as global warming: the appropriate policy may need to be implemented before conclusive proof of the damage appears, because of the cumulative effects of some types of environmental damage over time.

Nevertheless, some international agreements have been reached . . . and, if the significant increase in articles, studies and conferences on transfrontier pollution is any indication, there will be additional pressures to find new ways to deal with the increasing problem of transfrontier pollution.

NORTH-SOUTH ISSUES

One of the main reasons environmental policy affects trade is because countries are at different levels of industrialization and thus have different income levels, which can cause their optimal levels of pollution to differ. Because the interests between high- and low-income countries may differ, it is important to look more closely at these so-called North-South issues.

Currently the industrialized countries, in general, are greater polluters than less industrialized countries and thus tend to put a relatively greater demand on worldwide assimilative capacity. One concern heard in developing countries is that industrial economies, rather than reducing their own demand for assimilative services, could impose their environmental standards on developing countries without any assistance in paying for them, thereby reducing the opportunity for less-industrialized countries to grow. . . .

Other types of environmental issues have a particular North-South nature. For example, many of the world's nature preserves are in developing countries in Africa. Currently, trade in elephant hides and ivory, along with other endangered species, is prohibited under the Convention on International Trade in Endangered Species (CITES). At a recent conference on CITES in Kyoto, Japan, several African countries argued that their elephant herds are large enough to be culled without endangering the species. In addition, they argued, revenue generated by the sale of ivory and other elephant products is needed to fund future preservation.

Here, the interest of the industrialized countries, who do not have a native elephant population, is to protect an endangered species. The African countries, however, face a trade-off between the benefits of protecting the species and the loss of revenue associated with the prohibition of trade in elephant products. As a result, less-industrialized countries are putting increased pressure on industrialized countries to help pay for the services they are providing (such as species diversity).

In March 1992, the General Agreement on Tariffs and Trade (GATT), the main body regulating international trade, released a report entitled *Trade and the Environment,* that takes a non-traditional approach to North-South problems. One hotly debated issue concerns the protection of the rainforests, most of which are located in Latin America. Industrialized countries have moved to bar wood imports from Brazil and Thailand, for example, as a way to reduce deforestation in those countries. GATT argues that, rather than barring imports of wood products (much of which is GATT-illegal), the industrialized countries should compensate rainforest countries for providing "carbon absorption services."

Although this approach is novel, its advantage is that poorer countries are assisted with financing environmental protection, so that it does not come at the expense of economic development. This approach also reduces the free-rider problem that enables much of the world to benefit from the carbon absorption services provided by rainforests and the diversity of species provided by countries that are not the primary users of the environment. In addition, the approach directly protects the rainforests, rather than barring certain types of wood products in the hopes that doing so will cause the exporting countries to protect them.

Other approaches taken to improve environmental standards in lower-income, less-industrialized countries include debt-for-nature swaps. Here, foreign debt is purchased by environmental groups and sold back to the issuing governments in exchange for investment in local environmental projects, including the purchase of land that is then turned into environmental preserves.

CURRENT INTERNATIONAL REGULATIONS

At present, international agreements do not allow a country to discriminate against products based on their production techniques. Under GATT, barring imports because the production methods used do not meet the standards of the importing country is illegal. This rule has come under fire recently, particularly in light of the controversial tuna-dolphin dispute between the United States and Mexico.

The justification for prohibiting trade restrictions based on the production method is to prevent countries from using such restrictions to protect domestic industries. Unfortunately, GATT was not designed to address some of the more complicated issues of environmental protection, particularly regarding production methods that could have transborder or global effects. . . .

GATT's recently released report on the environment attempts to address some of these issues. Some have suggested, in addition, that GATT focus the next round of talks on environmental issues (assuming the current "Uruguay Round" of talks is successfully completed). The United Nations–sponsored "Earth Summit" in Rio de Janeiro [held in spring 1992, was] also an attempt to increase international cooperation on protecting the environment, particularly in regard to North-South issues.

CONCLUSION

This article examines the role of environmental policy on international trade. Environmental policy is justified because of the nature of externalities associated with using the environment. When the divergence between the social and private costs of using the environment is ignored, polluting activities receive an implicit subsidy. Environmental regulations may change international trade, but enhance social welfare by removing this subsidy. The optimal amount of environmental protection, however, can differ significantly across countries because of differences in preferences, income and assimilative capacities.

One important concern is that countries will use environmental policies as an excuse to establish protectionist policies. As environmental protection and environmental use take on a more transnational nature and the assimilative capacity is reduced worldwide, new agreements will have to be designed to both protect scarce resources and protect countries from being discriminated against because of how they choose to use their environmental endowments domestically. As the recent GATT report suggested, however, it is possible to protect the environment without distorting trade flows. Thus, free trade and environmental policy are not mutually exclusive but can work together to encourage both economic growth and environmental quality worldwide.

30

Globalization and the Changing Logic of Collective Action
PHILIP G. CERNY

Globalization is purported to have many effects. In this article, Philip Cerny argues that globalization is transforming states — the basic units of the international political economy — in profound ways. As the scale of markets widens and economic organizations become more complex, Cerny posits, current states are becoming insufficient to provide the range of public goods demanded by their citizens. Rather than creating a single "superstate," however, he identifies a series of overlapping political arenas that are developing at the local, intermediate, and transnational levels. States continue to have great cultural force, Cerny concludes, and will not soon disappear. However, they may suffer a crisis of legitimacy.

In both modern domestic political systems and the modern international system, the state has been the key structural arena within which collective action has been situated and undertaken, as well as exercising structural and relational power as an actor in its own right. However, the state is being not only eroded but also fundamentally transformed within a wider structural context. The international system is no longer simply a states system; rather, it is becoming increasingly characterized by a plural and composite — or what I [call] "plurilateral" — structure. This transformation has significant consequences for the logic of collective action. The word "globalization" often is used to represent this process of change. Globalization is neither uniform nor homogeneous; its boundaries are unclear and its constituent elements and multidimensional character have not as yet been adequately explored. But by reshaping the structural context of rational choice itself, globalization transforms the ways that the basic rules of the game work in politics and international relations and alters the increasingly complex payoff matrices faced by actors in rationally evaluating their options. . . .

. . . In the modern study of international relations, the state has constituted the key unit of collective action, while the interaction of states has been the very object of inquiry; similarly, in the domestic arena, the state has both encompassed the political system and constituted a potentially autonomous collective agent within that field.

Globalization, however, is changing all that. Globalization is defined here as a set of economic and political structures and processes deriving from the changing character of the goods and assets that comprise the base of the international political economy — in particular, the increasing structural differentiation of those goods and assets. "Structures" are more or less embedded sets — patterns — of constraints and opportunities confronting decision-making agents ("institutions" simply being more formalized structures); "processes" are dynamic patterns of interaction and change that take place on or across structured fields of action. Structural differentiation increasingly is spreading across borders and economic sectors, driving other changes and resulting in the increasing predominance of political and economic structures and processes that (1) are frequently (although not always) more transnational and multinational in scale (i.e., are in significant ways more inclusive) than the state, (2) potentially have a greater impact on outcomes in critical issue-areas than does the state (i.e., may in effect be more "sovereign"), and (3) may permit actors to be decisionally autonomous of the state. In particular, I argue that the more that the scale of goods and assets produced, exchanged, and/or used in a particular economic sector or activity diverges from the structural scale of the national state — both from above (the global scale) and from below (the local scale) — and the more that those divergences feed back into each other in complex ways, then the more that the authority, legitimacy, policy-making capacity, and policy-implementing effectiveness of states will be challenged from both without and within. A critical threshold may be crossed when the cumulative effect of globalization in strategically decisive issue-areas undermines the general capacity of the state to pursue the common good or the capacity of the state to be a true civil association; even if this threshold is not crossed, however, it is arguable that the role of the state both as playing field and as unit becomes structurally problematic.

The analysis here will focus on the changing nature and scale of public goods and private goods (expanding on the work of Mancur Olson) and on the relationship between specific assets and nonspecific assets (expanding on the work of Oliver Williamson) as the bases of both political-institutional and industrial market structure. . . .

This article focuses on the development of . . . "political economies of scale." In small-scale societies, goods and assets — and the structures and institutions that stabilize and regulate them — remain relatively undifferentiated. However, as the scale of goods and assets expands, major structural gaps can develop between different types of assets and between public goods and private goods. In particular, as European societies and economies grew in the late feudal and early capitalist periods, such a gap was filled by the emergence of the modern nation-state as an organizational form for providing public goods across both domestic and international arenas. Moreover, the development of scale economies in both the economic system and the political order during the nineteenth and early twentieth centuries dramatically reinforced and expanded the scope of this institutional isomorphism. A powerful structural convergence developed between the second industrial revolution economy, on the one hand, and the bureaucratic state, on the other. . . . In recent decades, however, an accelerating divergence has taken place between the structure of the state and the structure of industrial and financial markets in the complex, globalizing world of the third industrial revolution. There is a new disjuncture between institutional capacity to provide public goods and the structural characteristics of a much larger-scale, global economy. I suggest here that today's "residual state" faces crises of both organizational efficiency and institutional legitimacy. . . .

GOODS, ASSETS, AND POLITICAL ECONOMIES OF SCALE

The development of the modern state and the growth of capitalism involve a complex process of interaction, . . . first, between politics and economics, and, second, between market and hierarchy. Central to such developments are "political economies of scale," in which specific political structures . . . appear to be more or less efficient in stabilizing, regulating, controlling, or facilitating particular economic activities. Different economic processes are said to be characterized by different minimum efficient scales, given existing technology and size of market demand. Some optimal plant sizes remain small; others exhibit increasing returns to scale — that is, greater efficiency the bigger the factory or distribution system. Thus, in some cases, big is economically the most efficient, whereas in other cases small is beautiful. In the case of political economies of scale, the concept is expanded to include the scale of state structures, institutions, and processes and the economic tasks, roles, and activities they perform. Optimal political economies of scale therefore continually shift, adjusting to technological, sociological, and political change. Indeed, they have been shifting dramatically in the late twentieth century, both upward to the transnational and global levels and downward to the local level. In this more fluid environment, actors' choices have significant consequences for the changing structure of the state and, indeed, for the wider evolution of politics and society.

It is mistaken to assume that state structures are overwhelmingly hierarchical and bureaucratic in some inherent way, while economic structures are based essentially on market exchange. On the contrary, both state and economy are complex compounds of market and hierarchy as well as the outcome of the interaction between politics and economics. Evolution of political-economic structures results from the interaction of independent changes along each dimension (market/hierarchy and politics/economics) and from complex feedback effects that occur as the consequence of that interaction. For a state to approximate an overarching public role of the classical type would require it to have real and effective organizational capacity to shape, influence, and/or control designated economic activities (that is, those perceived to be the most socially significant such activities). In other words, it must stabilize, regulate, promote, and facilitate economic activity generally as well as exercise other forms of politically desired and/or structurally feasible control over more-specific targeted processes of production and exchange. The core of this [problem] lies in the character of the different kinds of . . . resources and values that are needed and/or desired by individuals and by society. . . . Identifying the structural characteristics of different goods and/or assets is crucial to understanding what rational players are likely to do in different situations.

I begin, like others, by distinguishing between two main polar types of good or asset. The best-known is [the] contrast between public goods (those that are non-divisible in crucial ways and from the use of which specific people cannot be easily or effectively excluded), on the one hand, and private goods (those that are both divisible and excludable), on the other. Note that "public" and "private" in this context do not refer to who *owns* the goods but to the specific structural features of the goods themselves: (1) whether the good(s) in question can in practice be divided between different users/owners, or whether they are composed of inseparable parts of a wider, inherently integrated entity; and (2) whether some people can be effectively excluded or prevented from using/owning the good(s) in question, or whether to make them available for one is to make them available to all.

A second distinction, found in institutional economics, is . . . between specific and nonspecific assets. This distinction is based upon two dimensions. The first is that of economies of scale in production, distribution, or exchange. Where returns to scale are high, then the more units of a good that are produced in a single integrated production process, the lower will be the marginal unit cost of production compared with smaller separate production processes; in asset terms, this means that the value of the entity kept as a whole would in theory be far more valuable than its "breakup" price. The second dimension is that of transaction costs, i.e., those costs incurred in the process of attempting to fix an efficiency price for an asset and actually to exchange it for another substitute asset. Transaction costs normally include negotiation costs, monitoring costs, enforcement costs, and the like. A specific asset is one for which there is no easily available substitute. Its exchange would involve high transaction costs, high economies of scale, or both, leading to difficulty in finding efficiency prices and ready markets. In turn, different types of good or asset are said to be more or less efficiently provided through distinct sets of structural arrangements or institutions, rather than simply through abstract economic processes. Markets in the real world are institutions — not spontaneous, unorganized activities. . . . [P]ublic goods cannot be provided in optimal amounts through a market, for free riders will not pay their share of the costs. Only authoritative structures and processes make it possible for costs to be efficiently recouped from the users of public goods. . . . [S]pecific assets are also more efficiently organized and managed authoritatively, through hierarchy. . . . Such authoritative allocation is done through long-term contracting (keeping the same collaborators) and decision making by managerial fiat (integration, merger, cartelization, etc.) rather than through the short-term, "recurrent contracting" of marketable, easily substitutable, nonspecific assets. Whereas efficient regulation of the market for the latter merely requires post hoc legal adjudication through contract law and the courts, the former requires increasing degrees of proactive institutionalized governance in the allocation of resources and values. Different kinds of structural integration — distinct mixes of market and hierarchy — may be judged to suit particular mixes of specific and nonspecific assets.

The sort of legitimate, holistic political authority characteristic of the traditional state reflects either an institutionalized commitment to provide public goods efficiently, or the presence of extensive specific assets, or both. The latter are mainly embodied in people (human capital), immobile factors of capital such as infrastructure, and the promotion of certain types of large-scale integrated industrial processes. Of course, traditional conceptions of the state also extend to other specific factors, especially national defense (the capacity to wage war being particularly public and specific); promotion of a common culture, national ideology, or set of constitutional norms; preservation of collective unity in the face of the "other"; and maintenance of a widely acceptable and functioning legal system. These sorts of tasks and activities also would normally be more efficiently carried out through predominantly hierarchical institutions (a classic conundrum of decision making in a liberal democracy). However, in the real world, most economic and political processes involve either a mix of market and hierarchy or goods having mixed public and private characteristics. In this context, it is important to remember that politics involves not only constructing relatively efficient structures within which to provide public goods and minimize transaction costs in the maintenance of specific assets but also managing the overarching system within which both types of goods and assets are produced and exchanged — this system itself constituting a public good.

THE HISTORICAL EVOLUTION
OF POLITICAL ECONOMIES OF SCALE

Such complex political-economic structures develop mainly through a continuing process . . . of tinkering. Occasional paradigmatic change does occur however when the requirements for providing . . . both public goods and private goods in some workable combination increase beyond the capacity of the institutional structure to reconcile the two over the medium-to-long term. Such major transformations are reflected in historical changes from small-scale to large-scale societies. At one end of the spectrum, the smaller the scale of an economy/society the more the public and private are likely to overlap and coincide. Such mechanisms remain relatively undifferentiated. The outstanding exemplar of how this management system works can be seen in the role of kinship as studied by anthropologists. Subsistence and early surplus production and reproduction in small, relatively isolated communities usually involve the emergence of a single, relatively homogeneous institutional structure in which economic and political power are part of the same more or less hierarchical system. . . .

In contrast, however, the larger and more complex the structural scale of a society/economy, the more assets and goods become differentiated. The scale of existing social and political arrangements for the stabilization and regulation of production, exchange, and consumption — i.e., for the provision of public goods — is likely to be suboptimal for the scale of public goods required and of specific assets involved. Furthermore, some former public goods and specific assets may be more readily and efficiently provided by the market, given the

between these economic sectors was interwoven with political and ideological clashes across a range of social and economic groups supporting different forms and combinations of authoritarianism and democracy. The internal control span of the state qua hierarchy was continually under challenge, even in the most outwardly authoritarian of states, and failures of hierarchy to work efficiently were commonplace.

Even more important in the long run was the interaction of these endogenous tensions with exogenous ones. On the exogenous level, the principal forms of tension between different types of goods or asset structures were those between the nationalization of warfare (and the production system necessary for modern total war), on the one hand, and the gradual, but uneven, internationalization of civilian production and exchange, on the other. Until World War I, the dynamics of economic competition and those of military rivalry were not so different with regard to many key issues, such as the development of dual-use railway systems, steel industries, and shipbuilding industries. Additionally, the nation-state constituted the predominant (although not the only) organizational unit for both types of activities. The international economic instability of the 1920s and the Great Depression of the 1930s, however, represented a fundamental loss of control by states, both authoritarian and liberal, over international economic processes. The immediate result was, of course, the attempt to reassert previously existing forms of control in more intensified forms — more potent authoritarian autarchic empires and the withdrawal of even liberal states behind trade barriers — as all major states tried to recapture hierarchical control over their economic processes.

Thus the story of capitalism in the second industrial revolution was one of uneven internationalization if not yet of globalization. . . .

. . . [A]lthough political consciousness remained overwhelmingly national, both security and economic structures — especially the latter — became increasingly internationalized. The later stages of the second industrial revolution itself — the so-called long boom — saw the beginnings of the decay of the second industrial revolution state. . . .

GLOBALIZATION AND THE CHANGING PUBLIC GOODS PROBLEM

The most important dimension of convergence between political and economic structures in the second industrial revolution state was the dominance of national-level organizational apparatuses in each sphere and the development of complex organized interfaces cutting across and linking the two spheres. . . . [A] fundamental transformation has taken place in the structure of public goods in today's global era, making both their pursuit and their provision through the nation-state more problematic.

Those traditionally conceived public goods have been primarily of three kinds. The first involves the establishment of a workable market framework for the ongoing operation of the system as a whole — regulatory public goods. These include the establishment and protection of private (and public) property rights, a stable currency, the abolition of internal barriers to production and exchange, standardization of weights and measures, a legal system to sanction and enforce contracts and to adjudicate disputes, a more specific regulatory system to stabilize and coordinate economic activities, a system of trade protection, and other systems that could be mobilized to counteract system-threatening market failures (such as lender of last resort facilities and emergency powers provisions). The second involves specific state-controlled or state-sponsored activities of production and distribution — productive/distributive public goods. Among these are full or partial public ownership of certain industries, direct or indirect provision of infrastructure and public services, direct or indirect involvement in finance capital, and myriad public subsidies. The third type of public goods are redistributive public goods, especially those resulting from the expanding political and public policy demands of emerging social classes, economic interests, and political parties and the responses of state actors to those demands. Redistributive goods include health and welfare services, employment policies, corporatist bargaining processes (although these often have had a significant regulatory function as well), and environmental protection—indeed, the main apparatus of the national welfare state. The provision of all three kinds of public goods in second industrial revolution states was dependent on the interweaving of large-scale specific assets between bureaucratic structures and structures of capital.

In a globalizing world, however, national states have difficulty supplying or fostering all of these categories of public good. Regulatory public goods are an obvious case. In a world of relatively open trade, financial deregulation, and the increasing impact of information technology, property rights are more difficult for the state to establish and maintain. For example, cross-border industrial espionage, counterfeiting of products, copyright violations, and the like have made the multilateral protection of intellectual property rights a focal point of international disputes and a bone of contention in the Uruguay Round of the General Agreement on Tariffs and Trade (now the World Trade Organization). International capital flows and the proliferation of offshore financial centers and tax havens have rendered firm ownership and firms' ability internally to allocate resources through transfer pricing and the like increasingly opaque to national tax and regulatory authorities. Traditional forms of trade protectionism, too, are both easily bypassed and counterproductive. Currency exchange rates and interest rates are increasingly set in globalizing marketplaces, and governments attempt to manipulate them at their peril. Legal rules are increasingly easy to evade, and attempts to extend the legal reach of the national state through the development of extraterritoriality are ineffective and hotly disputed. Finally, the ability of firms, market actors, and competing parts of the national state apparatus itself to defend and expand their economic and political turf through activities such as transnational policy networking and regulatory arbitrage — the capacity of industrial and financial sectors to whipsaw the state apparatus by pushing state agencies into a process of competitive deregulation or what economists call competition in laxity — has both undermined the control span of the state from without and fragmented it from within.

Furthermore, real or potential inefficiencies in the provision of regulatory public goods have much wider ramifications than merely for the provision of public goods per se, because they constitute the framework, the playing field, within which private goods as well as other public goods are provided in the wider economy and society. In other words, actors seeking to pursue regulatory public goods today are likely to see traditional state-based forms of regulation as neither efficient nor sufficient in a globalizing world. Perhaps a more familiar theme in the public goods literature, however, has been the impact of globalization on the capacity of the state to provide productive/distributive public goods. The most visible aspect of this impact has been the crisis of public ownership of strategic industries and the wave of privatization that have characterized the 1980s and 1990s. Once again, both political and economic scale factors are at work. At one level, such industries are no longer perceived as strategic. Steel, chemicals, railroad, motor vehicles, aircraft, shipbuilding, and basic energy industries were once seen as a core set of industries over which national control was necessary for both economic strength in peacetime and survival in wartime. Today, internationalization of the asset structure of these industries, of the goods they produce, and of the markets for those products — with foreign investment going in both directions— has caused the internationalization of even high-technology industries producing components for weaponry.

At the same time, the state is seen as structurally inappropriate for the task of directly providing productive/distributive goods. Public ownership of industry is thought so inherently inefficient economically (the "lame duck syndrome") as to render ineffectual its once-perceived benefits of permitting national planning, providing employment, or enlarging social justice. Third World countries increasingly reject delinkage and import substitution industrialization and embrace export promotion industrialization, thereby imbricating their economies even more closely with the global economy. Even where public ownership has been expanded, its ostensible rationale has been as part of a drive for international competitiveness and not an exercise in national exclusiveness, as in France in the early 1980s. The same can be said for more traditional forms of industrial policy, such as state subsidies to industry, public procurement of nationally produced goods and services, or trade protectionism. Monetarist and private sector supply-side economists deny that the state has ever been in a position to intervene in these matters in an economically efficient way and argue further that the possibility of playing such a role at all in today's globalized world has utterly evaporated in the era of "quicksilver capital" flowing across borders. However, even social liberal and other relatively interventionist economists nowadays regard the battle to retain the homogeneity of the national economy to be all but lost and argue that states are condemned to tinkering around the edges.

The outer limits of effective action by the state in this environment are usually seen to comprise its capacity to promote a relatively favorable investment climate for transnational capital — [that is], by providing an increasingly circumscribed range of goods that retain a national-scale (or subnational-scale) public character or of a particular type of still-specific assets described as immobile factors of capital. Such potentially manipulable factors include: human capital (the skills, experience, education, and training of the work force); infrastructure (from public transportation to high-technology information highways); support for a critical mass of research and development activities; basic public services necessary for a good quality of life for those working in middle- to high-level positions in otherwise footloose (transnationally mobile) firms and sectors; and maintenance of a public policy environment favorable to investment (and profit making) by such companies, whether domestic or foreign-owned. I [call] this mixture the "competition state."

Finally, of course, globalization has had a severe impact, both direct and indirect, on the possibility for the state efficiently to provide redistributive public goods. With regard to labor market policy, for example, corporatist bargaining and employment policies are everywhere under pressure — although somewhat unevenly, depending less on the country than on the sector concerned — in the face of international pressure for wage restraint and flexible working practices. The provision of education and training increasingly is taking priority over direct labor market intervention, worker protection, and incomes policies. With regard to the welfare state, although the developed states generally have not been able to reduce the overall weight of welfare spending in the economy, a highly significant shift from maintaining freestanding social and public services to merely keeping up with expanding existing commitments has occurred in many countries. Unemployment compensation and entitlement programs have ballooned as a consequence of industrial downsizing, increasing inequalities of wealth, homelessness, and the aging of the population in industrial societies, thereby tending to crowd out funding for other services. Finally, the most salient new sector of redistributive public goods, environmental protection, is especially transnational in character; pollution and the depletion of natural resources do not respect borders. Therefore, in all three of the principal categories of second industrial revolution public goods, globalization has undercut the policy capacity of the national state in all but a few areas. . . .

SCALE SHIFT AND THE THIRD INDUSTRIAL REVOLUTION

In addition to the changing scale of public goods, the changing technological and institutional context in which all goods are increasingly being produced and exchanged has been central to this transformation. The third industrial revolution has many characteristics, but those most relevant to our concern with scale shift involve five trends in particular, each bound up with the others. The first is the development of flexible manufacturing systems and their spread not only to new industries but to older ones as well. The second is the changing hierarchical form of firms (and bureaucracies) to what has been called "lean management." The third is the capacity of decision-making structures to monitor the actions of all levels of management and of the labor force far more closely through the use of information technology. The fourth is the segmentation of markets in a more complex consumer society. Finally, the third industrial revolution has been profoundly shaped by the emergence of increasingly autonomous transnational financial markets and institutions. . . .

. . . [F]inance embodies each of the main characteristics of the third industrial revolution. . . . In product terms, it has become the exemplar of a flexible industry, trading in notional and infinitely variable financial instruments. Financial innovation has been rapid and far-reaching, affecting all parts of the financial services industry and shaping every industrial sector. Furthermore, product innovation has been matched by process innovation. Traders and other financial market actors and firms are expected to act like entrepreneurs (or intrapreneurs) as a matter of course. Financial globalization has been virtually synonymous with the rapid development of electronic computer and communications technology. The ownership and transfer of shares and other financial instruments increasingly are recorded only on computer files, without the exchange of paper certificates — what the French call dematerialization — although written documentation can always be provided for financial controllers, auditors, or regulators (in principle, at least although in practice fraud adapts quickly). With increasing globalization of production and trade, market demand for financial services products continually is segmenting, too.

Probably the most important consequence of the globalization of financial markets is their increasing structural hegemony in wider economic and political structures and processes. In a more open world, financial balances and flows increasingly are dominant — with the volume of financial transactions variously estimated as totaling twenty to forty times the value of merchandise trade. This gap is growing rapidly as private international capital markets expand. Exchange rates and interest rates, as essential to business decision making as to public policymaking, increasingly are determined by world market conditions. In addition, as trade and production structures in the third industrial revolution go through the kinds of changes outlined earlier, they will be increasingly coordinated through the application of complex financial controls, accounting techniques, and financial performance indicators. . . . These strictures are applicable to a range of organizations, including government bureaucracies. Financial markets epitomize, in Williamson's terms, the structural ascendancy of almost purely nonspecific assets over specific assets in the global economy, pushing and pulling other economic sectors and activities unevenly into the global arena.

COLLECTIVE ACTION AND THE RESIDUAL STATE

The economic and political world of the third industrial revolution revolves around a central paradox. On the one hand, globalization would seem to entail the shift of the world economy to an even larger structural scale. This perception of globalization was what led observers a decade or two ago to misinterpret the significance of multinational corporations, which were seen as involving the worldwide integration of specific assets. Of course, many such firms, and some problems like environmental pollution, do resemble this model of an upward shift in scale, potentially requiring transnational-level institutions for effective regulation. However, economic restructuring has involved a more complex process, altering the composition of public goods and specific assets and even involving the privatization and marketization of the political-economic structure itself. These processes lead in turn to the whipsawing of states between structural pressures and organizational levels that they cannot control in a complex, circular fashion. Thus economic globalization contributes not to the supersession of the state by a homogeneous world order as such but to the differentiation of the existing national and international political orders, as well. Indeed, globalization leads to a growing disjunction between the democratic, constitutional, and social aspirations of people — which continue to be shaped by and understood through the framework of the territorial state — and the increasingly problematic potential for collective action through state political processes. . . .

Despite these changes, of course, states retain certain vital political and economic functions at both the domestic and international levels. Indeed, some of these have paradoxically been strengthened by globalization. But the character of these functions is changing. New collective action problems undermine the constraining character of previously dominant political and economic games. As a result, policymakers everywhere are seeking to restructure the state so that it can play new roles in the future. While the state retains a crucial role in the political-economic matrix of a globalizing world, however, its holistic and overarching character . . . may be increasingly compromised. The state today is a potentially unstable mix of civil association and enterprise association — of constitutional state, pressure group, and firm — with state actors, no longer so autonomous, feeling their way uneasily in an unfamiliar world. . . .

The structural coherence, power, and autonomy of states themselves clearly have become problematic in recent years. Over the past four centuries, the state has become the repository of probably the most important dimension of human society — social identity, and in this case, national identity. This sense of national identity has been reinforced both by nationalism and by the spread of democratic institutions and processes. Indeed, liberal democracy has constituted the most important linkage or interface between social identity on the one hand and state structures and processes on the other. Therefore, the first main bulwark of the state, even in a globalizing world, is found in the deep social roots of *gemeinschaftlich* national identity that have developed through the modern nation-state. Such identities are bound to decline to some extent, both through the erosion of the national public sphere from above and from the reassertion of substate ethnic, cultural, and religious identities from below. Thus the decay of the cultural underpinnings of the state — of rain-or-shine loyalty — will be uneven, and in economically stronger states this decay is likely to proceed more slowly than in weaker ones.

This will be particularly true if the potential capacity of the more developed states to provide infrastructure, education systems, workforce skills, and quality-of-life amenities (usually classed among the immobile factors of capital) to attract mobile, footloose capital of a highly sophisticated kind is effectively mobilized. On the one hand, the ability of states to control development planning, to collect and use their own tax revenues, to build infrastructure, to run education and training systems, and to enforce law and order gives actors continuing to work through the state a capacity to influence the provision of immobile factors of capital in many highly significant ways. If Europe, Japan, and the United States along with perhaps some others are better able to provide these advanced facilities, then *gemeinschaftlich* loyalty in those states may recede more slowly or even stabilize, maintaining the civil-associational character of the state even as many of its narrower functions are eroded. On the other hand, mobile international capital may well destabilize less-favored states, whose already fragile governmental systems will be torn by groups attempting to recast those *gemeinschaftlich* bonds through claims for the ascendancy of religious, ethnic, or other grassroots loyalties. The extent to which richer states are able to avoid such destabilization in the long run remains problematic, however.

State-based collective action continues to have a major role to play in the provision of certain crucial types of public goods and in the management of a range of significant specific assets, even if it must do so in a context where the authoritative power of the state as a whole is weaker and more circumscribed than it has been in the past. But rather than the state being directly responsible for market outcomes that guarantee the welfare of its citizens, the main focus of this competition state in the world . . . is the proactive promotion of economic activities, whether at home or abroad, that will make firms and sectors located within the territory of the state competitive in international markets. The state itself becomes an agent for the commodification of the collective, situated in a wider, market-dominated playing field. In David Andrews's terms, the competition state will increasingly "cheat" or ride free on opportunities created by autonomous transnational market structures and other public goods provided not by other states or the states system but by increasingly autonomous and private transnational structures, such as financial markets. The state is thus caught in a bind in which maintaining a balance between its civil-association functions and its enterprise-association functions will become increasingly problematic.

In this new context, the logic of collective action is becoming a heterogeneous, multilayered logic, derived not from one particular core structure, such as the state, but from the structural complexity embedded in the global arena. Globalization does not mean that the international system is any less structurally anarchic; it merely changes the structural composition of that anarchy from one made up of relations between sovereign states to one made up of relations between functionally differentiated spheres of economic activity, on the one hand, and the institutional structures proliferating in an ad hoc fashion to fill the power void, on the other. Different economic activities — differentiated by their comparative goods/assets structures — increasingly need to be regulated through distinct sets of institutions at different levels organized at different optimal scales. Such institutions, of course, overlap and interact in complex ways, but they no longer sufficiently coincide on a single optimal scale in such a way that they could be efficiently integrated into a multitask hierarchy like the nation-state. Some are essentially private market structures and regimes, some are still public intergovernmental structures, and some are mixed public-private.

The paths taken in the future in terms of both democratic accountability and political legitimacy will be crucial for the reshaping of the logic of collective action, especially where the state is no longer capable of being an effective channel for democratic demands. What sort of complex overall pattern of conflict and stability, competition and cooperation, will emerge from this process — in particular, whether the state will, despite its changing roles, remain a key element in a stabilizing, plurilateral web of levels and institutions or whether its decay will exacerbate a long-term trend toward greater instability — is not yet clear. We are only now in the first stages of a complex, worldwide evolutionary process of institutional selection.

31

Sense and Nonsense
in the Globalization Debate
DANI RODRIK

Many observers worry that globalization, a product of free markets and intense international competition, is undermining the
social welfare state in the advanced industrial countries. Dani
Rodrik questions the extent of globalization. He also demonstrates that since 1945, social welfare programs and openness
to trade have grown hand-in-hand, each reinforcing the other.
The social insurance programs carried out by governments have
helped mitigate the disruptions caused by international trade and
solidified coalitions in favor of economic openness. If vital social
safety nets are allowed to deteriorate, Rodrik concludes, the
domestic consensus in support of open markets will erode, protectionist pressures will soar, and political support for globalization itself will be threatened.

Globalization, Thomas Friedman of the *New York Times* has observed, is "the next
great foreign policy debate." Yet as the debate expands, it gets more confusing. Is
globalization a source of economic growth and prosperity, as most economists
and many in the policy community believe? Or is it a threat to social stability and
the natural environment, as a curious mix of interests ranging from labor advocates to environmentalists — and including the unlikely trio of Ross Perot,
George Soros, and Sir James Goldsmith — argue? Has globalization advanced so
far that national governments are virtually powerless to regulate their economies
and use their policy tools to further social ends? Is the shift of manufacturing
activities to low-wage countries undermining global purchasing power, thus creating a glut in goods ranging from autos to aircraft? Or is globalization no more than
a buzzword and its impact greatly exaggerated?

There are good reasons to be concerned about the quality of the globalization
debate. What we are witnessing is more a dialogue of the deaf than a rational
discussion. Those who favor international integration dismiss globalization's
opponents as knee-jerk protectionists who do not understand the principle of
comparative advantage and the complexities of trade laws and institutions.
Globalization's critics, on the other hand, fault economists and trade specialists
for their narrow, technocratic perspective. They argue that economists are too
enamored with their fancy models and do not have a good handle on how the real

world works. The result is that there is too much opponent bashing — and too little learning — on each side.

Both sides have valid complaints. Much of the popular discussion about globalization's effect on American wages, to pick one important example, ignores the considerable research that economists have undertaken. A reasonably informed reader of the nation's leading op-ed pages could be excused for not realizing that a substantial volume of literature on the relationship between trade and inequality exists, much of which contradicts the simplistic view that Americans or Europeans owe their deteriorating fortunes to low-wage competition from abroad. The mainstream academic view actually is that increased trade with developing countries may account for at most 20 percent of the reduction in the earnings of low-skilled American workers (relative to highly skilled workers) but not much more. One has to look elsewhere — to technological changes and deunionization, for example — to explain most of the increase in the wage gap between skilled and unskilled workers.

It is also true, however, that economists and proponents of trade have either neglected or pooh-poohed some of the broader complications associated with international economic integration. Consider the following questions: To what extent have capital mobility and the outsourcing of production increased the *substitutability* of domestic labor across national boundaries, thereby aggravating the economic insecurity confronting workers (in addition to exerting downward pressure on their wages)? Are the distributional implications of globalization — and certainly there are some — reconcilable with domestic concepts of distributive justice? Does trade with countries that have different norms and social institutions clash with and undermine long-standing domestic social bargains? To what extent does globalization undermine the ability of national governments to provide the public goods that their citizenries have come to expect, including social insurance against economic risks?

These are serious questions that underscore the potential of globally expanding markets to come into conflict with social stability, even as these markets provide benefits to exporters, investors, and consumers. Some of these questions have not yet been seriously scrutinized by economists. Others cannot be answered with economic and statistical analysis alone. But the full story of globalization cannot be told unless these broader issues are addressed as well.

THE LIMITS OF GLOBALIZATION

Even with the revolution in transportation and communication and the substantial progress made in trade liberalization over the last three decades, national economies remain remarkably isolated from each other. This isolation has a critical implication, which has been repeatedly emphasized by economist Paul Krugman: Most governments in the advanced industrial world are not nearly as shackled by economic globalization as is commonly believed. They retain substantial autonomy in regulating their economies, in designing their social policies, and in maintaining institutions that differ from those of their trading partners.

The supposition that domestic economies are now submerged in a seamless, unified world market is belied by various pieces of evidence. Take the case of North America. Trade between Canada and the United States is among the freest in the world and is only minimally hampered by transport and communications costs. Yet a study by Canadian economist John McCallum has documented that trade between a Canadian province and a U.S. state (that is, *international* trade) is on average 20 times smaller than trade between two Canadian provinces (that is, *intranational* trade). Clearly, the U.S. and Canadian markets remain substantially delinked from each other. And if this is true of U.S.-Canadian trade, it must be all the more true of other bilateral trade relationships.

The evidence on the mobility of physical capital also contradicts current thought. Popular discussions take it for granted that capital is now entirely free to cross national borders in its search for the highest returns. As economists Martin Feldstein and Charles Horioka have pointed out, if this were true, the level of investment that is undertaken in France would depend only on the profitability of investment in France, and it would have no relationship to the available savings in France. Actually, however, this turns out to be false. Increased savings in one country translate into increased investments in that country almost one for one. Despite substantial crossborder money flows, different rates of return among countries persist and are not equalized by capital moving to higher-return economies.

One can easily multiply the examples. U.S. portfolios tend to be remarkably concentrated in U.S. stocks. The prices of apparently identical goods differ widely from one country to another despite the fact that the goods can be traded. In reality, national economies retain a considerable degree of isolation from each other, and national policymakers enjoy more autonomy than is assumed by most recent writings on the erosion of national sovereignty.

The limited nature of globalization can perhaps be better appreciated by placing it into historical context. By many measures, the world economy was more integrated at the height of the gold standard in the late 19th century than it is now. In the United States and Europe, trade volumes peaked before World War I and then collapsed during the interwar years. Trade surged again after 1950, but neither Europe nor the United States is significantly more open today (gauging by ratios of trade to national income) than it was under the gold standard. Japan actually exports less of its total production today than it did during the interwar period.

GLOBALIZATION MATTERS

It would be a mistake to conclude from this evidence that globalization is irrelevant. Due to the increased importance of trade, the options available to national policymakers have narrowed appreciably over the last three decades. The oft-mentioned imperative of maintaining "international competitiveness" now looms much larger and imparts a definite bias to policymaking.

Consider labor market practices. As France, Germany, and other countries have shown, it is still possible to maintain labor market policies that increase the cost of labor. But globalization is raising the overall social cost of exercising this option.

European nations can afford to have generous minimum wages and benefit levels if they choose to pay the costs. But the stakes — the resulting unemployment levels — have been raised by the increased international mobility of firms.

The consequences are apparent everywhere. In Japan, large corporations have started to dismantle the postwar practice of providing lifetime employment, one of Japan's most distinctive social institutions. In France and Germany, unions have been fighting government attempts to cut pension benefits. In South Korea, labor unions have taken to the streets to protest the government's relaxation of firing restrictions. Developing countries in Latin America are competing with each other in liberalizing trade, deregulating their economies, and privatizing public enterprises.

Ask business executives or government officials why these changes are necessary, and you will hear the same mantra repeated over and over again: "We need to remain (or become) competitive in a global economy." As some of these changes appear to violate long-standing social bargains in many countries, the widespread populist reaction to globalization is perhaps understandable.

The anxieties generated by globalization must be seen in the context of the demands placed on national governments, which have expanded radically since the late 19th century. At the height of the gold standard, governments were not yet expected to perform social-welfare functions on a large scale. Ensuring adequate levels of employment, establishing social safety nets, providing medical and social insurance, and caring for the poor were not parts of the government agenda. Such demands multiplied during the period following the Second World War. Indeed, a key component of the implicit postwar social bargain in the advanced industrial countries has been the provision of social insurance and safety nets at home (unemployment compensation, severance payments, and adjustment assistance, for example) in exchange for the adoption of freer trade policies.

This bargain is clearly eroding. Employers are less willing to provide the benefits of job security and stability, partly because of increased competition but also because their enhanced global mobility makes them less dependent on the goodwill of their local work force. Governments are less able to sustain social safety nets, because an important part of their tax base has become footloose because of the increased mobility of capital. Moreover, the ideological onslaught against the welfare state has paralyzed many governments and made them unable to respond to the domestic needs of a more integrated economy.

MORE TRADE, MORE GOVERNMENT

The postwar period has witnessed two apparently contradictory trends: the growth of trade and the growth of government. Prior to the Second World War, government expenditures averaged around 20 per cent of the gross domestic products (GDPs) of today's advanced industrialized countries. By the mid-1990s, that figure had more than doubled to 47 per cent. The increased role of government is particularly striking in countries like the United States (from 9 to 34 per cent), Sweden (from 10 to 69 per cent), and the Netherlands (from 19 to 54 per cent).

The driving force behind the expansion of government during this period was the increase in social spending — and income transfers in particular.

It is not a coincidence that social spending increased alongside international trade. For example, the small, highly open European economies like Austria, the Netherlands, and Sweden have large governments in part as a result of their attempts to minimize the social impact of openness to the international economy. It is in the most open countries like Denmark, the Netherlands, and Sweden that spending on income transfers has expanded the most.

Indeed, there is a surprisingly strong association across countries between the degree of exposure to international trade and the importance of the government in the economy. . . . At one end of the distribution we have the United States and Japan, which have the lowest trade shares in GDP and some of the lowest shares of spending on social protection. At the other end, Luxembourg, Belgium, and the Netherlands have economies with high degrees of openness and large income transfers. This relationship is not confined to OECD economies: Developing nations also exhibit this pattern. Furthermore, the extent to which imports and exports were important in a country's economy in the early 1960s provided a good predictor of how big its government would become in the ensuing three decades, regardless of how developed it was. All the available evidence points to the same, unavoidable conclusion: The social welfare state has been the flip side of the open economy.

International economic integration thus poses a serious dilemma: Globalization increases the demand for social insurance while simultaneously constraining the ability of governments to respond effectively to that demand. Consequently, as globalization deepens, the social consensus required to keep domestic markets open to international trade erodes.

Since the early 1980s, tax rates on capital have tended to decrease in the leading industrial nations, while tax rates on labor have continued generally to increase. At the same time, social spending has stabilized in relation to national incomes. These outcomes reflect the tradeoffs facing governments in increasingly open economies: The demands for social programs are being balanced against the need to reduce the tax burden on capital, which has become more globally mobile.

By any standard, the postwar social bargain has served the world economy extremely well. Spurred by widespread trade liberalization, world trade has soared since the 1950s. This expansion did not cause major social dislocations and did not engender much opposition in the advanced industrial countries. Today, however, the process of international economic integration is taking place against a backdrop of retreating governments and diminished social obligations. Yet the need for social insurance for the vast majority of the population that lacks international mobility has not diminished. If anything, this need has grown.

The question, therefore, is how the tension between globalization and the pressure to mitigate risks can be eased. If the vital role that social insurance played in enabling the postwar expansion of trade is neglected and social safety nets are allowed to dwindle, the domestic consensus in favor of open markets will be eroded seriously, and protectionist pressures will soar.

THE GLOBAL TRADE IN SOCIAL VALUES

In the markets for goods, services, labor, and capital, international trade creates arbitrage — the possibility of buying (or producing) in one place at one price and selling at a higher price elsewhere. Prices thus tend to converge in the long run, this convergence being the source of the gains from trade. But trade exerts pressure toward another kind of arbitrage as well: arbitrage in national norms and social institutions. This form of arbitrage results, indirectly, as the costs of maintaining divergent social arrangements go up. As a consequence, open trade can conflict with long-standing social contracts that protect certain activities from the relentlessness of the free market. This is a key tension generated by globalization.

As the technology for manufactured goods becomes standardized and diffused internationally, nations with different sets of values, norms, institutions, and collective preferences begin to compete head on in markets for similar goods. In the traditional approach to trade policy, this trend is of no consequence: Differences in national practices and social institutions are, in effect, treated just like any other differences that determine a country's comparative advantage (such as endowments of physical capital or skilled labor).

In practice, however, trade becomes contentious when it unleashes forces that undermine the social norms implicit in domestic practices. For example, not all residents of advanced industrial countries are comfortable with the weakening of domestic institutions through the forces of trade, such as when child labor in Honduras replaces workers in South Carolina or when cuts in pension benefits in France are called for in response to the requirements of the Treaty on European Union. This sense of unease is one way of interpreting the demands for "fair trade." Much of the discussion surrounding the new issues in trade policy — e.g., labor standards, the environment, competition policy, and corruption — can be cast in this light of procedural fairness.

Trade usually redistributes income among industries, regions, and individuals. Therefore, a principled defense of free trade cannot be constructed without addressing the question of the fairness and legitimacy of the practices that generate these distributional "costs." How comparative advantage is created matters. Low-wage foreign competition arising from an abundance of workers is different from competition that is created by foreign labor practices that violate norms at home. Low wages that result from demography or history are very different from low wages that result from government repression of unions.

From this perspective it is easier to understand why many people are often ill at ease with the consequences of international economic integration. Automatically branding all concerned groups as self-interested protectionists does not help much. This perspective also prepares us not to expect broad popular support for trade when trade involves exchanges that clash with (and erode) prevailing domestic social arrangements.

Consider labor rules, for example. Since the 1930s, U.S. laws have recognized that restrictions on "free contract" are legitimate to counteract the effects of unequal bargaining power. Consequently, the employment relationship in the

United States (and elsewhere) is subject to a multitude of restrictions, such as those that regulate working hours, workplace safety, labor/management negotiations, and so forth. Many of these restrictions have been put in place to redress the asymmetry in bargaining power that would otherwise disadvantage workers vis-à-vis employers.

Globalization upsets this balance by creating a different sort of asymmetry: Employers can move abroad, but employees cannot. There is no substantive difference between American workers being driven from their jobs by their fellow *domestic* workers who agree to work 12-hour days, earn less than the minimum wage, or be fired if they join a union — all of which are illegal under U.S. law — and their being similarly disadvantaged by *foreign* workers doing the same. If society is unwilling to accept the former, why should it countenance the latter? Globalization generates an inequality in bargaining power that 60 years of labor legislation in the United States has tried to prevent. It is in effect eroding a social understanding that has long been settled.

Whether they derive from labor standards, environmental policy, or corruption, differences in domestic practices and institutions have become matters of international controversy. That is indeed the common theme that runs the gamut of the new issues on the agenda of the World Trade Organization (WTO). Conflicts arise both when these differences create trade — as in the cases of child labor or lax environmental policies — and when they reduce it — as industrial practices in Japan are alleged to do. As the *New York Times* editorialized on July 11, 1996, in connection with the Kodak-Fuji dispute on access to the photographic film market in Japan, "the Kodak case asks the WTO, in effect, to pass judgment on the way Japan does business."

The notions of "fair trade" and "leveling the playing field" that lie behind the pressures for putting these new issues on the trade agenda have been ridiculed by economists. But once it is recognized that trade has implications for domestic norms and social arrangements and that its legitimacy rests in part on its compatibility with these, such notions are not so outlandish. These sentiments are ways of addressing the concerns to which trade gives rise. Free trade among countries with different domestic practices requires an acceptance of either an erosion of domestic structures or the need for some degree of harmonization or convergence.

If this is the appropriate context in which demands for "fair trade" or "leveling the playing field" must be understood, it should also be clear that policymakers often take too many liberties in justifying their actions along such lines. Most of the pricing policies that pass as "unfair trade" in U.S. antidumping proceedings, for example, are standard business practice in the United States and other countries. While there may not be a sharp dividing line between what is fair and unfair in international trade, one clear sign that pure protectionism is at the root of a trade dispute is the prevalence of practices within the domestic economy that are identical or similar to those being protested in the international arena. Fairness cannot be eliminated from thinking about trade policy; but neither can it be invoked to justify trade restrictions when the practice in question does not conflict with domestic norms as revealed by actual practice.

MISUNDERSTANDING TRADE

The tensions created by globalization are real. They are, however, considerably more subtle than the terminology that has come to dominate the debate. "Low-wage competition," "leveling the playing field," and "race to the bottom" are catchy phrases that often muddle the public's understanding of the real issues. A more nuanced debate and more imaginative solutions are badly needed.

A broader approach to this debate, one that takes into account some of the aspects discussed here, provides more credibility to the defenders of free trade in their attempts to clear up the misunderstandings that the opponents of trade often propagate. Journalist William Greider's recent book, *One World, Ready or Not — The Manic Logic of Global Capitalism,* illustrates the appeal that many of these misunderstandings retain in the minds of popular commentators on trade.

One of the main themes of this book — that the global expansion of markets is undermining social cohesion and is inexorably leading toward a major economic and political crisis — could be viewed as a more boldly expressed version of the potential danger that is highlighted above. Many of Greider's concerns — the consequences for low-skilled workers in the advanced industrial countries, the weakening of social safety nets, and the repression of political rights in some leading exporters like China and Indonesia — are indeed valid. However, the disregard for sound economic analysis and systematic empirical evidence that characterizes Greider's book makes it both a very unreliable guide to understanding what is taking place and a faulty manual for setting things right.

A popular fallacy perpetuated in works like Greider's is that low wages are the driving force behind today's global trade. If that were so, the world's most formidable exporters would be Bangladesh and a smattering of African countries. Some Mexican or Malaysian exporting plants may approach U.S. levels in labor productivity, while local wages fall far short. Yet what is true for a small number of plants does not extend to economies as a whole and therefore does not have much bearing on the bulk of world trade.

... There is almost a one-to-one relationship between [economy-wide labor productivity (GDP per worker) and labor costs in manufacturing in a wide range of countries], indicating that wages are closely related to productivity. Low-wage economies are those in which levels of labor productivity are commensurately low. This tendency is of course no surprise to anyone with common sense. Yet much of the discourse on trade presumes a huge gap between wages and productivity in the developing country exporters.

Similarly, it is a mistake to attribute the U.S. trade deficit to the restrictive commercial policies of other countries — policies that Greider calls the "unbalanced behavior" of U.S. trading partners. How then can we explain the large U.S. deficit with Canada? If trade imbalances were determined by commercial policies, then India, as one of the world's most protectionist countries until recently, would have been running large trade surpluses.

Another misconception is that export-oriented industrialization has somehow failed to improve the livelihood of workers in East and Southeast Asia. Contrary to the impression one gets from listening to the opponents of globalization, life is significantly better for the vast majority of the former peasants who now toil in Malaysian or Chinese factories. Moreover, it is generally not the case that foreign-owned companies in developing countries provide working conditions that are inferior to those available elsewhere in the particular country; in fact, the reverse is more often true.

Perhaps the most baffling of the antiglobalization arguments is that trade and foreign investment are inexorably leading to excess capacity on a global scale. This is Greider's key argument and ultimately the main reason why he believes the system will self-destruct. Consider his discussion of Boeing's outsourcing of some of its components to the Xian Aircraft Company in China:

> When new production work was moved to Xian from places like the United States, the global system was, in effect, swapping highly paid industrial workers for very cheap ones. To put the point more crudely, Boeing was exchanging a $50,000 American machinist for a Chinese machinist who earned $600 or $700 a year. Which one could buy the world's goods? Thus, even though incomes and purchasing power were expanding robustly among the new consumers of China, the overall effect was an erosion of the world's potential purchasing power. If one multiplied the Xian example across many factories and industrial sectors, as well as other aspiring countries, one could begin to visualize why global consumption was unable to keep up with global production.

An economist would rightly point out that the argument makes little sense. The Chinese worker who earns only a tiny fraction of his American counterpart is likely to be commensurately less productive. Even if the Chinese worker's wages are repressed below actual productivity, the result is a transfer in purchasing power — to Boeing's shareholders and the Chinese employers — and not a diminution of global purchasing power. Perhaps Greider is thinking that Boeing's shareholders and the Chinese employers have a lower propensity to consume than the Chinese workers. If so, where is the evidence? Where is the global surplus in savings and the secular decline in real interest rates that we would surely have observed if income is going from low savers to high savers?

It may be unfair to pick on Greider, especially since some of his other conclusions are worth taking seriously. But the misunderstandings that his book displays are commonplace in the globalization debate and do not help to advance it.

SAFETY NETS, NOT TRADE BARRIERS

One need not be alarmed by globalization, but neither should one take a Panglossian view of it. Globalization greatly enhances the opportunities available to those who have the skills and mobility to flourish in world markets. It can help poor countries to escape poverty. It does not constrain national autonomy nearly as much as popular discussions assume. At the same time, globalization does exert downward pressure on the wages of underskilled workers in industrialized countries, exacerbate economic insecurity, call into question accepted social arrangements, and weaken social safety nets.

There are two dangers from complacency toward the social consequences of globalization. The first and more obvious one is the potential for a political backlash against trade. The candidacy of Patrick Buchanan in the 1996 Republican presidential primaries revealed that protectionism can be a rather easy sell at a time when broad segments of American society are experiencing anxieties related to globalization. The same can be said about the political influence of Vladimir Zhirinovsky in Russia or Jean-Marie Le Pen in France — influence that was achieved, at least in part, in response to the perceived effects of globalization. Economists may complain that protectionism is mere snake oil and argue that the ailments require altogether different medicine, but intellectual arguments will not win hearts and minds unless concrete solutions are offered. Trade protection, for all of its faults, has the benefit of concreteness.

Perhaps future Buchanans will ultimately be defeated, as Buchanan himself was, by the public's common sense. Even so, a second, and perhaps more serious, danger remains: The accumulation of globalization's side effects could lead to a new set of class divisions — between those who prosper in the globalized economy and those who do not; between those who share its values and those who would rather not; and between those who can diversify away its risks and those who cannot. This is not a pleasing prospect even for individuals on the winning side of the globalization divide: The deepening of social fissures harms us all. . . .

Globalization is not occurring in a vacuum: It is part of a broader trend we may call marketization. Receding government, deregulation, and the shrinking of social obligations are the domestic counterparts of the intertwining of national economies. Globalization could not have advanced this far without these complementary forces at work. The broader challenge for the 21st century is to engineer a new balance between the market and society — one that will continue to unleash the creative energies of private entrepreneurship without eroding the social bases of cooperation.

It is a violation of the law to reproduce these selections by any means whatsoever without the written permission of the copyright holder.

Stephen D. Krasner. "State Power and the Structure of International Trade." From *World Politics,* 28, 3 (April 1976). Reprinted by permission of The Johns Hopkins University Press.

Barry Eichengreen. "The Political Economy of the Smoot-Hawley Tariff." From *Research in Economic History,* Vol. 12 (1989), pp. 1–43. Reprinted by permission of JAI Press.

Douglass C. North. "Institutions and Economic Growth: An Historical Introduction." *World Development,* Vol. 17 (1989), pp. 1319–1332. Reprinted with permission from Elsevier Science.

Susan Strange. "States, Firms, and Diplomacy." This is an edited text of an article which first appeared in *International Affairs,* London, Vol. 68, No. 1 (January 1992), pp. 1–15, and is reproduced with permission.

Charles P. Kindleberger. "The Rise of Free Trade in Western Europe." From *The Journal of Economic History,* 35, 1 (1975), pp. 20–55. Copyright © 1975 by The Economic History Association. Reprinted with the permission of Cambridge University Press.

Peter Alexis Gourevitch. "International Trade, Domestic Coalitions, and Liberty: Comparative Responses to the Crisis of 1873–1896." Reprinted from *The Journal of Interdisciplinary History,* VIII (1977), 281–313, with the permission of the editors of *The Journal of Interdisciplinary History* and the MIT Press, Cambridge, Massachusetts. Copyright © 1977 by The Massachusetts Institute of Technology and the editors of *The Journal of Interdisciplinary History.*

Jeffry A. Frieden. "International Investment and Colonial Control: A New Interpretation." *International Organization,* 48:4 (Autumn, 1994), pp. 559–593. Copyright © 1994 by The IO Foundation and The Massachusetts Institute of Technology.

David A. Lake. "British and American Hegemony Compared: Lessons for the Current Era of Decline." Reproduced from Michael Fry, ed. *History, The White House & The Kremlin: Statesmen as Historians,* 1991, pp. 106–122 by permission of Pinter Publishers Ltd.

Richard E. Caves. "The Multinational Enterprise as an Economic Organization." From "The Multinational Enterprise as an Economic Organization" by R.E. Caves in R.E. Caves, *Multinational Enterprise and Economic Analysis,* Second Edition, Copyright © 1996, Cambridge University Press. Reprinted with permission.

Shah M. Tarzi. "Third World Governments and Multinational Corporations: Dynamics of Host's Bargaining Power." This first appeared as an article in *International Relations,* vol. X, no. 3 (May 1991), pp. 237–249. Reprinted by permission of The David Davies Memorial Institute of International Studies.

David Fieldhouse. "'A New Imperial System'? The Role of the Multinational Corporations Reconsidered." From Wolfgang Mommsen and Jurgen Osterhammel, eds. *Imperialism and*

472   Acknowledgments

After, Allen & Unwin, 1986, pp. 225–240. Copyright © The German Historical Institute. Reprinted by permission.

Jeffry A. Hart and Aseem Prakash. "Strategic Trade and Investment Policies: Implications for the Study of International Political Economy." *The World Economy,* Vol. 20 (1997), pp. 457–476. Reprinted by permission of Blackwell Publishers.

Lawrence Broz. "The Domestic Politics of International Monetary Order: The Gold Standard." From *Contested Social Orders and International Politics,* edited by David Skidmore (Nashville: Vanderbilt University Press, 1997), pp. 53–91. Copyright © 1997 by Vanderbilt University Press.

Barry Eichengreen. "Hegemonic Stability Theories of the International Monetary System." From *Can Nations Agree? Issues in International Economic Cooperation* (Washington: The Brookings Institution), 1989, pp. 255–98. Reprinted by permission of The Brookings Institution.

Benjamin J. Cohen. "The Triad and the Unholy Trinity: Problems of International Monetary Cooperation." From Richard Higgott, Richard Leaver, and John Ravenhill, eds. *Pacific Economic Relations in the 1990s: Cooperation or Conflict?* Allen & Unwin, 1993, pp. 133–158. Reprinted by permission.

Jeffry A. Frieden. "Exchange Rate Politics." *Review of International Political Economy,* Vol. 1, No. 1 (1994), pp. 81–98 plus notes. Reprinted by permission of Routledge Ltd.

Charles Wyplosz. "EMU: Why and How It Might Happen." *The Journal of Economic Perspectives,* Vol. 11, No. 4 (Fall 1997), pp. 3–22. Copyright © American Economic Association. Reprinted by permission of Charles A. Wyplosz.

John B. Goodman and Louis W. Pauly. "The Obsolescence of Capital Controls? Economic Management in an Age of Global Markets." From *World Politics,* Vol. 46, No. 1 (1993), pp. 50–82. Reprinted by permission of the authors and The Johns Hopkins University Press.

Cletus C. Coughlin, K. Alec Chrystal, and Geoffrey E. Wood. "Protectionist Trade Policies: A Survey of Theory, Evidence, and Rationale." Federal Reserve Bank of St. Louis.

Ronald Rogowski. "Commerce and Coalitions: How Trade Affects Domestic Political Alignments." Copyright © 1989 by Princeton University Press. Reprinted by permission of Princeton University Press.

James E. Alt and Michael Gilligan. "The Political Economy of Trading States: Factor Specificity, Collective Action Problems, and Domestic Political Institutions." *Journal of Political Philosophy,* Vol. 2, No. 2 (1994), pp. 165–192. Reprinted by permission of Blackwell Publishers.

Richard B. Freeman. "Are Your Wages Set in Beijing?" From *Journal of Economic Perspectives,* Vol. 9 No. 3 (1995), pages 15–31. Copyright © American Economic Association. Reprinted by permission of Dr. Richard B. Freeman.

Edward E. Mansfield and Marc L. Busch. "The Political Economy of Nontariff Barriers: A Cross-national Analysis." *International Organization,* Vol. 49, No. 4 (1995), pp. 723–749. © 1995 by The IO Foundation and The Massachusetts Institute of Technology.

Ronald W. Cox. "Explaining Business Support for Regional Trade Agreements." From *Business and the State in International Relations,* edited by Ronald Cox (Westview Press, 1996). Originally appeared in *Competition and Change,* Vol. 1:1 (1995), pp. 9–127. © OPA (Overseas Publishers Association) N.V.

Joseph E. Stiglitz and Lyn Squire. "International Development: Is It Possible?" Reprinted with permission from *Foreign Policy* No. 110 (1998), pp. 138–151. Copyright by The Carnegie Endowment for International Peace.

Robin Broad, John Cavanagh, and Walden Bello. "Development: The Market Is Not Enough." Reprinted by permission from *Foreign Policy* 81 (Winter 1990–91). Copyright © 1990 by The Carnegie Endowment for International Peace.

Jeffrey A. Williamson. "Globalization and Inequality, Past and Present" from *World Bank Research Observer,* 12:2 (1997), pp. 117–135. Reprinted by permission of The World Bank.

Stephan Haggard. "Inflation and Stabilization." From Gerald M. Meier, ed. *Politics and Policy Making in Developing Countries: Perspectives on the New Political Economy.* The International Center for Economic Growth, ICS Press, 1991, pp. 233–249. Reprinted by permission of ICS Press.

Alison Butler. "Environmental Protection and Free Trade: Are They Mutually Exclusive?" Federal Reserve Bank of St. Louis. May/June 1992.

Philip G. Cerny. "Globalization and the Changing Logic of Collective Action." *International Organization,* Vol. 49, No. 4 (1995), pp. 595–625. © 1995 by The IO Foundation and The Massachusetts Institute of Technology.

Dani Rodrik. "Sense and Nonsense in the Globalization Debate." Reprinted with permission from *Foreign Policy* No. 107 (1997), pp. 19–37. Copyright © by the Carnegie Endowment for International Peace.

INDEX